TEACHING YOUNG ADOLESCENTS

W9-AYQ-608

TEACHING YOUNG ADOLESCENTS

A Guide to Methods and Resources

Fourth Edition

Richard D. Kellough

Noreen G. Kellough

California State University at Sacramento

Merrill
Prentice Hall

Upper Saddle River, New Jersey
Columbus, Ohio

Library of Congress Cataloging in Publication Data

Kellough, Richard D. (Richard Dean)
    Teaching young adolescents: a guide to methods and resources / Richard D. Kellough,
  Noreen G. Kellough.—4th ed.
      p. cm.
    Rev. ed. of: Middle school teaching. 3rd ed. c1999.
    Includes bibliographical references and index.
    ISBN 0-13-061708-3 (pbk.)
      1. Middle school teaching—United States. 2. Middle schools—United States. I.
  Kellough, Noreen G. II. Kellough, Richard D. (Richard Dean) Middle school teaching.
  III. Title.

    LB1735.5 .K45 2003
    373.236'0973—dc21   2001058675

Vice President and Publisher: Jeffery W. Johnston
Executive Editor: Debra A. Stollenwerk
Assistant Editor: Daniel J. Parker
Production Editor: Kimberly J. Lundy
Production Coordination: Marilee Aschenbrenner, Carlisle Publishers Services
Design Coordinator: Diane C. Lorenzo
Cover Design: Ali Mohrman
Cover Image: Corbis Stock Market
Text Design and Illustrations: Carlisle Publishers Services
Photo Coordinator: Valerie Schultz
Production Manager: Pamela D. Bennett
Director of Marketing: Ann Castel Davis
Marketing Manager: Krista Groshong
Marketing Services Manager: Tyra Cooper

This book was set in New Baskerville by Carlisle Communications, Ltd., and was printed and bound by Banta Book Group. The cover was printed by The Lehigh Press, Inc.

Photo Credits: Cindy Charles/PhotoEdit, p. 25; Scott Cunningham/Merrill, pp. 189, 231; Anthony Magnacca/Merrill, pp. 47, 85, 305, 329, 347, 349, 386; URS Architectural Design, photo by Jeff Garland, p. 3; Anne Vega/Merrill, pp. 1, 83, 233; Tom Watson/ Merrill, p. 133; Todd Yarrington/Merrill, p. 258.

Earlier editions were entitled *Middle School Teaching: A Guide to Methods and Resources.*

Pearson Education Ltd.
Pearson Education Australia Pty. Limited
Pearson Education Singapore Pte. Ltd.
Pearson Education North Asia Ltd.
Pearson Education Canada, Ltd.
Pearson Educación de Mexico, S. A. de C. V.
Pearson Education—Japan
Pearson Education Malaysia Pte. Ltd.
Pearson Education, *Upper Saddle River, New Jersey*

Copyright © 2003, 1999, 1996, 1993 by Pearson Education, Inc., Upper Saddle River, New Jersey 07458. All rights reserved. Printed in the United States of America. This publication is protected by Copyright and permission should be obtained from the publisher prior to any prohibited reproduction, storage in a retrieval system, or transmission in any form or by any means, electronic, mechanical, photocopying, recording, or likewise. For information regarding permission(s), write to: Rights and Permissions Department.

Merrill
Prentice Hall

10 9 8 7 6 5 4 3 2 1
ISBN 0-13-061708-3

Preface

Welcome to the fourth edition of *Teaching Young Adolescents: A Guide to Methods and Resources*. The primary purpose of this textbook is to provide a practical, concise, criterion-referenced, performance-based, mastery learning model for college and university students who are in a methods course or in the field component of teacher education, learning how to teach young adolescent students regardless of where or how those students are housed or of the cognomen of the school in which they are housed. The term *young adolescents* refers to children ranging in age from 9 to 14 who are in the traditional middle level grades of 5 through 8.

Others who will find the guide useful are experienced teachers who want to continue developing their teaching skills, and curriculum specialists and school administrators who want a current, practical, and concise text of methods, guidelines, and resources for teaching young adolescents.

NEW TO THIS EDITION

Exemplary middle level programs are those that are rooted in celebrating and building upon the diverse characteristics and needs of young adolescents. To become and to remain exemplary, teachers in such programs must be in a continual mode of inquiry, reflection, and change. It is no different for us as the authors of this book. In a continuing effort to prepare a comprehensive and exemplary book that focuses on teaching young adolescents, we are in a *continual mode of inquiry* into the latest findings in research and practice, in *constant reflection* as we listen to and assess the comments from practitioners in the field and from users and reviewers of the book, and in *steady change* as we prepared each edition.

Changes for this fourth edition were substantial as we continue with our focus to respond to the challenge of providing a comprehensive and concise coverage of methods and resources for teaching young adolescents in the classroom, regardless of whether that classroom is housed, for example, in a middle school or in a K–8 elementary school. That focus resulted in this book's new title. Other changes include:

- We revisited and rewrote the entire book to assure a strong and consistent focus and the most current research base possible on teaching the young adolescent learner.
- Although separated in this book for reasons of organizational clarity, the component on planning the classroom learning environment is an integral and ongoing component of planning and implementing curriculum and instruction. The former section about establishing a supportive classroom learning environment, now titled "Planning the Classroom Learning Environment," has been moved from Part I to Part II where it is the first of three chapters about "Planning for Instruction," the title of Part II. The other two chapters in Part II are "Curriculum Planning" and "Preparing an Instructional Plan."
- Part III underwent organizational and content changes and now includes four rather than the previous three chapters.
- Despite the blue-ribbon commissions, authors, and politicians who vilify what they perceive as the failures of middle level school education in particular and public school education in general, thousands of committed teachers, administrators, parents, guardians, and community representatives struggle daily, year after year, to provide young adolescents with a quality education. So that readers can learn about or visit exemplary middle level programs, many are recognized and identified by name throughout this text.

Other changes made for this edition are mentioned in the paragraphs that follow.

OUR BELIEFS: HOW AND WHERE THEY ARE REFLECTED IN THIS BOOK

In preparing this book, we saw our task *not* as making the teaching job easier for you—effective teaching is never easy—but as improving your teaching effectiveness and providing relevant guidelines and current resources. You may choose from these resources and build upon what works best for you. Nobody can tell you what will work with your students; you will know them best. We do share what we believe to be the best of middle level practice, the most useful of recent research findings, and the richest of experiences. Although both of us are former middle level classroom teachers who now work with other middle level teachers, preparing this new edition presented us with an opportunity to reflect, reexamine, and share our own beliefs about working with young adolescents in the classroom. The boldface italic statements present our beliefs and explain how they are embraced in this resource guide.

The best learning occurs when the learner actively participates in the process, which includes having ownership in both the process and the product of the learning. Consequently, this book is designed to engage you in hands-on and minds-on learning about effective teaching of young adolescents in the classroom. For example, rather than simply reading a chapter devoted to the important topic of cooperative learning, in each chapter you will become involved in cooperative and collaborative learning. In essence, via the exercises found in every chapter, you will practice cooperative learning, talk about it, practice it some more, and finally, through the process of doing it, learn a great deal about it. This book *involves* you in cooperative learning.

The best strategies for learning about teaching young adolescents in the classroom are those that model those very strategies. As you will learn, integrated learning is the cornerstone of the most effective teaching of young adolescents, and that is a premise upon which this resource guide is designed.

To be most effective today a teacher must use an eclectic style in teaching. Rather than focusing your attention on particular models of teaching, we emphasize the importance of an eclectic model—that is, one in which you select and integrate the best from various instructional approaches. For example, sometimes you will want to use a direct, expository approach, perhaps through a minilecture; more often you will want to use an indirect, social-interactive, or student-centered approach, perhaps through project-based learning. This book not only provides guidelines to help you decide which approach to use at a particular time but also develops your skill in using specific approaches. Equally important, you will learn of the importance of being able to combine both direct and indirect approaches, of using what we refer to as *multilevel instruction*.

Learning should be active, pleasant, fun, meaningful, and productive. Our desire is to present this resource guide in an enthusiastic, positive, and cognitive-humanistic way, in part by providing rich experiences in social-interactive learning. How this is done is perhaps best exemplified by the active learning exercises found throughout the book and on the Companion Website at www.prenhall.com/kellough. Exercises were developed to ensure that you become an active participant in learning the methods and procedures that are most appropriate in facilitating learning by active, responsive young adolescents.

Teaching skills can be learned. In medicine, certain knowledge and skills must be learned and developed before the student physician is licensed to practice with patients. In law, certain knowledge and skills must be learned and developed before the law student is licensed to practice with clients. So it is in teacher preparation: knowledge and skills must be learned and developed before the teacher candidate is licensed to practice the art and science of teaching young people. We would never allow an untrained person to treat our child's illness or to defend us in a legal case: the professional education of teachers is no less important! Receiving a professional education on how to teach young people is absolutely necessary, and certain aspects of that education must precede any interaction with students if teachers are to become truly competent professionals.

ORGANIZATION OF THIS BOOK: AN OVERVIEW

Competent teaching of young adolescents in the classroom is a kaleidoscopic, multifaceted, eclectic process. When preparing and writing a book for use in teacher preparation, by necessity one must separate that kaleidoscopic process into separate parts, which is not always possible to do in a way that makes the most sense to everyone using the book. This overview explains how we have done it.

We believe that ***there are developmental components involved in becoming a competent teacher.*** This book is organized around four developmental components: *why*—the rationale to support the components that follow; *what*—the content, processes, and skills you will be helping young adolescent students learn; *how*—how you will do it; and *how well*—how well you are doing it. These are represented by the four parts of the book. Each part is introduced with the goals of the chapters that follow and with reflective thoughts relevant to topics addressed in its chapters. The following visual map illustrates how these four developmental elements are divided.

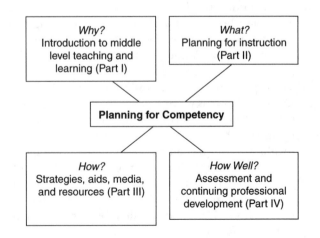

Each chapter begins with a brief introduction to that chapter followed by its major learning targets or objectives.

Throughout, we provide information that is useful for the teacher as a decision maker. You will find exercises to practice handling concepts in ways that facilitate metacognitive thinking. All exercises require you to deal in some descriptive, analytical, or self-reflective manner with text concepts and actual practice. Most of the exercises here in the text and on the Companion Website are adaptable for cooperative/collaborative group processing.

Part I: Introduction to Middle Level Teaching and Learning

The three chapters of Part I reflect the *why* component, the reality and challenge of teaching young adolescents today.

Chapter 1 presents an overview of that reality and challenge. Chapter 2 focuses on the unique and varied characteristics and developmentally appropriate ways of working with young adolescents in the classroom. *Regardless of their individual differences, every student must have an equal opportunity to participate and learn in the classroom.* Beginning with the first chapter, this belief is reflected throughout this book—sometimes in a very direct fashion and other times indirectly. This attention and overall sensitivity to diversity is intended to model not only our belief but also how to be inclusive to people of diverse backgrounds in many ways.

Chapter 3 reflects the expectations, responsibilities, and behaviors that are characteristic of competent middle level teachers.

Part II: Planning for Instruction

Effective teaching is performance based and criterion referenced. This book is constructed in this manner. Because we believe that teaching, indeed living, must allow for serendipity, encourage the intuitive, and foster the most creative aspects of one's thinking, we cannot always be specific about what students will learn as a result of our instruction. Hence, the occasional ambiguity must be expected. The three chapters in Part II reflect the planning, or *what*, component.

To teach young adolescents most effectively, you must recognize, appreciate, and understand them and be able to establish and maintain a safe and supportive classroom learning environment. Guidelines for accomplishing that are presented in Chapter 4.

Chapter 5 provides a focus on the curriculum and the programs that make it up, and on the rationale for planning and selecting the content of the curriculum; provides information about the national, state, and local documents that include benchmarks for learning and that guide content selection; and describes preparing goals and learning targets and using them to plan for and assess learning.

Chapter 6 deserves your time and attention as you use this book to move toward becoming a competent teacher of young adolescents. It presents detailed information and step-by-step guidelines for integrating the students' learning, selecting developmentally appropriate learning activities, and preparing various types of instructional units with lessons.

Part III: Strategies, Aids, Media, and Resources for Effective Instruction

Although it is very difficult to predict what 9- to 14-year-olds of today will need to know to be productive citizens in the middle of this century, we believe *they will always need to know how to learn, how to read, how to think productively, and how to communicate effectively and work together cooperatively.* We believe that young adolescents need to acquire skills in how to gain knowledge and how to process information, and they need learning experiences that foster effective communication and productive, cooperative behaviors. We hope all children feel good about themselves, about others, and about their teachers, schools, and communities. We emphasize the importance of helping students develop those skills, feelings, and attitudes. Teachers of all grades and subjects share in the responsibility for teaching skills in reading, writing, thinking, working cooperatively, and communicating effectively. This responsibility is no less important for teachers of young adolescents and is reflected clearly throughout this resource guide.

The appropriate teaching methods for reaching these goals incorporate thoughtful planning, acceptance of the uniqueness of each individual, honesty, trust, sharing, risking, collaboration, communication, and cooperation. Furthermore, we believe that students learn these skills and values best from teachers who model the same. Our book continues to be faithful to that hope and to that end.

Part III, the *how* component, is presented in four chapters. Chapter 7 focuses your attention on one significantly important teaching and learning strategy—questioning.

Chapter 8 presents guidelines for grouping students; using project-centered teaching, assignments, and homework; ensuring classroom equity; and writing across the curriculum. To help you learn how you can practically and effectively individualize the learning for every student, we added an exercise that clearly leads you through the development of your first self-instructional module. Chapter 8 ends with a section you may find useful for years to come—a popular and updated annotated listing of 100 motivational strategies and ideas for lessons, interdisciplinary teaching, transcultural studies, and student projects, followed by an extended listing of Internet sites for teaching ideas. This resource guide is intended to be useful to you not only while you are in phases of teacher preparation but well into your first several years as a teacher.

Chapter 9 presents guidelines for using formal and informal teacher talk; demonstrations; direct teaching of thinking, discovery, and inquiry; and educational games. Throughout the book, but especially in Part III, and with a focus in Chapter 10, you will find an emphasis on the importance of students using visual and technological tools to access information and to make sense of it.

Part IV: Assessment and Continuing Professional Development

In two chapters, Part IV addresses the fourth component of teaching and learning—*how well* the students are learning and how well the teacher is teaching. Although separated in this book for reasons of organizational clarity, the assessment component of teaching and learning is an integral and ongoing component of the total curriculum.

Chapter 11 focuses attention on the assessment of what students know or think they know before, during, and following the instructional experience. To complete your instructional planning (Chapter 6), you will necessarily be referring to the content of Chapter 11. Chapter 11 also provides practical guidelines for parent/guardian and teacher collaboration and for grading and reporting student achievement.

Chapter 12, the final chapter, focuses on how well you are doing—the assessment of teaching effectiveness. In addition, it provides guidelines that you will find useful during your student teaching, and for finding a teaching position and for continued professional growth. These guidelines and this book will be useful for you as a reference for years beyond a methods course.

FEATURES OF THE TEXT

To achieve professional competency, you need guided learning, guided practice, productive feedback, encouragement, opportunity for intelligent reflection, and positive reinforcement. To provide you with the resources and encouragement to make you an effective and confident teacher, this book is organized with the following features.

- **A strong, current, and broad research base.** This is evidenced by the footnotes throughout the text, which for this edition are arranged at the bottom of text pages for your immediate reference and clarification.
- **Advance organizers.** The four parts, the goals and reflective thoughts at the beginning of each part, and the objectives found at the beginning of each chapter serve as advance organizers; that is, they establish a mind-set.

- **Exercises for active learning.** Found throughout are exercises we believe are fundamental to your learning. All exercises require you to deal in some descriptive, analytical, or self-reflective manner with text concepts and actual practice. Each is designed to encourage continual assessment of and reflection on your progress in building your competencies and skills for teaching, and involve you in collaborative and cooperative learning. It is unlikely that all exercises in this book and those on the Companion Website could be (or should be) completed in a one-semester course. Since some exercises necessitate a school visit, review the exercises early so you can plan your visits and work schedule. In fact, because certain exercises build upon previous ones or suggest that help be obtained from teachers in the field, we advise that all exercises be reviewed at the outset of your course.
- **Perforated pages.** Pages of the book are perforated for easy removal of the exercises. Exercises and some forms that are likely to be removed begin on separate pages so they can be removed without disturbing text.
- **Performance assessment.** Assessment of your developing competencies is encouraged by three micro peer teaching exercises found in Chapters 7 (Exercise 7.7), 9 (Exercise 9.1), and 12 (Exercise 12.2).
- **Situational case studies, teaching vignettes, and questions for class discussion.** For extended class discussions, situational case studies—some new to this edition—are presented in Chapter 4. Teaching vignettes are distributed throughout. Questions for Class Discussion appear at the end of each chapter.
- **Outstanding practices and exemplary programs.** To let you gain further insight or to visit exemplary programs, schools recognized as having exemplary programs are identified throughout the text.
- **Internet resources.** In relevant locations throughout the book, you will find current lists of Internet sites and Internet references that we can recommend.
- **Suggested readings.** At the conclusion of each chapter are additional sources, both current and classic, to deepen and broaden your understanding of particular topics.
- **Glossary and index.** The text concludes with a glossary of terms, a name index, and a subject index.

COMPANTION WEBSITE

The **Companion Website** contains additional information for students and instructors to use in an on-line environment. For more information on what the Companion Website provides, please see the "Discover the Companion Website Accompanying This Book" section following the preface.

ACKNOWLEDGMENTS

We would never have been able to complete this book had it not been for the valued help of many individuals, including former students in our classes, teachers who have shared their experiences with us, administrators and colleagues who have talked and debated with us, and authors and publishers who have graciously granted permission to reprint materials and who are acknowledged in the book. To each we offer our warmest thanks.

Although we take full responsibility for any errors or omissions in this book, we are deeply grateful to others for their cogent comments and important contributions that led to the development of this book. We thank Karen Bosch, Virginia Wesleyan College; Edward N. Brazee, University of Maine; Toni Briegel, Southwest Missouri State University; Barbara Kacer, Western Kentucky University; and Sheila Wright, Minnesota State University, Mankato.

We express our deepest admiration for and appreciation to the highly competent professionals at Merrill/Prentice Hall with whom we have had a long and rewarding relationship.

We are indeed indebted and grateful to all the people in our lives, now and in the past, who have interacted with us and reinforced what we have known since the days we began our careers as teachers: teaching is the most rewarding profession of all.

Richard D. Kellough
Noreen G. Kellough

Discover the Companion Website Accompanying This Book

THE PRENTICE HALL COMPANION WEBSITE: A VIRTUAL LEARNING ENVIRONMENT

Technology is a constantly growing and changing aspect of our field that is creating a need for content and resources. To address this emerging need, Prentice Hall has developed an online learning environment for students and professors alike—Companion Websites—to support our textbooks.

In creating a Companion Website, our goal is to build on and enhance what the textbook already offers. For this reason, the content for each user-friendly website is organized by topic and provides the professor and student with a variety of meaningful resources. Common features of a Companion Website include:

For the Professor

Every Companion Website integrates **Syllabus Manager™,** an online syllabus creation and management utility.

- **Syllabus Manager™** provides you, the instructor, with an easy, step-by-step process to create and revise syllabi, with direct links into Companion Website and other online content without having to learn HTML.
- Students may logon to your syllabus during any study session. All they need to know is the web address for the Companion Website and the password you've assigned to your syllabus.
- After you have created a syllabus using **Syllabus Manager™,** students may enter the syllabus for their course section from any point in the Companion Website.
- Clicking on a date, the student is shown the list of activities for the assignment. The activities for each assignment are linked directly to actual content, saving time for students.
- Adding assignments consists of clicking on the desired due date, then filling in the details of the assignment—name of the assignment, instruc-

tions, and whether it is a one-time or repeating assignment.
- In addition, links to other activities can be created easily. If the activity is online, a URL can be entered in the space provided, and it will be linked automatically in the final syllabus.
- Your completed syllabus is hosted on our servers, allowing convenient updates from any computer on the Internet. Changes you make to your syllabus are immediately available to your students at their next logon.

For the Student

- **Topic Overviews**—outline key concepts in topic areas.
- **Web Links**—a wide range of websites provide useful and current information related to each topic area.
- **Lesson Plans**—links to lesson plans for appropriate topic areas.
- **Projects on the Web**—links to projects and activities on the Web for appropriate topic areas.
- **Education Resources**—links to schools, online journals, government sites, departments of education, professional organizations, regional information, and more.
- **Electronic Bluebook**—send homework or essays directly to your instructor's email with this paperless form.
- **Message Board**—serves as a virtual bulletin board to post—or respond to—questions or comments to/from a national audience.
- **Chat**—real-time chat with anyone who is using the text anywhere in the country—ideal for discussion and study groups, class projects, etc.

To take advantage of these and other resources, please visit the Companion Website that accompanies *Teaching Young Adolescents: A Guide to Methods and Resources,* Fourth Edition, at

www.prenhall.com/kellough

Brief Contents

Contents

PART III STRATEGIES, AIDS, MEDIA, AND RESOURCES FOR EFFECTIVE INSTRUCTION / 231

Chapter 7 Using Questioning for Teaching and Learning / 233

Chapter 8 Using Grouping and Assignments for Positive Interaction and Quality Learning / 258

NOTE: Every effort has been made to provide accurate and current Internet information in this book. However, the Internet and information posted on it are constantly changing, so it is inevitable that some of the Internet addresses listed in this textbook will change.

Part I

INTRODUCTION TO MIDDLE LEVEL TEACHING AND LEARNING

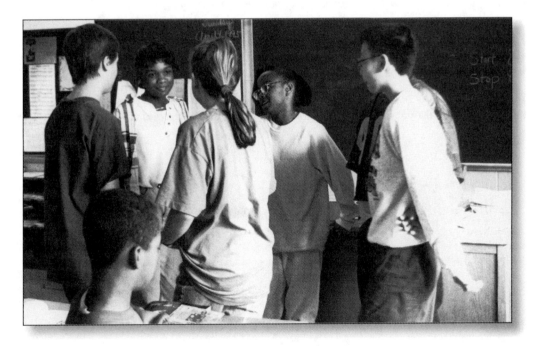

Part I responds to your needs concerning:

▶ Creation of your professional resources file.
▶ Development of a personal instructional strategies repertoire.
▶ Expectations, responsibilities, competencies, and fundamental teaching behaviors of a middle grades classroom teacher.
▶ Guidelines for recognizing and providing for student differences.
▶ Home, school, and community connections.
▶ Teaching for positive character development.
▶ The importance of developing an eclectic teaching style.
▶ The *middle school concept.*

▶ The realities of teaching young adolescents today.
▶ The teacher as a reflective decision maker.

REFLECTIVE THOUGHTS

Wherever and however the students are housed, and regardless of other responsive practices, in the end it is the dedication, commitment, and nature of the understanding of the involved adults—the teachers, administrators, bus drivers, cooks, grounds crew, security staff, custodial staff, and support personnel—that remains the incisive element. That, in our opinion, is the fundamental characteristic of exemplary middle level education—that is, to celebrate and build upon the diverse characteristics and needs of young adolescent students.

During one school year, you will make literally thousands of decisions, many of which can and will affect the lives of students for years to come. You may see this as an awesome responsibility, which it is.

A teacher who, for all students, uses only one style of teaching in the same classroom setting day after day is shortchanging students who learn better another way.

Like intelligences, teaching style is neither absolutely inherited nor fixed. Your teaching style will change, develop, and emerge throughout your career.

The efforts to transform schools into caring and responsive learning environments has as its sole purpose that of helping every student make the transitions necessary to succeed in school and in life.

To become and to remain exemplary, a school must be in a continual mode of inquiry, reflection, and change.

The advantage from using a combination of practices concurrently is usually greater in helping all students succeed in school than is the gain from using any singular practice by itself.

History brims with examples of how relatively few, but positive, moments with a truly caring and knowledgeable teacher can drastically alter for the better the life of a student who until then had a history of mostly negative experiences.

1

Today's Middle Level Schools

Welcome to the exciting and ever-changing world of teaching young adolescents. Whether you are in your early twenties and starting your first career or older and beginning a new career, this book is for you—that is, for any person interested in becoming a classroom teacher of young adolescents. Young adolescents are children who are experiencing the developmental stage of early adolescence, generally who are in the age range of from 9 to 14. Let us begin this journey with the following clarification of terms and purpose.

CLARIFICATION OF TERMS AND PURPOSE

Young adolescents typically are found in schools in what traditionally have been referred to as grades 5 to 8. Those grades today in the United States may be housed in a number of ways. The **elementary school,** for example, sometimes includes students from kindergarten through grade 8, although more often it stops with grade 5 or 6. An **intermediate school** commonly houses children of grades 4–6. **Middle schools** most often house children of grades 6 through 8. There are, as you will learn in this chapter, other arrangements.

Regardless of where or how young adolescents are housed or of the cognomen of the school in which they are housed, this resource guide is about preparing you to teach those children in the classroom. Most often, when referring to grades and schools that house young adolescents, we use the term *middle level.* This is not in any way to be construed that we, the authors of this resource guide, are not supporters of the middle school concept because WE ARE! However, the purpose of this book is to help you in your pursuit of excellence as a teacher of young adolescents, not to explain everything you might want or need to know about the middle school. There are other good sources for that.[1]

If you are now in a program of teacher preparation, then perhaps near the completion of the program you will be offered your first teaching contract. If that happens, you will be excited and eager to sign the contract and begin your new career. Yet after the initial excitement, you will have time to reflect, and many questions will begin to form in your mind. If in a multiple-school district, to which school will I be assigned? Will it be an elementary school, an intermediate school, a junior high school, or a middle school?

Will it be a traditional school or will it be a *magnet school,* that is, a school that specializes in a particular academic area? It might be a *charter school,* an independent public school that is freed from many of the usual rules but accountable for results.[2] Or perhaps a *full-service school* that serves as a hub for quality education and comprehensive social services all under one roof.[3] An *International Baccalaureate Middle School* is one with a curriculum approved by the International Baccalaureate Organization (IBO), a worldwide nonprofit educational foundation based in Switzerland.[4] A *Comer School,* based on James Comer's School Development Program, is designed specifically as a way to improve the educational experiences of underprivileged children.[5] Or perhaps you will be assigned to another type or a combination of these, such as a for-profit charter school or a charter-magnet school. In different ways and with various terminology, the historical practice of providing different routes for students with different needs and different vocational and academic aspirations continues.

Will it be a school that has its start in the fall, as is traditional, or will it be an extended-year (one that extends longer than the usual 180 days) or a year-round school? Which subjects will I be assigned to teach? What specific grade levels will I have? How many different preparations will I have? Will I be a member of a teaching team? Will I have core curriculum teaching responsibilities? What advisory and supervision responsibilities might I have? What will the students be like? What will their parents or guardians be like? How will I get along with the rest of the faculty? What textbooks and curricular materials will I use, and when can I expect to see them? How should I prepare? How can I prepare when there are so many unanswered questions? What school district policies do I need to learn about now? What support services can I expect? How extensive are the school's rules and regulations? Will there be an orientation and an induction program for new and beginning teachers? How can I prepare for students I know nothing about?

Those questions, and many others, are often the concerns of beginning teachers. To guide you through this initial experience and to help answer some of your questions, this chapter offers a first glimpse into today's world of middle level teaching. This chapter and the two that follow in Part I provide a basis for your planning and selecting learning activities presented in subsequent chapters. Enjoy your quest toward becoming the best teacher you can be.

OBJECTIVES

Upon completion of this chapter, you should be able to

1. Define middle school.
2. Describe essential characteristics that characterize a middle level school as being exemplary.

---

[1]See, for example, J. Wiles and J. Bondi, *The New American Middle School,* 3rd ed. (Upper Saddle River, NJ: Merrill/Prentice Hall, 2001) and P. George; G. Lawrence; and D. Bushnell, *Handbook for Middle School Teaching,* 2nd ed. (New York: Addison Wesley Longman, 1998).

[2]B. V. Manno, et al., "Beyond the Schoolhouse Door," *Phi Delta Kappan* 81(10):736–744 (June 2000), p. 737. Connect to the charter school home pages via the United States Charter School Website at http://www.uscharterschools.org/. For additional information and for a copy of the *National Charter School Directory,* contact the Center for Education Reform (CER) at 800-521-2118; see the Website at http://edreform.com/research/css9697.htm.

[3]See, for example, H. Raham, "Full-Service Schools," *School Business Affairs* 64(6):24–28 (June 1998); J. G. Dryfoos, "Full Service Schools: Revolution or Fad?" *Journal of Research on Adolescence* 5(2):147–172 (1995); and, A. W. Jackson and G. A. Davis, *Turning Points 2000: Educating Adolescents in the 21st Century* (New York: A Report of Carnegie Corporation of New York, Teachers College Press, 2000), pp. 215–217.

[4]In addition to a Diploma Program for students in the final two years of high school, IBO offers a Primary Years Program (for children ages 3 to 12) and a Middle Years Program (for students ages 11 to 16). See IBO's site on the Internet at http://www.ibo.org. See also M. Tolan, "Global Horizons: International Baccalaureate Program Helps Students See Beyond Their Boundaries," *Middle Ground* 4(5):26–30 (April 2001).

[5]See, for example, W. Malloy and J. Rayle, "Using the Comer Process to Create a Successful Middle School," *Middle School Journal* 31(5):12–18 (May 2000).

3. Describe the middle school concept, how it came to be, and its contributions to public K–12 education.
4. Describe similarities and differences between the exemplary middle school and the traditional junior high school.
5. Describe the purposes and characteristics of the school-within-a-school (SWAS) concept.
6. Demonstrate understanding of the term developmentally appropriate.
7. Describe current trends, problems, and issues in middle level education.

THE MIDDLE SCHOOL

When you receive your state teaching credential, you may or may not be certified to teach at the middle school level. In some states an elementary school credential certifies a person to teach in any grade, kindergarten through grade 8. In some states a secondary school credential certifies a person to teach a particular subject at any grade level, kindergarten through grade 12. In other states such a credential qualifies a person to teach only grades 7 through 12. At least 33 states provide a middle school teaching credential to candidates who have successfully completed a program specifically designed to prepare teachers for that level.

As a starting point, you should note that there are two sometimes quite different types of schools, both of which may be called middle schools. One is the traditional junior high school with perhaps a few minor changes, such as changing its name to middle school. The second is the exemplary middle school, which is, as shown in Table 1.1, quite different from the traditional junior high school. To understand the significance of what has become known as the **middle school concept,** certain background information may prove helpful.

The Middle School Concept and Philosophy

Used historically from about 1880, the term junior high school most commonly refers to schools having grades 7 and 8 or grades 7, 8, and 9, in which a program is designed to approximate the type of education commonly found in traditional high schools. Thus, a junior high school might be considered a "not-quite-yet-but-trying-to-be" high school. Students graduating from a junior high school often would then move on to a senior high school.

The term middle school gained favor as a result of the movement away from the concept of "junior" high school. Reasons for the reorganization away from the concept of junior high school and the adoption of a middle school education include (a) to provide a program specifically designed for young adolescents, (b) to set up a more effective transition between the elementary school and the high school, and (c) to move ninth graders to the high school or, as has happened in some school districts in recent years, to a location designed

Table 1.1   Summary of Differences between Middle Schools and Traditional Junior High Schools

Characteristic	*Junior High School*	*Middle School*
Most common grade-span organization	7–8 or 7–9	6–8
Scheduling	Traditional 50-minute periods, six-period day	Flexible, usually block
Subject organization	Departmentalized	Integrated and thematic; interdisciplinary, usually language arts, math, science, and social studies
Guidance/counseling	Separate sessions with counselor on individual or "as needed" basis; full-time counselors	Advisor-advisee relationship between teacher and student in homeroom or home base
Exploratory curriculum	Electives by individual choice	Common "wheel" of experiences for all students
Teachers	Subject-centered; grades 7–12 certification	Interdisciplinary teams; student-centered; grades K–8 or 6–8 certification
Instruction	Traditional; lecture, skills, and repetition	Thematic units; discovery techniques; study skills
Athletics	Interscholastic sports emphasizing competition	Intramural programs emphasizing participation

solely for ninth-graders, known as a ninth-grade center or academy.[6,7]

Although any combination of grades 5 through 9 may be included in a middle school, the most common configuration is grades 6 through 8. Including sixth graders and excluding ninth graders is a reflection of the recommendation of the National Middle School Association in its official position paper, *This We Believe*.[8]

The term **middle level education** identifies school organizations that are based on a philosophy that incorporates curricula and instructional practices specifically designed to meet the developmental needs of young adolescent students, that is, of students "between the ages of 10 and 15."[9] This philosophy is referred to as the middle school concept. The notion that greater and more specific attention should be given to the special needs of young adolescents became known as the **middle school movement**. Basic to the movement is the continued belief that middle level school teachers need specialized training to work most effectively with young adolescents.[10]

The middle school movement began to grow in the 1960s, especially with the publication of W. M. Alexander's, "The Junior High: A Changing View," in *Readings in Curriculum*, edited by G. Hass and K. Wiles (Boston: Allyn and Bacon, 1965), D. H. Eichhorn's *The Middle School* (New York: The Center for Applied Research in Education, 1966), and W. M. Alexander's, ed., *The Emergent Middle School* (New York: Holt, Rinehart and Winston, 1969).

Since the emergence of the middle school concept in the 1960s, the needs of young adolescents have been studied, researched, and analyzed in greater detail and sophistication than ever before. Over the years, youngsters of middle school age have been designated by various nomenclatures, including transescent, preadolescent,

preteen, prepubescent, in-betweenager, and tweenager, defined as the stage of development that begins before the onset of puberty and extends through the early stages of adolescence. Although the term used is perhaps inconsequential, some understanding of the various developmental stages associated with this group of youngsters is essential if an educational program and its instruction are to be appropriately tailored to address their needs. That understanding is the focus of Chapter 2.

In recent years, some school districts, especially large inner city school districts, have equated low achievement test scores with the middle school concept. As a result, they have looked for ways to improve the academic achievement of their young adolescent students, such as closing their middle schools and returning to the neighborhood K-8 elementary school concept. Their reasoning includes (a) teachers get to know children better and can more effectively share important information about the children and about the curriculum when children are at the same school for eight or nine years rather than just three or four, (b) children in a K–8 school can be continuously assessed and will therefore progress more smoothly and successfully through the curriculum than when there is a break due to their changing schools, (c) more effective modeling behaviors occur as the young adolescents realize their responsibility that results from the younger children adulating them, and (d) the stress of early adolescence is less magnified than when only young adolescents are together in a school.

Two things remain clear to us: regardless of organizational patterns, to become and to remain an exemplary school, there must be a continual mode of inquiry, reflection, and change; and the advantage from using a combination of practices concurrently is usually greater in helping all students succeed in school than is the gain from using any singular practice by itself. The bottom line? Schools must constantly change; there is no single shoe that best fits all children in all neighborhoods.

So, what does all this mean to you, the teacher soon to be? Let's first take a look at middle level school organization, especially the aspects of that organization that are important to you as a beginning teacher.

MIDDLE LEVEL ORGANIZATION

The rapid and dramatic changes occurring throughout modern society, as well as what has been learned in recent years about intelligence and learning, are reflected in the equally rapid and dramatic changes occurring in today's schools. The school in which you soon will be teaching may bear little resemblance to the school that you attended—in its curriculum, its student body, its methods of instruction, or its physical appearance. From the moment you set foot onto a school campus for this teacher-preparation program until later, when you

---

[6]K. Brooks and F. Edwards, *The Middle School in Transition: A Research Report on the Status of the Middle School Movement* (Lexington: College of Education, University of Kentucky, 1978).

[7]See, for example, the story of Oregon City High School, a ninth-grade-only school since 1990, in C. Paglin and J. Fager, *Grade Configuration: Who Goes Where?* (Portland, OR: Northwest Regional Educational Laboratory, 1997), pp. 29–31; the West Orange High School (Orlando, FL) Ninth Grade Center, opened in 1993, the Scott County Schools (Georgetown, KY) Ninth Grade Center, opened in 1996, on the Internet at http://www.scott.k12.ky.us; and the ninth grade academy at James F. Rhodes High School (Cleveland, OH) and at Hartford Public High School (Hartford, CT) both opened in 1999.

[8]National Middle School Association, *This We Believe* (Columbus, OH: Author, 1982, reissued in 1995).

[9]*This We Believe*, 1995, p. 5.

[10]See, for example, Chapter 5 ("Expert Teachers for Middle Grades Schools: Pre-service Preparation and Professional Development," pp. 94–120) of A. W. Jackson and G. A. Davis, *Turning Points 2000*.

obtain your first paid teaching job, you will want to keep your sensory input channels wide open to learn as much as you can about the school, its organization, its students, and its support staff. Although it is perhaps only the beginning to your learning about teaching, this resource guide offers information and resources that you will want to refer to time and again, long after the initial course for which it is used is over.

Orientation Meetings: Start of the School Year

As a beginning teacher, you will likely be expected to participate in orientation meetings designed to help you get off to a good beginning. When not in meetings, you will have time to prepare your assigned classroom(s) for instruction.

Some school districts start the school year with a district-wide orientation, whereas others schedule on-site orientations at each school. Many school districts do both, with perhaps a district-wide morning meeting followed by school on-site meetings in the afternoon. Such meetings provide you with the opportunity to meet other teachers and establish new collegial friendships and professional relationships. Many school districts sponsor beginning-teacher induction programs that provide special assistance to new teachers (discussed in the final chapter of this resource guide). Of course, the scheduling and planning of orientation meetings will vary, district by district and school by school. The objectives for all orientation meetings, however, should be similar to those described in the following paragraphs.

You should become familiar with the district's (or school's) written statement of its unique beliefs and goals—its *statement of mission* (or philosophy or vision)—and what that statement means to the people affiliated with the district or school. [*Note:* Although the terms mission statement, philosophy statement, and vision statement are often used interchangeably, and while in our opinion the first two are synonymous, the vision statement is or should be a statement of intention that goes beyond the immediate mission of the school and gives future direction to the school's stated mission.] See sample missions statements in Figure 1.1.

You will be encouraged to become familiar with the policies of the school and district. Numerous policies often cover a wide range of circumstances. There are policies for procedures relating to students who are injured at school; for what to do during natural disasters, such as earthquakes, flood, and severe storms; regarding students who need to take prescribed medications; for finding illegal drugs and weapons; for parking on campus; for leaving campus during the school day; for classroom conduct; for school programs, field trips, and parties in the classroom; for mandatory testing and grading practices; for completing absentee and tardy forms; for

sending students to the office; and for chaperoning and sponsoring student activities. And these examples are just the beginning.

You will learn about the myriad forms that teachers must fill out. There are forms for injuries that occur while at school, for textbook loans, for key loans, for attendance, for student academic deficiencies, for working with students with special needs, for sponsoring student activities, for field trips, and for referrals of students for inappropriate behavior, to name just a few.

You will learn about the approved curriculum that defines what teachers are mandated to teach and what students are expected to learn. This means that you must familiarize yourself with the curriculum frameworks and learning benchmarks, courses of study, curriculum guides, resource units, teacher's manuals, student textbooks, media programs, and supplementary materials—all of which should reflect the school's mission statement and approved curriculum. You will learn about the school or district plan for monitoring, assessing, and supervising implementation of the curriculum; and about available resource materials and equipment, as well as procedures for reserving and using them on certain dates.

You will learn about the school library/media resource center, and its personnel and procedures, and you will meet district and school personnel and become familiar with the many services that support you in the classroom. You will meet campus security personnel, resource officers, and other ancillary personnel and learn about their functions and locations.

As a student in a program for teacher preparation, you may be expected to participate in an orientation meeting at your college or university. The meeting may be held at the beginning of the program or just before the beginning of your field experiences, or both times. Perhaps this meeting will be a function of one of your college or university courses. You will receive your school assignment, including the name of the school and the school district, the school's location, the date when you should report to that assignment, the name of your cooperating teacher(s), the grade level(s), the subject(s), and perhaps the name of your college or university supervisor. You will probably be encouraged to follow many of the objectives just discussed as well as to meet other teacher candidates.

When you arrive at your assigned school and after introductions have been made, you should begin to become familiar with the school campus and the way that the school is organized. Walk around the campus, perhaps with a copy of the school map, and learn the location of your classroom(s). Also locate the nearest rest rooms for girls, for boys, and for faculty men or women. You may be loaned one or several keys—one for the classroom, one for the faculty rest room, and perhaps

Figure 1.1   Sample middle school mission statements. (Reprinted by permission).

- The **Aspen Middle School** (Aspen, CO) is dedicated to creating an experiential environment where all individuals can succeed and take risks in developing the mind, body, and spirit. We strive to develop a caring school community that is safe, supportive, and flexible to encourage the individual growth of its members with respect for others. This environment will encourage individuals to take responsibility and ownership of their own lives while developing an enthusiasm for life-long learning and an appreciation for democratic values.
- The mission of **Dawson County Middle School** (Dawsonville, GA) is to provide a safe school where individuals are given encouragement, support, and respect and are provided opportunities and resources to develop knowledge and skills necessary for the future.
- The mission of **Elliott Grant Middle School** (Corpus Christi, TX) is to evoke and nurture a community of learners by creating opportunities that: develop the mind, heart, and spirit of every student; develop skills for gathering, analyzing, and communicating information in a way that is constructive and for the good of humankind; promote perseverance; and embody service to others.
- The faculty and staff of **Litchfield Middle School** (Akron, OH) believe that it is our mission to create an atmosphere which encourages all students to develop the desire, the knowledge, and the technological skills necessary for lifelong learning. In order to achieve this, we will strive for a positive environment which includes (a) involved parents and community, (b) capable, enthusiastic staff, (c) abundant and relevant instructional resources, (d) collaborative planning, (e) high expectations for all students, (f) measurement of student progress, and (g) recognition and reward of achievement. It is our belief that the multicultural educational experiences of our students will prepare them for productive futures.
- The **Lux Middle School** (Lincoln, NE) community appreciates and welcomes the uniqueness of middle level students, promotes academic, creative and interpersonal success for all students, encourages responsibility, affirms diversity and pursues lifelong learning.
- At **Plainview Middle School** (Ardmore, OK) we believe it is our mission to empower all students to become responsible, productive citizens in an everchanging global society.
- **Timothy Edwards Middle School** (South Windsor, CT) is a place where children are inspired to grow and learn in an atmosphere of respect, love, and caring. We believe that our charge as educators is (a) to offer intellectual challenge in order to promote academic development, (b) to address the needs of each student as an individual, (c) to foster in each child a sense of belonging and appreciation for self and others, and (d) to help students to become contributing citizens of the world. We . . . are committed to these goals—the keys to a healthy, interesting, and prosperous environment where a child's positive self-concept is cultivated through academic, physical, and social/emotional growth.

one for a faculty workroom. Become familiar with areas such as the teacher's workroom, the faculty room, and the faculty lunch room, which may or may not be a single area. A large school may have several faculty rooms scattered around the campus.

Thoroughly investigate this campus environment. Where do students eat their lunches? Is there a multipurpose room—a room used for lunch as well as for educational purposes? Is there a school nurse? Where is the nurse's room? When is the nurse available? Where is the nearest first aid and emergency equipment? How do you notify maintenance personnel quickly and efficiently? Where are the written procedures for fire drills and other emergencies? Where is information about the school's emergency warning system? Is there a plan posted in a conspicuous place for all to see? Where are the various administrative offices? Where are the counseling and guidance offices? Is there an office of student activities? Where are the library, the media center, the resources room, the gymnasium, and the auditorium? Where are textbooks stored, and how are they used by

students? Are they to be checked out and distributed? If so, how? Where is the attendance office? Are there resource specialists and, if there are, what are their functions and where are their offices located? If a K–8 school, where are the separate playground areas for the middle grades children?

At an orientation session, you may meet the grade level or department chairperson or the team leader and members of that team. How can you discover where those persons are to be found at various times during the school day? Where are teaching materials and laboratory supplies kept, and how do you obtain them? Have you located your faculty mailbox and the place to check in or out when you arrive at school or leave at the end of the day? What procedures do you follow if you are absent because of illness or if you know you are going to arrive late? Do you have the necessary phone numbers? Not least in importance, if you drive a vehicle to school, where do you park? Otherwise, what is the best local transportation available for getting to and from school each day?

After becoming familiar with the school campus and obtaining answers to some of your more urgent questions, you will want to focus your attention on the various school schedules and particularly your own teaching schedule.

The School Calendar Year

School years vary from state to state, from district to district, and from school to school. Most school years begin in mid- to late-August or early-September and continue through late-May or mid-June. However, to accommodate more students without a significant increase in capital costs and to better sustain student learning, an increasing number of schools are eliminating the traditional long summer break by switching to year-round education (YRE), which, by the way, has been around for more than half a century.[11] Nevertheless, whether the school follows a year-round schedule or not, for teachers and students in the United States the school year still approximates 180 days.

In a school with year-round operation, a teacher might teach for three-quarters of the year and be off for one-quarter or teach in a 45/15 program, which means nine weeks of school (45 days) "on track" followed by three weeks of school (15 days) "off track" throughout the year. In a 45/15 arrangement, teachers and students are on tracks, referred to as A Track, B Track, and so on, with starting and ending times that vary depending on the track and time of year. At any given time, at least one track is on vacation. Intersession programs may be held during off-track time, at which time students might participate in classes designed for remediation, exploration, or enrichment.

Beginning about 8:00 A.M., the school day lasts until about 3:00 or 4:00 P.M. During hot summer months, some schools begin earlier, say at 7:15, and end around 2:00. District and state laws vary, but generally teachers are expected to be in the classroom no less than 15 minutes prior to the start of school and to remain in their classrooms no less than 15 minutes after final dismissal of students.

Drawing upon studies of adolescent sleep patterns as well as the need to find ways to deal with crowded schools or to cut transportation expenses by reducing the number of buses and drivers needed, some schools are experimenting with later than usual starting times or, because no single schedule can accommodate the desires and needs of everyone, with multiple starting times.[12]

Teaching Teams

Traditionally, elementary school teachers taught their groups of children in self-contained classrooms for most of the school day, and junior high and senior high school teachers taught their subject disciplines as often as seven or eight times each day to as many groups of students. At all levels, teachers taught in their assigned classrooms, fairly isolated from other teachers and school activities—not unlike the parallel play of preschool children, that is, playing side-by-side but not really together. In some schools, that is still the case. Increasingly, however, teachers are members of a collaborative **teaching team** in which several teachers work together to reflect, plan, and implement a curriculum for a common cohort of students. [*Note:* A distinction must be made between teaching teams and team teaching; **team teaching** refers to two or more teachers simultaneously providing instruction to students in the same classroom. Members of a teaching team may participate in team teaching.]

The teaching team may comprise only a few teachers, for example, all seventh-grade teachers or all the teachers who teach the same cohort of sixth-grade students. They may meet periodically to plan a curriculum and learning activities around a common theme. Sometimes teaching teams comprise one teacher each from English/reading/language arts (known also as literacy), history/social studies/geography, mathematics, and science. These four areas are known as the **core curriculum.** In addition to teachers of the core subjects, specialty-area teachers may be part of the team, including teachers of physical education, the visual and performing arts, and even special education teachers and at-risk specialty personnel or school counselors. As a visiting or continuing member of this interdisciplinary team organization (ITO), a team may invite a community-resource person (see, for example, the School Vignette later in the chapter. Because the core and specialty subjects cross different disciplines of study, these teams are commonly called interdisciplinary teaching teams or simply **interdisciplinary teams.**

The School-within-a-School

An interdisciplinary teaching team and its common cohort of students is referred to as the **school-within-a-school** (also called village, pod, academy, family, house, or sometimes just team), or SWAS concept, where each team of teachers is assigned each day to the same cohort of students for a common block of time. Within this block of time, teachers on the team are responsible for many professional decisions, such as how school can be made developmentally responsive, that is, most meaningful, to students' lives; what specific responsibilities each teacher has each day; what guidance activities need to be implemented; which students need special attention; and how

---

[11]K. Rasmussen, "Year-Round Education," *Education Update* 42(2):1, 4–5 (March 2000).

[12]See, for example, M. Lawton, "For Whom the School Bell Tolls," *School Administrator* 56(3):6–12 (March 1999).

students will be grouped for instruction. Members of such a team become "students of their students" and thereby build the curriculum and instruction around their students' interests, perspectives, and perceptions. Because they "turn on" learning, the school and its classrooms become exciting places to be and to learn. In contrast, "symptoms of turned-off learning include students' seeming inability to grasp concepts, to exert effort, or to display enthusiasm; repeated lateness or absence; boredom; and work that is sloppy or of poor quality."[13]

The SWAS concept helps students make important and meaningful connections among disciplines. It also provides them with both peer and adult group identification, which provides an important sense of belonging. In some schools, using an arrangement called **looping** (also referred to as banding, multiyear grouping, multiyear instruction, multiyear placement, and teacher-student progression), the cohort of students and teachers remain together as a group for several or for all the years a student is at that school.[14] Spending more than the usual one school year with a group of children allows their teacher or the teaching team to acquire greater knowledge of the students' personalities, learning styles and capacities, and needs. Students in looping classes scored substantially higher on standardized tests of reading and mathematics than did students in regular classes, even when both groups were taught by the same teacher.[15]

The advantages to being a member of a teaching team in a school-within-a-school learning environment are numerous. For example, the combined thinking of several teachers creates an expanded pool of ideas, enhances individual capacities for handling complex problems, and provides intellectual stimulation and emotional support. The combination of talents produces an energy that has a positive impact on the instructional program. A beginning teacher who joins a team has the benefit of support from more experienced teammates. When a team member is absent, other members of the team work closely with the substitute, resulting in less loss of instructional time for students. More and better planning for students occurs as teachers discuss, argue, and reach agreement on behavioral expectations, curriculum emphasis, instructional approaches, and materials.

COMMON PLANNING TIME

For a teaching team to plan effectively and efficiently, members must meet together frequently. This is best accomplished when they share a common planning time, preferably a minimum of four hours a week.[16] This means that in addition to each member's daily preparation time (discussed in the next section), members of a team share a common planning time to plan curriculum and to discuss the progress and needs of individual students within the cohort.

Each team assigns a member to be team facilitator, or **lead teacher.** The lead teacher organizes the meetings and facilitates discussions during the common planning time. Usually, this teacher also acts as a liaison with the administration to assure that the team has the necessary resources to put its plans into action. A team's lead teacher (or another member designated by the team) may also serve on the school *leadership team,* a group of teachers, administrators, and sometimes students designated by the principal or elected by the faculty (and student body) to assist in the leadership of the school.

Nontraditional Scheduling

For some middle level teachers, the school day consists of the traditional seven or eight periods, each period lasting about 50 minutes. This traditional schedule includes teaching three or four classes before lunch and three or four following lunch. One of these periods is a preparation period, referred to sometimes as the conference or planning period. Most teachers are quite busy during their preparation periods, reading and grading student papers, preparing classrooms and materials, meeting in conferences, or preparing instructional tools.

To maximize the learning time, to allow for more instructional flexibility, and to accommodate common planning time for teachers, many schools use some form of **block scheduling.**[17] Block scheduling means that for at least part of the school day or part of the week, blocks of time ranging from 70 to 140 or more minutes replace the traditional structure of 50-minute-long classes. The possible variations are nearly limitless.[18]

---

[13] The phrases "students of their students" and "turn on learning" are borrowed from C. A. Grant and C. E. Sleeter, *Turning on Learning* (Upper Saddle River, NJ: Prentice Hall, 1989), p. 2.

[14] See, for example, A. W. Jackson and G. A. Davis, *Turning Points 2000,* pp. 133–134, and A. Pyle, "In the Loop," *Middle Ground* 1(1):15 (August 1997).

[15] J. Gaustad, *Implementing Looping,* ERIC Digest 123 (Eugene, OR: ED429330, ERIC Clearinghouse on Educational Management, 1998).

---

[16] See, for example, A. C. Howe and J. Bell, "Factors Associated with Successful Implementation of Interdisciplinary Curriculum Units," *Research in Middle Level Education Quarterly* 21(2):39–52 (Winter 1998), and N. Flowers, et al., "How Teaming Influences Classroom Practices," *Middle School Journal* 32(2):52–59 (November 2000).

[17] See, for example, W. J. Ullrich and J. T. Yeamen, "Using a Modified Block Schedule to Create a Positive Learning Environment," *Middle School Journal* 31(1):14–20 (September 1999).

[18] See, for example, W. J. DiBiase and J. A. Queen, "Middle School Social Studies on the Block," *Clearing House* 72(6):377–384 (July 1999).

For example, the school year for some schools consists of three 12-week long trimesters with each school day divided into five 70-minute-long class periods. Such a schedule is referred to as a 5×7 block plan. Some schools use a 4×4 block plan, whereby students take four 85 to 90-minute-long macroperiods (or macroclasses) every day of each semester.[19] Other schools use an alternating-day block plan, sometimes called the A–B plan, where classes meet every other day for the entire school year for 90-minute blocks.

Using extended periods, or macroperiods, allows the teacher to supervise and assist students with assignments; project work; and reading, writing, thinking, and study skills. Macroperiods provide more time for student inquiry, project work, and interactive and interdisciplinary thematic instruction that might otherwise be difficult or impossible to accomplish in shorter class periods.

BLOCK SCHEDULING: ADVANTAGES AND DISADVANTAGES

Research of schools using block scheduling, where students and teachers work together in longer but fewer classes at a time, consistently report greater satisfaction among teachers and administrators and improvement in both the behavior and the learning of all students.[20] Students do more writing, pursue issues in greater depth, enjoy classes more, feel more challenged, and gain deeper understandings. In addition, teachers get to know the students better and are therefore able to respond to a student's needs with greater care. In studies of schools using block scheduling, as opposed to traditional scheduling, researchers report equal or better mastery and retention of material, and a significant reduction in suspension and dropout rates.[21]

Other reported benefits of the block plans over a traditional seven- or eight-period daily schedule include the following: in one school year the total hours of instruction is significantly greater; each teacher teaches fewer courses during a semester and is responsible for fewer students; therefore, student-teacher interaction is more productive and the school climate is positive with fewer discipline problems; and, because planning periods are longer, teachers have more time to plan and to interact with parents and guardians.

Block scheduling arrangements often produce serendipitous benefits. For example, students may not have to carry as many books and may go to their lockers

fewer times a day to exchange textbooks and materials between blocks. In many middle level schools, except perhaps in physical education and shop classes, student lockers are not used at all. Also, the reduction of bells ringing from as many as eight times a day to only two or three times a day or not at all creates less disturbance.

Because students are not roaming halls for 3 to 5 minutes five or six times a day, teachers can more easily supervise unstructured time. This allows better control over portions of the unplanned and subtle message systems within schools that are referred to as the **hidden curriculum.** The messages of the hidden curriculum are the school climate, the feelings that are projected from the teacher and other adults to students and from the students to one another. These are evident not only in classrooms but before and after school; at social events, school programs, and club meetings; in the halls, rest rooms, and lunch areas; and other places on the school campus that are not monitored as closely as are the classrooms.

Nontraditional school schedules are not without their problems, which may include the following: there may be a mismatch between content actually covered and that expected by state-mandated tests and the dates those tests are given to students; content coverage in a course may be less than that which was traditionally covered (certainly neither of which is an unimportant issue in this day of high stakes exterior-developed academic achievement testing); teachers may be unhappy, especially teachers of mathematics if classes meet less frequently than in the traditional once a day, five days a week schedule; and, when the instructional strategy is developmentally inappropriate (such as when a teacher uses a lecture for the entire length of a macroperiod), students are likely to become bored, restless, and mischievous.

By using a modified block schedule, some schools have successfully combined schedules, thus satisfying teachers who prefer block scheduling and those who prefer a traditional schedule. A modified block schedule can provide both traditional 40-minute periods (sometimes called split-block periods) that meet daily and longer blocks. A modified block schedule centers on seven or eight 40- or 45-minute periods per day along with alternate longer blocks. In a modified block schedule all students might start the day with a 30- or 40-minute long first period, which serves as a homebase (known also as homeroom or advisor/advisee) time. From there, some students continue the morning attending traditional-length periods while others move into a morning block class. Throughout the day, teachers and students may pass from block classes to those of traditional length or vice versa.

Some schools use a flexible block schedule. The daily schedule is a seven-period day with all seven classes meeting on Monday. Periods one through four meet for 75 minutes, while periods five through seven meet for

[19]See, for example, R. B. Cobb; S. Abate; and D. Baker, "Effects on Students of a 4×4 Junior High School Block Scheduling Program," *Education Policy Analysis Archives* v7 n3 (1999).

[20]See, for example, S. Black, "Learning on the Block." *American School Board Journal* 185(1):32–34 (January 1998).

[21]See, for example, T. L. Shortt and Y. V. Thayer, "Block Scheduling Can Enhance School Climate," *Educational Leadership* 56(4):76–81 (December 1998/January 1999).

30 minutes. Periods one through four meet for 105 minutes each on Tuesdays and Thursdays, and periods five through seven meet for 120 minutes each on Wednesdays and Fridays. A 30-minute homebase period is held at the same time each day, perhaps the first thing in the morning or immediately after lunch.

There is little doubt that longer blocks of instructional time with young adolescents is a positive factor contributing to students' meaningful learning, especially when combined with some form of year-round education, curriculum integration and interdisciplinary thematic instruction (discussed in Chapter 5), and the use of project-based learning (discussed in Chapter 8).

QUALITY EDUCATION FOR EVERY STUDENT

Nontraditional scheduling is one part of the effort to organize schools in a way that will deliver quality education for all students. The curriculum of a quality education school is seen by students as having meaning and usefulness in their lives and is delivered by activity-oriented instruction. Rather than dictating procedures, ordering students to work, and berating them when they do not, in a quality school the teachers provide a stimulating learning environment and are seen by the children as being encouraging and helpful.

Sometimes it may appear that more energy is devoted to organizational change (how and where the curriculum is delivered) than to school curriculum (what is taught). However, the two are inseparable, as will be discussed in Chapter 5. School organization has a direct effect on what students learn; if it did not, educators would not be spending so much valuable time trying to organize their schools to effect the most productive (and cost-effective) delivery of the curriculum.

Organizational changes are often referred to as school restructuring, a term that has a variety of connotations, including site-based management, collaborative decision making, school choice, personalized learning, integrated curricula, and collegial staffing. School restructuring has been defined as "activities that change fundamental assumptions, practices, and relationships, both within the organization and between the organization and the outside world, in ways leading to improved learning outcomes."[22] No matter how it is defined, educators agree on the following point: the design and functions of schools should reflect the needs of students of the twenty-first century rather than a nineteenth-century factory model.

Exemplified by efforts mentioned in the preceding discussions, the movement to year-round operation and the redesigning of schools into smaller cohorts or "houses" represents a movement that is becoming increasingly common across the country. With this redesign, the intention is that schools will better address the needs and capabilities of each unique student. To that end, a number of specific trends have developed, which are discussed later in this chapter. As a teacher in the twenty-first century, you will undoubtedly help accomplish many of those changes.

School Restructuring and Students at Risk

Although the focus in Chapter 2 is on specifics about working with particular groups of young adolescent learners, it is appropriate now to say a few words about school restructuring efforts and at-risk students. **At risk** is the term used by educators when referring to students who have a high probability of dropping out of formal education before graduating high school. Established in 1994 by the U.S. Department of Education, the National Institute on the Education of At-Risk Students defines "at-risk student" as one who "because of limited English proficiency, poverty, race, geographic location, or economic disadvantage, faces a greater risk of low educational achievement or reduced academic expectation."[23] Many students, at any one time, have risk factors from more than one of these categories.

It has been estimated that by the year 2020 the majority of students in the public schools in the United States will be at risk.[24] A nontraditional school schedule alone, without quality, personalized attention to each student, may be of no value in addressing the needs of children who are at risk of not finishing school. As emphasized in *Turning Points* and again in *Turning Points 2000*, "middle grades schools are potentially society's most powerful force to recapture millions of youth adrift."[25] (See discussions about working with at-risk students in Chapter 2, "There Are Success Stories" in Chapter 4, and "Strategies for Personalizing the Instruction" in Chapter 8.)

Today's movement to transform all schools, not just middle level schools, into caring and responsive learning environments has as its sole purpose that of helping all students, perhaps especially those at risk, to make the transitions necessary to succeed in school and in life.

Responsive Practices for Helping Every Student Succeed

The reorganization of schools and the restructuring of school schedules represent only two of the efforts to help all students to make successful transitions.

---

[22] D. T. Conley, "Restructuring In Search of a Definition," *Principal* 72(3):12 (January 1993).

[23] See http://www.ed.gov/offices/OERI/At-Risk/.

[24] R. J. Rossi and S. C. Stringfield, "What We Must Do for Students Placed at Risk," *Phi Delta Kappan* 77(1):73–76 (September 1995).

[25] *Turning Points 2000*, p. 229.

Other important responsive practices (including attitudes) are (a) a perception, shared by all teachers and staff, that all students can learn when they are given adequate support, although not all students need the same amount of time to learn the same thing; (b) high, although not necessarily identical, expectations for all students; (c) personal attention, adult advocacy, and scheduling and learning plans to help students learn in a manner by which they best learn—research clearly points out that achievement increases, students learn more, and students enjoy learning and remember more of what they have learned when individual learning styles and capacities are identified and accommodated—learning style traits are known that significantly discriminate between students who are at risk of dropping out of school and students who perform well, discussed in "Learning Modalities" and "Learning Styles" in Chapter 2; (d) engagement of parents and guardians as partners in their child's education; (e) extra time and guided attention to basic skills—especially those of literacy, thinking, and social—rather than on rote memory; (f) specialist teachers and smaller classes; (g) peer tutoring and cross-age coaching; and (h) attention and guidance in the development of coping skills.

THE FUNDAMENTAL CHARACTERISTIC OF EXEMPLARY MIDDLE LEVEL EDUCATION

Wherever and however the students are housed, and regardless of other responsive practices, in the end it is the dedication, commitment, and nature of the understanding of the involved adults—the teachers, administrators, bus drivers, cooks, grounds crew, security staff, custodial staff, and support personnel—that remains the incisive element. That, in our opinion, is the fundamental characteristic of exemplary middle level education—that is, to celebrate and build upon the diverse characteristics and needs of young adolescents. In fact, that is the title of the next chapter of this edition of our resource guide.

Committed Teachers

Middle level teachers represent myriad individual personalities that are perhaps impossible to capture in generalizations. Let us imagine that a teaching colleague mentions that Pat Washington, in Room 17, is a "fantastic teacher," "one of the best teachers in the district," "super," and "magnificent." What might be some of the characteristics you would expect to see in Pat's teaching behaviors? (A more detailed presentation of teacher responsibilities and behaviors is the topic of Chapter 3.)

Perhaps foremost is that Pat constructs positive, accepting, respectful, and trusting relationships with students and their families. Additionally, we can expect Pat to (a) be knowledgeable about the developmental char-

acteristics of the young adolescent; (b) be understanding of and committed to the school's statement of philosophy or mission; (c) know the curriculum and how best to teach it; (d) be enthusiastic, motivated, and well organized; (e) show effective communication and interpersonal skills; (f) be willing to listen to the students and to risk trying their ideas; and (g) to be a reflective and responsible decision maker.

Young adolescents need teachers who are well organized and who know how to establish and manage an active and supportive learning environment (the topic of Chapter 4), even with its multiple instructional demands. Young adolescents respond best to teachers who provide leadership and who enjoy their function as role models, advisors, mentors, and reflective decision makers.

Reflective Decision Making

During any school day, as a classroom teacher you will make hundreds of nontrivial decisions, many of them instantaneously. In addition, you will have already made many decisions in preparation for the teaching day. During one school year a teacher makes literally thousands of decisions, many of which can and will affect the lives of her or his students for years to come. This may seem to be an awesome responsibility; indeed it is.

Initially, of course, you will make errors in judgment, but you will also learn that your students are fairly resilient and that there are experts available who can guide you to help ensure that the students are not harmed severely by your mistakes. You can and should learn from your errors. Keep in mind that the sheer number of decisions you make each day will mean that not all will be the best decisions that could have been made had you had more time and better resources for planning.

GOOD TEACHING IS AS MUCH AN ART AS IT IS A SCIENCE

Although pedagogy is based on scientific principles, good classroom teaching is as much an art as it is a science. Few rules apply to every teaching situation. In fact, decisions about the selection of content, instructional objectives and materials, teaching strategies, a teacher's response to student misbehavior, and the selection of techniques for assessment of the learning experiences are all the result of subjective judgments. Although many decisions are made at a somewhat unhurried pace when you are planning for your instruction, many others will be made intuitively and immediately. Once the school day has begun, there is rarely time for making carefully thought-out judgments. At your best, you base your decisions on your teaching style, which, in turn, is based on your knowledge of school policies, pedagogical research, the curriculum, and the unique characteristics of the young adolescents in your classroom. You will also base your decisions on instinct, common sense, and reflective judgment. The better your understanding and experience with middle level schools, the curriculum, and the children, and the more time you have for thoughtful reflection, the more likely it will be that your decisions will result in the students meeting the educational goals. You will reflect upon, conceptualize, and apply understandings from one teaching experience to the next. As your understanding about your classroom experiences accumulate, your teaching will become more routinized, predictable, and refined. The topic of reflective decision making is presented more fully in Chapter 3. To learn more about the reality of teaching, do Exercise 1.1, "Conversation with a Middle Level Teacher."

EXERCISE 1.1: CONVERSATION WITH A MIDDLE LEVEL TEACHER

INSTRUCTIONS: For this exercise you are to interview one or more middle level teachers, perhaps one who is relatively new to the classroom and one who has been teaching for 10 years or more. For this you may duplicate blank copies of this form. Use the following questions to guide the interview; then share the results with your classmates.

1. Name and grade span of school: _____

2. Date of interview: _____

3. Name, grade level, and subject of teacher: _____

4. In which area(s) of the school curriculum do you work?

   Core? _____

   Exploratory? _____

   Advisory? _____

   Cocurricular? _____

   Other (specify)? _____

5. Why did you select teaching as a career? _____

   _____

   _____

   _____

   _____

6. Why are you teaching at this grade level? _____

   _____

   _____

   _____

   _____

7. What training did you have? _____

   _____

   _____

   _____

   _____

8. What advice about preparation can you offer me? _____

   _____

   _____

   _____

   _____

EXERCISE 1.1 (*continued*)

9. What do you like most about teaching? _____

_____

_____

_____

_____

_____

_____

_____

Least? _____

_____

_____

_____

_____

_____

_____

10. What do I most need to know to be an effective middle level classroom teacher? _____

_____

_____

_____

_____

_____

_____

11. What other specific advice do you have for those of us entering teaching at this level? _____

_____

_____

_____

_____

_____

_____

_____

The Principal Can Make a Difference

As a new or visiting member of the faculty, one of your tasks is to become familiar with the administrative organization of your school and district.

One person significantly responsible for the success of any school is its principal. What are the characteristics of an effective school principal? Perhaps foremost is that the principal has a vision of what a quality school is and strives to bring that vision to life. School improvement is the effective school principal's constant theme.[26]

The effective middle level school principal is well aware of the importance and ramifications, and is a proponent of, the key components of exemplary middle level school organization: (a) interdisciplinary teaming (as discussed earlier in this chapter and again in Chapter 6); (b) advisory programs (Chapter 5); (c) varied instruction (discussed throughout this guide, especially in Part III), including service learning; (d) exploratory programs (Chapter 5), and (e) transition programs (that is, programs that are designed to help children make the transitions from elementary to middle level schools, from one grade to the next, and from middle level school to high school, discussed throughout this guide).

The effective school principal establishes a collaborative climate in which teachers and students share the responsibility for determining the appropriate use of time and facilities. More than half of the middle level schools have a *site-based management team* that is comprised of teachers and administrators, and often parents/guardians too. About a third of the schools also include students on the team.[27]

Because exemplary middle level educators today believe in the innate potential of every child, rather than in the dumbing down standards and expectations, they modify the key variables of time, grouping, and instructional strategies to help individual students achieve mastery (see Chapter 8). This is nearly impossible to do without a supportive, and forward and positive thinking school principal.

In addition to the school principal there may be vice-principals or assistant principals with specific responsibilities and oversight functions, such as student activities, school discipline and security, transition programs, and curriculum and instruction. (Some large schools have the school site principal plus persons des-

ignated as grade level principals.)[28] Sometimes teachers who are department chairs or designated team leaders may also serve administrative functions. But the principal is (or should be) the person with the final responsibility for everything that happens at the school. Principals used to debate whether they were leaders or managers. Today there is no debate—to be most effective the principal must be both.

TELECOMMUNICATIONS NETWORKS, MEMBERS OF THE COMMUNITY, AND PARENT ORGANIZATIONS: VEHICLES FOR OBTAINING AND SHARING IDEAS AND INFORMATION

Today's exemplary middle level educators are making major efforts to enhance the connections among the home, the school, and local and global communities to promote the success of all students.

Home and School Connections

It is well known that parental and family involvement in a child's education can have a positive impact on the student's achievement at school. For example, when parents or guardians of at-risk students get involved, the student benefits with more consistent attendance at school, more positive attitudes and actions, better grades, and higher test scores.

Although not all schools have a parent organization, when school principals were given a list of community groups or organizations and asked to assess the influence each group had exerted on their school, the group that had the most influence was the parent-teacher organization (PTO) or parent-teacher association (PTA).[29] Recognizing the positive effect that parent and family involvement has on student achievement and success, the National PTA published *National Standards for Parent/Family Involvement Programs*.[30]

Many schools have adopted formal policies about home and community connections. These policies usually emphasize that parents/guardians should be included as partners in the educational program, and that teachers and administrators will inform parents/guardians about their child's progress, about the school's family involvement policy, and about any programs in

---

[26]To read how one middle school principal was instrumental in turning around an urban school, see A. Downs, "One Urban School's Adventure in Reform," *Harvard Education Letter* 16(2):2–3 (March/April 2000).

[27]U.S. Department of Education. National Center for Education Statistics. *In the Middle: Characteristics of Public Schools With a Focus on Middle Schools*, NCES 2000-312, by Martha Naomi Alt and Susan P. Choy. Project Officer: Charles H. Hammer. Washington, DC: 2000, pp. 19–20.

[28]For example, housing approximately 1,300 students, First Colony Middle School (Sugar Land, TX) has, in addition to its school site principal, principals for each grade level, 6–8.

[29]J. W. Valentine, et al., *Leadership in Middle Level Education. Vol. 1: A National Survey of Middle Level Leaders and Schools* (Reston, VA: National Association of Secondary School Principals, 1993), p. 98.

[30]See P. Sullivan, "The PTA's National Standards," *Educational Leadership* 55(8):43–44 (May 1998). For a copy of the standards, contact the National PTA, 330 N. Wabash Ave., Chicago, IL 60611–3690. Phone (312) 670-6782; Fax (312) 670-6783.

which family members can participate. Some middle level schools are members of the National Network of Partnership 2000 Schools. Middle level efforts to foster parent/guardian and community involvement are as varied as the people who participate. They include (a) student-teacher-parent contracts and assignment calendars, sometimes available via the school's Web page on the Internet; (b) home visitor programs; (c) involvement of community leaders in the classroom as mentors, aides, and role models; (d) newsletters, workshops, and electronic hardware and software for parents/guardians to help facilitate their children's learning; (e) homework hotlines; (f) regular phone calls and personal notes home about a student's progress; (g) enrollment of not only students but of entire families as members of a learning team; and (h) involvement of students in community service learning.[31]

Service Learning

A recommendation of the Carnegie Task Force 1989 publication *Turning Points* that was reaffirmed in *Turning Points 2000* is that "every middle grades school should include youth service—supervised activity helping others in the community or in school—in its core instructional program."[32] In service learning, students learn and develop through active participation in thoughtfully organized and curriculum-connected experiences that meet community needs. Here are a few examples of how middle schools incorporate service learning activities; see also Figure 1.2 and other examples near the end of Chapter 8.

- At Harmony Middle School (Bloomington, IN) students develop individual service projects of various sorts, which range from helping victims of flooding to working at a Head Start program, a recycling center, or a veterinarian's office.
- At MacArthur Barr Middle School (Nanuet, NY) eighth-grade students participate every day for 10 weeks at one of several sites in the community.
- At Redland Middle School (Homestead, FL) students enroll in a students-at-risk program to participate in conflict mediation/resolution activities and to work with fifth graders at feeder elementary schools.

---

[31]See B. Kleiner and C. Chapman, *Youth Service-Learning and Community Service among 6th- through 12th-Grade Students in the United States: 1996–1999. Statistics in Brief.* ED439086 (Washington, DC: National Center for Education Statistics, 2000); the May 2000 theme issue, "service learning," of *Phi Delta Kappan,* v81, n9, C. I. Fertman, et al., *Service Learning in the Middle School: Building a Culture of Service* (Westerville, OH: National Middle School Association, 1996); and J. A. Brough and J. L. Irvin, "Parental Involvement Supports Academic Improvement Among Middle Schoolers," *Middle School Journal* 32(5):56–61 (May 2001).

[32]Carnegie Task Force on Education of Young Adolescents, *Turning Points: Preparing Youth for the Twenty-First Century* (Washington, DC: Carnegie Council on Adolescent Development, 1989), p. 45, and A. W. Jackson and G. A. Davis, *Turning Points 2000,* p. 211.

Figure 1.2 Internet sources on community service learning.

- Big Dummy's Guide to Service-Learning at http://www.fiu.edu/~time4chg/Library/bigdummy.html
- National Service-Learning Clearinghouse at http://www.servicelearning.org/res/listserv.htm.

- At West Fargo Middle School (Fargo, ND) students make quilts, which are presented to local shelters. Math students calculate the dimensions and materials needed; home economics students cut the materials; reading students make quilt squares depicting favorite stories.
- Eighth-grade students at Westside Middle School (Omaha, NE) "adopted" the local home for veterans.

A PROFESSIONAL RESOURCE FILE

Community members, geographic features, buildings, monuments, historic sites, and other places in a school's geographic area constitute one of the richest instructional laboratories that can be imagined. To take advantage of this accumulated wealth of resources, as well as to build school-community partnerships, you should start a file of community resources as soon as you are hired by a school. For instance, you might include files about the skills of the students' parents and other family members, noting those that could be resources for the study occurring in your classroom. You might also include files on various resource people who could speak to the class, on free and inexpensive materials, on sites for field trips, and on what other communities of teachers, students, and adult helpers have done.

It is a good idea to start your professional resources file now and keep it going throughout your professional career; see Figure 1.3. Many resource ideas and sources are mentioned and listed throughout this resource guide. (The use of guest speakers and field trips is discussed in Chapter 10.)

Telecommunications Networks

To guide their students toward becoming autonomous thinkers, effective decision makers, and life-long learners; and to make their classrooms more student-centered, collaborative, interdisciplinary, and interactive, teachers are increasingly turning to telecommunications networks and to the community. See, for example, the vignette, "Interdisciplinary Thematic Instruction at West Salem Middle School." Webs of connected computers allow teachers and students from around the world to reach each other directly and gain access to quantities of information previously unimaginable. Students using networks learn and develop new inquiry and analytical

Figure 1.3   Beginning my professional resources file.

A professional resources file is a project that you could begin now and continue throughout your professional career. Begin your resources file either on a computer database program or on color-coded file cards that list (1) name of resource, (2) how and where to obtain the resource, (3) description of how to use the resource, and (4) evaluative comments about the resource.

Organize the file in a way that makes the most sense to you now. Cross-reference or color-code your system to accommodate the following categories of instructional aids and resources:

- Articles from print sources
- Compact disc titles
- Computer software titles
- Games
- Guest speakers and other community resources
- Internet resources
- Media catalogs
- Motivational ideas
- Pictures, posters, graphs

- Resources to order
- Sources of free and inexpensive materials
- Student worksheets
- Test items
- Thematic units and ideas
- Unit and lesson plans and ideas
- Videocassette titles
- Videodisc titles
- Miscellaneous

Figure 1.4   Sample internet sites for teachers and students.

- Classroom Connect http://www.classroomconnect.com. Resources for teachers.
- Education links http://www.execpc.com/,dboals/k-12.html.
- Education World http://www.education-world.com. Electronic version of *Education Week*.
- ENC http://www.enc.org.. Eisenhower National Clearinghouse for Mathematics and Science.
- FedWorld http://www.fedworld.gov. Access to information from government agencies.
- GEM, the Gateway to Educational Materials http://www.thegateway.org. Federal government's effort to provide access to Internet-based educational materials.
- Global Schoolnet Foundation http://www.gsn.org/. Global resources and expedition teams, and links.
- GLOBE (Global Learning and Observations to Benefit the Environment) Program http://www.globe.gov. An international environmental science and education partnership.
- HomeworkCentral http://www.bigchalk.com. Lesson plans and subject research.
- Kathy Schrock's Guide for Educators http://school.discovery.com/schrockguide/. Resources and information on education.
- Knowledge Loom http://www.knowledgeloom.org. Database of resources for teachers.
- Learning Network http://www.learningnetwork.com/. Informational resource links.
- Library of Congress http://lcweb.loc.gov/homepage. National Digital Library life history manuscripts from the WPA Federal Writers' Folklore Project, Civil War photographs, early motion pictures, legal information, and research sources.
- ClubMid http://www.ClubMid.phschool.com. Middle grades network.
- MiddleWeb http://www.middleweb.com/. Focuses on middle schools.
- National Consortium for School Networking http://cosn.org.
- Novagate reference site http://www.novagate.com/novasurf/onlinereference.html.
- On-Line Books http://digital.library.upenn.edu/books/.
- Study Web http://www.studyweb.com. Place for students and teachers to research topics.
- Teachers Helping Teachers http://www.pacificnet.net/-mandel/.
- Teacher Talk http://education.indiana.edu/cas/tt/tthmpg.html.
- United Nations' CyberSchool Bus http://www.un.org/Pubs/CyberSchoolBus/. Curriculum units and projects, databases on U.N. member states, and global trends.
- United States Department of Education http://www.ed.gov/index.html.
- Virtual Reference Desk, for Educators http://thorplus.lib.purdue.edu/reference/.
- Yahoo's Education Index http://www.yahoo.com/Education/.

skills in a stimulating environment, and gain an increased appreciation of their role as world citizens. Sample Web-site and addresses are shown in Figure 1.4; others are indicated throughout this guide, especially in Figures 8.3 of Chapter 8 (for subject-specific sites) and 10.2 of Chapter 10 (for sites about materials and technology). For a sample lesson plan illustrating student use of the Internet, see Figure 6.10 (Chapter 6).

SCHOOL VIGNETTE

Interdisciplinary Thematic Instruction at West Salem Middle School*

What began as an isolated, single-grade, telecommunications-dependent project for students at West Salem Middle School (Wisconsin) eventually developed into a longer-term cross-grade interdisciplinary program of students and adults working together to design and develop a local nature preserve. Students began their adventure by interacting with explorer Will Steger as he led the International Arctic Project's first training expedition. Electronic on-line messages, via the Internet, allowed students to receive and send messages to Will and his team in real time. Students delved into the Arctic world, researching the physical environment and the intriguing wildlife, reading native stories and novels about survival, keeping their own imaginary expedition journals, learning about the impact of industrialized society on the Arctic, and conversing with students from around the world. But something very important was missing—a connection between the students' immediate environment and the faraway Arctic.

West Salem Middle School's focus became the local 700-acre Lake Neshonoc, an impoundment of the LaCrosse River, a tributary of the Mississippi. Although many students had enjoyed its recreational opportunities, they had never formally studied the lake. The Neshonoc Partners, a committee of parents, community leaders, teachers, students, and environmentalists, was established to assist in setting goals, brainstorming ideas, and developing the program for a year's study of the lake. Right from the start, students showed keen interest in active involvement in the project. A second committee, involving parents, students, and the classroom teacher, met during lunch time on a weekly basis to allow for more intensive discussions about the lake and the overall project.

The team of teachers brainstormed ideas to further develop an interdisciplinary approach to the study of Lake Neshonoc. Special activities, including an all-day "winter survival" adventure, gave students a sense of what real explorers experience. Students learned about hypothermia, winter trekking by cross-country skiing, and building their own snow caves.

For several weeks, students learned about the ecosystem of Lake Neshonoc through field experiences led by local environmentalists and community leaders. Guest speakers told their stories about life on the lake and their observations about the lake's health. Student sketchbooks provided a place to document personal observations about the shoreline, water testing, animal and plant life, and the value of the lake. From these sketchbooks, the best student creations were compiled in books to share electronically with students with similar interests in schools from Russia, Canada, Missouri, South Carolina, Nevada, Wisconsin, and Washington, DC. The opportunity to share findings about their local watershed sparked discussions about how students can make a difference in their own community. Comparative studies gave students a chance to consider how humans and nature impact other watersheds.

West Salem students worked with the local County Parks and Recreation Department to assist in developing a sign marking the new County Park where the nature sanctuary will reside. Students brainstormed design ideas and then constructed a beautiful redwood sign with the help of a local technical educational teacher. Today the sign is a symbol of the partnership that has been established between the students and the community. It is a concrete reminder that together we can work for the common good of the community and the environment. Students celebrated the study of the lake with a closure. Will Steger, along with community leaders, parents, school board members, and staff, commended the students for what is sure to be the start of a long and enduring relationship—a partnership created out of common respect and appreciation for the value of our ecosystem.

*Source: J. Wee, "The Neshonoc Project: Profiles in Partnership," *World School for Adventure Learning Bulletin* (Fall 1993):2–3. Adapted by permission.

THE EMERGENT OVERALL PICTURE

Certainly, no facet of education receives more attention from the media, causes more concern among parents and teachers, or gets larger headlines than that of a decline (factual or fanciful) in students' achievement in the public schools. This has been no less true for middle schools in particular than for public schools in general. Reports are issued, polls taken, debates organized, and blue-ribbon commissions are formed. Community members write letters to local editors about it, news editors devote editorial space to it, television anchors comment about it, and documentaries and specials focus on it in full color. We read, "U.S. Students Lag Behind Other Nations in Science," "Middle Schools Fail to Make the Grade," and so on. What initiated this attention that began more than a quarter of a century ago and continues today? We are not sure, but it has never been matched in its political interest and participation, and it has affected and continues to affect both the public schools and the programs in higher education that are directly or indirectly related to teacher preparation and certification.[33]

In response to the reports, educators, corporations and local business persons, and politicians acted. Around the nation, their actions resulted in the following:

- Changes in standards for teacher certification. For example, model standards describing what prospective teachers should know and be able to do in order to receive a teaching license were prepared and released in 1992 by the Interstate New Teacher Assessment and Support Consortium (INTASC), which was a project of the Council of Chief State School Officers (CCSSO), in a document titled *Model Standards for Beginning Teacher Licensing and Development*. Representatives of at least 36 states and professional associations—including the National Education Association (NEA), the American Federation of Teachers (AFT), the American Association of Colleges for Teacher Education (AACTE), and the National Council for the Accreditation of Teacher Education (NCATE)—comprise the group. The standards are performance-based and revolve around a common core of principles of knowledge and skills that cut across disciplines. The INTASC standards were developed to be compatible with the National Board for Professional Teaching Standards (NBPTS). Specifically addressing middle level instruction, in 1997 the NBPTS released 11 categories of standards for certification as a Middle Childhood/Generalist. The 11 categories are (1) knowledge of students, (2) knowledge of content and curriculum, (3) learning environment, (4) respect for diversity, (5) instructional resources, (6) meaningful applications of knowledge, (7) multiple paths of knowledge, (8) assessment, (9) family involvement, (10) reflection, and (11) contributions to the profession.[34]

- Development of national education standards for all major subject areas (see Chapter 5).

- Emphasis on education for cultural diversity and ways of teaching language minority students.

- Emphasis on helping students make effective transitions from one level of schooling to the next and from school to life, with an increased focus on helping students make connections between what is being learned and real life, as well as connections between subjects in the curriculum and between academics and vocations.

- Emphasis on rising test scores, reducing dropout rates, increasing instructional time, and changing curricula.

- Emphasis on standards-based education.

- Improvement of school-home-community connections.

- School restructuring to provide more meaningful curriculum options.

Key Middle Level Trends and Practices Today

Key trends and practices today include the following:

- Deemphasizing traditional curriculum tracking and instead providing meaningful curriculum options with multiple pathways for academic success.[35]

- Dividing the student body and faculty into smaller cohorts, that is, the house concept, and using nontraditional scheduling.

- Encouraging the practices of reflective thinking and self-discipline.

- Facilitating students' social skills as they interact, relate to one another, solve meaningful problems, develop skills in conflict resolution, and foster peaceful relationships and friendships.

- Facilitating the development of students' values as related to their families, the community, and schools.

---

[33]See, for example, J. Norton, "Important Developments in Middle-Grades Reform," *Phi Delta Kappan* 81(10):K2–K4 (June 2000).

[34]Access the standards via Internet http://www.nbpts.org/. You may want to compare the 11 standards of the NBPTS document with the 22 competencies that are identified in Chapter 3 of this resource guide and with the 22 "components of professional practice" in C. Danielson, *Enhancing Professional Practice: A Framework for Teaching* (Alexandria, VA: Association for Supervision and Curriculum Development, 1996).

[35]See A. W. Jackson and G. A. Davis, *Turning Points 2000*, pp. 65–68, 83, 130, and 175; R. Mills, *Grouping Students for Instruction in Middle Schools* (Champaign, IL: ED419631, ERIC Clearinghouse on Elementary and Early Childhood Education, 1998); and W. Schwartz (Ed.), *New Trends in Language Education for Hispanic Students* (New York: ED442913, ERIC Clearinghouse on Urban Education, 2000).

- Holding high expectations, although not necessarily the same expectations, for all students by establishing benchmark academic standards and assessing student achievement against those standards.
- Integrating the curriculum.
- Involving parents/guardians and communities in the schools.
- Involving students in self-assessment.
- Movement away from the traditional "agrarian school calendar" to a 45/15 year-round calendar in order to reduce the effect of the so-called summer regression, which is the loss of skills and content knowledge during the nearly three-month summer layoff.
- Providing students with the time and the opportunity to think and be creative, rather than simply memorizing and repeating information.
- Redefining giftedness to include nonacademic as well as traditional academic abilities.
- Teaching and assessing for higher-order thinking skills.
- Using heterogeneous small-group learning, peer coaching, and cross-age tutoring as instructional strategies.
- Using the Internet in the classroom as a communication tool and learning resource.

Problems and Issues That Plague the Nation's Schools

Our nation's schools are plagued by major problems and issues, all of which in one way or another affect middle level education. Some of these are discussed in subsequent chapters (see index for topic locations). Perhaps you and members of your class can identify other issues and problems faced by our nation's schools, especially the middle level schools. Major problems and issues are as follows:

- Bias, prejudice, harassment, and violence in schools.[36]
- Buildings that are old and in need of repair and upgrading.[37]
- Controversy created by mandatory high stakes testing.[38]

- Continued controversy over ability grouping and curriculum tracking.[39]
- Debate regarding the value of the child-centered middle school concept versus a rigorous curriculum-centered approach.[40]
- Debate over the value of year-round as opposed to traditional school year.
- Debate over the value of extending the school year beyond the typical 180 school days.
- Debate over the value of grades 6–8 middle schools versus smaller grades K–8 neighborhood schools.
- Identification and development of programs that recognize, develop, and nurture talents in all children.[41]
- Recruiting and retaining school administrators.[42]
- Retention in grade versus social promotion and the search for alternatives to grade retention.[43]
- Using standardized test scores and statistics to judge and reward the performance of schools.
- Scarcity of teachers of color to serve as role models for students.[44]
- School security and the related problem of weapons, crime, violence, and drugs on school campuses and in nearby neighborhoods.[45]

---

[36]See, for example, S. L. Wessler, "Sticks and Stones," *Educational Leadership* 58(4):28–33 (December 2000/January 2001).

[37]See, for example, C. Rowand, *How Old Are America's Public Schools?* (Washington, DC: ED426586, National Center for Education Statistics, 1999).

[38]See, for example, *Turning Points 2000*, pp 220–221; S. Ohanian, "News from the Test Resistance Trail," *Phi Delta Kappan* 82(5):363–366 (January 2001); A. Kohn, "Fighting the Tests: A Practical Guide to Rescuing Our Schools," *Phi Delta Kappan* 82(5):349–357 (January 2001); and M. Sadowski, "Are High-Stakes Tests Worth the Wager?" *Harvard Education Letter* 16(5):1–5 (September/October 2000).

[39]See, for example, R. Mills, *Grouping Students for Instruction*, and T. Loveless, *The Tracking and Ability Grouping Debate*, Volume 2, Number 8 (Washington, DC: Thomas B. Fordham Foundation, 1998), and *Turning Points 2000*.

[40]See, for example, J. R. Belair and P. Freeman, "Providing a Responsive and Academically Rigorous Curriculum," *Middle School Journal* 32(1):5–6 (September 2000), and V. A. Anfara, Jr. and L. Waks, "Resolving the Tension Between Academic Rigor and Developmental Appropriateness," *Middle School Journal* 32(2):46–51 (November 2000).

[41]See, for example, J. Fulkerson and M. Horvich, "Talent Development: Two Perspectives," and J. VanTassel-Baska, "The Development of Academic Talent," both in *Phi Delta Kappan* 79(10):756–759 and 760–763 (respectively) (June 1998).

[42]See, for example, L. T. Fenwick and M. C. Pierce, "The Principal Shortage: Crisis or Opportunity," and L. Potter, "Solving the Principal Shortage," *Principal* 80(4):24–32 and 34–37 respectively (March 2001).

[43]See, for example, K. Kelly, "Retention vs. Social Promotion: Schools Search for Alternatives," *The Harvard Education Letter* 15(1):1–3 (January/February 1999).

[44]M. S. Lewis, *Supply and Demand of Teachers of Color* (Washington, DC: ED390875, ERIC Clearinghouse on Teaching and Teacher Education, 1996). See also "The Need for Minority Teachers" in P. R. Rettig and M. Khodavandi, *Recruiting Minority Teachers: The UTOP Program*, Fastback 436 (Bloomington, IN: Phi Delta Kappa Educational Foundation, 1998), pp. 13–21.

[45]See, for example, N. K. Bowen and G. I. Bowen, "Effects of Crime and Violence in Neighborhoods and Schools on the School Behavior and Performance of Adolescents," *Journal of Adolescent Research* 14(3):319–342 (July 1999). Intended to alert teachers and parents to the warning signs exhibited by troubled children is *Early Warning-Time Response: A Guide to Safe Schools*. Written by the National Association of School Psychologists and released in August 1998, the guide is available free by calling 1-877-4ED-PUBS or from the Internet at http://www.ed.gov/offices/OSERS/OSEP/Products/earlywrn.html.

- Schools that are too large.[46]
- Shortage of qualified teachers, especially in certain subjects and for schools located in areas of high poverty.[47]
- The education of teachers to work effectively with children who may be too overwhelmed by personal problems to focus on learning and to succeed in school.
- The number of children at risk of dropping out of school, especially Hispanics for whom the dropout rate has hovered around 30% for more than a quarter century.[48] However, see the Lennox Middle School following scenario.

LENNOX MIDDLE SCHOOL'S SUCCESS SCENARIO*

Countering the Hispanic Student Dropout Rate

Experience shows that specifically recruiting teachers and administrative staff who speak Spanish and are familiar with Hispanic culture increases achievement in schools with a large Hispanic student body. Thus, Lennox Middle School (Lennox, CA), whose student population is largely Hispanic, and which has high student achievement and a low dropout rate, requires that its staff be bilingual, that they are sensitive to students' culture, and that they demonstrate respect for the students by patiently supporting their efforts to learn.

*Source: W. Schwartz (Ed.), *New Trends in Language Education for Hispanic Students*, ERIC/CUE Digest Number 155 (New York: ED442913, ERIC Clearinghouse on Urban Education, 2000).

SUMMARY

In beginning to plan for developing your teaching competencies, you have read an overview of today's middle level schools and of the characteristics of some of the adults who work there, of trends and practices, and of problems and issues that continue to plague our nation's schools. That knowledge will be useful in your assimilation of the content explored in chapters that follow, beginning in the next chapter with the characteristics of young adolescents, how they learn, and strategies to use to effectively work with them.

Despite the many blue ribbon commissions, writers, and politicians that have and continue to vilify the failures of public education, thousands of committed teachers, administrators, parents, and members of the community struggle daily, year after year, to provide students with a quality education. Throughout the remaining chapters of this text, many exemplary middle schools and school programs are recognized and identified by name.

ADDITIONAL EXERCISES

See the companion Website http://www.prenhall.com/kellough for the following exercises related to the content of this chapter:

- Visiting a Middle School Parent-Teacher or Parent-Teacher-Student Organization Meeting
- Conversation with a Middle School Teacher Candidate

QUESTIONS FOR CLASS DISCUSSION

1. How would you know if you were at an exemplary middle school? Describe at least three characteristics of an exemplary middle school. Is it possible for a traditional junior high to also be an exemplary school? Explain why or why not.

2. One of the fastest growing demographic groups in the United States is the prison population. With more than one million individuals incarcerated, the United States now has the highest prison population in the world. The relationship between incarceration and education is perhaps more than coincidental: 82% of the country's prisoners are school dropouts. We spend roughly five times as much money to house a prisoner as we do to educate a child. Do you believe that this is the way it should be in America? Explain why or why not. If not, what can be done about it?

3. Describe evidence you can find that shows that middle level school children are involved in decision making about school activities. Describe evidence you can find that shows that middle level school teachers are involved in decision making about school activities. Describe evidence you can find that shows that parents and guardians are involved in decision making about school activities.

4. From your point of view, what societal influences affect today's young adolescents? Are crime, gangs, drugs, and images of professional athletes and musicians among those influences? Explain the effects.

5. Select one of the "Reflective Thoughts" from the introduction to Part I (page 2) that is specifically related to the content of this chapter. Research it and write a one-page essay explaining why you agree or disagree with the thought. Share your essay with members of your class for their thoughts.

6. If, during a job interview, you were asked to explain the "middle school concept," how would you do so?

7. If, during a job interview, you were asked whether you believe that the "middle school movement" is alive and well, how would you respond?

---

[46]See, for example, S. B. Mertens; N. Flowers; and P. F. Mulhall, "School Size Matters in Interesting Ways," *Middle School Journal* 32(5):51–55 (May 2001).

[47]See, for example, L. Olson, "Finding and Keeping Competent Teachers," *Quality Counts 2000: Education Week* 19(28):12–18 (January 13, 2000).

[48]See, for example, P. Kaufman, et al., *Dropout Rates in the United States, 1998*. Statistical Analysis Report (Washington, DC: ED438381, National Center for Education Statistics, 2000).

8. To improve instruction for middle level school children, districts in some states are participating in partnership schools programs. Partnership schools are members of networks in geographic areas. The focus is on connecting students to the goals and purposes of the school in positive ways to increase their academic performance and self-esteem. Each school works on this focus and shares its findings with other schools in the networks. Programs center on bilingual tutoring, at-risk students, cooperative learning, improving problem-solving skills, advisor-advisee relationships, young adolescent issues, skills and habits, moral and ethical problems facing middle level school children, and exploratory classes. After the findings are shared, the successful programs may be adopted statewide. Are similar programs being carried out in your state? If so, discuss them with others in your class.

9. From your current observations and fieldwork related to this teacher preparation program, clearly identify one specific example of educational practice that seems contradictory to exemplary practice or theory as presented in this chapter. Present your explanation for the discrepancy.

10. Do you have other questions generated by the content of this chapter? If you do, list them along with ways that answers might be found.

FOR FURTHER READING

Beane, J. A. "Middle Schools Under Siege: Points of Attack." *Middle School Journal* 30(4):3–9 (March 1999).

Briggs, T. H. *The Junior High School.* Boston: Houghton Mifflin, 1920.

Carnegie Council on Adolescent Development. *Great Transitions: Preparing Adolescents for a New Century.* Washington, DC: Author, 1995.

Clark, D. C., and Clark, S. N. "Developmentally Responsive Curriculum and Standards-based Reform: Implications for Middle Level Principals." *NASSP* (National Association of Secondary School Principals) *Bulletin* 84(615):1–13 (April 2000).

Consortium on Chicago School Research. *Social Support, Academic Press, and Student Achievement: A View from the Middle Grades in Chicago.* Chicago, IL: Improving Chicago's Schools, A Report of the Chicago Annenberg Research Project, 1990.

Downs, A. "Successful School Reform Efforts Share Common Features." *Harvard Education Letter* 16(2):1–5 (March/April 2000).

Elmore, R. "Leadership for Effective Middle School Practice." *Phi Delta Kappan* 82(4):269 (December 2000).

Erb, T. O. "Do Middle School Reforms Make a Difference?" *Clearing House* 73(4):194–200 (March/April 2000).

Flowers, N., Mertens, S. B.; and Mulhall, P. F. "What Makes Interdisciplinary Teams Effective?" *Middle School Journal* 31(4):53–56 (March 2000).

Gallagher, J. "Teaching in the Block." *Middle Ground* 2(3):10–15 (February 1999).

George, P. S. "The Evolution of Middle Schools." *Educational Leadership* 58(4):40–44 (December 2000/January 2001).

Gold, J. M.; Rotter, J. C.; Holmes, G. R.; and Motes, P. S. *Middle School Climate: A Study of Attitudes.* Fastback 455. Bloomington, IN: Phi Delta Kappa Educational Foundation, 1999.

Gruhn, W. T., and Douglass, H. R. *The Modern Junior High School.* New York: Roland Press, 1947.

Hansen, J. H., and Hearn, A. C. *The Middle School Program.* Chicago: Rand McNally, 1971.

Hope, W. C. "Service Learning: A Reform Initiative for Middle Level Curriculum." *Clearing House* 72(4):236–238 (March/April 1999).

Hopping, L. "Multi-Age Teaming: A Real-Life Approach to the Middle School." *Phi Delta Kappan* 82(4):270–272, 292 (December 2000).

Jackson, A. W., and Davis, G. A. *Turning Points 2000: Educating Adolescents in the 21st Century.* A Report of the Carnegie Corporation of New York. New York: Teachers College Press, 2000.

Kienholz, D. B. "From Dewey to Beane: Innovation, Democracy, and Unity Characterize Middle Level Education." *Middle School Journal* 32(3):20–24 (January 2001).

Koos, L. V. *The Junior High School.* Boston: Ginn and Co., 1927.

Lipsitz, J. *Successful Schools for Young Adolescents.* New Brunswick, NJ: Transaction, 1984.

Lounsbury, J. H. "The Middle School Movement: A Charge to Keep." *Clearing House* 73(4):193 (March/April 2000).

Loveless, T. *The Tracking Wars: State Reform Meets School Policy.* Washington, DC: Brookings Institution Press, 1999.

National Commission on Excellence in Education. *A Nation at Risk: The Imperative for Educational Reform.* Washington, DC: Government Printing Office, 1983.

National Middle School Association. *This We Believe: Developmentally Responsive Middle Level Schools.* Columbus, OH: National Middle School Association, 1995.

Norton, J., and Lewis, A. C. "Middle-Grades Reform." Kappan Special Report. *Phi Delta Kappan* 81(10):K1–K20 (June 2000).

Offenberg, R. M. "The Efficacy of Philadelphia's K–8 Schools Compared to Middle Grades Schools." *Middle School Journal* 32(4):23–29 (March 2001).

Ohanian, S. *Caught in the Middle: Nonstandard Kids and a Killing Curriculum.* Westport, CT: Heinemann, 2001.

Rosselli, H. C., and Irvin, J. L. "Differing Perspectives, Common Ground: The Middle School and Gifted Education Relationship." *Middle School Journal* 32(3):57–62 (January 2001).

Ruder, M. "The Mark of Leadership." *Middle Ground* 5(1):29–30 (August 2001).

Southern Regional Education Board. *Leading the Way: State Actions To Improve Student Achievement in the Middle Grades.* Atlanta, GA: Author, 1999.

Thornton, H. J. "The Meaning of National Board Certification for Middle Grades Teaching." *Middle School Journal* 32(4):46–54 (March 2001).

Tye, K. A. *The Junior High School: A School in Search of a Mission.* New York: University Press of America, 1985.

Wormeli, R. "Block Classes Change Instructional Practice—Carpe Diem!" *Middle Ground* 2(3):17–19 (February 1999).

Wormeli, R. "The Truth About Middle School Students." *Middle Ground* 4(2):23–25 (October 2000).

CHAPTER 2

Celebrating and Building upon the Diverse Characteristics and Needs of Young Adolescents

The bell rings and the students enter your classroom— a kaleidoscope of personalities, all peerless and idiosyncratic, each a packet of energy, with different focuses, experiences, dispositions, and learning capacities, and differing proficiencies in the use of the English language. What a challenge it is to understand and to teach 30 or so unique individuals all at once, and to do it for six hours a day, five days a week, 180 days a year! What a challenge it is today to be a middle grades classroom teacher. To prepare yourself for this challenge, consider the information provided in this chapter about the diverse characteristics and needs of young adolescents, for it is well known that their academic achievement is

greatly dependent upon how well their other developmental needs are understood and satisfied.

OBJECTIVES

Upon completion of this chapter, you should be able to

1. Demonstrate your growing understanding of the meaning of *developmentally appropriate practice.*
2. Demonstrate an understanding of the developmental characteristics of young adolescents and their implications for developmentally appropriate practice.

3. Demonstrate developing skills in recognizing, celebrating, and building upon student diversity.
4. Demonstrate an understanding of the significance of the concepts of learning modalities, learning styles, and learning capacities, and their implications for appropriate educational practice.
5. Demonstrate an understanding of the three-phase learning cycle and the types of learning activities that might occur in each phase.
6. Demonstrate an awareness of appropriate curriculum options and instructional practices for specific groups of learners.
7. Describe today's concept of middle level teaching and learning, and how it differs from that of the recent past.
8. Demonstrate your developing knowledge of practical ways of attending to student individual differences while working with a cohort of students.
9. Demonstrate the concept of *multilevel instruction* and how you would use multilevel instruction in your teaching.

YOUNG ADOLESCENT YEARS: TIME OF RAPID CHANGE AND GREAT VARIABILITY

Although generalizations are risky, from many years of experience and research experts have come to accept certain precepts about young adolescents. These are developmental characteristics of 10 to 14 year olds regardless of their individual genetic or cultural differences. They are presented here in five categories: intellectual, physical, emotional/psychological, social, and moral/ethical.[1] Each category is accompanied by practices that are developmentally appropriate for middle-level curriculum and instruction.[2]

Characteristics of Young Adolescents and Their Implications for Developmentally Appropriate Practice

It is important to emphasize that early adolescence is a period of tremendous variability among individuals of the same gender and chronological age, and that dissimilar rates of growth are common in all areas of development. It would be erroneous, for example, to draw a conclusion that states "All seventh graders are. . . ." In addition, the five areas of development are inexorably entwined.[3]

Intellectual Development. Young adolescents tend to

1. Be egocentric; argue to convince others; exhibit independent, critical thought.
2. Be intellectually at risk; that is, they face decisions that have the potential to affect major academic values with lifelong consequences.
3. Be intensely curious.
4. Consider academic goals as a secondary level of priority, whereas personal-social concerns dominate thoughts and activities.
5. Display a wide range of individual intellectual development as their minds experience change from the concrete-manipulatory stage to the capacity for abstract thought. This change makes possible
   a. Ability to project thought into the future, to expect, and to formulate goals.
   b. Analysis of the power of a political ideology.
   c. Appreciation for the elegance of mathematical logic expressed in symbols.
   d. Consideration of ideas contrary to fact.
   e. Insight into the nuances of poetic metaphor and musical notation.
   f. Insight into the sources of previously unquestioned attitudes, behaviors, and values.
   g. Interpretation of larger concepts and generalizations of traditional wisdom expressed through sayings, axioms, and aphorisms.
   h. Propositional thought.
   i. Reasoning with hypotheses involving two or more variables.
6. Experience the phenomenon of **metacognition**—that is, the ability to think about one's thinking, and to know what one knows and does not know.
7. Exhibit strong willingness to learn what they consider to be useful, and enjoy using skills to solve real-life problems.
8. Prefer active to passive learning experiences; favor interaction with peers during learning activities.

Implications for Developmentally Appropriate Practice (DAP). Regarding the intellectual development of young adolescents, developmentally appropriate actions include

- The use of a wide variety of approaches and materials for instruction, that is an eclectic approach (a theme found throughout this resource guide), including physical movement with small-group discussions and learning centers.

---

[1]These characteristics are adapted from *Caught in the Middle: Educational Reform for Young Adolescents in California Public Schools* (Sacramento, CA: California State Department of Education, 1987), 144–148. See also "Characteristics of Young Adolescents," *This We Believe: Developmentally Responsive Middle Level Schools* (Columbus, OH: National Middle School Association, 1995), pp. 35–40.

[2]The implications are adapted from *The New American Middle School* by Wiles/Bondi 3rd ed., pp. 33–36. a.2001 Reprinted by Permission of Pearson Education, Inc. Upper Saddle River, NJ 07458.

[3]*This We Believe*, p. 6.

- Curricula organized around real-life concepts (e.g., conflict, competition, peer-group influence). Activities in formal and informal situations that are designed to improve reasoning powers. Studies of the community and environment are particularly relevant for young adolescents.
- Organized discussions of ideas and feelings in peer groups to facilitate self-understanding. Provision of experiences for individuals to express themselves by writing and participating in creative dramatics.
- Opportunities for enjoyable studies in the arts. Encouragement of self-expression in all subjects.

Physical Development. Young adolescents tend to

1. Be concerned about their physical appearance.
2. Be physically at risk; major causes of death are homicide, suicide, accident, and leukemia.
3. Experience accelerated physical development marked by increases in weight, height, heart size, lung capacity, and muscular strength.
4. Experience bone growth faster than muscle development; uneven muscle/bone development results in lack of coordination and awkwardness; bones may lack protection of covering muscles and supporting tendons.
5. Experience fluctuations in basal metabolism, which at times can cause either extreme restlessness or listlessness.
6. Face responsibility for sexual behavior before full emotional and social maturity has occurred.
7. Have ravenous appetites and peculiar tastes; may overtax digestive system with large quantities of improper foods.
8. Lack physical health; have poor levels of endurance, strength, and flexibility; as a group are more overweight and less healthy.
9. Mature at varying rates of speed. Girls are often taller than boys for the first two years of early adolescence and are ordinarily more physically developed than boys are.
10. Reflect a wide range of individual differences that begin to appear in prepubertal and pubertal stages of development. Boys tend to lag behind girls at this stage, and there are marked individual differences in physical development for both boys and girls. The greatest variation in physiological development and size occurs at about age 13.
11. Show changes in body contour, including temporarily large noses, protruding ears, and long arms; have posture problems.

Implications for Developmentally Appropriate Practice.
Regarding the physical development of young adolescents, developmentally appropriate actions include

- A health and science curriculum that emphasizes self-understanding about body changes. Guidance counseling and community resource persons to help students understand what is happening to their bodies.
- Advising parents to insist that students get proper rest; overexertion should be discouraged.
- Providing an opportunity for daily exercise and a place where students can be children by playing and being noisy for short periods.
- Encouraging activities such as special-interest classes and hands-on learning. Students should be allowed to move about physically in classes and avoid long periods of passive work.
- Providing snacks to satisfy between-meal hunger as well as nutritional guidance specific to the needs of young adolescents.

Emotional/Psychological Development. Young adolescents tend to

1. Be easily offended and are sensitive to criticism of personal shortcomings.
2. Be erratic and inconsistent in their behavior; anxiety and fear are contrasted with periods of bravado; feelings shift between superiority and inferiority.
3. Be moody, restless; often feel self-conscious and alienated; lack self-esteem; be introspective.
4. Be optimistic, hopeful.
5. Be psychologically at risk; at no other point in human development is an individual likely to meet so much diversity in relation to self and others.
6. Be searching for adult identity and acceptance even in the midst of intense peer-group relationships.
7. Be searching to form a conscious sense of individual uniqueness—"Who am I?"
8. Be vulnerable to naive opinions, one-sided arguments.
9. Exaggerate simple occurrences and believe that personal problems, experiences, and feelings are unique to themselves.
10. Have an emerging sense of humor based on increased intellectual ability to see abstract relationships; appreciate the *double entendre.*
11. Have chemical and hormonal imbalances, which often trigger emotions that are frightening and poorly understood; may regress to more childish behavior patterns at this point.

Implications for Developmentally Appropriate Practice.
Regarding the psychological development of young adolescents, developmentally appropriate actions include

- Encouragement of self-assessment.
- Activities designed to allow students to play out their emotions.
- Helping students to understand their feelings of superiority and inferiority.
- Avoiding the pressuring of students by adults in the school to explain their emotions. Occasional childlike behavior is not ridiculed. Sarcasm by adults is avoided.

- Encouragement of students to assume leadership in group discussions and to experience frequent success and recognition for personal efforts and achievement.
- A general atmosphere of friendliness, relaxation, concern, and group cohesiveness.
- Numerous opportunities to release emotional stress.
- Use of sociodrama to enable students to see themselves as others see them.
- Readings that deal with problems similar to their own to help them see that many of their problems are not unique.

Social Development.   Young adolescents tend to

1. Act out unusual or drastic behavior at times; may be aggressive, daring, boisterous, and argumentative.
2. Be confused and frightened by new school settings that are large and impersonal.
3. Be fiercely loyal to peer-group values; sometimes cruel or insensitive to those outside the peer group.
4. Be impacted by the high level of mobility in society; may become anxious and disoriented when peer-group ties are broken because of family relocation.
5. Be rebellious toward parents but still strongly dependent on parental values; want to make their own choices, but the authority of the family is a critical factor in final decisions.
6. Be socially at risk. Adult values are largely shaped conceptually during adolescence; negative interactions with peers, parents, and teachers may compromise ideals and commitments.
7. Challenge authority figures; test limits of acceptable behavior.
8. Experience low-risk trust relationships with adults who show lack of sensitivity to adolescent characteristics and needs.
9. Experience often traumatic conflicts because of conflicting loyalties to peer group and family.
10. Refer to peers as sources for standards and models of behavior. Media heroes and heroines are also singularly important in shaping both behavior and fashion.
11. Sense the negative impact of adolescent behaviors on parents and teachers; realize the thin edge between tolerance and rejection. Feelings of adult rejection can drive the adolescent into the relatively secure social environment of the peer group.
12. Strive to define sex role characteristics; search to set up positive social relationships with members of the same and opposite sex.
13. Want to know and feel that significant adults, including parents and teachers, love and accept them; need frequent affirmation.

Implications for Developmentally Appropriate Practice. Regarding the social development of young adolescents, developmentally appropriate actions include

- Scheduling debates, plays, play days, and other activities to allow students to show off in a productive way.
- Role-playing and guidance exercises that provide the opportunity to act out feelings. Providing opportunities for social interaction between the sexes—parties and games, but not dances in the early grades of middle school.
- Establishing a student government so students can develop their own guidelines for dress and behavior. Adults should be encouraged not to react with outrage when students display extreme dress or mannerisms.
- Fostering peer teaching and community service projects.
- Planning large group activities rather than boy-girl events. Intramurals can be scheduled so students can interact with friends of the same or opposite sex.

Moral and Ethical Development.   Young adolescents tend to

1. Ask broad, unanswerable questions about the meaning of life; not expecting absolute answers but being turned off by trivial adult responses.
2. Be at risk in the development of moral and ethical choices and behaviors; depend on the influences of home and church for moral and ethical development; explore the moral and ethical issues that are met in the curriculum, in the media, and in daily interactions with their families and peer groups.
3. Be idealistic; have a strong sense of fairness in human relationships.
4. Be reflective, introspective, and analytical about their thoughts and feelings.
5. Experience thoughts and feelings of awe and wonder related to their expanding intellectual and emotional awareness.
6. Face hard moral and ethical questions for which they are unprepared to cope.

Implications for Developmentally Appropriate Practice. Regarding the moral and ethical development of young adolescents, developmentally appropriate actions include

- Encouraging mature value systems by providing opportunities for students to examine options of behavior and to study consequences of various actions.
- Providing opportunities to students to accept responsibility in setting standards for behavior.
- Helping students to develop values when solving their problems.

DIMENSIONS OF THE CHALLENGE

Young adolescents differ in many ways: physical characteristics, interests, home life, intellectual ability, learning capacities, motor ability, social skills, aptitudes and talents, language skills, experience, ideals, attitudes, needs, ambitions, hopes, and dreams. Having long recognized the importance of these individual differences, educators have made many attempts to develop systematic programs of individualized and personalized instruction. In the 1920s there were the "programmed" workbooks of the Winetka Plan. The 1960s brought a multitude of plans, such as IPI (Individually Prescribed Instruction), IGE (Individually Guided Education), and PLAN (Program for Learning in Accordance with Needs). The 1970s saw the development and growth in popularity of individual learning packages and the Individualized Education Program (IEP) for students with special needs. Although some of these efforts did not survive the test of time, others met with more success; some have been refined and are still being used. Today, for example, some schools, like Maryville Middle School (TN), report success using personalized learning plans for all students, not only those with special needs.[4] As stated in *This We Believe*, "in essence, every student needs an individualized educational plan."[5]

Furthermore, for a variety of reasons (e.g., learning styles and learning capacities, modality preferences, information-processing habits, motivational factors, and physiological factors) all persons learn in their own ways and at their own rates. Interests, background, innate and acquired abilities, and a myriad of other influences shape how and what a person will learn. From any particular learning experience no two persons ever learn exactly the same thing.

The Classroom in a Nation of Diversity and Shifting Demographics

Central to the challenge is the concept of **multicultural education,** the recognition and acceptance of students from a variety of backgrounds. An important goal of this concept

> is to educate citizens who can participate successfully in the workforce and take action in the civic community to help the nation actualize its democratic ideals . . . Schools should be model communities that mirror the kind of democratic society we envision [where] the curriculum reflects the cultures of the diverse groups within society, the languages and dialects that students speak are respected and valued, cooperation rather than competition is fostered among students and students from diverse racial, ethnic and social-class groups are given equal status.[6]

The variety of individual differences among middle level students requires that classroom teachers use teaching strategies and tactics that accommodate those differences. To most effectively teach students who are different from you, you need skills in (a) establishing a classroom climate in which all students feel welcome, can learn, and are supported in doing so (topic of Chapter 4), (b) techniques that emphasize cooperative and social-interactive learning and that deemphasize competitive learning (topics of Chapters 8 and 9), (c) building upon students' learning styles, capacities, and modalities, and (d) strategies and techniques that have proven successful for students of specific differences. The last two are topics of this chapter.

To help you meet the challenge, a wealth of information is available. As a licensed teacher you are expected to know, or at least to know where you can find, all necessary information, and to review it when needed. Certain information you have stored in memory will surface and become useful at the most unexpected times. While concerned about all students' safety and physical well being, you will want to remain sensitive to each student's attitudes, values, social adjustment, emotional well being, and cognitive development. You must be prepared not only to teach one or more subjects but to do it effectively with students of different cultural backgrounds, diverse linguistic abilities, and different learning styles, as well as with students who have been identified as having special needs. It is, indeed, a challenge! The statistics that follow make this even more clear.

The traditional two-parent, two-child family now constitutes only about 6 percent of U.S. households. Approximately one-half of the children in the United States will spend some years being raised by a single parent. Nationwide, an estimated one-third of all 12 year olds go home after school to places devoid of any adult supervision.[7] And on any given day, it is estimated that as many as a quarter million children have no place at all to call home. Even with all the nation's resources and wealth, still about one out of every ten children in the United States has a mental illness[8] and about one out of every five children lives in poverty, facts that are inexcusable in the wealthiest nation on Earth.[9]

By the year 2050, the nation's population is predicted to grow to 400 million (from 2001's approximately 283 million), a population boom that will be led by Hispanics and

---

[4]C. McCullen, "Using Data to Change Instruction," *Middle Ground* 4(3):7–9 (February 2001).

[5]*This We Believe*, p. 22.

[6]J. A. Banks, "Multicultural and Citizenship Education in the New Century," *School Administrator* 56(6):8–10 (May 1999). [Online 3/19/00 http://www.aasa.org/SA/may9901/htm] Now available at http://www.aasa.org/publications/sa/1999-05/banks.htm

[7]D. Pride, "Open After Hours: After-School Programs Extend the Learning of Young Adolescents," *Middle Ground* 3(1):20–23 (August 1999), p. 20.

[8]N. Shute, "Children in Anguish: A Call for Better Treatment of Kids' Mental Ills" [Online 1/8/01 http://www.usnews.com/usnews/issue/010115/kids.htm]

[9]H. Hodgkinson, "Educational Demographics: What Teachers Should Know," *Educational Leadership* 58(4):9 (December 2000/January 2001).

Asian Americans. Although, by then, non-white youths in the school-age population throughout the United States will average close to 40 percent, a steady increase in interracial marriages and interracial babies may challenge today's conceptions of multiculturalism and race.[10]

The United States truly is a multilingual, multiethnic, multicultural nation. Of children ages five to seven, approximately one out of every six speaks a language other than English at home. Many of these children have only limited proficiency in the English language (i.e., conversational speaking ability only). In many large school districts, as many as 100 languages are represented, with as many as 20 or more different primary languages found in some classrooms. An increasing ethnic, cultural, and linguistic diversity is affecting schools all across the country—not only the large urban areas but also traditionally homogeneous suburbs and small rural communities.

The overall picture that emerges is a diverse student population that challenges teaching skills. Teachers who traditionally have used direct instruction (see Chapter 6) as the dominant mode of instruction have done so with the assumption that their students were relatively homogeneous in terms of experience, background, knowledge, motivation, and facility with the English language. However, no such assumption can be made today in classrooms of such cultural, ethnic, and linguistic diversity. *As a classroom teacher today, you must be knowledgeable and skilled in using teaching strategies that recognize, celebrate, and build upon that diversity.* In a nutshell, that is your challenge.

STYLES OF LEARNING AND IMPLICATIONS FOR TEACHING

Teachers who are most effective are those who adapt their teaching styles and methods to their students, using approaches that interest the students, that are neither too easy nor too difficult, that match the students' learning styles and learning capacities, and that are relevant to the students' lives. This adaptation process is further complicated because each student is different from every other one. All do not have the same interests, abilities, backgrounds, or learning styles and capacities. As a matter of fact, not only do students differ from one another, but each student can change to some extent from one day to the next. What appeals to a young adolescent today may not have the same appeal tomorrow. Therefore, you need to consider both the nature of young adolescents in general and each student in particular. Since you probably have already experienced a recent course in the psychology of learning, what follows is only a brief synopsis of knowledge about learning.

Learning Modalities

Learning modality refers to the *sensory portal* (or *input channel*) by which a student prefers to receive *sensory reception (modality preference)*, or the actual way a student learns best *(modality adeptness)*. Some young adolescent students prefer learning by seeing, a *visual modality;* others prefer learning through instruction from others (through talk), an *auditory modality;* many others prefer learning by doing and being physically involved, the *kinesthetic modality;* and by touching objects, the *tactile modality.* A student's modality preference is not always that student's modality strength.

While primary modality strength can be determined by observing students, it can also be mixed and it can change as the result of experience and intellectual maturity. As one might suspect, modality integration (i.e., engaging more of the sensory input channels, using several modalities at once or staggered) has been found to contribute to better achievement in student learning. We return to this concept in Part II of this resource guide.

Because many young adolescents have neither a preference nor a strength for auditory reception, teachers should severely limit their use of the lecture method of instruction, that is, of too much reliance on formal teacher talk. Furthermore, instruction that uses a singular approach, such as auditory (e.g., talking to the students), cheats students who learn better another way. This difference can affect student achievement. For example, a teacher who only talks to the students or uses discussions day after day is shortchanging the education of learners who learn better another way, such as kinesthetic and visual learners.

Finally, if a teacher's verbal communication conflicts with his or her nonverbal messages, students can become confused and even resentful, and this too can affect their learning. And when there is a discrepancy between what the teacher says and what that teacher does, the teacher's nonverbal signal will win every time. Actions do speak louder than words! A teacher, for example, who emphasizes the importance of students getting their assignments in on time but then takes forever to read, evaluate, and return those same papers to the students is using inappropriate modeling. Or a teacher who has just finished a lesson on the conservation of energy and does not turn off the room lights upon leaving the classroom for lunch, has, by his or her inappropriate modeling behavior, created cognitive disequilibrium and sabotaged the real purpose for the lesson. And a teacher who asks students not to interrupt others when they are on task but who repeatedly interrupts students when they are on task, is confusing the students with his or her contradictory words and behavior. A teacher's job is not to confuse students. To avoid this, think through what it is that you really expect from your students and

---

[10]See "race facts," pp. 8–9 in H. Hodgkinson, "Educational Demographics: What Teachers Should Know."

then ensure that your own verbal and nonverbal behaviors are consistent with those expectations.[11]

As a general rule, most young adolescents prefer and learn best by touching objects, by feeling shapes and textures, by interacting with each other, and by moving things around. In contrast, learning by sitting and listening are difficult for many of them.

Some learning style traits significantly discriminate between students who are at risk of not finishing school and students who perform well. Students who are underachieving and at risk need (a) frequent opportunities for mobility; (b) options and choices; (c) a variety of instructional resources, environments, and sociological groupings, rather than routines and patterns; (d) to learn during late morning, afternoon, or evening hours, rather than in the early morning; (e) informal seating, rather than wooden, steel, or plastic chairs; (f) low illumination, because bright light contributes to hyperactivity; and (g) tactile/visual introductory resources reinforced by kinesthetic (i.e., direct experiencing and whole-body activities)/visual resources, or introductory kinesthetic/visual resources reinforced by tactile/visual resources.[12]

Regardless of the subject(s) you intend to teach, you are advised to use strategies that integrate the modalities. When well designed, thematic units and project-based learning incorporate modality integration. In conclusion, then, when teaching any group of young adolescents of mixed learning abilities, modality strengths, language proficiency, and cultural backgrounds, integrating learning modalities is a must for the most successful teaching.

Learning Styles

Related to learning modality is **learning style,** which can be defined as independent forms of knowing and processing information. While some students may be comfortable beginning their learning of a new idea in the abstract (e.g., visual or verbal symbolization), most need to begin with the concrete (e.g., learning by actually doing it). Many young adolescents prosper while working in groups, while others prefer to work alone. Some are quick in their studies, whereas others are slow, methodical, cautious, and meticulous. Some can sustain attention on a single topic for a long time, becoming more absorbed in their study as time passes. Others are slower starters and more casual in their pursuits but are capable of shifting with ease from subject to subject. Some

can study in the midst of music, noise, or movement, whereas others need quiet, solitude, and a desk or table. The point is this: students vary not only in their skills and preferences in the way knowledge is received, but also in how they mentally process that information once it has been received. This latter is a person's style of learning.

CLASSIFICATIONS OF LEARNING STYLES

It is important to note that learning style is *not* an indicator of intelligence, but rather an indicator of how a person learns. Although there are probably as many types of learning styles as there are individuals, David Kolb describes two major differences in how people learn: how they perceive situations and how they process information.[13] On the basis of perceiving and processing and on earlier work by Carl Jung on psychological types,[14] Bernice McCarthy has described four major learning styles, presented in the following paragraphs.[15]

The *imaginative learner* perceives information concretely and processes it reflectively. Imaginative learners learn well by listening and sharing with others, integrating the ideas of others with their own experiences. They often have difficulty adjusting to traditional teaching, which depends less on classroom interactions and on students' sharing and connecting of their prior experiences. In a traditional classroom, the imaginative learner is likely to be an at-risk student.

The *analytic learner* perceives information abstractly and processes it reflectively. Analytic learners prefer sequential thinking, need details, and value what experts have to offer. They do well in traditional classrooms.

The *common sense learner* perceives information abstractly and processes it actively. This learner is pragmatic and enjoys hands-on learning. Common sense learners sometimes find school frustrating unless they can see an immediate use for what is being learned. In the traditional classroom, the common sense learner is likely to be a learner who is at risk of not completing school, of dropping out.

The *dynamic learner* perceives information concretely and processes it actively. Dynamic learners also prefer hands-on learning and are excited by anything new. They are risk takers and are frustrated by learning if they see it as being tedious and sequential. In a traditional classroom, the dynamic learner also is likely to be an at-risk student.

---

[11]T. L. Good and J. E. Brophy, *Looking in Classrooms,* 8th ed. (New York: Addison Wesley Longman, 2000), p. 127.

[12]R. Dunn, *Strategies for Educating Diverse Learners,* Fastback 384 (Bloomington, IN: Phi Delta Kappa Educational Foundation, 1995), p. 9.

[13]D. A. Kolb, *Experiential Learning: Experience as the Source of Learning and Development* (Upper Saddle River, NJ: Prentice Hall, 1984).

[14]C. G. Jung, *Psychological Types* (New York: Harcourt Brace, 1923).

[15]See B. McCarthy, "A Tale of Four Learners: 4MAT's Learning Styles," *Educational Leadership* 54(6):47–51 (March 1997).

The Three-Phase Learning Cycle

To understand conceptual development and change, researchers in the 1960s developed a Piaget-based theory of learning where students are guided from concrete, hands-on learning experiences to the abstract formulations of concepts and their formal applications. This theory became known as the *three-phase learning cycle*.[16] Long a popular strategy for teaching science, the learning cycle can be useful in other disciplines as well.[17] The three phases are (1) the *exploratory hands-on phase*, where students can explore ideas and experience assimilation and disequilibrium that leads to their own questions and tentative answers, (2) the *invention* or *concept development phase*, where, under the guidance of the teacher, students invent concepts and principles that help them answer their questions and reorganize their ideas (that is, the students revise their thinking to allow the new information to fit), and (3) the *expansion* or *concept application phase*, another hands-on phase in which students try out their new ideas by applying them to situations that are relevant and meaningful to them.[18] During application of a concept the learner may discover new information that causes a change in the learner's understanding of the concept being applied. Thus, as discussed further in Chapter 9, the process of learning is cyclical.

Recent interpretations or modifications of the three-phase cycle include McCarthy's 4MAT.[19] With the 4MAT system developed by McCarthy, teachers employ a learning cycle of instructional strategies to try to reach each student's learning style. As stated by McCarthy, in the cycle learners "sense and feel, they experience, then they watch, they reflect, then they think, they develop theories, then they try out theories, they experiment. Finally, they evaluate and synthesize what they have learned in order to apply it to their next similar experience. They get smarter. They apply experi-

ence to experiences."[20] In this process, they are likely to be using all four learning modalities.

To evince *constructivist learning theory,* that is, that learning is a process involving the active engagement of learners who adapt the educative event to fit and expand their individual world view (as opposed to the behaviorist pedagogical assumption that learning is something done to learners)[21] and to accentuate the importance of student self-assessment, some variations of the learning cycle include a fourth phase, an *assessment phase*. However, because we, the authors of this book, believe that assessment of what students know or think they know should be a continual process, permeating all three phases of the learning cycle, we reject any treatment of assessment as a self-standing phase.

Learning Capacities: The Theory of Multiple Intelligences

In contrast to learning styles, Gardner introduced what he calls *learning capacities* exhibited by individuals in differing ways.[22] Originally called and sometimes still referred to as **multiple intelligences,** or *ways of knowing,* capacities identified thus far are

- *Bodily/kinesthetic:* ability to use the body skillfully and to handle objects skillfully.
- *Interpersonal:* ability to understand people and relationships.
- *Intrapersonal:* ability to assess one's emotional life as a means to understand oneself and others.
- *Logical/mathematical:* ability to handle chains of reasoning and to recognize patterns and orders.
- *Musical:* sensitivity to pitch, melody, rhythm, and tone.
- *Naturalist:* ability to draw on materials and features of the natural environment to solve problems or fashion products.
- *Verbal/linguistic:* sensitivity to the meaning and order of words.
- *Visual/spatial:* ability to perceive the world accurately and to manipulate the nature of space, such as through architecture, mime, or sculpture.

As discussed earlier, and as implied in the presentation of McCarthy's four types of learners, many educa-

---

[16]See R. Karplus, *Science Curriculum Improvement Study,* Teacher's Handbook (Berkeley: University of California, 1974).

[17]See, for example, M. M. Bevevino; J. Dengel; and K. Adams, "Constructivist Theory in the Classroom: Internalizing Concepts through Inquiry Learning," *Clearing House* 72(5):275–278 (May/June 1999), using the learning cycle in a history lesson about WWI; A. C. Rule, *Using the Learning Cycle to Teach Acronyms, a Language Arts Lesson* (ED383000, 1995); and, J. E. Sowell, "Approach to Art History in the Classroom," *Art Education* 46(2):19–24 (March 1993).

[18]The three phases of the learning cycle are comparable to the three levels of thinking, described variously by others. For example, in Elliot Eisner's *The Educational Imagination* (New York: Macmillan, 1979), the levels are referred to as "descriptive," "interpretive," and "evaluative."

[19]For information about 4MAT, contact Excel, Inc. at 23385 W. Old Barrington Road, Barrington, IL 60010 (847-382-7272) or at 6322 Fenworth Ct., Agoura Hills, CA 91301, (818-879-7442).

[20]B. McCarthy, "Using the 4MAT System to Bring Learning Styles to Schools," *Educational Leadership* 48(2):33 (October 1990).

[21]R. DeLay, "Forming Knowledge: Constructivist Learning and Experiential Education," *Journal of Experiential Education* 19(2):76–81 (August/September 1996).

[22]For Gardner's distinction between "learning style" and "intelligences," see: H. Gardner, "Multiple Intelligences: Myths and Messages," *International Schools Journal* 15(2):8–22 (April 1996) and the many articles in the "Teaching for Multiple Intelligences" theme issue of *Educational Leadership* 55(1) (September 1997).

CLASSROOM VIGNETTE
Using the Theory of Learning Capacities (Multiple Intelligences) and Multilevel Instruction

In one middle school classroom, during one week of a six-week thematic unit on weather, students were concentrating on learning about the water cycle. For this study of the water cycle, with the students' help the teacher divided the class into several groups of three to five students per group. The groups worked on six projects simultaneously to learn about the water cycle. (1) One group of students designed, conducted, and repeated an experiment to discover the number of drops of water that can be held on one side of a new one-cent coin versus the number that can be held on the side of a worn one-cent coin; (2) working in part with the first group, a second group designed and prepared graphs to illustrate the results of the experiments of the first group; (3) a third group of students created and composed the words and music of a song about the water cycle; (4) a fourth group incorporated their combined interests in mathematics and art to design, collect the necessary materials, and create a colorful and interactive bulletin board about the water cycle; (5) a fifth group read about the water cycle in materials they researched from the Internet and various libraries; and (6) a sixth group created a puppet show about the water cycle. On Friday, after each group had finished, the groups shared their projects with the whole class.

tors believe that many of the students who are at risk of not completing school are those who may be dominant in a cognitive learning style that is not in sync with traditional teaching methods. Traditional methods of instruction are largely of McCarthy's analytic style: information is presented in a logical, linear, sequential fashion. Traditional methods also reflect three of the Gardner types: verbal/linguistic, logical/mathematical, and intrapersonal. Consequently, to better synchronize methods of instruction with learning styles, some teachers and middle level schools have restructured the curriculum and instruction around Gardner's learning capacities,[23] or around Sternberg's Triarchic Theory.[24]

Sternberg identifies seven metaphors for the mind and intelligence—geographic, computational, biological, epistemological, anthropological, sociological, and systems—and proposes a theory of intelligence consisting of three elements: analytical, practical, and creative.[25]

See the Classroom Vignette above. Internet resources on learning styles and multiple intelligences are shown in Figure 2.1.

From the preceding information about learning, these two important facts are evident:

1. *Intelligence is not a fixed or static reality, but can be learned, taught, and developed.* This concept is important for students to understand also. When students understand that intelligence is incremental, something that is developed through use over time, they tend to be more motivated to work at learning than when they believe intelligence is a fixed entity.[26]

2. *Not all students learn and respond to learning situations in the same way.* A student may learn differently according to the situation or according to the student's ethnicity, cultural background, or socioeconomic status.[27] A teacher who uses only one style of teaching for all students or who teaches to only one or a few styles of learning day after day is short-changing those students who learn better another way.

---

[23]For example, see G. Gallagher, "Multiple Intelligences," *Middle Ground* 1(2):10–12 (October 1997).

[24]See, for example, R. J. Sternberg, "Teaching and Assessing for Successful Intelligence," and L. English, "Uncovering Students' Analytic, Practical, and Creative Intelligences: One School's Application of Sternberg's Triarchic Theory," *School Administrator* 55(1):26–27, 30–31, and 28–29, respectively (January 1998).

[25]See R. J. Sternberg, "Teaching and Assessing for Successful Intelligence," *School Administrator* 55(1):26–27, 30–31 (January 1998). See also R. J. Sternberg; E. L. Grigorenko; and L. Jarvin, "Improving Reading Instruction: The Triarchic Model," *Educational Leadership* 58(6):48–52 (March 2001).

---

[26]See, for example, R. J. Marzano, "20th Century Advances in Instruction," in R. S. Brandt (Ed.), *Education in a New Era*, (Alexandria, VA: ASCD Yearbook, Association for Supervision and Curriculum Development, 2000), p. 76, and A. W. Jackson and G. A. Davis, *Turning Points 2000: Educating Adolescents in the 21st Century* (New York: Teachers College Press, 2000), p. 66.

[27]See P. Guild, "The Culture/Learning Style Connection," *Educational Leadership* 51(8):16–21 (May 1994).

Figure 2.1   Internet resources on learning styles and multiple intelligences.

- ERIC link to multiple intelligences resources at http://www.indiana.edu/~eric_rec/ieo/bibs/multiple.html
- Howard Gardner's Project Zero web site at http://pzweb.harvard.edu
- Resources on learning styles at http://www.d.umn.edu/student/loon/acad/strat/lrnsty.html

MEETING THE CHALLENGE: RECOGNIZING AND PROVIDING FOR STUDENT DIFFERENCES

Assume that you are a middle school history teacher and that your teaching schedule consists of four sections of U.S. history. Three sections meet daily for 50 minutes each day. The fourth section follows a block schedule of 100 minutes two days a week and 40 minutes one day a week. Furthermore, assume that students at your school are tracked (as they are in many middle level schools). Of your three classes that follow the traditional schedule, one is a so-called accelerated class with 30 students. Another is a regular-education class with 35 students, 3 of whom have special needs because of disabilities. The third is a sheltered English class with 13 students—6 Hispanics with limited proficiency in English; 1 student from Russia and 2 from the Ukraine, all three of whom have very limited proficiency in English; and 4 Southeast Asians, 2 with no ability to use English. The class that follows the block schedule is a regular education class of 33 English-proficient students. Again, for all four sections, the course is U.S. history. Will one lesson plan using lecture and teacher-directed discussion as the primary instructional strategies work for all four sections? The answer is an emphatic no! How do you decide what to do? Before you finish this resource guide, we hope the answer to that question will become clear to you.

First consider the following general guidelines, most of which are discussed in further detail in later chapters as designated.

Instructional Practices That Provide for Student Differences: General Guidelines

To provide learning experiences that are consistent with what is known about ways of learning and knowing, consider the recommendations that follow and refer to them during the preactive phase of your instruction (discussed in Chapter 3).

- As frequently as is appropriate, and especially for skills development, plan the learning activities so they follow a step-by-step sequence from concrete to abstract (see "The Learning Experiences Ladder" in Chapter 6).
- Communicate with students in a clear, direct, and consistent manner (Chapters 2, 3, 5, and others).
- Concentrate on using student-centered instruction by using project-centered learning, discovery and inquiry strategies, simulations and role-play (Chapters 8 and 9).
- Establish multiple learning centers within the classroom (Chapter 8).
- Maintain high expectations, although not necessarily identical, for every student; establish high standards and teach toward them without wavering (see throughout).
- Plan interesting activities to bridge learning, activities that help the students connect what is being learned with their real world.
- Provide a structured learning environment with regular and understood procedures (Chapter 4).
- Provide ongoing and frequent monitoring of individual student learning, or **formative assessment** (discussed throughout).
- Provide variations in meaningful assignments, with optional due dates, that are based on individual student abilities and interests (Chapters 5 and 8).
- Use direct instruction to teach to the development of observation, generalization, and other thinking and learning skills (Chapter 9).
- Use interactive computer programs and multimedia (Chapter 10).
- Use multilevel instruction (see Figure 2.1 and Chapter 3).
- Use reciprocal peer coaching and cross-age tutoring (Chapter 8).
- Use small-group and cooperative learning strategies (Chapter 8).
- With students, collaboratively plan challenging and engaging classroom learning activities and assignments (see Chapters 5, 6, 8, and others).

Because social awareness is such an important and integral part of a young adolescent student's experience, exemplary school programs and much of their practices are geared toward some type of social interaction. Indeed, learning is a social enterprise among learners and their teachers. Although many of today's successful instructional practices rely heavily on social learning activities and interpersonal relationships, each teacher must be aware of and sensitive to individual student differences. For working with specific learners, consider the guidelines that follow and refer back to these guidelines often during your preactive phase of instruction.

Recognizing and Working with Students with Disabilities

Students with disabilities (referred to also as **exceptional students** and special-needs students) include those with disabling conditions or impairments in any one or more of the following categories: mental retardation, hearing, speech or language, visual, emotional, orthopedic, autism, traumatic brain injury, other health impairment, or specific learning disabilities. To the extent possible, students with special needs must be educated with their peers in the regular classroom. Public Law 94-142, the Education for All Handicapped Children Act (EAHCA) of 1975, mandates that all children have the right to a free and appropriate education, as well as to nondiscriminatory assessment. (Public Law 94-142 was amended in 1986 by P.L. 99-457, in 1990 by P.L. 101-476 at which time its name was changed to Individuals with Disabilities Education Act-IDEA, and in 1997 by P.L. 105-17.) Emphasizing normalizing the educational environment for students with disabilities, this legislation requires provision of the least-restrictive environment (LRE) for these students. An LRE is an environment that is as normal as possible.

Teachers today know that students with disabilities fall along a continuum of learner differences rather than in a separate category of student.[28] Because of their wide differences, students identified as having special needs may be placed in the regular classroom for the entire school day. This is called *full inclusion.*[29] Those students may also be in a regular classroom the greater part of the school day, called *partial inclusion,* or only for designated periods. Although there is no single, universally accepted definition of the term, **inclusion** is the concept that students with disabilities should be integrated into general education classrooms regardless of whether they can meet traditional academic standards.[30] (The term *inclusion* has largely replaced use of an earlier and similar term, mainstreaming.) As a classroom teacher you will need information and skills specific to teaching learners with special needs who are included in your classes.

Generally speaking, teaching students who have special needs requires more care, better diagnosis, greater skill, more attention to individual needs, and an even greater understanding of the students. The challenges of teaching students with special needs in the regular classroom are great enough that to do it well you need specialized training beyond the general guidelines presented here. At some point in your teacher preparation, you should take one or more courses in working with special-needs learners in the regular classroom.

When a student with special needs is placed in your classroom, your task is to deal directly with the differences between this student and other students in your classroom. To do this, you should develop an understanding of the general characteristics of different types of special-needs learners, identify the student's unique needs relative to your classroom, and design lessons that teach to different needs at the same time. This is called *multilevel teaching,* or *multitasking.* Remember that just because a student has been identified as having one or more special needs does not preclude that person from being gifted or talented.

Congress stipulated in P.L. 94-142 that an Individualized Educational Program (IEP) be devised annually for each special-needs child. According to that law, an IEP is developed for each student each year by a team that includes special education teachers, the child's parents or guardians, and the classroom teachers. The IEP contains a statement of the student's present educational levels, the educational goals for the year, specifications for the services to be provided and the extent to which the student should be expected to take part in the regular education program, and the evaluative criteria for the services to be provided. Consultation by special and skilled support personnel is essential in all IEP models. A consultant works directly with teachers or with students and parents. As a classroom teacher, you may play an active role in preparing the specifications for the special-needs students assigned to your classroom and assume a major responsibility for implementing the program.

GUIDELINES FOR WORKING WITH SPECIAL-NEEDS STUDENTS IN THE REGULAR CLASSROOM

Although the guidelines represented by the paragraphs that follow are important for teaching all students, they are especially important for working with special-needs students.

Familiarize yourself with exactly what the special needs of each learner are. Privately ask the special-needs student whether there is anything he or she would like for you to know about the learner or anything that you specifically can do to facilitate his or her learning.

Adapt and modify materials and procedures to the special needs of each student. For example, a student who has extreme difficulty sitting still for more than a few minutes will need planned changes in learning activities. When establishing student seating arrangements in the classroom, give preference to students according to their special needs. Try to incorporate activities into lessons that engage all learning modalities—visual, auditory, tactile, and kinesthetic. Be flexible in your classroom procedures. For example, allow the use of tape recorders for note taking and test taking when students have trouble with the written language.

---

[28]A. Meyer and D. H. Rose, "Universal Design for Individual Differences," *Educational Leadership* 58(3):39–43 (November 2000), p. 40.

[29]See, for example, M. L. Yell, "The Legal Basis of Inclusion," *Educational Leadership* 56(2):70–73 (October 1998).

[30]E. Tiegerman-Farber and C. Radziewicz, *Collaborative Decision Making: The Pathway to Inclusion* (Upper Saddle River, NJ: Merrill/Prentice Hall, 1998), pp. 12–13.

Provide high structure and clear expectations by defining the learning objectives in behavioral terms (discussed in Chapter 5). Teach students the correct procedures for everything (Chapter 4). Break complex learning into simpler components, moving from the most concrete to the abstract, rather than the other way around. Check frequently for student understanding of instructions and procedures, and for comprehension of content. Use computers and other self-correcting materials for drill and practice and to provising immediate, constructive, and private feedback to the student.

Develop your **withitness** (discussed in Chapters 3 and 4), which is your awareness of everything that is going on in the classroom at all times, monitoring students for signs of restlessness, frustration, anxiety, and off-task behaviors. Be ready to reassign individual learners to different activities as the situation warrants. Established classroom learning centers (discussed in Chapter 8) can be a big help.

Have all students maintain assignments for the week or some other period of time in assignment books or in folders that are kept in their notebooks. This is a requirement in many middle schools. Post assignments in a special place in the classroom (and perhaps on the school's website) and frequently remind students of assignments and deadlines.

Maintain consistency in your expectations and in your responses. Special-needs learners, particularly, can become frustrated when they do not understand a teacher's expectations and when they cannot depend on a teacher's reactions.

Plan interesting activities to bridge learning. Activities that help the students connect what is being learned with their real world helps to motivate students and to keep them on task.

Plan questions and questioning sequences and write them into your lesson plans (discussed in Chapters 6 and 7). Plan questions to ask special-needs learners so that they are likely to answer them with confidence. Use signals to let students know that you are likely to call on them in class (e.g., prolonged eye contact or mentioning your intention to the student before class begins). After asking a question, give the student adequate time to think and respond. Then, after the student responds, build upon the student's response to indicate that the student's contribution was accepted as being important.

Provide for and teach toward student success. Offer students activities and experiences that ensure each individual student's success and mastery at some level. Use of student portfolios (discussed in Chapter 11) can give evidence of progress and help build student confidence and self-esteem.

Provide guided or coached practice and time in class for students to work on assignments and projects. During this time, you can monitor the work of each student while looking for misconceptions, thus ensuring that students get started on the right track (discussed in Chapter 6).

Provide help in the organization of students' learning. For example, give instruction in the organization of notes and notebooks. Have a three-hole punch available in the classroom so students can put papers into their notebooks immediately, thus avoiding disorganization and their loss of papers. During class presentations use an overhead projector with transparencies so students who need more time can copy material from them. Ask students to read their notes aloud to each other in small groups, thereby aiding their recall and understanding, and encouraging them to take notes for meaning rather than for rote learning. Encourage and provide for peer support, peer tutoring or coaching, and cross-age teaching (Chapter 8). Ensure that the special-needs learner is included in all class activities to the fullest extent possible.

Recognizing and Working with Students of Diversity and Differences

Quickly determine the language and ethnic groups represented by the students in your classroom. A major problem for newcomers, as well as some ethnic groups, is learning a second (or third or fourth) language. While in many schools it is not uncommon for more than half the students to come from homes where the spoken language is not English, standard English is a necessity in most communities of this country if a person is to become vocationally successful and enjoy a full life. Learning to communicate reasonably well in English can take an immigrant student at least a year and probably longer; some authorities say three to seven years. By default, then, an increasing percentage of teachers are teachers of English language learning. Helpful to the success of teaching students who are English Language Learners (ELL's), that is, who have limited proficiency in English language usage, is the demonstration of respect for students' cultural backgrounds, long-term teacher-student cohorts (such as, for example, in looping), and the use of active and cooperative learning.[31]

There are numerous programs specially designed for English language learners. Most use the acronym LEP (limited English proficiency) with five number levels from LEP 1 that designates non-English-speaking, although the student may understand single sentences and speak simple words or phrases in English, to LEP 5, sometimes designated FEP (fluent English proficient), for the student who is fully fluent in English. However, the student's overall academic achievement may still be less than desired because of language or cultural differences.

---

[31] See P. Berman, et al., *School Reform and Student Diversity, Volume II: Case Studies of Exemplary Practices for LEP Students* (Berkeley, CA: National Center for Research on Cultural Diversity and Second Language Learning, 1995).

Some schools use a "pullout" approach, where part of the student's school time is spent in special bilingual classes and the rest of the time the student is placed in regular classrooms. In some schools, LEP students are placed in academic classrooms that use a simplified or "sheltered" English approach. Regardless of the program, specific techniques recommended for teaching ELL students include

- Allowing more time for learning activities than one normally would.
- Allowing time for translation by a classroom aide or by a classmate and allowing time for discussion to clarify meaning, encouraging the students to transfer into English what they already know in their native language.
- Avoiding jargon or idioms that might be misunderstood. See the scenario that follows.

CLASSROOM SCENARIO

A Humorous Scenario Related to Idioms: A Teachable Moment

While Elina was reciting she had a little difficulty with her throat (due to a cold) and stumbled over some words. The teacher jokingly commented, "That's okay Elina, you must have a horse in your throat." Quickly, Mariya, a recent immigrant from the Ukraine, asked, "How could she have a horse in her throat?" The teacher ignored Mariya's question. Missing this teachable moment, he continued with his planned lesson.

- Dividing complex or extended language discourse into smaller, more manageable units.
- Giving directions in a variety of ways.
- Giving special attention to key words that convey meaning, and writing them on the board.
- Maintaining high expectations of each learner.
- Reading written directions aloud and then writing the directions on the board.
- Speaking clearly and naturally but at a slower than normal pace.
- Using a variety of examples and observable models.
- Using simplified vocabulary but without talking down to students.[32]

ADDITIONAL GUIDELINES FOR WORKING WITH LANGUAGE-MINORITY STUDENTS

While they are becoming literate in English language usage, LEP students can learn the same curriculum in the various disciplines as native English-speaking students.

Although the guidelines presented in the following paragraphs are important for teaching all students, they are especially important when working with language-minority students.

Present instruction that is concrete, that includes the most direct learning experiences possible. Use the most concrete (least abstract) forms of instruction.

Build upon (or connect with) what the students already have experienced and know. Building upon what students already know, or think they know, helps them to connect their knowledge and construct their understandings.

Encourage student writing. One way is by using student journals (see Chapters 8 and 11). Two kinds of journals that are appropriate when working with LEP students are dialogue journals and response journals. *Dialogue journals* are used for students to write anything that is on their minds, usually on the right page. Teachers, parents, and classmates then respond on the left page, thereby "talking with" the journal writers. *Response journals* are used for students to write (record) their responses to what they are reading or studying.

Help students learn the vocabulary. Assist the ELL students in learning two vocabulary sets: the regular English vocabulary needed for learning and the new vocabulary introduced by the subject content. For example, while learning science a student is dealing with both the regular English language vocabulary and the special vocabulary of science.

Involve parents, guardians, or older siblings. Students whose primary language is not English may have other differences about which you will also need to become knowledgeable. These differences are related to culture, customs, family life, and expectations. To be most successful in working with language minority students, you should learn as much as possible about each student. To this end it can be valuable to solicit the help of the student's parent, guardian, or even an older sibling. Parents (or guardians) of new immigrant children are usually truly concerned about the education of their children and may be very interested in cooperating with you in any way possible. In a study of schools recognized for their exemplary practices with language-minority students, the schools were recognized for being "parent friendly," that is, for welcoming parents in a variety of innovative ways.[33]

Plan for and use all learning modalities. As with teaching young adolescents in general, in working with language-minority students in particular you need to use multisensory approaches—learning activities that involve students in auditory, visual, tactile, and kinesthetic learning activities.

---

[32]D. R. Walling, *English as a Second Language: 25 Questions and Answers,* Fastback 347 (Bloomington, IN: Phi Delta Kappa Educational Foundation, 1993), p. 26.

[33]C. Minicucci, et al., "School Reform and Student Diversity," *Phi Delta Kappan* 77(1):77–80 (September 1995), p. 78.

Use small group cooperative learning. Cooperative learning strategies are particularly effective with language-minority students because they provide opportunities for students to produce language in a setting that is less threatening than speaking before the entire class.

Use the benefits afforded by modern technology. For example, computer networking allows the language minority students to write and communicate with peers from around the world as well as to participate in "publishing" their classroom work.

ADDITIONAL GUIDELINES FOR WORKING WITH STUDENTS OF DIVERSE BACKGROUNDS

To be compatible with, and to be able to teach, students who come from backgrounds different from yours, you need to believe that, given adequate support, all students *can* learn—regardless of gender, social class, physical characteristics, language, and ethnic or cultural backgrounds. You also need to develop special skills that include those in the following guidelines, each of which is discussed in detail in other chapters. To work successfully and most effectively with students of diverse backgrounds, you should do the following:

- Build the learning around students' individual learning styles. Personalize learning for each student, much like what is done by using the IEP with special-needs learners. Involve students in understanding and in making important decisions about their own learning, so that they feel ownership (i.e., a sense of empowerment and connectedness) of that learning. As was said at the start of this chapter, some schools report success using personalized learning plans for all students, not only those with special needs.
- Communicate positively with every student and with the student's parents or guardians, learning as much as you can about the student and the student's culture, and encouraging family members to participate in the student's learning. Involve parents, guardians, and other members of the community in the educational program so that all have a sense of ownership and responsibility, and feel positive about the school program.
- Establish and maintain high expectations, although not necessarily the same expectations, for each student. Both you and your students must understand that intelligence is not a fixed entity, but a set of characteristics that, through a feeling of "I can" and with proper coaching, can be developed. (See, for example, Characteristics of Intelligent Behavior, in Chapter 9.)
- Teach to individuals by using a variety of strategies to achieve an objective or by using a number of different objectives at the same time (multilevel teaching).
- Use techniques that emphasize collaborative and cooperative learning—that de-emphasize competitive learning.

Recognizing and Working with Students Who Are Gifted

Historically, educators have used the term *gifted* when referring to a person with identified exceptional ability in one or more academic subjects, and *talented* when referring to a person with exceptional ability in one or more of the visual or performing arts.[34] Today, however, the terms more often are used interchangeably as if they are synonymous, which is how they are used for this resource guide.

Sometimes, unfortunately, in the regular classroom gifted students are neglected.[35] At least part of the time, it is likely to be because there is no singularly accepted method for identification of these students. In other words, students who are gifted in some way or another may go unidentified as such. For placement in special classes or programs for the gifted and talented, school districts traditionally have used grade point averages and standard intelligence quotient (IQ) scores. However, because IQ testing measures linguistic and logical/mathematical aspects of giftedness (refer to earlier discussion in this chapter—Learning Capacities: The Theory of Multiple Intelligences), it does not account for others and thus gifted students sometimes are unrecognized. They can also be among the students most at risk of dropping out of school.[36] It is estimated that between 10 and 20 percent of school dropouts are students who are in the range of being intellectually gifted.[37]

To work most effectively with gifted learners, their talents first must be identified. This can be done not only with tests, rating scales, and auditions but also by observations in and out of the classroom, and from knowledge about the student's personal life. With those information sources in mind, here is a list of indicators of superior intelligence:[38]

- Ability to assume adult roles and responsibilities at home or at work.
- Ability to cope with school while living in poverty.
- Ability to cope with school while living with dysfunctional families.

---

[34]See the discussion in G. Clark and E. Zimmerman, "Nurturing the Arts in Programs for Gifted and Talented Students," *Phi Delta Kappan* 79(10):747–751 (June 1998).

[35]See, for example, J. F. Feldhusen, "Programs for the Gifted Few or Talent Development for the Many?" *Phi Delta Kappan* 79(10):735–738 (June 1998).

[36]C. Dixon, L. Mains, and M. J. Reeves, *Gifted and At Risk*, Fastback 398 (Bloomington, IN: Phi Delta Kappa Educational Foundation, 1996), p. 7.

[37]S. B. Rimm, "Underachievement Syndrome: A National Epidemic," in N. Colangelo and G. A. Davis (Eds.), *Handbook of Gifted Education*, 2nd ed. (Needham Heights, MA: Allyn & Bacon, 1997), p. 416.

[38]S. Schwartz, *Strategies for Identifying the Talents of Diverse Students*, ERIC/CUE Digest, Number 122 (New York: ED410323, ERIC Clearinghouse on Urban Education, May 1997).

- Ability to extrapolate knowledge to different circumstances.
- Ability to lead others.
- Ability to manipulate a symbol system.
- Ability to reason by analogy.
- Ability to retrieve and use stored knowledge to solve problems.
- Ability to think and act independently.
- Ability to think logically.
- Creativity and artistic ability.
- Strong sense of self, pride, and worth.
- Understanding of one's cultural heritage.

To assist you in understanding gifted children who may or may not yet have been identified as being gifted, following are some types of students and the kinds of problems to which they may be prone, that is, personal behaviors that may identify them as being gifted but academically disabled, bored, and alienated.

- *Antisocial* students, alienated by their differences from peers, may become bored and impatient troublemakers.
- *Creative, high achieving* students often feel isolated, weird, and depressed.
- *Divergent thinking* students can develop self-esteem problems when they provide answers that are logical to them but seem unusual and off-the-wall to their peers. They may have only a few peer friends.
- *Perfectionists* may exhibit compulsive behaviors because they feel as though their value comes from their accomplishments. When their accomplishments do not live up to expectations—their own, their parents', or their teachers—anxiety and feelings of inadequacy arise. When other students do not live up to the gifted student's high standards, alienation from those students is probable.
- *Sensitive* students who also are gifted may become easily depressed because they are so aware of their surroundings and of their differences.
- *Students with special needs* may be gifted. Attention deficit disorder, dyslexia, hyperactivity, and other learning disorders sometimes mask giftedness.
- *Underachieving* students can also be gifted students but fail in their studies because they learn in ways that are seldom or never challenged by classroom teachers. Although often expected to excel in everything they do, most gifted students can be underachievers in some areas. Having high expectations of themselves, underachievers tend to be highly critical of themselves and develop a low self-esteem, and can become indifferent and even hostile.[39]

Curriculum Tracking: Not a Viable Option

All students, not only those who have been identified as gifted, need a challenging academic environment. Although grouping and tracking students into classes based on interest and demonstrated ability is still widely practiced (such as reading groups, grade level retention, accelerated groups, and special education placement), an overwhelming abundance of sources in the literature adamantly opposes the homogeneous grouping of students according to ability, or *curriculum tracking*, as it has long been known. Grouping and tracking do not seem to increase overall achievement of learning, but they do promote inequity.[40]

Although many, perhaps most, research studies lead one to conclude that tracking, as it has been traditionally practiced, should be discontinued because of its discriminatory and damaging effects on students, many schools continue using it. Direct examples are counseling students into classes according to evidence of ability and the degree of academic rigor of the program. Tracking also results indirectly by designating certain classes and programs as "academic" or "accelerated" and others as "non-academic" or "standard" and allowing students some degree of latitude to choose, either partly or wholly, from one or the other.

Meaningful Curriculum Options: Multiple Pathways to Success

Because of what is now known about learning and intelligence, the trend today is to assume that each student, to some degree and in some area of learning and doing, has the potential for giftedness, and to provide sufficient curriculum options, or multiple pathways, so each student can reach those potentials. For example, that is why, in schools' mission statements (see Figure 1.1 of Chapter 1) today there is usually reference to the school's belief that all students can succeed. Clearly, achievement in school increases, students learn more, and they enjoy learning and remember more of what they have learned when individual learning capacities, styles, and modalities are identified and accommodated.[41]

To provide relevant curriculum options, a trend in exemplary schools is to eliminate from the school curriculum what have traditionally been the lower and general curriculum tracks and instead provide curriculum options to try to assure success for every student. While attempting to diminish the discriminatory and damaging effects on

---

[39]Adapted from Dixon, Mains, and Reeves, pp. 9–12. By permission of the Phi Delta Kappa Educational Foundation.

[40]See J. Oakes, et al., "Equity Lessons from Detracking Schools," Chapter 3 of A. Hargreaves (Ed.), *Rethinking Educational Change With Heart and Mind* (Alexandria, VA: ASCD 1997 Yearbook, Association for Supervision and Curriculum Development, 1997) (pp. 43–72); W. Schwartz (Ed.), *New Trends in Language Education for Hispanic Students* (New York: ED442913, ERIC Clearinghouse on Urban Education, 2000); and *Turning Points 2000*, pp. 65–68 and 175.

[41]Dixon, Mains, and Reeves, p. 21.

students that are believed to be caused by tracking and homogeneous ability grouping, educators have devised and are refining numerous other seemingly more productive ways of attending to student differences, of providing a more challenging but supportive learning environment, and of stimulating the talents and motivation of each student. Because the advantage gained from using a combination of responsive practices concurrently is generally greater than is the gain from using any singular practice by itself, in many instances in a given school the practices overlap and are used simultaneously. These practices are shown in Figure 2.2, and most are discussed in various places throughout this resource guide. Check the index for topic locations.

ADDITIONAL GUIDELINES FOR WORKING WITH GIFTED STUDENTS

When working in the regular classroom with a student who has special gifts and talents, you are advised to

- Collaborate with students in some planning of their own objectives and activities for learning.

Figure 2.2   Multiple pathways to success: productive ways of attending to student differences, of providing a more challenging learning environment, and of stimulating the talents and motivation of each student.

- Advisory programs and adult advocacy relationships for each student
- Students being allowed to attend a high school class while still in middle grades
- Students being allowed to skip a traditional grade level, thereby accelerating the time it takes for a student to pass through the grades
- Bilingual programs that are intellectually stimulating and designed for integration with mainstream education
- Community service learning that is connected to some portion of the academic program
- Cooperative learning in the classroom
- Curriculum compacting
- Extra effort to provide academic help
- Flexible block scheduling
- High expectation for every student
- Individualized educational plans and instruction
- Integrating new technologies into the curriculum
- Interdisciplinary teaming and thematic instruction
- Looping
- Peer and cross-age teaching
- Personal problems assistance provision at school
- Second opportunity recovery strategies
- Specialized and/or smaller schools or schools-within-a-school
- Ungraded or multi-age grouping
- Within-class and across discipline student-centered projects

- Emphasize skills in critical thinking, problem solving, and inquiry.
- Identify and showcase the student's special gift or talent.
- Involve the student in selecting and planning activities, encouraging the development of the student's leadership skills.
- Plan assignments and activities that challenge the students to their fullest abilities. This does *not* mean overloading them with homework or giving identical assignments to all students (see "tiered assignments" in Chapter 7). Rather, carefully plan so that the students' time spent on assignments and activities is quality time on meaningful learning.
- Provide in-class seminars for students to discuss topics and problems that they are pursuing individually or as members of a learning team.
- Provide independent and dyad learning opportunities. Gifted and talented students often prefer to work alone or with another gifted student.
- Use *curriculum compacting,* a process that allows a student who already knows the material to pursue enriched or accelerated study. Plan and provide optional and voluntary enrichment activities. Learning centers, special projects, and computer and multimedia activities are excellent tools for providing enriched learning activities.
- Use preassessments (diagnostic evaluation) for reading level and subject content achievement so that you are better able to prescribe objectives and activities for each student.

Recognizing and Working with Students Who Take More Time but Are Willing to Try

Students who are slower to learn typically fall into one of two categories: (1) those who try to learn but simply need more time to do it, and (2) those who do not try, referred to variously as underachievers, recalcitrant, or reluctant learners. Practices that work well with students in one category are often not those that work well with students in the other—making life difficult for a teacher of 30 students, half of whom try and half who don't. It is worse still for a teacher of a group of 30 students in which some try but need time, one or two are academically talented, one or two have special needs, a few are LEP students, and several not only seem unwilling to try but are also disruptive in the classroom.

Remember that just because a student is slow to learn does not mean that the student is less intelligent; some students just plain take longer, for any number of reasons. The following guidelines may be helpful when working with a student who is slow but willing to try:

- Adjust the instruction to the student's preferred learning style, which may be different from yours and from other students in the group.

- Be less concerned with the amount of content coverage than with the student's successful understanding of content that is covered.
- Discover something the student does exceptionally well, or a special interest, and try to build on that.
- Emphasize basic communication skills, such as speaking, listening, reading, and writing, to ensure that the student's skills in these areas are sufficient for learning the intended content.
- Help the student learn content in small sequential steps with frequent checks for comprehension.
- If necessary, help the student to improve his or her reading skills, such as pronunciation and word meanings.
- If using a single textbook, be certain that the reading level is adequate for the student; if it is not, use other more appropriate reading materials for that student.
- Maximize the use of in-class, on-task work and cooperative learning, with close monitoring of the student's progress. Avoid relying much on successful completion of traditional out-of-class assignments unless you can supply coached guidance to the student in the classroom.
- Vary the instructional strategies, using a variety of activities to engage the visual, verbal, tactile, and kinesthetic modalities.
- When appropriate, use frequent positive reinforcement with the intention of increasing the student's self-esteem.

Recognizing and Working with Recalcitrant Learners

When working with recalcitrant learners you can use many of the guidelines from the preceding list. You should understand, however, that the reasons for these students' behaviors may be quite different from those for the other category of slow learners. Slower-learning students who are willing to try may be slow because of their learning style, genetic factors, or a combination of those and any number of other reasons. They are simply slower at learning. But they can and will learn. Recalcitrant learners, on the other hand, may be generally quick and bright thinkers but reluctant even to try because of a history of failure, a history of boredom with school, a poor self-concept, severe personal problems that distract from school, or any variety and combination of reasons, many of which are psychological in nature.

Whatever the case, you need to know that a student identified as being a slow or recalcitrant learner might, in fact, be quite gifted or talented in some way, but because of personal problems, may have a history of increasingly poor school attendance, poor attention to schoolwork, and poor self-confidence, and may have an attitude problem. Consider the following guidelines when working with recalcitrant learners:

- As the school year begins, learn as much about each student as you can. Be cautious in how you do it, though, because many of these students will be suspicious of any interest you show in them. Be businesslike, trusting, genuinely interested, and patient. A second caution: although you should learn as much as possible about each student, what has happened in the past is history. Use that information not as ammunition, something to be held against the student, but as insight to help you work more productively with the student.
- Avoid lecturing to these students; it won't work.
- Early in the school term, preferably with the help of adult volunteers (e.g., professional community members acting as mentors have worked well to help change a student's attitude from one of rebellion to one of hope, challenge, and success), work out a personalized education program with each student.
- Engage the students in learning by using interactive media, such as the Internet.
- Engage the students in active learning with real-world problem solving and perhaps community service projects.
- Forget about trying to "cover the subject matter," concentrating instead on the student's learning some things well. A good procedure is to use thematic teaching and to divide the theme into short segments. Because school attendance for these students is sometimes sporadic, try to individualize their assignments so that they can pick up where they left off and move through the course in an orderly fashion, even when they have been absent excessively. Try to assure some degree of success for each student.
- Help students develop their studying and learning skills, such as concentrating, remembering, and comprehension. Mnemonics, for example, is a device these students respond to positively, and they are often quick to create their own (for examples, see Chapter 8).
- If using a single textbook, see if the reading level is appropriate (discussed in Chapter 5); if it is not, discard the book and select other more appropriate reading materials for that student.
- Make sure your classroom procedures and rules are understood at the beginning of the school term and be consistent about following them (see Chapter 4).
- Maximize the use of in-class, on-task work and cooperative learning, with close monitoring of the student's progress. Do not rely on successful completion of traditional out-of-class assignments unless the student gets coached guidance from you before leaving your classroom.
- Use simple language in the classroom. Be concerned less about the words the students use and the way they use them and more about the ideas they are expressing. Let the students use their own idioms without carping too much on grammar and syntax. Always take care, though, to use proper and professional English yourself.

- When appropriate, use frequent positive reinforcement, with the intention of increasing the student's sense of personal worth. When using praise for reinforcement, however, try to direct your praise to the deed rather than the student.

TEACHING TOWARD POSITIVE CHARACTER DEVELOPMENT

In what appears to be a cycle, arising in the 1930s, in the late 1960s, in the 1990s, and continuing today, interest is high in the development of students' values, especially those of honesty, kindness, respect, and responsibility. Today this interest is in what some refer to as **character education.** Whether defined as ethics, citizenship, moral values, or personal development, character education has long been part of public education in this country.[42] Stimulated by a perceived need to act to reduce students' antisocial behaviors and to produce more respectful and responsible citizens, many schools and districts recently have developed or are developing curricula in character education with the ultimate goal of "developing mature adults capable of responsible citizenship and moral action."[43]

As a teacher at the middle level, you can teach toward positive character development in two general ways (both of which are discussed further in Chapters 3, 4, and 5): by providing a conducive classroom atmosphere where students actively and positively share in the decision making; and by being a model that students can proudly emulate. Acquiring knowledge and developing understanding can enhance the learning of attitudes. Nevertheless, changing an attitude is often a long and tedious process, requiring the commitment of the teacher and the school, assistance from the community, and the provision of numerous experiences that will guide students to new convictions. Here are some specific practices, most of which are, as indicated, discussed further in later chapters:

- Build a sense of community in the school and in the classroom with shared goals, optimism, cooperative efforts, and clearly identified and practiced procedures for reaching those goals (see Chapter 4).
- Collaboratively plan, with students, action- and community-oriented projects that relate to curriculum themes; solicit students' family members and community members to assist in projects (see Chapters 1, 5, 8, and others).
- Teach students to negotiate; practice and develop skills in conflict resolution such as empathy, problem solving, impulse control, and anger management (see Chapter 4).[44]
- Share and highlight examples of class and individual cooperation in serving the classroom, school, and community (see throughout).
- Make student service projects visible in the school and community (Chapters 5 and 8).
- Promote higher-order thinking about value issues through the development of students' skills in questioning (Chapters 7 and 9).
- Sensitize students to issues and teach skills of conflict resolution through debate, role play, simulations, and creative drama (Chapters 8 and 9).

See Figure 2.3 for resources on character education. When compared with traditional instruction, one characteristic of exemplary middle level instruction today is the teacher's encouragement of dialogue among students in the classroom to debate, discuss, and explore their own ideas. Modeling the very behaviors we expect of teachers and students in the classroom is, as promised in the Preface, a constant theme throughout this resource guide. One purpose of Exercise 2.1 is, in a similar fashion, to start that dialogue. Complete that exercise now.

---

[44]See D. W. Johnson and R. T. Johnson, *Reducing School Violence Through Conflict Resolution* (Alexandria, VA: Association for Supervision and Curriculum Development, 1995).

Figure 2.3   Selected resources on character education.

- Character Education Institute, 8918 Tesoro Drive, San Antonio, TX 78217 (800-284-0499).
- Character Education Partnership, 918 16th Street NW, Suite 501, Washington, DC 20006 (800-988-8081). Web site http://www.character.org.
- Character Education Resources, P.O. Box 651, Contoocook, NH 03229.
- Developmental Studies Center, 111 Deerwood Place, San Ramon, CA 94583 (415-838-7633).
- Ethics Resource Center, 1120 G Street NW, Washington, DC 20005 (202-434-8465).
- Jefferson Center for Character Education, 202 S. Lake Avenue, Pasadena, CA 91101 (818-792-8130).
- Josephine Institute of Ethics, 310 Washington Boulevard, Marina Del Rey, CA 90292 (310-306-1868).
- C. Martin and J. Lehr, *The Start Curriculum: An Interactive and Experiential Curriculum for Building Strong Character and Healthy Relationships in Middle and High Schools* (Minneapolis, MN: Educational Media Corporation, 1999). For information via e-mail: emedia@usinternet.com.
- Texas Education Agency, *Building Good Citizens for Texas: Character Education Resource Guide. Middle School* (Austin, TX: Author, 2000). Available online at http://www.tea.state.tx.us.

---

[42]See K. Burrett and T. Rusnak, *Integrated Character Education*, Fastback 351 (Bloomington, IN: Phi Delta Kappa Educational Foundation, 1993).

[43]Burrett and Rusnak, p. 15.

EXERCISE 2.1: REFLECTING UPON MY OWN SCHOOL EXPERIENCES

INSTRUCTIONS: The purpose of this exercise is to share with others in your class your reflections on your own experiences during your middle grade years.

1. What school(s) did you attend at this age (10–14)? Where and when? _____

_____

_____

2. What do you remember most about how this school level differed from your elementary and high school

experiences? _____

_____

_____

_____

_____

_____

3. What do you remember most about your teachers? _____

_____

_____

_____

_____

_____

_____

4. What do you remember most about other students? _____

_____

_____

_____

_____

_____

5. What do you remember most about school life? _____

_____

_____

_____

_____

_____

EXERCISE 2.1 (*continued*)

6. What grade (or class) do you specifically recall with fondness? Why? _____

_____

_____

_____

7. What grade (or class) would you particularly like to forget? Why? _____

_____

_____

_____

_____

8. What do you recall about peer and parental pressures? _____

_____

_____

_____

_____

_____

9. What do you recall about your own feelings during these years? _____

_____

_____

_____

_____

_____

10. Is there any other aspect of your attendance at a middle or junior high school you wish to share with others?

_____

_____

_____

_____

SUMMARY

Teachers and other adults in a school can collaborate in the promotion of harmony among young adolescents and within the school community by encouraging and providing experiences that recognize and celebrate student differences and cultural identities and establish close friendships with and positive opinions of others, and by promoting a sense of empathy, trust, integrity, and fairness.

As a classroom teacher, you must acknowledge that students in your classroom have different ways of receiving information and processing that information—different ways of knowing and of constructing their knowledge. These differences are unique and important and, as you will learn in Part II of this resource guide, they are central considerations in curriculum development and instructional practice.

You must try to learn as much as you can about how each student learns and processes information. But because you can never know everything about each student, the more you dialogue with your colleagues, vary your teaching strategies, and assist students in integrating their learning, the more likely you are to reach more of the students more of the time. In short, to be an effective middle level classroom teacher you should (a) learn as much about your students and their preferred styles of learning as you can, (b) develop an eclectic style of teaching that is flexible and adaptable, and (c) integrate the disciplines, thereby helping students make bridges or connections between their lives and all that is being learned.

ADDITIONAL EXERCISE

See the companion Website http://www.prenhall. com/ kellough for the following exercise related to the content of this chapter:

- Interviewing a Young Adolescent

QUESTIONS FOR CLASS DISCUSSION

1. Explain why knowledge of learning styles, learning capacities, and teaching styles is or should be important to you.
2. Kelly, a social studies teacher, has a class of 33 eighth-graders who, during her lecture, teacher-led discussion, and recitation lessons are restless and inattentive, creating a problem for her in classroom management. At Kelly's invitation, the school psychologist tests the students for learning modality and finds that of the 33 students, 29 are predominately kinesthetic learners. Of what value is this information to Kelly? Describe what, if anything, Kelly should try as a result of this information.
3. What concerns you most about teaching the diverse students you are likely to have in a classroom? Share those concerns with others in your class. Categorize your group's concerns. By accessing an Internet teacher bulletin board see what kinds of problems classroom teachers are currently concerned about. Are block scheduling, thematic instruction, grading, group learning, and classroom management high in frequency of concern? Are the concerns of teachers as expressed on the Internet similar to yours? As a class, devise a plan and time line for attempting to ameliorate your concerns.
4. Give an example of how and when you would use multilevel instruction. Of what benefit is its use to students? To teachers? What particular skills must a teacher have in order to effectively implement multilevel instruction?
5. Select one of the "Reflective Thoughts" from the introduction to Part I (page 2) that is specifically related to the content of this chapter, research it, and write a one-page essay explaining why you agree or disagree with the thought. Share your essay with members of your class for their thoughts.
6. Explain why many educators and researchers discourage the use of curriculum tracking or homogeneous grouping. What strategies are recommended in the place of traditional tracking?
7. Prepare an argument either for or against the following statement and present your argument to your classmates: Since teaching about citizenship, ethics, and moral values are unavoidable, a school should plan and do it well.
8. Describe any prior concepts you held that changed as a result of your experiences with this chapter. Describe the changes.
9. From your current observations and fieldwork, as related to this teacher preparation program, clearly identify one specific example of educational practice that seems contradictory to exemplary practice or theory as presented in this chapter. Present your explanation for the discrepancy.
10. Do you have other questions generated by the content of this chapter? If you do, list them along with ways answers might be found.

FOR FURTHER READING

Allsopp, D. H. "Using Modeling, Manipulatives, and Mnemonics with Eighth-Grade Students." *Teaching Exceptional Children* 32(2):74–81 (November/December 1999).

Bempechat, J. "Learning from Poor and Minority Students Who Succeed in School." *Harvard Education Letter* 15(3):1–3 (May/June 1999).

Bond, B. "Using Standards-Based Performance Assessment with At-Risk Students." *Middle Ground* 4(3):36–39 (February 2001).

Brame, P. B. "Using Picture Storybooks to Enhance Social Skills Training of Special Needs Students." *Middle School Journal* 32(1):41–46 (September 2000).

Brisk, M. E., and Harrington, M. M. *Literacy and Bilingualism: A Handbook for ALL Teachers.* Mahwah, NJ: Lawrence Erlbaum, 2000.

Campbell, L., and Campbell, B. *Multiple Intelligences and Student Achievement: Success Stories From Six Schools.* Alexandria, VA: Association for Supervision and Curriculum Development, 1999.

Holland, H. "Diversity Defined: Supportive Middle Schools Search for the Beauty Within." *Middle Ground* 3(3):6–10 (December 1999).

Jensen, E. "Moving with the Brain in Mind." *Educational Leadership* 58(3):34–37 (November 2000).

Kwon, Y-J, and Lawson, A. E. "Linking Brain Growth with the Development of Scientific Reasoning Ability and Conceptual Change during Adolescence." *Journal of Research in Science Teaching* 37(1):44–62 (January 2000).

Langer, J. A. "Turning Obstacles into Opportunity." *Harvard Education Letter* 17(2):6–7 (March/April 2001).

Lawton, M. "The 'Brain-Based' Ballyhoo." *Harvard Education Letter* 15(4):5–7 (July/August 2000).

Manning, M. L. "Developmentally Responsive Multicultural Education for Young Adolescents." *Childhood Education* 76(2):82–87 (Winter 1999–2000).

McCoy, K. M. "Helping Middle School Students Overcome Common Dysfunctional Behaviors Which Impede Academic Success." *Middle School Journal* 31(4):42–46 (March 2000).

Meinbach, A. M. "Seeking the Light: Welcoming a Visually Impaired Student." *Middle School Journal* 31(2):10–17 (November 1999).

Meyer, A., and Rose, D. H. "Universal Design for Individual Differences." *Educational Leadership* 58(3):39–43 (November 2000).

Morgan, R. R.; Ponticell, J. A.; and Gordon, E. E. *Rethinking Creativity.* Fastback 458. Bloomington, IN: Phi Delta Kappa Educational Foundation, 2000.

Myers, J., and Boothe, D. "Cultural and Language Diversity in the Middle Grades." *Clearing House* 73(4):230–234 (March/April 2000).

Ohanian, S. *Caught in the Middle.* Westport, CT: Heinemann, 2001.

Reed, D. F., and Rossi, J. A. "My Three Wishes: Hopes, Aspirations, and Concerns of Middle School Students." *Clearing House* 73(3):141–144 (January/February 2000).

Renzulli, J. S., and Richards, S. "Meeting the Enrichment Needs of Middle School Students." *Principal* 79(4):62–63 (March 2000).

Rosselli, H. C., and Irvin, J. L. "Differing Perspectives, Common Ground: The Middle School and Gifted Education Relationship." *Middle School Journal* 32(3):57–62 (January 2001).

Sprenger, M. *Learning & Memory: The Brain in Action.* Alexandria, VA: Association for Supervision and Curriculum Development, 1999.

Stephen, C. *Working with Second Language Learners: Answers to Teachers' Top Ten Questions.* Westport, CT: Heinemann, 2000.

Stronge, J. H., and Reed-Victor, E., eds. *Educating Homeless Students: Promising Practices.* Larchmont, NY: Eye on Education, 2000.

Teemant, A., Berhardt, E. B., Rodriquez-Muñoz, M., and Aiello, M. "A Dialogue Among Teachers that Benefits Second Language Learners." *Middle School Journal* 32(2):30–37 (November 2000).

Van Hoose, J., and Strahan, D. B. *Young Adolescent Development and School Practices: Promoting Harmony.* Westerville, OH: National Middle School Association, 1998.

Voltz, D. L. "Empowering Diverse Learners at the Middle Level." *Middle School Journal* 30(4):29–36 (March 1999).

Waldron, K. A., and Allen, L. "Successful Strategies for Inclusion at the Middle Level." *Middle School Journal* 30(4):18–28 (March 1999).

Whitbread, K. "Inclusion: Making It Work for Students and Teachers." *Middle Ground* 2(4):10–16 (April 1999).

3

The Expectations, Responsibilities, and Facilitating Behaviors of a Middle Level Teacher

The primary expectation of any teacher is to facilitate student learning. As an effective middle level teacher, your professional responsibilities will extend well beyond the ability to work competently in a classroom from approximately 8:00 A.M. until midafternoon. In this chapter, you will learn about the many responsibilities you will assume and the competencies and behaviors necessary for fulfilling them. Four categories of responsibilities and 22 competencies are identified.

The four categories are (a) responsibility as a reflective decision maker, (b) commitment to children and to the profession, (c) noninstructional responsibil-

ities, and (d) instructional responsibilities and fundamental teaching behaviors. As these categories and the 22 competencies are presented, you are guided through the reality of these expectations as they exist for today's middle level classroom teacher.

OBJECTIVES

Upon completion of this chapter, you should be able to

1. Describe the decision-making and thought-processing phases of instruction and the types of decisions you must make during each.

2. Describe the importance of the concept of locus of control and its relationship to your professional responsibilities.

3. Demonstrate your understanding of the depth and breadth of the responsibilities of being a middle level teacher.

4. Demonstrate an understanding of the concept of *meaningful learning*.

5. Compare and contrast the two phrases, **hands-on** and **minds-on learning.**

6. Contrast teacher use of praise and of encouragement, and describe situations in which each is more appropriate.

7. Compare and contrast teacher **facilitating behaviors** with *instructional strategies*.

8. Demonstrate your growing understanding of the concept of teaching style and its relevance to middle level instruction.

9. Demonstrate your understanding of the importance of reflection to the process of constructing skills and understandings.

THE TEACHER AS A REFLECTIVE DECISION MAKER

During any single school day you will make hundreds, perhaps thousands, of decisions. Some decisions will have been made prior to meeting your students for instruction, others will be made during the instructional activities, and still others will be made later as you reflect on the instruction for that day. Let us consider further these decision-making and thought-processing phases of instruction.

Decision-Making Phases of Instruction

Instruction can be divided into four decision-making and thought-processing phases: (a) the planning or *preactive phase,* (b) the teaching or *interactive phase,* (c) the analyzing and evaluating or *reflective phase,* and (d) the application or *projective phase.*[1]

The preactive phase consists of all those intellectual functions and decisions you will make prior to actual instruction. This includes decisions about goals and objectives, homework assignments, what students already know and can do, appropriate learning activities, questions to be asked (and possible answers), and the selection and preparation of instructional materials.

The interactive phase includes all the decisions made during the immediate and spontaneous teaching act. This includes maintaining student focus, questions to be asked, types of feedback given to the students, and ongoing adjustments to the lesson plan. As said before,

decisions made during this phase are likely to be more intuitive, unconscious, and routine than those made during the planning phase.

The reflective phase is the time you will take to reflect on, analyze, and judge the decisions and behaviors that occurred during the interactive phase. (See questions for self-reflection in Figure 6.11 in Chapter 6.) It is during reflection that you make decisions about student learning, student grades, feedback given to parents/guardians, and adjustments on what to teach next.

As a result of this reflection, decisions are made to use what was learned in subsequent teaching actions. At this point, you are in the projective phase, abstracting from your reflection and projecting your analysis into subsequent teaching behaviors.

Reflection, Locus of Control, and Teacher Responsibility

During the reflective phase, teachers have a choice of whether to assume full responsibility for the instructional outcomes or whether to assume responsibility for only the positive outcomes of the planned instruction while placing the blame for the negative outcomes on outside forces (e.g., parents and guardians, society in general, peers, other teachers, administrators, or textbooks). Where the responsibility for outcomes is placed is referred to as *locus of control.*

Just because a teacher thinks that he or she is a competent teacher does not mean it is so. If many of a teacher's students are not learning, then that teacher is not competent. In the words of the late Madeline Hunter, "To say that I am an effective teacher, and acknowledge that my students may not be learning is the same as saying I am a great surgeon, but most of my patients die."[2] Teachers who are intrinsically motivated and competent tend to assume full responsibility for instructional outcomes, regardless of whether or not the outcomes are as intended from the planning phase.

Of course every teacher realizes that there are factors the teacher cannot control, such as the negative effects on children from poverty, gangs, alcohol, and drug abuse, so they must do what they can within the confines of the classroom and resources of the school and district. History brims with examples of how a relatively few, but positive, moments with a truly caring and knowledgeable adult can drastically change for the better the life of a young person who, until then, had a history of mostly negative experiences.

Proceed now to Exercises 3.1 and 3.2 to learn more about the teacher and decision making, and the preactive phase of instruction.

---

[1]See A. L. Costa, *The School as a Home for the Mind* (Palatine, IL: Skylight Publishing, 1991), pp. 97–106.

[2]In R. A. Villa and J. S. Thousands, (Eds.), *Creating an Inclusive School* (Alexandria, VA: Association for Supervision and Curriculum Development, 1995), p. 36.

EXERCISE 3.1: THE TEACHER AS REFLECTIVE DECISION MAKER

INSTRUCTIONS: The purpose of this exercise is to learn more about the nature of the decisions and the decision-making process used by teachers. To accomplish this, you are to observe one middle level teacher for one hour while that teacher is teaching. Tabulate as accurately as possible the number of decisions the teacher makes during that time period, then share the results with your classmates. Obtain permission from a cooperating teacher by explaining the purpose of your observations. You will need to have a follow-up discussion with the cooperating teacher regarding your tabulations. A follow-up thank-you letter is appropriate.

School, teacher, and class observed: _____

_____

_____

_____

_____

1. Use the following format for your tabulations. You may first want to make your tabulations on a separate blank sheet of paper and then organize and transfer those tabulations to this page. Tabulate and identify each decision. To tabulate the decisions made before and after instruction, confer with the teacher after class.

DECISION MADE BEFORE INSTRUCTION

Examples:
- Objectives of lesson
- Amount of time to be devoted to particular activities
- Classroom management procedures

_____

_____

_____

_____

_____

_____

DECISIONS MADE DURING INSTRUCTION

Examples:
- Called on Roberta to answer a question
- Teacher remained silent until students in back corner got quiet
- Talked with tardy student

_____

_____

_____

_____

_____

_____

☞

EXERCISE 3.1 (*continued*)

DECISIONS MADE AFTER INSTRUCTION

Examples:
- To review a particular concept tomorrow
- To arrange a conference with Sean to talk with him about his hostility in class
- To make a revision in Friday's homework assignment

_____

_____

_____

_____

_____

2. What was the total number of decisions made by this teacher

   before instruction? _____ during instruction? _____ after instruction? _____

   Compare your results with those of others in your class.

3. Did you observe any evidence that this teacher assumed full responsibility for the learning outcomes of this

   class session? Describe the evidence. _____

_____

_____

_____

_____

4. What percentage of all decisions by this teacher

   were planned? _____ were spontaneous? _____

5. Did you share your results of this exercise with the cooperating teacher? His or her reaction? _____

_____

_____

_____

_____

6. Your conclusions from this exercise: _____

_____

_____

_____

_____

EXERCISE 3.2: THE PREACTIVE PHASE OF INSTRUCTION

INSTRUCTIONS: Mentally rehearsing your actions before meeting the students is absolutely essential for effective teaching and learning. The purpose of this exercise is to stress the importance of clearly and fully thinking about what you will do and say in the classroom and to demonstrate how mental rehearsal of a lesson can identify possible problems. Follow these steps:

1. Select a grade level (5–8) you are currently teaching or that you would like to teach. _____

_____

2. Objective of lesson: Students will design name tags for their desks during a 20-minute time frame.

3. *Without looking ahead at step 4,* on separate paper write a lesson plan for this activity. (Although you have not yet learned the details of lesson planning, outline the steps you would follow and things you would say to your students in order to accomplish the objective of step 2.)

4. To analyze the thoroughness of your preactive thinking, respond to the following questions.

   a. Are materials listed in your plan? _____

   b. Are those materials readily available in your classroom? _____

   c. Will paper or tagboard need to be precut? _____

   d. How large can the name tags be? _____

   e. How and where will they be attached to each desk? _____

   _____

   f. Should they be flat or three-dimensional? _____

   g. Will you supply markers or crayons, or are the students expected to have them? _____

   h. Will students need scissors? _____

   i. Will you have left-handed scissors available if needed? _____

   j. Should name tags have first name, last name, last initial? _____

   _____

   k. Can other words or designs be added? _____

   l. When and how will materials be distributed? Collected? _____

   _____

   m. What plan do you have for absent or tardy students? _____

   _____

5. Share the results of your steps 1–4 with others in your class. Did members of your class come up with other questions relevant and necessary to the preplanning for this instructional period? If so, share them with the rest of the class. _____

_____

Conclusion: A teacher who practices thorough preactive planning should have planned answers for each of these questions.

FOR YOUR NOTES

TEACHING STYLE

Teaching style is the way teachers teach, which includes their distinctive mannerisms complemented by their choices of teaching behaviors and strategies. A teacher's style affects the way that teacher presents information and interacts with the students. The manner and pattern of those interactions with students clearly determines a teacher's effectiveness in promoting student learning, positive attitudes about learning, and students' self-esteem.

A teacher's style is determined by the teacher's personal characteristics (especially the teacher's own learning style), experiences, and knowledge of research findings about how young adolescents learn. Teaching style can be altered, intentionally or unintentionally, as a result of changes in any of these three areas.

While there are other ways to label and to describe teaching styles, we consider two contrasting styles—the **traditional** and the **facilitating** styles—(see Table 3.1) to emphasize that although today's middle level teacher must use aspects from each (that is, be eclectic in style choice), there must be a strong inclination toward the facilitating style.

Multilevel Instruction

As emphasized in Chapter 2, students in your classroom have their own independent ways of knowing and learning. It is important to try to attend to how each student best learns and to where each student is developmentally, that is, to individualize both the content and the methods of learning. In essence, although perhaps not as detailed as those prepared for special education students, at various times during the school year you will be developing personalized educational programs for each student. These may be prepared in collaboration with members of your teaching team. To accomplish this individual teaching, you can use multitasking or multilevel instruction (as discussed in Chapter 2) in which individual students and groups of students are working at different tasks to accomplish the same objective or at different tasks to accomplish different objectives. For example, while some students may be working independently of the teacher—that is, within the facilitating mode—others may be receiving direct instruction—that is, more within the traditional mode.

When integrating student learning, as you will be learning in Part II of this guide, multitasking is an

Table 3.1 A Contrast of Two Teaching Styles

		Traditional Style	*Facilitating Style*
Teacher		Autocratic	Democratic
		Curriculum-centered	Student-centered
		Direct	Indirect
		Dominative	Interactive
		Formal	Informal
		Informative	Inquiring
		Prescriptive	Reflective
Classroom		Teacher-centered	Student-centered
		Linear (seats facing front)	Grouped or circular
Instructional modes		Abstract learning	Concrete learning
		Teacher-centered discussion	Discussions
		Lectures	Peer and cross-age coaching
		Competitive learning	Cooperative learning
		Some problem solving	Problem solving
		Demonstrations by teacher	Student inquiries
		From simple to complex	Start with complex tasks and use instructional scaffolding and dialogue
		Transmission of information from teacher to students	Reciprocal teaching (using dialogue) between teacher and a small group of students, then among students

important and useful, perhaps even necessary, strategy. Project-centered teaching (discussed in Chapter 8) is an instructional method that easily allows for the provision of multilevel instruction.

The Theoretical Origins of Teaching Styles and Their Relation to Constructivism

Constructivist teaching and the integration of curriculum are not new to education. The importance of constructivism and of curriculum integration approaches are found, for example, in the writings of John Dewey,[3] Arthur W. Combs,[4] and Jean Piaget.[5]

Instructional styles are deeply rooted in certain theoretical assumptions about learners and their development. Although it is beyond the scope of our intent for this resource guide to explore deeply those assumptions, three major theoretical positions with research findings, each of which is based on certain philosophical and psychological assumptions, suggest different ways of working with children. The theoretical positions are described in the next three paragraphs.

Tied to the theoretical positions of *romanticism-maturationism* is the assumption that the learner's mind is neutral-passive to good-active, and that the main focus in teaching should be the addition of new ideas to a subconscious store of old ones. Key persons include Jean J. Rousseau and Sigmund Freud; key instructional strategies include classic lecturing with rote memorization.

Tied to the theoretical position of **behaviorism** is the assumption that the learner's mind is neutral-passive with innate reflexes and needs, and that the main focus in teaching should be on the successive, systematic changes in the learner's environment to increase the possibilities of desired behavior responses. Key persons include John Locke, B. F. Skinner, A. H. Thorndike, Robert Gagné, and John Watson; key instructional strategies include practice and reinforcement as in workbook drill activities and programmed instruction.

Tied to the theoretical position of *cognitive-experimentalism* (including **constructivism**) is the assumption that the learner is a neutral-interactive purposive individual in simultaneous interaction with physical and biological environments. The main focus in teaching should be on facilitating the learner's gain and construction of new perceptions that lead to desired behavioral changes and ultimately to a more fully functioning individual.[6] Key persons are John Dewey, Lev Vygotsky, Jerome Bruner, Jean Piaget, and Arthur W. Combs; key instructional strategies include discovery, inquiry, project-centered teaching, cooperative and social-interactive learning, and integrated curriculum.

It is our opinion that to be most effective, a teacher with a diversity of students must be eclectic, but with a strong emphasis toward cognitive-experimentalism-constructivism because of its divergence in learning and the importance given to learning as a change in perceptions—using at appropriate times the best of strategies and knowledgeable instructor behaviors. This is true regardless of whether individually they can be classified within any style dichotomy, such as "direct vs. indirect," "formal vs. informal," "traditional vs. progressive," or "didactic vs. facilitative."

Now, to further your understandings do Exercises 3.3 and 3.4.

---

[3]J. Dewey, *How We Think* (Boston, MA: Heath, 1933).

[4]A. W. Combs (Ed.), *Perceiving, Behaving, Becoming: A New Focus for Education* (Arlington, VA: 1962 ASCD Yearbook, Association for Supervision and Curriculum Development, 1962). See also H. J. Freiberg, (Ed.), *Perceiving, Behaving, Becoming: Lessons Learned* (Alexandria, VA: Association for Supervision and Curriculum Development, 1999).

[5]J. Piaget, *Science of Education and the Psychology of the Child* (New York: Orion, 1970).

---

[6]A person with a "fully functioning self" can be described only in terms of ideal behavior. As described by Earl C. Kelley, those characteristics are thinks well of himself and of others; sees his stake in others; sees himself as a part of a world in movement—in process of becoming; sees the value of mistakes; develops and holds human values and knows of no other way to live except in keeping with his values; sees himself as cast in a creative role. From pp. 17–20 of E. C. Kelley, "The Fully Functioning Self," chapter 3 (pp. 9–20) of A. W. Combs (Ed.), *Perceiving, Behaving, Becoming*, 1962. See same in pp. 13–16 of H. J. Freiberg, (Ed.), *Perceiving, Behaving, Becoming: Lessons Learned*, 1999.

EXERCISE 3.3: USING OBSERVATION OF CLASSROOM INTERACTION TO ANALYZE ONE MIDDLE GRADE TEACHER'S STYLE*

INSTRUCTIONS: The purpose of this exercise is to visit a classroom to observe and identify the instructional style for that particular day. Be certain first to obtain permission and then to explain to the teacher that you are observing, not evaluating, for teaching style. The host teacher may be interested in discussing with you the results of your observation. A follow-up thank-you letter is appropriate.

1. Class, grade level, and school visited: _____

2. Date of visit: _____

3. From the start of your classroom observation, observe at 1-minute intervals for a period of 10 minutes what the teacher is doing at that very moment, marking the appropriate traditional or facilitating teacher behavior on the chart below. Continue for the entire class meeting for as many 10 minute intervals as you can.

					Minutes						
Traditional teacher behaviors	*1*	*2*	*3*	*4*	*5*	*6*	*7*	*8*	*9*	*10*	*Totals*
Prescribing (giving advice or directions; being critical, evaluative; offering judgments)											
Informing (giving information; lecturing; interpreting)											
Confronting (directly challenging students)											

Traditional Behaviors Total   _____

Facilitating teacher behaviors	*1*	*2*	*3*	*4*	*5*	*6*	*7*	*8*	*9*	*10*	*Totals*
Relaxing (releasing tension; using humor)											
Mediating (asking for information; being reflective; encouraging self-directed problem solving)											
Supporting (approving; confirming; validating; listening)											

Facilitating Behaviors Total   _____

4. Total traditional (T) behaviors divided by total facilitating (F) behaviors = T/F ratio.

   T/F ratio for this observation = _____

5. Conclusions about the host teacher's style on this day: _____

   _____

   _____

   _____

   _____

   _____

6. Did you discuss your observations with the host teacher? _____

*Adapted from J. Heron, *Six Category Intervention Analysis* (Guildford, England: Centre of Adult Education, University of Surrey, 1975).

FOR YOUR NOTES

EXERCISE 3.4: USING A QUESTIONNAIRE TO DEVELOP A PROFILE AND A STATEMENT ABOUT MY OWN EMERGING TEACHING STYLE

INSTRUCTIONS: The purpose of this exercise is to help you clarify and articulate your own assumptions about teaching and learning. You will develop a profile of your emerging teaching style, and from that a statement representative of your current thinking about teaching and learning especially about teaching young adolescents. Proceed with the following five steps.*

Step 1.   Read each of the 50 statements and rate your feelings about each, giving a *1* if you strongly agree, a *2* if you are neutral, and a *3* if you strongly disagree.

Remember: *1* = strongly agree; *2* = neutral; *3* = strongly disagree

_____ 1. Most of what students learn, they learn on their own.

_____ 2. Students should be concerned about other students' reactions to their work in the classroom.

_____ 3. An important part of schooling is learning to work with others.

_____ 4. Students learn more by working on their own than by working with others.

_____ 5. Students should be given opportunities to participate actively in class planning and implementation of lessons.

_____ 6. In an effective learning environment, grades are inappropriate.

_____ 7. Students enjoy working in a classroom that has clearly defined learning objectives and assessment criteria.

_____ 8. I favor teaching methods and classroom procedures that maximize students' independence to learn from their own experiences.

_____ 9. Most of what students learn is learned from other students.

_____ 10. Students should be concerned with getting good grades.

_____ 11. An important part of teaching and learning is learning how to work independently.

_____ 12. A teacher should not be contradicted or challenged by a student.

_____ 13. Interchanges between students and a teacher can provide ideas about content better than those found in a textbook.

_____ 14. For students to get the most out of a class, they must be aware of the primary concerns and biases of the teacher.

_____ 15. Students should not be given high grades unless they are clearly earned.

_____ 16. Learning should help the student to become an independent thinker.

_____ 17. Most of what students learn is learned from their teachers.

_____ 18. A teacher who makes students do things they don't want to do is an ineffective teacher.

_____ 19. Learning takes place most effectively under conditions in which students are in competition with one another.

_____ 20. A teacher should try to persuade students that particular ideas are valid and exciting.

_____ 21. To do well in school, students must be assertive.

*Adapted from William H. Berquist and Steve R. Phillips, *A Handbook for Faculty Development* (Washington, DC: The Council for Independent Colleges, June 1975), 25–27.

☞

EXERCISE 3.4 (*continued*)

_____ 22. Facts in textbooks are usually accurate.

_____ 23. I favor the use of teaching methods and classroom procedures that maximize students and teacher interaction.

_____ 24. Most of what students learn is learned from books.

_____ 25. A teacher who lets students do whatever they want is incompetent.

_____ 26. Students can learn more by working with an enthusiastic teacher than by working alone.

_____ 27. I favor the use of teaching methods and classroom procedures that maximize students learning of basic subject matter content.

_____ 28. Ideas of other students are useful for helping a student understand the content of lessons.

_____ 29. A student should study what the teacher says is important and not necessarily what is important to that student.

_____ 30. A teacher who does not motivate students' interest in subject content is incompetent.

_____ 31. An important part of education is learning how to perform under testing and evaluation conditions.

_____ 32. Students can learn more by sharing their ideas than by keeping their ideas to themselves.

_____ 33. Teachers tend to give students too many assignments that are trivial.

_____ 34. Ideas contained in the textbook should be the primary source of the content taught.

_____ 35. Students should be given high grades as a means of motivating them and increasing their self-esteem.

_____ 36. The ideas a student brings into a class are useful for helping him or her to understand subject content.

_____ 37. Students should study what is important to them and not necessarily what the teacher claims is important.

_____ 38. Learning takes place most effectively under conditions in which students are working independently of one another.

_____ 39. Teachers often give students too much freedom of choice in content, methods, and procedures.

_____ 40. Teachers should clearly explain what it is they expect from students.

_____ 41. Students' ideas about content are often better than those ideas found in textbooks.

_____ 42. Classroom discussions are beneficial learning experiences.

_____ 43. A student's education should help the student to become a successful and contributing member of society.

_____ 44. Learning takes place most effectively under conditions in which students are working cooperatively with one another.

_____ 45. Teachers often are too personal with their students.

_____ 46. A teacher should encourage students to disagree with or challenge that teacher in the classroom.

_____ 47. Students have to be able to work effectively with other people to do well in school.

_____ 48. For students to get the most out of school, they must assume at least part of the responsibility for their learning.

_____ 49. Students seem to enjoy discussing their ideas about learning with the teacher and other students.

_____ 50. A student's education should help him or her to become a sensitive human being.

EXERCISE 3.4 (*continued*)

Step 2.   From the list of 50 items, write the items (by their number) in two columns, those with which you held strong agreement, and those with which you strongly disagreed, ignoring those items you gave a *2* (were neutral).

Strongly agreed   *Strongly disagreed*

Step 3.   In groups of three or four, discuss your lists (in Step 2) with your classmates. From the discussion, you may rerank any items you wish.

Step 4.   You now have a finalized list of those items with which you were in agreement, and those with which you disagreed. On the basis of those two lists, write a paragraph that summarizes your philosophy about teaching and learning. It should be no longer than one-half page in length. That statement is a theoretical representation of your present philosophy about teaching, especially about teaching young adolescents.

_____

_____

_____

_____

_____

_____

_____

_____

☞

EXERCISE 3.4 (*continued*)

_____

_____

_____

_____

_____

_____

Step 5.   Compare your philosophical statement with the three theoretical positions as discussed prior to this exercise. Can you clearly identify your position? Name it: _____

_____

_____

Explain your rationale: _____

_____

_____

_____

_____

_____

_____

_____

_____

_____

_____

_____

_____

At the completion of this course, you may wish to revisit your philosophical statement, perhaps even to make revisions to it. It will be useful to have your educational philosophy firmly implanted in your memory for teaching job interviews at a later date (see Chapter 12).

COMMITMENT AND PROFESSIONALISM

The classroom teacher is expected to demonstrate commitment to the school's mission (discussed in Chapter 1), and to both the personal and intellectual development of the students (discussed in Chapter 2). Not only do the most effective middle level teachers expect, demand, and receive positive results in learning from their students while in the classroom, they are also interested and involved in the activities of the students outside the classroom, willing to sacrifice personal time to give them attention and guidance.

Noninstructional Responsibilities

The aspect of the teacher as a decision maker with professional commitments takes on a very real dimension when you consider specific noninstruction-related and instruction-related responsibilities of the classroom teacher. Shown in Figure 3.1 are 13 categories of items that should alert you to the many noninstructional matters with which you should become familiar, especially during your first year of teaching. Their importance and the amount of time they require are often underestimated by beginning teachers.

Instructional Responsibilities

The items illustrated in Figure 3.2 introduce you to or remind you of the instructional responsibilities you will have as a classroom teacher which are the primary focus of study of the remainder of this resource guide. After you have reviewed the lists of instructional and noninstructional responsibilities of the classroom teacher, do Exercise 3.5, which is a model of cooperative learning for the beginning teacher.

Figure 3.1   Noninstructional responsibilities of the classroom teacher.

1. Knowledgeable about activities of interest to the students.
2. Familiarity with the school campus and community.
3. Acquainted with members of the faculty and the support staff.
4. Knowledgeable about school and district policies.
5. Familiar with the backgrounds of the students.
6. Knowledgeable about procedures for such routine matters as planning and scheduling of before- and after-school activities; rest room regulations; distribution and collection of textbooks and other school materials; class dismissal; ordering of supplies; fire drills and severe weather; daily attendance records; school assemblies; sharing of instructional space with other teachers; arranging for and preparing displays for common areas of the school.
7. Expected role in teaching common elements of the curriculum, such as reading, writing, thinking, social skills, and study skills.
8. Expected role in the advisory program.
9. Classroom duties such as maintaining a cheerful, pleasant, and safe environment; obtaining materials needed for each lesson; keeping supplies orderly; supervising students who are helpers.
10. Expected role in the parent-teacher organization and other community participation activities.
11. The many conferences that will be needed, such as those between teacher and teacher; teacher and student; teacher and parent or guardian; teacher, student, and parent/guardian; teacher and administrator; and teacher and community representative.
12. Professional meetings, such as those of the interdisciplinary teaching team; other school and district committees; parent-teacher and community groups; and local, regional, state, and national professional organizations.
13. Time to relax and enjoy family, friends, and hobbies.

Figure 3.2   Instructional responsibilities of the classroom teacher.

1. Planning units and daily lessons.
2. Learning the interests of the students so lessons will reflect those interests.
3. Incorporating the individual learning styles, capacities, and modalities of the students in lesson plans.
4. Reading student papers.
5. Assessing and recording student progress.
6. Preparing the classroom.
7. Providing classroom instruction.
8. Thinking about professional growth and development, which may include attending university courses, attending workshops and other presentations offered by the school district or professional organizations, and reading professional literature.
9. Developing a firm but fair classroom management system.
10. Reacquainting yourself with the developmental characteristics of young adolescents.
11. Learning the background of students with special problems who might cause concerns in the learning environment.
12. Developing techniques and plans for cross-age tutoring, peer coaching, cooperative learning, project-based learning, and other developmentally appropriate teaching strategies.
13. Identifying resources and sources.
14. Devoting time to team planning.
15. Conferencing with individual students.

EXERCISE 3.5: REVIEWING THE PROFESSIONAL RESPONSIBILITIES OF A FIRST-YEAR MIDDLE LEVEL TEACHER

INSTRUCTIONS: The purpose of this exercise is to review the responsibilities of a first-year teacher. Have the class of teacher candidates divide into groups of four. Within each group, one member should play each of the following roles: (1) group facilitator, (2) recorder, (3) materials manager, and (4) reporter. Each group is to choose one of these six categories of responsibilities:

1. Audiovisual/media

2. Classroom environment

3. Clerical

4. Instructional

5. Professional activities

6. Advisory/supervision

Each group then read the responsibilities for their selected category listed on the following cards and arrange them in prioritized order, beginning with the most important. The group facilitator will lead this discussion. Under the guidance of the materials manager, the group may cut the cards apart so they can be physically manipulated as priorities are discussed. The recorder should take notes of the groups's work, which can then be discussed in order to develop the report that will be made to the class.

After a prearranged discussion time, recall the entire class and ask each reporter to share the group's (1) prioritized order of responsibilities and (2) estimate of the amount of time that a beginning teacher might devote to these responsibilities each week.

As each group reports, all members of the class should enter its list of priorities and time estimates on the Recap Sheet.

After completion of this exercise, the class may wish to discuss the group dynamics of this model of cooperative learning (see Chapter 8). For discussion in either large or small groups, key questions might be

1. Would you use this form of discussion in your own teaching?

2. How would you divide a class into groups of four?

Other questions may be generated by the group work.

FOR YOUR NOTES

CARDS FOR EXERCISE 3.5

Audiovisual/Media Responsibilities

Selecting, ordering, and returning cassettes, films, videodiscs, and other materials

Preparing and operating equipment	Reviewing selected materials
Planning class introduction to the audiovisual materials	Other audiovisual responsibilities as determined

Estimated hours a beginning teacher will devote to audiovisual/media responsibilities each week = _____

CARDS FOR EXERCISE 3.5

Classroom Environment Responsibilities

Planning and constructing displays	Preparing bulletin boards
Reading, announcing, and posting class notices	Managing a classroom library
Opening and closing windows, arranging furniture, cleaning the writing board	Other classroom environment responsibilities as determined

Estimated hours a beginning teacher will devote to classroom environment responsibilities each week = _____

CARDS FOR EXERCISE 3.5

Clerical Responsibilities

Maintaining attendance and tardy records	Entering grades, scores, or marks into a record book or onto the computer
Preparing progress and grade reports	Typing, drawing, and duplicating instructional materials
Locating resource ideas and materials to support lessons	Other clerical responsibilities as determined

Estimated hours a beginning teacher will devote to clerical responsibilities each week = _____

FOR YOUR NOTES

CARDS FOR EXERCISE 3.5

Instructional Responsibilities

Giving additional instruction (e.g., to students who need one-to-one attention, those who have been absent, or small review groups)	Correcting student work
Preparing special learning materials	Preparing, reading, and scoring tests; helping students self-evaluate
Writing information on the board	Preparing long-range and daily lesson plans
Grouping for instruction	Other instructional responsibilities as determined

Estimated hours a beginning teacher will devote to instructional responsibilities each week = _____

CARDS FOR EXERCISE 3.5

Professional Activities Responsibilities

Researching and writing teacher reports	Attending teachers' and school district meetings
Planning and attending parent-teacher meetings	Attending local teachers' organization meetings
Attending state, regional, and national professional organizations; taking university classes	Other professional activities responsibilities as determined

Estimated hours a beginning teacher will devote to professional activities each week = _____

CARDS FOR EXERCISE 3.5

Advisory/Supervision Responsibilities

Supervising before- or after-school activities	Supervising hallways, lunchrooms, and bathrooms
Supervising student assemblies	Advisory meetings
Supervising laboratory activities	Settling students' disputes

Other supervision responsibilities as determined

Estimated hours a beginning teacher will devote to supervision responsibilities each week = _____

FOR YOUR NOTES

EXERCISE 3.5: RECAP SHEET

AUDIOVISUAL/MEDIA RESPONSIBILITIES

1. _____
2. _____
3. _____
4. _____
5. _____

   Estimated hours = _____

CLASSROOM ENVIRONMENT RESPONSIBILITIES

1. _____
2. _____
3. _____
4. _____
5. _____
6. _____

   Estimated hours = _____

CLERICAL RESPONSIBILITIES

1. _____
2. _____
3. _____
4. _____
5. _____
6. _____

   Estimated hours = _____

INSTRUCTIONAL RESPONSIBILITIES

1. _____
2. _____
3. _____
4. _____
5. _____
6. _____
7. _____
8. _____

   Estimated hours = _____

EXERCISE 3.5 (*continued*)

PROFESSIONAL ACTIVITIES RESPONSIBILITIES

1. _____

2. _____

3. _____

4. _____

5. _____

6. _____

    Estimated hours = _____

ADVISORY/SUPERVISION RESPONSIBILITIES

1. _____

2. _____

3. _____

4. _____

5. _____

6. _____

7. _____

    Estimated hours = _____

FROM THE VIEWPOINT OF YOUNG ADOLESCENTS
What Makes a Great Teacher

Here are the replies of young adolescents when asked the question "What makes a great teacher?"

Approachable and inspiring.

A 14 year old said, "A great teacher is someone you can talk to about things. Someone who takes time out to help give you a better understanding with problems that seem impossible. Who will not allow you to settle for a C but inspires you to strive for an A."

Respectful and communicates what is needed.

A 13 year old said that a great teacher "respects students and appreciates them, and makes them learn a lot and tells us what we need to do to have a good job in life."

Educated, attentive, willing to reach out to students and to make learning fun.

A 13 year old replied that a great teacher "has patience and treats everyone equally. . .is attentive to what's going on in the classroom and makes school fun and exciting."

IDENTIFYING AND BUILDING YOUR INSTRUCTIONAL COMPETENCIES

The overall purpose of this resource guide is to assist you in building your instructional competencies. In order to do that, we need a starting place and this is it, our presentation of 22 specific competencies.[7] (See also "From the Viewpoint of Young Adolescents" about what makes a great teacher.)

Characteristics of the Competent Classroom Teacher: An Annotated List

Please do not feel overwhelmed by the following list; it may well be that no teacher expertly models all the characteristics that follow. The characteristics do, however, represent an ideal to strive for. You will continue to reflect on and to build upon these competencies through your study of the remaining chapters of this book and, indeed, throughout your professional career.

1. *The teacher is knowledgeable about the subject matter.* You should have both historical understanding and current knowledge of the structure of those subjects you are expected to teach, and of the facts, principles, concepts, and skills needed for those subjects. This does not mean you need to know everything about the subject, but more than you are likely to teach.

2. *The teacher is an "educational broker."* You will learn where and how to discover information about content you are expected to teach. You cannot know everything there is to know about each subject—indeed, you will not always be able to predict all that is learned—but you should become knowledgeable about where and how to best research it, and how to assist your students in developing those same skills. Among other things, this means that you should be computer literate, that is, have the ability to understand and use computers for research and writing, paralleling reading and writing in verbal literacy.

3. *The teacher is an active member of professional organizations; reads professional journals; dialogues with colleagues; and maintains currency about methodology, the students, and the subject content the teacher is expected to teach.* While this resource guide offers valuable information about teaching and learning, it is much closer to the start of your professional career than it is to the end. As a teacher, you are a learner among learners. Plan to spend your career in a perpetual mode of learning through workshops, advanced course work, coaching and training, reading and study, and collaboration with and role-modeling of significant and more experienced colleagues.

4. *The teacher understands the processes of learning.* You will ensure that students understand the lesson objectives, your expectations, and the classroom procedures. They must feel welcome in your classroom and involved in learning activities, and they should have some control over the pacing of their own learning. Furthermore, when preparing your lessons, you will (a) consider the unique learning characteristics of each student; (b) see that content is presented in reasonably small doses—and in a logical and coherent sequence—while using visual, verbal, tactile, and kinesthetic learning activities

---

[7]You may want to compare the 22 competencies that are identified here with the INTASC standards via Internet http://www.ccsso.org/intascst.html.gen.html and with the 22 "components of professional practice" in C. Danielson, *Enhancing Professional Practice: A Framework for Teaching* (Alexandria, VA: Association for Supervision and Curriculum Development, 1996).

with opportunities for coached practice and reinforcement; and (c) frequently check for student comprehension to assure the students are learning. Checks for comprehension can be accomplished in many ways, such as by the questions you and the students ask during the lesson, by your awareness and understanding of student facial expressions and body language, and by various kinds of checklists (see Chapter 11).

5. *The teacher uses effective modeling behaviors.* Your own behaviors must be consistent with those expected of your students. If, for example, you want your students to demonstrate regular and punctual attendance, to have their work done on time, to have their materials each day for learning, to demonstrate cooperative behavior and respect for others, to maintain an open and inquisitive mind and attitude, to demonstrate critical thinking, and to use proper communication skills, then you will do likewise, modeling those same behaviors and attitudes for the students. As a middle level teacher, you serve as a very important role model for your students. Whether you realize it or not, your behavior sends important messages to students that complement curriculum content. You serve your students well when you model inclusive and collaborative approaches to learning. Presented later in this chapter are specific guidelines for effective modeling. The importance of effective modeling is one of several recurring themes throughout this resource guide.

6. *The teacher is open to change, willing to take risks and to be held accountable.* If there were no difference between what is and what can be, then formal schooling would be of little value. A competent teacher knows not only about historical and traditional values and knowledge, but also about the value of change. Thus, he or she is willing to carefully plan and experiment, to move between that which is known and that which is not. Realizing that little of value is ever achieved without a certain amount of risk and employing personal strength of convictions, the competent teacher stands ready to be held accountable, as the teacher undoubtedly will be, for assuming such risks. As stated so clearly elsewhere, "no coward ever got the Great Teacher Award."[8]

7. *The teacher is nonprejudiced toward gender, sexual preference, ethnicity, skin color, religion, physical disabilities, socioeconomic status, learning disabilities, or national origin.* Among other things, this means no sexual innuendoes, religious or ethnic jokes, or racial slurs. It means being cognizant of how teachers, male and female, knowingly or unknowingly, have historically mistreated female students, and of how to avoid those same errors in your own teaching. (Chapter 8 offers specific guidelines.) It means learning about and attending to the needs of individual students in your classroom. It means having

high, although not necessarily identical, expectations for all students.

8. *The teacher organizes the classroom and plans lessons carefully.* Long-range plans, no matter whether they include interdisciplinary thematic units or standards units; and daily lessons, no matter whether they are student-centered or teacher-centered; are prepared thoughtfully, reflected on, revised, and competently implemented with creative, motivating, and effective strategies and skill. Much of this resource guide is devoted to assisting in your development of this competency.

9. *The teacher is a capable communicator.* The competent teacher uses thoughtfully selected words, carefully planned questions, expressive voice inflections, useful pauses, meaningful gestures, and productive and non-confusing body language. Some of these expressions are carefully and thoughtfully planned during the preactive phase of instruction, and others, through practice and reflection, become second-nature skills. Throughout this book you will find useful suggestions for your development of this competency.

10. *The teacher functions effectively as a decision maker.* The exemplary middle level classroom is a complex place, busy with fast-paced activities. In a single day you may engage in a thousand or more interpersonal exchanges with students, to say nothing about the numerous exchanges possible with the many adults with whom you will be in contact. The competent teacher is in control of classroom events rather than being controlled by them. The teacher initiates, rather than merely reacts, and is proactive and in control of her or his interactions, having learned how to manage time to analyze and develop effective interpersonal behaviors. (For this purpose it can be valuable to videotape a class period for later analysis of your interactions.)

11. *The teacher is in a perpetual learning mode, striving to further develop a repertoire of teaching strategies.* Competent teachers are good students, continuing their own learning by reflecting on and assessing their work; attending workshops; studying the work of others; and talking with students, parents and guardians, and colleagues, sometimes through Internet bulletin boards. (While the development of your strategy repertoire is the essence of the focus of Parts II and III of this resource guide, the topic of ongoing professional development is a major topic of the final chapter.)

12. *The teacher demonstrates concern for the safety and health of the students.* The competent teacher consistently models safety procedures, ensuring precautions necessary to protect the health and the psychological and physical safety of the students. The teacher strives to maintain a comfortable room temperature with adequate ventilation and to prevent safety hazards in the classroom. Students who are ill are encouraged to stay home and to get well. If a teacher suspects that a student may be ill or may be suffering from neglect or abuse at

---

[8]S. Wassermann, "Shazam! You're a Teacher," *Phi Delta Kappan* 80(6):464, 466–468 (February 1999), p. 468.

home (see Chapter 4), the teacher appropriately and promptly acts upon that suspicion by referring it to the appropriate school official.

13. *The teacher demonstrates optimism for the learning of every student, while providing a constructive and positive environment for learning.* Much of this resource guide is devoted to providing specific guidelines and resources for developing this competency. Both common sense and research tell us clearly that young adolescents enjoy and learn better from a teacher who is positive and optimistic, encouraging, nurturing, and happy, rather than from a teacher who is negative and pessimistic, discouraging, uninterested, and grumpy.

14. *The teacher demonstrates confidence in each student's ability to learn.* For a student, nothing at school is more satisfying than a teacher who demonstrates confidence in that student's abilities. Unfortunately, for some students, a teacher's show of confidence may be the only positive indicator that student ever receives. Each of us can recall with admiration a teacher (or other significant person) who demonstrated confidence in our ability to accomplish seemingly formidable tasks. A competent teacher demonstrates this confidence with each and every student. This does not mean that you must personally like every student with whom you come into contact; it does mean that you accept each one as a person of dignity who is worthy of receiving your respect and professional skills.

15. *The teacher is skillful and fair in the employment of strategies for the assessment of student learning.* The competent teacher is knowledgeable about the importance of providing immediate intensive intervention when learning problems become apparent, implementing appropriate learning assessment tools while avoiding the abuse of power afforded by the assessment process. Assessment is the focus of Chapter 11.

16. *The teacher is skillful in working with parents and guardians, colleagues, administrators, and the support staff, and maintains and nurtures friendly and ethical professional relationships.* Teachers, parents and guardians, administrators, cooks, custodians, secretaries, security personnel, and other adults of the school community all share one common purpose, and that is to serve the education of the students. It is done best when it is done cooperatively.

17. *The teacher demonstrates continuing interest in professional responsibilities and opportunities.* Knowing that ultimately each and every school activity has an effect upon the classroom, the competent teacher assumes an active interest in the school community. The purpose of the school is to serve the education of the students, and the classroom is the primary, but not only, place where this occurs. Every committee meeting, school event, advisory meeting, faculty meeting, school board meeting, office, program, and other planned function that is related to school life shares in the ultimate purpose of better serving the education of the students who attend that school.

18. *The teacher exhibits a wide range of interests.* This includes interest in the activities of the students and in the many aspects of the school and its surrounding community. The competent teacher is interesting because of his or her interests; a teacher with varied interests more often motivates and captures the attention of more students. A teacher with no interests outside his or her subject area and the classroom is likely, for young adolescents, to be an exceedingly dull person.

19. *The teacher shares a healthy sense of humor.* The positive effects of appropriate humor (that is, humor that is not self-deprecating or disrespectful of others) on learning are well established. It increases immune system activity and decreases stress-producing hormones; causes a drop in the pulse rate; reduces feelings of anxiety, tension, and stress; activates T-cells for the immune system, which are antibodies that fight against harmful microorganisms, and gamma interferon, a hormone that fights viruses and regulates cell growth; and increases blood oxygen. Because of these effects, humor is a stimulant not only to healthy living, but to creativity and higher-level thinking. As they should, young adolescents appreciate and learn more from a teacher who shares a sense of humor and laughs with them.

20. *The teacher is quick to recognize a student who may be in need of special attention.* A competent teacher is alert to recognize any child who demonstrates behaviors indicating a need for special attention, guidance, or counseling. The teacher knows how and where to refer the student, and does so with minimal class disruption and without embarrassment to the child. For example, a pattern of increasingly poor attendance or of steady negative-attention seeking behaviors are two of the more obvious early signals of the student who is potentially at risk of dropping out of school.

21. *The teacher makes specific and frequent efforts to demonstrate how the subject content may be related to the students' lives.* A potentially dry and dull topic is made significant and alive when taught by a competent teacher. Regardless of the topic, somewhere competent teachers are teaching that topic. One of the significant characteristics of their effectiveness is they make the topic alive and relevant to themselves and to their students, helping the students make relevant connections. Time and again studies point out what should be obvious: Students do not learn much from dull, meaningless "drill and kill" exercises and assignments. Such uninspired teaching may be at the root of why some children lose interest in formal schooling. Obtaining ideas from professional journals; attending workshops; communicating with colleagues either personally or via electronic bulletin boards and Websites; and using project-based and interdisciplinary thematic instruction are ways of discovering how to make a potentially dry and boring topic interesting and alive for students (and for the teacher).

22. *The teacher is reliable.* The competent teacher can be relied on to fulfill professional responsibilities, promises, and commitments. A teacher who cannot be relied on is quick to lose credibility with the students and with colleagues and administrators. Regardless of a teacher's potential for effectiveness, an unreliable teacher is an incompetent teacher. No matter the reason, a teacher who is chronically absent from his or her teaching duties is an "at-risk" teacher.

Specific teacher behaviors are discussed in the following section; guidelines and resources to assist you in your development of these competencies permeate this resource guide.

TEACHER BEHAVIORS NECESSARY TO FACILITATE STUDENT LEARNING

Your ability to perform your instructional responsibilities effectively is directly dependent upon your knowledge of young adolescents and how they best learn and on your knowledge of and the quality of your teaching skills. As we said at the beginning of this chapter, development of your strategy repertoire along with your skills in using specific strategies should be ongoing throughout your teaching career. To be most effective, you need a large repertoire from which to select a specific strategy for a particular goal with a distinctive group of students. In addition, you need skill in using that strategy. This section is designed to help you begin building your specific strategies repertoire and to develop your skills in using these strategies. Like intelligences, teaching style is neither absolutely inherited nor fixed, but continues to develop and emerge throughout one's professional career.

First, you must know why you have selected a particular strategy. An unknowing teacher is likely to use the teaching strategy most common in college classes—the lecture. However, as many beginning teachers have discovered the hard way, the traditional lecture is seldom if ever an effective or appropriate way to instruct young adolescents. As a rule, unlike many college and university students, not many young adolescents are strong auditory learners by preference and by adeptness. For most of them, learning by sitting and listening is difficult. Instead, they learn best when physically (hands-on) and intellectually (minds-on) active—that is, when using tactile and kinesthetic experiences, such as touching objects, feeling shapes and textures, and moving objects, and when together they are able to talk about and share what they are learning.

Second, basic teacher behaviors create the conditions needed to enable students to think and to learn, whether the learning is a further understanding of concepts, the internalization of attitudes and values, the development of cognitive processes, or the actuating of the most complex behaviors. The basic teacher behaviors are those that produce the following results: (a) students are physically and mentally engaged in the learning activities, (b) instructional time is efficiently used, and (c) classroom distractions and interruptions are minimal.

Third, the effectiveness with which a teacher carries out the basic behaviors can be measured by how well the students learn (this is the topic of Chapter 11).

The basic teacher behaviors that facilitate student learning, which are discussed next, are structuring the learning environment; accepting and sharing instructional accountability; demonstrating withitness and overlapping; providing a variety of motivating and challenging lessons; modeling appropriate behaviors; facilitating student acquisition of data; creating a psychologically safe environment; clarifying whenever necessary; using periods of silence; and questioning thoughtfully.

Facilitating Behaviors and Instructional Strategies: A Clarification

Clearly, at least some of the 10 behaviors are also instructional strategies. Questioning is one example. The difference is that while the behaviors must be in place for the most effective teaching to occur, strategies (discussed in Part III) are more or less discretionary; that is, they are pedagogical techniques from which you may select but may not be obligated to use. For example, questioning and the use of silence are fundamental teaching behaviors, whereas lecturing and showing videos are not. Thus, you see, your task is two-fold: (1) develop your awareness of and skills in using the fundamental teaching behaviors, and (2) develop your repertoire and skills in selecting and using appropriate instructional strategies.

Starting now and continuing throughout your teaching career, you will want to evaluate your developing competency for each of the 10 fundamental facilitating behaviors and improve in areas where you need help. Consider the following descriptions and examples, and discuss them with your classmates.

Structuring the Learning Environment

Structuring the learning environment means establishing an intellectual, psychological, and physical environment that enables all students to act and react productively. Specifically, you

- Attend to the organization of the classroom as a learning laboratory to establish a positive, safe, and efficient environment for student learning.
- Establish and maintain clearly understood classroom procedures, definitions, instructions, and expectations. Help students to clarify the learning expectations and to establish clearly understood learning objectives.

- Help students assume tasks and responsibilities, thereby empowering them in their learning.
- Organize the students, helping them to organize their learning. Help students in identifying and understanding time and resource constraints. Provide instructional scaffolds, such as building bridges to student learning by helping students connect what is being learned with what the students already know or think they know and have experienced.
- Plan and implement techniques for schema building, such as providing content and process outlines, visual diagrams, and opportunities for thinking process mapping (discussed in Chapter 9).
- Use techniques for students' metacognitive development, such as *think-pair share,* in which students are asked to think about an idea, share thoughts about it with a partner, and then share the pair's thoughts with the entire class; *think-write-pair-share,* in which each student writes his or her ideas about the new word and then shares in pairs before sharing with the entire class; and *jigsaw,* in which individuals or small groups of students are given responsibilities for separate tasks that lead to a bigger task or understanding, thereby putting together parts to make a whole (as was done in Exercise 3.5).
- Plan units and lessons that have clear and concise beginnings and endings with at least some of the planning done collaboratively with the students.
- Provide frequent summary reviews, often by using student self-assessment of what is being learned. Structure and facilitate ongoing formal and informal discussion based on a shared understanding of rules of discourse.

Accepting and Sharing Instructional Accountability

While holding students accountable for their learning, the teacher is willing to be held accountable for the effectiveness of the learning process and outcomes (the "locus of control" discussed at the start of this chapter). Specifically, you

- Assume a responsibility for professional decision making and the risks associated with that responsibility. You also share some responsibility for decision making and risk taking with the students. A primary goal in the students' education must be to see that they become accountable for themselves as learners and as citizens. Middle level teachers are advised to work with their students as *partners* in their learning and development. One dimension of the partnership is shared accountability. An effective way of doing that is by using student portfolios (discussed in Chapters 5 and 11).
- Communicate clearly to parents/guardians, administrators, and colleagues.

- Communicate to the students that accomplishment of learning goals and objectives is a responsibility they share with you.
- Plan exploratory activities that engage students in the learning.
- Provide continuous cues for desired learning behaviors and incentives contingent upon desired performance, such as grades, points, rewards, and privileges. Establish a clearly understood and continuous program of assessment that includes reflection and self-assessment.
- Provide opportunities for the students to demonstrate their learning, to refine and explore their questions, to inquire, and to share their thinking and results.

Demonstrating Withitness and Overlapping

Withitness and overlapping, first described by Jacob Kounin, are separate but closely related behaviors.[9] **Withitness** is your awareness of the whole group. **Overlapping** is your ability to attend to several matters simultaneously. (Further discussion and guidelines for developing these two skills are presented in Chapter 4.) Specifically, you

- Attend to the entire class while working with one student or with a small group of students, communicating this awareness with eye contact, hand gestures, body position and language, and clear but private verbal cues.
- Continually and simultaneously monitor all classroom activities to keep students at their tasks and to provide students with assistance and resources.
- Continue monitoring the class during any distraction, such as when a visitor enters the classroom or while the students are on a field trip.
- Demonstrate an understanding of when comprehension checks and instructional transitions are appropriate or needed.
- Dwell on one topic only as long as is necessary for the students to understand.
- Quickly intervene and redirect potential undesirable student behavior (see Chapter 4).
- Refocus or shift activities for a student when that student's attention begins to fade.

Providing a Variety of Motivating and Challenging Activities

The effective teacher uses a variety of activities that motivate and challenge all students to work to the utmost of their abilities, and that engage and challenge the preferred

---

[9] J. S. Kounin, *Discipline and Group Management in Classrooms* (New York: Holt, Rinehart and Winston, 1970).

learning styles and learning capacities of more of the students more of the time. Specifically, you

- Demonstrate optimism toward each student's ability.
- Demonstrate an unwavering expectation that each student will work to the best of his or her ability.
- Show pride, optimism, and enthusiasm in learning, thinking, and teaching.
- View teaching and learning as an organic and reciprocal process that extends well beyond what can be referred to as the traditional 2 by 4 by 6 curriculum—that is, a curriculum that is bound by the two covers of the textbook, the four walls of the classroom, and the six hours of the school day.
- Collaborate with the students to plan exciting and interesting learning activities, including those that engage the students' natural interest in the mysterious and the novel.

Modeling Appropriate Behaviors

Effective teachers model the very behaviors expected of their students. Specifically, you

- Are prompt in returning student papers and offer comments that provide instructive and encouraging feedback.
- Arrive promptly in the classroom and demonstrate on-task behaviors for the entire class meeting just as is expected of the students.
- Demonstrate respect for all students. For example, you do not interrupt when a student is showing rational thinking, even though you may disagree with or frown upon the words used or the direction of the students' thinking.
- Demonstrate that making "errors" is a natural event in learning and during problem solving, and readily admit and correct a mistake made by yourself.
- Model and emphasize the skills, attitudes, and values of higher-order intellectual processes. Demonstrate rational problem-solving skills and explain to the students the processes being engaged while problem solving.[10]
- Model professionalism by spelling correctly, using proper grammar, and writing clearly and legibly.
- Practice communication that is clear, precise, and to the point. For example, use "I" when referring to yourself, "we" when "we" is meant. Rather than responding to student contributions with simply "good" or "okay," tell specifically what about the response was good, or what made it okay.
- Practice moments of silence (see "Using Periods of Silence" that follows), thus modeling thoughtfulness, reflectiveness, and restraint of impulsiveness.

- Realize that students are also models for other students, and therefore reinforce appropriate student behaviors and intervene when behaviors are not appropriate (discussed in Chapter 4).

Facilitating Student Acquisition of Data

The teacher makes sure that data are accessible to students as input that they can process. Specifically, you

- Create a responsive classroom environment with direct learning experiences (discussed early in Chapter 6).
- Ensure that major ideas receive proper attention and emphasis.
- Ensure that sources of information are readily available to students for their use. Select books, media, and materials that facilitate student learning. Assure that equipment and materials are readily available for students to use. Identify and use resources beyond the walls of the classroom and the boundaries of the school campus.
- Provide clear and specific instructions.
- Provide feedback and feedback mechanisms about each student's performance and progress. Encourage students to organize and maintain devices to self-monitor their progress in learning and thinking. (Discussed in Chapter 11).
- Select anchoring (also called model or benchmark) examples of student work that help students bridge what is being learned with what they already know and have experienced.
- Serve as a resource person and use cooperative learning (discussed in Chapter 8), thus regarding students as resources too.

Creating a Psychologically Safe Environment

To encourage the positive development of student self-esteem, to provide a psychologically safe learning environment, and to encourage the most creative thought and behavior, the teacher provides an attractive and stimulating classroom environment and appropriate nonjudgmental responses. (Chapter 4 is devoted to this theme.) Specifically, you

- Avoid negative criticism. Criticism is often a negative value judgment, and "when a teacher responds to a student's ideas or actions with such negative words as "poor," "incorrect," or "wrong," the response tends to signal inadequacy or disapproval and ends the student's thinking about the task."[11]

---

[10]See, for example, J. W. Astington, "Theory of Mind Goes to School," *Educational Leadership* 56(3):46–48 (November 1998).

[11]Costa, *The School*, 1991, p. 54.

Figure 3.3   Statements of praise versus encouragement.

Statement of Praise	*Statement of Encouragement*
1. Your painting is excellent.	1. It is obvious that you enjoy painting.
2. I am delighted that you behaved so well on our class field trip.	2. I am so delighted that we all enjoyed the class field trip.
3. You did a good job on those word problems.	3. I can tell that you have been working and are enjoying it more.
4. Your oral report on your project was well done.	4. I can tell that you got really interested in your topic for the oral report on your project.
5. Great answer Louis!	5. Louis, your answer shows that you gave a lot of thought to the question.

- Frequently use minimal reinforcement (that is, non-judgmental acceptance behaviors, such as nodding head, writing a student's response on the board, or saying "I understand"). Whereas elaborate or strong praise is generally unrelated to student achievement, minimal reinforcement, using words like "right," "okay," "good," "uh-huh," and "thank you," does correlate with achievement.

  However, as implied previously in the discussion about "modeling," be careful with a too frequent and thereby ineffective and even damaging use of the single word "good" following student contributions during a class discussion. Use the word only when the contribution was truly that—good—and better yet, say not only "good" but tell what specifically was good about the student's contribution. That provides a more powerful reinforcement by demonstrating that you truly heard the student's contribution and you indeed thought it was good.

- Infrequently use elaborate or strong praise. By the time students are in middle grades, teacher praise, a positive value judgment, has little or no value as a form of positive reinforcement. When praise is used for young adolescents it should be mild, private, and for student accomplishment, rather than for effort. For each child, the frequency of using praise should be gradually reduced. When praise is reduced, a more diffused sociometric pattern develops; that is, more of the children become directly and productively involved in the learning. Praise should be simple and direct, delivered in a natural voice without dramatizing.[12] Young adolescents see overly done theatrics as insincere.

  Let us take pause to consider this point. Probably no statement in this resource guide raises more eyebrows than the statement that praise for most young adolescents has little or no value as a form of positive rein-

forcement. After all, praise may well motivate some people. However, at what cost? Praise and encouragement are often confused and considered to be the same (see Figure 3.3), but they are not, and they do not have the same long-term results. This is explained as follows:

> For many years there has been a great campaign for the virtues of praise in helping children gain a positive self-concept and improve their behavior. This is another time when we must "beware of what works." Praise may inspire some children to improve their behavior. The problem is that they become pleasers and approval "junkies." These children (and later these adults) develop self-concepts that are totally dependent on the opinions of others. Other children resent and rebel against praise, either because they don't want to live up to the expectations of others or because they fear they can't compete with those who seem to get praise so easily. The alternative that considers long-range effects is encouragement. The long-range effect of encouragement is self-confidence. The long-range effect of praise is dependence on others.[13]

In summary, while being cautious with the use of praise, do reinforce student efforts by recognizing specific personal accomplishments.[14]

- Perceive your classroom as the place where you work and students learn, and make it and the tools available a place of pride—as stimulating and practical as possible.
- Plan behaviors, within the lessons, that show respect for the cultures, experiences, and ideas of individual students.
- Provide positive individual student attention as often as possible. Write sincere reinforcing personalized comments on student papers. Provide incentives and

---

[12]T. L. Good and J. E. Brophy, *Looking in Classrooms,* 8th ed. (New York: Addison Wesley Longman, 2000), p. 142.

[13]J. Nelsen, *Positive Discipline* (New York: Ballantine Books, 1987), p. 103. See also L. A. Froyen, *Classroom Management: The Reflective Teacher-Leader,* 2nd ed. (Upper Saddle River, NJ: Prentice Hall, 1993), pp. 294–298.

[14]See the discussion titled "Research and theory on providing recognition," pp. 53–59 of R. J. Marzano, et al., *Classroom Instruction That Works* (Alexandria, VA: Association for Supervision and Curriculum Development, 2001).

rewards for student accomplishments. (See discussion in Chapter 4 about using rewards.)

- Use nonverbal cues to show awareness and acceptance of individual students. Use paraphrasing and reflective listening. Use empathic acceptance of a student's expression of feelings; demonstrate by words and gestures that you understand the student's position.

Clarifying Whenever Necessary

Your responding behavior seeks further elaboration from a student about that student's idea or comprehension. Specifically, you

- Help students to connect new content to that previously learned. Help them relate content of a lesson to their other school and nonschool experiences. Help students make learning connections between disciplines. (Much of Part III of this resource guide is devoted to this theme.)
- Politely invite a student to be more specific and to elaborate on or rephrase an idea, or to provide a concrete illustration of an idea.
- Provide frequent opportunity for summary reviews.
- Repeat or paraphrase a student's response, allowing the student to correct any other person's misinterpretation of what the student said or implied.
- Select instructional strategies that help students correct their prior notions about a topic.

Using Periods of Silence

Use periods of silence in the classroom. Specifically, you

- Actively listen when a student is talking.

- Allow sufficient think-time, sometimes as long as nine seconds, after asking a question or posing a problem. (See "wait-time" in Chapter 7.)
- Keep silent when students are working quietly or are attending to a visual display, and maintain classroom control by using nonverbal signals and indirect intervention strategies.
- Pause while talking to allow for thinking and reflection.
- Use teacher silence, supported by body language and nonverbal gesturing (i.e., a nod of the head, a thumbs up), to stimulate group discussion.

Questioning Thoughtfully

Use thoughtfully worded questions to induce learning and to stimulate thinking and the development of students' thinking skills. (Questioning is the topic of Chapter 7). Specifically, you

- Encourage student questioning without judging the quality or relevancy of a student's question. Attend to student questions, and respond and encourage other students to respond, often by building upon the content of a student's questions and student responses.
- Help students develop their own questioning skills and provide opportunities for students to explore their own ideas, to obtain data, and to find answers to their own questions and solutions to their problems.
- Plan questioning sequences that elicit a variety of thinking skills, and that maneuver students to higher levels of thinking and doing.
- Use a variety of types of questions.
- Use questions to help students to explore their knowledge, to develop new understandings, and to discover ways of applying their new understandings.

KNOW ENOUGH FOR NOW, BY TINA HUMPHREY*

A Middle School Teacher's Reflections on Her First Year—the Funny, Frustrating, Sad, and Happy Moments—as She Learns What She Needs to Know to Survive and Grow as an Educator.

As a first-year teacher I must have heard a thousand times in the past nine months, "Wait until winter break . . . ," and "If you can just make it until spring break . . . ," and, "You'll be amazed at what an expert teacher you'll feel like when you return from summer break." And so *finally* I've reached the summer break and I have a chance to not do anything even remotely related to school; and yet, I'm finding this desire to reflect on my first real year of teaching and where I'm at now in my career. I ask my students to do this all the time; shouldn't I do the same?

*Source: Tina Humphrey, "Knowing Enough for Now," *Reading Today* 18(1):4 (August/September 2000). By permission of middle level teacher Tina Humphrey and the editors of *Reading Today*, published by the International Reading Association.

Well, it's safe to say that I've got the basic patterns and habits down that work for me:

- Put the desks in rows for attendance and daily activities; move to groups or circles when necessary.
- Don't check my voice mail messages until the end of the day; a disgruntled parent will only vampirize all of my energy first thing in the morning.
- Dress like a professional so that I *feel* like a professional.
- Laugh a lot—I mean a *lot*—because none of my peers get to hear a 13-year-old's amazing views on flag football statistics and what the latest nail polish trend is on a daily basis like I do.
- Take time for *myself* every single day—school will absolutely engulf me if I don't.
- Seek out a mentor and use her, test her, question her, probe her, hug her.
- Be nice to the copy ladies.
- Always remember that first and foremost, these are 12- and 13-year-old kids and yes, they honestly do believe that their Friday night plans are much, much more important than proper nouns and Tom Sawyer.
- And I also need to remember that first and foremost, I am still just a 24-year-old person trying to balance my checkbook and send my rent check in on time.

And so, I've finally gotten that stuff figured out (maybe). I also don't turn down the wrong hallways any more looking for my classroom, I know where the teachers' restrooms are, I've learned to write down assignments in *at least* three different places in the classroom, I've learned that being "cool" with the students doesn't make one a good teacher, and most importantly, I've learned that all 120 of my kids are as different as snowflakes—and that's precisely why it's not easy being a novice teacher (or an expert teacher for that matter).

I also know what I *should* do. I know all about differentiation, tiered assignments, and learning stations. I've read a million books. I've looked at charts and plans and other teachers' lessons. I've given up my own free reading time with a cheesy mystery novel in order to review old college textbooks on educational psychology in order to be the best teacher I can possibly be.

But I also know about state standards and CSAP results and the fact that I have empty filing cabinets to pull lessons from. I know what a failed lesson looks like. I know what it means to have seventh grade gifted and talented students performing at a level beyond my own, and I know what it means to have eighth graders who don't seem to know what a paragraph is—all in one day. And I know what I *should* have done—it just wasn't going to happen in those first few months.

I know what it's like to have the desire to save the world and be the best teacher there ever was. And I know how crushing it is to realize that's not going to happen—at least not the first year. And I know what it's like to cry at school because I'm too overwhelmed and exhausted to deal with grades and attendance slips. And I know what it's like to cry before I go to bed because I can't figure out how to reach that one student.

And it was only my first year.

And so, in other words, what I feel like I *know* is what it's truly like to be a teacher—not a good teacher, or a bad teacher, or a student teacher any more, but a *real* teacher. I now know about the hoops we're required to jump through on a daily basis and I now know more than ever that the salary truly, truly, truly isn't enough. (And yet it doesn't really matter somehow.)

After my first year of teaching I can say that I have a vision—certainly not an answer or a solution—but a vision nonetheless. I can visualize myself with individualized learning plans, a class full of students all reading different novels, music playing, kids laughing, and behind me will rest full filing cabinets to refer to. I can really see that. But until that vision comes true, I will strive day-to-day to survive, to laugh, to love, to be patient—and to move up from there. And I need to feel safe in the knowledge that that is enough for now.

SUMMARY

You have reviewed the realities of the responsibilities of today's classroom teacher. Being a good teacher takes time, commitment, concentrated effort, and just plain hard work. Nobody truly knowledgeable about it ever said that good teaching was easy.

You have learned that your professional responsibilities as a middle level teacher will extend well beyond the four walls of the classroom, the six hours of the school day, the five days of the school week, and the 180 or so days of the school year. You learned of the many expectations (a) to demonstrate effective decision making; (b) to be committed to young adolescents, to the school's mission, and to the profession; (c) to develop facilitating behaviors and to provide effective instruction; and (d) to fulfill numerous noninstructional responsibilities. As you have read and discussed these responsibilities, you should have begun to fully comprehend the challenge and reality of being a competent middle level teacher.

Teaching style is the way teachers teach, their distinctive mannerisms complemented by their choices of teaching behaviors and strategies. Style develops from tradition, from one's beliefs and experiences, and from one's knowledge of research findings. You analyzed your own beliefs, observed one teacher and that teacher's style for that lesson, and began the development of your philosophy about teaching and learning, a philosophical statement that should be useful to you during later job interviews (see Chapter 12).

Exciting research findings continue to emerge from several, related areas—about learning, conceptual development, and thinking styles—and from neurophysiology. The findings continue to support the hypothesis that a middle level classroom teacher's best teaching style choice is eclectic with a strong bent toward the facilitating, at least until the day arrives when students of certain thinking styles can be practically matched to teachers with particular teaching styles. Future research will undoubtedly shed additional light on the relationships among pedagogy, pedagogical styles, and student thinking and learning.

Today, there seems to be much agreement that the essence of the learning process is a combination of self-awareness, self-monitoring, and active reflection. Young adolescents learn these skills best when exposed to teachers who themselves effectively model those same behaviors. For young adolescents, the most effective teaching and learning is an interactive process, which involves not only learning, but also thinking about learning and learning how to learn.

This completes our introduction to middle level teaching and learning. You are now ready to begin Part II, planning for instruction. The first chapter of Part II presents ways of establishing an effective learning environment where you can carry out your professional responsibilities.

ADDITIONAL EXERCISES

See the companion Website http://www.prenhall.com/kellough for the following exercises related to the content of this chapter:

- My Perceptions of How I Learn: Sources of Motivation
- My Perceptions of How I Learn: Techniques Used

QUESTIONS FOR CLASS DISCUSSION

1. Explain the meaning of each of the following two concepts and why you agree or disagree with each. (a) The teacher should hold high, although not necessarily identical, expectations for all students and never waver from those expectations. (b) The teacher should not be controlled by a concern to "cover" the content of the textbook by the end of the school term.
2. More than a third of a century ago, a publication entitled *Six Areas of Teacher Competencies* (Burlingame, CA: California Teachers Association, 1964) identified six roles of the classroom teacher: director of learning, counselor and guidance worker, mediator of the culture, link with the community, member of the school staff, and member of the profession. When compared with that, have the roles changed for today's classroom teacher? If so, how?
3. Identify a middle level teacher whom you consider to be competent and compare what you recall about that teacher's classroom with the characteristics of competent teachers as presented in this chapter. Share your comparison with others in the class.
4. Before studying this chapter, were you fully aware of the extent of a middle level teacher's responsibilities? Explain your response.
5. Compare the teacher's use of praise and of encouragement for student work; describe specific classroom situations in which each is more appropriate.
6. Select one of the "Reflective Thoughts" from the beginning of Part I (page 2) that is specifically related to the content of this chapter, research it, and write a one-page essay explaining why you agree or disagree with the thought. Share your essay with members of your class for their thoughts.
7. Explain how you now feel about being a middle level teacher—for example, motivated, excited, enthusiastic, befuddled, confused, depressed. Explain and discuss your current feelings with your classmates. Sort out common concerns and design avenues for dealing with any negative feelings you might have.
8. Describe any prior concepts you held that changed as a result of your experiences with this chapter. Describe the changes.
9. From your current observations and fieldwork related to this teacher preparation program, clearly identify one specific example of educational practice that seems contradictory to exemplary practice or theory as presented in this chapter. Present your explanation for the discrepancy.
10. Do you have other questions generated by the content of this chapter? If you do, list them along with ways answers might be found.

FOR FURTHER READING

Bailey, D. L. and Helms, R. G. *The National Board Certified Teacher.* Fastback 470. Bloomington, IN: Phi Delta Kappa Educational Foundation, 2000.

Cornell, C. "I Hate Math! I Couldn't Learn It, and I Can't Teach It!" *Childhood Education* 75(4):225–230 (Summer 1999).

Cornett, C. *Learning Through Laughter . . . Again.* Fastback 487. Bloomington, IN: Phi Delta Kappa Educational Foundation, 2001.

Freiberg, H. J. (ed.). *Perceiving, Behaving, Becoming: Lessons Learned.* Alexandria, VA: Association for Supervision and Curriculum Development, 1999.

Hodgkinson, H. "Educational Demographics: What Teachers Should Know." *Educational Leadership* 58(4):6–11 (December 2000/January 2001).

Krogness, M. M. "Ten Remarkable Middle School Language Arts Teachers (Middle Ground)." *English Journal* 87(1):98–101 (January 1998).

Linkous, V. "Simply Speaking. Issues in Education." *Childhood Education* 76(3):161 (Spring 2000).

Rea, D.; Millican, K. P.; and Watson, S. W. "The Serious Benefits of Fun in the Classroom." *Middle School Journal* 31(4):23–28 (March 2000).

Stodolsky, S. S., and Grossman, P. L. "Changing Students, Changing Teaching." *Teachers College Record* 102(1):125–172 (February 2000).

Stroka, S. R. "Education is Not a Laughing Matter! Or is it?" *Middle Ground* 3(4):32–34 (February 2000).

Wasley, P. "Teaching Worth Celebrating." *Educational Leadership* 56(8):8–13 (May 1999).

Wassermann, S. "Shazam! You're a Teacher." *Phi Delta Kappan* 80(6):464, 466–468 (February 1999).

Part II

PLANNING FOR INSTRUCTION

Part II responds to your needs concerning:

▶ An effective, safe, and supportive classroom environment.
▶ Collaborative planning.
▶ Curriculum integration and the interdisciplinary thematic unit.
▶ Dealing with content and issues that may be controversial.
▶ Direct and indirect instruction.
▶ Documents that provide guidance for curriculum planning.
▶ Domains of learning.
▶ Goals, objectives, and learning outcomes.
▶ Levels of curriculum planning.
▶ National Educational Goals and national curriculum standards.

- Productive ways to start the school term.
- Selected legal guidelines for the classroom teacher.
- Selecting and developing appropriate learning activities.
- Selecting and sequencing content.
- Using textbooks.

REFLECTIVE THOUGHTS

A caring and responsive learning environment has as its sole purpose that of helping all students to make the transitions necessary to succeed in school and in life.

As a teacher, you are a professional who deals in matters of human relations and who must exercise professional judgment.

A classroom teacher is responsible for planning at three levels–the year, the units, and the lessons–with critical decisions to be made at each level. Failing to prepare is preparing to fail.

The obsolescence of many past instructional practices has been substantiated repeatedly by those researchers who have made recent studies of exemplary educational practices.

Your challenge is to use performance-based criteria with a teaching style that encourages the development of intrinsic sources of student motivation, and that provides for coincidental learning, which goes beyond what might be considered predictable, immediately measurable, and having minimal expectations.

Teachers must be clear about what they expect their students to learn and about the kind of evidence needed to verify their learning, and they must communicate those things to the students so they are clearly understood.

Curriculum integration refers to a way of thinking, a way of teaching, and a way of planning and organizing the instructional program so the discrete disciplines of subject matter are related to one another in a design that (a) matches the developmental needs of the learners and (b) helps to connect their learning in ways that are meaningful to their current and past experiences.

No matter what else you are prepared to teach, you are primarily a teacher of literacy and of thinking, social, and learning skills.

4

Planning the Classroom Learning Environment

Effective teaching does not just happen. It begins with (a) the deliberative planning and arranging of the learning environment and continues with (b) the thoughtful planning of each phase of the learning process. This chapter deals with the first of these two aspects of planning for effective teaching—the planning, establishing, and managing of a supportive classroom learning environment.

To become and to remain an effective teacher with a minimum of distractions in the classroom, you must (a) apply your knowledge of the characteristics and needs of the young adolescent students with whom you work (Chapters 1 and 2), (b) practice the behaviors that facili-

tate their learning (Chapter 3), and (c) do so in a conducive learning environment. The latter is the principal focus of this chapter. The planning, establishment, and managing of a conducive classroom learning environment derives from one's knowledge about young adolescents and how they learn, and from careful thought and planning. It should not be left for the beginning teacher to learn on the job in a sink-or-swim situation.

A conducive classroom learning environment is one that is psychologically safe, that helps the students to perceive the importance of what is being taught, that helps them realize they can achieve, and that is instructive in the procedures for doing it. While it is important that they learn to control their impulses and to delay their need for gratification (see "characteristics of intelligent behavior" in Chapter 9), students are more willing to spend time on a learning task when they perceive value or reward in doing so, when they possess some ownership in planning and carrying out the task, and when they feel they can accomplish the task. Thoughtful and thorough planning of your procedures for classroom management is as important a part of your preactive-phase of instruction (discussed in Chapter 3) as is the preparation of units and lessons (discussed in Chapters 5 and 6). Indeed, an analysis of 50 years of research studies shows that classroom management is the single most important factor influencing student learning.[1]

This chapter presents guidelines and resources that will help you to establish and manage a classroom environment that is safe for the students and favorable to their learning.

OBJECTIVES

Upon completion of this chapter, you should be able to

1. As related to classroom management, distinguish between the concepts of *consequences* and *punishment*.
2. Demonstrate knowledge of basic legal guidelines for the classroom teacher.
3. Describe a teacher's reasonable first reaction to each of the following students: one who is aggressively violent, one who habitually lies, one who is defiant, one who tosses paper from across the room at the wastebasket, and one who is sitting and staring out the window.
4. Describe by examples how each of the following contributes to effective classroom control: a positive approach, well-planned lessons, a good start of the school term, classroom procedures and rules, consistency but with professional judgment in enforcing procedures and rules, correction of student misbehavior, and classroom management.
5. Describe means you can use to help students establish self-control.
6. Describe important perceptions that must be in place and why.
7. Describe planning you would do for the first week of school.
8. Describe the advantages and disadvantages of studying students' school records for the purpose of discovering which students have a history of causing trouble in the classroom.
9. Describe the characteristics of an effective instructional transition.
10. Describe the meaning and give an example of sequenced consequences as used in response to inappropriate student behavior.
11. Differentiate between direct and indirect intervention to refocus a student and describe situations where you would be most likely to use each.
12. Explain how you will know if you have classroom control and if you are an effective manager of students' learning.
13. Identify characteristics of a classroom environment that is both safe for students and favorable to their learning.
14. Prepare an initial draft of your proposed management system.

PERCEPTIONS AND THEIR IMPORTANCE

Unless you believe that your students can learn, they will not. Unless you believe that you can teach them, you will not. Unless your students believe that they can learn and until they want to learn, they will not.

We all know or have heard of teachers who get the very best from their students, even from those students that many teachers find to be the most challenging to teach. Regardless of individual circumstances, those teachers (a) *know* that, when given adequate support, all students can learn; (b) *expect* the best from each student; (c) establish a classroom environment that motivates students to do their best, and (d) manage their classrooms so class time is efficiently used; that is, with the least amount of distraction to the learning process.

Regardless of how well planned you are for the instruction, certain perceptions by students must be in place to support the successful implementation of those plans. Students must perceive (a) the classroom environment as being supportive of their efforts, (b) that you care about their learning and that they are welcome in your classroom, (c) the expected learning as being challenging but not impossible, and (d) the anticipated learning outcomes as being worthy of their time and effort to try to achieve.[2]

CLASSROOM CONTROL—ITS MEANING—PAST AND PRESENT

Classroom control frequently is of the greatest concerns to beginning teachers—and they have good cause to be concerned. Even experienced teachers sometimes find control difficult, particularly in middle level schools where so many students come to school with so much

---

[1]M. C. Want; G. D. Haertel; and H. J. Walberg, "What Helps Students Learn?" *Educational Leadership* 51(4):74–79 (December 1993/January 1994).

[2]See, for example, R. W. Roeser and J. S. Eccles, "Adolescents' Perceptions of Middle School: Relation to Longitudinal Changes in Academic and Psychological Adjustment," *Journal of Research on Adolescence* 8(1):123–158 (1998).

psychological baggage and have already become alienated as the result of negative experiences in their lives.

In one respect, being a classroom teacher is much like being a truck driver who must remain alert while going down a steep and winding grade; otherwise, the truck most assuredly will get out of control, veer off the highway, and crash. This chapter has been thoughtfully designed to help you with your concerns about control—and to help you avoid a crash.

Historical Meaning of Classroom Control

To set the stage for your comprehension, consider what the term *classroom control* has meant historically and what it means today. In the 1800s, instead of classroom control, educators spoke of *classroom discipline,* and that meant punishment. Such an interpretation was consistent with the then-popular learning theory that assumed children were innately bad and that inappropriate behavior could be prevented by strictness or treated with punishment. Schools of the mid-1800s have been described as being "wild and unruly places," and "full of idleness and disorder."[3]

By the early 1900s, educators were asking, "Why are the children still misbehaving?" The accepted answer was that the children were misbehaving *because* of the rigid punitive system. On this point, the era of progressive education began, providing students more freedom to decide what they would learn. The teacher's job, then, became one of providing a rich classroom of resources and materials to stimulate the student's natural curiosity. And since the system no longer would be causing misbehavior, punishment would no longer be necessary. Classes of the 1930s that were highly permissive, however, turned out to cause more anxiety than the restrictive classes of the 1800s.

Today's Meaning of Classroom Control and the Concept of Classroom Management

Today, rather than classroom discipline, educators talk of **classroom control,** the process of controlling student behavior in the classroom. The most effective teacher is one who is in control of classroom events rather than controlled by them. Classroom control is an important aspect of the broader concept of classroom management. Classroom control is part of a management plan designed to (a) prevent inappropriate student behaviors, (b) help students develop self-control, and (c) suggest procedures for dealing with inappropriate student behaviors.

Effective teaching requires a well-organized, businesslike classroom in which motivated students work diligently at their learning tasks, free from distractions and interruptions. Providing such a setting for learning requires careful thought and preparation, and is called effective **classroom management.** Effective classroom management is the process of organizing and conducting a classroom so that it maximizes student learning.

A teacher's procedures for classroom control reflect that teacher's philosophy about how young adolescents learn and the teacher's interpretation and commitment to the school's stated mission. In sum, those procedures represent the teacher's concept of classroom management. Although often eclectic in their approaches, today's teachers share a concern for selecting management techniques that enhance student self-esteem and that help students learn how to assume control of their behavior and ownership of their learning.

Although some middle level schools subscribe heavily to one approach or another, such as the Fred Jones model or Gordon's Teacher Effectiveness Training (TET) model, many others are more eclectic, having evolved from the historical works of several leading authorities. Let's consider what some authorities have said. To assist your understanding, refer to Table 4.1, which illustrates the main ideas of each authority and provides a comparison of their recommended approaches. The guidelines and suggestions that are presented throughout this chapter represent an eclectic approach, borrowing from many of these authorities.

Classroom Management: Contributions of Some Leading Authorities

You are probably familiar with the term *behavior modification,* which describes several high-control techniques for changing behavior in an observable and predictable way; with **B. F. Skinner's** (1904–1990) ideas about how students learn and how behavior can be modified by using reinforcers (rewards); and with how his principles of behavior shaping have been extended by others.[4]

Behavior modification begins with four steps: (a) identify the behavior to be modified; (b) record how often and under what conditions that behavior occurs: (c) cause a change by reinforcing a desired behavior with a positive reinforcer (a reward); (d) choose the type of positive reinforcers to award. These include *activity or privilege reinforcers* such as choice of playing a game, running the projection equipment for the teacher, caring for a classroom pet, decorating the classroom, choosing a learning center, being freed without

---

[3]I. A. Hyman and J. D'Allessandro, "Oversimplifying the Discipline Problem," *Education Week* 3(29):24 (April 11, 1984).

[4]See B. F. Skinner, *The Technology of Teaching* (New York: Appleton-Century-Crofts, 1968) and *Beyond Freedom and Dignity* (New York: Knopf, 1971).

Table 4.1   Comparing Approaches to Classroom Management

Authority	To Know What Is Going On	To Provide Smooth Transitions
Canter/Jones	Realize that the student has the right to choose how to behave in your class with the understanding of the consequences that will follow his or her choice.	Insist on decent, responsible behavior.
Dreikurs/Nelsen/Albert	Realize that the student wants status, recognition, and a feeling of belonging. Misbehavior is associated with mistaken goals of getting attention, seeking power, getting revenge, and wanting to be left alone.	Identify a mistaken student goal; act in ways that do not reinforce these goals.
Ginott	Communicate with the student to find out his/her feelings about a situation and about him/herself.	Invite student cooperation.
Glasser/Gordon	Realize that the student is a rational being; he/she can control his/her own behavior.	Help the student make good choices; good choices produce good behavior, and bad choices produce bad behavior.
Kounin	Develop *withitness,* a skill enabling you to see what is happening in all parts of the classroom at all times.	Avoid jerkiness, which consists of thrusts (giving directions before your group is ready), dangles (leaving one activity dangling in the verbal air, starting another one, and then returning to the first activity), flip-flops (terminating one activity, beginning another one, and then returning to the first activity you terminated).
Skinner	Realize value of nonverbal interaction (i.e., smiles, pats, and handshakes) to communicate to students that you know what is going on.	Realize that smooth transitions may be part of your procedures for awarding reinforcers (i.e., points and tokens) to reward appropriate behavior.

penalty from doing an assignment or test, running an errand for the teacher; *social reinforcers* such as verbal attention or private praise, nonverbal attention such as proximity of teacher to student, and facial (such as a wink) or bodily (such as a handshake or pat on the back) expressions of approval; *graphic reinforcers* such as numerals and symbols like those made by rubber stamps; *tangible reinforcers,* such as candy and other edibles, badges, certificates, stickers, books; or *token rein-*forcers, such as points, stars, or script or tickets that can be accumulated and cashed in later for a tangible reinforcer, such as a trip to the pizza parlor or ice cream store with the teacher.

Lee Canter and **Marlene Canter** developed an *assertive discipline* model. Using an approach that emphasizes both reinforcement for appropriate behaviors *and* punishment or consequences for inappropriate behaviors, their model emphasizes four major points. First, as a

To Maintain Group Alertness	To Involve Students	To Attend to Misbehavior
Set clear limits and consequences; follow through consistently; state what you expect; state the consequences, and why the limits are needed.	Use firm tone of voice; keep eye contact; use nonverbal gestures as well as verbal statements; use hints, questions, and direct messages in requesting student behavior; give and receive compliments.	Follow through with your promises and the reasonable, previously stated consequences that have been established in your class.
Provide firm guidance and leadership.	Allow students to have a say in establishing rules and consequences in your class.	Make it clear that unpleasant consequences will follow inappropriate behavior.
Model the behavior you expect to see in your students.	Build student's self-esteem.	Give a message that addresses the situation and does not attack the student's character.
Understand that class rules are essential.	Realize that classroom meetings are effective means for attending to rules, behavior, and discipline.	Accept no excuses for inappropriate behavior; see that reasonable consequences always follow.
Avoid slowdowns (delays and time wasting) that can be caused by overdwelling (too much time spent on explanations) and by fragmentation (breaking down an activity into several unnecessary steps). Develop a group focus (active participation by all students in the group) through accountability (holding all students accountable for the concept of the lesson) and by attention (seeing all the students and using unison responses as well as individual responses).	Avoid boredom by providing a feeling of progress for the students, by offering challenges, by varying class activities, by changing the level of intellectual challenge, by varying lesson presentations, and by using many different learning materials and aids.	Understand that teacher correction influences behavior of other nearby students (the ripple effect).
Set rules, rewards, and consequences; emphasize that responsibility for good behavior rests with each student.	Involve students in "token economies," in contracts, and in charting own behavior performance.	Provide tangibles to students who follow the class rules; represent tangibles as "points" for the whole class to use to "purchase" a special activity.

teacher, you have professional rights in your classroom and should expect appropriate student behavior. Second, your students have rights to choose how to behave in your classroom, and you should plan limits for inappropriate behavior. Third, an assertive discipline approach means you clearly state your expectations in a firm voice and explain the boundaries for behavior. And fourth, you should plan a system of positive consequences (e.g., positive messages home, awards and rewards, special privileges) for appropriate behavior and establish consequences (e.g., time out, withdrawal of privileges, parent/guardian conference) for inappropriate student misbehavior and follow through in a consistent way.[5]

With a *logical consequences approach*, **Rudolf Dreikurs** (1897–1972) emphasized six points. First, be fair, firm,

---

[5]See L. Canter and M. Canter, *Assertive Discipline: Positive Behavior Management for Today's Schools*, rev. ed. (Santa Monica, CA: Lee Canter & Associates, 1992).

and friendly, and involve your students in developing and implementing class rules. Second, students need to clearly understand the rules and the logical consequences for misbehavior. For example, a logical consequence for a student who has painted graffiti on a school wall would be to either clean the wall or pay for a school custodian to do it. Third, allow the students to be responsible not only for their own actions but also for influencing others to maintain appropriate behavior in your classroom. Fourth, encourage students to show respect for themselves and for others, and provide each student with a sense of belonging to the classroom. Fifth, recognize and encourage student goals of belonging, gaining status, and gaining recognition. And sixth, recognize but do not reinforce correlated student goals of getting attention, seeking power, and taking revenge.[6]

Continuing the work of Dreikurs, **Linda Albert** has developed *cooperative discipline*. The cooperative discipline model makes use of Dreikurs' fundamental concepts, with emphasis added on Three C's: capable, connect, and contribute.[7] Also building upon the work of Dreikurs, **Jane Nelsen** provides guidelines for helping children to develop positive feelings of self. Key points made by Nelsen that are reflected throughout this resource guide are to (a) use natural and logical consequences as a means to inspire a positive classroom atmosphere; (b) understand that children have goals that drive them toward misbehavior (attention, power, revenge, and assumed adequacy); (c) use kindness (student retains dignity) and firmness when administering consequences for a student's misbehavior; (d) establish a climate of mutual respect; (e) use class meetings to give students ownership in problem solving; and (f) offer encouragement as a means of inspiring self-evaluation and focusing on the student's behaviors.[8]

William Glasser developed his concept of *reality therapy* (i.e., the condition of the present, rather than of the past, contributes to inappropriate behavior) for the classroom. Glasser emphasizes that students have a responsibility to learn at school and to maintain appropriate behavior while there. He stresses that with the teacher's help, students can make appropriate choices about their behavior in school—can, in fact, learn self-control.[9] Finally, he suggests holding classroom meetings that are devoted to establishing class rules, and identifying standards for student behavior, matters of misbehavior, and the consequences of misbehavior. Since the publication of his first book in 1965, Glasser has expanded his message to include the student needs of belonging and love, control, freedom, and fun, asserting that if these needs are ignored and unattended to at school, students are bound to fail.[10]

Today's commitment to *quality education* (see Chapter 8) is largely derived from the recent work of Glasser and the corresponding concept of the *personal-centered classrooms* as advanced by **Carl Rogers** and **H. Jerome Freiberg** in their 1994 book *Freedom to Learn* (Columbus, OH: Merrill). In schools committed to quality education and the person-centered classroom, students feel a sense of belonging, enjoy some degree of self-discipline, have fun learning, and experience a sense of freedom in the process.[11]

Haim G. Ginott (1922–1973) emphasized ways for teacher and student to communicate in his *communication model*. He advised a teacher's sending a clear message (or messages) about situations rather than about a child. And he emphasized that teachers must model the behavior they expect from students.[12] Ginott's suggested messages are those that express feelings appropriately, acknowledge students' feelings, give appropriate direction, and invite cooperation.

Thomas Gordon emphasizes influence over control and decries use of reinforcement (i.e., rewards and punishment) as ineffective tools for achieving a positive influence over a child's behavior.[13] Rather than using reinforcements for appropriate behavior and punishment for inappropriate behaviors, Gordon advocates encouragement and development of student self-control

[6]See R. Dreikurs and P. Cassel, *Discipline Without Tears* (New York: Hawthorne Books, 1972), and R. Dreikurs; B. B. Grunwald; and F. C. Pepper; *Maintaining Sanity in the Classroom: Classroom Management Techniques*, 2nd ed. (New York: Harper & Row, 1982).

[7]L. Albert, *A Teacher's Guide to Cooperative Discipline: How to Manage Your Classroom and Promote Self-Esteem* (Circle Pines, MN: American Guidance Service, 1989, revised 1996).

[8]J. Nelsen, *Positive Discipline*, 2nd ed. (New York: Ballantine Books, 1987) and J. Nelsen, L. Lott, and H. S. Glenn, *Positive Discipline in the Classroom: How to Effectively Use Class Meetings and Other Positive Discipline Strategies* (Rocklin, CA: Prima Publishing, 1993).

[9]See, for example, W. Glasser, "A New Look at School Failure and School Success," *Phi Delta Kappan* 78(8):597–602 (April 1997).

[10]See W. Glasser, *Reality Therapy: A New Approach to Psychiatry* (New York: Harper & Row, 1965), *Schools Without Failure* (New York: Harper & Row, 1969), *Control Theory in the Classroom* (New York: Harper & Row, 1986), *The Quality School* (New York: Harper & Row, 1990), and *The Quality School Teacher* (New York: HarperPerennial, 1993).

[11]See H. J. Freiberg (Ed.), *Beyond Behaviorism: Changing the Classroom Management Paradigm* (Boston: Allyn & Bacon, 1997). See also H. J. Freiberg (Ed.), *Perceiving, Behaving, Becoming: Lessons Learned* (Alexandria, VA: Association for Supervision and Curriculum Development, 1999), and "Consistency Management and Cooperative Discipline," on pp. 172–173 of A. W. Jackson and G. A. Davis, *Turning Points 2000: Educating Adolescents in the 21st Century* (New York: A Report of Carnegie Corporation of New York, Teachers College Press, 2000).

[12]See H. G. Ginott, *Teacher and Child* (New York: Macmillan, 1971).

[13]T. Gordon, *Discipline That Works: Promoting Self-Discipline in the Classroom* (New York: Penguin, 1989).

and self-regulated behavior. To have a positive influence and to encourage self-control, the teacher (and school) should provide a rich and positive learning environment with rich and stimulating learning activities. Specific teacher behaviors include active listening, sending I-messages (rather than you-messages), shifting from I-messages to listening when there is student resistance to an I-message, clearly identifying ownership of problems to the student when such is the case (i.e., not assuming ownership if it is a student's problem), and encouraging collaborative problem solving.

Fredric Jones also promotes the idea of helping students support their own self-control, but by way of a negative reinforcement method—rewards follow good behavior.[14] Preferred activity time (PAT), for example, is an invention derived from the Jones Model. The Jones Model makes four recommendations. First, you should properly structure your classroom so students understand the **rules** (the expectation standards for classroom behavior) and **procedures** (the means for accomplishing routine tasks). Second, you should maintain control by selecting appropriate instructional strategies. Third, build patterns of cooperative work. Finally, develop appropriate backup methods for dealing with inappropriate student behavior.

Jacob Kounin is well known for his identification of the ripple effect (i.e., the effect of a teacher's response to one student's misbehavior on students whose behavior was appropriate) and of **withitness** (i.e., the teacher's ability to remain alert in the classroom, to spot quickly and redirect potential student misbehavior, which is analogous to having "eyes in the back of your head").[15] In addition to being alert to everything that is going on in the classroom, another characteristic of a "withit" teacher is the ability to attend to the right student.

GUIDELINES FOR DEVELOPING WITHITNESS

Consider the following guidelines for developing withitness:

- Avoid spending too much time with any one student or group; longer than 30 seconds may be approaching "too much time."
- Avoid turning your back to all or a portion of the students, such as when writing on the writing board.
- If two or more errant behaviors are occurring simultaneously in different locations, attend to the most serious first, while giving the other(s) a nonverbal gesture showing your awareness (such as by eye contact) and displeasure (such as by a frown).

- Involve all students in the act, not just any one student or group. Avoid concentrating on only those who appear most interested or responsive, sometimes referred to as the "chosen few."
- Keep students alert by calling on them randomly, asking questions and calling on an answerer, circulating from group to group during team learning activities, and frequently checking on the progress of individual students.
- Maintain constant visual surveillance of the entire class, even when talking to or working with an individual or small group of students and when meeting a classroom visitor at the door.
- Move around the room. Be on top of potential misbehavior and quietly redirect student attention before the misbehavior occurs or gets out of control.
- Try during whole-class direct instruction to establish eye contact with each student about once every minute. It initially may sound impossible to do, but it is not; it is a skill that can be developed with practice.

A prerequisite to being withit is the skill to attend to more than one matter at a time. This is referred to as *overlapping ability*. The teacher with overlapping skills uses body language, body position, and hand signals to communicate with students. Consider the following examples of overlapping ability:

- Rather than bringing their papers and problems to her desk, the teacher expects students to remain seated and to raise their hands as he or she circulates in the room monitoring and attending to individual students.
- The teacher takes care of attendance while visually and/or verbally monitoring the students during their warm-up activity.
- While attending to a messenger who has walked into the room, the teacher demonstrates verbally or by gestures that he expects the students to continue their work.
- While working in a small group, a student raises his hand to get the teacher's attention. The teacher, while continuing to work with another group of students, signals with her hand to tell the student that she is aware that he wants her attention and will get to him quickly, which she does.
- Without missing a beat in her talk, the teacher aborts the potentially disruptive behavior of a student by gesturing, making eye contact, or moving closer to the student (proximity control).

Developing Your Own Effective Approach to Classroom Management

As you review these classic contributions to today's approaches to effective classroom management, the expert opinions as well as the research evidence will remind you

---

[14]F. Jones, *Positive Classroom Discipline* and *Positive Classroom Instruction* (both New York: McGraw-Hill, 1987).

[15]J. S. Kounin, *Discipline and Group Management in Classrooms* (New York: Holt, Rinehart and Winston, 1977).

of the importance of doing the following: (a) concentrating your attention on desirable student behaviors; (b) quickly and appropriately attending to inappropriate behavior; (c) maintaining alertness to all that is happening in your classroom; (d) providing smooth transitions, keeping the entire class on task, preventing dead time (i.e., time when students have nothing to do); (e) involving students by providing challenges, class meetings, ways of establishing rules and consequences, opportunities to receive and return compliments, and chances to build self-control and self-esteem.

Using the criteria of your own perceptions, philosophy, feelings, values, and knowledge, you are encouraged to construct a classroom environment and management system that is positive and effective for you and your students, and then to consistently apply it while still being willing to modify it as time and circumstances dictate.

PROVIDING A SUPPORTIVE LEARNING ENVIRONMENT

It is probably no surprise to hear that teachers whose classrooms are pleasant, positive, and challenging but supportive places to be, find that their students learn and behave better than do the students of teachers whose classroom atmospheres are harsh, negative, repressive, and unchallenging. What follows are specific suggestions for making your classroom a pleasant, positive, and challenging place; that is, an environment that supports the development of meaningful understandings.

Consider the Physical Layout

There is much in the arrangement of the classroom that can either contribute to or help prevent classroom management problems. There is no one best way to arrange a classroom. To the extent allowed by the room, the arrangement should be kept flexible so student may be deployed in the ways most suitable for accomplishing specific tasks.

The guideline is simple. Just as is true with adults, when young adolescents are seated side by side or facing one another, it is perfectly natural for them to talk to each other. Therefore, if your purpose is to encourage social interaction, as when using small-group learning, seat the students in the groups close together; if you would rather they work alone such as when taking independent achievement tests, separate them.

Some teachers have students design individual space dividers at the beginning of the school year to provide privacy during testing. Attaching three approximately 8 × 10-inch rectangular sections of cardboard can make privacy providers or space dividers. The divider stands in front of the student making it impossible for neighboring students to see over or around. Dividers can be made from cardboard boxes or heavy folders of various sorts. Each student could design and make an individual space divider that would be stored in the classroom for use on test days. Students enjoy being allowed to personalize their dividers.

It is unreasonable to place students in situations that encourage maximum interaction and then to admonish or berate them for whispering and talking. Sometimes, in order to not disturb the learning going on in neighboring classrooms, you may need to remind the students to keep their voices down.

You will not (or should not) be seated much of the time during the instructional period; therefore, it matters little where your teacher's desk is located except that it is out of the way.

Create a Positive Classroom Atmosphere

All students should feel welcome in your classroom and accepted by you as individuals of worth and dignity. Although these feelings and behaviors should be reciprocal, that is, expected of the students as well, they may have to begin with your frequent modeling of the behaviors expected of the students. You must help students know that any denial by you of a student's specific behavior is *not* a denial of that individual as a worthwhile person. He or she is still welcome to come to your class to learn as long as the student agrees to follow expected procedures.

Specific things you can do to create a positive classroom environment, some of which are repeated from preceding chapters and others that are addressed in later chapters, are to

- Admonish behavior, not persons.
- Assure that no bias or prejudice is ever displayed against any individual student.
- Attend to the classroom's physical appearance and comfort—it is your place of work; show pride in that fact. Consider this: a recent study with eighth-grade students suggests that in a classroom atmosphere that is enhanced with a pleasant fragrance, students require fewer redirections of their behavior from the teacher.[16]
- Be an interesting person and an optimistic and enthusiastic teacher.
- Encourage students to set high yet realistic goals for themselves, and then show them how to work in increments toward meeting their goal—letting each know that you are confident of their ability to achieve.
- Help students develop the skills necessary for interactive and cooperative learning.
- Involve students in every aspect of their learning, including the planning of learning activities, thereby

---

[16]A. E. Gabriel, "Brain-Based Learning: The Scent of the Trail," *Clearing House* 72(5):288–290 (May-June 1999).

giving them part ownership and responsibility in their learning.

- Make the learning fun, at least to the extent possible and reasonable.
- Send positive and easily understood messages home to parents or guardians, even if you have to get help to write the message in the language of the student's home.
- Recognize and reward truly positive behaviors and individual successes, no matter how meager they might seem to be.
- Use varied, interesting, and motivating learning activities.

BEHAVIORS TO AVOID

Two items in the preceding list are statements about giving encouragement. When using encouragement to motivate student learning, there are a few important behaviors that you should *avoid* because they inhibit learning.

- Avoid comparing one student with another, or one class of students with another.
- Avoid encouraging competition among students.
- Avoid giving up or appearing to give up on any student.
- Avoid telling a student how much better he or she could be.
- Avoid using qualifying statements, such as "I like what you did, but . . ." or "It's about time."

Get to Know Your Students as People

For classes to move forward smoothly and efficiently, they should fit the learners' learning styles, learning capacities, developmental needs, and interests. To make the learning meaningful and the most long lasting, build curriculum around student interests, capacities, perceptions, and perspectives (as you will learn to do in the remaining chapters of Part II). Therefore, you need to know your students well enough to be able to provide learning experiences that they will find interesting, valuable, intrinsically motivating, challenging, and rewarding. Knowing your students is as important as knowing your subject. The following paragraphs describe a number of things you can do to get to know your students as people.

QUICKLY LEARN AND USE STUDENT NAMES

Like everyone else, young adolescents appreciate being recognized and addressed by name. Quickly learning and using their names is an important motivating strategy. One technique for learning names quickly is to take photographs of each student on the first day. Later, students could use the photographs as a portion of the covers of their portfolios. Another technique for learning names quickly is to use a seating chart. Laminate the seating chart onto an attractive neon-colored clipboard

that you can carry with you in class. Many teachers prefer to assign permanent seats and then make seating charts from which they can unobtrusively check the roll while students are doing seatwork. It is usually best to get your students into the lesson before taking roll and before doing other housekeeping chores. Ways of assigning student seating are discussed later in this chapter (see "The First Day").

Addressing students by name every time you speak to them helps you to learn and remember their names. Be sure to quickly learn to pronounce their names correctly; that helps in making a good impression. Another helpful way to learn student names is to return papers yourself by calling student names and then handing the papers to them, paying careful attention to look at each student and make mental notes that may help you to associate names with faces.

CLASSROOM SHARING DURING THE FIRST WEEK OF SCHOOL

During the first week of school many teachers take time each day to have students present information about themselves and/or about the day's assignment. For instance, five or six students might be selected each day to answer questions such as "What name would you like to be called by?" "Where did you attend school last year?" "Tell us about your hobbies and other interests." "What interested you about last night's reading, or yesterday's lesson?"

Still another useful approach with young adolescents is the "me-in-a-bag" activity. With this, each student is to bring one large paper grocery bag to school that contains items from home that represent that person. The student then is given time in class to share the items brought. [*Note:* It is a good idea to alert parents/guardians of the assignment so nothing of value from home gets lost in the process.]

How the student answers such questions or participates in such activities can be as revealing about the student as is the information (or the lack thereof) that the student shares. From the sharing, you sometimes get clues about additional information you would like to obtain about the student.

OBSERVE STUDENTS IN THE CLASSROOM— DEVELOP AND PRACTICE YOUR WITHITNESS

During learning activities, the wise teacher is constantly moving around the classroom and is alert to the individual behavior (nonverbal and verbal) of each student in the class, whether the student is on task or is gazing off and perhaps thinking about other things. Be cautious, however; just because a student is gazing out the window does not mean that the student is not thinking about the learning task. During group work is a particularly good time to observe students and get to know more about each one's skills and interests.

OBSERVATIONS OF AND CONVERSATIONS WITH STUDENTS OUTSIDE THE CLASSROOM

Another way to learn more about students is by observing them outside class, for example at athletic events, dances, performing arts presentations, lunch time (finding it to be an excellent time to get to know their students as well as to provide informal guidance/counseling, some teachers open their classrooms at noon for a brown-bag lunch with any students who wish to come), intramural activities, and during advisory or homeroom, in the hallways, and at club meetings. Observations outside the classroom can give information about student personalities, friendships, interests, and potentialities. For instance, you may find that a student who seems phlegmatic, lackadaisical, or uninterested in the learning activities in your classroom is a real fireball on the playing field or at some other student gathering.

CONFERENCES AND INTERVIEWS WITH STUDENTS

Conferences with students, and sometimes with family members as well, afford yet another opportunity to show that you are genuinely interested in each student as a person as well as a student. Some teachers and teaching teams plan a series of conferences during the first few weeks in which, individually or in groups of three or four, students are interviewed by the teacher or by the teaching team. Block scheduling is especially conducive to teacher-parent/guardian-student conferences. Such conferences and interviews are managed by using open-ended questions. The teacher indicates by the questions, by listening, and by nonjudgmental and empathic responses (i.e., being able to "step into the shoes" of the student, thereby understanding from where the student is coming) a genuine interest in the students. Keep in mind, however, that students who feel they have been betrayed by prior adult associations may at first be distrustful of your sincerity. In such instances, don't force it. Be patient, but do not hesitate to take advantage of the opportunity afforded by talking with individual students outside of class time. Investing a few minutes of time in a positive conversation with a student, during which you indicate a genuine interest in that student, can pay real dividends when it comes to that student's interest and learning in your classroom.

When using interviews with students, consider having the students individually write one or two questions that they would like to ask you in the interview. This ensures that the student is an active participant in the interview.

STUDENT WRITING AND QUESTIONNAIRES

Much can be learned about students by what they write. It is important to encourage writing in your classroom, and (with varying degrees of intensity) to read everything that students write, and to ask for clarification when needed. Journals and portfolios are useful for this. They are discussed in Chapters 5, 9, and 11.

Some teachers use open-ended interest-discovering and/or autobiographical questionnaires. Student responses to these questionnaires can provide ideas about how to tailor assignments for individual students. However, you must assure students that their answers are optional and that you are not invading their privacy.

In an *interest-discovering questionnaire,* students are asked to answer questions such as "When you read for fun or pleasure, what do you usually read?" "What are your favorite movies, videos, or TV shows?" "Who are your favorite music video performers?" "Athletes?" "Describe your favorite hobby or other nonschool-related activity." "What are your favorite sport activities to participate in and to watch?"

In an *autobiographical questionnaire,* the student is asked to answer questions such as "Where were you born?" "What do you hope to do following high school?" "Do you have responsibilities at home; what are they?" "How do you like to spend your leisure time?" "Do you like to read?" "What do you like to read?" "Do you have a favorite hobby; what is it?" Many teachers model the process by reading their own autobiographical answers to the students before they begin.

CUMULATIVE RECORD, DISCUSSIONS WITH COLLEAGUES, AND EXPERIENTIAL BACKGROUNDS

The cumulative record for each student is held in the school office. It contains information recorded from year to year by teachers and other school professionals. The information covers the student's academic background, standardized test scores, and extracurricular activities. However, the Family Educational Rights and Privacy Act (FERPA) of 1974, its subsequent amendments, and local policies may forbid your reviewing the record, except perhaps in collaboration with an administrator or counselor when you have a legitimate educational purpose for doing so. Although you must use discretion before arriving at any conclusion about information contained in the cumulative record, the record may afford information for getting to know a particular student better. Remember, though, a child's past is history and should not be held against that student. It should be used only as a means for improved understanding of a child's experiences and current perceptions.

To better understand a student, it is sometimes helpful to talk with the student's other teachers, advisor, or counselor to learn about their perceptions and experiences with the student. As discussed in Chapter 1, one of the advantages of schools that use looping or that are divided into "houses," or both, is that teachers and students get to know one another better.

Another way of getting to know your students is to spend time in the neighborhoods in which they live. Observe and listen, finding and noting things that you can use as examples, as bridges, or as learning activities.

PREPARATION PROVIDES CONFIDENCE AND SUCCESS

For successful classroom management, beginning the school term well may make all the difference in the world. Remember that you have only one opportunity to make a first and lasting impression. Therefore, you should appear at the first class meeting as well prepared and as confident as possible.

Perhaps in the beginning you will feel nervous and apprehensive, but being ready and well prepared will help you to at least appear to be confident. It is likely that every beginning teacher is, to some degree, nervous and apprehensive; the secret is to not appear to be nervous. Being well prepared provides the confidence necessary to cloud feelings of nervousness. A slow under-the-breath counting to 10 at the start can be helpful, too. Then, if you proceed in a businesslike, matter-of-fact way, the impetus of your well-prepared beginning will, most likely, cause the day, week, and year to proceed pretty much as desired.

Effective Organization and Administration of Activities and Materials

In a well-managed classroom, student movement is routinized, controlled, and purposeful to the learning activities; students know what to do, have the materials needed to do it well, and stay on task while doing it. The classroom atmosphere is supportive; the assignments and procedures for doing them are clear; the instruction materials are current, interesting, and readily available; and the classroom proceedings are businesslike. At all times, the teacher is in control of events, rather than controlled by them, seeing that students are spending their time on appropriate tasks. For your teaching to be effective, you must be skilled in managing the classroom.

Natural Interruptions and Disruptions to Routine

As you devise and prepare to implement your management system, you must also be aware of your own moods and high-stress days, and anticipate that your own tolerance levels may vary. Students, too, are susceptible to personal problems that can be the sources of high stress. As you come to know your students well, you will be able to ascertain when certain students are under an inordinate amount of stress and anxiety, come to school sleepy or hungry, or are emotionally distraught from unfortunate happenings at home or elsewhere.

You must understand that classroom routines may be interrupted occasionally, especially on certain days and at certain times during the school year. Students will not have the same motivation and energy level on each and every day. Energy level also varies throughout the school day. Your anticipation of periods of high or low energy levels, and your thoughtful and careful planning for them during the preactive phase of instruction, will

help protect your own mental health. Depending on a number of factors, periods of high energy level might include (a) the beginning of each school day; (b) before a field trip, holiday, or school event such as a dance, picture day, athletic event, or school assembly; (c) the day of a holiday, (d) the day following a holiday, (e) grade report day, (f) the time immediately before and/or after lunch, (g) a minimum day or the day a substitute teacher is present, (h) the time approaching the end of each school day, the end of school each Friday afternoon, and the end of the school term or year.

Although there may be no hard evidence, many experienced teachers will tell you that days when there is a strong north wind or a full moon are particularly troublesome for classroom control. One teacher jokingly (we suspect) said that on days with both a strong north wind and a full moon, she calls in sick.

How should you prepare for these so-called high-energy days? There are probably no specific guidelines that will work for all teachers in all of the situations listed. However, these are days to which you need to pay extra attention during your planning, days that students could possibly be restless and more difficult to control, days when you might need to be especially forceful and consistent in your enforcement of procedures, or even more compassionate and tolerant than usual. Plan instructional activities that might be more readily accepted by the students. It is not our intent to imply that learning ceases and play time takes over. What little instructional time is available to a teacher during a school year is too precious for that ever to happen.

CLASSROOM PROCEDURES AND GUIDELINES FOR ACCEPTABLE BEHAVIOR

It is impossible to overemphasize the importance of getting the school term off to a good beginning, so we start this section by discussing how that is done.

Starting the School Term Well

There are three important keys to getting the school term off to a good beginning. First, be *prepared* and be *fair.* Preparation for the first day of school should include determining your classroom procedures and basic expectations for the behavior of the students while they are under your supervision. The procedures and expectations must be consistent with school policy and seem reasonable to your students, and in enforcing them you must be a fair and consistent professional. However, being coldly consistent is not the same as being fair and professional. As a teacher, you deal in matters of human relations and must exercise professional judgment. You are not a robot, nor are any of your students. Human beings differ from one another, and seemingly similar situations can vary substantially because the people involved are different. Consequently, your response, or lack of response, to each of two separate but quite similar situations may differ. To be most effective, learning must be enjoyable for students; it cannot be enjoyable when a teacher consistently acts like a marine drill sergeant. If a student infracts upon a rule, rather than assuming why, seeming not to care why, or overreacting to the infraction, find out why before deciding your response. See, for example, "Classroom Vignette: Late Homework Paper from an At-Risk Student" in Chapter 8.

Second, in preparing your classroom management system, remember that too many rules and detailed procedures at the beginning can be a source of trouble. To avoid trouble, it is best at first to present only the minimum number of procedural expectations necessary for an orderly start to the school term. By the time students are in the middle grades, unless they are newcomers to this country, they likely already know the expected procedures; that is, the general rules of expected behavior, although some of their prior teachers may not always have been consistent or even fair about applying them. However, by establishing and sticking to a few explained general expectations (see discussion that follows under The First Day) and to those that may be specific to your subject area, you can leave yourself some room for judgments and maneuvering.

Third, consequences for not following established procedures must be reasonable, clearly understood, and fairly applied. The procedures should be quite specific so that students know exactly what is expected and what is not, and what the consequences are when procedures are not followed.

Procedures Rather than Rules; Consequences Rather than Punishment

To encourage a constructive and supportive classroom environment, we encourage you (and your students) to practice thinking in terms of *procedures* (or *expectations* or *standards and guidelines*)[17] rather than of "rules," and of *consequences* rather than *punishment*. The rationale is this: to many people, the term *rules* has a more negative connotation than does the term *procedures*. When working with a cohort of students, some rules are necessary but some people feel that using the term *procedures* has a more positive ring to it. For example, a classroom rule might be that when one person is talking we do not interrupt that person until he or she is finished. When that rule is broken, rather than reminding students of the rule, the emphasis can be changed to a procedure simply by reminding the students by asking, "What is our procedure (or expectation) when someone is talking?"

Although some people will disagree, we concur with the contention that thinking in terms of and talking about *procedures* and *consequences* is more likely to contribute to a positive classroom atmosphere than using the terms *rules* and *punishment*. Of course, some argue that by the time students are in middle grades, you might as well tell it like it is. Especially if your group of students is linguistically and culturally mixed, you will need to be as direct and clear as possible to avoid sending confusing or mixed signals. Like always, after considering what experienced others have to say, the final decision is one of many that you must make that will be influenced by your own thinking and situation. It might be a decision made in collaboration with members of your teaching team. It is, however, important that expectations are communicated clearly to the students and followed consistently by you and other members of your teaching team.

Once you have decided your initial expectations, you are ready to explain them to your students and to begin rehearsing a few of the procedures on the very first day of class. You will want to do this in a positive way. Students work best in a positive atmosphere, in which teacher expectations are clear to them; procedures are stated in positive terms, are clearly understood and agreed upon, and have become routine; and when consequences for behaviors that are inappropriate are reasonable, clearly understood, and fairly applied.

The First Day

On the first day, you will want to cover certain major points of common interest to you and the students. The following paragraphs offer guidelines and suggestions for meeting your students the first time.

GREETING THE STUDENTS AND FIRST ACTIVITY

While standing at the door, welcome your students with a smile as they arrive, and then welcome the entire class with a friendly but businesslike demeanor. You should not be frowning or off in a corner of the room doing something else as students arrive. As you greet the students, tell them to take a seat and start on the first activity at their desk.

After your greeting, begin immediately with some sort of assignment, preferably a written assignment already on each student's desk. This assures that students have something to do as soon as they arrive at your classroom. That first assignment might be a questionnaire each student completes. This is a good time to instruct students on the expected standard for heading their papers. After giving instructions on how papers are to be handed in, rehearse the procedure by collecting this first assignment.

STUDENT SEATING

One option for student seating is to have students' names on the first assignment paper placed at their seats

---

[17]See J. A. Queen, et al., *Responsible Classroom Management for Teachers and Students* (Upper Saddle River, NJ: Merrill/Prentice Hall, 1997), especially "Standards and Guidelines Versus Rules" and "Replacing Rules With Standards," pp. 110 and 111–112 respectively.

when they arrive for the first class meeting. That allows you to have a seating chart ready on the first day, from which you can quickly take attendance and begin learning student names. Another option, not exclusive of the first, is to tell students that by the end of the week each should be in a permanent seat (either assigned by you or self-selected), from which you will make a seating chart that will help you to quickly learn their names and efficiently take attendance each day. Let them know, too, that from time to time you will change the seating arrangement (if that is true).

INFORMATION ABOUT THE CLASS

After the first assignment has been completed, discussed, and collected, talk to the students about the class—what they will be learning and how they will learn it (covering work and study habits and your expectations regarding the quantity and quality of their work). This is a time where you may choose to get student input into the course content (discussed in Chapter 5), to give students some empowerment. We advise you to put this information in a course syllabus (discussed in Chapter 6), give each student a copy, and review it with them. Specifically discuss the teacher's expectations about how books will be used; about student notebooks, journals, portfolios, and assignments; about what students need to furnish; and about the location of resources in the classroom and elsewhere.

CLASSROOM PROCEDURES AND ENDORSED BEHAVIOR

Now discuss in a positive way your expectations regarding classroom behavior, procedures, and routines. Students work best when teacher expectations are well understood and there are established routines. In the beginning, it is important that there be no more procedures than necessary to get the class moving effectively for daily operation. Five or fewer expectations should be enough, such as arrive promptly and stay on task until excused by the teacher (the teacher, not a bell, excuses students), listen attentively, show mutual respect, use appropriate language, and appreciate the rights and property of others.

Too many procedural expectations at first can be restricting and even confusing to students. Most students already know these things so you should not have to spend much time on the topic, except for items specific to your course, such as dress and safety expectations for laboratory courses, shop and art classes, and physical education. Be patient with yourself on this; finding and applying the proper level of control for a given group of students is one of the skills that you will develop from experience.

Although many schools traditionally have posted in the halls and in the classrooms a list of prohibited behaviors, exemplary middle level schools tend to focus on the positive, on endorsed attitudes and behaviors. Displaying a list of *do nots* does not encourage a positive school or classroom atmosphere; a list of *dos* does. For example, at Constellation Community Middle School (Long Beach, CA), all students receive regular daily reminders when, after reciting the Pledge of Allegiance, they recite the school's five core principles: (1) Anything that hurts another person is wrong. (2) We are each other's keepers. (3) I am responsible for my own actions. (4) I take pride in myself. (5) Leave it better than when you found it.[18]

FIRST HOMEWORK ASSIGNMENT AND DISMISSAL

End the first class meeting with a positive statement about being delighted to be working with them and then give the first homework assignment. The first homework assignment should perhaps be one that will not take too much student time and that each student can achieve a perfect score on with minimal effort. Be sure to allow yourself sufficient time to demonstrate where assignments will regularly be posted, and to make assignment instructions clearly understood by every student. Include a reminder about how you expect students to head their papers.

When you are ready to dismiss students on this first day and every day thereafter, our advice is for you to do so by moving to the classroom exit and then verbally excusing the students, giving each a smile and a high five as they leave the classroom.

Establishing Classroom Expectations, Procedures, and Consequences

When establishing classroom behavior expectations and procedures, remember this point: the learning time needs to run efficiently (i.e., with no "dead spots," or time when students have nothing to do), smoothly (i.e., routine procedures are established and transitions between activities are smooth), and with minimum distraction. As discussed in the preceding section, when stating your expectations for student classroom behavior, try to do so in a positive manner, emphasizing procedures and desired attitudes and behaviors, stressing what students should *do* rather than what they should *not* do.

What Students Need to Understand from the Start

As you prepare the guidelines, standards, and expectations for classroom behavior, you (and, if relevant, your teaching team) should consider some of the specifics about what students need to understand from the start. These specific points, then, should be reviewed and rehearsed with the students, sometimes several times,

---

[18]D. Harrington-Lueker, "Emotional Intelligence," *High Strides* 9(4):1 (March/April 1997).

A CLASSROOM SCENARIO
Rules in a Community of Learners[19]

Rules must be designed to equally support and value all members of the learning community, including teachers.

Some say students should not be allowed to drink or eat in the classroom because of the potential for a mess. From that concern, a common rule that often puts teachers and students at odds is that eating and drinking are not allowed in the classroom. The teacher who bans eating and drinking by students but keeps a cup of coffee handy is flagrantly violating the rules.

However, helping students learn how to clean up after themselves and how to react to spills is a worthwhile lesson that can be applied for the rest of an individual's life. For example, Miss Andrews, a science teacher, allows her students to drink from water bottles they bring to class. On the first day of class she tells the students that they can bring bottled water to class and then she instructs them about what to do when a water bottle spills in the classroom. When the inevitable spill does occur, Miss Andrews does not interrupt her teaching for even one minute. While she continues to teach, her students know where to find extra paper towels and how to mop up the water. The students have been taught how to clean up after themselves, so a spill is not a problem. Her students, rather than Miss Andrews, assume responsibility for their actions.

during the first week of school and then followed *consistently* throughout the school term. Important and specific things that students need to know from the start will vary considerably depending on your specific situation, but the following paragraphs describes things that all students generally need to understand from the beginning.

SIGNALING FOR YOUR ATTENTION AND HELP

At least at the start of the school term, most middle level teachers who are effective classroom managers expect students to raise their hands until the teacher acknowledges (usually by a nonverbal gesture, such as eye contact and a nod) that the student's hand has been seen. With that acknowledgment, the recommended procedure is that the student should lower his or her hand and return to work.

There are a number of important reasons for expecting children to raise their hands before speaking. Two are that it allows you to (a) control the noise and confusion level and (b) be proactive in deciding who speaks. The latter is important if you are to be in control of classroom events, rather than be controlled by them, and you are to manage a classroom with equality—that is, with equal attention to individuals regardless of their gender, ethnicity, proximity to the teacher, or other personal characteristics. We are not talking here about students having to raise their hands before talking with their peers during group work. We are talking about not allowing students to shout across the room to get your attention; boisterously talk out freely; and rudely interrupt others during whole-class discussions and instruction.

Another important reason for expecting students to raise their hands and be recognized before speaking is to discourage impulsive outbursts and to grow emotionally and intellectually. An instructional responsibility shared by all teachers is to help students develop intelligent behaviors (discussed in Chapter 9). Learning to control impulsivity is an intelligent behavior. Teaching children to control their impulsivity is a highly important responsibility that, in our opinion, is too often neglected by too many teachers (and too many parents and guardians). To us, the ramifications of this are frightening.

Some teachers employ the *three-before-me* procedure to avoid dependence on the teacher, to avoid having too many students raising their hands for the teacher's attention, and to encourage positive interaction among the students. The procedure is this: When a student has a question or needs help, the student must quietly ask up to three peers before seeking help from the teacher. Again, as a beginning teacher, you need to try ideas and find what works best for you in your unique situation.

ENTERING AND LEAVING THE CLASSROOM

From the time the class is scheduled to begin, teachers who are effective classroom managers expect students to

---

[19]From Barbara McEwan, *The Art of Classroom Management: Effective Practices for Building Equitable Learning Communities.* (Upper Saddle River, NJ: Merrill/Prentice Hall, 2000), p. 39. Adapted and reprinted by permission of Pearson Education, Inc., Upper Saddle River, NJ 07458.

be in their assigned seats or at their assigned learning stations and to be attentive to the teacher or to the learning activity until excused by the teacher. And, remember, teachers, not bells, excuse students. (See the discussion in the paragraph titled First Homework Assignment and Dismissal.) For example, students should not be allowed to begin meandering toward the classroom exit in anticipation of the passing bell or the designated passing time; otherwise their meandering toward the door will begin earlier and earlier each day and the teacher will increasingly lose control. Besides, it is a waste of a very valuable and very limited resource—instructional time.

MAINTAINING, OBTAINING, AND USING MATERIALS FOR LEARNING AND ITEMS OF PERSONAL USE

Students need to know where, when, and how to store, retrieve, and care for items such as their coats, backpacks, books, pencils, and medicines; how to get papers and materials; and when to use the pencil sharpener and wastebasket. Classroom control is easiest to maintain when (a) items that students need for class activities and for their personal use are neatly and safely arranged (for example, backpacks stored under tables or chairs rather in aisles) and located in places with minimum foot traffic, (b) there are established procedures that students clearly expect and understand, (c) there is the least amount of student off-task time, and (d) students do not have to line up to wait for anything. Therefore, you will want to plan the room arrangement, equipment and materials storage, preparation of equipment and materials, and transitions between activities to avoid needless delays, confusion, and safety hazards. Remember this well: problems in classroom control will most certainly occur whenever some or all students have nothing to do, even if only briefly.

LEAVING CLASS FOR A PERSONAL MATTER

Normally, students should be able to get a drink of water or go to the bathroom between classes; however sometimes they do not, or, for medical reasons or during long block classes, they cannot. Reinforce the notion that they should do those things before coming into your classroom or during the scheduled times, but be flexible enough for the occasional student who has an immediate need. Whenever you permit a student to leave class for a personal reason, follow established school procedures, which may, for reasons of personal security, mean that students can only leave the room in pairs and with a hall pass, or when accompanied by an adult.

REACTING TO A VISITOR OR AN INTERCOM ANNOUNCEMENT

Unfortunately, class interruptions do occur, and in some schools they occur far too often and for reasons that are not as important as interrupting a teacher and students' learning would imply. When there is an important reason, the principal, a vice-principal, or some other person from the school's office may interrupt the class to see the teacher or a student, or to make an announcement to the entire class. Students need to understand what behavior is expected of them during those interruptions. When there is a visitor to the classroom, the expected procedure should be for students to continue their learning task unless directed otherwise by you. To learn more about class interruptions, do Exercise 4.1 now.

FOR YOUR NOTES

EXERCISE 4.1: OBSERVING A CLASSROOM FOR FREQUENCY OF EXTERNAL INTERRUPTIONS

INSTRUCTIONS: The purpose of this exercise is for you to observe a classroom for frequency of externally caused interruptions to the learning. A second and perhaps even more important purpose is described at the end of the next paragraph. It is disconcerting to realize how often teachers and, therefore, student learning in the classrooms of some schools are interrupted by an announcement over the intercom, a phone call, or a visitor at the door. After all, no one would even consider interrupting a surgeon during the most climactic moments of an open heart operation, nor a defense attorney at the climax of her or his summation. Far too often, though, teachers are interrupted at a critical point in a lesson just when they have their students in "the palm of their hand". Once lost because of an interruption, student attention and that teachable moment are nearly impossible to recapture.

School administrators and office personnel must sometimes be reminded that the most important thing going on in the school is what teachers have been hired to do—teach—and that the act of teaching must not be frivolously interrupted. Except for absolutely critical reasons, teachers should never be interrupted after the first five minutes of a class period or before the last five minutes. That policy should be established and rigidly adhered to. Otherwise, after many years of being a student, the lesson learned is that the least important thing going on at the school is what is going on in the classroom. No wonder then that it is so difficult for teachers in some schools to gain student attention and respect. That respect must be shown, beginning with the school's central office. The need to turn around and refocus on this is the reason for this exercise.

Arrange to visit a classroom (grade 5–8) and observe for interruptions created from outside the classroom.

1. School and class (including grade level) visited:

   _____

2. Time (start and end of class period):

3. Interruptions (tally for each interruption):
   a. intercom:
   b. phone:
   c. visitor at door:
   d. emergency drill:
   e. other (specify):

4. Total number of interruptions: _____

5. My conclusion:

6. Share and compare your results with your classmates.

7. Describe any further conclusion (and resolve) that you and your classmates draw as a result of sharing your experiences with this exercise.

FOR YOUR NOTES

WHEN LATE TO CLASS OR LEAVING EARLY

You must abide by school policies on early dismissals and late arrivals. Make your own procedures routine so students clearly understand what they are to do if they must leave your class early (e.g., for a medical appointment) or when they arrive late. Procedures in your classroom, and indeed throughout the school, should be such that late-arriving and early-dismissal students do not disturb you or other teachers, or the learning in progress.

When students are allowed to interrupt the learning in progress repeatedly and regularly because the teacher has not established such procedures, then the covert message conveyed, in that classroom if not by the hidden curriculum of the entire school, is that academic instruction is relatively low in importance.

CONSEQUENCES FOR INAPPROPRIATE BEHAVIOR

Most teachers who are effective classroom managers routinize their procedures for handling inappropriate behavior and assure that the students understand the consequences for inappropriate behavior. The consequences, which should be consistent throughout the school, are posted in the classroom and may be similar to the five-step model shown in Figure 4.1.

A teacher, members of a teaching team or department, or the entire faculty must decide whether offenses subsequent to the first are those that occur on the same day or within a designated period of time, such as one week. And, of course, it is quite clear in the policy of most schools that there are some offenses (such as having a weapon at school) for which there is zero tolerance; that is they will result in direct suspension or expulsion even though it is a first offense.

EMERGENCY SITUATIONS, PRACTICE AND REAL

Students need to clearly understand what to do, where to go, and how to behave in emergency conditions, such as a fire, storm, or earthquake, or because of a disruptive campus intruder. Students (and teachers, too) must behave well during practice drills, as well as in real emergencies.

RETURNING TO SCHOOL AFTER AN ABSENCE

Students need to know what to do upon their return to your classroom after being absent. They basically need to know how to make up what they missed. See Figure 4.2 for the procedure established by one middle school teacher for returning students that least disrupts the teacher or disturbs other students.

To further your understanding of classroom management and to begin the development of your own management system, do Exercises 4.2 and 4.3.

Figure 4.1 Model of consequences for inappropriate student behavior.

First offense results in a direct but unobtrusive (often it is nonverbal) reminder to the student.

Second offense results in a private but direct verbal reminder of expected behavior and the consequences of continued inappropriate behavior.

Third offense results in the student's being given a time out in a supervised isolation area followed by a private teacher-student conference and the student's subsequent return to class.

Fourth offense results in a suspension from class until there is a student-parent/guardian-teacher (and perhaps the counselor or a school administrator) conference.

Fifth offense results in the student being referred to the vice-principal, principal, or counselor's office (depending on the school), sometimes followed by a limited or permanent suspension from that class or an expulsion from school.

Figure 4.2   Procedure established by one teacher for students returning to class after being absent.

I WAS ABSENT–NOW WHAT DO I DO?

1. Go to the back of the room.
2. Check calendar on wall.
3. Open file folder in agenda file box that labels the day you were absent. In this file you will find the *overhead* agenda used that day with the *list of activities, warm-ups, vocabulary, and homework assigned*—this is **very** important so please *refile* this agenda for other students to use as soon as you are finished.
4. Copy warm-ups and vocabulary.
5. *Take one copy of each ditto*—check to make sure you have claimed all of them.
6. Read the agenda on the overhead.
7. Match goals/homework to dittos—did you get everything you need?
8. Record all due dates on your calendar.
9. Ask questions about work after doing 1–8.
10. *Work should be turned in within two days of absence*—multiple days of absences simply means that you can turn in one day's work every two days. After that work is considered late unless we have made arrangements—so *talk* to me.

You are the one who is responsible for claiming and making up work when you are absent. The file is for your convenience. Do not claim you missed an assignment because you were absent—it doesn't wash in this class!!!!

Other students may have been absent the same day. If you do not find the overhead agenda in the file, check to see if anyone in the class has the agenda. Also, sometimes the agendas are misfiled—check the day before and day after if you don't see the overhead (this is called critical thinking!).

I wonder where that agenda went?

Courtesy: Patricia A. Nelson

EXERCISE 4.2: TEACHERS' CLASSROOM MANAGEMENT SYSTEMS

INSTRUCTIONS: The purpose of this exercise is to interview two teachers (grades 5–8) to discover how they manage their classrooms. Use the outline format that follows, conduct your interviews, and then share the results with your classmates, perhaps in small groups. You may duplicate blank copies of this form.

1. Teacher interviewed: _____

2. Date: _____ 4. School: _____

3. Grade level: _____ 5. Subject(s): _____

6. Please describe your classroom management system. Specifically, I would like to know your procedures for the following:

   a. How are students to signal that they want your attention and help? _____

   _____

   _____

   b. How do you call on students during question and discussion sessions? _____

   _____

   _____

   c. How and when are students to enter and exit the classroom? _____

   _____

   _____

   d. How are students to obtain the materials for instruction? _____

   _____

   _____

   e. How are students to store their personal items? _____

   _____

   _____

   f. What are the procedures for students going to the drinking fountain or bathroom? _____

   _____

   _____

   g. What are the procedures during class interruptions? _____

   _____

   _____

   h. What are the procedures for tardies or early dismissal? _____

   _____

   _____

EXERCISE 4.2 (*continued*)

    i. What are the procedures for turning in homework? _____

_____

_____

7. Describe your expectations for classroom behavior and the consequences for misbehavior. _____

_____

_____

_____

_____

_____

In a discussion with classmates following the interviews, consider the following:

Many modern teachers advocate the use of a highly structured classroom, and then, as appropriate over time during the school year, they share more of the responsibility with the students. Did you find this to be the case with the majority of teachers interviewed? Was it more or less the case with any particular grade level or subject areas?

EXERCISE 4.3: BEGINNING THE DEVELOPMENT OF MY CLASSROOM MANAGEMENT SYSTEM

INSTRUCTIONS: The purpose of this exercise is to begin preparation of the management system that you will explain to your students during the first day or week of school. Answer the questions that follow and share those answers with your peers for their feedback. Then make changes as appropriate. (Upon completion of this chapter, you may want to revisit this exercise to make adjustments to your management plan, as you will from time to time throughout your professional career.)

1. My teaching subject area and anticipated grade level: _____

   _____

2. Attention to procedures. Use a statement to explain your procedural expectation for each of the following:

   a. How are students to signal that they want your attention and help? _____

      _____

      _____

   b. How do you call on students during question and discussion sessions? _____

      _____

      _____

   c. How and when are students to enter and exit the classroom? _____

      _____

      _____

   d. How are students to obtain the materials for instruction? _____

      _____

      _____

   e. How are students to store their personal items? _____

      _____

      _____

   f. What are the procedures for students going to the drinking fountain or bathroom? _____

      _____

      _____

   g. What are the procedures during class interruptions? _____

      _____

      _____

   h. What are the procedures for tardies or early dismissal? _____

      _____

      _____

EXERCISE 4.3 (*continued*)

   i. What are the procedures for turning in homework? _____

_____

_____

3. List of student behavior expectations that I will present to my class (no more than five):

Rule 1: _____

_____

_____

Rule 2: _____

_____

_____

Rule 3: _____

_____

_____

Rule 4: _____

_____

_____

Rule 5: _____

_____

_____

4. Explanation of consequences for broken rules: _____

_____

_____

_____

_____

5. How procedures, rules, or consequences may vary (if at all) according to the grade level taught or according to any other criteria, such as in team teaching: _____

_____

_____

_____

_____

_____

USING POSITIVE REWARDS

Reinforcement theory contends that a person's gratification derived from receiving a reward strengthens the tendency for that person to continue to act in a certain way, while the lack of a reward (or the promise of a reward) weakens the tendency to act that way. For example, according to the theory, if students are promised a reward of "preferred activity time (PAT) on Friday" if they work well all week long, then the students are likely to work toward that reward, thus improving their standards of learning. Some educators argue that (a) once the *extrinsic* reinforcement (i.e., the reward from outside the learner) has been removed, the desired behavior tends to diminish; and that (b) rather than *extrinsic* sources of reinforcement, focus should be on increasing the student's internal sense of accomplishment, an *intrinsic reward.* Further, rewarding students for complying with expected/standard behavior sends the wrong message. It reinforces the mentality of, "What do I get for doing what I am supposed to do?" If this is a common school practice, it carries over into home situations and eventually into adulthood. A principal does not reward a teacher for showing up on time, attending a faculty meeting, or having report cards prepared on time. Those are expected/standard behaviors. Perhaps, for the daily work of a teacher in a classroom of many diverse young adolescents, the practical reality is somewhere between. After all, the reality of classroom teaching is less than ideal, and all activities cannot be intrinsically rewarding. Further, for many young adolescents intrinsic rewards are often too remote to be effective.

The promise of extrinsic rewards is not always necessary or beneficial. Students generally will work harder to learn something because they want to learn it (i.e., intrinsic motivation) than they will merely to earn PAT, points, grades, candy, or some other form of reward. In addition, many young adolescents are so preoccupied with "the here and now" that for them the promise on Monday of PAT on Friday probably will have little desired effect on their behavior on Monday. To them, on Monday, Friday seems a long way off.

Activities that are interesting and intrinsically rewarding are not further served by the addition of extrinsic rewards. This is especially true when working with students who are already highly motivated to learn. Adding extrinsic incentives to learning activities that are already highly motivating tends to reduce student motivation. For most young adolescents, the use of extrinsic motivators should be minimal. They are probably most useful in skills learning, where there is likely to be a lot of repetition and the potential for boredom. If students are working diligently on a highly motivating student-initiated project of study, extrinsic

rewards are not necessary and could even have negative effects.[20]

MANAGING CLASS MEETINGS

The guidelines for the first meeting with your students hold true for every meeting thereafter. When it is time for the class period to begin, you should start the learning activities at once, with no delay. This discourages the kind of fooling around and time wasting that might otherwise occur. To minimize problems with classroom control, you must practice this from the very first day of your teaching career. [*Note:* At the beginning of your student teaching, you may need to follow the opening procedures already established by your cooperating teacher. If your cooperating teacher's procedures for classroom management are largely ineffective, then you should talk with your university supervisor about a different placement.]

Once class has begun, the pace of activities should be lively enough to keep students alert and productively busy, and without dead time, but not so fast as to discourage or lose some students. The effective teacher runs a businesslike classroom; at no time does any student sit or stand around with nothing to do. To maintain a smooth and brisk pace, to lessen distractions, and to prevent dead time, consider the guidelines that follow.

Opening Activities

Although some schools no longer use a bell system to denote the beginning and ending of every class period, some teachers still refer to the initial class activity as the *bell activity.* More frequently, perhaps, it is referred to as the *warm up activity* or simply as the *opener.*

At the beginning of each class period, in order to take attendance and to attend to other routine administrative matters, most teachers expect the students to be in their assigned seats. You should greet the students warmly and start their learning quickly. (Unless you really want responses, it is best to avoid greeting students with a rhetorical question such as "How was your weekend?" See "rhetorical questioning" at the beginning of Chapter 7.) If you are teaching in a school where you must monitor attendance at the beginning of each class period and you are not yet comfortable with your overlapping skill, an effective management procedure is to have the overhead projector on each day when students arrive in class. The day's agenda and immediate assignment or warm-up activity is clearly written on a transparency and displayed on the screen, which then is referred to after your greeting. Once administrative

---

[20]See, for example, A. Kohn, *Punished by Rewards* (New York: Houghton Mifflin, 1993).

CLASSROOM SCENARIO

Beginning the Class Period in Mr. Scott's Class

On the first day of school, two students arrived a half-minute late to Mr. Scott's class. On the second day, three students were a minute late, and Mr. Scott waited to begin class until they were in their seats. On the third day, four students were each from one to three minutes late, and again Mr. Scott waited to begin class. By the end of the first week, Mr. Scott was delaying the start of the class for seven minutes after the bell because students continued to amble in throughout this time period.

Questions for Class Discussion

1. What do you predict will be the situation by the end of the second week? Why?
2. What alternatives are open to Mr. Scott for Monday of the second week?
3. Which of the alternatives are likely to lead to a worse situation? Why?
4. Which of the alternatives promise to lead to improvement? Why?

matters are completed (usually in a matter of a minute or two), the day's lesson should begin, which could mean that students will move to other stations within the classroom.

When there are no announcements or other administrative matters to cover, you should try to begin the day's lesson immediately. Then, within a few minutes after the students have begun their lesson activities, take attendance. Perhaps the best routine, one that requires practice and overlapping skill, is to do both simultaneously—take attendance while starting the day's instructional activities. Whichever the case, once the class period has begun, routines and lesson activities should move forward briskly and steadily until the official end of the class period or, in the case of extended class periods or blocks, until a scheduled break.

Warm-up activities include a variety of things, such as a specific topic or question that each student responds to by writing in his or her journal or a topic or question that pairs (dyads) of students discuss and write about in their journals. Other activities include a problem to be solved by each student or student pair, the exchange and discussion of a homework assignment, the completion of the write-up of a laboratory activity, and the writing of individual or student dyad responses to textbook questions.

Now do Exercise 4.4 to learn further how experienced teachers open their class meetings.

EXERCISE 4.4: OBSERVATION AND ANALYSIS OF HOW EXPERIENCED TEACHERS OPEN CLASS MEETINGS

INSTRUCTIONS: The purpose of this exercise is to learn how experienced teachers open class meetings and, from that, to begin building your own repertoire of options. Select three experienced teachers, all of the same grade level (grade 5, 6, 7, or 8) and subject, and observe how they begin their class meetings. Observe only the first 10 minutes of each period. After collecting these data, share, compile, and discuss the results as follows:

1. Grade level and subject discipline I observed: _____

2. Normal time duration of class period: (example 9:00–10:50 A.M.) _____

   Time that I observed:(example, 9:00–9:10 A.M.) _____

3. Make a check for each of the following observations that you make. For each teacher indicate by numbering 1, 2, 3, etc., the things that he or she did first, second, third, etc., during the initial 10 minutes from the time students began entering the classroom until after the official clock start of class (i.e., when class is supposed to begin).

	✓	Teacher 1	Teacher 2	Teacher 3
Greeting the students	____	____	____	____
Warm and friendly?	____	____	____	____
Giving an assignment (i.e., a warm-up activity)	____	____	____	____
Taking attendance	____	____	____	____
Talking with another adult	____	____	____	____
Talking with one or a few students	____	____	____	____
Readying materials or equipment	____	____	____	____
Working at desk	____	____	____	____
Handing out student papers or materials	____	____	____	____
Other (specify)	____	____	____	____

4. For these three teachers, was there a common way in which they began class?

5. Compile your results with those of your classmates. Write the results here.

6. Compare the results of observations for all similar subjects/grade level combinations. What are the similarities and differences?

7. As a group can you reach any conclusions about teachers of particular grade levels and subject disciplines, and how they spend the first 10 minutes of the class meeting?

FOR YOUR NOTES

Smooth Implementation of the Lesson

Lessons should move forward briskly and purposefully, with natural transitions from one lesson activity to the next and with each activity starting and ending conclusively, especially when using direct (teacher-centered) instruction. Transitions (discussed in the section that follows), in particular, are a most troublesome time for many beginning teachers.

When giving verbal instructions to students, do so quickly and succinctly, without talking too long and giving so much detail that students begin to get restless and bored.

Once students are busy at their learning tasks, avoid interrupting them with additional verbal instructions, statements, or announcements that distract and get them off task, and that could as easily be written on the board or overhead transparency. Interventions should be communicated to a student privately without disturbing the rest of the class. Most young adolescents are easily distracted; do not be the cause of their distractions.

With whole-class instruction, before starting a new activity, be sure that most students have satisfactorily completed the present one. Students who finish early can work on an *anchor* or *transitional activity* (described later). End each activity conclusively before beginning a new activity. With a relevant and carefully prepared transition, bridge the new activity with the previous one, so students understand the connection. Helping students understand connections is a continuing focus and theme for every classroom teacher.

With skill in withitness, you will carefully and continuously monitor all students during the entire class period. If one or two students become inattentive and begin to behave inappropriately, quietly (i.e., using indirect or unobtrusive intervention) redirect their attention without distracting and interrupting the learning activities of the rest of the students.

To help prevent dead time and management problems, especially when using multiple learning tasks and indirect (student-centered) instruction, you will want to establish and rehearse the students in the use of anchor or transitional activities. These are ongoing, relevant tasks that students automatically move to whenever they have completed their individual or small group classroom learning activities. Examples of an anchor activity are working on a portfolio, writing in a journal, or working on an aspect of a long-term project.

Transitions: A Difficult Skill for Beginning Teachers

Transitions are the moments in lessons between activities or topics—times of change. It will probably take you a while to sharpen the skill of smooth transitions. Planning and consistency are important in mastering this important skill. With careful planning, a dependable schedule, and consistent routines, transitions usually occur efficiently, automatically, and without disruption. Still, it is probable that for classroom teachers the greatest number of discipline problems occur during times of transitions, especially when students must wait for the next activity. To avoid problems during transitions, eliminate wait times by thinking and planning ahead. During the preactive phase of instruction, plan your transitions and write them into your lesson plan.

Transitions in lessons are of two types. The first is achieved by the teacher's connecting one activity to the next so that students understand the relationship between the two activities. That is a *lesson transition*. The second type of transition occurs when some students have finished a learning activity but must wait for others to catch up before starting the next. This we call an *anchor* or *transitional activity*. The transitional (or anchor) activity is intended to keep all students academically occupied, allowing no time when students have nothing to do but wait. A common example is when, during testing, some students finish the test before others. The wise and effective teacher plans a transitional activity and gives instructions or reminders for that activity or an ongoing activity before students begin the test.

During the preactive phase of instruction, you should plan and rehearse nearly every move you and the students will make, thinking ahead to anticipate and avoid problems in classroom control. Transitions are planned and students are prepared for them by clearly established transition routines. While waiting for the start of the next activity, students engage in these transitional activities. You can plan a variety of these activities relevant and appropriate to the topics being studied, although not necessarily related to the next activity of that particular day's lesson. Transitional activities may include any number of meaningful activities such as journal writing, worksheet activity, lab reports, portfolio work, homework, project work, and even work for another teacher's class.

As a beginning teacher, it will take time to develop finesse in your application of these guidelines for effective lesson management. During your student teaching experience, your cooperating teacher and college or university supervisor will understand this and will help you develop and hone your skills.

SELECTED LEGAL GUIDELINES

Among teachers and teacher candidates, the topic of teacher and student rights generates discussions and concerns. You are, or will be, interested in teacher tenure laws, retirement laws, professional organizations, collective bargaining, legal requirements concerning student discipline, teacher liability and insurance, and teacher negligence, topics this resource guide cannot pursue or discuss in depth.

Nevertheless, you must be knowledgeable about legal matters regarding teaching and supervising minors. Such knowledge can minimize the possibility of making errors that abuse the rights of students, that cause emotional or physical trauma to a student, and that could result in litigation and an abrupt and unpleasant break or end to your teaching career. The content that follows gives only some very basic information.

Title IX: Student Rights

Resulting from legislation that occurred more than three decades ago—Federal law Title IX of the Education Act Amendments of 1972, P.L. 92-318—a teacher is prohibited from discriminating among students on the basis of their gender. In all aspects of school, male and female students must be treated the same. This means, for example, that a teacher must not pit males against females in a subject content quiz game—or for any other activity or reason. Further, no teacher, student, administrator, or other school employee should make sexual advances toward or sexually harass a student (i.e., speaking or touching in a sexual manner). The school atmosphere must be one of trust, dignity, and respect among students and the adult staff.

Students should be informed by their schools of their rights under Title IX, and they should be encouraged to report any suspected violations of their rights to the school principal or other designated person. Many middle level schools provide students with a publication of their rights as students. See Figure 4.3 for resources.

Teacher Liability and Insurance

Credentialed teachers and student teachers in public schools are usually protected by their school districts against personal injury litigation (i.e., a negligence suit filed as the result of a student being injured at school or at a school-sponsored activity). Student teachers and credentialed teachers should investigate carefully the extent of their tort (i.e., any private or civil wrong for which a civil suit can be brought) liability coverage in districts where they work. You may decide that the coverage provided is insufficient. Additional liability coverage can be obtained through private insurance agents and through affiliation with national teacher's organizations.

Teachers sometimes find themselves in situations where they are tempted to transport students in their own private automobiles, such as for field trips and other off-campus activities. Before ever transporting students in your automobile—or in private automobiles driven by others—you and other drivers should inquire from your insurance agents whether you have adequate automobile insurance liability coverage to do that and if any written permissions or release from liability is needed. Our advice is not to use private automobiles for transporting students for school events; after all, if it is

Figure 4.3   Resources on sexual harassment in schools.

- L. A. Brown, et al., *Student-Student Sexual Harassment: A Legal Guide for Schools* (Alexandria, VA: Council of School Attorneys, National School Boards Association, 1998).
- G. Crisci, "When No Means No: Recognizing and Preventing Sexual Harassment in Your Schools," *American School Board Journal* 186(6):25–29 (June 1999).
- M. V. Henderson, et al., *Preventive Law Curriculum Guide* (Baton Rouge, LA: Louisiana State Board of Regents, 1999).
- B. Goorian, *Sexual Misconduct by School Employees,* ERIC Digest Number 134 (Eugene, OR: ERIC Clearinghouse on Educational Management, 1999).
- A. Hassenpflug, "Courts and Peer Sexual Harassment by Middle School Students," *Middle School Journal* 31(2):49–56 (November 1999).
- K. Herr, "Institutional Violence in the Everyday Practices of School: The Narrative of a Young Lesbian," *Journal for a Just and Caring Education* 5(3):242–255 (July 1999).
- W. Hughes, "School Liability for Sexual Harassment," *American Secondary Education* 28(2):23–26 (Winter 1999).
- Iowa State Department of Education, *No Big Deal: A Sexual Harassment Training Manual for Middle School and High School Students* (Des Moines, IA: Author, 1998).
- R. Jones, "I Don't Feel Safe Here Anymore," *American School Board Journal* 186(11):26–31 (November 1999).
- National Association of Attorneys General, *Protecting Students from Harassment and Hate Crime: A Guide for Schools* (Washington, DC: Office for Civil Rights, 1999).
- S. Rubin and J. S. Biggs, *Teachers That Sexually Abuse Students: An Administrative and Legal Guide* (Lancaster, PA: Technomic, 1999).
- N. Stein, *Classrooms and Courtrooms: Facing Sexual Harassment in K–12 Schools* (New York: Teachers College Press, 1999).

an important educational activity, then the school district should provide proper transportation support.

Inevitably, teachers take personal items to school—purses, cameras, CD players, and so on. It is unlikely that the school's insurance policy covers your personal items if stolen or damaged. A homeowner's or apartment renter's policy might. Our advice: avoid taking valuable personal items to school.

Child Abuse and Neglect

Child abuse and neglect (e.g., physical abuse, incest, malnutrition, improper clothing, and inadequate dental care) is a grave matter of pressing national concern. *In all 50 states, teachers are legally mandated to report any suspicion of child abuse.* It is a serious moral issue not to report such suspicion; lawsuits have been brought against educators for negligence for not doing so. To report your suspicion of child abuse, you can telephone toll free on the national 24-hour hotline at 1-800-4-A-CHILD or on the hotline for your state (see Internet site at http://www.kidsafe-caps.org/report.html). Proof of abuse is not necessary.

Although physical abuse is the easiest to spot, other types of abuse and neglect can be just as serious. General characteristics of children who are abused or neglected are (a) below normal height and weight; (b) exhibiting destructive behaviors; (c) exhibiting hyperactive or aggressive behavior; (d) exhibiting short attention spans and lack of interest in school activities; (e) exhibiting sudden and dramatic changes in behavior; (f) fear of everyone and everything; (g) fear of going home after school; (h) fear of their parent/guardians and other adults; (i) frequent sickness and absence from school; (j) frequent tiredness and often falling asleep in class; (k) smelling of alcohol, (l) smelling of body wastes, unclean; (m) unexpected crying; (n) unexplained lacerations and bruises; (o) withdrawing from adult contact; and (p) withdrawing from peer interaction.[21] A student who comes to your classroom abused or neglected needs to feel welcome and secure while in the classroom. For additional guidance in working with such a student, contact experts from your local school district (e.g., the school psychologist), or request guidelines from your state department of education or the local Children's Protective Services (CPS) agency.

First Aid and Medication

Accidents and resulting injuries to students while at school do occur. While doing a laboratory experiment, a student is burned by an acid or a flame. A student is injured by glass from a falling window pane when the teacher attempts to open a stuck window. A student falls on the school grounds and is injured by an automatic sprinkler head that failed to retract into the ground when the system shut down. While on a field trip a student falls and is injured while climbing on rocks. Do you know what you should do when a student is injured in your presence?

First, you should give first aid *only* when necessary to save a limb or life. When life or limb are not at risk, then you should follow school policy by referring the student immediately to professional care. When immediate professional care is unavailable and you believe that immediate first aid is necessary, then you can take prudent action, as if you were that student's parent or legal guardian. But you must always be cautious and knowledgeable about what you are doing so you do not cause further injury.

Unless you are a licensed medical professional, you should *never* give medication to a minor, whether prescription or over-the-counter. Students who need to take personal medication should bring from home a written parental statement of permission and instructions. Follow school policy on this matter.

INAPPROPRIATE STUDENT BEHAVIOR

Inappropriate student behavior in the classroom can range from minor acts to very serious ones. Sometimes student behaviors seen by the teacher as inappropriate are simply the demonstration of behaviors that are learned and even encouraged in the child's home. Sometimes the causes of student misbehavior are problems that originated outside the classroom and spilled over into it. Others are simply misbehaviors that result from the fact that whenever a group of young adolescents are together for a period of time, mischief or fooling around will likely result. Still others are the result of something the teacher did or did not do. Read attentively the guidelines and hints in the remaining pages of this chapter.

Categories of Student Misbehavior

Described next, in order of increasing seriousness, are categories of student misbehavior that teachers sometimes have to contend with.

TRANSIENT NONDISRUPTIVE BEHAVIORS

This least-serious category includes these common and usually nondisruptive behaviors: seeming inattentive and staring off into space or out the window, chatting with a neighbor and momentarily being off task, or fooling around but not really bothering anyone else. Fortunately, in most instances, this type of behavior is transient, and sometimes it is even best to pretend for a

---

[21]D. G. Gil, *Violence Against Children: Physical Child Abuse in the United States* (Cambridge, MA: Rand McNally, 1970).

moment or so not to be aware of it.[22] If it persists, all it may take to get the student back on task is an unobtrusive (silent and private) redirection. Examples of silent and private redirection techniques include a stare or a stare accompanied by a frown (when eye contact with the student is made). If this does not work, go to a third-level intervention by calling on the student by name and reminding the student of the correct procedure or of what he or she is supposed to be doing.

Avoid asking an off-task student any question (such as a content question like, "John, what are the raw material of photosynthesis?" when you know full well that John is not paying attention; or making an inquiry ("John, why are you doing that?" John probably doesn't know why). Avoid also making a threat such as, "John, if you don't turn around and get to work I will send you out into the hall." It is important you not make "mountains out of molehills," or you could cause more problems than you would resolve. Maintain the students' focus on the lesson rather than on the off-task behavior.

Examples of trivial misbehaviors that you need not worry about unless they become disruptive include emotionally excited student behavior because the student is really "into the lesson"; brief whispering during a lesson; or short periods of inattentiveness, perhaps accompanied by visual wandering or daydreaming. Teacher responses to student behavior and enforcement of procedures such as raising hands and being recognized before speaking will naturally vary depending on the particular subject, lesson activity, and maturity of the students.

DISRUPTIONS TO LEARNING

This category includes incessant talking out of turn, walking around the room aimlessly and without permission, clowning, and tossing objects, all of which are behaviors that students know are unacceptable in the classroom. In responding to such misbehaviors, it is important that you have explained their consequences to students, and then that, following your stated procedures, you promptly and consistently deal with the violations. Too many beginning teachers (and veteran teachers as well) tend to ignore these class disruptions (seemingly in hope that, if not recognized, they will discontinue). You must *not* ignore minor infractions of this type, for if you do, they most likely will escalate beyond your worst nightmare. Without displaying any anger (otherwise students are winning the battle for control), simply and quickly enforce your consequences and keep the focus on the lesson, not the inappropriate behavior. In other words, maintain your control of classroom events, rather than being controlled by them.

There is sometimes a tendency among beginning teachers, especially when they have a problem with students goofing off and being disruptive, to assume that the entire group of students is being unruly, when, in fact, it is usually only one or two or maybe three students. You want to avoid saying to the entire group of students anything that implies you perceive them all as being unruly if, in fact, they are not. Such a false accusation will only serve to alienate the majority of the students who are being attentive to the learning task.

DEFIANCE, CHEATING, LYING, AND STEALING

When a student refuses to do what you say, the student's defiance may be worthy of temporary or permanent removal from the class. Depending upon your judgment of the seriousness of the act of defiance, you may simply give the student a time-out. Or you may suspend the student from class until there has been a conference about the situation, perhaps involving you, members of your teaching team, the student, the student's parent or guardian, and a school official.

Any cheating, lying, and stealing may be an isolated act, and the student may only need a one-on-one talk to find out what precipitated the incident and what might be done to prevent it from ever happening again. A student who habitually exhibits any of these behaviors may need to be referred to a specialist. Whenever you have reason to suspect immoral behavior, you should discuss your concerns with members of your teaching team and a school official.

SEXUAL MISCONDUCT, FIGHTING, AND VIOLENCE

It seems that more and more often today, teachers are confronted with major problems of misbehavior that have ramifications beyond the classroom or that begin elsewhere and spill over into the classroom. If this happens, you may need to ask for help, and for the safety of your students and yourself you should not hesitate to do so. For that reason, every classroom teacher should have immediate access to a phone. As a teacher, you must stay alert. In the words of Johnson and Johnson,

> Teaching is different from what it used to be. Fifty years ago, the main disciplinary problems were running in halls, talking out of turn, and chewing gum. Today's transgressions include physical and verbal violence, incivility, and in some schools, drug abuse, robbery, assault, and murder. The result is that many teachers spend an inordinate amount of time and energy managing classroom conflicts. When students poorly manage their conflicts with each other and with faculty, aggression results. Such behavior is usually punished with detentions, suspensions, and expulsions. As violence increases, pressure for safe and orderly schools increases. Schools are struggling with what to do.[23]

---

[22]See, for example, T. L. Good and J. E. Brophy, *Looking in Classrooms*, 8th ed. (New York: Addison-Wesley/Longman, 2000), p. 165.

[23]D. W. Johnson and R. T. Johnson, *Reducing School Violence Through Conflict Resolution* (Alexandria, VA: Association for Supervision and Curriculum Development, 1995), p. 1.

Today's schools are adopting a variety of types of school-wide and classroom procedures and instructional programs designed to reduce or eliminate violent, aggressive, student behaviors.[24]

There Are Success Stories

Some schools report success using what is called a Prescriptive Discipline Plan that separates misbehaviors into three categories of seriousness with related consequences: minor misbehaviors that are handled by classroom teachers; intermediate offenses (cheating, disrespect, and insubordination) handled by administrators; and serious offenses (fighting, assault, sexual misconduct) invoking automatic suspension from school.

After instituting nontraditional scheduling (see Chapter 1), it is not uncommon for schools to report an improved school climate with significant improvement in student behavior, attendance, and academic success.[25]

After instituting looping (keeping students with the same teacher for multiple years) and creating a focus on character development, Kennedy Middle School (Eugene, OR) reports higher student achievement and improved student behavior.[26]

When teachers, counselors, students, parents, and community representatives work together, it is not uncommon for a school to report improved student attendance and a decline in the dropout rate. A successful effort at helping students make a connection with the value and goals of school has been through school and business partnerships. A special form of partnership called **mentoring** has had success with at-risk students as they become more receptive to schooling. The mentoring component of the partnership movement is a one-on-one commitment by community volunteers to improve the self-esteem, attitudes, and attendance of youngsters. Around the country there are a number of successful mentoring programs.[27]

Principals can make a difference. In the 1980s, after it had become a run-down school in a run-down neighborhood, the Boston School Committee considered shutting down Lewenberg Middle School. But a new principal arrived and turned the school around, making it an "exciting, effective, and attractive learning environment." Lewenberg Middle School went from the least-chosen school in the city of Boston to one of the best, to "a school that is 'overchosen' by parents."[28]

Combined successful strategies include incorporating modern technology, making classes more student-centered, eliminating the lower curriculum track and raising expectation standards for all students, intelligent teamwork and linking the school with parents and community representatives. Time and again it is reported that schools that have used these combined strategies experience a decline in suspensions and an increase in student attendance and academic success, with a decrease in the rate of student dropout and failure. The school becomes a positive force in enhancing students' lives, and in improving their academic achievement and their desire to come to and remain in school.[29] For more success stories, see the suggested readings at the end of the chapter.

Teacher Response to Student Misbehavior: Direct and Indirect Intervention

Rather than to punish, the goal in responding to student misbehavior should be to intervene and redirect the student's focus, and to do so successfully with the least amount of classroom disturbance. Typically, teachers respond to student classroom misbehaviors in one of three ways: hostile, assertive, or nonassertive. Hostile and nonassertive responses should be avoided. Unlike a hostile response, an assertive response is not abusive or derogatory to the student. Unlike a nonassertive response, an assertive response is a timely and clear communication to the student of what the teacher wants and an indication that the teacher is prepared to back that want with action.[30]

Too often, teachers intervene with verbal commands—direct intervention—when nonverbal gesturing such as eye contact, proximity, gesturing (e.g., finger to the lips or raised hand), and body language—indirect and unobtrusive intervention strategies—are less disruptive and often more effective in redirecting a misbehaving student. Although the offense might be identical, the teacher's intervention for one student might have to be direct, while for another student indirect intervention is enough to stop the inappropriate behavior.

[24]See, for example, S. M. Banks, "Addressing Violence in Middle Schools," *Clearing House* 73(4):209–210 (March/April 2000).

[25]See examples in Southern Regional Education Board, *1995 Outstanding Practices* (Atlanta, GA: Southern Regional Education Board, 1995.)

[26]"National Schools of Character Awards," on The Character Education Partnership Website http://www.character.org/schools/index.cgi?detail:schools, online January 30, 2000.

[27]S. G. Weinberger, *How to Start a Student Mentor Program,* Fastback 333 (Bloomington, IN: Phi Delta Kappa Educational Foundation, 1992), p. 8.

[28]M. D. O'Donnell, "Boston's Lewenberg Middle School Delivers Success," *Phi Delta Kappan* 78(7):508–512 (March 1997).

[29]See, for example, D. K. Schnitzer and M. J. Caprio, "Academy Rewards," *Educational Leadership* 57(1):48 (September 1999).

[30]C. H. Edwards, *Classroom Discipline and Management,* 2nd ed. (Upper Saddle River, NJ: Prentice Hall, 1997), pp. 71–72.

ORDER OF BEHAVIOR INTERVENTION STRATEGIES

To redirect a student's attention, your usual *first effort* should be indirect intervention (e.g., proximity, eye contact, gesturing, silence). Your *second effort* could be the simplest (that is, the most private) direct intervention (e.g., "Marco, please follow procedures"). Your *third effort,* one that in time interval closely follows the second (i.e., within the same class period), should follow your rules and procedures as outlined in your management system. This might mean a time out (as discussed earlier in this chapter) or detention and a phone call to the student's parent or guardian (in private, of course). Normally, such a third effort is not necessary. A *fourth effort,* still rarer, is to suspend the student from class (and/or school) for some period of time until decisions about the future of the student in that school are made by school officials, in consultation with the student, the parents or guardians, and other professionals such as the school psychologist.

Direct intervention should be reserved for repetitive and serious misbehavior. When using direct intervention, you should give a direct statement, either reminding the student of what he or she is supposed to be doing or telling the student what to do. You should avoid asking rhetorical questions, such as "David, why are you doing that?" When giving students directions about what they are supposed to be doing, you may be asked by a student, "Why do we have to do this?" To that question, you may give a brief academic answer, but do not become defensive or make threats. And rather than spending an inordinate amount of time on the misbehavior, try to focus the student's attention on a desired behavior.

One reason that direct intervention should be held in reserve is that, by interrupting the lesson to verbally intervene, you are doing exactly what the student who is being reprimanded was doing—interrupting the lesson. Not only is that poor modeling but it can create a host of management problems beyond your wildest nightmares. Another reason for saving direct intervention is that, when used too frequently, direct intervention loses it effectiveness.

TEACHER-CAUSED STUDENT MISBEHAVIOR

As a classroom teacher, one of your major responsibilities is to model appropriate behavior and *not* to contribute to or be the cause of problems in the classroom. Some student misbehaviors and problems in classroom control are caused or escalated by the teacher and could have been prevented or easily rectified had the teacher behaved or acted differently. Consider the information that follows, first in scenarios for case study review and then in a presentation of fifty mistakes to avoid.

Scenarios for Case Study Review

In addition to sometimes ignoring certain transient student behaviors, you should also avoid using negative methods of rule enforcement and ineffective forms of punishment, such as those exemplified by the following scenarios. You and your classmates might decide to treat these scenarios as case studies for small groups to consider and then to discuss before the whole class.

- *Capricious.* Because of her arbitrary and inconsistent enforcement of classroom rules, Fran Fickle, an eighth-grade language arts teacher, has lost the respect and trust of her students as well as the control of her classes. Students are constantly testing Fran to see what they can get away with.
- *Extra Assignments.* When students in Margaret Malopropros's seventh-grade reading class misbehave, she habitually assigns extra reading and written work as punishment, even for the most minor offenses. This behavior has simply reinforced the view of many of her students that school is drudgery, so they no longer look forward to her classes. Behavior problems in her class have steadily increased since the beginning of the school year.
- *Embarrassment.* When eighth-grade social studies teacher Denise Degradini was having difficulty controlling the behavior of one of her students, she got on the classroom phone and called the student's parent. While the entire class of 33 students could hear the conversation, she told the parent about her child's behavior in class and how she was going to have to give the student a referral if the student's behavior did not improve. From that one act Denise lost all respect of her students. Class academic achievement grades plummeted for the rest of the year.
- *Group Punishment.* Because Fred Flock has not developed his withitness and overlapping skills, he has the unfortunate habit of punishing the entire group for every instance of misbehavior. Yesterday, for example, because some students were noisy during a video presentation, he gave the entire class an unannounced quiz on the content of the film. He has lost the respect of the students, students are hostile toward him, and his problems with classroom control are steadily growing worse.
- *Harsh and Humiliating Punishment.* Vince Van Pelt, a physical education teacher, has lost control of his classes and the respect of his students. His thrashing, whipping, tongue-lashing, and use of humiliation are ineffective and indicative of his loss of control. Parents have complained and one is suing him. The district has given Mr. Van Pelt official notice of the nonrenewal of his contract.
- *Loud Talk.* The noisiest person in Steve Shrill's class is Mr. Shrill. His constant and mistaken efforts to talk over the classes have led to his own yelling and

screaming, to complaints from neighboring teachers about the noise in his classes, and to a reprimand from the principal.

- *Lowered Marks.* Eunice Erudite, an eighth-grade language arts/social studies teacher, has a policy of writing a student's name on the board each time the person is reprimanded for misbehavior. When a student has accumulated five marks on the board, she lowers his or her academic grade by one letter. As a result of her not separating their academic and social behaviors, her students are not doing as well as they were at the start of the year. Parents and students have complained about this policy to the administration, arguing that the grades Ms. Erudite is giving do not reflect the students' academic progress or abilities.

- *Nagging.* Paul Peck's continual and unnecessary scolding and criticizing of students upsets the recipient students and arouses resentment from their peers. His nagging resolves nothing, and, like a snowball building in size as it rolls down the hill, causes Mr. Peck, a social studies teacher, more and more problems in the classroom.

- *Negative Direct Intervention.* In the seventh-grade humanities block class, Joshua swears more and more frequently and with graphic and startling language. Other students are beginning to behave similarly. Rather than giving Joshua alternative ways of expressing his feelings, Polly Premio, one team teacher, verbally reprimands Joshua each time this happens and threatens to call his parents about it. Ms. Premio doesn't realize that by giving her attention to Joshua's swearing she is rewarding, reinforcing, and causing the increase in Joshua's unacceptable behavior.

- *Negative Touch Control.* When Ezzard, an eighth-grade bully, pushes and shoves other students out of his way for no apparent reason other than to physically manipulate them, his teacher, Tony Trenchant, grabs Ezzard and yanks him into his seat. What "roughneck" Tony the teacher does not realize is that he is using the very behavior (physical force) that he is trying to stop Ezzard from using. This simply confuses students and teaches them (especially Ezzard) that the use of physical force is okay if you are bigger or older than the recipient of that force. In this situation, unfortunately, hostility begets hostility.

- *Overreaction.* Randall was reading a magazine in his language arts class when his teacher, Harriet Harshmore, grabbed it from Randall's hands, called it "pornographic," and ripped out the offending pages and tossed them into a waste basket. The magazine was *National Geographic,* and the "pornographic article" was on evolution and included drawings of unclothed humans. Harriet was later reprimanded by the school superintendent who said that although he supported her right to put a stop to what she considered a class disruption, Ms. Harshmore had crossed the line when she damaged the magazine. The magazine, apparently a rare collector's issue, had been brought from Randall's home at his teacher's encouragement to bring reading material from home.

- *Physical Punishment.* Mr. Fit, a geography teacher, punishes students by making them go outside and run around the school track when they misbehave in his class. Last week he told Sebastian to go out and run four laps for "mouthing off in class." Sebastian collapsed and died while running. Mr. Fit has been placed on paid leave and is being sued for negligence by Sebastian's parents.

- *Premature Judgments and Actions.* Because of Kathy Kwik's impulsiveness, she does not think clearly before acting, and more than once she has reprimanded the wrong student. Because of her hasty and faulty judgments, students have lost respect for her. For them, her mathematics class has become pure drudgery.

- *Taped Mouths.* Miss Ductless taped the mouths of 20 of her sixth grade students in order to keep them quiet. Later in the school day, several of the students went to the school nurse complaining of allergic reactions caused by the duct tape. Until a full investigation is made, Miss Ductless has been relieved of her teaching duties.

- *Threats and Ultimatums.* Threats and ultimatums from math teacher Bonnie Badger are known to be empty; because she does not follow through, her credibility with the students has been lost. Like wildfire, the word has spread—"We can do whatever we want in old Badger's class."

- *Too Hesitant.* Because Tim Timideo is too hesitant and slow to intervene when students get off task, his classes have gotten further and further out of his control, and it is still early in the school year. As a result, neighbor teachers are complaining about the noise from his classroom, and Tim has been writing more and more referrals.

- *Writing as Punishment.* Because they were "too noisy," science teacher Sam Scribe punished his class of 28 students by making each one hand-copy 10 pages from encyclopedias. When they submitted this assignment, he tore up the pages in front of the class and said, "Now, I hope you have learned your lesson and from now on will be quiet." Upon hearing about this, all six teachers in the school's English department signed and filed a complaint with the principal about Mr. Scribe's use of writing for punishment.

Preventing a Ship from Sinking Is Much Easier Than Saving a Sinking One: Fifty Mistakes to Avoid

During your beginning years of teaching, no one, including you, should expect you to be perfect. You should, however, be aware of common mistakes teachers make that

CLASSROOM SCENARIO

Upon Entering the Classroom the Students Have Nothing to Do

Ms. Roberts is standing by the door as students enter the classroom. Because she has not prepared an opening activity, the students have nothing to do until class officially starts. A couple of students start kicking each other in the corner. Others have not stopped talking since entering the classroom. One student falls asleep. Then the bell sounds, and Ms. Roberts announces that class is beginning. Some of the students continue talking because they have not heard her. One student wakes up and starts looking in his backpack for a book. Another student asks to sharpen a pencil. Yet another asks to be excused to go to the bathroom. Ms. Roberts makes two more requests for attention and gives a couple of detentions to let the class know that she is serious. At that point a student enters the classroom tardy, with numerous apologies as to why he is late. No problem; he hasn't missed anything. After 10 minutes, the students finally settle down to work. Ms. Roberts begins with a short activity to focus them, but by now she has two students with after-school detentions, several evening phone calls to make to parents/guardians, and some potential office referrals.

Source: E. Varner, "Turn Discipline Problems into Opportunities to Improve Instruction," *Middle Ground* 2(4):27–28 (April 1999), p. 27. Adapted by permission.

often are the causes of student inattention and misbehavior. We estimate that as much as 95% of classroom control problems are teacher-caused or teacher-aggravated and are preventable. In this section, you will find descriptions of mistakes commonly made by beginning (and even experienced) teachers. To have a most successful beginning to your career, you will want to develop your skills so you avoid these mistakes. To avoid making these mistakes requires both knowledge of the potential errors and a reflection upon one's own behaviors in relation to them.

The items are mostly grade-level and subject-matter neutral, although clearly some may be more relevant to you than others, depending on your own particular teaching situation.

1. *Inadequately attending to long-range and daily planning.* A teacher who inadequately plans ahead is heading for trouble. Inadequate long-term planning and unimaginative, sketchy, inadequate lesson planning is a precursor to ineffective teaching and, eventually, to teaching failure. Students are motivated best by teachers who clearly are working hard and intelligently for them.

Many beginning teachers plan their lessons carefully at first and their students respond well. Then, after finding a few strategies that seem to work, their lesson planning becomes increasingly sketchy. They fall into a rut of doing pretty much the same thing day after day—lecture, discussion, videos, and worksheets are common for these teachers. They fail to consider and plan for individual student differences. By mid-semester they have stopped growing professionally and begin to experience increasing numbers of problems with students.

2. *Emphasizing the negative.* Too many warnings to students for their inappropriate behavior—and too little recognition for their positive behaviors—do not help to establish the positive climate needed for the most effective learning to occur. Reminding students of procedures is more positive and will bring quicker success than reprimanding them when they do not follow procedures.

Too often, teachers try to control students with negative language, such as "There should be no talking," and "No gum or candy in class or else you will receive detention," and "No getting out of your seats without my permission." Teachers sometimes allow students, too, to use negative language on each other, such as "Shut up!" Negative language does not help instill a positive classroom climate. To encourage a positive atmosphere, use concise, positive, language. Tell students precisely what they are supposed to do rather than what they are not supposed to do. Disallow the use of disrespectful and negative language in your classroom.

3. *Not requiring students to raise hands and be acknowledged before responding.* While ineffective teachers often are ones who are controlled by class events, competent teachers are those who are in control of class events. You cannot be in control of events and your interactions with students if you allow students to shout out their comments, responses, and questions whenever they feel like it. The most successful beginning teacher is one who quickly establishes control of classroom events.

In addition, indulging their natural impulsivity is not helping students to grow intellectually. When students develop impulse control, they think before acting. Students can be taught to think before acting or shouting out an answer. One of several reasons that teachers should insist on a raised hand before a student is acknowledged is to discourage students from the impulsive, disruptive, and irritating behavior of shouting out in class.[31]

4. *Allowing students' hands to be raised too long.* When students have their hands raised for long periods before you recognize them and attend to their questions or responses, you are providing them with time to fool around. Although you do not have to call on every student as soon as he or she raises a hand, you should acknowledge him or her quickly, such as with a nod or a wave of your hand, so the student can lower the hand and return to work. Then you should get to the student as quickly as possible. Procedures for this should be clearly understood by the students and consistently practiced by you.

5. *Spending too much time with one student or one group and not monitoring the entire group.* Spending too much time with any one student or a small group of students is, in effect, ignoring the rest of the students. As a novice teacher you cannot afford to ignore the rest of the class, even for a moment.

6. *Beginning a new activity before gaining the students' attention.* A teacher who consistently fails to insist that students follow procedures and who does not wait until all students are in compliance before starting a new activity is destined for major problems in classroom control. You must establish and maintain classroom procedures. Starting an activity before all students are in compliance is, in effect, telling the students that they do not have to follow expected procedures. You cannot afford to tell students one thing and then do another. In the classroom, your actions will always speak louder than your words.

7. *Pacing teacher talk and learning activities too fast.* Pacing of the instructional activities is one of the most difficult skills for beginning teachers to master. Students need time to disengage mentally and physically from one activity before engaging in the next. You must remember that this takes more time for a room of 25 or so students than it does for just one person—you. This is one reason that transitions need to be planned and written into your lesson plan (discussed in Chapter 6).

8. *Using a voice level that is always either too loud or too soft.* A teacher's voice that is too loud day after day can become irritating to some students, just as one that cannot be heard or understood can become frustrating.

9. *Assigning a journal entry without giving the topic careful thought.* If the question or topic about which students are supposed to write is ambiguous or obviously hurriedly prepared—without your having given thought to how students will interpret and respond to it—students

will judge that the task is busywork (e.g., something to keep them busy while you take attendance). If they do it at all, it will be with a great deal of commotion and much less enthusiasm than if they were writing on a topic that had meaning to them.

10. *Standing too long in one place.* Most of the time in the classroom, you should be mobile, schmoozing, "working the crowd."

11. *Sitting while teaching.* Unless you are physically unable to stand, in most situations there is no time to sit while teaching. It is difficult to monitor the class while seated, and you cannot afford to appear that casual.

12. *Being too serious and no fun.* Without a doubt, good teaching is serious business. But students are motivated by and respond best to teachers who obviously enjoy working with them and helping them learn.

13. *Falling into a rut by using the same teaching strategy or combination of strategies day after day.* A teacher in such a rut is likely to become boring to students. Because of the multitude of differences, students are motivated by and respond best to a variety of well-planned and meaningful learning activities.

14. *Inadequately using silence (wait time) after asking a content question.* When students are expected to think deeply about a question, they need time to do so. A teacher who consistently allows insufficient time for students to think is teaching only superficially and at the lowest cognitive level, and is destined for problems in student motivation and classroom control.

15. *Poorly or inefficiently using instructional tools.* The ineffective use of teaching tools such as books, the overhead projector, writing board, and computer says to students that you are not a competent teacher. Would you want an auto mechanic who did not know how to use the tools of the trade to service your automobile? Would you want a brain surgeon who did not know how to use the tools of the trade to remove your tumor? Working with children in a classroom is no less important. Like a competent automobile mechanic or a competent surgeon, a competent teacher selects and effectively uses the best tools available for the job to be done.

16. *Ineffectively using facial expressions and body language.* Your gestures and body language communicate more to students than your words do. For example, one teacher did not understand why his class of seventh graders would not respond to his repeated expression of "I need your attention." In one 15-minute segment, he used that expression eight times. Studying videotape of that class period helped him understand the problem. His dress was very casual, and he stood most of the time with his right hand in his pocket. At five foot, eight inches, with a slight build, a rather deadpan facial expression, and a nonexpressive voice, he was not a commanding presence in the classroom. After seeing himself on tape, he returned to the class wearing a tie, and began using his hands and face more expressively.

---

[31]For further reading about the relationship between impulse control and intelligence, see D. Goleman, *Emotional Intelligence: Why It Can Matter More Than IQ* (New York: Bantam Books, 1995), and D. Harrington-Lueker, "Emotional Intelligence," *High Strides* 9(4):1, 4–5 (March/April 1997).

Rather than saying "I need your attention," he waited in silence for the students to become attentive. It worked.

17. *Relying too much on teacher talk for classroom control.* Beginning teachers have a tendency to rely too much on teacher talk. Too much teacher talk can be deadly. Unable to discern between the important and the unimportant verbiage, students will quickly tune a teacher out.

Some teachers rely too much on verbal interaction and too little on nonverbal intervention techniques. Verbally reprimanding a student for his or her interruptions of class activities is reinforcing the very behavior you are trying to stop. In addition, verbally reprimanding a student in front of his or her peers can backfire on you. Instead, develop your indirect, silent intervention techniques such as eye contact, mobility, frown, silence, body stance, and proximity.

18. *Inefficiently using teacher time.* During the preactive phase of your instruction (the planning phase), think carefully about what you are going to be doing every minute, and then plan for the most efficient and therefore the most productive use of your time in the classroom. Consider the following example. During a language arts brainstorming session a teacher is recording student contributions on a large sheet of butcher paper that has been taped to the wall. She solicits student responses, acknowledges those responses, holds and manipulates the writing pen, walks to the wall, and writes on the paper. Each of those actions requires decisions and movements that consume precious instructional time and that can distract her from her students. An effective alternative would be to have a reliable student helper do the writing while the teacher handles the solicitation and acknowledgment of student contributions. That way she has fewer decisions and fewer actions to distract her, and she does not lose eye contact and proximity with the students.

19. *Talking to and interacting with only half the class.* While leading a class discussion, there is a tendency among some beginning teachers to favor (by their eye contact and verbal interaction) only 40 to 65 percent of the students, sometimes completely ignoring the others for an entire class period. Knowing that they are being ignored, those students will, in time, become uninterested and perhaps unruly. Remember to spread your interactions and eye contact throughout the entire class.

20. *Collecting and returning student papers before assigning students something to do.* If, while turning in papers or waiting for their return, students have nothing else to do, they get restless and inattentive. Students should have something to do while papers are being collected or returned.

21. *Interrupting students while they are on task.* It is not easy to get an entire class of students on task. Once they are on task, you do not want to distract them. Try to give all instructions before students begin their work. The detailed instructions should be written in your lesson plan; that way you are sure not to forget anything. Once on task, if there is an important point you wish to make, write it on the board. If you want to return papers while students are working, do it in a way and at a time that is least likely to interrupt them from their learning task.

22. *Using "Shhh" as a means of quieting students.* When you do that, you simply sound like a balloon with a slow leak. The sound should be deleted from your professional vocabulary. Quiet finger to the lips is a useful substitute.

23. *Using poor body positioning.* Develop your skill of withitness by always positioning your body so you can continue to visually monitor the entire class, even while talking to and working with one student or a small group. Avoid turning your back to even a portion of the class.

24. *Settling for less when you should be trying for more—not getting the most from student responses.* The most successful schools are those with teachers who expect and get the most from all students. Don't hurry a class discussion; "milk" student responses for all you can, especially when discussing a topic that students are obviously interested in. Ask a student for clarification or reasons for his or her response. Ask for verification. Have another student paraphrase what a student said. Pump students for deeper thought and meaning. Too often, the teacher will ask a question, get an abbreviated (often one word and low cognitive level) response from a student, and then move on to another subject. Instead, follow up a student's response to your question with a sequence of questions, prompting and cueing to elevate the student's thinking to higher levels.

25. *Using threats.* Avoid making threats of any kind. One teacher, for example, told her class that if they continued with their inappropriate talking they would lose their break time. She should have had that consequence as part of the understood procedures and consequences and then taken away the break time for some students if warranted.

26. *Avoid punishing the entire class for the misbehavior of a few.* Although the rationale behind such action is clear (i.e., to get group pressure working for you), often the result is the opposite. Students who have been behaving well are alienated from the teacher because they feel they have been punished unfairly for the misbehavior of others. Those students expect the teacher to be able to handle the misbehaving students without punishing those who are not misbehaving, and they are right!

27. *Using global praise.* Global praise is pretty useless. An example is, "Class, your rough drafts were really wonderful." This is hollow and says little except that the teacher has a limited vocabulary or is generally well pleased. The statement is too general and is another instance of verbalism from the teacher that is unnecessary or does not effectively inform students. Instead, be specific—tell what it was about their drafts that made them so wonderful. As another example, after a student's oral response to the class, rather than simply saying "Very good," tell what was so good about the student's response.

28. *Using color meaninglessly.* The use of color on transparencies and the writing board is nice but will shortly lose its effectiveness unless the colors have meaning. If, for example, everything in the classroom is color-coded and students understand the meaning of the code, then using color can serve as an important mnemonic to student learning.

29. *Verbally reprimanding a student from across the room.* This is yet another example of the needless interruption of all students. In addition, because of peer pressure (students tend to support one another) it increases the "you versus them" syndrome. Reprimand when necessary, but do it quietly and as privately as possible.

30. *Interacting with only a "chosen few" students rather than spreading interactions around to all.* As a beginning teacher, especially, it is easy to fall into a habit of interacting with only a few students, especially those who are vocal and who have significant contributions. Your job, however, is to teach all the students. To do that, you must be proactive, not reactive, in your interactions.

31. *Not intervening quickly enough during inappropriate student behavior.* When allowed to continue, inappropriate student behavior only gets worse, not better. It will not go away by itself. It is best to nip it in the bud quickly and resolutely. A teacher who ignores inappropriate behavior, even briefly, is, in effect, approving it. In turn, that approval reinforces the continuation and escalation of inappropriate behaviors.

32. *Not learning and using student names.* To expedite your success, you should quickly learn the students' names and then refer to them by their names. A teacher who does not know or use names when addressing students is, in effect, viewed by the students as impersonal and uncaring.

33. *Reading student papers only for correct (or incorrect) answers and not for process and student thinking.* Reading student papers only for correct responses reinforces the false notion that the process of arriving at answers or solutions is unimportant and that alternative solutions or answers are impossible or unimportant. In effect, it negates the importance of the individual and the very nature and purpose of learning.

34. *Not putting time plans on the board for students.* Yelling out how much time is left for an activity interrupts student thinking and, in effect, says their thinking is unimportant. Again, avoid interrupting students once they are on task. Show respect for their on-task behavior. In this instance, before the activity begins write on the board how much time is allowed for it and the time it is to end. If, during the activity, you decide to change the end time, then write the changed time on the board.

35. *Asking global questions that nobody likely will answer.* Examples are "Does everyone understand?" and "Are there any questions?" and "How do you all feel about . . . ?" It is a brave young soul who, in the presence of peers, is willing to admit ignorance. It is a waste of precious instructional time to ask such questions. If you truly want to check for student under-

standing or opinions, then do a spot check by asking specific questions, allowing think time, and then calling on individuals.

36. *Failing to do frequent comprehension checks (every few minutes during most direct instruction situations) to see if students are understanding.* Too often, teachers simply plow through a big chunk of the lesson, or the entire lesson, assuming that students are understanding it. Or, in the worst case scenario, teachers rush through a lesson without even caring if students are getting it. Students are quick to recognize teachers who don't care.

37. *Using poorly worded, ambiguous questions.* Key questions you will ask during a lesson should be planned and written into your lesson plan. Refine and make precise the questions by asking them to yourself or a friend, and try to predict how students will respond to a particular question.

38. *Trying to talk over student noise.* This simply tells students that their making noise while you are talking is acceptable behavior. When this happens, everyone, teacher included, usually gets increasingly louder during the class period. All that you will get is a sore throat by the end of the school day and, over a longer period of time, the potential for nodules on your vocal cords.

39. *Wanting to be liked by students.* Forget it. If you are a teacher, then teach. Respect is earned as a result of your effective teaching. Liking you may come later.

40. *Permitting students to be inattentive to an educationally useful media presentation.* This usually happens because the teacher has failed to give the students a written handout of questions or guidelines for what they should acquire from the program. Sometimes students need an additional focus. Furthermore, a media presentation is usually audio and visual. To reinforce student learning, add the kinesthetic, such as writing, by using a handout of questions. This provides minds-on and hands-on activities that enhance learning.

41. *Using stutter starts.* A stutter start is when the teacher begins an activity, is distracted, begins again, is distracted again, tries again to start, and so on. During stutter starts, students become increasingly restless and inattentive and sometimes even amused by the teacher's futility, making the final start almost impossible for the teacher to achieve. Avoid stutter starts. Begin an activity clearly and decisively. This is done best when lesson plans are prepared thoughtfully and in detail.

42. *Introducing too many topics simultaneously.* It is important that you not overload students' capacity to engage mentally by introducing different topics simultaneously. For example, during the first 10 minutes of class a teacher started by introducing a warm-up activity, which was a journal write with instructions clearly presented on the overhead. The teacher also verbally explained the activity, although she could have simply pointed to the screen, thereby nonverbally instructing students to begin work on the activity (without disrupting the thinking of those who had already begun). One minute later, the teacher told students about their quarter grades and how later in the

period they would learn more about those grades. Then she returned to the warm-up activity, explaining it a second time (a third time if you count the detailed explanation already on the screen). Next she reminded students of the new tardy rules (thereby introducing a third topic). At this time, however, most of the students were still thinking and talking about what she had said about quarter grades, few were working on the warm-up activity, and hardly any were listening to the teacher talking about the new tardy rules. There was a lot of commotion among the students. The teacher had tried to focus student attention on too many topics at once, thus accomplishing little and losing control of the class in the process.

43. *Failing to give students a pleasant greeting on Monday or following a holiday or to remind them to have a pleasant weekend or holiday.* Students are likely to perceive such a teacher as uncaring or impersonal.

44. *Sounding egocentric.* Whether you are or are not egocentric, you want to avoid appearing so. Sometimes the distinction is subtle, although apparent, such as when a teacher says, "What I am going to do now is. . . ." rather than "What we are going to do now is. . . ." If you want to strive for group cohesiveness—a sense of "we-ness"—then teach not as if you are the leader and your students are the followers, but rather in a manner that empowers your students in their learning.

45. *Taking too much time to give verbal instructions for an activity.* Students become impatient and restless during long verbal instructions from the teacher. It is better to give brief instructions (two or three minutes should do it) and get the students started on the task. For more complicated activities, teach three or four students the instructions and then have those students do workshops with five or six students in each workshop group. This frees you to monitor the progress of each group.

46. *Taking too much time for an activity.* No matter what the activity, during your planning think carefully about how much time students can effectively attend to it. A general rule for most classes (age level and other factors will dictate variation) is when only one or two learning modalities are involved (e.g., auditory and visual), the activity should not extend beyond about 15 minutes; when more than 2 modalities are engaged (e.g., add tactile or kinesthetic), the activity might extend longer, say for 20 or 30 minutes.

47. *Being uptight and anxious.* Consciously or subconsciously, students are quick to detect a teacher who is afraid that events will not go well. And if you are uptight and anxious, it will be like a contagious disease— your students will likely become so, too. To prevent such emotions, at least to the extent that they damage your teaching and your students' learning, you must prepare lessons carefully, thoughtfully, and thoroughly. Unless there is something personal going on in your life that is making you anxious, you are more likely to be in control and confident in the classroom when you have lessons that are well prepared. How do you know if your lesson is well prepared? You will know! It is when you develop a written lesson plan that you are truly excited about and looking forward to implementing, and then before doing so, you review it one more time.

If you do have a personal problem in your life that is distracting and making you anxious (and occasionally most of us do), you need to concentrate on ensuring that your anger, hostility, fear, or other negative emotions do not adversely affect your teaching and your interactions with students. Regardless of your personal problems, your classes of students will face you each day expecting to be taught reading, mathematics, history, science, physical education, or whatever it is you are supposed to be helping them to learn.

48. *Failing to apply the best of what is known about how young adolescents learn.* Too many teachers unrealistically seem to expect success by having all 33 students doing the same thing at the same time rather than having several alternative activities simultaneously occurring in the classroom (called multilevel teaching or multitasking). For example, a student who is not responding well (i.e., being inattentive and disruptive) to a class discussion might behave better if given the choice of moving to a quiet reading center in the classroom or to a learning center to work alone. If, after trying an alternative activity, the student continues to be disruptive, then you may have to try still another alternative activity. You may have to send the student to another supervised location (out of the classroom, to a place previously arranged by you) until you have time (after class or after school) to talk with the student about the problem.

49. *Overusing punishment for classroom misbehavior— jumping to the final step without trying alternatives.* Teachers sometimes mistakenly either ignore inappropriate student behavior (see number 31) or they skip steps for intervention, resorting too quickly to punishment. They immediately send the misbehaving student outside to stand in the hall (not a wise choice if the student is not supervised) or too quickly assign detention (a usually ineffective consequence). Being quick in the use of punishment is not a lesson we should be teaching young people. In-between steps to consider include the use of alternative activities in the classroom (as in number 48). It is good to keep in mind that every child is a work in progress. When a child errs, it is important that the child has the opportunity to recover and to learn from the error.

50. *Being inconcise and inconsistent.* Perhaps one of the most frequent causes of problems in classroom control for beginning teachers is failing to say what is meant or to mean what is said. A teacher who gives only vague instructions or who is inconsistent in his or her behaviors only confuses students (e.g., does not enforce his or her own classroom procedural expectations). A teacher's job is not to confuse students.

Now do Exercise 4.5.

EXERCISE 4.5: IDENTIFYING TEACHER BEHAVIORS THAT CAUSE STUDENT MISBEHAVIOR—A SELF-CHECK EXERCISE

INSTRUCTIONS: The purpose of this exercise is to practice your awareness of the kinds of teacher behaviors to avoid—namely, those that tend to reinforce or cause student misbehavior. Place a check next to each of the following situations you believe illustrate teacher behaviors that cause or reinforce student misbehavior. Then identify what the teacher should do instead. Share your responses with your classmates. An answer key follows.

_____   1. Ms. Rodriquez is nearly always late in arriving to her eighth-grade English class that meets immediately after lunch, seldom beginning class until at least five minutes past the time it is supposed to start.

_____   2. Mr. Beyer ignores brief whispering between two students during a quiet activity in his seventh-grade history class.

_____   3. While lecturing to her biology class, Ms. Whyte ignores brief talking between two students.

☞

EXERCISE 4.5 (*continued*)

_____ 4. During a class discussion in Mr. Stephen's social studies class, one student appears to be daydreaming and just staring out the window.

_____ 5. During quiet study time in Mr. Orey's seventh-grade reading class, Mr. Orey asks for everyone's attention, verbally reprimands two students for horsing around, and then writes out a referral for each of the two students.

_____ 6. Ms. Fueyo advises her students to pay attention during the viewing of a film or else she will give them a quiz on the film's content.

_____ 7. Ms. Lee tells a student that because of his behavior in class today he must come in after school and be detained with her for ten minutes, the same amount of time that he disturbed the class.

EXERCISE 4.5 (*continued*)

_____   8. When Mr. Murai sees a student cheating on a science test, he walks over to the student, picks up the student's test paper, and tears it up in front of the student and the rest of the class.

_____   9. While Ms. Wong is talking to her eighth-grade language arts class, the school principal walks into the room. Ms. Wong stops her lecture and walks over to greet the principal and find out what the principal wants.

_____   10. While a student learning team is giving its oral report to the health science class, Mr. Edwards, the teacher, begins a conversation with several students in the back of the room.

☞

EXERCISE 4.5 (*continued*)

Answer Key

You should have checked situations 1, 3, 5, 6, 7, 8, 9, and 10; these are teacher behaviors that reinforce or cause student misbehavior. For some situations, reasonable teachers will disagree. You should talk about these disagreements with your classmates and arrive at common understandings. Here are some thoughts on each of the ten situations:

1. Ms. Rodriquez's behavior is poor modeling for her students. She must model what she expects—as well as what the school expects—of students. In this instance, she should model arriving and starting on time.
2. Minor infractions, such as this, are often best ignored, as long as the whispering is brief and not disturbing.
3. This should not be ignored. Students are expected to give their attention to the teacher or whoever has the floor at the moment—a show of common courtesy. By not attending to these students (perhaps by eye contact, proximity, name dropping, or some other form of indirect intervention), Ms. Whyte is saying that it is OK for students to be discourteous and to talk during the teacher's lecture. In this instance, Ms. Whyte is not following through with classroom behavioral expectations. Her lack of follow-through will cause further and increasingly disturbing management problems.
4. Minor infractions are sometimes best ignored. Perhaps the student is really thinking about ideas presented in the discussion.
5. By his disruption of the class learning activity, Mr. Orey is reinforcing the very behavior he considers inappropriate from his students. This lack of consistency will cause continued problems in management for Mr. Orey.
6. Threats are unacceptable behaviors, from students or from teachers. And tests should never be administered as punishment. Ms. Fueyo could recommend that students take notes (mental or written) during the film, and that these notes will serve as a focus for discussion after the film's showing. And she could advise them that there will be a follow-up quiz later.
7. By giving the student even more individual attention after school, Ms. Lee is reinforcing and rewarding the student's misbehavior that caused the problem in the first place. Besides, this may not be safe for Ms. Lee to do. Detention, supervised by someone other than this teacher, is a better alternative.
8. Mr. Murai has taken no time to diagnose and to prescribe and thus is reacting too hastily and with hostility. This sort of teacher behavior reinforces the notion that the student is guilty until proven innocent and the notion that process is of greater importance than is the individual student. In addition, Mr. Murai violated this student's right to due process.
9. The error here is that by stopping her lesson, Ms. Wong and the principal are reinforcing the notion that classroom disruptions are acceptable—that the act of teaching is less important than other school business.
10. Mr. Edwards's behavior is both disrespectful and an example of poor modeling. Mr. Edwards and his class should be giving their full attention to the student's report. Mr. Edwards is not modeling the very behavior that he undoubtedly expects from his students when he is leading the class.

SITUATIONAL CASE STUDIES FOR ADDITIONAL REVIEW

To provide further insight into the day-by-day events that occur in teaching, as well as to stimulate your thinking about what you might do in similar situations, the following 10 case studies are presented. Each is a situation that actually occurred. Analyze and discuss these in your class, using the accompanying questions to guide your thinking.

☐ CASE 1 The Boy Who Hangs Around

Background

Bill is male, age 13, in life science. He is tall and awkward and has poor skin. His classmates consider him "crazy." He has minor police offenses and is apparently in conflict with his father. He has taken a liking to the life science teacher and spends many extra hours in the classroom. He is energetic and displays an inquisitive nature. He is quick to get interested in projects but almost as quick to lose interest. He likes to run the film projector for the teacher, but he does not like to participate in discussions with the rest of the class. He likes personal chats with the teacher but feels that the other students laugh at him.

The Situation

Bill's IQ is recorded to be 95. The teacher attempted to work with Bill in improving his feelings of inadequacy and had frank talks with him about his gangliness and his acne. What follows is actual material as written by Bill during the first semester of school:

September: "I want to make the best out of the time I am on earth. I want to be somebody, not just exist either. . . . The members of this class influence me and what I think of doing. . . . They also make me feel real low. Their teasing me has changed me. . . . The teacher of my science class has helped me very much. . . . My greatest problem is in holding my head up and fighting for myself. . . ."

October: "I have made a lot of headway in the past weeks. . . . I think I have done a good choice in the subject I am studying. . . . I also thank my teacher's actions toward me, that we may get to be very good friends, and learn a lot to know that teachers are human too, that they also have problems to solve and goals to head for."

November: "I don't have to fear anybody or anything on the idea of getting up and saying what I feel I have accomplished in this class and I have learned to make my own decisions on what I will study or maybe do when I get out of school."

December: "I have learned that I have confidence in others only when I have confidence in myself."

January: "I have my report on the affect of geabriilic acid on plants. . . . I told (the class) about all my failures and they were quite interested. I told them that I had failed four times . . . that my science teacher told me I should not give up at this point and that a seintice [scientist] does not give up. I had no longer stated that fact and they all seemed like they could help in some way. I think the report went over well."

So the student developed courage to stand in front of his peers, holding his head high, and confidently reporting to the class how he kept at his plant experiment, even after four failures. He was proud of what he had learned about the work of the scientist. And he was even more proud that the students no longer teased and laughed at him.

Questions for Class Discussion

1. How did you feel after reading this case?
2. Did Bill learn anything that semester? What?
3. Did he learn science?
4. What did the teacher do to facilitate Bill's learning?
5. What is ahead for Bill in school?

☐ CASE 2 The Bully

Background

Tony is considered by his peers to be one of the "tough guys." He is 14 and in the eighth grade at Green Middle School. Tony is prone to bullying, frequently quarreling with his fellow students and teachers, and is considered by his parents to be disobedient. He has a record of minor offenses that range from truancy to destruction of property to drunkenness and offensive behavior. In general, Tony gets satisfaction in ways that are damaging and unfair to others.

It is obvious to school officials that Tony is beyond parental control. Tony's mother has no apparent ability to control Tony's behavior. His father frequently beats him.

Tony is not a member of any school organization, nor does he participate in co-curricular activities. His midterm progress shows that he is failing in three subjects.

The Situation

One of the subjects Tony is failing is English. Tony is a discipline problem in class, and although it makes the teacher feel guilty, she cannot help but be pleased when Tony is absent from class.

Questions for Class Discussion

1. Where is the problem?
2. Where is Tony heading?
3. What can and should be done, if anything? By whom?
4. What is the role for Tony? His teachers? His peers? The school administration? His parents? Society in general?
5. Is it too late for Tony?

☐ CASE 3 The Problem of Mary

Background

Mary has been characterized by her peers and by her teachers as being lonely, indifferent, and generally unhappy. She avoids both students and teachers. She will lie and cheat to avoid attention. Her "close" friends describe her as thoughtless and unkind. She often uses damaging remarks about members of her class, calling them conceited, teacher's pets, and so on. She considers members of her class to be thoughtless, unkind, and uninterested in her.

Mary will do what she has to do to achieve average success in her studies. Her association with adults, her parents, and her teachers would be described as one of "getting along," doing what "I have to do in order not to get too much attention."

The Situation

One of Mary's friends is another 14-year-old girl, Jane. Jane is an above-average student in school, seemingly well adjusted, and interested in people. She has gotten to know Mary because they are neighbors and walk together to school. Because of Jane's interest in other people and her closeness to Mary, she has become interested in "trying to bring Mary out of her shell."

Mary has told Jane that she feels her teachers are unreasonably severe. Mary said, "The teachers are only interested in the popular kids." Jane disagreed. Mary said, "You only disagree because you are pretty and popular." At this point, the conversation was broken by a boy running up and saying, "Hey, Jane, you're late for the council meeting."

Questions for Class Discussion

1. Where is the problem?
2. What if you were Mary's teacher?
3. How did you feel after reading this case?

☐ CASE 4 The Stabbing Victim

Ron King, who claims he was stabbed in the back during a class, wants $100,000 in damages from his school and student Richard Decarlo.

According to the action, filed by King's mother, the incident occurred last February. King says he was stabbed by Decarlo and lost his spleen as a result.

The suit says there was no teacher in the classroom when the stabbing took place and that the school was negligent in not providing supervision.

The action also contends that school officials knew that Decarlo secretly carried deadly weapons with him on the school grounds.

Question for Class Discussion

1. After reading this case, how did you feel and what were you thinking?

☐ CASE 5 From a Deadly Dare

In a life science class the students were just starting a lab involving the dissection of triple latex-injected formaldehyde-preserved bullfrogs. While the teacher was busy talking with a few students off to one side of the room—answering their questions and helping them get started on their work—she heard screaming and a com-

motion from the far side of the room. She looked up and immediately saw Robert vomiting and convulsing. On a dare from other students, he had eaten one of the preserved bullfrogs, completely devouring it. Immediately the teacher sent a runner to the office (there was no phone in the classroom). Someone dialed 911, and an ambulance and paramedics soon arrived to take Robert to a nearby hospital, where his stomach was pumped and other treatment was administered. For the next 24 hours Robert was listed in serious condition.

Questions for Class Discussion

1. What were your thoughts after reading this case?
2. Could the incident have been prevented?

☐ CASE 6 Student Has a Crush on Teacher

During his first year of teaching it had become obvious that one of Mr. Kline's female seventh-grade students had developed a serious crush on him. One day, after class was over and all other students had left the room, she approached Mr. Kline and politely asked him if he had a photograph of himself that she could have.

Questions for Class Discussion

1. Is this a potentially serious situation?
2. How should Mr. Kline respond to the student's request?

☐ CASE 7 Science Teacher Solicits Students for Marijuana for Experiment

A teacher gave $30 to a student for a quantity of marijuana with the intention of putting the marijuana in a bowl with goldfish so students could study the effects on the fish. Before the experiment ever took place, other students reported the teacher's action to the school principal. The teacher was placed on administrative leave. After pleading guilty to charges of contributing to the delinquency of a minor, the teacher was sentenced to 45 days in jail and two years of probation. Apparently, the experiment was to be a repeat of one done earlier at the school by police officers, but with cutbacks and restraints the teacher decided to use her own money to repeat the experiment.

Questions for Class Discussion

1. After reading this, what were your thoughts?
2. What, if anything, did you learn from this situation that might be helpful to you during your own teaching career?[32]

☐ CASE 8 Student Complains to a Student Teacher about Continued Sexual Harassment by a Peer

During the first week after John began his student teaching in eighth-grade history, one of his female students

---

[32]Perhaps the teacher should have searched for an alternative active. For example, see R. N. Russo and S. Parrish, "Toxicology for the Middle School," *Journal of Chemical Education* 72(1):49–50 (January 1995).

came to him after class and complained that a boy in the class has continued to sexually harass her even after she had reported it to the school vice-principal. She says that the harassment is beyond just verbal abuse and she wants it stopped.

Questions for Class Discussion

1. After reading this case, what were your thoughts?
2. What, if anything, should John do?
3. What, if anything, did you learn from this situation that might be helpful to you during your own teaching career?

□ CASE 9 **Students Use the Internet for Extracurricular Activity**

During project work time in a seventh-grade language arts/social studies block, the classroom teacher discovers a group of three students at a computer workstation viewing a graphic sex Website.

Questions for Class Discussion

1. After reading this, what were your immediate thoughts?
2. What should the teacher do?
3. How could the problem have been avoided?
4. What, if anything, did you learn from this case that might be helpful to you during your own teaching career?

□ CASE 10 **Violence at School**

Consider the following events:

• December 1, 1997 (Paducah, Kentucky), a 14-year-old boy shot and killed three students at school.

• March 24, 1998 (Jonesboro, Arkansas), two boys, ages 11 and 13, shot and killed one teacher and four students at school.

• April 25, 1998 (Edinboro, Pennsylvania), a 14 year old shot and killed a teacher.

• May 21, 1998 (Springfield, Oregon), two students are killed by a 15-year-old student.

• April 20, 1999 (Littleton, Colorado), two high school students shot and killed 12 other students, one teacher, and themselves, and seriously wounded more than a dozen other students.

• March 5, 2001 (Santee, California) two students at school are shot and killed and at least 13 other people are wounded by a 15 year old.

Questions for Class Discussion

1. After reading this chronology, how did you feel? What were you thinking?
2. What do you suppose causes students to commit such acts as these?

3. What precautions, if any, can and should teachers, schools, and communities take to protect themselves and their students from such acts.

SUMMARY

In this chapter, you learned ways to cope with the daily challenges of classroom teaching, guidelines for effectively managing students in the classroom, and some legal rights and responsibilities of students and teachers. Within that framework, your attention was then focused on specific approaches and additional guidelines for effective classroom management and control of the learning environment. You were offered advice for setting up and maintaining a classroom environment that is favorable to student learning, and for establishing procedures for efficiently controlling student behavior and encouraging student learning. To become an accomplished classroom manager takes thoughtful and thorough planning, consistent and confident application, and reflective experience. Be patient with yourself as you accumulate the prerequisite knowledge and practice and hone the necessary skills.

From this knowledge about establishing the most effective learning environment, in the remaining two chapters of this part we guide you through important considerations for selecting the content and planning units of instruction and lessons.

ADDITIONAL EXERCISES

See the companion Website http://www.prenhall.com/kellough for the following exercises related to the content of this chapter:

• An Analysis of What I Know about Legal Guidelines in My State
• Applying Measures of Control
• Reinforcing Positive Student Behavior
• Selecting Measures of Control
• Sending a Positive Word Home

QUESTIONS FOR CLASS DISCUSSION

1. Is it better to be strict with students at first and then relax once your control has been established, or to be relaxed at first and then tighten the reins later if students misbehave, or does it matter? Explain your answer.
2. Some educators argue that good classroom managers are not necessarily good teachers. Do you agree or disagree with that position? Why? Is the reverse true; that is, are good teachers necessarily good classroom managers? Explain why or why not.
3. Explain why it is important to try to prevent behavior problems before they occur. Describe at least five preventive steps you will take to reduce the number of management problems you will have.
4. Explain what you would do if two errant behaviors occurred simultaneously in different locations in your classroom.

5. Explain what you would do if a student from one of your classes came to you and reported that fellow students were harassing him by throwing objects at him, slapping him, pulling his chair out from under him, and pretending to rape him.

6. An historical review of disciplinary practices used in the nation's classrooms shows that corporal punishment has been a consistent and conspicuous part of schooling since the beginning. Many educators are concerned about the increased violence in schools, represented by possession of weapons, harassment, bullying, intimidation, gang or cult activity, arson, and the continued use of corporal punishment of students. They argue that schools are responsible for turning a student's behavior into an opportunity to teach character and self-control. When self-disciplined adults create a problem, they apologize, accept the consequences, make restitution, and learn from their mistakes. We have a responsibility for teaching children to do the same. An important characteristic of exemplary schooling is that of maintaining respect for a student's dignity even when responding to the student's inappropriate behavior. Saturday School may be an acceptable alternative to more harmful disciplinary practices, as well as a step toward developing more internal rather than external student control methods. Are there any such programs in your geographic area? What is your opinion about using corporal punishment at any level of schooling? Organize a class debate on the issue.

7. You have undoubtedly read and heard much about the importance of being consistent in implementing the expected classroom procedures and the consequences for inappropriate behavior. When it comes to procedures and consequences, is there danger in a teacher being too rigid or inflexible? Explain your answer.

8. Select one of the "Reflective Thoughts" from the introduction to Part II (page 84) that is specifically related to the content of this chapter, research it, and write a one-page essay explaining why you agree or disagree with the thought. Share your essay with members of your class for their thoughts.

9. From your current observations and field work relating to this teacher preparation program, clearly identify one specific example of educational practice that seems contradictory to exemplary practice or theory as presented in this chapter. Present your explanation for the discrepancy.

10. Do you have questions generated by the content of this chapter? If you do, list them along with ways answers might be found.

FOR FURTHER READING

Bicard, D. F. "Using Classroom Rules to Construct Behavior." *Middle School Journal* 31(5):37–45 (May 2000).

Bowers, R. S. "A Pedagogy of Success: Meeting the Challenges of Urban Middle Schools." *Clearing House* 73(4):235–238 (March/April 2000).

Cornell, C. "I Hate Math! I Couldn't Learn It, and I Can't Teach It!" *Childhood Education* 75(4):225–230 (Summer 1999).

Curwin, R. L., and Mendler, A. N. *As Tough as Necessary: Countering Aggression, Violence, and Hostility in Schools.* Alexandria,

VA: Association for Supervision and Curriculum Development, 1999.

DiGiulio, R. *Positive Classroom Management,* 2nd ed. Thousand Oaks, CA: Corwin, 2000.

Freiberg, H. J. (Ed.). *Beyond Behaviorism: Changing the Classroom Management Paradigm.* Needham Heights: Allyn & Bacon, 1999.

Gibbs, J. L. "Value-Based Discipline in a Fifth Grade Classroom." *Middle School Journal* 31(5):46–50 (May 2000).

Gibson, B. P., and Govendo, B. L. "Encouraging Constructive Behavior in Middle School Classrooms: A Multiple-Intelligences Approach." *Intervention in School and Clinic* 35(1):16–21 (September 1999).

Gold, J. M.; Rotter, J. C.; Holmes, G. R.; and Motes, P. S. *Middle School Climate: A Study of Attitudes.* Fastback 455. Bloomington, IN: Phi Delta Kappa Educational Foundation, 1999.

Gordon, D. T. "Rising to the Discipline Challenge." *Harvard Education Letter* 15(5):1–4 (September/October 1999).

Hardin, C. J., and Harris, E. A. *Managing Classroom Crises.* Fastback 465. Bloomington, IN: Phi Delta Kappa Educational Foundation, 2000.

Hassenpflug, A. "Courts and Peer Sexual Harassment by Middle School Students." *Middle School Journal* 31(2):49–56 (November 1999).

Holland, H. "Effective Classroom Management Strategies Keep Bad Behavior at Bay." *Middle Ground* 5(1):18–22 (August 2001).

Kalichman, S. C. *Mandated Reporting of Suspected Child Abuse: Ethics, Law, Policy,* 2nd ed. Washington, DC: American Psychological Association, 2000.

Landau, B. M. and Gathercoal, P. "Creating Peaceful Classrooms: Judicious Discipline and Class Meetings." *Phi Delta Kappan* 81(6):450–452, 454 (February 2000).

McEwan, B. *The Art of Classroom Management: Effective Practices for Building Equitable Learning Communities.* Upper Saddle River, NJ: Merrill/Prentice Hall, 2000.

Nissman, B. S. *Teacher-Tested Classroom Management Strategies.* Upper Saddle River, NJ: Merrill/Prentice Hall, 2000.

O'Donnell, R., and White, G. P. "Teaching Realistic Consequences to the Most Angry and Aggressive Students." *Middle School Journal* 32(4):40–45 (March 2001).

Rea, D.; Millican, K. P.; and Watson, S. W. "The Serious Benefits of Fun in the Classroom." *Middle School Journal* 31(4):23–28 (March 2000).

Skiba, R., and Peterson, R. "The Dark Side of Zero Tolerance: Can Punishment Lead to Safe Schools?" *Phi Delta Kappan* 80(5):372–376, 381–382 (January 1999).

Tomal, D. R. *Discipline by Negotiation: Methods for Managing Student Behavior.* Lancaster, PA: Technomic, 1999.

Tomlinson, C. A. *The Differentiated Classroom.* Chapter 4. Alexandria, VA: Association for Supervision and Curriculum Development, 1999.

Urban, V. D. "Eugene's Story: A Case for Caring." *Educational Leadership* 56(6):69–70 (March 1999).

Walters, L. S. "What Makes a Good School Violence Prevention Program?" *The Harvard Education Letter* 15(1):4–5 (January/February 1999).

Wolfgang, C. H.; Bennett, B. J.; and Irvin, J. L. *Strategies for Teaching Self-Discipline in the Middle Grades.* Boston, MA: Allyn and Bacon, 1999.

Curriculum Planning

Effective teaching does not just happen; it is produced through the thoughtful planning of each phase of the learning process. Most effective teachers begin their planning months before meeting their students for the first time. Daily lessons form parts of a larger scheme, which is designed to accomplish the teacher's long-range goals for the semester or year and to mesh with the school's mission and goals standards.

If learning is defined only as the accumulation of bits and pieces of information, then we already know everything about how to teach and how students learn. But the accumulation of pieces of information is at the lowest end of a spectrum of types of learning. Discover-

ies are still being made about the processes involved in higher forms of learning—that is, for meaningful understanding and the reflective use of that understanding. The results of recent research support the use of instructional strategies that help students make connections as they learn. These strategies include discovery learning, inquiry, cooperative learning, interdisciplinary thematic instruction, and project-based learning, with a total curriculum that is integrated and connected to the student's life experiences.

Like the construction of a bridge, meaningful learning is a gradual and sometimes painstakingly slow process. When compared with traditional instruction,

133

teaching in a constructivist mode is slower, involving more discussion and debate, and the re-creation of ideas. Rather than following clearly defined and previously established steps, the curriculum evolves. Such a curriculum depends heavily on materials and, to a great extent, the student's interests and questions determine it.

The methodology uses *hands-on* and *minds-on* learning—that is, the learner is learning by doing and is thinking about what she or he is learning and doing. When thoughtfully coupled, these approaches help construct, and often reconstruct, the learner's perceptions. Hands-on learning engages the learner's mind, causing questioning, and turning a learner's mind on. Hands-on/minds-on learning encourages students to question and then, with the teacher's guidance, to devise ways of investigating satisfactory, although sometimes only tentative, answers to their questions.

As a classroom teacher, your instructional task is twofold: (1) to plan hands-on experiences, providing the materials and the supportive environment necessary for student's meaningful exploration and discovery, and (2) to know how to facilitate the most meaningful and longest lasting learning possible once the learner's mind has been engaged by the hands-on learning. To accomplish this requires your knowledge about varied and developmentally appropriate methods of instruction and your competence in using them. To assist you in the acquisition of that knowledge and competence is the primary purpose of this book.

Competent middle level teaching is a kaleidoscopic, multifaceted, eclectic process. When writing a book to prepare one to teach, authors must separate that kaleidoscopic process into separate topics, which is not always possible to do in a way that makes the most sense to everyone using the book. So, here is our plan and our advice for you. The remaining two chapters in Part II of the book address the instructional planning aspect—first the necessary planning of the curriculum in this chapter and then, in Chapter 6, the detailed instructional planning that is necessary to bring the planned curriculum to fruition. As you proceed through these chapters and begin to develop your instructional plans, from time to time you will want to refer to particular topics in Part III and also to the topic of assessment of student learning in Chapter 11. For now, the rationale for careful planning and the components of that planning are the topics of this chapter.

OBJECTIVES

Upon completion of this chapter, you should be able to

1. Anticipate controversial topics and issues that may arise while teaching and what you might do if and when they do arise.

2. Demonstrate ability to plan the sequence of content for instruction in a particular subject that is typically taught in middle level schools.
3. Demonstrate an understanding of the purpose and process of curriculum integration.
4. Demonstrate an understanding of the rationale for planning for instruction, the levels of planning, and the components of a total instructional plan.
5. Demonstrate knowledge of the value of various types of documents that can be resources for curriculum and instructional planning.
6. Demonstrate understanding of how to help students develop meaningful understandings while still scoring well on mandated standardized achievement tests.
7. Demonstrate understanding of the concept of integrated curriculum, and its relevance to curriculum and instruction.
8. Demonstrate an understanding of the value and limitations of a syllabus, textbook, and other print resources for student learning.
9. Demonstrate understanding of the value of and tools used for the diagnostic and formative assessment of student learning as related to planning for curriculum and instruction.
10. Describe the relationship of instructional planning to the preactive and reflective thought-processing phases of instruction.
11. Differentiate among diagnostic assessment, formative assessment, and summative assessment and explain the place and use of each in instructional planning.
12. Explain both the value and the limitations afforded by using instructional objectives.
13. Explain the difference and the relationship between *hands-on* and *minds-on* learning.
14. Explain the relationship among curriculum standards, instructional objectives, and assessment of student learning.
15. Explain the value of students being empowered with some decision making about course planning.
16. Prepare learning objectives for each of the three domains of learning at various levels within each domain.

PROGRAM ORGANIZATION: PROVIDING SUCCESSFUL TRANSITIONS FOR MIDDLE GRADES CHILDREN

Within the framework of middle level school organization lie several components that form a comprehensive, albeit ever-changing, program. Central to the school's purpose and its organizational structure is the concerted effort to see that all students make successful *transitions* from one level to the next and from one grade to the next. Every aspect of the school program is, in some way, designed to help students make those transitions. Combining to form the program that students experience are **curriculum** and **instruction**. Before going further let us clarify the meaning of each of these frequently encountered terms as they are used in this textbook.

Curriculum and Instruction: Clarification of Terms

Curriculum is defined in various ways. Some define it as the planned subject-matter content and skills to be presented to students. Others say that the curriculum is only that which students actually learn. Still others hold the broad definition that the curriculum is all of the experiences students encounter, whether planned or unplanned, learned or unlearned.

Four programs are identified that contribute in different ways to student learning, that do, in fact, comprise the broadest definition of curriculum: (a) the program of studies (courses offered), (b) the program of student activities (sports, clubs, and organizations), (c) the program of services (transportation, meals, counseling, nurse station), and (d) the hidden curriculum (i.e., the unplanned and subtle message systems within schools as discussed in Chapter 1).

A working definition that adheres to the middle school philosophy is one that considers curriculum as the *entire school program*. Accepting this broad definition of curriculum, the National Middle School Association describes curriculum of developmentally responsive middle level schools as being all that is intentionally designed to accomplish a school's mission. The curriculum embraces every planned aspect of a school's educational program, including the classes that are designed specifically to advance skills and knowledge as well as schoolwide services such as guidance, clubs and interest groups, visual and performing arts productions, student government, and athletic programs.[1]

Instruction, too, has several definitions, some of which are not clearly distinguishable from *curriculum*. Whereas curriculum is usually associated with the what or content of the learning, instruction is associated with the how, or *methods*—that is, with ways of presenting content, conveying information, and facilitating student learning. Obviously, curriculum and instruction must be in tandem to affect student learning.

Curriculum Domains and Their Components

Looking at the total school program (the curriculum) and analyzing its various component parts, or domains, you can readily see the importance of studying curriculum and instruction. In one such study, Hough found that young adolescent student learning experiences are affected by six domains.[2] The six domains and their components are shown in Figure 5.1.

Although the six domains do not address the hidden (unplanned) curriculum, it is understood that various amounts and degrees of unplanned learning occur within each of the domains. In addition, whereas some schools include certain specialty classes as part of the core curriculum, others do not. In other words, any school's philosophy forms the underpinnings for the development of its curriculum. The middle school philosophy asserts that the needs of young adolescents are different from those of other stages of human development and require a curriculum that attends to these needs. Based on this principle, the various parts of middle school curricula can be grouped into three areas that combine all programs, components, and domains into a comprehensive and challenging middle school educational program. The three areas are the core curriculum, exploratories, and co-curricular student activities. A brief review of each of these three areas follows.

Core Curriculum

The core subjects of the curriculum are English/language arts/reading (also referred to as "literacy"), history/ social studies/geography, mathematics, and science. It is within these classes, individually or in some combination, that **interdisciplinary thematic units** (ITUs) are taught. The purpose of teaching subject matter on a central theme is to avoid a departmentalized mentality that all too often communicates the wrong message to students— that learning is piecemeal and separate from one experience to another. On the contrary, the **core curriculum** facilitates the integration of subjects of the thematic units taught in tandem by the core teaching team. Specialty subject teachers, although not usually part of the core,[3] often cooperate with the core team in developing and implementing thematic units.

Exploratory Opportunities

The purpose of exploratory opportunities is to provide a variety of experiences to help students discover areas of interest for future pursuit that will perhaps develop

---

[1] National Middle School Association, *This We Believe: Developmentally Responsive Middle Level Schools* (Columbus, OH: Author, 1995), p. 20.

[2] D. L. Hough, *Middle Level Education in California: A Survey of Programs and Organizations* (Riverside, CA: University of California, Educational Research Cooperative, 1989).

[3] Some writers, including us, believe that the visual and performing arts should be considered core subjects. Unfortunately, current emphasis on high stakes achievement testing, especially in reading, mathematics, and science, will likely put a restraint on any movement to include the arts as core subjects.

Figure 5.1   Middle school curriculum domains and their components.

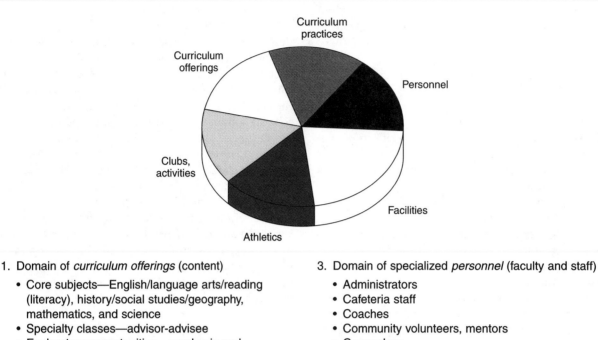

1. Domain of *curriculum offerings* (content)
   - Core subjects—English/language arts/reading (literacy), history/social studies/geography, mathematics, and science
   - Specialty classes—advisor-advisee
   - Exploratory opportunities—academic and nonacademic, graded and nongraded classes, sometimes taught for a shorter period of time by teachers, parents, and community members and designed to provide special opportunities for students to discover learning outside the core and the traditional academic format. Exploratories include foreign languages, intramural sports, health, clubs, student government, home economics, technological arts, independent study projects, music, art, speech, drama, careers, hunter safety, yearbook and newspaper, consumer education, creative writing, computer, captive breeding, film study, calligraphy, and many more.

2. Domain of *curriculum practices* (instruction)
   - Cooperative learning
   - Electives
   - Individual development
   - Interdisciplinary
   - Learning how to learn
   - Mastery learning
   - Mini-classes and experimental projects
   - Mission statement
   - Parental and community involvement
   - Project-centered
   - Service learning (see Chapter 1)

3. Domain of specialized *personnel* (faculty and staff)
   - Administrators
   - Cafeteria staff
   - Coaches
   - Community volunteers, mentors
   - Counselors
   - Custodial and grounds crew staff
   - Hall monitors and security personnel
   - Librarians
   - Nurse and other health specialists
   - Physical education teachers
   - Visual and performing arts teachers

4. Domain of *clubs and activities*
   - Assemblies
   - Cheerleading
   - Clubs
   - Dances and parties
   - School newspaper and yearbook
   - Student government

5. Domain of *athletics*
   - Interscholastic (competitive between schools)
   - Intramural (noncompetitive and open to all students of the school)

6. Domain of *facilities*
   - Auditorium
   - Athletic field
   - Concession stand
   - Grounds
   - Gymnasium
   - Nature area

into a lifelong passion. Allowing young adolescents opportunities to discover and explore unusual topics can spawn or rekindle interests in life and school. Exposing them to a range of academic, vocational, and recreational subjects for career options, community service, enrichment, and enjoyment, exploratories build on the intrinsic curiosity of young adolescents.

Middle schools have devised a variety of approaches to providing exploratory experiences.[4] However, in the

[4]See, for example, the several articles in the section titled "Spotlight on Exploratory Courses," *Middle Ground* 3(5):33–40 (April 2000), and J. S. Renzulli, "Academies of Inquiry and Talent Development," *Middle School Journal* 32(2):5–14 (November 2000).

opinion of the National Middle School Association, the entire curriculum, not just certain courses or activities, should be exploratory in nature, thereby enabling young adolescents to discover their particular abilities, talents, interests, values, and preferences; discover opportunities for making contributions to society; and develop enriching, healthy, leisure-time pursuits.[5] This means, of course, that students should be an integral part of the decision making about course goals and objectives.

Co-Curricular versus Extracurricular

Traditionally, in junior high schools and high schools, student activities involving, for example, clubs and athletics, have been commonly referred to as *extracurricular.* That is because they are considered separate from the academic learning of the regular school day. However, in exemplary middle level education many activities are significant components of the total educational program and are *co-curricular,* rather than extracurricular. *Co-curricular* means that regardless of whether they occur before, during, or after school, or in some combination, the activities are essential to the total curriculum. They are integral to the total school experience and to the needs of young adolescents; they are not simply add-ons or extras. Three co-curricular program components are intramurals, study skills, and advisory.

INTRAMURAL VERSUS INTERSCHOLASTIC SPORTS

The sports program in the exemplary middle level school emphasizes intramural participation rather than interscholastic competition. Some middle level schools try to offer both, but most experts of middle level curricula agree that emphasis on an intramural program is better suited to the needs of all young adolescents.[6] Intramural sports programs are developed to promote participation by all students. The emphasis is on fun, teamwork, socialization, and peer relationships in an unthreatening and relaxed environment. Assessment is based on a student's willingness to cooperate with others and to participate, rather than on the student's skill or performance. Through intramurals, all students can recognize and feel that they are part of a cohesive group, that they are of value as individuals, and that regular physical exercise is more important than skilled performance.

Unfortunately, in recent years there has been a decline in the number of middle level schools implementing intramural sports programs. In place of intramurals, many middle school interscholastic sports programs make every effort to include any student who chooses to participate. The focus, then, is on participation rather than on winning. Sometimes a middle school interscholastic sports committee is appointed, with the responsibility of regulating all competitive sports and designing innovative ways to nurture the "athletic elite" without excluding those students who are less skilled.

STUDY SKILLS

Study skills are integral to the learning process. The young adolescent needs practical application of study skills in all content areas, but can also benefit from an intensive two- to three-week exploratory class. The study skills program should provide each student with an exploratory study skills course, emphasize organizational skills and learning techniques in each core subject, maintain continuous direction and adherence to study skills components throughout the school year, and provide peer or cross-age tutoring or adult mentors where and when appropriate. Study skills are also addressed in the advisory program, demonstrating to students that their homebase teacher is interested in their personal and academic development.

ADVISORY PROGRAM

The advisory (also called *homebase*) program is usually a separate class, comprised ideally of 8 to 12 students, although, in reality, closer to 15 to 25. It meets daily for no less than 20 minutes, without interruptions, at the beginning of the school day. The primary purpose of the advisory program is to ensure adult advocacy for each child, that each child is known well by at least one adult who can give positive and constructive individual attention to that child.[7] In fact, in some middle level schools the homebase teacher remains with the same students throughout their years at that school. All teachers should be expected to participate in the advisory program.

The advisory program should promote a student's feeling of belonging to a group and is not intended to be used for mechanical tasks (although, in reality, it is often a time for announcements, attendance taking, and other maintenance tasks). Before implementation, careful preparation of homebase teachers and parents is necessary. The program is for purposeful individual and small-group activities that deal with students' social relationships, transitioning, health education, and emotional development. The program should be a vehicle for dealing with students' affective needs and for

---

[5] *This We Believe,* 23–24.

[6] See, for example, Chapter 9, "Intramural and Interscholastic Sports," in C. K. McEwin, et al., *America's Middle Schools: A 25 Year Perspective* (Columbus, OH: National Middle Schools Association, 1996.)

[7] *This We Believe,* 16–17.

teaching skills in organization and studying; thinking, problem solving, and decision making; and for ensuring meaningful contacts with parents.[8]

PLANNING FOR INSTRUCTION

As a classroom teacher, planning for instruction is a major part of your job. You will be responsible for planning at three levels—the school year, the units, and the lessons—with critical decisions to be made at each level.

You need not do all your instructional planning from scratch, and you need not do all your planning alone. In many schools, as discussed in Chapter 1, a team of teachers develops the curricula. Teams of teachers collectively plan special programs for their specific cohorts of students. Team members either plan together or split the responsibilities and then share their individual plans. A final plan is then developed collaboratively.

The heart of good planning is good decision making. For every plan at each of the three levels, you and your team must make decisions about the educational goals and learning objectives to be set, the subject to be introduced, the materials and equipment to be used, the methods to be adopted, the assessments to be made, and the tools to be used for those assessments. This decision-making process is complicated because so many options are available at each level. Decisions made at all three levels result in a total plan.

Although the planning process continues term after term, year after year, the task becomes somewhat easier after the first year as you learn to recycle plans. The process is also made easier via research and communication—by reviewing documents and sharing ideas and plans with other teachers.

Teacher-Student Collaborative Team Planning

Exemplary middle level classrooms today tend to be more project-oriented and student- and group-centered than the traditional teacher- and subject-centered classroom of the past, in which the teacher served as the primary provider of information. Although the teacher today is no less a determiner of what is ultimately learned by the children, today's middle level students participate more actively in their learning in collabora-

tion with the teacher.[9] The teacher provides some structure and assistance, but the collaborative approach requires that students inquire and interact, generate ideas, seriously listen and talk with one another, and recognize that their thoughts and experiences are valuable and essential to learning that is most meaningful and longest lasting.

Many exemplary middle level teachers and teaching teams encourage their students to participate in the planning of some phase of their learning. Such participation tends to give students a proprietary interest in the activities, to satisfy the developmental need to explore knowledge, and to give them a sense of ownership of their learning, thereby increasing their motivation for learning. What students have contributed to the plan often seems more meaningful to them than what others have planned for them. And students like to see their own plans succeed. Thus, teacher-student collaboration in planning can be an effective motivational tool.

Reasons for Planning

Planning is done for a number of reasons, perhaps foremost of which is to ensure *curriculum coherence*, that is to ensure that what is supposed to be taught is, in fact, taught. Periodic lesson plans are an integral part of a larger plan, represented by school- and district-wide mission statements and target goals, and by grade level and course goals and objectives. Students' learning experiences are thoughtfully planned in sequence and then orchestrated by teachers who understand the rationale for their respective positions in the curriculum. Such plans do not preclude, of course, an occasional diversion from predetermined activities.

Another reason for planning is, as discussed in Chapter 2, to assure that the curriculum is developmentally appropriate for the education of young adolescents, that is to give considerations to students' experiential backgrounds, developmental needs, learning capacities and styles, reading abilities, and special needs. Without careful planning, it would be impossible for any teacher to personalize the instruction, and to adequately attend to the students' needs and differences.

Planning is necessary to ensure efficient and effective teaching with a minimum of classroom-control problems. After deciding *what* to teach, you face the important task of deciding *how* to teach it. To efficiently use precious instructional time, planning should be accomplished with two goals in mind: to not waste anyone's time during the time allotted for instruction, and to select strategies that

[8]See, for example: J. P. Galassi, et al., "Planning and Maintaining Sound Advisory Programs," *Middle School Journal* 28(5):35–41 (May 1997); D. F. Brown, "The Value of Advisory Sessions: Perceptions of Young Adolescents at an Urban Middle School," *Research in Middle Level Education Quarterly* 22(4):41–58 (Summer 1999); and S. MacLaury, "Teaching Prevention by Infusing Health Education into Advisory Programs," *Middle School Journal* 31(5):51–56 (May 2000).

[9]See, for example, the many examples in J. Weasmer and A. M. Woods, "Shifting Classroom Ownership to Students," *Middle School Journal* 32(2):15–20 (November 2000).

most effectively promote the anticipated student learning. As emphasized throughout this resource guide, a large portion of the instruction will be via student-centered indirect instruction, but not exclusive of direct instruction. (See, for example, the discussion "Degrees of Directness" in Chapter 6.)

Planning helps ensure program continuation. The program must continue even if you are absent and a substitute teacher is needed. Planning provides a criterion for reflective practice and self-assessment. After a learning activity and at the end of a school term, you can reflect on and assess what was done and how it affected student learning. Planning provides a means to evaluate your teaching. Your plans represent a criterion recognized and evaluated by supervisors and administrators.

From the preceding you realize there are many reasons a teacher must plan and must do it carefully. With those experienced in such matters, it is clear that inadequate planning is usually a precursor to incompetent teaching. Put simply, failing to plan is planning to fail.

Components of an Instructional Plan

A total instructional plan has six major components, described as follows.

Rationale component. This is a statement about why the content of the plan is important and about how students will learn it. The statement should be consistent with the school's mission statement and with the school district's benchmark standards.

Goals and objectives (standards) component. The goals and objectives represent the learning targets, that is, the knowledge, skills, and attitudes to be gained from the study. The plan's learning targets should be consistent with the rationale statement.

Articulation component. The articulation component shows the plan's relationship to the learning that preceded it and the learning and experiences that will follow. This is referred to as *vertical articulation*. The plan should also indicate its *horizontal articulation*, which is its connectedness with other learning and activities that are occurring simultaneously across grade level. Writing, reading, thinking skills development, and character education are examples. Vertical and horizontal articulation are usually represented in curriculum documents and programs by scope and sequence charting.

Learning activities component. This is the presentation of organized and sequential units and lessons appropriate for the subject or grade level, and for the age and diversity of the learners.

Resources component. This is a listing of anticipated resources needed, such as print and electronic resources, realia, guest speakers, and field trips.

Assessment component. This is the appraisal of student learning, which occurs (a) before the start of the instruction with a diagnostic or preassessment of what students already know or think they know about the topic, (b) during the instruction to find out if students are learning what is intended (formative assessment), and (c) at the end of the instruction to determine to what extent the students actually did learn (summative assessment).

Planning the Scope of the Curriculum: Documents That Provide Guidance

Whether for a semester or a school year or some other period of time, when planning the scope of the curriculum you should decide what is to be accomplished in that period of time. To help in setting goals, you should examine school and other resource documents for mandates and guidelines; communicate with colleagues to learn of common expectations; and probe, analyze, and translate your own convictions, knowledge, and skills into behaviors that foster the intellectual and psychological, and in some instances the physical, development of your students.

With the guidance of Exercises 5.1–5.3, you will examine major documents that help guide you in selecting the content of your curriculum. These are national and state curriculum standards, school or district benchmark standards, curriculum frameworks and courses of study, and school-adopted materials. Sources for your examination of these documents include the Internet (see Figure 5.2), your college or university library, and personnel at local schools.

Figure 5.2   Internet resources on national and state curriculum standards and frameworks.

General and multiple disciplines

- http://www.mcrel.org
- http://www.enc.org/reform/fworks/index.htm

Discipline-specific national standards

- Economics http://www.ncee.org
- English/reading http://www.ncte.org
- Mathematics http://www.nctm.org
- Physical education http://www.aahperd.org
- Science http://www.nsta.org
- Social studies http://www.ncss.org
- Theatre http://www.byu.edu/tma/arts-ed
- Technology http://www.iteawww.org
- Visual and performing arts http://www.amc-music.com

Standards state by state, discipline by discipline

- http://www.statestandards.com

CURRICULUM STANDARDS

What are curriculum standards? **Curriculum standards** are a definition of what students should know (content) and be able to do (process and performance). At the national level, curriculum standards did not exist until they were developed and released for mathematics education by the National Council of Teachers of Mathematics in 1989 (revised in 2000). Shortly after the release of the mathematics standards, support for national goals in education was endorsed by the National Governors Association, and the National Council on Education Standards and Testing. They recommended that in addition to those for mathematics, national standards for subject matter content in K–12 education be developed for the arts, civics/social studies, English/language arts/reading, geography, history, and science. The U.S. Department of Education provided initial funding for the development of national standards. In 1994 the U.S. Congress passed the *Goals 2000: Educate America Act,* which was amended in 1996 with an Appropriations Act that encouraged states to set curriculum standards. Long before, however, as was done for mathematics, national organizations devoted to various disciplines, were already defining standards.

What are the *national standards?* The national standards represent the best thinking by expert panels, including teachers from the field, about what the essential elements are of a basic subject knowledge that all K–12 students should acquire. They serve not as national mandates but rather as voluntary guidelines to encourage curriculum development that promotes higher student achievement. It is at the discretion of state and local curriculum developers to decide the extent to which the standards are used.

Strongly influenced by the national standards, nearly all 50 states have completed state standards for the various disciplines. For example, standards for the state of Massachusetts are found in seven Curriculum Frameworks: Arts, English/Language Arts, Health, Mathematics, Science and Technology, Social Studies, and World Languages. For the state of Montana, Content and Performance Standards are found in documents for Reading, Mathematics, Speaking and Listening, Media Literacy, Writing, Literature, Health Enhancement, Science, Technology, World Languages, Arts, Library Media, Social Studies, and Work Place Competencies. The North Carolina Standard Course of Study presents curriculum in Arts Education, Computer/ Technology Skills, English/Language Arts, Healthful Living, Mathematics, Science, Second-Language Studies, Social Studies, and Work-Force Development (which includes sections on Planning, The Middle Grades, Agricultural Education, Business Education, Family and Consumer Sciences, Health Occupations, Marketing Education, Career De-

velopment, Technical Education, and Trade and Industrial Education). For the state of Texas, the Texas Essential Knowledge and Skills (TEKS) are in the foundations areas of English Language Arts and Reading, Mathematics, Science, Social Studies, and Spanish Language Arts and English as a Second Language, and in the enrichment areas of Languages Other Than English, Fine Arts, Health, Physical Education, and Technology Applications (which includes Agricultural Science and Technology, Business Education, Health Science Technologies, Home Economics Education, Technology Education/Industrial Technology Education, Marketing Education, Trade and Industrial Education, and Career Orientation).

Both national and state standards, accessible on the Internet (see Figure 5.2), provide guidance to the developers of the standardized tests used in what is referred to today as high stakes testing, that is, the tests being used at various grade levels to determine student achievement, promotion, rewards to schools and even to individual teachers, and in an increasing number of states as a requirement for graduation from high school.

National Curriculum Standards by Content Area

The following paragraphs describe K–12 national standards development for content areas relevant to the middle grades curriculum. (In 1999, the American Psychological Association [APA] released national standards for what students should be taught in high school psychology courses.)

Arts (visual and performing). Developed jointly by the American Alliance for Theater and Education, the National Art Education Association, the National Dance Association, and the Music Educators National Conference, the *National Standards for Arts Education* were completed and released in 1994.

Economics. Developed by the National Council on Economic Education, standards for the study of economics were completed and released in 1997.

English/language arts/reading. Developed jointly by the International Reading Association, the National Council of Teachers of English, and the University of Illinois Center for the Study of Reading, standards for English education were completed and released in 1996.

Foreign languages. Standards for Foreign Language Learning: Preparing for the 21st Century was completed and released by the American Council on the Teaching of Foreign Languages (ACTFL) in 1996.[10]

---

[10]Contact ACTFL, Six Executive Plaza, Yonkers, NY 10701-6801.

Geography. Developed jointly by the Association of American Geographers, the National Council for Geographic Education, and the National Geographic Society, standards for geography education were completed and released in 1994.[11]

Health. Developed by the Joint Committee for National School Health Education Standards, *National Health Education Standards: Achieving Health Literacy* was published in 1995.[12]

History/civics/social studies. The Center for Civic Education and the National Center for Social Studies developed standards for civics and government, and the National Center for History in the Schools developed the standards for history, all of which were completed and released in 1994.

Mathematics. In 1989, the National Council of Teachers of Mathematics (NCTM) completed and released *Curriculum and Evaluation Standards for School Mathematics.* Revised standards were developed and released in 2000. See the NCTM mathematics site in Figure 5.2.

Physical education. In 1995, the National Association of Sport and Physical Education (NASPE) published *Moving Into the Future: National Standards for Physical Education.*

Science. In 1995, with input from the American Association for the Advancement of Science and the National Science Teachers Association, the National Research Council's National Committee on Science Education Standards and Assessment published the standards for science education.

Technology. With initial funding from the National Science Foundation and the National Aeronautics and Space Administration, and in collaboration with the International Technology Education Association, National Educational Technology Standards (NETS) were released in 2000.

Supplements to the national standards are available from the Bureau of Indian Affairs for the arts (dance, music, theater, and visual), civics and government, geography, health, language arts, mathematics, science, and social studies.[13] The *American Indian Supplements* may be used by Indian nations as guides in their preparation of tribally specific local standards. They are also useful to school districts serving American Indian children in adapting state standards to be more culturally relevant to their communities.

Proceed now to Exercises 5.1, 5.2, 5.3, and 5.4, through which you will explore national, state, and local curriculum documents.

---

[11]Contact National Geographic Society, PO Box 1640, Washington, DC 20013-1640.

[12]Contact the American Alliance for Health, Physical Education, Recreation and Dance (AAHPERD), 1900 Association Drive, Reston, VA 22091.

[13]Bureau of Indian Affairs, 1849 C St, NW, Washington, DC 20240-0001. Phone 202-208-3710; http://www.doi.gov/bureau-indian-affairs.html.

FOR YOUR NOTES

EXERCISE 5.1: EXAMINING NATIONAL CURRICULUM STANDARDS

INSTRUCTIONS: The purpose of this exercise is to become familiar with national curriculum standards for the subject(s) that you intend to teach. Using the addresses provided in the preceding section of the text and the Internet sites in Figure 5.2, review the standards that interest you. Use the following questions as a guideline for subject-area small group discussions. Following the small group discussion, share the big ideas about the standards and perceptions of your group with the rest of your class.

Subject area _____

1. Name of the standards documents reviewed, year of publication, and development agency for each document.

2. What are the major educational goals as specified by the national standards?

3. Are the standards specific as to subject-matter content for each level of schooling, K–12? Explain.

4. Do the standards offer specific strategies for instruction? Describe.

5. Do the standards offer suggestions for teaching students who are culturally different, for students with special needs, and for students who are intellectually gifted and talented? Describe.

6. Do the standards offer suggestions or guidelines for dealing with controversial topics and issues?

7. Do the standards documents or their accompanying materials offer suggestions for specific resources? Describe.

☞

EXERCISE 5.1 (*continued*)

8. Do the standards refer to assessment? Describe.

9. Do the standards documents make any reference to what and how the subject has been traditionally taught in the United States? Describe.

10. Is there anything else about the standards you would like to discuss and present?

EXERCISE 5.2: EXAMINING STATE CURRICULUM STANDARDS

INSTRUCTIONS: The purpose of this exercise is to become familiar with your state's curriculum standards for the subject(s) that you intend to teach. Using the addresses provided in the preceding section of the text and the Internet sites in Figure 5.2, review the standards that interest you. Use the following questions as a guideline for subject-area small group discussions. Following the small group discussion, share the big ideas about the standards and perceptions of your group with the rest of your class.

Subject area _____

1. Name of the standards documents reviewed, year of publication, and development agency for each document.

2. What are the major educational goals as specified by the state standards?

3. Are the standards specific as to subject-matter content for each level of schooling, K–12? Explain.

4. Do the standards offer specific strategies for instruction? Describe.

5. Do the standards offer suggestions for teaching students who are culturally different, for students with special needs, and for students who are intellectually gifted and talented? Describe.

6. Do the standards offer suggestions or guidelines for dealing with controversial topics or issues?

☞

EXERCISE 5.2 (*continued*)

7. Do the standards documents or their accompanying materials offer suggestions for specific resources? Describe.

8. Do the standards refer to assessment? Describe.

9. Do the standards documents make any reference to what and how the subject has been traditionally taught? Describe.

10. Is there anything else about the standards you would like to discuss and present?

EXERCISE 5.3: EXAMINING STATE CURRICULUM FRAMEWORKS

INSTRUCTIONS: The purpose of this exercise is to become familiar with curriculum documents published by your state department of education. You must determine if that department publishes a curriculum framework for various subjects taught in schools. State frameworks provide valuable information about both content and process, and teachers need to be aware of these documents. You may want to duplicate this form so you can use it to evaluate several documents. After examining documents that interest you, use the following questions as a guideline for small- or large-group class discussions.

1. Are there state curriculum documents available and relevant to middle school teachers for your state? If so, describe them and explain how they can be obtained.

   Title of document:

   Source:

   Most recent year of publication:

   Other pertinent information:

2. Examine how closely the document follows the components presented in this chapter. Are any components omitted? Are there additional components? Specifically, check for these components:

	Yes	*No*
a. Rationale?	_____	_____
b. Goals, and objectives?	_____	_____
c. Schemes for vertical articulation?	_____	_____
d. Schemes for horizontal articulation?	_____	_____
e. Recommended instructional procedures?	_____	_____
f. Recommended resources?	_____	_____
g. Assessment strategies?	_____	_____

   Other:

3. Are the documents specific as to subject-matter content for each grade level? Describe evidence of both vertical and horizontal articulation schemes.

4. Do the documents offer specific strategies for instruction? If yes, describe.

EXERCISE 5.3 (*continued*)

5. Do the documents offer suggestions and resources for working with students who are culturally different, for students with special needs, and for students who are intellectually gifted and talented? Describe.

6. Do the documents offer suggestions or guidelines for dealing with controversial topics? If so, describe.

7. Do the documents distinguish between what shall be taught (mandated) and what can be taught (permissible)?

8. Do the documents offer suggestions for specific resources?

9. Do the documents refer to assessment strategies? Describe.

10. Is there anything else about the documents you would like to discuss in your group?

EXERCISE 5.4: EXAMINING LOCAL CURRICULUM DOCUMENTS

INSTRUCTIONS: The purpose of this exercise is to become familiar with curriculum documents prepared by local school districts. A primary resource for what to teach is referred to as a *curriculum guide,* or *course of study,* which normally is developed by teachers in a school or district. Samples may be available in your university library or in a local school district resource center. Or perhaps you could borrow them from teachers you visit. Obtain samples from a variety of sources and then examine them using the format of this exercise. (You may duplicate this form for each document examined.) An analysis of several documents will give you a good picture of expectations. If possible, compare documents from several school districts and states.

Title of document: _____

District or school: _____

Date of document: _____

1. Does the document contain the following?

	Yes	*No*
a. Statement of rationale?	_____	_____
b. Goals and objectives?	_____	_____
c. Schemes for vertical articulation?	_____	_____
d. Schemes for horizontal articulation?	_____	_____
e. Recommended instructional procedures?	_____	_____
f. Recommended resources?	_____	_____
g. Assessment strategies?	_____	_____

2. Does the document list expected learning outcomes? If so, describe what they are. _____

_____

_____

_____

3. Does the document contain detailed unit plans? If so, describe them by answering the following questions:

   a. Are the units interdisciplinary? _____

   b. Do they contain initiating activities (how to begin a unit)? _____

   c. Do they contain specific learning activities? _____

   d. Do they contain suggested enrichment activities (as for gifted and talented students)? _____

   e. Do they contain culminating activities (activities that bring a unit to an end)? _____

   f. Do they contain assessment procedures (for determining student achievement)? _____

   g. Do they contain activities for learners with special needs? or for learners who are different in other

   respects? _____

EXERCISE 5.4 (*continued*)

4. Does it provide bibliographic entries for

   • The teacher? _____

   _____

   _____

   _____

   _____

   • The students? _____

   _____

   _____

   _____

   _____

5. Does it list audiovisual, media, and other materials needed? _____

   _____

   _____

   _____

   _____

   _____

   _____

6. Does the document clearly help you understand what the teacher is expected to teach? _____

   _____

   _____

   _____

   _____

   _____

7. Are there questions not answered by your examination of this document? If so, list them for class discussion.

   _____

   _____

   _____

   _____

   _____

   _____

STUDENT TEXTBOOKS

For several reasons—the recognition of the diversity of learning styles, capacities, and modalities of students; changing concepts about literacy and habits of thought; enhanced graphics capabilities; economic pressures in the publishing industry; and the availability of electronic and other nonprinted materials—textbook appearance, content, and use has changed considerably in recent years and in all likelihood will continue to change.

Within the span of your teaching career, you will likely witness and even be a part of a revolution in the continuing redesign of school textbooks. Already some schools allow teachers in certain disciplines the option of choosing between traditional printed textbooks and interactive computer programs. With the continuing developments in electronics and microcomputer chip technology, textbooks may take on a whole new appearance. With that will come dramatic changes in the importance and use of text, as well as new problems for the teacher, some that are predictable, others that we cannot even imagine. On the positive side, it is probable that the classroom teacher will have available a variety of "textbooks" to better address the reading levels, interests, abilities, and perhaps even the primary language of individual students. Because of these changes, the distribution and maintenance of reading materials could create a greater demand on the teacher's time. Regardless, dramatic and exciting events have begun to affect the teaching tool that had not changed much throughout the twentieth century. The textbook of the twenty-first century may become a palm-size, handheld, multimedia, interactive, and personal tool that encompasses digitized text, sound, and video and allows for global communications.

Still, today, it may be that printed textbooks regulate as much as 90% of all learning activity in the classroom. School districts periodically adopt new textbooks, usually every five to eight years. If you are a student teacher or a first-year teacher, this will most likely mean that someone will tell you, "Here are the textbooks you will be using."

Benefit of Student Textbooks to Student Learning

It is unlikely that anyone could rationally argue that textbooks are of no benefit to student learning. Text-books can provide (a) an organization of basic or important content for the students, (b) a basis for deciding content emphasis, (c) previously tested activities and suggestions for learning, (d) information about other readings and resources to enhance student learning, and (e) a foundation for building higher-order thinking activities (e.g., inquiry discussions and student research) that help develop critical thinking skills. The textbook, however, should not be the "be all and end all" of the instructional experiences.

Problems with Reliance on a Single Textbook

The student textbook is only one of many teaching tools, and not the ultimate word. Of the many ways that you can use textbooks for student learning, the *least* acceptable is to show a complete dependence on a single book and require students simply to memorize material from it. This is the lowest level of textbook use and learning; furthermore, it implies that you are unaware of other significant resources and have nothing more to contribute to student learning.

Another potential problem brought about by reliance on a single textbook is that, because textbook publishers prepare books for national or statewide use—a state- and district-adopted book may not adequately address issues of special interest and importance to the community in which you teach. That is one reason why some teachers and schools provide supplementary printed and nonprinted resources.

Still another problem brought about by reliance upon a single source is that the adopted textbook may not be at the appropriate reading level for many students. In today's heterogeneous classrooms, the level of student reading can vary by as much as two-thirds of the chronological age of the students. This means that if the chronological age is 12 years (typical for seventh-graders), then the reading-level range would be 8 years—that is, the class may have some students reading at only the pre-school level, if at all, while others have college-level reading ability.

Examine student textbooks and teacher's editions of those books by doing Exercise 5.5.

FOR YOUR NOTES

EXERCISE 5.5: EXAMINING STUDENT TEXTBOOKS AND TEACHERS' EDITIONS

INSTRUCTIONS: The purpose of this exercise is to become familiar with textbooks that you may be using in your teaching. Student textbooks are usually accompanied by a teacher's edition that contains specific objectives, teaching techniques, learning activities, assessment instruments, test items, and suggested resources. Your university library, local schools, and cooperating teachers are sources for locating and borrowing these enhanced textbooks. For your subject field of interest, select a textbook that is accompanied by a teacher's edition and examine the contents of both, using the following format. If there are no standard textbooks available for your teaching field (such as might be the case for art, music, and physical education), then select a field in which there is a possibility you might teach. Beginning teachers are often assigned to teach in more than one field—sometimes, unfortunately, in fields for which they are untrained or have only minimal training. After completion of this exercise, share the book and your analysis of it with your colleagues.

Title of book: _____

Author(s): _____

Publisher: _____

Date of most recent publication: _____

	Yes	*No*
1. Analyze the teacher's edition for the following elements:		
a. Are its goals consistent with the goals of local and state curriculum documents?	_____	_____
b. Are there specific objectives for each lesson?	_____	_____
c. Does the book have scope and sequence charts for teacher reference?	_____	_____
d. Are the units and lessons sequentially developed, with suggested time allotments?	_____	_____
e. Are there any suggested provisions for individual differences?	_____	_____
for reading levels?	_____	_____
for students with special needs?	_____	_____
for students who are gifted and talented?	_____	_____
for students who have limited proficiency in English?	_____	_____
f. Does it recommend specific techniques and strategies?	_____	_____
g. Does it have listings of suggested aids, materials, and resources?	_____	_____
h. Are there suggestions for extension activities (to extend the lessons beyond the usual topic or time)?	_____	_____
i. Does the book have specific guidelines for assessment of student learning?	_____	_____
2. Analyze the student textbook for the following elements:		
a. Does it treat the content with adequate depth?	_____	_____
b. Does it treat ethnic minorities and women fairly?*	_____	_____
c. Is the format attractive?	_____	_____
d. Does the book have good quality binding with suitable type size?	_____	_____

☞

EXERCISE 5.5 (*continued*)

	Yes	No
e. Are illustrations and visuals attractive and useful?	_____	_____
f. Is the reading clear and understandable for the students?	_____	_____

3. Would you like to use this textbook? Give reasons why or why not.

_____

_____

_____

_____

_____

_____

_____

_____

_____

_____

_____

_____

_____

_____

_____

_____

_____

_____

_____

_____

_____

_____

_____

_____

_____

* For a detailed procedure that is more specific to subject areas, see Carl A. Grant and Cristine E. Sleeter, *Turning on Learning: Five Approaches for Multicultural Teaching Plans for Race, Class, Gender, and Disability* (Upper Saddle River, NJ: Prentice Hall, 1989), 104–109.

Guidelines for Textbook Use

Generally speaking, students benefit by having their own copies of textbooks in the current edition. However, because of budget constraints, this may not always be possible. The book may be outdated; quantities may be limited. When the latter is the case, students may not be allowed to take the books home or perhaps may only occasionally do so. In some high-poverty area schools in particular, students are not allowed to take textbooks from the classroom at all because of the replacement costs of books. In other classrooms, because of inadequate funding, there may be no textbooks at all.

Encourage students to respect books by covering and protecting them and not marking in them. In many schools this is a rule; at the end of the term, students who have damaged or lost their books are charged a fee. As a matter of fact, this is why in some high-poverty area schools books are not issued at all. If their students lose or damage their books and are charged a fee, the fee goes unpaid because neither the students nor their parents/guardians can afford to pay it.

Yet, in the classrooms of some school districts, there are *two* sets of the textbooks, one set that remains for use in the classroom and another set that is assigned to students to keep at home to use for home studying. With that arrangement, students do not have to carry heavy books around in their backpacks for the many subjects taught in today's middle schools. The paragraphs that follow offer general guidelines for using the textbook as a learning tool.

Progressing through a textbook from the front cover to the back in one school term is not necessarily an indicator of good teaching. The textbook is one resource; to enhance their learning, students should be encouraged to use a variety of resources. Encourage students to search additional sources to update the content of the textbook. This is especially important in certain disciplines such as the sciences and social sciences, where the amount of new information is growing rapidly and students may have textbooks that are several years old. The library and sources on the Internet should be researched by students for the latest information on certain subjects, always keeping in mind, however, that just because something is found in print or on the Net does not mean that the information is accurate or even true. Maintain supplementary reading materials for student use in the classroom. School and community librarians and resource specialists usually are delighted to cooperate with teachers in the selection and provision of such resources.

Individualize the learning for students of various reading abilities. Consider differentiated reading and workbook assignments in the textbook and several supplementary sources (see multitext and multireadings approaches, which follow). Except to make life simpler for the teacher, there is no advantage to having all students working out of the same book and doing the same exercises. Some students benefit from the drill, practice, and reinforcement afforded by workbooks or software programs that accompany textbooks, but this is not true for all students, nor do all benefit from the same activity. In fact, the traditional printed workbook may eventually become extinct, as it is replaced by the modern technology afforded by electronic software. Computers and other interactive media provide students with a psychologically safer learning environment in which they have greater control over the pace of the instruction, can repeat instruction if necessary, and can ask for clarification without the fear of having to do so publicly.

Teachers have invented several methods to help students develop their higher-level thinking skills and their comprehension of expository material. Some of these methods are shown in Figure 5.3.

Encourage students to be alert for errors in the textbook, both in content and printing—perhaps giving them some sort of credit reward, such as points, when they bring an error to your attention. This helps students develop the skills of critical reading, critical thinking, and healthy skepticism. For example, a history book is reported to have stated that the first person to lead a group through the length of the Grand Canyon was John Wesley Powell. Critically thinking students were quick to make the point that perhaps Powell was only the first white person to do this, that Native Americans had traveled the length of the Grand Canyon for centuries.[14]

Multitext and Multireadings Approach

Rather than a single textbook approach, consider using a strategy that incorporates many readings that vary in difficulty, detail, and vocabulary but that have a common focus. This multiple reading source strategy gives students a choice in what they read. Especially useful for interdisciplinary thematic instruction, the strategy also allows for differences in reading ability and interest level, and stimulates the sharing of what is being read and learned. By using a teacher's guide, such as the sample in Figure 5.4, all the students can be directed toward specific information and concepts, but they do not have to all read the same selections.

---

[14]R. Reinhold, "Class Struggle," *The New York Times Magazine,* September 29, 1991, p. 46.

Figure 5.3 Methods for helping students develop their higher-level thinking skills and their comprehension of expository material.[15]

- **KWL:** Students recall what they already know (K) about a topic, determine what (W) they want to learn, and later assess what they have learned (L).
- **KWLQ:** Students record what they already know (K) about a topic, formulate questions about what (W) they want to learn about the topic, search for answers to their questions to learn (L), and ask questions (Q) for further study.
- **POSSE:** *Predict* ideas, *organize* ideas, *search* for structure, *summarize* main ideas, and *evaluate* understanding.
- **PQRST:** *Preview, question, read, state* the main idea, and *test* yourself by answering the questions you posed earlier.
- **RAP:** *Read* paragraphs, *ask* questions about what was read, and *put* it in your own words.
- **Reciprocal teaching:** Students are taught and practice the reading skills of summarizing, questioning, clarifying, and predicting.
- **SQ3R:** *Survey* the chapter, ask *questions* about what was read, *read, recite,* and *review.*
- **SQ4R:** *Survey* the chapter, ask *questions* about what was read, *read* to answer the questions, *recite* the answers, *record* important items from the chapter into their notebooks, then *review* it all.
- **SRQ2R:** *Survey, read, question, recite,* and *review.*

BEGINNING TO THINK ABOUT THE SEQUENCING OF CONTENT

As you have reviewed the rationale and components of instructional planning, and have examined national and state curriculum standards, state and local curriculum documents, and student reading materials, you have undoubtedly reflected on your own opinion regarding content that should be included in a subject at a particular grade level. Now it is time to obtain some practical experience in long-range planning.

While some authors believe that the first step in preparing to teach is to prepare the objectives, others believe that a more logical starting point is to prepare a sequential topic outline—the next step in this chapter—from which you can then prepare the major target objectives (Chapter 6). With today's pressure on teachers to work from established and mandated benchmark standards (target objectives) it may well be that many teachers today do, in fact, begin their curriculum development from those objectives.

Regardless of the approach used, experts agree that the curriculum plan should (a) be organized around important ideas, concepts, and questions, all of which should correlate with mandated content standards, (b) reflect the interests and concerns of young adolescents, and (c) be oriented toward the assessments and tasks that will be used for students in demonstrating what they have learned.[16]

The curriculum plans, topic outlines, and instructional objectives may be presented to most beginning teachers with the expectation that they will teach from them. For you this may be the case, but someone had to write those outlines and objectives and that someone was a classroom teacher or more than one. As a new teacher, you must know how this is done; someday it will be your task. To experience preparing a full semester content outline for a subject and grade level that you intend to teach, do Exercise 5.6 now.

---

[15]Source of KWL: D. M. Ogle, "K-W-L: A Teaching Model That Develops Active Reading of Expository Text," *Reading Teacher* 39(6):564–570 (February 1986). Source of POSSE: C. S. Englert and T. V. Mariage, "Making Students Partners in the Comprehension Process: Organizing the Reading 'POSSE'," *Learning Disability Quarterly* 14(1):23–138 (September 1991). Source of PQRST: E. B. Kelly, *Memory Enhancement for Educators,* Fastback 365 (Bloomington, IN: Phi Delta Kappa Educational Foundation, 1994), p. 18. Source of RAP: J. B. Schumaker, et al, *The Paraphrasing Strategy* (Lawrence, KS: Edge Enterprises, 1984). Source of SQ3R: F. P. Robinson, *Effective Study* (rev. ed.), New York: Harper & Brothers, 1961). The original source of SQ4R is unknown. For SRQ2R, see M. L. Walker, "Help for the 'Fourth-Grade Slum'—SRQ2R Plus Instruction in Text Structure or Main Idea," *Reading Horizons* 36(1):38–58 (1995). About reciprocal teaching, see C. J. Carter, "Why Reciprocal Teaching?" *Educational Leadership* 54(6):64–68 (March 1997); and T. L. Good and J. E. Brophy, *Looking in Classrooms,* 8th ed. (New York: Addison Wesley Longman, 2000), pp. 431–433.

[16]G. A. Davis and A. W. Jackson, "Turning Points a Decade Later," *Middle Ground* 4(2):10–13, 15–16 (October 2000), p. 11.

Figure 5.4   Sample multiple readings guide and student's book bibliography to assist
students in multiple readings about America's Revolutionary times in 1776.

- Purpose: To engage students in multiple readings, critical thinking, and problem solving related to America's Revolutionary times in 1776.
- Activities:

1. By reading and browsing through several books and by carefully observing several illustrations of people in this particular time period and geographic area, the students can engage in critical thinking and problem solving by working in small groups. The bibliography that follows includes books related to America in 1776 that are suitable for a wide range of reading levels. Students can respond to the following focus questions after multitext reading:
   a. What features of the land (features of government, society, etc.) seem to be important to the people in 1776?
   b. What occupations seem to be most important? What inventions (tools, machines) appear to be most useful?
   c. What do the answers to these questions tell us about the way of life of the people who lived in this time period (geographic area)?
2. Back with the whole group, have the students from each group report on the responses to the questions. Engage students in dictating or writing a paragraph summarizing the responses to the questions.
3. Students can meet with response partners to read their individually written paragraphs aloud to one another and provide suggestions to each other for rewriting the paragraphs.

- Bibliography [*Note:* the bibliography shown here is not intended to be inclusive, only to show how a multiple readings guide might appear]:

African American

Davis, B. *Black Heroes of the American Revolution.* (San Diego: Harcourt J, 1976). Nonfictional account depicting contributions of African Americans during the Revolutionary War. Includes drawings, etchings, bibliography, and an index.

Hansen, J. *The Captive.* (New York: Scholastic, 1994). Based on a journal written in the late 1700s, this is about Kofi, the 12-year-old son of an Ashanti chief. Kofi is sold and sent to America after a family slave murders his father. Kofi and others escape from the farmer in Massachusetts and return to Africa. An epilogue relates his good life when he returned to Africa.

Millender, D. H. *Crispus Attucks: Black Leader of Colonial Patriots.* (New York: Macmillan, 1986). Biographical portrayal of the life of a Colonial African American and his contribution to the American Revolution.

European

Wade, M. D. *Benedict Arnold.* (New York: Franklin Watts, 1995). Biographical story of Arnold's life; his heroic deeds, including his leadership at the battle of Saratoga; his later traitorous actions; and his death in London. Includes information about his wife, Peggy Shippen.

Female Image

DePaul, L. G. *Founding Mothers: Women in America in the Revolutionary Era.* (Boston: Houghton Mifflin, 1975). Nonfictional account of the contributions of women during the revolution.

McGovern, A. *Secret Soldier: The Story of Deborah Sampson.* (New York: Scholastic, 1991). Story of a young woman who disguised herself as a boy and joined the army to serve in America's War for Independence.

Latino/Hispanic

Anderson, J. *Spanish Pioneers of the Southwest.* Illustrated by G. Ancona. (New York: Dutton, 1989). Nonfictional account of the lives of the colonists on the east coast contrasted with the lives of the members of a pioneer family in a Spanish community in New Mexico in the 1700s and the family's hard work, harsh living conditions, and traditions.

Native American

Hudson, J. *Dawn Rider.* (New York: Putnam, 1990). Fictional account of 16-year-old Kit Fox, a Blackfoot, forbidden to ride horses. She disobeys and her riding skills help her people when their camp is attacked.

Kinsey-Warock, N. *Wilderness Cat.* Illustrated by Mark Graham. (Minneapolis: Cobblehill, 1992). Lives of colonists are contrasted with the lives of Serena's family members when they moved to Canada in the 1700s. Even though the family trades with the Indians, they do not have enough to eat; Papa and Serena's brother leave to find work. Historical fiction.

Religious Minority

Faber, D. *The Perfect Life: The Shakers in America.* (New York: Farrar, Straus, & Givoux, 1974). Escaping from England, Mother Ann and several followers voyage to America and set up the first settlement in New York in 1776. Nonfictional account detailing the Shaker influence on furniture construction, mechanical inventions, and their religious beliefs.

FOR YOUR NOTES

EXERCISE 5.6: PREPARING A FULL SEMESTER CONTENT OUTLINE

INSTRUCTIONS: The purpose of this exercise is for you to organize your ideas about subject content and the sequencing of content for one semester. Unless instructed otherwise by your instructor, you should select the subject (e.g., algebra, science, English/language arts) and the grade level (5–8).

With *three levels of headings* (see the example that follows), prepare a sequential topic outline (on a separate piece of paper, as space is not provided here) for a subject and grade level you intend to teach. Identify the subject by title, and clearly state the grade level. This is an outline of topic content only and does *not* need to include student activities associated with learning that content (i.e., do not include experiments, assignments, or assessment strategies).

For example, for the study of earth science, three levels of headings might include

I. The earth's surface

    A. Violent changes in earth's surface

        1. Earthquakes

        2. Volcanoes

    B. Earth's land surface

        1. Rocks
          etc.

If the study of earth science is just one unit for a grade level's study of the broader area of "science," then three levels of headings for that study might include

I. Earth science

    A. The earth's surface

        1. Violent changes in earth's surface
          etc.

Share your completed outline to obtain feedback from your colleagues and university instructor. Because content outlines are never to be "carved in stone," make adjustments to your outline when and as appropriate.

CONTENT OUTLINE ASSESSMENT CHECKLIST

For the development of your own outline and the assessment of outlines by others, following is a content outline assessment checklist:

- Does the outline align with relevant curriculum standards? Yes _____ No _____

  Comment: _____

  _____

- Does the outline follow a logical sequence, with each topic logically leading to the next? Yes _____

  No _____ Comment: _____

  _____

- Does the content assume prerequisite knowledge or skills that the students are likely to have? Yes _____

  No _____ Comment: _____

  _____

- Is the content inclusive, and to an appropriate depth? Yes _____ No _____ Comment: _____

☞

EXERCISE 5.6 (*continued*)

- Does the content consider individual student differences? Yes _____ No _____ Comment: _____

  _____

- Does the content allow for interdisciplinary studies? Yes _____ No _____ Comment: _____

  _____

- Is the outline complete? Yes _____ No _____ Are there serious content omissions? Yes _____
  No _____ Comment: _____

  _____

- Is there content that is of questionable value for this level of instruction? Yes _____ No _____
  Comment: _____

Save your content outline and this completed exercise for later when you are working on Exercise 5.12 and Exercises 6.4 and 6.5 in Chapter 6.

PREPARING FOR AND DEALING WITH CONTROVERSY

Controversial content and issues abound in most disciplines in teaching. For example, in English, over the use of certain books—see Exercise 5.7B; in mathematics, over the use of calculators;[17] in social studies, over values and moral issues; in science, over biological evolution. As a general rule, if you have concern that a particular topic or activity might create controversy, it probably will. During your teaching career, you undoubtedly will have to make decisions about how you will handle such matters. When selecting content that might be controversial, consider the paragraphs that follow as guidelines.

Maintain a perspective regarding your own goal, which is at the moment to obtain your teaching credential, and then a teaching job, and then tenure. Student teaching, in particular, is not a good time to become involved in controversy. If you communicate closely with your cooperating teacher and your college or university supervisor, you should be able to prevent major problems dealing with controversial issues.

Sometimes, during normal discussion in the classroom, a controversial subject will emerge spontaneously, catching the teacher off guard. If this happens, think before saying anything. You may wish to postpone further discussion until you have a chance to talk over the issue with members of your teaching team or your supervisors. Controversial topics can seem to arise from nowhere for any teacher, and this is perfectly normal. Your young adolescent students are in the process of developing their moral and value systems, and they need and want to know how adults feel about issues that are important to them, particularly those adults they hold in esteem—their teachers. Young adolescents need to discuss issues that are important to society, and there is absolutely nothing wrong with dealing with those issues as long as certain guidelines are followed.

First, students should learn about all sides of an issue. Controversial issues are open-ended and should be treated as such. They do not have "right" answers or "correct" solutions. If they did, there would be no controversy. (As used in this book, an "issue" differs from a "problem" in that a problem generally has a solution, whereas an issue has many opinions and several alternative solutions.) Therefore, the focus should be on process as well as on content. A major goal is to show students how to deal with controversy and to mediate wise decisions on the basis of carefully considered information. Another goal is to help students learn how to disagree without being disagreeable—how to resolve conflict. To that end students need to learn the difference between conflicts that are destructive and those that can be constructive, in other words, to see that conflict (disagreement) can be healthy, and that it can have value. Yet another goal, of course, is to help students learn about the content of an issue so, when necessary, they can make decisions based on knowledge, not on ignorance.

Second, as with all lesson plans, dealing with a topic that could lead to controversy should be well thought out ahead of time. Potential problem areas and resources must be carefully considered and prepared for in advance. Problems for the teacher are most likely to occur when the plan has not been well thought out.

Third, at some point all persons directly involved in an issue have a right to input: students, parents and guardians, community representatives, and other faculty. This does not mean, for example, that people outside of the school have the right to censor a teacher's plan, but it does mean that parents or guardians and students should have the right *sans penalty* to not participate and to select an alternate activity. Most school districts have written policies that deal with challenges to instructional materials. As a beginning teacher, you should become aware of the policies of your school district. In addition, professional associations such as the NCTE, NCSS, NBTA, and NSTA have published guidelines for dealing with controversial topics, materials, and issues.

Fourth, there is nothing wrong with students knowing a teacher's opinion about an issue as long as it is clear that the students may disagree without reprisal or academic penalty. However, it is probably best for a teacher to wait and give her or his opinion only after the students have had full opportunity to study and report on facts and opinions from other sources. Sometimes it is helpful if you assist students in separating facts from opinions on a particular issue being studied by setting up on the overhead or writing board a fact-opinion table. See Figure 5.5, with the issue stated at the top and then two parallel columns, one for facts, the other for related opinions.

Figure 5.5 Fact/opinion table.

Issue: _____	
FACTS	OPINIONS

[17]See, for example, M. E. Schmidt, "Middle Grades Teachers' Beliefs about Calculator Use: Pre-project and Two Years Later," *Focus on Learning Problems in Mathematics* 21(1):18–34 (Winter 1999).

A characteristic that has made this nation so great is the freedom for all its people to speak out on issues. This freedom should not be excluded from public school classrooms. Teachers and students should be encouraged to express their opinions about the great issues of today, to study the issues, to suspend judgment while collecting data, and then to form and accept each other's reasoned opinions. We must understand the difference between teaching truth, values, and morals, and teaching *about* truth, values, and morals.

As a public school teacher, there are limits to your academic freedom, much greater than are the limits, for example, on a university professor. You must understand this fact. The primary difference is that the students with whom you will be working are not yet adults; because they are juveniles they must be protected from dogma and allowed the freedom to learn and to develop their values and opinions, free from coercion by those who have power and control over their learning.

Now that you have read our opinion and suggested guidelines, what do you think about this topic, which should be important to you as a teacher? Use Exercises 5.7A and 5.7B for the development and expression of your opinion.

EXERCISE 5.7A: DEALING WITH CONTROVERSIAL CONTENT AND ISSUES

INSTRUCTIONS: The purpose of this exercise is for you to discover controversial content and issues that you may face as a teacher and to consider what you can and will do about them. After completing this exercise, share it with members of your class.

1. After studying current periodicals and talking with colleagues in the schools you visit, list two potentially controversial topics that you are likely to encounter as a teacher. (Two examples are given for you.)

Issue	*Source*
Racial or ethnic profiling	*New York Times, March 11, 2001*
Human cloning	*New York Times, August 22, 2001*

2. Take one of these issues, and identify opposing arguments and current resources. _____

    _____

    _____

    _____

    _____

    _____

3. Identify your own positions on this issue. _____

    _____

    _____

    _____

    _____

    _____

4. How well can you accept students (and parents or guardians) who assume the opposite position? _____

    _____

    _____

    _____

    _____

5. Share the preceding with other teacher candidates. Note comments that you find helpful or enlightening.

    _____

    _____

    _____

    _____

    _____

EXERCISE 5.7B: CENSORSHIP: BOOKS THAT ARE SOMETIMES CHALLENGED

INSTRUCTIONS: Continuing with the topic introduced in Exercise 5.7A, this exercise concentrates on certain books that, although frequently used in public schools, are sometimes challenged by members of some communities. Book censorship becomes a concern when literature is the base for integrated teaching since there may be attempts to censor and ban books and curricular materials in the schools. Books that have been challenged include the following:

A Light in the Attic (Shel Silverstein)
Adventures of Huckleberry Finn, The (Mark Twain)
Annie on My Mind (Nancy Garden)
Are You There, God? It's Me, Margaret (Judy Blume)
Arizona Kid, The (Ron Koertge)
Blubber (Judy Blume)
Bridge to Terabithia (Katherine Paterson)
Catcher in the Rye, The (J. D. Salinger)
Chocolate War, The (Robert Cormier)
Christine (Stephen King)
Color Purple, The (Alice Walker)
Fallen Angels (Walter Dean Myer)
Flowers for Algernon (Daniel Keyes)
Flowers in the Attic (V. C. Andrews)
Forever (Judy Blume)
Giver, The (Lois Lowry)

Go Ask Alice (Anonymous)
Handmaids's Tale, The (Margaret Atwood)
I Know Why the Caged Bird Sings (Maya Angelou)
Kaffir Boy: The True Story of a Black Youth's Coming of Age in Apartheid South Africa (Mark Mathabane)
Lord of the Flies (William Golding)
My Brother Sam is Dead (James Lincoln Collier and Christopher Collier)
Of Mice and Men (John Steinbeck)
Outsiders, The (S. E. Hinton)
Running Loose (Chris Crutcher)
Scary Stories to Tell in the Dark (Alvin Schwartz)
Slaughterhouse-Five (Kurt Vonnegut)
To Kill a Mockingbird (Harper Lee)
Witches, The (Roald Dahl)

We leave the organization of this exercise for your class to decide; we recommend that you assign small groups to review certain books, then report to the entire class so that all the books on the list are addressed.

AIMS, GOALS, AND OBJECTIVES: THE ANTICIPATED LEARNING OUTCOME

Now that you have learned of the components of the middle level school organization, have examined content typical of the curriculum, have experienced preparing a tentative content outline for a subject that you intend to teach, and understand some important guidelines for dealing with controversial topics, you are ready to write instructional objectives for that content learning.

Instructional objectives are statements describing what the student will be able to do upon completion of the planned learning experience. Whereas historically some authors distinguish between *instructional objectives* (referring to objectives that are *not* behavior specific) and **behavioral** or **performance objectives** (objectives that *are* behavior specific), the terms are used here as if they are synonymous to emphasize the importance of writing instructional objectives in terms that are measurable. *Terminal objective* is sometimes used to distinguish between instructional objectives that are intermediate and those that are final, or "terminal" to an area of learning.

As a teacher, you frequently will encounter *goals and objectives*, as you likely found in the curriculum documents that you reviewed (Exercises 5.1–5.4). A distinction needs to be made and understood. The easiest way to understand the difference between the two words, *goals* and *objectives*, is to look at your *intent*.

Goals are ideals that you intend to reach, that is, ideals that you would like to accomplish. Goals may be stated as **teacher goals,** as student goals, or, collaboratively, as team goals. Ideally, in all three, the goal is the same. If, for example, the goal is to improve students' reading skills, it could be stated as follows:

"To help students develop   *Teacher or*
their reading skills"   *course goal*

    or

"To improve my reading   *Student goal*
skills"

Educational goals are general statements of intent and are prepared early in course planning. [*Note:* Some writers use the phrase "general goals and objectives," but that is incorrect usage. Goals *are* general; objectives are specific.] Goals are useful when planned cooperatively with students and/or when shared with students as advance mental organizers to establish a mind-set. The students then know what to expect and will begin to prepare mentally to learn it. From the goals, objectives are prepared. Objectives are *not* intentions. They are the actual behaviors that students are expected to display. In short, objectives are what students *do*.

The most general educational objectives are often called *aims;* the objectives of schools, curricula, and courses are called *goals;* the objectives of units and lessons are called *instructional objectives*. Aims are more general than goals, goals are more general than objectives. Instructional objectives are quite specific. Aims, goals, and objectives represent the targets, from general to specific statements of learning expectations, to which curriculum is designed and instruction is aimed.

Instructional Objectives and Their Relationship to Aligned Curriculum and Authentic Assessment

As implied in the preceding paragraphs, goals guide the instructional methods; objectives drive student performance. Assessment of student achievement in learning should be an assessment of that performance. When the assessment procedure does match the instructional objectives, that is sometimes referred to as assessment that is *aligned* or *authentic* (discussed in Chapter 11). (If the term *authentic assessment* sounds rather silly to you, we concur. After all, if the objectives and assessment do not match, then that particular assessment should be discarded or modified until it does match. In other words, assessment that is not authentic is poor assessment and should not be used.) When objectives, instruction, and assessment match the stated goals we have what is referred to as an *aligned curriculum*. (Again, a curriculum that does not align is nonsensical and should be corrected or discarded.)

Goals are general statements, usually not even complete sentences and often beginning with the infinitive "to," that identify what the teacher intends the students to learn. Objectives, stated in performance terms, are specific actions and should be written as complete sentences that include the verb "will" *to indicate what each student is expected to be able to do as a result of the instructional experience*. This is emphasized because, when writing instructional objectives for their unit and lesson plans, one of the most common errors made by beginning teachers is to state what *they*, the teachers, intend to do rather than what the anticipated student performance is. The value of stating learning objectives in terms of student performance is well documented by research.[18]

While instructional goals may not always be quantifiable (that is, readily measurable), instructional objectives should be measurable. Furthermore, those objectives then become the essence of what is measured for in instruments designed to assess student learning; they are the learning targets. Consider the examples shown in Figure 5.6.

LEARNING TARGETS AND GOAL INDICATORS

One purpose for writing objectives in performance terms is to be able to assess with precision whether the instruction has resulted in the desired behavior. In many

---

[18]See, for example, J. C. Baker and F. G. Martin, *A Neural Network Guide to Teaching*, Fastback 431 (Bloomington, IN: Phi Delta Kappa Educational Foundation, 1998, and T. L. Good and J. E. Brophy, *Looking in Classrooms*, 8th ed. (New York: Addison Wesley Longman, 2000), p. 252–253.

Figure 5.6 Examples of goals and objectives.

Goals

1. To acquire knowledge about the physical geography of North America.
2. To develop an appreciation for music.
3. To develop enjoyment for reading.

Objectives

1. On a map, the student will identify specific mountain ranges of North America.
2. The student will identify 10 different musical instruments by listening to a tape recording of the Boston Pops Symphony Orchestra and identify which instrument is being played at specified times as determined by the teacher.
3. The student will read two books, three short stories, and five newspaper articles at home, within a two-month period. The student will maintain a daily written log of these activities.

schools the educational goals are established as *learning targets*, competencies that the students are expected to achieve that were derived from the district and state curriculum standards. These goals or learning targets are then divided into performance objectives, sometimes referred to as *goal indicators*. Instruction is designed to teach toward those objectives. When students perform the competencies called for by these objectives, their education is considered successful. As discussed further in Chapters 8 and 11, this is known variously as *criterion-referenced, competency-based, performance-based, results-driven,* or *outcome-based education*. Expecting students to achieve one set of competencies before moving on to the next set is called **mastery learning** (discussed further in Chapter 8). The success of the student achievement, the teacher performance, and the school may each be assessed according to these criteria.

OVERT AND COVERT PERFORMANCE OUTCOMES

Assessment is not difficult to accomplish when the desired performance outcome is *overt behavior*, which can be observed directly. Each of the sample objectives of the preceding section is an example of an overt objective. Assessment is more difficult to accomplish for *covert behavior*, that is, when it is not directly observable. Although certainly no less important, behaviors that call for "appreciation," "discovery," or "understanding," for example, are not directly observable because they occur within a person, and so are covert behaviors. Since covert behavior cannot be observed directly, the only way to tell whether the objective has been achieved is to observe behavior that may be indicative of that achievement. The objective, then, is written in overt language, and evaluators can only assume or trust that the ob-

served behavior is, in fact, reasonably close to being indicative of the expected learning outcome.

Furthermore, when assessing whether an objective has been achieved—that learning has occurred—the assessment device must be consistent with the desired learning outcome. Otherwise, the assessment is not aligned; it is invalid. When the measuring device and the learning objective are compatible, we say that the assessment is authentic. For example, a person's competency to teach specific skills in physical education to middle school students is best measured (i.e., with highest reliability) by directly observing that person *doing* that very thing—teaching specific skills in physical education to middle school students. Using a standardized paper-and-pencil test of multiple-choice items to determine a person's ability to teach specific physical education skills to middle school students is *not* authentic assessment.

Balance of Behaviorism and Constructivism

While behaviorists (behaviorism) assume a definition of learning that deals only with changes in overt behavior, constructivists hold that learning entails the construction or reshaping of mental schemata and that mental processes mediate learning. Thus, people who adhere to constructivism or cognitivism are concerned with both overt and covert behaviors.[19] Does this mean that you must be one or the other, a behaviorist or a constructivist? Probably not. For now, the point is that when writing instructional objectives, you should write most or all of your basic expectations (minimal competency expectations) in overt terms (the topic of the next section). On the other hand, you cannot be expected to foresee all learning that occurs nor to translate all that is learned into performance terms—most certainly not before it occurs.

Teaching toward Multiple Objectives, Understandings, and Appreciations: The Reality of Classroom Instruction

Any effort to write all learning objectives in performance terms is, in effect, to neglect the individual learner for whom it purports to be concerned; such an approach does not allow for diversity among learners. Learning that is most meaningful to young adolescents is not so neatly or easily predicted or isolated. Rather than teaching one objective at a time, much of the time you should direct your teaching toward the simultaneous learning of multiple objectives, understandings, and appreciations. However, when you assess for learning, assessment

[19]See, for example, the many articles in "The Constructivist Classroom," the November 1999 theme issue of *Educational Leadership*, Volume 57, number 3; D. R. Geelan, "Epistemological Anarchy and the Many Forms of Constructivism," *Science and Education* 6(1–2):15–28 (January 1997); and R. DeLay, "Forming Knowledge: Constructivist Learning and Experiential Education," *Journal of Experiential Education* 19(2):76–81 (August/September 1996).

is cleaner when objectives are assessed one at a time. More on this matter of objectives and their use in teaching and learning follows later in this chapter. We will now review how objectives are prepared.

PREPARING INSTRUCTIONAL OBJECTIVES

When preparing instructional objectives, you must ask yourself, "How is the student to demonstrate that the objective has been reached?" The objective must include an action that demonstrates that the objective has been achieved. Inherited from behaviorism, this portion of the objective is sometimes called the *anticipated measurable performance.*

Components

When completely written in performance terms, an instructional objective has four components, although in practice you are unlikely to use all four. To aid your understanding and as a mnemonic for remembering, you can refer to these components as the ABCDs of writing objectives.

One component is the *audience.* The *A* of the ABCDs refers to the student for whom the objective is intended. To address this, sometimes teachers begin their objectives with the phrase "The student will be able to . . ." or, to personalize the objective, "You will be able to. . . ." [*Note:* To conserve space and to eliminate useless language, in the examples that follow we eliminate the use of "be able to,"

Figure 5.7 Verbs to avoid when writing overt objectives.

appreciate	enjoy	indicate	like
believe	familiarize	know	realize
comprehend	grasp	learn	understand

and write simply "The student will. . . ." As a matter of fact, we prefer eliminating the use of "be able to" and simply use "will." For brevity, writers of objectives sometimes use the abbreviation "TSWBAT . . ." for "The student will be able to . . ." or more simply "TSW . . ." for "The student will. . . ."]

The second component is the expected *behavior,* the *B* of the ABCDs. It is this second component that represents the learning target. The expected behavior (or performance) should be written with verbs that are measurable—that is, with action verbs—so that it is directly observable that the objective, or target, has been reached. As discussed in the preceding section, some verbs are too vague, ambiguous, and not clearly measurable. When writing overt objectives, you should avoid verbs that are not clearly measurable, covert verbs such as "appreciate," "comprehend," and "understand." (See Figure 5.7.) For the three examples given in Figure 5.6, for Objectives 1 and 2 the behaviors (action or overt verbs) are "will *identify,*" and, for Objective 3, the behaviors are "will *read* and *maintain.*"

Now do Exercise 5.8 to assess and further your understanding.

EXERCISE 5.8: RECOGNIZING VERBS THAT ARE ACCEPTABLE FOR OVERT OBJECTIVES—A SELF-CHECK EXERCISE

INSTRUCTIONS: The purpose of this exercise is to check your recognition of verbs that are suitable for use in overt objectives. In the list of verbs below, circle those that *should not* be used in overt objectives—that is, those verbs that describe covert behaviors that are not directly observable and measurable. Check your answers against the answer key that follows. Discuss any problems with the exercise with your classmates and instructor.

1. apply
2. appreciate
3. believe
4. combine
5. comprehend
6. compute
7. create
8. define
9. demonstrate
10. describe

11. design
12. diagram
13. enjoy
14. explain
15. familiarize
16. grasp*
17. identify
18. illustrate
19. indicate
20. infer

21. know
22. learn
23. name
24. outline
25. predict
26. realize
27. select
28. solve
29. state
30. understand

Answer Key for Exercise 5.8: The following verbs should be circled: 2, 3, 5, 13, 15, 16, 21, 22, 26, 30. If you missed more than a couple, then you need to read the previous sections again and discuss your errors with your classmates and instructor.

*Note: words in English often have more than one meaning. For example, *grasp* as listed here could mean *to take hold,* or it could mean *to comprehend.* For the former it would be an acceptable verb for use in overt objectives; for the latter it would not.

Most of the time, for reasons to be explained, when writing objectives for your unit and lesson plans, you will not bother yourself with including the next two components. However, as you will learn, they are important for assessment.

The third component is the *conditions*, the *C* of the ABCDs, the setting in which the behavior will be demonstrated by the student and observed by the teacher. Conditions are forever changing; although the learning target should be clearly recognizable long before the actual instruction occurs, the conditions may not be. Thus, conditions are not often included in the objectives that teachers write. For the first sample objective in Figure 5.6, the conditions are "on a map." For the second sample objective, the conditions are "by listening to a tape recording of the Boston Pops Symphony Orchestra" and "specified times as determined by the teacher." For the third sample, for "the student will read . . ." the conditions are "at home within a two-month period."

The fourth component that, again, is not always included in objectives written by teachers, is the *degree (or level) of expected performance*—the *D* of the ABCDs. This is the ingredient that allows for the assessment of student learning. When mastery learning is expected, the level of expected performance is usually omitted (because it is understood). In teaching for mastery learning, the performance-level expectation is 100%. In reality, however, the performance level will most likely be 85 to 95 percent, particularly when working with a group of students, rather than an individual student. The 5 to 15 percent difference allows for human error, as can occur when using written and oral communication. Like conditions, the level of performance will vary depending on the situation and purpose and, therefore, is not normally included in the unit and lessons that teachers prepare. Now, to reinforce your comprehension, do Exercise 5.9.

EXERCISE 5.9: RECOGNIZING THE PARTS OF CRITERION-REFERENCED INSTRUCTIONAL OBJECTIVES—A SELF-CHECK EXERCISE

INSTRUCTIONS: The purpose of this exercise is to practice your skill in recognizing the four components of an instructional objective. In the following two objectives, identify the parts of the objectives by underlining

once the *audience,*

twice the *performance (behavior),*

three times the *conditions,* and

four times the *performance level* (that is, the degree or standard of performance).

Check your answers against the answer key that follows, and discuss any problems with this exercise with your classmates and instructor.

1. Given a metropolitan transit bus schedule, at the end of the lesson the student will be able to read the schedule well enough to determine at what times buses are scheduled to leave randomly selected locations, with at least 90 percent accuracy.
2. Given five rectangular figures, you will correctly compute the area in square centimeters of at least four, by measuring the length and width with a ruler and computing the product using an appropriate calculation method.

Answer Key for Exercise 5.9:

	Objective 1	*Objective 2*
Audience	the student	you
Behavior	will be able to read the schedule	will compute
Conditions	given a metropolitan transit bus schedule	given five rectangular figures
Performance level	well enough to determine (and) with at least 90 percent accuracy	correctly compute the area in square centimeters of at least four (80 percent accuracy)

Performance level is used to assess student achievement, and sometimes to evaluate the effectiveness of the teaching. Student grades might be based on performance levels; evaluation of teacher effectiveness might be based on the level of student performance. Indeed, with today's use of state-mandated standardized testing (see Chapter 11) schools are evaluated on the basis of student performance on those tests.

Now try your skill at recognizing student learning objectives that are measurable in Exercise 5.10

EXERCISE 5.10: RECOGNIZING OBJECTIVES THAT ARE MEASURABLE— A SELF-CHECK EXERCISE

INSTRUCTIONS: The purpose of this exercise is to assess your ability to recognize objectives that are measurable. Place an *X* before each of the following that is an overt, student-centered behavioral objective, that is, a learning objective that is clearly measurable. Although "audience," "conditions," or "performance levels" may be absent, ask yourself, "As stated, is this a student-centered and measurable objective?" If it is, place an *X* in the blank. A self-checking answer key follows. After checking your answers, discuss any problems you had with the exercise with your classmates and instructor.

_____   1. To develop an appreciation for literature.

_____   2. To identify those celestial bodies that are known as planets.

_____   3. To provide meaningful experiences for the students.

_____   4. To recognize antonym pairs.

_____   5. To convert Celsius temperatures to Fahrenheit.

_____   6. To analyze and compare patterns of data or specific quartile maps.

_____   7. To develop skills in inquiry.

_____   8. To identify which of the four causes is most relevant to the major events leading up to the Civil War.

_____   9. To use maps and graphs to identify the major areas of world petroleum production and consumption.

_____ 10. To know the causes for the diminishing ozone concentration.

Answer Key for Exercise 5.10:

You should have marked items 2, 4, 5, 6, 8, and 9.

Items 1, 3, 7, and 10 are inadequate because of their ambiguity. Item 3 is not even a student learning objective; it is a teacher goal. "To develop" and "to know" can have too many interpretations. Although the conditions are not given, items 2, 4, 5, 6, 8, and 9 are clearly measurable. The teacher would have no difficulty recognizing when a learner had reached those objectives. Discuss any problem you had with this exercise with your classmates and instructor.

Classifying Instructional Objectives

When planning instructional objectives, it is useful to consider the three domains of learning objectives:

Cognitive domain—involves intellectual operations from the lowest level of the simple recall of information to complex, high-level thinking processes.

Affective domain—involves feelings, emotions, attitudes, and values, and ranges from the lower levels of acquisition to the highest level of internalization and action.

Psychomotor domain—ranges from the simple manipulation of materials to the communication of ideas, and finally to the highest level of creative performance.

The Domains of Learning and the Developmental Needs of Young Adolescents

Educators attempt to design learning experiences to meet the five areas of developmental needs of the young adolescent that were discussed in Chapter 2: intellectual, physical, emotional/psychological, social, and moral/ethical. As a teacher, you must include objectives that address learning within each of these categories of needs. While the intellectual needs are primarily within the cognitive domain and the physical are within the psychomotor, the other needs mostly are within the affective domain.

Too frequently, teachers focus on the cognitive domain while assuming that the psychomotor and affective will take care of themselves. With the renewed national focus on standardized achievement testing, this may become even more the case. Many experts argue, however, that teachers should do just the opposite; that when the affective is directly attended to, the psychomotor and cognitive naturally develop. There is little doubt that, as stated by Linda Hopping, executive director of the Georgia Middle School Association, "if the social and emotional needs of children this age are ignored, little happens cognitively."[20] Whether the domains are attended to separately or simultaneously, you should plan your teaching so your students are guided from the lowest to the highest levels of operation within each of the domains.

The three developmental hierarchies are discussed next to guide your understanding of each of the five areas of needs. Notice the illustrative verbs within each hierarchy. These verbs help you fashion objectives when you are developing unit plans and lesson plans. (To see how goals and objectives are fit into one lesson plan, see Figure 6.10,

Figure 5.8 Sometimes the same action verb may be used appropriately in objectives at different cognitive levels.

> The student will identify the correct definition of the term *osmosis.* (knowledge)
>
> The student will identify examples of the principle of osmosis. (comprehension)
>
> The student will identify the osmotic effect when a cell is immersed into a hypotonic solution. (application)
>
> The student will identify the osmotic effect on turgor pressure when the cell is placed in a hypotonic solution. (analysis)

"Multiple-day, project-centered, interdisciplinary and transcultural lesson using world-wide communication via the Internet.") However, caution must be urged, for there can be considerable overlap among the levels at which some action verbs may appropriately be used. For example, as shown in Figure 5.8, the verb "identify" is appropriate in each of the four objectives at different levels (identified in parentheses) within the cognitive domain.

Cognitive Domain Hierarchy

In a widely accepted taxonomy of objectives, Bloom and his associates arranged cognitive objectives into classifications according to the complexity of the skills and abilities they embodied.[21] The result was a ladder ranging from the simplest to the most complex intellectual processes. Within each domain, prerequisite to a student's ability to function at one particular level of the hierarchy is the ability to function at the preceding level or levels. In other words, when a student is functioning at the third level of the cognitive domain, that student is automatically also functioning at the first and second levels. Rather than an orderly progression from simple to complex mental operations, as illustrated by Bloom's taxonomy, other researchers prefer an organization of cognitive abilities that ranges from simple information storage and retrieval, through a higher level of discrimination and concept attainment, to the highest cognitive ability to recognize and solve problems.[22]

The six major categories (or levels) in Bloom's taxonomy of cognitive objectives are (a) *knowledge*—recognizing and recalling information; (b) *comprehension*—understanding the meaning of information; (c) *application*—

[20]L. Hopping, "Multi-Age Teaming: A Real-Life Approach to the Middle School," *Phi Delta Kappan* 82(4):270–272, 292 (December 2000), p. 271.

[21]B. S. Bloom (Ed.). *Taxonomy of Educational Objectives, Book 1, Cognitive Domain* (White Plains, NY: Longman, 1984).

[22]See R. M. Gagné; L. J. Briggs; and W. W. Wager, *Principles of Instructional Design,* 4th ed. (New York: Holt, Rinehart and Winston, 1994).

using information; (d) *analysis*—dissecting information into its component parts to comprehend their relationships; (e) *synthesis*—putting components together to generate new ideas; and (f) *evaluation*—judging the worth of an idea, notion, theory, thesis, proposition, information, or opinion. In this taxonomy, the top four categories or levels—application, analysis, synthesis, and evaluation—represent what are called *higher-order cognitive thinking skills.*[23]

While space does not allow elaboration here, Bloom's taxonomy includes various subcategories within each of these six major categories. It is probably less important that an objective be absolutely classified than it is to be cognizant of hierarchies of thinking and doing and to understand the importance of attending to student intellectual behavior from lower to higher levels of operation in all three domains. Discussion of each of Bloom's six categories follows.

KNOWLEDGE

The basic element in Bloom's taxonomy concerns the acquisition of knowledge—that is, the ability to recognize and recall information. (As discussed in Chapter 8, this is similar to the *input level* of thinking and questioning.) Although this is the lowest of the six categories, the information to be learned may not be of a low level. In fact, it may be of an extremely high level. Bloom includes knowledge of principles, generalizations, theories, structures, and methodology, as well as knowledge of facts and ways of dealing with facts.

Action verbs appropriate for this category include *choose, complete, cite, define, describe, identify, indicate, label, list, locate, match, name, outline, recall, recognize, select,* and *state.*

The following are examples of objectives at the knowledge level. Note especially the verb (in italics) used in each example:

- From memory, the student *will recall* the letters in the English alphabet that are vowels.
- The student *will list* the organelles found in animal cell cytoplasm.

The remaining five categories of Bloom's taxonomy of the cognitive domain deal with the *use* of knowledge. They encompass the educational objectives aimed at developing cognitive skills and abilities, including comprehension, application, analysis, synthesis, and evaluation of

knowledge. As stated earlier, the last four—application, analysis, synthesis, and evaluation—are referred to as *higher-order thinking skills,* as are the higher categories of the affective and psychomotor domains.

COMPREHENSION

Comprehension includes the ability to translate, explain, or interpret knowledge and to extrapolate from it to address new situations. Action verbs appropriate for this category include *change, classify, convert, defend, describe, discuss, distinguish, estimate, expand, explain, generalize, give example, infer, interpret, paraphrase, predict, recognize, retell, summarize,* and *translate.* Examples of objectives in this category are

- From a sentence, the student *will recognize* the letters that are vowels in the English alphabet.
- The student *will describe* each of the organelles found in animal cell cytoplasm.

APPLICATION

Once learners understand information, they should be able to apply it. Action verbs in this category of operation include *apply, calculate, compute, demonstrate, develop, discover, exhibit, manipulate, modify, operate, participate, perform, plan, predict, relate, show, simulate, solve,* and *use.* Examples of objectives in this category are

- The student *will use* in a sentence a word that contains at least two vowels.
- The student *will predict* the organelles found in plant cell cytoplasm.

ANALYSIS

This category includes objectives that require learners to use the skills of analysis. Action verbs appropriate for this category include *analyze, arrange, break down, categorize, classify, compare, contrast, debate, deduce, diagram, differentiate, discover, discriminate, group, identify, illustrate, infer, inquire, organize, outline, relate, separate,* and *subdivide.* Examples of objectives in this category include

- From a list of words, the student *will differentiate* those that contain vowels from those that do not.
- Under the microscope, the student *will identify* the organelles found in animal cell cytoplasm.

SYNTHESIS

This category includes objectives that involve such skills as designing a plan, proposing a set of operations, and deriving a series of abstract relations. Action verbs appropriate for this category include *arrange, assemble, categorize, classify, combine, compile, compose, constitute, create, design, develop, devise, document, explain, formulate, generate, hypothesize, imagine, invent, modify, organize, originate, plan, predict, produce, rearrange, reconstruct, revise, rewrite,*

---

[23]Compare Bloom's higher-order cognitive thinking skills with R. H. Ennis's, "A Taxonomy of Critical Thinking Dispositions and Abilities," and E. Quellmalz's "Developing Reasoning Skills," both in J. B. Barron and R. J. Sternberg (Eds.), *Teaching Thinking Skills: Theory and Practice* (New York: W. H. Freeman, 1987), and with Marzano's "Complex Thinking Strategies" in R. J. Marzano, *A Different Kind of Classroom: Teaching with Dimensions of Learning* (Alexandria, VA: Association for Supervision and Curriculum Development, 1992).

summarize, synthesize, tell, transmit, and *write.* Examples of objectives in this category are

- From a list of words, the student *will rearrange* them into several lists according to the vowels contained in each.
- The student *will devise* a classification scheme of the organelles found in animal cell and plant cell cytoplasm according to their functions.

EVALUATION

This, the highest category of Bloom's cognitive taxonomy, includes offering opinions and making value judgments. Action verbs appropriate for this category include *appraise, argue, assess, choose, compare, conclude, consider, contrast, criticize, decide, describe, discriminate, estimate, evaluate, explain, interpret, judge, justify, predict, rank, rate, recommend, relate, revise, standardize, summarize, support,* and *validate.* Examples of objectives in this category are

- The student *will listen to and evaluate* other students' identifications of vowels from sentences written on the board.
- While observing living cytoplasm under the microscope, the student *will justify* his or her interpretation that certain structures are specific organelles of a plant or animal cell.

Affective Domain Hierarchy

Krathwohl, Bloom, and Masia developed a useful taxonomy of the affective domain.[24] The following are their major levels (or categories), from least internalized to most internalized: (a) *receiving*—being aware of the affective stimulus and beginning to have favorable feelings toward it; (b) *responding*—taking an interest in the stimulus and viewing it favorably; (c) *valuing*—showing a tentative belief in the value of the affective stimulus and becoming committed to it; (d) *organizing*—placing values into a system of dominant and supporting values; and, (e) *internalizing*—demonstrating consistent beliefs and behavior that have become a way of life. Although there is considerable overlap from one category to another within the affective domain, these categories do give a basis by which to judge the quality of objectives and the nature of learning within this area. A discussion of each of the five categories follows.

RECEIVING

At this level, which is the least internalized, the learner exhibits willingness to give attention to particular phenomena or stimuli, and the teacher is able to arouse, sustain, and direct that attention. Action verbs appro-

[24]D. R. Krathwohl; B. S. Bloom; and B. B. Masia, *Taxonomy of Educational Goals, Handbook 2, Affective Domain* (New York: David McKay, 1964).

priate for this category include *ask, choose, describe, differentiate, distinguish, give, hold, identify, locate, name, point to, recall, recognize, reply, select,* and *use.* Examples of objectives in this category are

- The student *listens attentively* to the instructions for the project assignment.
- The student *demonstrates sensitivity* to the property, beliefs, and concerns of others.

RESPONDING

At this level, learners respond to the stimulus they have received. They may do so because of some external pressure, because they find the stimulus interesting, or because responding gives them satisfaction. Action verbs appropriate for this category include *answer, applaud, approve, assist, command, comply, discuss, greet, help, label, perform, play, practice, present, read, recite, report, select, spend (leisure time in), tell,* and *write.* Examples of objectives at this level are

- The student *completes* the project assignment.
- The student *cooperates* with others.

VALUING

Objectives at the valuing level deal with learner's beliefs, attitudes, and appreciations. The simplest objectives concern the acceptance of beliefs and values; the higher ones involve learning to prefer certain values and finally becoming committed to them. Action verbs appropriate for this level include *argue, assist, complete, describe, differentiate, explain, follow, form, initiate, invite, join, justify, propose, protest, read, report, select, share, study, support,* and *work.* Examples of objectives in this category include

- The student *justifies* an inquiry approach.
- The student *argues* a position against abortion or pro-choice for women.

ORGANIZING

This fourth level in the affective domain concerns the building of a personal value system. Here the learner is conceptualizing and arranging values into a system that recognizes their relative importance. Action verbs appropriate for this level include *adhere, alter, arrange, balance, combine, compare, defend, define, discuss, explain, form, generalize, identify, integrate, modify, order, organize, prepare, relate,* and *synthesize.* Examples of objectives in this category are

- The student *recognizes* the value of serendipity when problem-solving.
- The student *defends* the values of a particular subculture.

INTERNALIZING

This is the last and highest category within the affective domain, at which the learner's behaviors have become consistent with his or her beliefs. Action verbs appropriate for this level include *act, complete, discriminate, display, influence, listen, modify, perform, practice, propose, qualify, question, revise, serve, solve,* and *verify.* Examples of objectives in this category are

- The student's behavior *displays* self-assurance in working alone.
- The student *practices* cooperative behaviors in group activities.

Psychomotor Domain Hierarchy

Whereas identification and classification within the cognitive and affective domains are generally agreed upon, there is less agreement on the classification within the psychomotor domain. Originally, the goal of this domain was simply to develop and categorize proficiency in skills, particularly those dealing with gross and fine muscle control. The classification of the domain presented here follows this lead, but includes at its highest level the most creative and inventive behaviors, thus coordinating skills and knowledge from all three domains. Consequently, the objectives are in a hierarchy ranging from simple gross locomotor control to the most creative and complex, requiring originality and fine locomotor control—for example, from simply turning on a computer to designing a software program. From Harrow we offer the following taxonomy of the psychomotor domain: (a) *moving,* (b) *manipulating,* (c) *communicating,* and (d) *creating.*[25]

MOVING

This level involves gross motor coordination. Action verbs appropriate for this level include *adjust, carry,*

clean, *grasp, jump, locate, obtain,* and *walk.* Sample objectives for this category are

- The student *will jump* a rope 10 times without missing.
- The student *will carry* the microscope to the desk correctly.

MANIPULATING

This level involves fine motor coordination. Action verbs appropriate for this level include *assemble, build, calibrate, connect, play, thread,* and *turn.* Sample objectives for this category are

- The student *will assemble* a kite.
- The student *will turn* the fine adjustment until the microscope is in focus.

COMMUNICATING

This level involves the communication of ideas and feelings. Action verbs appropriate for this level include *analyze, ask, describe, draw, explain,* and *write.* Sample objectives for this category are

- The student *will draw* what he or she observes on a slide through the microscope.
- The student *will describe* his or her feelings about cloning.

CREATING

Creating is the highest level of this domain and of all other domains, and represents the student's coordination of thinking, learning, and behaving in all three domains. Action verbs appropriate for this level include *create, design,* and *invent.* Sample objectives for this category are

- The student *will create, choreograph,* and *perform* a dance pattern.
- The student *will design* and *build* a kite pattern.

Now, using Exercise 5.11, assess your recognition of performance objectives according to which domain they belong. Then, with Exercise 5.12, begin writing your own objectives for use in your teaching. You may want to correlate your work on Exercise 5.12 with Exercises 5.6, 6.4, 6.5, and 12.2.

---

[25]A. J. Harrow, *Taxonomy of the Psychomotor Domain* (New York: Longman, 1977). A similar taxonomy for the psychomotor domain is that of E. J. Simpson, *The Classification of Educational Objectives in the Psychomotor Domain. The Psychomotor Domain: Volume 3* (Washington, DC: Gryphon House, 1972).

EXERCISE 5.11: ASSESSING RECOGNITION OF OBJECTIVES ACCORDING TO DOMAIN—A SELF-CHECK EXERCISE

INSTRUCTIONS: The purpose of this exercise is to assess your ability to identify objectives correctly according to their domain: For each of the following instructional objectives, identify by the appropriate letter the domain involved: *(C)* cognitive; *(A)* affective; *(P)* psychomotor. Check your answers, and discuss the results with your classmates and instructor.

_____ 1. The student will shoot free throws until he or she can complete 80 percent of the attempts.

_____ 2. The student will identify on a map the mountain ranges of the eastern United States.

_____ 3. The student will summarize the historical development of the Democratic Party in the United States.

_____ 4. The student will demonstrate a continuing desire to learn more about using the classroom computer for word processing by volunteering to work at it during free time.

_____ 5. The student will volunteer to tidy up the storage room.

_____ 6. After listening to several recordings, the student will identify their respective composers.

_____ 7. The student will translate a favorite Cambodian poem into English.

_____ 8. The student will calculate the length of the hypotenuse.

_____ 9. The student will indicate an interest in the subject by voluntarily reading additional library books about earthquakes.

_____ 10. The student will successfully stack five blocks.

Answer Key for Exercise 5.11: 2, 3, 6, 7, 8 = C; 1, 10 = P; 4, 5, 9 = A

EXERCISE 5.12: PREPARING MY OWN INSTRUCTIONAL OBJECTIVES

INSTRUCTIONS: The purpose of this exercise is to begin the construction of objectives for your own teaching. For a subject content and grade level of your choice (perhaps from your content outline, Exercise 5.6), prepare 10 specific objectives. (Audience, conditions, and performance level are not necessary unless requested by your course instructor.) Exchange completed exercises with your classmates; then discuss and make changes where necessary.

Subject Field: _____   Grade Level (5–8): _____

1. Cognitive knowledge:

   _____

   _____

   _____

   _____

   _____

2. Cognitive comprehension:

   _____

   _____

   _____

   _____

   _____

3. Cognitive application:

   _____

   _____

   _____

   _____

   _____

4. Cognitive analysis:

   _____

   _____

   _____

   _____

   _____

5. Cognitive synthesis:

   _____

   _____

   _____

EXERCISE 5.12 (*continued*)

_____

_____

_____

6. Cognitive evaluation:

_____

_____

_____

_____

_____

7. Affective (low level):

_____

_____

_____

_____

_____

8. Affective (highest level):

_____

_____

_____

_____

_____

9. Psychomotor (low level):

_____

_____

_____

_____

_____

10. Psychomotor (highest level):

_____

_____

_____

_____

_____

USING THE TAXONOMIES

Theoretically, the taxonomies are constructed so that students achieve each lower level before they are ready to move to the higher levels. However, because categories and behaviors overlap, as they should, this theory does not always hold in practice. Furthermore, as explained by others, feelings and thoughts are inextricably interconnected; they cannot be neatly separated as the taxonomies might seem to imply.[26]

The taxonomies are important in that they emphasize the various levels to which instruction and learning must aspire. For learning to be worthwhile, you must formulate and teach to objectives from the higher levels of the taxonomies as well as from the lower ones. Student thinking and behaving must be moved from the lowest to the highest levels of thinking and behavior. When it is all said and done, it is, perhaps, the highest level of the psychomotor domain (creating) to which we aspire.

In using the taxonomies, remember that the point is to formulate the best objectives for the job to be done. Results-driven education models (see page 166 for synonyms) describe levels of mastery standards *(rubrics)* for each outcome. The taxonomies provide the mechanism for assuring that you do not spend a disproportionate amount of time on facts and other low-level learning. They can be of tremendous help where teachers are expected to correlate learning activities to one of the school or district's outcome standards (See Figure 5.9).

Preparing objectives is essential to the preparation of good items for the assessment of student learning. Clearly communicating your performance expectations to students and then specifically assessing student learning against those expectations makes the teaching most efficient and effective, and it makes the assessment of the learning closer to being authentic. This does not mean to imply that you will always write performance objectives for everything taught, nor will you always be able to accurately measure what students have learned. Learning that is meaningful to students is not as easily compartmentalized as the taxonomies of educational objectives would imply.

Observing for Connected (Meaningful) Learning: Logs, Portfolios, and Journals

In learning that is most important and that has the most meaning to students, the domains are inextricably interconnected. Consequently, when assessing for student learning, both during instruction (formative assessment) and at the conclusion of the instruction (summative assessment) you must look for those connections.

[26]R. N. Caine and G. Caine, *Education on the Edge of Possibility* (Alexandria, VA: Association for Supervision and Curriculum Development, 1997), pp. 104–105.

Figure 5.9   Sample school district-expected learning outcome standards.

Results-driven education helps produce people who are life-long learners, who are effective communicators, who have high self-esteem, and who are:

Problem Solvers

- Are able to solve problems in their academic and personal lives
- Demonstrate higher-level analytical thinking skills when they evaluate or make decisions
- Are able to set personal and career goals
- Can use knowledge, not just display it
- Are innovative thinkers

Self-Directed Learners

- Are independent workers
- Can read, comprehend, and interact with text
- Have self-respect, with an accurate view of themselves and their abilities

Quality Producers

- Can communicate effectively in a variety of situations (oral, aesthetic/artistic, nonverbal)
- Are able to use their knowledge to create intelligent, artistic products that reflect originality
- Have high standards

Collaborative Workers

- Are able to work interdependently
- Show respect for others and their points of view
- Have their own values and moral conduct
- Have an appreciation of cultural diversity

Community Contributors

- Have an awareness of civic, individual, national, and international responsibilities
- Have an understanding of basic health issues
- Have an appreciation of diversity

Ways of looking for connected learning include (a) maintaining a teacher's (or team's) log with daily or nearly daily entries about the progress of each student, (b) having students maintain personal learning journals in which they reflect on and respond to their learning, and (c) having students assemble individual learning portfolios that document students' thinking, work, and learning experiences.

Dated and chronologically organized items that students place in their portfolios can include notes and communications; awards; brainstorming records; photos of bulletin board contributions and charts; posters, displays, and models made by the student; records of peer coaching; visual maps; learning contract; record of debate contributions, demonstrations, and presentations;

mnemonics created by the student; peer evaluations; reading record; other contributions made to the class or to the team; record of service work; and test and grade records.

The use of portfolios and student journals is discussed further in Chapter 11.

Character Education

Related especially to the affective domain, although not exclusive of the cognitive and psychomotor domains, is an interest in the development of students' values, especially those of honesty, kindness, respect, and responsibility, which is sometimes called *character education* (see discussion and list of resources in Chapter 2). For example, Wynne and Ryan state that "transmitting character, academics, and discipline—essentially, 'traditional' moral values—to pupils is a vital educational responsibility."[27] If one agrees with that interpretation, then the teaching of moral values is the transmission of character, academics, and discipline and clearly implies learning that transcends the three domains of learning presented in this chapter. Stimulated by a perceived need to reduce student antisocial behaviors (such as drug abuse and violence) and to produce more respectful and responsible citizens, with a primary focus on the affective domain, many middle level schools are developing curricula in character education, and instruction in conflict resolution. Often it is a function of the advisory program to promote character education, life skills training, conflict resolution skills, and other strategies for seeking peaceable solutions to problems. The ultimate goal of those efforts is to develop values in students that lead to responsible citizenship and moral action.

Learning That Is Not Immediately Observable

Unlike behaviorists, constructivists do not limit the definition of learning to that which is observable behavior—nor should you. Bits and pieces of new information are stored in short-term memory, where the new information is "rehearsed" until ready to be stored in long-term memory. If the information is not rehearsed, it eventually fades from short-term memory. If it is rehearsed and made meaningful through connections with other stored knowledge, then this new knowledge is transferred to and stored in long-term memory, either by building existing schemata or by forming new schemata. As a teacher, your responsibility is to provide learning experiences that will result in the creation of new schemata as well as the modification of existing schemata.

To be an effective middle level teacher, the challenge is to use performance-based criteria simultaneously with a teaching style that encourages the development of intrinsic sources of student motivation, and that allows, provides, and encourages coincidental learning—learning that goes beyond what might be considered predictable, immediately measurable, and representative of minimal expectations.

It has become quite clear to many teachers that to be most effective in helping young adolescents to develop meaningful understandings, much of the learning in each discipline can be made more effective and longer lasting when it is integrated with the whole curriculum, and made meaningful to the lives of the students, rather than simply being taught as an unrelated and separate discipline at the same time each day.

As we noted at the start of this chapter, if learning is defined only as the accumulation of bits and pieces of information, we already know how to learn and how to teach. However, the accumulation of pieces of information is at the lowest end of the spectrum of types of learning. For higher levels of thinking and for learning that is most meaningful and longest lasting, the results of research support using (a) a curriculum where disciplines are integrated and (b) instructional techniques that involve the learners in social interactive learning, such as project-centered learning, cooperative learning, peer tutoring, and cross-age teaching.

INTEGRATED CURRICULUM

When learning about *integrated curriculum (IC)*, it is easy to be confused by the plethora of terms that are used, such as *integrated studies, thematic instruction, multidisciplinary teaching, interdisciplinary curriculum,* and *interdisciplinary thematic instruction.* In essence, regardless of which of these terms is being used, the reference is to the same thing.

Because it is not always easy to tell where the term *curriculum* leaves off and the term *instruction* begins, let's assume for now that, for the sake of better understanding the meaning of *integrated curriculum,* there is no difference between what is curriculum and what is instruction. In other words, for this discussion, *integrated curriculum* and *integrated instruction* will refer to the same thing.

Definition of Integrated Curriculum

The term **integrated curriculum (IC)** (or any of its synonyms) refers to both a way of teaching and a way of planning and organizing the instructional program so the discrete disciplines of subject matter are related to one another in a design that (a) matches the developmental needs of the learners and (b) helps to connect their learning in ways that are meaningful to their cur-

---

[27]E. A. Wynne and K. Ryan, *Reclaiming Our Schools: Teaching Character, Academics, and Discipline,* 2e (Upper Saddle River, NJ: Prentice Hall, 1997), p. 1.

rent and past experiences. In that respect, IC is the antithesis of traditional disparate subject-matter-oriented teaching and curriculum designations.

Integrated Curricula: Past and Present

The reason for the varying terminology is, in part, because the concept of an integrated curriculum is not new. In fact, it has had a roller-coaster ride throughout most of the history of education in this country. Over time those, efforts to integrate student learning have had various labels.

Today's interest in curriculum integration has risen from at least five inextricably connected sources: (a) the success at curriculum integration that has been enjoyed by middle level schools since the beginning of the middle school movement in the 1960s, (b) the literature-based, whole-language movement in reading and language arts that began in the 1980s,[28] (c) the diversity of learners in the regular classroom coupled with growing acceptance of the philosophy that a certain percentage of school dropouts is not a viable assumption, (d) recent research in cognitive science and neuroscience demonstrating the necessity of helping young adolescent learners establish bridges between school and life, knowing and doing, content and context, with a parallel rekindled interest in constructivism as opposed to a strictly behaviorist philosophical approach to teaching and learning.

An integrated curriculum approach may not necessarily be the best approach for every school or for all learning for every student, nor is it necessarily the manner by which every middle grades teacher should or must always plan and teach. As evidenced by practice, the truth of this statement becomes obvious. And, as you should be well aware now, it is our belief that a teacher's best choice as an approach to instruction—and to classroom management—is one that is eclectic.

The Spectrum of Integrated Curriculum

In attempts to connect students' learning with their experiences, efforts fall at various places on a spectrum or continuum, from the least integrated instruction (level 1) to the most integrated (level 5), as illustrated in Figure 5.10. It is not our intent that this illustration be interpreted as going from "worst case scenario" (far left) to "best case scenario" (far right), although some people may interpret it exactly that way. The fact is that there are various interpretations to curriculum integration and teachers must make their own decisions about their use. Figure 5.10 is meant solely to show how efforts to integrate fall on a continuum of sophistication and complexity. The following is a description of each level of the continuum.

Level 1 curriculum integration. Level 1 curriculum integration is the traditional organization of curriculum and classroom instruction, where teachers plan and arrange the subject-specific scope and sequence in the format of topic outlines, much as you did for Exercise 5.6. If there is an attempt to help students connect their experiences and their learning, then it is up to individual classroom teachers to do it. A student in a school and classroom that has subject-specific instruction at varying

---

[28]Various movements and approaches have been used over the years to try to find the most successful approach to teaching English and the language arts—movements with names such as *whole language, integrated language arts, communication arts and skills, literature-based,* and so forth. Whatever the cognomen, certain common elements and goals prevail: student choice in materials to be read, student reading and writing across the curriculum, time for independent and sustained silent reading in the classroom, use of integrated language arts skills across the curriculum, and use of nonprint materials.

Figure 5.10   Levels of curriculum integration.

Least Integrated *Level 1*	*Level 2*	*Level 3*	*Level 4*	*Most Integrated* *Level 5*
Subject-specific topic outline	Subject-specific	Multidisciplinary	Interdisciplinary thematic	Integrated thematic
No student collaboration in planning	Minimal student input	Some student input	Considerable student input in selecting themes and in planning	Maximum student and teacher collaboration
Teacher solo	Solo or teams	Solo or teams	Solo or teams	Solo or teams
Student input into decision making is low.		Student input into decision making is high.		Student input into decision making is very high.

times of the day (e.g., language arts at 8:00, mathematics at 9:00, social studies at 10:30, and so on) from one or more teachers is likely learning at a level 1 instructional environment, especially when what is being learned in one subject has little or no connection with content being learned in another. The same applies for a student, as found in many junior high schools, who moves during the school day from classroom to classroom, teacher to teacher, subject to subject, from one topic to another. A topic in science, for example, might be "earthquakes." A related topic in social studies might be "the social consequences of natural disasters." These two topics may or may not be studied by a student at the same time.

Level 2 curriculum integration. If the same students are learning English/language arts, or social studies/history, or mathematics, or science using a thematic approach rather than a topic outline, then they are learning at level 2. At this level, themes for one discipline are not necessarily planned and coordinated to correspond or integrate with themes of another or to be taught simultaneously. At level 2, the students may have some input into the decision making involved in planning themes and content from various disciplines. Before going further in our presentation of the levels of curriculum integration, let's stop and consider what is a topic and what is a theme.

Integrated Thematic Unit: Topic versus Theme. The difference between a topic and a theme is not always clear. For example, "earthquakes" and "social consequences of natural disasters" are topics, but "a survival guide to local natural disasters" could be the theme or umbrella under which these two topics could fall. In addition, themes are likely to be problem-based statements or questions; they often result in a product and are longer in duration than are topics. A theme is the point, the message, or the idea that underlies a study. When compared to a topic, a theme is more dynamic; the theme explains the significance of the study. It communicates to the student what the experience means. Although organized around one theme, many topics make up an interdisciplinary thematic unit (ITU). Often the theme of a study becomes clearer to students when an overall guiding question is presented and discussed, such as "What could we do to improve our living environment?" or "What happens in our community after natural disasters?"

Some educators say that the integrated curriculum of the future will be based on broad, unchanging, and unifying concepts (that is, on conceptual themes).[29] If

so, it would be a recycling of an approach of the 1960s, as supported by the writings of Jerome Bruner[30] and implemented in some of the National Foundation-sponsored curriculum projects of that era. In fact, there is already action in that direction. For example, forming the basis for the national curriculum standards (discussed earlier in this chapter) for social studies are 10 "thematic strands," including "people, places, and environments," and "power, authority, and governance." The national standards for science education are centered on unifying conceptual schemes, such as "systems, order, and organization," and "form and function."

Level 3 curriculum integration. When the same students are learning two or more of their core subjects (English/language arts, social studies/history, mathematics, and science) around a common theme, such as "natural disasters," from one or more teachers, they are learning at level 3 integration. At this level, teachers agree on a common theme and then *separately* deal with it in their individual subject areas, usually at the same time during the school year. So what the student is learning from a teacher in one class is related to and coordinated with what the student is concurrently learning in another or several others. At level 3, students may have some input into the decision making involved in selecting and planning themes and content. Some authors may refer to levels 2 or 3 as *coordinated* or *parallel curriculum*.

Level 4 curriculum integration. When teachers and students collaborate on a common theme and its content, and when discipline boundaries begin to disappear as teachers teach about this common theme, either solo or as an *interdisciplinary teaching team*, level 4 integration is achieved.

Level 5 curriculum integration. Level 5 occurs when teachers and their students have collaborated on a common theme and its content, discipline boundaries are truly blurred during instruction, and teachers of several grade levels and of various subjects teach toward student understanding of aspects of the common theme. This is an *integrated thematic approach*.[31]

Guidelines for integrating topics and for planning and developing an interdisciplinary thematic unit are presented in the next chapter.

INTEGRATED CURRICULUM IN A STANDARDS-BASED ENVIRONMENT

Although it is still too early to obtain reliable data on how students in integrated curriculum programs fare on mandatory state-wide achievement tests, it should be

[29]See, for example, E-M Lolli, "Creating a Concept-Based Curriculum," *Principal* 76(1):26–27 (September 1996); T. L. Riley, "Tools for Discovery: Conceptual Themes in the Classroom," *Gifted Child Today Magazine* 20(1):30–33, 50 (January/February 1997); and C. A. Tomlinson, "For Integration and Differentiation Choose Concepts over Topics," *Middle School Journal* 30(2):3–8 (November 1998).

[30]J. S. Bruner, *Process of Education* (Cambridge, MA: Harvard University Press, 1960).

[31]For detailed accounts of teaching at this level of integration, see C. Stevenson and J. F. Carr, eds., *Integrated Studies in the Middle Grades* (New York: Teachers College Press, 1993).

reassuring to today's classroom teacher to know that from their analysis of recent data Vars and Beane conclude that "almost without exception, students in any type of interdisciplinary or integrative curriculum do as well as, and often better than, students in a conventional departmentalized program. These results hold whether the combined curriculum is taught by one teacher in a self-contained or block-time class or by an interdisciplinary team."[32]

PLANNING FOR INSTRUCTION: A THREE-LEVEL AND SEVEN-STEP PROCESS

Earlier in the chapter we noted that complete planning for instruction occurs at three levels: the year, the units, and the lessons. There are seven steps in the process. They are as follows:

1. *Course, grade level, and school goals.* Consider and understand your curriculum goals and their relationship to the mission and goals of the school. Your course is not isolated on Jupiter but is an integral part of the total school curriculum.

2. *Expectations.* Consider topics, knowledge, and skills that you are expected to teach, such as those found in the district-wide standards and the course of study.

3. *Academic year, semester, trimester, or quarter plan.* Think about the goals you want the students to reach months from now. Working from your tentative content outline (Exercise 5.6) and with the school calendar in hand, you will begin by deciding the amount of time (e.g., the number of days) to be devoted to each topic (or unit), and then penciling those times onto the outline. (Unless you are doing your planning at a computer, you may wish to use pencil because the times are likely to be modified frequently).

4. *Course schedule.* This schedule becomes a part of the course syllabus that is presented to students at the beginning of the course (discussed in the next and final section of this chapter). However, the schedule *must* remain flexible to allow for the unexpected, such as the cancellation or interruption of a class meeting, or an extended study of a particular topic.

5. *Plans for each class meeting.* Working from the calendar plan or the course schedule, you are ready to prepare plans for each class meeting, keeping in mind the abilities and interests of your students while making decisions about appropriate strategies and learning experiences. The preparation of daily plans takes considerable time and continues throughout the year as you arrange and prepare instructional notes; demonstrations; discussion topics and questions; classroom ex-

ercises; learning centers; guest speakers; audiovisual materials and media equipment; field trips; and tools for the assessment of student learning. Because the content of each class meeting is often determined by the accomplishments of the preceding one and by your reflections on it, your lessons are never "set in concrete" but need your continual revisiting and assessment.

6. *Instructional objectives.* Once you have the finalized schedule and as you prepare daily plans, you will complete your preparation of the instructional objectives (begun in Exercise 5.12). Those objectives are critical for proper development of the next and final step.

7. *Assessment.* The final step is that of deciding how to assess for student achievement. Included in this component are your decisions about how you will accomplish diagnostic or preassessment (that is the assessment of what students know or think they know at the start of a new unit of study or a new topic), formative assessment (the ongoing assessment of what the students are learning that takes place almost daily during a unit of study) and summative assessment (the assessment of learning at the conclusion of a unit of study on what the students learned). Also included in the assessment component are your decisions about assignments (discussed in Chapter 8) and the grading procedures (discussed in Chapter 11).

In Chapter 6, the next and final chapter of Part II, you will proceed through these steps as you develop your first instructional plan. However, before starting that, let's consider one more topic relevant to the overall planning of the course—the syllabus.

THE SYLLABUS

A syllabus is a written statement of information about the workings of a particular class or course. (See sample in Figure 5.11.) As a student in postsecondary education, you have seen a variety of syllabi written by professors, each with their individual ideas and personal touches about what general and specific logistic information is most important for students to know about a course. Some instructors, however, err in thinking that a course outline constitutes a course syllabus; a course outline is only one component of a syllabus.

Not all middle grades teachers use a course syllabus, at least as it is described here, but, for reasons we will explore in this discussion, we believe they should. Related to that belief are several questions that are answered next: "Why should teachers use a syllabus?" "What value is it?" "What use can be made of it?" "What purpose does it fulfill?" "How do I develop one?" "Can students have input into its contents and participate in its development?" "Where do I start?" "What information should be included?" "When should it be distributed?" "To whom should it be distributed?" and "How rigidly should it be followed?"

---

[32]G. F. Vars and J. A. Beane, *Integrative Curriculum in a Standards-Based World* (Champaign, IL: ED441618, ERIC Clearinghouse on Elementary and Early Childhood Education, 2000).

Figure 5.11   Sample course syllabus.

English 8   *Room 23, Mrs. Biletnikoff*

Course Description

English 8 is a course designed to provide instruction in the areas of reading, analyzing, and writing about literature, while using texts that support the History 8 coursework. Essay writing, especially descriptive writing, is emphasized. In addition to intensive vocabulary study, students will be writing on a daily basis. Also, the students will read one million words of outside texts, in addition to their assigned reading. The readings for English 8 are an eclectic mix. The novels that the class will be reading this semester are *April Morning, The Giver,* and *The Diary of Anne Frank.*

Materials Required

Students are required to bring pen, pencil, and paper to class each day. Journal binder should be a 2-pocket, 3-prong paper binder. The school provides the vocabulary text and all literary texts.

Goals

• To understand and recognize the various aspects of literature: character, setting, plot, point of view, and theme.
• To increase vocabulary, preparing students for more advanced writing.
• To develop and enhance students' descriptive writing and organizational skills.
• To increase oral and listening skills.

Objectives

• Students will participate in projects, class discussions, journal writing, quizzes, essay writing, and tests that are designed to help them grasp the concepts of plot, setting, character, theme, and other literary devices. Through these activities, students will demonstrate improvement in their writing and oral/listening skills.
• Students will participate in class activities such as sustained silent reading (SSR), reading aloud, and project development to help in their learning of the material.

Assignments

There are weekly vocabulary quizzes. There is also weekly vocabulary homework. Throughout the course, students will be writing journal entries, quickwrites, and essays. All completed and graded work is returned to the corresponding class file. Students are free to check the file before or after class.

Assessment Criteria

• Students will complete weekly vocabulary quizzes.
• Quizzes are administered when the teacher needs to check the students' progress.
• Test dates will be announced in class and class time is used for test preparation.
• Class participation accounts for 15% of the student's grade, therefore absences and tardiness can negatively affect this assessment component.
• Group work is graded, therefore lack of participation can negatively affect the student's grade.

Method of Evaluation

Evaluation is done through oral and written quizzes and tests. In addition, students are evaluated on class participation, assignments, projects, and class discussions. All grades are based on a point system.

Papers, quizzes, and tests   = 50% of total points
Homework   = 20% of total points
Journals   = 15% of total points
Group work and class participation = 15% of total points

Grading Scale

90–100% of total points   = A   50–69% = D
80–89%   = B   <50%   = F
70–79%   = C
Grades are posted (by codes, not names) biweekly.

Figure 5.11   *(continued)*

Classroom Behavior and Consequences for Inappropriate Behavior

Students are expected to be prompt, prepared, polite, productive, and positive (the 5Ps). Students may earn 5 points per day by observing the 5Ps guidelines. Students may forfeit their citizenship points by excessive bathroom requests, tardiness, or leaving class without the teacher's approval.
Consequences for inappropriate behavior:

1st infraction = verbal warning
2nd infraction = 15 minutes at time out and a phone call to parent or guardian
3rd infraction = referral to administration or a call home
4th infraction = administrative referral and possible suspension
Note: Any step in the above process may be skipped at the teacher's discretion.

Attendance

Regular attendance is crucial for success. It enables the student to understand assignments and to take advantage of the guidance provided by the teacher and others. In addition, the students will receive immediate feedback regarding their progress. If a student needs to leave early or enter late, please make arrangements with the teacher beforehand if possible.

Tardiness

Students are tardy when they are not in their seats when the tardy bell rings. Any student who elects to leave the classroom for any reason takes a tardy for that period. Tardiness affects citizenship as well as the privilege to participate in extra-curricular activities before and after school.

Bathroom Privileges

Students are allowed two bathroom passes per quarter. Each pass is redeemed at the time of use. If the student does not use the two passes for the quarter, the student receives 5 extra points per pass with a total of 10 points possible towards their citizenship grade. If a student chooses to use the bathroom beyond the two-pass limit, then that student forfeits the citizenship points (5) for the day.

Make-up

Students may make up assignments one day after returning from an excused absence. All other work is accepted at the teacher's discretion.

Extra Credit Work

There is no "extra credit" work in this class.

Instructional Schedule for English 8, Fall Semester

    Unit I Introduction to the short story (2 weeks)
    Vocabulary, journal, SSR, and outside readings begin
    Unit II *April Morning* (4–5 weeks)
    Unit III *The Giver* (4–5 weeks)
    Unit IV *Diary of Anne Frank* (4–5 weeks)

Source: Courtesy of Angela Biletnikoff.

Use and Development of a Syllabus

The syllabus is printed information about the class or the course that is usually presented to the students on the first day or during the first week of school. The syllabus may be developed completely by you or in collaboration with members of your teaching team. It can also be developed collaboratively with students. As always, the final decision about its development is yours to make. However it is developed, the syllabus should be designed so that it helps establish a rapport among students, parents or guardians, and the teacher; helps stu-dents feel at ease by providing an understanding of what is expected of them; and helps them to organize, conceptualize, and synthesize their learning experiences.

The syllabus should provide a reference, helping eliminate misunderstandings and misconceptions about the nature of the class—its rules, expectations, procedures, requirements, and other policies. It should provide students with a sense of connectedness (often by allowing students to work collaboratively in groups and actually participate in fashioning *their* course syllabus).

The syllabus should also serve as a plan to be followed by the teacher and the students, and it should serve as a resource for substitute teachers and, when relevant, members of a teaching team. Each team member should have a copy of every other member's syllabus. In essence, the syllabus stands as documentation for what is taking place in the classroom for those outside the classroom (i.e., parents or guardians, school board members, administrators, other teachers, and students). For access by parents and other interested persons, some teachers include at least portions of their course syllabus, such as homework assignment specifications and due dates, on the school's website.

Usually at least portions of the syllabus are prepared by the teacher long before the first class meeting. If you maintain a syllabus template on your computer, then it is a simple task to customize it for each group of students you teach. You may find it is more useful if students participate in the development of the syllabus, thereby having an ownership of it and a commitment to its contents.

By having input into the workings of a course and knowing that their opinions count, students usually will take more interest in what they are doing and learning. Some teachers give students a brief syllabus on the first day (see Figure 5.12) and then, collaboratively with the students and other members of the teaching team, develop a more detailed syllabus during the initial days of the start of school. Shown in Figure 5.13 are steps you can take to provide a collaborative learning experience where students spend time during the first (or an early) class meeting brainstorming content of their syllabus.

Content of a Syllabus

A syllabus should be concise, matter-of-fact, uncomplicated, and brief—perhaps no more than two pages—and, to be thorough and most informative, include the following information:

Descriptive information about the course. This includes the teacher's name, the course or class title, class period,

Figure 5.12 A boxed scenario: how one teacher welcomes students and their parents or guardians.

To Student and Parent/Guardian

Welcome to Sixth Grade—Carmichael School

Your Homeroom will be: Room 18   Your Homeroom Teacher will be: Mrs. Craine

Welcome back! We are looking forward to a productive year of interesting learning experiences to prepare each student for the transition to middle school. The following information will help students and parents/guardians to understand the classroom policies and procedures.

Materials Needed:

Pens (black or blue ink), a binder, dividers, and pencils. Colored pens or pencils are optional but nice to have. Textbooks need to be covered the night the students receive them.

Homework:

Students will have from one to two hours of homework every night, 15 minutes of which will be quiet reading. Please provide a quiet area and a regular study time for your child to complete daily homework assignments. The homework reminder sheet *must* be signed each night. If homework is not ready the next day (1) the student will receive a slip called "unprepared," (2) an area in the classroom will be provided for the student to complete the unfinished work, and (3) when a student receives five unprepareds, an office referral will be given and a phone call made to the parent/guardian.

Rules:

Listen carefully; follow directions; stay on task; respect others and be kind with your words and actions; and turn in homework and classwork on time and be responsible for it being completed and neatly done.

Consequences for breaking a classroom rule:

1. Student receives verbal warning.
2. Student's name is written on the clipboard.
3. If inappropriate behavior continues, student receives a blue card.
4. If two blue cards are received in one week, student receives an orange card and is referred to the office.
5. If inappropriate behavior continues, student receives a purple card, is referred to the office, and is suspended from school.

Source: Courtesy of Shirley Craine.

days of class meetings, beginning and ending times, and room number.

Importance of the course. This information should describe the course, cite how students will profit from it, tell whether the course is a required course and (if relevant) from which program in the curriculum—for example, a core course, an elective, exploratory, or some other arrangement.

Learning targets. This should include major goals and a few objectives.

Materials required. Explain what materials are needed—such as a textbook, notebook, binder, calculator, supplementary readings, apron, and safety goggles—and specify which are supplied by the school, which must be supplied by each student, and what materials must be available each day.

Types of assignments that will be given. These should be clearly explained in as much detail as is possible this early in the school term. There should be a statement of your estimate of time required (if any) for homework each night. There should also be a statement about where daily assignments will be posted in the classroom (a regular place each day), and about the procedures for completing and turning in assignments and (if relevant) for making corrections to assignments already turned in. Include your policy regarding late work. Also, parents may need to know your expectations of them regarding helping with assignments. (Homework is discussed in Chapter 8.)

Attendance expectations. Explain how attendance is related to achievement grades and to promotion (if relevant) and the procedure for making up missed work.

Figure 5.13   Steps for involving students in the development of their course syllabus.

Step 1

Sometime during the first few days of the course, arrange students in heterogeneous groups (mixed abilities) of three or four members to brainstorm the development of their syllabus.

Step 2

Instruct each group to spend five minutes listing everything they can think of that they would like to know about the course. Tell students that a group *recorder* must be chosen to write their list of ideas on paper and then, when directed to do so, to transfer the list to the writing board or to sheets of butcher paper to be hung in the classroom for all to see (or on an overhead transparency—a transparency sheet and pen are made available to each group). Tell them to select a group *spokesperson* who will address the class, explaining the group's list. Each group could also appoint a *materials manager,* whose job is to see that the group has the necessary materials (e.g., pen, paper, transparency, chalk), and a *task master,* whose job is to keep the group on task and to report to the teacher when each task is completed.

Step 3

After five minutes, have the recorders prepare their lists. When a transparency or butcher paper is used, the lists can be prepared simultaneously while recorders remain with their groups. If using the writing board, then recorders, one at a time, write their lists on areas of the board that you have designated for each group's list.

Step 4

Have the spokesperson of each group explain the group's list. As this is being done, you should make a master list. If transparencies or butcher paper are being used rather than the writing board, you can ask for either as backup to the master list you have made.

Step 5

After all spokespersons have explained their lists, ask the class collectively for additional input. "Can anyone think of anything else that should be added?"

Step 6

You now take the master list and design a course syllabus, being careful to address each question and to include items of importance that students may have omitted. However, your guidance during the preceding five steps should ensure that all bases have been covered.

Step 7

At the next class meeting, give each student a copy of the final syllabus. Discuss its content. (Make copies to distribute to colleagues, especially those on your teaching team; interested administrators; and parents and guardians at back-to-school night.)

Typical school policy allows that for an excused absence, missed work can be completed without penalty if done within a reasonable period of time after the student returns to school.

Assessment and marking/grading procedures. Explain the assessment procedures and the procedures for determining grades. Will there be quizzes, tests, homework, projects, and group work? What will be their formats, coverage, and weights in the procedure for determining grades? For group work, how will the contributions and learning of individual students be evaluated?

Other information specific to the course. Field trips? Special privileges? Computer work? Parental expectations? Homework hotline? Classroom procedures and expectations (discussed in Chapter 4) should be included here.

If you are a beginning teacher or are new to the school, to confirm that the policies indicated in the first draft of your syllabus are not counter to any existing school policies, you should probably share it with members of your team or the department chairperson for their feedback.

SUMMARY

In your comparison and analysis of courses of study and teachers' editions of student textbooks, you probably discovered that many are accompanied by sequentially designed resource units from which the teacher can select and build specific teaching units. A resource unit usually consists of an extensive list of objectives, a large number and variety of activities, suggested materials, and extensive bibliographies for teacher and students.

As you may also have found, some courses of study contain actual teaching units that have been prepared by teachers of the school district. Beginning teachers and student teachers often ask, "How closely must I follow the school's curriculum guide or course of study?" To find out, you must talk with teachers and administrators of the school before you begin teaching.

In conclusion, your final decisions about what content to teach are guided by (a) discussions with other teachers; (b) review of state curriculum documents, local courses of study, and articles in professional journals; (c) your personal convictions, knowledge, and skills; and (d) the unique characteristics of your students.

In this chapter, you learned of the differences among the terms *aims, goals,* and *objectives.* Regardless of how these terms are defined, the important point is this: *teachers must be clear about what it is they want their students to learn and about the kind of evidence needed to verify their learning, and they must communicate those things to the students so they are clearly understood.*

Many teachers do not bother to write specific objectives for all the learning activities in their teaching plans. However, when teachers do prepare specific ob-

jectives (by writing them themselves or by borrowing them from textbooks and other curriculum documents), teach toward them, and assess students' progress against them, student learning is enhanced; this is called performance-based teaching and criterion-referenced measurement. It is also known as an aligned curriculum. In schools using results-driven education mastery learning models, those models describe levels of mastery standards or rubrics for each outcome or learning target. The taxonomies are of tremendous help in schools where teachers are expected to correlate learning activities to the school's outcome standards.

As a teacher, you will be expected to (a) plan your lessons well, (b) convey specific expectations to your students, and (c) assess their learning against that specificity. However, because it tends toward high objectivity, there is the danger that such performance-based teaching could become too objective, which can have negative consequences. If students are treated as objects, then the relationship between teacher and student becomes impersonal and counterproductive to real learning. Highly specific and impersonal teaching can be discouraging to serendipity, creativity, and the excitement of discovery, to say nothing of its possibly negative impact on the development of students' self-esteem.

Performance-based instruction works well when teaching toward mastery of basic skills, but the concept of mastery learning is inclined to imply that there is some foreseeable end to learning, an assumption that is obviously erroneous. With performance-based instruction, the source of student motivation tends to be extrinsic. Teacher expectations, marks and grades, society, and peer pressures are examples of extrinsic sources that drive student performance. To be a most effective teacher, your challenge is to use performance-based criteria together with a teaching style that encourages the development of intrinsic sources of student motivation and that allows for, provides for, and encourages coincidental learning—learning that goes beyond what might be considered as predictable, immediately measurable, and representative of minimal expectations. With a knowledge of the content of the school curriculum and the value of instructional objectives, you are now ready to prepare detailed instructional plans with sequenced lessons, the subject of the next chapter.

ADDITIONAL EXERCISE

See the companion Website http://www.prenhall.com/kellough for the following exercise related to the content of this chapter:

- Preparing a Course Syllabus: An Exercise in Collaborative Thinking

QUESTIONS FOR CLASS DISCUSSION

1. Explore a school library or resource center. Are the student books current? Does this place and its books appear attractive for students and user-friendly? Share your conclusions with your classmates.

2. It is sometimes said that teaching less is better. Explain the meaning and significance of that statement. Explain why you agree or disagree with the concept.

3. Recall your own middle level schooling. What do you really remember? Most likely you remember projects, your presentations, the lengthy research you did, and your extra effort doing art work to accompany your presentation. Maybe you remember a compliment by a teacher or a pat on the back by peers. Most likely you do *not* remember the massive amount of factual content that was covered. Discuss this and your feelings about it with your classmates.

4. Describe the concept of "integrated curriculum" as you would to a person who knew nothing about it.

5. Some people say that it is easier to write performance objectives after a lesson has been taught. What is the significance of that notion?

6. Should a teacher encourage serendipitous (coincidental) learning. If no, why not? If so, describe ways that a teacher can do it.

7. Describe the relationship between goals and objectives. Describe the relationship between scope and sequence, and between instructional goals and objectives. To what extent should students have a say in what the course objectives are to be? At any time during your teaching, should you ignore the planned scope and sequence, goals and objectives? If so, explain why, when, and to what extent. If not, explain why not.

8. Select one of the "Reflective Thoughts" from the introduction to Part II (page 84) that is specifically related to the content of this chapter, research it, and write a one-page essay explaining why you agree or disagree with the thought. Share your essay with members of your class for their thoughts.

9. From your current observations and field work as related to this teacher preparation program, clearly identify one specific example of educational practice that seems contradictory to exemplary practice or theory as presented in this chapter. Present your explanation for the discrepancy.

10. Do you have questions generated by the content of this chapter? If you do, list them along with ways answers might be found.

FOR FURTHER READING

Brown, D. F. "The Value of Advisory Sessions for Urban Young Adolescents." *Middle School Journal* 32(4):14–22 (March 2001).

Brown, R. G. "Middle School Social Studies and the Cognitive Revolution." *Clearing House* 72(6):327–330 (July 1999).

Burns, P. C., and Roe, B. D. *Informal Reading Inventory: Preprimer to Twelfth Grade*, 5th ed. Wilmington, MA: Houghton Mifflin, 1999.

Carr, J. F., and Harris, D. E. *Succeeding with Standards: Linking Curriculum, Assessment, and Action Planning*. Alexandria, VA: Association of Supervision and Curriculum Development, 2001.

Clark, D. C., and Clark, S. N. "Appropriate Assessment Strategies for Young Adolescents in an Era of Standards-Based Reform." *Clearing House* 73(4):201–204 (March/April 2000).

Erlandson, C., and McVittie, J. "Student Voices on Integrative Curriculum." *Middle School Journal* 33(2):28–36 (November 2001).

Flowers, N.; Mertens, S. B.; and Mulhall, P. F. "What Makes Interdisciplinary Teams Effective?" *Middle School Journal* 31(4):53–56 (March 2000).

Goodlad, J. I. "Teachers as Moral Stewards of Our Schools." *Journal for a Just and Caring Education* 5(3):237–242 (July 1999).

Hargreaves, A., and Moore, S. "Curriculum Integration and Classroom Relevance: A Study of Teachers' Practice." *Journal of Curriculum and Supervision* 15(2):89–112 (Winter 2000).

Harmon, J. M., and Wood, K. D. "The TAB Book Club Approach: Talking (T) About (A) Books (B) in Content Area Classrooms." *Middle School Journal* 32(3):51–56 (January 2001).

Hennessey, B., and Irvin, J. L. "What Research Says About Middle School Foreign Language Programs." *Middle School Journal* 31(1):55–59 (September 1999).

Hepburn, M. A. "Media Literacy: A Must for Middle School Social Studies." *Clearing House* 72(6):352–356 (July 1999).

Hereford, N. "A Good Sport! Middle School Athletics Can Help Kids Put Their Best Foot Forward." *Middle Ground* 3(1):25–28 (August 1999).

Hume, H. D. *A Survival Kit for the Elementary/Middle School Art Teacher.* Paramus, NJ: Prentice Hall, 2000.

Hynd, C. R. "Teaching Students to Think Critically Using Multiple Texts in History." *Journal of Adolescent & Adult Literacy* 42(6):428–436 (March 1999).

Ivey, G., and Broaddus, K. "Tailoring the Fit: Reading Instruction and Middle School Readers." *The Reading Teacher* 54(1):68–78 (September 2000).

Jehlen, A. "Science Texts Flunk the Test." *NEA Today* 18(7):29 (April 2000).

Katims, D. S., and Harmon, J. M. "Strategic Instruction in Middle School Social Studies: Enhancing Academic and Literacy Outcomes for At-Risk Students." *Intervention in School and Clinic* 35(5):280–289 (May 2000).

Kellough, R. D.; Cangelosi, J. S.; Collette, A. T.; Chiappetta, E. L.; Souviney, R. J.; Trowbridge, L. W.; and Bybee, R. W. *Integrating Mathematics and Science for Intermediate and Middle School Students.* Englewood Cliffs, NJ: Merrill/Prentice Hall, 1996.

Kellough, R. D.; Jarolimek, J.; Parker, W. C.; Martorella, P. H.; Tompkins, G. E.; and Hoskisson, K. *Integrating Language Arts and Social Studies for Intermediate and Middle School Students.* Englewood Cliffs, NJ: Merrill/Prentice Hall, 1996.

Loftis, N. "Communications Cove: A Vital Part of the Exploratory Program at Chapin Middle School." *Quill and Scroll* 73(4):9–11 (April/May 1999).

Martin, B. L., and Briggs, L. J. *The Affective and Cognitive Domains.* Englewood Cliffs, NJ: Educational Technology Publications, 1986.

Mayer, R. H. "Use the Story of Anne Hutchinson To Teach Historical Thinking." *Social Studies* 90(3):105–109 (May/June 1999).

McElroy, C. "Middle School Programs That Work." *Phi Delta Kappan* 82(4):277–279, 292 (December 2000).

Moore, D. W.; Alvermann, D. E.; and Hinchman, K. A. (Eds.). *Struggling Adolescent Readers: A Collection of Teaching Strategies.* Newark, DE: International Reading Association, 2000.

Ohanian, S. *One Size Fits Few: The Folly of Educational Standards.* Portsmouth, NH: Heinemann, 1999.

Reid, L., and Golub, J. N. (Eds.). *Reflective Activities: Helping Students Connect with Texts. Classroom Practices in Teaching English, Volume 30.* Urbana, IL: National Council of Teachers of English, 1999.

Roberts, P. L., and Kellough, R. D. *A Guide for Developing Interdisciplinary Thematic Units,* 2nd ed. Upper Saddle River, NJ: Merrill/Prentice Hall, 2000.

Rottier, J. "Teaming in the Middle School: Improve It or Lose It." *Clearing House* 3(4):214–216 (March/April 2000).

Sanacore, J. "Promoting the Lifetime Reading Habit in Middle School Students." *Clearing House* 73(3):157–161 (January/February 2000).

Shirley, L. "Twentieth-Century Mathematics: A Brief Review of the Century." *Mathematics Teaching in the Middle School* 5(5):278–285 (January 2000).

Smith, C. "Addressing Standards Through Curriculum Integration." *School Journal* 33(2):5–6 (November 2001).

Stix, A. "Bridging Standards Across the Curriculum with Portfolios." *Middle School Journal* 32(1):15–25 (September 2000).

Strauss, S. E., and Irvin, J. L. "Exemplary Literacy Learning Programs." *Middle School Journal* 32(1):56–59 (September 2000).

Taylor, B. M.; Graves, M. F.; and van den Broek, P. (Eds.). *Reading for Meaning: Fostering Comprehension in the Middle Grades.* Language and Literacy Series. Newark, DE: International Reading Association, 2000.

Taylor, H. E., and Larson, S. "Social and Emotional Learning in Middle School." *Clearing House* 72(6):331–336 (July 1999).

Thompson, S. "The Authentic Standards Movement and Its Evil Twin." *Phi Delta Kappan* 82(5):358–362 (January 2001).

Vars, G. "Can Curriculum Integration Survive in an Era of High-Stakes Testing?" *Middle School Journal* 33(2):7–17 (November 2001).

Victor, E., and Kellough, R. D. *Science for the Elementary and Middle School,* 9th ed. Upper Saddle River, NJ: Prentice Hall, 2000.

Vontz, T. S., and Nixon, W. A. *Issue-Centered Civic Education in Middle Schools.* ERIC Digest 429929. Bloomington, IN: ERIC Clearinghouse for Social Studies/Social Science Education, 1999.

Weilbacher, G. "Is Curriculum Integration an Endangered Species?" *Middle School Journal* 33(2):18–27 (November 2001).

Wolk, S. "The Benefits of Exploratory Time." *Educational Leadership* 59(2):56–59 (October 2001).

6

Preparing an Instructional Plan

The teacher's edition of the student textbook you use and other resource materials may expedite your planning but should not be a substitute for it. You must know how to create a good instructional plan. In this chapter you will learn how it is done.

OBJECTIVES

Upon completion of this chapter, you should be able to

1. Complete a unit of instruction with sequential lesson plans.

2. Demonstrate understanding of the significance of the planned unit of instruction and the concept of planning curriculum and instruction as an organic process.

3. Describe the similarities and differences between two types of instructional units—the conventional unit and the integrated thematic unit.

4. Demonstrate understanding of the place and role of each of the four decision-making and thought-processing phases in unit planning and implementation.

5. Demonstrate understanding of self-reflection as a common thread that is important to the reciprocal process of teaching and learning.

6. Demonstrate an understanding of the differences between direct and indirect instruction and the advantages and limitations of each.

7. Give examples of learning experiences for a discipline and grade level from each of these categories, know when and why you would use each one and give examples of how, why, and when they could be combined: verbal, visual, vicarious, simulated, and direct.

THE INSTRUCTIONAL UNIT

The instructional unit is a major subdivision of a course (for one course there are several to many units of instruction) and is comprised of learning activities that are planned around a central theme, topic, issue, or problem. Organizing the content of the semester or year into units makes the teaching process more manageable than when a teacher has no plan or only makes random choices.

The instructional unit is not unlike a chapter in a book, an act or scene in a play, or a phase of work when undertaking a project such as building a house. Breaking down information or actions into component parts and then grouping the related parts makes sense out of learning and doing. The unit brings a sense of cohesiveness and structure to student learning and avoids the piecemeal approach that might otherwise unfold. You can learn to articulate lessons within, between, and among unit plans and focus on important elements while not ignoring tangential information of importance. Students remember "chunks" of information, especially when those chunks are related to specific units.

Although the steps for developing any type of instructional unit are basically the same, units can be organized in a number of ways. For this resource guide, we will consider two basic types of units—the standard unit and the integrated thematic unit, both of which you are likely to use as a middle level teacher.

A *standard unit* (known also as a *conventional* or *traditional unit*) consists of a series of lessons centered on a topic, theme, major concept, or block of subject matter. Each lesson builds on the previous lesson by contributing additional subject matter, providing further illustrations, and supplying more practice or other added instruction, all of which are aimed at bringing about mastery of the knowledge and skills on which the unit is centered.

When a standard unit is centered on a central theme (see "Integrated Thematic Unit: Topic versus Theme" in Chapter 5) the unit may be referred to as a **thematic unit.** When, by design, the thematic unit integrates disciplines, such as combining the learning of science and mathematics, or social studies and English/ language arts, or combining all four core (or any other) disciplines, then it is called an *integrated* (or *interdisciplinary*) *thematic unit (ITU),* or simply, an integrated unit.

Planning and Developing Any Unit of Instruction

Whether for a standard unit or an integrated thematic unit, steps in planning and developing the unit are the same and are described in the following paragraphs.

1. *Select a suitable theme, topic, issue, or problem.* These may be already laid out in your course of study or textbook or already have been agreed to by members of the teaching team. Many schools change their themes or add new ones from year to year.

2. *Select the goals of the unit and prepare the overview.* The goals are written as an overview or rationale, covering what the unit is about and what the students are to learn. In planning the goals, you should (a) become as familiar as possible with the topic and materials used; (b) consult curriculum documents, such as courses of study, state frameworks, and resource units for ideas; (c) decide the content and procedures (i.e., what the students should learn about the topic and how); (d) write the rationale or overview, where you summarize what you expect the students will learn about the topic; and (e) be sure your goals are congruent with those of the course or grade level program.

3. *Select suitable instructional objectives.* In doing this, you should (a) include understandings, skills, attitudes, appreciations, and ideals; (b) be specific, avoiding vagueness and generalizations; (c) write the objectives in performance terms; and (d) be as certain as possible that the objectives will contribute to the major learning described in the overview.

4. *Detail the instructional procedures.* These procedures include the subject content and the learning activities, established as a series of lessons. Proceed with the following steps in your initial planning of the instructional procedures.

   a. Using curriculum documents, resource units, and colleagues as resources, gather ideas for learning activities that might be suitable for the unit.

   b. Check the learning activities to make sure that they will actually contribute to the learning designated in your objectives, discarding ideas that do not.

   c. Make sure that the learning activities are feasible. Can you afford the time, effort, or expense? Do you have the necessary materials and equipment? If not, can they be obtained? Are the activities suited to the intellectual and maturity levels of your students?

   d. Check available resources to be certain that they support the content and learning activities.

   e. Decide how to introduce the unit. Provide *introductory activities* that will arouse student interest;

inform students of what the unit is about; help you learn about your students—their interests, abilities, experiences, and present knowledge of the topic; provide transitions that bridge this topic with what students have already learned; and involve the students in the planning.

    f. Plan *developmental activities* that will sustain student interest, provide for individual student differences, promote the learning as cited in the specific objectives, and promote a project.

    g. Plan *culminating activities* that will summarize what has been learned, bring together loose ends, apply what has been learned to new situations, provide students with the opportunity to demonstrate their learning, and provide transfer to the unit that follows.

    5. *Plan for preassessment and assessment of student learning.* Preassess what students already know or think they know. Assessment of student progress in achievement of the learning objectives (formative evaluation) should permeate the entire unit (that is, as often as possible, assessment should be a daily component of lessons). Plan to gather information in several ways, including informal observations, checklist observations of student performance and their portfolios, and paper and pencil tests. As discussed in Chapters 5 and 11, assessment must be congruent with the instructional objectives.

    6. *Provide for the materials and tools of instruction.* The unit cannot function without materials. Therefore, you must plan long before the unit begins for media equipment and materials, references, reading materials, reproduced materials, and community resources. Librarians and media center personnel are usually more than willing to assist in finding appropriate materials to support a unit of instruction.

Unit Format, Inclusive Elements, and Time Duration

Follow those six steps to develop any type of unit. In addition, two general points should be made. First, although there is no single best format for a teaching unit, there are minimum inclusions. Particular formats may be best for specific disciplines, topics, and types of activities. During your student teaching, your college or university program for teacher preparation and/or your cooperating teacher(s) may have a format that you will be expected to follow. Regardless of the format, the following seven elements should be evident in any unit plan: (1) identification of grade level, subject, topic, and time duration of the unit; (2) statement of rationale and general goals for the unit; (3) major objectives of the unit; (4) materials and resources needed; (5) lesson plans; (6) assessment strategies; and (7) a statement of how the unit will attend to variations in students' reading levels, experiential backgrounds, and special needs.

Second, there is no set time duration for a unit plan, although for specific units, curriculum guides will recommend certain time spans. Units may extend for a minimum of several days (for example, the Indian Trail Junior High School "prom night" integrated unit discussed in Chapter 8 is a five-day unit) or, as in the case of some interdisciplinary thematic units, for several weeks to an entire semester or even a school year. However, be aware that when standard units last more than two or three weeks, they tend to lose the character of clearly identifiable units. For any unit of instruction, the exact time duration will be dictated by several factors, including the topic, problem, or theme; the interests and maturity of the students; and the scope of the learning activities.

THEORETICAL CONSIDERATIONS FOR THE SELECTION OF INSTRUCTIONAL STRATEGIES

As you prepare to detail your instructional plan you will be narrowing in on selecting and planning the instructional activities. In Chapter 3, you learned about specific teacher behaviors that must be in place for students to learn—structuring the learning environment, accepting and sharing instructional accountability, demonstrating withitness and overlapping, providing a variety of motivating and challenging activities, modeling appropriate behaviors, facilitating students' acquisition of data, creating a psychologically safe environment, clarifying whenever necessary, using periods of silence, and questioning thoughtfully. In the paragraphs that follow, you will learn more, not only about how to implement some of those fundamental behaviors, but also about the large repertoire of other strategies, aids, media, and resources available to you (See Figure 6.1). You will learn how to select and implement from this repertoire.

Decision Making and Strategy Selection

You must make a myriad of decisions to select and implement a particular teaching strategy effectively. The selection of a strategy depends in part upon whether you decide to deliver information directly (direct, expository, or didactic teaching) or to provide students with access to information (indirect or facilitative teaching). Direct teaching tends to be teacher-centered, while indirect teaching is more student-centered. To assist in your selection of strategies, it is important that you understand basic principles of learning summarized as follows.

Direct and Indirect Instruction: A Clarification of Terms

You are probably well aware that professional education is rampant with its own special jargon, which can be confusing to the neophyte. The use of the term **direct teaching** (or its synonym, *direct instruction*) and its antonym,

Figure 6.1 Instructional strategies.

Assignment	Lecture
Autotutorial	Library/resource center
Brainstorming	Metacognition
Coaching	Mock-up
Collaborative learning	Multimedia
Cooperative learning	Panel discussion
Debate	Problem solving
Demonstration	Project
Diorama	Questioning
Discovery	Review and practice
Drama	Role play
Drill	Script writing
Expository	Self-instructional
Field trip	module
Game	Simulation
Group work	Study guide
Guest speaker	Symposium
Homework	Telecommunication
Individualized instruction	Term paper
Inquiry	Textbook
Interactive media	Think-pair-share
Journal writing	Tutorial
Laboratory investigation	
Laser videodisc or compact disc	

direct experiences, are examples of how confusing the jargon can be. The term *direct teaching* (or *direct instruction, expository teaching,* or *teacher-centered instruction*) can also have a variety of definitions, depending on who is doing the defining. For now, you should keep this distinction in mind—do not confuse the term *direct instruction* with the term *direct experience.* The two terms indicate two separate (though not incompatible) instructional modes. The dichotomy of pedagogical opposites shown in Figure 6.2 provides a useful visual distinction of the opposites. While terms in one column are similar if not synonymous, they are near or exact opposites of those across from them in the other column.

DEGREES OF DIRECTNESS

Rather than thinking and behaving in terms of opposites, as may be suggested by Figure 6.2, more likely your teaching will be distinguished by "degrees of directness," or "degrees of indirectness." For example, directions for a culminating project may be given by the teacher in a di-

rect or expository minilesson, followed by a student-designed inquiry that leads to the final project.

Rather than focus your attention on the selection of a particular model of teaching, we emphasize the importance of an eclectic model—selecting the best from various models or approaches. As indicated by the example of the preceding paragraph, there will be times when you want to use a direct, teacher-centered approach, perhaps by a minilecture or a demonstration. There will be many more times when you want to use an indirect, student-centered or social-interactive approach, such as cooperative learning and investigative projects. And there may be even more times when you do both at the same time; for example, use a teacher-centered approach to work with one small group of students, perhaps giving them direct instruction, while another group or several groups of students, in areas of the classroom, work on their project studies (a student-centered approach). The information that follows and specific descriptions in Part III will help you make decisions about when each approach is most appropriate and will provide guidelines for their use.

Principles of Classroom Instruction and Learning: A Synopsis

A student does not learn to write by learning to recognize grammatical constructions of sentences. Neither does a person learn to play soccer solely by listening to a lecture about soccer. Learning is superficial unless the instructional methods and learning activities are (a) developmentally appropriate for the learners and (b) intellectually appropriate for the understanding, skills, and attitudes desired. Memorizing, for instance, is not the same as understanding. Yet far too often, memorization seems all that is expected of students in many classrooms. The result is low-level learning, a mere verbalism or mouthing of poorly understood words and sentences. The orchestration of short-term memory exercises is not intellectually appropriate, and it is not teaching. A mental model of learning that assumes that a brain is capable of doing only one thing at a time is invidiously incorrect.[1]

---

[1]See, for example, E. Jensen, *Teaching With the Brain in Mind* (Alexandria, VA: Association for Supervision and Curriculum Development, 1998), and J. C. Baker and F. G. Martin, *A Neural Network Guide to Teaching,* Fastback 431 (Bloomington, IN: Phi Delta Kappa Educational Foundation, 1998).

Figure 6.2 Pedagogical opposites.

Delivery mode of instruction	versus	Access mode of instruction
Didactic instruction	versus	Facilitative teaching
Direct instruction	versus	Indirect instruction
Direct teaching	versus	Direct experiencing
Expository teaching	versus	Discovery learning
Teacher-centered instruction	versus	Student-centered instruction

When selecting the mode of instruction, you should bear in mind the following basic principles of classroom instruction and learning.

- Although young adolescent students differ in their styles of learning and in their learning capacities, all can learn.
- Learning is most meaningful and longest lasting when it is connected to real-life experiences.
- No matter what else you are prepared to teach, you are primarily a teacher of literacy and of thinking, social, and learning skills.
- Physical activity enhances learning.[2] As recommended by teachers from Crabapple Middle School (Roswell, GA), every lesson should include an activity involving the kinesthetic learning modality.[3]
- Students must be actively involved in their own learning and in the assessment of their learning.
- Students need constant, understandable, positive, and reliable feedback about their learning.
- Students should be engaged in both independent study and cooperative learning and should give and receive tutorial instruction.
- To a great degree, it is the mode of instruction that determines what is learned and how well it is learned.
- You must hold high expectations for the learning of each student (but not necessarily identical expectations for every student) and not waiver from those expectations.

CONCEPTUAL AND PROCEDURAL KNOWLEDGE

Conceptual knowledge refers to the understanding of relationships and abstractions, whereas procedural knowledge entails the recording in memory of the meanings of symbols, rules, and procedures needed in order to accomplish tasks. Unless it is connected in meaningful ways for the formation of conceptual knowledge, the accumulation of memorized procedural knowledge is fragmented and ill fated and will be maintained in the brain for only a brief time.

To help young adolescents establish conceptual knowledge, their learning must be meaningful. To help make learning meaningful for your students, you should use direct and real experiences as often as practical and possible. Vicarious experiences are sometimes necessary to provide students with otherwise unattainable knowledge; however, direct experiences that engage all the student's senses and all their learning modalities are more powerful. Students learn to write by writing and by receiving coaching and feedback about

their progress in writing. They learn to play soccer by experiencing playing soccer and by receiving coaching and feedback about their developing skills and knowledge in playing the game. They learn these things best when they are actively (hands-on) and mentally (minds-on) engaged in doing them. This is real learning that is meaningful; it is *authentic learning*.

Direct vs. Indirect Instructional Modes: Strengths and Weaknesses of Each

When selecting an instructional strategy, there are two distinct modes from which you must choose. Should you deliver information to students directly or should you provide students with access to information? (Refer to the comparison of "pedagogical opposites" in Figure 6.2.)

The *delivery mode* (known also as the *didactic, expository,* or *traditional* style) is to deliver information. Knowledge is passed on from those who know (the teachers, with the aid of textbooks) to those who do not (the students). Within the delivery mode, traditional and time-honored strategies are textbook reading, lecture (formal teacher talk), questioning, and teacher-centered or teacher-planned discussions.

With the *access mode,* instead of direct delivery of information and direct control over what is learned, you provide students with access to information by working *with* them. In collaboration with the students, experiences are designed that facilitate their building of existing schemata and obtaining new knowledge and skills. Within the access mode, important instructional strategies include cooperative learning, inquiry, and investigative student-centered project learning. Each of these most certainly uses questioning, although the questions more frequently come from the students than from you or the textbook or some other source extrinsic to the student. Discussions and lectures on particular topics also may be involved. But when used in the access mode, discussions and lectures occur during or after (rather than before) direct, hands-on learning by the students. In other words, rather than preceding student inquiry, discussions and lectures *result from* student inquiry, and then may be followed by further student investigation.

You are probably more experienced with the delivery mode. To be most effective as a middle level classroom teacher, however, you must become knowledgeable and skillful in using access strategies. You should appropriately select and effectively use strategies from both modes, but with a strong tendency toward access strategies. Strategies within the access mode clearly facilitate students' positive learning and acquisition of conceptual knowledge and help build their self-esteem. From your study of the chapters that follow in Part III, you will become knowledgeable about specific techniques so you can make intelligent choices

---

[2]See, for example, E. Jensen, "Moving with the Brain in Mind," *Educational Leadership* 58(3):34–37 (November 2000).

[3]S. Moss and M. Fuller, "Implementing Effective Practices," *Phi Delta Kappan* 82(4):273–276 (December 2000), p. 274.

Figure 6.3 Delivery mode: Its strengths and weaknesses.

DELIVERY MODE

Strengths

- Much content can be covered within a short span of time, usually by formal teacher talk, which then may be followed by an experiential activity.
- The teacher is in control of what content is covered.
- The teacher is in control of time allotted to specific content coverage.
- Strategies within the delivery mode are consistent with competency-based instruction.
- Student achievement of specific content is predictable and manageable.

Potential Weaknesses

- The sources of student motivation are mostly extrinsic.
- Students have little control over the pacing of their learning.
- Students make few important decisions about their learning.
- There may be little opportunity for divergent or creative thinking.
- Student self-esteem may be inadequately served.

Figure 6.4 Access mode: Its strengths and weaknesses.

ACCESS MODE

Strengths

- Students learn content, and in more depth.
- The sources of student motivation are more likely intrinsic.
- Students make important decisions about their own learning.
- Students have more control over the pacing of their learning.
- Students develop a sense of personal self-worth.

Potential Weaknesses

- Breadth of content coverage may be more limited.
- Strategies are time-consuming.
- The teacher has less control over content and time.
- The specific results of student learning are less predictable.
- The teacher may have less control over class procedures.

concerning the best strategy to use for particular goals and objectives for your own discipline, and for the interests, needs, and maturity level of your unique group of students.

Figures 6.3 and 6.4 provide an overview of the specific strengths and weaknesses of each mode. By comparing those figures you can see that the strengths and weaknesses of one mode are nearly exact opposites of the other. As noted earlier, as a teacher you should be skillful in the use of strategies from both modes, but for the most developmentally appropriate teaching you should concentrate more on using strategies from the access mode. Strategies within that mode are more student-centered, hands-on, and concrete; students interact with one another and are actually doing or are closer to doing what they are learning—that is, the learning is likely more authentic. Learning that occurs from using that mode is longer lasting (fixes into long-term memory). And, as the students interact with one another and with their learning, they develop a sense of "can do," which enhances their self-esteem.

SELECTING LEARNING ACTIVITIES THAT ARE DEVELOPMENTALLY APPROPRIATE

Returning to our soccer example, can you imagine a soccer coach teaching students the skills and knowledge needed to play soccer but without ever letting them experience playing the game? Can you imagine a science

teacher instructing students on how to read a thermometer without ever letting them actually read a real thermometer? Can you imagine a geography teacher teaching students how to read a map without ever letting them put their eyes and hands on a real map? Can you imagine a piano teacher teaching a student to play piano without ever allowing the student to touch a real keyboard? Unfortunately, even in middle level schools too many teachers still do almost those exact things— they try to teach students to do something without letting the students practice doing it.

In planning and selecting developmentally appropriate learning activities, an important rule to remember is to select activities that are as close to the real thing as possible—learning through direct experiencing. When students are involved in direct experiences, they are using more of their sensory input channels, which are their learning modalities (i.e., auditory, visual, tactile, kinesthetic). And when all the senses are engaged, learning is more integrated and is most effective, meaningful, and longest lasting. This "learning by doing" is *authentic learning*—or, as referred to earlier, *hands-on/minds-on learning*.

The Learning Experiences Ladder

Figure 6.5 shows the Learning Experiences Ladder, a visual depiction of a range of kinds of learning experiences from which a teacher may select. Hands-on/minds-on learning is at the bottom of the ladder. At the top are abstract experiences, where the learner is exposed only to symbolization (letters and numbers) and uses only one or two senses (auditory or visual). The teacher lectures while the students sit and watch and hear. Visual and verbal symbolic experiences, although impossible to avoid when teaching, are

Figure 6.5   The Learning Experiences Ladder.

Note: Earlier versions of this concept were Charles F. Hoban, Sr., et al., *Visualizing the Curriculum* (New York: Dryden, 1937), p. 39; Jerome S. Bruner, *Toward a Theory of Instruction* (Cambridge: Harvard University Press, 1966), p. 49, Edgar Dale, *Audio-Visual Methods in Teaching* (New York: Holt, Rinehart & Winston, 1969), p. 108; and Eugene C. Kim and Richard D. Kellough, *A Resource Guide for Secondary School Teaching*, 2nd ed. (Upper Saddle River, NJ: Prentice Hall, 1978), p. 136.

A B S T R A C T ↑

Verbal Experiences

Teacher talk, written words; engaging only one sense; using the most abstract symbolization; students physically inactive. *Examples:* (a) Listening to the teacher talk about tide pools. (b) Listening to a student report about the Grand Canyon. (c) Listening to a guest speaker talk about how the state legislature functions.

Visual Experiences

Still pictures, diagrams, charts; engaging only one sense; typically symbolic; students physically inactive. *Examples:* (a) Viewing slide photographs of tidel pools. (b) Viewing drawings and photographs of the Grand Canyon. (c) Listening to a guest speaker talk about the state legislature and show slides of it in action.

Vicarious Experiences

Laser videodisc programs; computer programs; video programs; engaging more than one sense; learner indirectly "doing"; may be some limited physical activity. *Examples:* (a) Interacting with a computer program about wave action and life in tidel pools. (b) Viewing and listening to a video program about the Grand Canyon. (c) Taking a field trip to observe the state legislature in action.

Simulated Experiences

Role-playing; experimenting; simulations; mock-up; working models; all or nearly all senses engaged; activity often integrating disciplines; closest to the real thing. *Examples:* (a) Building a classroom working model of a tidel pool. (b) Building a classroom working model of the Grand Canyon. (c) Designing a classroom role-play simulation patterned after the operating procedure of the state legislature.

Direct Experiences

Learner actually doing what is being learned; true inquiry; all senses engaged; usually integrates disciplines; the real thing. *Examples:* (a) Visiting and experiencing a tidal pool. (b) Visiting and experiencing the Grand Canyon. (c) Designing an elected representative body to oversee the operation of the school-within-the-school program that is patterned after the state legislative assembly.

↓ C O N C R E T E

less effective in assuring that planned and meaningful learning occurs. This is especially so with learners who have special needs, learners with ethnic and cultural differences, and English language learning (ELL) students. Thus, when planning learning experiences and selecting instructional materials, you are advised to select activities that engage the students in the most direct experiences possible and that are developmentally and intellectually appropriate for your specific group of students.

As can be inferred from the Learning Experiences Ladder, when teaching about tide pools (the first example for each step) the most effective mode is to take the students to a tide pool (direct experience), where students can see, hear, touch, smell, and perhaps even taste (if not polluted with toxins) the tide pool. The least effective mode is for the teacher to merely talk about the

tide pool (verbal experience, the most abstract and symbolic experience), engaging only one sense—auditory.

Of course, for various reasons—such as time, matters of safety, lack of resources, geographic location of your school—you may not be able to take your students to a tide pool. You cannot always use the most direct experience, so sometimes you must select an experience higher on the ladder. Self-discovery teaching is not always appropriate. Sometimes it is more appropriate to build upon what others have discovered and learned. Although learners do not need to "reinvent the wheel," the most effective and longest-lasting learning is that which engages most or all of their senses. On the Learning Experiences Ladder, those are the experiences that fall within the bottom three categories—direct, simulated, and vicarious.

Direct, Simulated, and Vicarious Experiences Help Connect Student Learning

Another value of direct, simulated, and vicarious experiences is that they tend to be interdisciplinary; that is, they blur or bridge subject-content boundaries. That makes those experiences especially useful for teachers who want to help students connect the learning of one discipline with that of others and to bridge what is being learned with their own life experiences. Direct, simulated, and vicarious experiences are more like real life. That means that the learning resulting from those experiences is authentic.

Now do Exercises 6.1 and 6.2.

EXERCISE 6.1: RECALLING MY OWN LEARNING EXPERIENCES IN SCHOOL

INSTRUCTIONS: The purpose of this exercise is to recall and share learning experiences from your own school days. You should reflect on them with respect to their relationship to the Learning Experiences Ladder and the discussion of the access and delivery modes of instruction.

1. Recall one vivid learning experience from each level of your schooling and identify its position on the Learning Experiences Ladder.

   Middle Level Experience: _____

   _____

   _____

   _____

   _____

   _____

   _____

   Position on Ladder: _____

   _____

   High School Experience: _____

   _____

   _____

   _____

   _____

   _____

   _____

   Position on Ladder: _____

   _____

   College Experience: _____

   _____

   _____

   _____

   _____

   _____

   _____

   Position on Ladder: _____

   _____

EXERCISE 6.1 (*continued*)

2. Share with classmates in small groups. After sharing your experiences with others of your group, what, if anything, can your group conclude? Write those conclusions here and then share them with the entire class.

_____

_____

_____

_____

_____

_____

_____

_____

_____

_____

_____

_____

_____

_____

_____

_____

_____

_____

_____

_____

_____

_____

_____

_____

_____

_____

_____

EXERCISE 6.2: CONVERSION OF AN ABSTRACT LEARNING EXPERIENCE TO A DIRECT ONE

INSTRUCTIONS: This exercise is to tax your creative imagination. Select from your outline a topic that is typically taught by the use of symbolization (at or near the top of the Learning Experiences Ladder), then devise a technique by which, with limited resources, that same content would be taught more directly (at or close to the bottom of the ladder). Upon completion of this exercise, share your proposal with your colleagues for their feedback.

1. Grade Level: _____

2. Topic: _____

3. Traditional way of teaching this topic: _____

_____

_____

_____

_____

_____

4. Detailed description of how to teach this topic using direct learning experiences: _____

_____

_____

_____

_____

_____

_____

_____

5. Statement about why you believe a direct way of teaching this topic is uncommon: _____

_____

_____

_____

_____

_____

_____

6. Ideas resulting from sharing your proposal with others in your class: _____

_____

_____

_____

_____

_____

_____

FOR YOUR NOTES

SCHOOL VIGNETTE

A Seventh-Grade ITU at Albert F. Ford Middle School

Seventh-grade students at Ford Middle School (Acushnet, MA) work all year on various projects that constitute a thematic unit about hot air ballooning. The title of the unit is "The Great Balloon Craze." Students read *The Great Balloon Craze,* a nonfiction selection about women who were active in hot air ballooning more than a century ago, and *Airy-Go-Round,* an adventure story of a retired math teacher whose balloon went down and was washed ashore on the island of Krakatoa. Students plot an imaginary journey of their own, create a comic strip, design an imaginary machine, and study and calculate information about three record-breaking balloon voyages. They watch the movie *Around the World in 80 Days* and attend a live theater production of the same title. Students design posters that use persuasive techniques, and that act as ads inviting people in the early 1800s to witness Madame Blanchard's first balloon flight in Paris. A local balloonist gives a live presentation. Students experiment with creating hot air balloon soft sculptures and create watercolors of landscapes and hot air balloons.

Source: Adapted by permission from the Ford Middle School (Acushnet, MA) Web page [Online]. Available at http://www.ultranet.com/~fordms/news.html (March 1, 2001).

PLANNING AND DEVELOPING AN INTERDISCIPLINARY THEMATIC UNIT

The six steps outlined earlier in this chapter are essential for planning any type of teaching unit. That includes the interdisciplinary thematic unit (ITU), which may consist of smaller subject-specific conventional units. Because developing interdisciplinary thematic units is an essential task for many of today's middle level teachers, you should learn this process now.

The primary responsibility for the development of ITUs can depend on a single teacher or upon the cooperation of several teachers, who represent several disciplines. A teaching team may develop from one to several interdisciplinary thematic units a year. Over time, then, a team will have several units that are available for implementation. However, the most effective units are often those that are the most current or the most meaningful to students. This means that ever-changing global, national, and local topics provide a veritable smorgasbord from which to choose, and teaching teams must constantly update old units and develop new and exciting ones.

One teaching team's unit should not conflict with others at the same or another grade level. If a school has two or more teams at the same grade level that involve the same disciplines, the teams may want to develop units on different themes and share their products. For example, a seventh-grade team must guard against developing a unit quite similar to one that the students had or will have at another grade level. Open lines of communication within, between, and among teams and schools within a school district are critical to the success of interdisciplinary thematic teaching.[4] Consider the steps that follow.

Steps for Developing an Interdisciplinary Thematic Unit

Following are ten steps to guide you in developing an ITU:

1. *Agree on the nature or source of the unit.* Team members should view the interdisciplinary approach as a collaborative effort in which all members (and other faculty) can participate if appropriate. Write what you want the students to receive from interdisciplinary instruction. Troubleshoot potential stumbling blocks.

2. *Discuss subject-specific standards, goals, and objectives; curriculum guidelines; textbooks and supplemental materials; and units already in place for the school year.* Focus on what you are obligated or mandated to teach, and explain the scope and sequence of the teaching so all team members understand the constraints and limitations.

3. *Choose a theme topic and develop a time line.* From the information provided by each subject-specialist teacher in step 2, start listing possible theme topics that can be drawn from within the existing course outlines. Give-and-take is essential here, as some topics will fit certain subjects better than others. (See "Integrated Thematic Unit: Topic versus Theme," in Chapter 5.) The chief goal is to find a topic that can be adapted to each subject without detracting from the educational plan already in place. This may require choosing and merging content from two or more other units previously planned. The theme is then drawn from the topic.

---

[4]See G. Quinn and L. N. Restine, "Interdisciplinary Teams: Concerns, Benefits, and Costs," *Journal of School Leadership* 6(5):494–511 (September 1996).

Sometimes themes are selected by the teacher or by a teaching team before meeting the students for the first time. Other times they are selected by the teachers in collaboration with students. Even when the theme is preselected, with guidance from the teacher, students still should be given major responsibility for deciding the final theme title (name), topics, and corresponding learning activities. Integrated thematic instruction works best when students have ownership in the study, that is, when they have been empowered with major decision-making responsibility.

The basis for theme selection should satisfy two criteria: the theme should (a) fit within the expected scope and sequence of mandated content and (b) be of interest to the students. Regarding the first criterion, many teachers have said that when they and their students embarked on an interdisciplinary thematic study, they did so without truly knowing where the study would go or what the learning outcomes would be—and they were somewhat frightened by that. But when the unit was completed, their students had learned everything (or nearly everything) that the teacher would have expected them to learn were the teacher to use a more traditional approach. And, it was more fun!

See Figure 6.6 for important questions to ask when selecting a theme.

The second criterion is easy to satisfy when students are truly empowered with decision-making responsibility for what and how they learn. So, once a general theme is selected (one that satisfies the first criterion), its final title, subtopics, and corresponding procedural activities should be finalized in collaboration with the students. (See Step 7.)

Figure 6.6 Questions to ask when selecting a theme.

- Is the theme within the realm of understanding and experience of the teachers involved?
- Will the theme interest all members of the teaching team?
- Do we have sufficient materials and resources to supply information we might need?
- Does the theme lend itself to active learning experiences?
- Can this theme lead to a unit that is of the proper duration—not too short and not too long?
- Is the theme helpful, worthwhile, and pertinent to the instructional objectives?
- Will the theme be of interest to students, and will it motivate them to do their best?
- Is the theme one with which teachers are not already so familiar that they cannot share in the excitement of the learning?

4. *Establish two time lines.* The first is for the team only and is to ensure that the deadlines for specific work required in developing the unit will be met by each member. The second time line is for both students and teachers and shows the intended length of the unit, when it will start, and in which classes it will be taught.

5. *Develop the scope and sequence for content and instruction.* To develop the unit, follow the six steps for planning and developing a unit of instruction outlined earlier in this chapter. This should be done by each team member as well as by the group during common planning time so members can coordinate dates and activities in logical sequence and depth. This is an organic process and will generate both ideas and anxiety. Under the guidance of the team leader, members should strive to keep this anxiety at a level conducive to learning, experimenting, and arriving at group consensus.

6. *Share goals and objectives.* Each team member should have a copy of the goals and target objectives of every other team member. This helps to refine the unit and lesson plans and to prevent unnecessary overlap and confusion.

7. *Give the unit a name.* The unit has been fashioned and is held together by the theme that is chosen. Giving the theme a name and using that name communicates to the students that this unit of study is integrated, important, and meaningful to school and to life.

8. *Share subject-specific units, lesson plans, and printed and nonprinted materials.* Exchange the finalized unit to obtain one another's comments and suggestions. Keep a copy of each teacher's unit(s) as a resource, and see if you could present a lesson using it as your basis (some modification may be necessary).

9. *Field test the unit.* Beginning at the scheduled time and date, present the lessons. Team members may trade classes from time to time. Team teaching may take place if and when two or more classes can be combined for instruction (if a large enough classroom space is available).

10. *Reflect, assess, and perhaps adjust and revise the unit.* During planning time, team members should share and discuss their successes and failures and determine what needs to be changed and how and when that should be done to make the unit successful. Adjustments can be made along the way and revisions for future use can be made after the unit.

The preceding 10 steps are not absolutes and should be viewed only as guides. Differing teaching teams and levels of teacher experience and knowledge make the strict adherence to any one plan less productive than the use of group-generated plans. For instance, some teachers have found that the last point in Figure 6.6 could state exactly the opposite; they recommend that the topic for an interdisciplinary unit should be one that a teacher or a teaching team already knows well. In practice, the process that works well—one that results in meaningful learning for the students and positive feelings about themselves, about learning, and about school—is the appropriate process. For example, at Collins Middle School (Salem, MA) teachers use what is sometimes called a *backward design* for their curriculum planning. The procedure is as follows: (a) first the teachers study the state standards; (b) from the standards they establish goals for their students; (c) they think of projects that will provide opportunities for their students to demonstrate that they have gained the expected understandings and skills; and (d) finally they select instructional activities that will support their plan.[5]

Developing the Learning Activities: The Heart and Spirit of the ITU

Activities that engage the students in meaningful learning constitute the heart and spirit of the ITU. Activities that start a unit into motion, that initiate the unit are *initiating activities;* activities that comprise the heart of the unit are *ongoing developmental activities;* and, activities that bring the unit to a natural close are *culminating activities.*

THE COMMON THREAD

Central to the selection and development of all learning activities for interdisciplinary thematic instruction is a common thread of four tightly interwoven components: (a) the instruction is centered around a big and meaningful idea (theme) rather than on factitious subject areas, (b) the students and the teacher share in the decision making and responsibility for learning, (c) the learning activities are selected so all students are actively engaged in their learning—that is, they are both physically active (hands-on learning) and mentally active (minds-on learning), and (d) there is steady reflection on and frequent sharing of what is being done and what is being learned.

INITIATING ACTIVITIES

An ITU can be initiated in a limitless variety of ways. You must decide which ways are appropriate for your educational goals and objectives, your intended time duration, and your own unique group of students, considering their interests, abilities, and skills. You might start with a current event, a community problem, an artifact, a book, a media presentation, or something interesting you found on the Internet.

ONGOING DEVELOPMENTAL ACTIVITIES

Once the ITU has been initiated, students become occupied with a variety of ongoing activities. In working with students in selecting and planning the ongoing learning activities, you will want to keep in mind the concept represented by the Learning Experiences Ladder (Figure 6.5) as well as the predetermined goals and target objectives (Chapter 5).

---

[5]G. A. Davis and A. W. Jackson, "Backward Design: Putting Standards into the Curriculum," *Middle Ground* 4(2):13–14 (October 2000).

CULMINATING ACTIVITY

Just as with other types of unit plans, an ITU is brought to close with a culminating activity. Such an activity often includes an exhibition or sharing of the product of the students' study. You could accept the students' suggestions for a culminating activity if it engages them in summarizing what they have learned with others. A culminating activity that brings closure to a unit can give the students an opportunity for synthesis (by assembling, constructing, creating, inventing, producing, or incorporating something) and even an opportunity to present that synthesis to an audience, such as by establishing an Internet website, or sharing their product on an existing school website.

A culminating activity can provide an opportunity for the students to move from recording information to reporting on their learning. For example, one activity might be for students to take field trips to study something related to the theme and then synthesize their learning after the trip in a way that culminates the study. On field trips, students should be given notepads similar to the ones reporters use and asked to take notes and make sketches of what they learn. They can discuss the questions they have on the ride to the site. They can discuss what they liked and did not like on the ride back to school. After the trip, each student can choose something he or she saw and then build it to scale, so the students can have scale models of the things they saw on the trip that caught their interest. The students could then invite other classes in to examine the scale models and listen to student reports about why the objects interested them. Students might also present an art show of drawings about the unit's theme, with a narration that informs others about their study. You might also schedule a culminating activity that asks students to report on individual projects—the aspect each student formerly reserved for individual study.

Culminating activities are opportunities for students to proudly demonstrate and share their learning and creativity in different and individual ways. Examples of actual culminating activities and products of an ITU are endless. As just one successful example, students at King Middle School (Portland, ME) studied the shore life of Maine's Casco Bay for a year. The culminating activity of their study was their writing and publishing a book that includes student-drawn illustrations and scientific descriptions of the flora and fauna found along the shore. The book is now in all the city's libraries where it can be borrowed and used by anyone taking a walk along the shore.

PREPARING LESSON PLANS: RATIONALE AND ASSUMPTIONS

As described at the beginning of this chapter, step 4 of the six steps of instructional planning is the preparation for class meetings. The process of designing a lesson is important in learning to provide the most efficient use of valuable and limited instructional time and the most effective learning for the students, to meet the unit goals.

Notice the title of this section does not refer to the "*daily* lesson plan," but rather, "the lesson plan." The focus is on how to prepare a lesson plan, and that plan may, in fact, be a daily plan, or it may not. In some instances, a lesson plan may extend for more than one class period or days, perhaps two or three (as, for example, the lesson shown later in this chapter in Figure 6.10). In other instances, the lesson plan is in fact a daily plan and may run for an entire class period. In block scheduling, one lesson plan may run for part or all of a two-hour block of time. See "The Problem of Time" later in this chapter.

Effective teachers are always planning for their classes. For the long range, they plan the scope and sequence, and develop content. Within this long-range planning, they develop units, and within units, they design the activities to be used and the assessments of learning to be done. They familiarize themselves with books, materials, media, and innovations in their fields of interest. Yet, despite all this planning activity, the lesson plan remains pivotal to the planning process.

Consider now the rationale, description, and guidelines for writing detailed lesson plans.

Rationale for Preparing Written Plans

First, *carefully prepared and written lesson plans show everyone—first and foremost your students, then your colleagues, your administrator, and, if you are a student teacher, your college or university supervisor—that you are a committed professional.* Sometimes beginning teachers are concerned about being seen by their students using a written plan in class, thinking it may suggest that they have not mastered the material. On the contrary, a lesson plan is tangible evidence that you are working at your job, and it demonstrates respect for the students, yourself, and for the profession. A written lesson plan shows that preactive thinking and planning have taken place. There is absolutely no excuse for appearing before a class without evidence of being prepared.

Written and detailed lesson plans provide an important sense of security, which is especially useful to a beginning teacher. Like a rudder of a ship, it helps keep you on course. Without it, you are likely to drift aimlessly. Sometimes a disturbance in the classroom can distract from the lesson, causing the teacher to get "off track" or forget an important part of the lesson. A detailed, written lesson plan provides a road map to guide you and help keep you on track.

Written lesson plans help you to be or become a reflective decision maker. Without a written plan, it is difficult or impossible to analyze how something might have been planned or implemented differently after the lesson has been taught. Written lesson plans serve as resources for the next time you teach the same or a similar lesson and are useful for teacher self-evaluation and for the evaluation of student learning and the curriculum.

Written lesson plans help you organize material and search for "loopholes," "loose ends," or incomplete content. Careful and thorough planning during the preactive phase of instruction includes anticipation of how the lesson activities will develop as the lesson is being taught. During this anticipation you will actually visualize yourself in the classroom teaching your students, using that visualization to anticipate possible problems.

Written plans help other members of the teaching team understand what you are doing and how you are doing it. This is especially important when implementing an interdisciplinary thematic unit. *Written lesson plans also provide substitute teachers with a guide to follow if you are absent.*

Those reasons clearly express the need to write detailed lesson plans. The list is not exhaustive, however, and you may discover additional reasons why written lesson plans are crucial to effective teaching. In summary, two points must be made: (a) lesson planning is an important and ongoing process and (b) teachers must take time to plan, reflect, write, test, evaluate, and rewrite their plans to reach optimal performance. In short, preparing written lesson plans is important work.

Assumptions about Lesson Planning

Not all teachers need elaborate written plans for every lesson. Sometimes effective, skilled, experienced teachers need only a sketchy outline. Sometimes they may not need written plans at all. Veteran teachers who have taught the topic many times in the past may need only the presence of a class of students to stimulate a pattern of presentation that has often been successful (though frequent use of old patterns may lead one into the rut of unimaginative and uninspiring teaching). You probably do not need to be reminded that the obsolescence of many past classroom practices has been substantiated repeatedly by those researchers who have made serious and recent studies of exemplary educational practices.

Considering the diversity among middle level teachers, their instructional styles, and their students, and what research has shown, certain assumptions can be made about lesson planning.

- A plan is more likely to be carefully and thoughtfully plotted during the preactive phase of instruction when the plan is written out.
- Although not all teachers need elaborate written plans for all lessons, all effective teachers do have clearly defined goals and objectives in mind and a planned pattern of instruction for every lesson, whether that plan is written out or not.
- Beginning teachers need to prepare detailed written lesson plans—failing to prepare is preparing to fail.
- The depth of knowledge a teacher has about a subject or topic influences the amount of planning necessary for the lessons.

CLASSROOM VIGNETTE

A Teachable Moment

At Harriet Eddy Middle School (Elk Grove, CA), Casey was teaching an eighth-grade humanities block, a two-hour block course that integrates student learning in social studies, reading, and language arts. On this particular day, while Casey and her students were discussing the topic of Manifest Destiny, one of the students raised his hand and, when acknowledged by Casey, asked, "Why aren't we [referring to the United States] still adding states? [that is, adding territory to the United States]." Casey immediately replied with, "There aren't any more states to add." By responding too quickly, Casey missed one of those "teachable moments," moments when the teacher has the students right where she wants them, that is; when the students are the ones who are thinking and asking questions. What could Casey have done? When was Hawaii added as a state? Why hasn't Puerto Rico become a state? Guam? etc. Aren't those possibilities? Why *aren't* more states or territories being added? What are the political and social ramifications today and how do they differ from those of the 1800s?

• The diversity of students within today's middle level classroom necessitates careful and thoughtful consideration about individualizing the instruction—these considerations are best implemented when they have been thoughtfully written into lesson plans.

• The skill a teacher has in remaining calm and in following a trend of thought in the presence of distraction will influence the amount of detail necessary when planning activities and writing the lesson plan.

• There is no particular pattern or format that all teachers need to follow when writing out plans. Some teacher-preparation programs have agreed on certain lesson-plan formats for their teacher candidates; you need to know if this is the case for your program.

In summary, then, well-written lesson plans provide many advantages: they give a teacher an agenda or outline to follow in teaching a lesson; they give a substitute teacher a basis for presenting appropriate lessons to a class—thereby retaining lesson continuity in the regular teacher's absence; they are certainly very useful when a teacher is planning to use the same lesson again in the future; they provide the teacher with something to fall back on in case of a memory lapse, an interruption, or a distraction such as a call from the office or a fire drill; they demonstrate to students that you care and are working for them; and, above all, they provide beginners with security. With a carefully prepared plan, a beginning teacher can walk into a classroom with confidence and professional pride gained from having developed a sensible framework for that day's instruction.

Therefore, as a beginning teacher, you should make considerably detailed lesson plans. Naturally, this will require a great deal of work for at least the first year or two, but the reward of knowing that you have prepared and presented effective lessons will compensate for that effort. You can expect a busy first year of teaching.

A Continual Process

Lesson planning is a continual process even for experienced teachers, for there is always a need to keep materials and plans current and relevant. Because no two classes of students are ever identical, today's lesson plan will need to be tailored to the peculiar needs of each classroom of students. Moreover, because the content of instruction and learning will change as each distinct group of students provides input about their needs and interests, new thematic units are developed, new developments occur, or new theories are introduced, your objectives and the objectives of the students, school, and teaching faculty will change.

For these reasons, lesson plans should be in a constant state of revision—never "set in concrete." Once the basic framework is developed, however, the task of updating and modifying becomes minimal. If your plans are maintained on a computer, making changes from time to time is even easier.

Well Planned but Open to Last-Minute Change

The lesson plan should provide a tentative outline of the time period given for the lesson but should always remain flexible. A carefully worked out plan may have to be set aside because of the unpredictable, serendipitous effect of a "teachable moment" (see the vignette above) or because of unforeseen circumstances, such as a delayed school bus, an impromptu school assembly program, an emergency drill, or the cancellation of school due to inclement weather conditions. Student teachers often are appalled at the frequency of interruptions during a school day and disruptions to their lesson planning that occur. A daily lesson planned to cover six aspects of a given topic may end with only three of the points having been considered. Although they are far more frequent than is necessary in too many schools (recall Exercise 4.1?), these occurrences are natural in a school setting and the teacher and the plans must be flexible enough to accommodate this reality.

IMPLEMENTATION OF TODAY'S LESSON MAY NECESSITATE CHANGES IN TOMORROW'S PLAN

Although you may have your lesson plans completed for several consecutive lessons, as can be inferred by the vignette involving Casey and her students, what actually transpires during the implementation of today's lesson may necessitate last minute adjustments to the lesson you had planned for tomorrow. Rick Wormeli, an award-winning middle school teacher has said, "I've thrown out the rest of the week's lessons because the feedback I received on Tuesday indicated that students didn't understand the basic steps well enough to move on to more complex applications."[6]

Consequently, during student teaching in particular, it is neither uncommon nor unwanted to have last-minute changes penciled in your lesson plan. If, however, penciled-in modifications are substantial and might be confusing to you during implementation of the lesson, then you should rewrite the lesson plan.

The Problem of Time

A lesson plan should provide enough materials and activities to consume the entire class period or time allotted. As mentioned earlier, in planning for teaching, you need to plan for every minute of every class period. The lesson plan, then, is more than a plan for a lesson to be taught; it is a plan that accounts for the entire class period or time that you and your students are together in the classroom. Planning is a skill that takes years of experience to master, especially when teaching a block of time that may extend for 90 or more minutes and that involves more than one discipline and perhaps more than one teacher. Therefore, as a beginning teacher, rather than run the risk of having too few activities to occupy the time the students are in your classroom, you should overplan. One way of assuring that you overplan is to include "if time remains" activities in your lesson plan (see example in Figure 6.7).

When a lesson plan does not provide sufficient activity to occupy the entire class period or the time that the students are available for the lesson, a beginning teacher often loses control of the class as behavior problems mount. Therefore, it is best to prepare more than you likely can accomplish in a given period of time. This is not to imply that you should involve the students in meaningless busywork. Students can be very perceptive

when it comes to a teacher who has finished the plan and is attempting to bluff through the minutes that remain before dismissal. And, they are not usually favorably responsive to meaningless busywork.

If you ever do get caught short—as most teachers do at one time or another—one way to avoid embarrassment is, as discussed in Chapter 4, to have students work on what is known as an *anchor activity* (or transitional activity). This is an ongoing assignment, and students understand that whenever they have spare time in class, they should be working on it. Example anchor activities include reviewing material that has been covered that day or during the past several days, allowing students to work on homework, journal writing, portfolio organization, and long-term project work. Regardless of how you handle time remaining, it works best when you plan for it and write that aspect into your lesson plan. Make sure students understand the purpose and procedures for these anchor assignments.

A Caution about "The Daily Planning Book"

A distinction needs to be made between actual lesson plans and the book for daily planning that many schools require teachers to maintain and even submit to their supervisors a week in advance. Items that a teacher writes into the boxes in a daily planning book (see Figure 6.8) most assuredly are not lesson plans. Rather, the pages are a layout of boxes in which the teacher writes the lessons that will be taught during the day, week, month, or term. Usually the book provides only a small lined box for each day of the week. These books are useful for outlining the topics, activities, and assignments projected for the week or term, and supervisors sometimes use them to check the adequacy of teachers' course plans. But they are not lesson plans. Teachers and their supervisors who believe that the notations in the daily planning book are actual lesson plans are fooling themselves. Student teachers should not use these in place of authentic lesson plans.

CONSTRUCTING A LESSON PLAN: FORMAT, COMPONENTS, AND SAMPLES

Although it is true that each teacher develops a personal system of lesson planning—the system that works best for that teacher in each unique situation—a beginning teacher needs a more substantial framework from which to work. For that, this section provides a "preferred" lesson plan format (Figure 6.9). Nothing is hallowed about this format, however. Review the preferred format and samples and, unless your program of teacher preparation insists otherwise, use it with your own modifications until you find or develop a better model. All else being equal, you are encouraged, however, to begin your teaching by following as closely as possible this "preferred" format.

---

[6]R. Wormeli, "Aim for More Authentic Assessment," *Middle Ground* 4(3):10–15 (February 2001), pp. 25–28.

Figure 6.7   Lesson plan sample with alternative activities. (*Source:* Courtesy of Michelle Yendrey.)

LESSON PLAN

Descriptive Course Data
Instructor: Michelle Yendrey   *Class:* Social Studies   *Period:* 1
Grade level: 7–8   *Unit:* History of Religion   *Topic:* Persecution of Christians

Objectives
Upon completion of this lesson, students will be able to
1. Make connections between persecutions today and persecutions that occurred approximately 2,000 years ago.
2. Describe the main teachings of Christianity and how the position of Christianity within the Roman Empire changed over time.
3. Share ideas in a positive and productive manner.

Instructional Components
Activity 1 (Anticipatory Set: 10 minutes) Write on overhead: You have until 8:40 (5 minutes) to write a defense to one of the following statements. (Remember, there are no right or wrong answers. Support your position to the best of your ability.)

- A. The recent hate crimes in our city can be related to our current unit on the history of religion.
- B. The recent hate crimes in our city cannot be related to our current unit on the history of religion.

Activity 2 (3–5 minutes) Students will be asked to indicate, by a show of hands, how many chose statement A and how many chose statement B. Some reasons for each will be shared orally and then all papers will be collected.

Activity 3 (3–5 minutes) Return papers of previous assignment. Give students new seat assignments for the activity that follows, and have them assume their new seats.

Activity 4 (15 minutes) The students are now arranged into seven groups. Each group will write a paragraph using the concepts from certain assigned words (for their definition sheets of Section 3 of Chapter 7, "Christianity spread through the empire") to answer the essay question(s) at the end of the definition sheet.

Each group will select a
Task master to keep members of the group on task
Recorder to write things down
Spokesperson to present the results
Timekeeper to keep group alert so task is completed on time
In addition, some groups will have a
Source master to look up or ask about any questions that arise

Activity 5 (15–20 minutes) Each group's spokesperson will come to the front of the classroom and present the group's result for activity 4.

Alternate Activity (Plan B: 5–10 minutes) Should the activities run more quickly than anticipated, the students will take out their "Religion Comparison Sheets." Using Chapter 2, Section 2, "Jews worshiped a single God," and Chapter 7, Section 3 definition sheets. With the teacher's direction, the students will fill in the boxes for "similar" and "different" with regard to Christianity and Judaism.

Second Alternate Activity (Plan C: 25–30 minutes) In the unlikely event that timing is really off, each student will be given a blank grid and assigned ten vocabulary words from the definition sheets. Students will be directed to create a crossword puzzle using the definitions as clues and the words as answers. After 15–20 minutes, the crosswords will be collected and distributed to different students to solve. If not completed in class, students will finish and hand them in later along with their essays, for a few points of extra credit. Students will be required to write their names in the appropriate spaces marked "Created By" and "Solved By."

Activity 6 (7–10 minutes) Collect the overhead sheets and pens. Hand out the take-home essay test. Explain and take questions about exactly what is expected from the essay. (This is their first take-home test.)

Materials and Equipment Needed
Overhead projector and transparency sheets (7) and transparency markers (7); 36 copies of the essay question plus directions; 36 copies of the blank grid sheets.

Assessment, Reflection, and Plans for Revision

Figure 6.8 Daily planning book.

DAILY PLANNING BOOK

Class _____ Lesson _____ Teacher _____

Date	Content	Materials	Procedure	Evaluation
Monday				
Tuesday				
Wednesday				
Thursday				
Friday				

1. Descriptive Data

Teacher _____ Class _____ Date _____ Grade level _____

Room number _____ Period _____ Unit _____

Lesson Number _____ Topic _____

Anticipated noise level (high, moderate, low)

2. Goals and Objectives

Instructional Goals:

Specific Objectives:

Cognitive:

Affective:

Psychomotor:

3. Rationale

4. Procedure (Procedure with modeling examples, transitions, coached practice, etc.)

Content:

_____ minutes. Activity 1: Set (introduction)

_____ minutes. Activity 2:

Figure 6.9   Preferred lesson plan format with seven components.   *(continued)*
This blank lesson plan format is placed alone so that if you choose, you may remove it from the book
and make copies for use in your teaching.

_____ minutes. Activity 3: (the exact number of activities in the procedures will vary)

_____ minutes. Final Activity (lesson conclusion or closure):

If time remains:

5. **Assignments and Reminders of Assignments**

   Special notes and reminders to myself:

6. **Materials and Equipment Needed**
   Audiovisual:

   Other:

7. **Assessment, Reflection, and Revision**
   Assessment of student learning:

   Reflective thoughts about lesson:

   Suggestions for revision:

Figure 6.9 (continued)

For Guidance, Reflection, and Reference

While student teaching and during your first few years as a beginning teacher, your lesson plans should be printed from a computer or typewritten, or, if that is not possible, then written out in an intelligible style. If you have a spelling problem, use a spell check and print your plans from the computer. There is good reason to question teachers who say they have no need for a written plan because they have their lessons planned "in their heads." The hours and periods in a school day range from several to many, as do the numbers of students in each class. When multiplied by the number of school days in a week, a semester, or a year, the task of keeping so many things in one's head becomes mind-boggling. Few persons could effectively do that. Until you have considerable experience, you need to prepare and maintain detailed lesson plans for guidance, reflection, and reference.

Basic Elements in a Lesson Plan

The lesson plan format we recommend contains the following basic elements: (1) descriptive course data, (2) goals and objectives, (3) rationale, (4) procedure, (5) assignments and assignment reminders, (6) materials and equipment, and (7) a section for assessment of student learning, reflection on the lesson, and ideas for lesson revision. These seven components need not be present in every written lesson plan, nor must they be presented in any particular order. Nor are they inclusive or exclusive. You might choose to include additional components or subsections. Figure 6.10 displays a completed multiple-day lesson that includes the seven components and also incorporates many of the developmentally appropriate learning activities discussed in this resource guide.

Following are descriptions of the seven major components of the preferred format, with examples and explanations of why each is important.

Descriptive Data

A lesson plan's descriptive data is demographic and logistical information that identifies details about the class. Anyone reading this information should be able to identify when and where the class meets, who is teaching it, and what is being taught. Although as the teacher you know this, someone else may not. Members of the teaching team, administrators, and substitute teachers (and, if you are the student teacher, your university supervisor and cooperating teacher) appreciate this information, especially when asked to fill in for you, even if only for a few minutes during a class session. Most teachers find out which items of descriptive data are most beneficial in their situation and then develop their own

identifiers. Remember this: The mark of a well-prepared, clearly written lesson plan is the ease with which someone else (such as another member of your teaching team or a substitute teacher) could implement it.

As shown in the sample plans of Figures 6.7 (social studies), 6.10 (English/science), and 6.12 (physical science), the descriptive data include the following:

1. *Name of course or class.* These serve as headings for the plan, and facilitate orderly filing of plans.
   Social Studies
   Language Arts/Science (integrated block course)
   Physical Science
2. *Name of the unit.* Inclusion of this facilitates the orderly control of the hundreds of lesson plans a teacher constructs. For example
   Social Studies
       Unit: History of Religion
   Language Arts/Science
       Unit: Investigative Research and Generative Writing
   Physical Science
       Unit: What's the Matter?
3. *Topic to be considered within the unit.* This is also useful for control and identification. For example

Social Studies	*Unit: History of Religion*	*Topic: Persecution of Christians*
Language Arts/Science	*Unit: Investigative Research and Generative Writing*	*Topic: Writing Response and Peer Assessment via the Internet*
Physical Science	*Unit: What's the Matter?*	*Topic: Density of Solids*

ANTICIPATED NOISE LEVEL

Although not included in the sample lesson plans in this resource guide, the teacher might include in the descriptive data, the category of "anticipated classroom noise level," such as "high," "moderate," "low." Its inclusion, or at least consideration, is useful during the planning phase of instruction to think about how active and noisy the students might become during the lesson, how you might prepare for that, and whether you should warn an administrator and teachers of neighboring classrooms.

Goals and Objectives

The instructional goals are general statements of intended accomplishments from that lesson. Teachers and students need to know what the lesson is designed to accomplish. In clear, understandable language, the general goal statement provides that information. From the sample in Figure 6.10, the goals are

- To collaborate and prepare response papers to peers from around the world who have shared the results of

1. Descriptive Data

Teacher _____   Class _English/Language Arts/Science_   Date _____   Grade level _5–8_

Unit: _Investigative Research and Generative Writing_

Lesson Topic: _Writing Response and Peer Assessment via Internet_

Time duration: _several days_

2. Goals and Objectives of Unit

Instructional Goals:

2.1. One goal of this lesson is for students to collaborate and prepare response papers for peers around the world who have shared the results of their own experimental research findings and research papers about ozone concentrations in the atmosphere.

2.2. The ultimate goal of this unit is for students around the world to prepare and publish, for worldwide dissemination, a final paper about global ozone levels in the atmosphere.

Objectives:

Cognitive:

a. Through cooperative group action, students will conduct experimental research to collect data about the ozone level of air in their environment. (application)

b. In cooperative groups, students will analyze the results of their experiments. (analysis)

c. Students will compile data and infer from their experimental data. (synthesis and evaluation)

d. Through collaborative writing groups, the students will prepare a final paper that summarizes their research study of local atmospheric ozone levels. (evaluation)

e. Through sharing via the Internet, students will write response papers to their peers at other locations in the world. (evaluation)

f. From their own collaborative research and worldwide communications with their peers, the students will draw conclusions about global atmospheric ozone levels. (evaluation)

Affective:

a. Students will respond attentively to the response papers of their peers. (attending)

b. Students will willingly cooperate with others during the group activities. (responding)

c. Students will offer opinions about the atmospheric level of ozone. (valuing)

d. Students will form judgments about local, regional, and worldwide ozone levels. (organizing)

e. Students will communicate accurately their findings and attend diligently to the work of their worldwide peers. (internalizing)

Psychomotor:

a. Students will manipulate the computer so that their e-mail communications are transmitted accurately. (manipulating)

b. In a summary to the study, students will describe their feelings about atmospheric ozone concentrations. (communicating)

c. The students will ultimately create a proposal for worldwide dissemination. (creating)

3. Rationale

3.1. Important to improvement in one's writing and communication skills are the processes of selecting a topic, decision making, arranging, drafting, proofing, peer review, commenting, revising, editing, rewriting, and publishing the results—processes that are focused on in the writing aspect of this unit.

3.2. Student writers need many readers to respond to their work. Through worldwide communication with peers and dissemination of their final product, this need can be satisfied.

3.3. Students learn best when they are actively pursuing a topic of interest and meaning to them. Resulting from brainstorming potential problems and arriving at their own topic, this unit provides such a topic.

3.4. Real-world problems are interdisciplinary and transcultural; involving writing (English), science, mathematics (data collecting, graphing, etc.), and intercultural communication, this unit is an interdisciplinary transcultural unit.

Figure 6.10 Lesson plan sample: multiple-day, project-centered, interdisciplinary, and transcultural lesson using worldwide communication via the Internet.

4. Procedure

Content:

At the start of this unit, collaborative groups were established via Intercultural E-mail Classroom Connections (IECC)— (http://www.stolaf.edu/network/iecc)—with other classes from schools around the world. These groups of students conducted several scientific research experiments on the ozone levels of their local atmospheric air. To obtain relative measurements of ozone concentrations in the air, students set up experiments that involved stretching rubber bands on a board, then observing the number of days until the bands broke. Students maintained daily journal logs of the temperature, barometric pressure, wind speed/direction, and the number of days it took for bands to break. (Information about the science experiment on the ozone levels of the local atmospheric air is from R. J. Ryder and T. Hughes, *Internet for Educators* [Upper Saddle River, NJ: Prentice Hall, 1997], 98.) After compiling their data and preparing single-page summaries of their results, via the Internet, students exchanged data with other groups. From data collected worldwide, students wrote a one-page summary of what conditions may account for the difference in levels of ozone. Following the exchange of students' written responses and their subsequent revisions based on feedback from the worldwide peers, students are now preparing a final summary report about the world's atmospheric ozone level. The intention is to disseminate worldwide (to newspapers and via the Internet) this final report.

Activity 1: Introduction (10 minutes)

Today, in think-share-pairs, you will prepare initial responses to the e-mail responses we have received from other groups around the world. (Teacher shares the list of places from which e-mail has been received.) Any questions before we get started?

   As we discussed earlier, here are the instructions: in your think-share-pairs (each pair is given one response received via e-mail), prepare written responses according to the following outline: (a) note points or information you would like to incorporate in the final paper to be forwarded via Internet; (b) comment on one aspect of the written response you like best; (c) provide questions to the sender to seek clarification or elaboration. I think you should be able to finish this in about 30 minutes, so let's try for that.

Activity 2: (30 minutes, if needed)

Preparation of dyad responses

Activity 3: (open)

Let's now hear from each response pair.

Dyad responses are shared with whole class for discussion of inclusion in response paper to be sent via Internet.

Activity 4: (open)

Discussion, conclusion, and preparation of final drafts to be sent to each e-mail corresponder to be done by cooperative groups (the number of groups is decided by the number of e-mail corresponders at this time).

Activity 5: (open)

Later, as students receive e-mail responses from other groups, the responses will be printed and reviewed. The class then responds to each, using the same criteria as before, and returns this response to the e-mail sender.

Closure:

The process continues until all groups (from around the world) have agreed upon and prepared the final report for dissemination.

5. Assignments and Reminders

Remind students of important dates and decisions to be made.

6. Materials and Equipment Needed

School computers with Internet access, printers, copies of e-mail responses.

7. Assessment, Reflection, and Revision

Assessment of student learning for this lesson is formative: journals, daily checklist of student participation in groups, writing drafts.

Reflective thoughts about lesson and suggestions for revision:

_____

_____

_____

their own experimental research findings and research papers about ozone concentrations in the atmosphere.

- For students worldwide to prepare and publish for worldwide dissemination a final paper about global ozone levels in the atmosphere.

And, from the sample unit of Figure 6.12, goals are

- To understand that all matter is made of atoms.
- To develop a positive attitude about physical science.

Because the goals are also included in the unit plan, sometimes a teacher may include only the objectives in the daily lesson plan but not the goals. As a beginning teacher, it usually is a good idea to include both.

SETTING THE LEARNING OBJECTIVES

A crucial step in the development of any lesson plan is setting the objectives. It is at this point that many lessons go wrong and many beginning teachers have problems.

A Common Error and How to Avoid It

As was stated in Chapter 5, teachers sometimes confuse "learning activity" (*how* the students will learn it) with the "learning objective" (*what* the student will learn as a result of the learning activity). For example, teachers sometimes mistakenly list what *they* intend to do—such as "lecture on photosynthesis" or "lead a discussion on the causes of the Civil War." They fail to focus on just what the learning objectives in these activities truly are—that is, what the students will be able to do (performance) as a result of the instructional activity. Or, rather than specifying what the student will be able to do as a result of the learning activities, the teacher mistakenly writes what the students will do in class (the learning activity)—such as "in pairs the students will do the 10 problems on page 72"—as if that were the learning objective. While solving the problems correctly may well be the objective, "doing the 10 problems" is not. At the risk of sounding trite or belaboring the point, we emphasize the importance of the teacher being an accurate communicator. If the teacher's stated expectations are fuzzy, then the students may never get it.

When you approach this step in your lesson planning, to avoid error, ask yourself, "What should students learn *as a result* of the activities of this lesson?" Your answer to that question is your objective! Objectives of the lesson are included then as specific statements of performance expectations, detailing precisely what students will be able to do as a result of the instructional activities.

No Need to Include All Domains and Hierarchies in Every Lesson

We have seen beginning teachers worrying needlessly over trying to include objectives from all three domains (cognitive, affective, and psychomotor) in every lesson they write. Please understand that not all three domains are necessarily represented in every lesson plan. As a matter of fact, any given lesson plan may be directed to only one, two, or a few specific objectives. Over the course of a unit of instruction, however, all domains and most if not all levels within each, should be addressed.

From the lesson shown in Figure 6.10, sample objectives, and the domain and level (in parentheses) within that domain, are

- *Through cooperative group action, students will conduct experimental research to collect data about the ozone level of air in their environment.* (cognitive, application)
- *Through the Internet, students will write and share response papers to their peers from other locations in the world.* (cognitive, evaluation)
- *Students will form judgments about local, regional, and world ozone levels.* (affective, organizing)
- *Students will create a proposal for worldwide dissemination.* (psychomotor, creating)

And, from the lesson illustrated in Figure 6.12, sample objectives are

- *Determine the density of a solid cube* (cognitive, application)
- *Communicate the results of their experiments to others in the class* (psychomotor, communicating)

Rationale

The rationale is an explanation of why the lesson is important and why the instructional methods chosen will achieve the objectives. Parents, students, teachers, administrators, and others have the right to know why specific content is being taught and why the methods employed are being used. Prepare yourself well by setting a goal for yourself of always being prepared with intelligent answers to those two questions.

Teachers become reflective decision makers when they challenge themselves to think about *what* (the content) they are teaching, *how* (the learning activities) they are teaching it, and *why* (the rationale) it must be taught. As illustrated in the sample unit of Figure 6.12, sometimes the rationale is included within the unit introduction and goals, but not in every lesson plan of the unit. Some lessons are carryovers or continuations of a lesson; there is no reason to repeat the rationale for a continuing lesson.

Procedure

The procedure consists of the instructional activities for a scheduled period of time. The substance of the lesson—the information to be presented, obtained, and learned—is the *content*. Appropriate information is selected to meet the learning objectives, the level of competence of the students, and the grade level or course requirements. To be sure your lesson actually covers what it should, you should write down exactly what minimum content you intend to cover. This material may be placed in a separate section or combined with the procedure section. The important thing is to be sure that your information is written down so you can refer to it quickly and easily when you need to.

If, for instance, you intend to conduct the lesson using discussion, you should write out the key discussion questions. Or, if you are going to introduce new material using a 10-minute lecture, then you need to outline the content of that lecture. The word "outline" is not used casually—you need not have pages of notes to sift through; nor should you ever read declarative statements to your students. You should be familiar enough with the content so that an outline (in as much detail as you believe necessary) will be sufficient to carry out the lesson, as in the following example of a content outline:

Causes of Civil War
  A. Primary causes
      1. Economics
      2. Abolitionist pressure
      3. Slavery
      4. etc.
  B. Secondary causes
      1. North-South friction
      2. Southern economic dependence
      3. etc.

The procedure or procedures to be used, sometimes referred to as the *instructional components,* comprise the *procedure* component of the lesson plan. It is the section that outlines what you and your students will do during the lesson. Appropriate instructional activities are chosen to meet the objectives, to match the students' learning styles and special needs, and to assure that all students have an equal opportunity to learn. Ordinarily, you should plan this section of your lesson as an organized entity having a beginning (an introduction or set), a middle, and an end (called the *closure*) to be completed during the lesson. This structure is not always needed, because some lessons are simply parts of units or long-term plans and merely carry on activities spelled out in those long-term plans. Still, most lessons need to include in the procedure (a) an *introduction,* the process used to prepare the students mentally for the lesson, sometimes referred to as the set, or initiating activity; (b) *lesson development,* the detailing of *activities* that occur between the beginning and the end of the lesson, including the transitions that connect activities (see discussion regarding transitions in Chapter 4); (c) plans for *practice,* sometimes referred to as the follow-up, that is, ways that you intend to have students interact in the classroom—such as with individual practice, in dyads, or in small groups—receiving guidance or coaching from each other and from you; (d) the *lesson conclusion* (or closure), the planned process of bringing the lesson to an end,

thereby providing students with a sense of completeness and, with effective teaching, accomplishment and comprehension by helping students to synthesize the information learned from the lesson; (e) a *timetable* that serves simply as a planning and implementation guide; (f) a plan for what to do if you finish the lesson and time remains; and (g) *assignments,* that is, what students are instructed to do as follow-up to the lesson, either as homework or as in-class work, providing students an opportunity to practice and enhance what is being learned. Let's now consider some of those elements in detail.

INTRODUCTION TO THE LESSON

Like any good performance, a lesson needs an effective beginning. In many respects, the introduction sets the tone for the rest of the lesson by alerting the students that the business of learning is to begin. The introduction should be an attention-getter. If it is exciting, interesting, or innovative, it can create a favorable mood for the lesson. In any case, a thoughtful introduction serves as a solid indicator that you are well prepared. Although it is difficult to develop an exciting introduction to every lesson taught each day, there are always a variety of options available by which to spice up the launching of a lesson. You might, for instance, begin the lesson by briefly reviewing the previous lesson, thereby helping students connect the learning. Another possibility is to review vocabulary words from previous lessons and to introduce new ones. Still another possibility is to use the key point of the day's lesson as the introduction and then again as the conclusion. Sometimes teachers begin a lesson by demonstrating a discrepant event (i.e., an event that is contrary to what one might expect), or as sometimes referred to, a "hook." Yet another possibility is to begin the lesson with a writing activity on some controversial aspect of the ensuing lesson. Following are some sample introductions:

For U.S. history, study of westward expansion:

- The teacher asks "Who has lived somewhere else other than (*name of your state)?*" After students show hands and answer, the teacher asks individuals why they moved to (*name of your state*). The teacher then asks students to recall why the first European settlers came to the United States, then moves into the next activity.

For science, study of the science process skill of predicting:

- The teacher takes a glass filled to the brim with colored water (colored so it is more visible) and asks students to discuss and predict (in dyads) how many pennies can be added to the glass before any water spills over the rim of the glass.

In short, you can use the introduction of the lesson to review past learning, tie the new lesson to the previous lesson, introduce new material, point out the objectives of the new lesson, help students connect their learning with other disciplines or with real life (such as with the Indian Trail Junior High School "prom night" unit discussed in Chapter 8), or—by showing what will be learned and why the learning is important—inducing in students motivation and a mindset favorable to the new lesson.

LESSON DEVELOPMENT

The developmental activities that comprise the bulk of the plan are the specifics by which you intend to achieve your lesson objectives. They include activities that present information, demonstrate skills, provide reinforcement of previously learned material, and provide other opportunities to develop understanding and skill. Furthermore, during lesson development the teacher models, by actions and words, the behaviors expected of the students. Students need such modeling. By effective modeling, the teacher can exemplify the anticipated learning outcomes. Activities of this section of the lesson plan should be described in some detail so (a) you will know exactly what it is you plan to do and (b) during the intensity of the class meeting, you do not forget important details and content. This is why you should consider, for example, noting answers (if known) to questions you intend to ask and solutions (if known) to problems you intend to have students solve.

LESSON CONCLUSION

Having a concise closure to the lesson is as important as having a strong introduction. The concluding activity should summarize and bind together what has ensued in the developmental stage and should reinforce the principal points of the lesson. One way to accomplish these ends is to restate the key points of the lesson. Another is to briefly outline the major points. Still another is to review the major concept. Sometimes the closure is not only a review of what was learned but also a summary of a question left unanswered that signals a change in your plan of activities for the next day. In other words, it becomes a *transitional closure*.

TIMETABLE

To estimate the time factors in any lesson can be very difficult, especially for the beginning teacher. A good procedure is to gauge the amount of time needed for each learning activity and note that alongside the activity and strategy in your plan, as shown in the preferred sample lesson plan format. Placing too much faith in your time estimate may be foolish—an estimate is more for your guidance during the preactive phase of instruction than for anything else. Beginning teachers frequently find that their planned discussions and presentations do not last as long as was expected. To avoid being embarrassed by running out of material, try to make sure you have planned enough meaningful work to consume the en-tire class period. Another important reason for including a time plan in your lesson is to give information to students about how much time they have for a particular activity, such as a quiz or a group activity.

Assignments

When an assignment is to be given, it should be noted in your lesson plan. When to present an assignment to the students is optional, but it should never be yelled as an afterthought as the students are exiting the classroom at the end of the period. Whether they are to be started and completed during class time or done outside of class, assignments should be written on the writing board, in a special place on the bulletin board, on the school Website, in each student's assignment log maintained in a binder, or on a handout. Make sure that assignment specifications are clear to the students. Many teachers give assignments to their students on a weekly or other periodic basis. When given on a periodic basis, rather than daily, assignments should still show in your daily lesson plans to remind yourself to remind students of them.

Once assignment specifications and due dates are given, it is best not to make major modifications to them, and it is especially important to not change assignment specifications several days after an assignment has been given. Last-minute changes in assignment specifications can be very frustrating to students who have already begun or completed the assignment; it shows little respect to those students. (See also "assignments and homework" in Chapter 8.)

Understand the difference between assignments and procedures. An assignment tells students *what* is to be done, while procedures explain *how* to do it. Although an assignment may include procedures, spelling out procedures alone is not the same thing as giving an academic assignment. When students are given an assignment, they need to understand the reasons for doing it as well as have some notion of ways the assignment might be done.

Allowing time in class for students to begin work on homework assignments and long-term projects is highly recommended; it provides an opportunity for the teacher to give individual attention to students and to coach them. The benefits of *coached practice* include being able to (a) monitor student work so a student does not go too far in a wrong direction, (b) help students to reflect on their thinking, (c) assess the progress of individual students, (d) provide for peer tutoring, and (e) discover or create a "teachable moment." For example, while observing and monitoring student practice the teacher might discover a commonly shared student misconception. The teacher stops and discusses it, and attempts to clarify the misconception or collaboratively with students plans a subsequent lesson focusing on the common misconception.

Special Notes and Reminders

In the lesson plan format, we recommend that you have a regular place for special notes and reminders, perhaps, as our preferred format shows, in the same location as assignments. In that special section, you can place reminders concerning such things as announcements to be made, school programs, assignment due dates, and makeup work or special tasks for certain students.

Materials and Equipment to Be Used

Materials of instruction include books, media, handouts, and other supplies necessary to accomplish the lesson's learning objectives. You must be *certain* that the proper and necessary materials and equipment are available for the lesson. To be certain requires planning. Teachers who, for one reason or another, have to use class time to look for materials or equipment that should have been readied before class began are likely to experience classroom control problems. Plus, if it happens very often, it demonstrates incompetency and the teacher loses credibility with the students. Teachers want students to be prepared; students expect competent teachers to be prepared.

Assessment, Reflection, and Revision

Details of how you will assess how well students *are* learning (formative assessment) and how well they *have learned* (summative assessment) should be included in your lesson plan. This is not meant to imply that both types of assessment will be in every daily plan. Comprehension checks for formative assessment can be in the form of questions that both you and the students ask during the lesson (in the procedural section), as well as various kinds of checklists.

For summative assessment, teachers typically use review questions at the end of a lesson (as a closure) or the beginning of the next lesson (as a review or transfer introduction), independent practice or summary activities at the completion of a lesson, and tests.

In most lesson plan formats, for the reflective phase of instruction (see "Decision-Making Phases of Instruction" in Chapter 3) there is a section reserved for the teacher to make notes or reflective comments about the lesson. Many student teachers seem to prefer to write their reflections at the end or on the reverse page of their lesson plans. As well as being useful to yourself, reflections about the lesson are useful for those who are supervising you if you are a student teacher or a teacher being mentored or considered for tenure. Sample reflective questions you might ask yourself are shown in Figure 6.11.

Writing and later reading your reflections can not only provide ideas that may be useful if you plan to use the lesson again at some later date, but can also offer catharsis, easing the tension caused from teaching. To continue working effectively at a challenging task (that is, to prevent intellectual downshifting, by reverting to earlier learned, lower cognitive level behaviors) requires significant amounts of reflection.

If you have reviewed the sample lesson plan formats, proceed now to Exercise 6.3, where you will analyze a lesson that failed; then, as instructed by your course instructor, do Exercises 6.4 and 6.5.

Figure 6.11 Questions for self-reflection for the reflective phase of instruction.

- What is my overall feeling about today's lesson—good, fair, or bad? What made me feel this way?
- Did students seem to enjoy the lesson? What makes me think so?
- Did the objectives seem to be met? What evidence do I have?
- What aspects of the lesson went well? What makes me believe so?
- Were I to repeat the lesson, what changes might I make?
- Which students seemed to do well? Which ones should I give more attention to? Why and how?
- To what extent was this lesson individualized according to student learning styles, abilities, interests, talents, and needs? Could I do more in this regard? If so, what? If not, then why not?
- Did the students seem to have sufficient time to think and apply? Why or why not?
- Would I have been proud had the school district superintendent been present to observe this lesson? Why or why not?

UNIT PLAN SAMPLE WITH A DAILY LESSON

Course _Science_

Teacher _____   **Duration of Unit** _10 days_

Unit Title _What's the Matter?_   **Grade Level** _Grades 5–8_

Purpose of the Unit

This unit is designed to develop students' understanding of the concept of matter. At the completion of the unit, students should have a clearer understanding of matter and its properties, of the basic units of matter, and of the source of matter.

Rationale of the Unit

This unit topic is important for building a foundation of knowledge for subsequent courses in science. This can increase students' chances of success in those courses, and thereby improve their self-confidence and self-esteem. A basic understanding of matter and its properties is important because of daily decisions that affect the manipulation of matter. The hands-on laboratory activities in this unit will help students develop their understanding. It is more likely that students will make correct and safe decisions when they understand what matter is, how it changes form, and how its properties determine its use.

Goals of the Unit

The goals of this unit are for students to
1. Understand that all matter is made of atoms.
2. Understand that matter stays constant and that it is neither created nor destroyed.
3. Develop certain basic physical science laboratory skills.
4. Develop a positive attitude about physical science.
5. Look forward to taking other science courses.
6. Understand how science is relevant to their daily lives.

Instructional Objectives of the Unit

Upon completion of this unit of study, students should be able to
1. List at least 10 examples of matter.
2. List the four states of matter, with one example of each.
3. Calculate the density of an object when given its mass and volume.
4. Describe the properties of solids, liquids, and gases.
5. Demonstrate an understanding that matter is made of elements and that elements are made of atoms.
6. Identify and explain one way that knowledge of matter is important to their daily lives.
7. Demonstrate increased self-confidence in pursuing laboratory investigations in physical science.
8. Demonstrate skill in communicating within the cooperative learning group.
9. Demonstrate skill in working with the triple-beam balance.

Unit Overview

Throughout this unit, students will be developing a concept map of matter. Information for the map will be derived from laboratory work, class discussions, lectures, student readings, and research. The overall instructional model is that of concept attainment. Important to this is an assessment of students' concepts about matter at the beginning of the unit. The preassessment and the continuing assessment of their concepts will center on the following:
1. What is matter and what are its properties? Students will develop the concept of matter by discovering the properties that all matter contains (that is, it has mass and takes up space).
2. Students will continue to build on their understanding of the concept of matter by organizing matter into its four major states (that is, solid, liquid, gas, plasma). The concept development will be used to define the attributes of each state of matter, and students will gather information by participating in laboratory activities and class discussions.
3. What are some of the physical properties of matter that make certain kinds of matter unique? Students will experiment with properties of matter such as elasticity, brittleness, and density. Laboratory activities will allow students to contribute their observations and information to the further development of their concept of matter. Density activities enable students to practice their lab and math skills.

Figure 6.12   Sample integrated unit plan with one daily lesson for lab science.
(*Source:* Courtesy of Will Hightower.)

4. What are the basic units of matter, and where did matter come from? Students will continue to develop their concept of matter by working on this understanding of mixtures, compounds, elements, and atoms.

Assessment of Student Achievement

For this unit, assessment of student achievement will be both formative and summative. Formative evaluation will be done daily by checklists of student behavior, knowledge, and skills. Summative evaluation will be based on the following criteria:

1. Student participation as evidenced by completion of daily homework, class work, laboratory activities, and class discussions, and by the information on the student behavior checklists.
2. Weekly quizzes on content.
3. Unit test.

Lesson Number _____   **Duration of Lesson** _1–2 hours_____

Unit Title ___*What's the Matter?*_____   **Teacher** _____

Lesson Title ___*Mission Impossible*_____   **Lesson Topic** _*Density of Solids*_____

Objectives of the Lesson

Upon completion of this lesson, students should be able to

1. Determine the density of a solid cube.
2. Based on data gathered in class, develop their own definition of density.
3. Prepare and interpret graphs of data.
4. Communicate the results of their experiments to others in the class.

Materials Needed

1. Two large boxes of cereal and two snack-size boxes of the same cereal
2. Four brownies (two whole and two cut in halves)
3. Four sandboxes (two large plastic boxes and two small boxes, each filled with sand)
4. Two triple-beam balances
5. Several rulers
6. Six hand-held calculators
7. Eighteen colored pencils (six sets with three different colors per set)
8. Copies of lab instructions (one copy for each student)

Instructional Procedure with Approximate Time Line

ANTICIPATORY SET (10–15 MINUTES)

Begin class by brainstorming to find what students already know about density. Place the word on the board or overhead, and ask students if they have heard of it. Write down their definitions and examples. Hold up a large box of cereal in one hand and the snack-size box in the other. Ask students which is more dense. Allow them time to explain their responses. Then tell them that by the end of this lesson they will know the answer to the question and that they will develop their own definition of density.

LABORATORY INVESTIGATION (30–60 MINUTES)

Students are divided into teams of four students of mixed abilities. Each member has a role:

1. *Measure master:* In charge of the group's ruler and ruler measurements
2. *Mass master:* In charge of the group's weighings
3. *Engineer:* In charge of the group's calculator and calculations
4. *Graph master:* In charge of plotting the group's data on the graph paper

Each team has eight minutes before switching stations. Each team completes three stations and then meets to make its graphs and to discuss results.

Station 1: Cereal Box Density. Students calculate the density of a large and a small box of cereal to determine whether a larger and heavier object is more dense. The masses versus the volumes of the two boxes are plotted on graph paper using one of the pencil colors.

(continued)

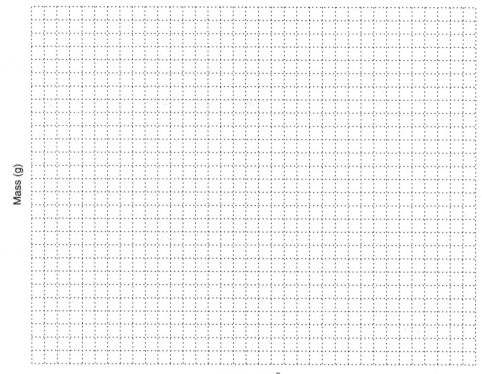

Instructions

1. The density of any object is determined by dividing its mass by its volume. Density in grams is divided by volume in cubic centimeters. Example: 20 g/10 cm^3 ÷ 2 g/cm^3.
2. Measure the volume of the small cereal box (length × width × height), and use the balance to determine its mass in grams. The engineer can do the calculations on the calculator. The graph master should graph the results of each trial and connect two points with a straight line.
3. Repeat the procedure using the large box of cereal.
4. The engineer computes the density of both cereal boxes with the calculator and records the results on the proper blank below the graph.

   a. Density of large box of cereal _____

   b. Density of small box of cereal _____

   c. Density of large brownie _____

   d. Density of small brownie _____

   e. Density of large sandbox _____

   f. Density of small sandbox _____

Station 2: Brownie Density. Students calculate the density of a full-size brownie and a half-size brownie. Results are plotted on the same graph as in Station 1, but with the second color.

Instructions

1. The density of any object is determined by dividing its mass by its volume. Density in grams is divided by volume in cubic centimeters. Example: 20 g/10 cm^3 ÷ 2 g/cm^3.
2. Measure the volume of a small brownie (length × width × height), and use the balance to determine its mass in grams. The engineer can do the calculations on the calculator. The graph master should graph the results of each trial and connect two points with a straight line.

Figure 6.12   *(continued)*

3. Repeat the procedure using the large brownie.
4. The engineer computes the density of both brownies and records the result on the proper blank.

***Station 3:* Sandbox Density.** Students calculate the density of a large and a small box filled with sand. Results are plotted on the graph, but with the third color.

Instructions

1. The density of any object is determined by dividing its mass by its volume. Density in grams is divided by volume in cubic centimeters. Example: 20 g/10 cm^3 ÷ 2 g/cm^3.
2. Measure the volume of the small sandbox (length × width × height), and use the balance to determine its mass in grams. The engineer can do the calculations on the calculator. The graph master should graph the results of each trial and connect two points with a straight line.
3. Repeat the procedure using the large sandbox.
4. The engineer computes the density of both boxes and records the results on the proper blank.

Lab Worksheet. Teams return to their seats to do the graphing, analyze the results, and answer the following questions from their lab sheets:

1. Is a larger, heavier object more dense than its smaller counterpart? Explain your evidence.
2. What is your definition of density?
3. Which is more dense, a pound of feathers or a pound of gold? Explain your answer.

LESSON CLOSURE (10 MINUTES OR MORE)
When all teams are finished, teams should display their graphs, and share and discuss the results.

Concepts

1. Density is one of the properties of matter.
2. Mass and volume are related.
3. Density is determined by dividing mass by volume.

Extension Activities

1. Use a density graph to calculate the mass and volume of a smaller brownie.
2. Explore the story of Archimedes and the king's crown.

Evaluation, Reflection, and Revision of Lesson

Upon completion of this lesson and of the unit, revision in this lesson may be made on the basis of teacher observations and student achievement.

Figure 6.12   (*continued*)

FOR YOUR NOTES

EXERCISE 6.3: ANALYSIS OF A LESSON THAT FAILED

INSTRUCTIONS: The planning and structure of a lesson are often predictors of the success of its implementation. The purpose of this exercise is to read the following synopsis of the implementation of a lesson, answer the discussion questions individually, and use your responses as a basis for class discussion in small groups about the lesson.

The Setting: Seventh-grade life science class; 1:12–2:07 P.M., spring semester

Synopsis of Events

1:12   Bell rings.

1:12–1:21 Teacher directs students to read from their texts, while he takes attendance.

1:21–1:31 Teacher distributes a photocopy to each student; students are now to label the parts of a flower shown on the handout.

1:31–1:37 Silent reading and labeling of photocopy.

1:37–1:39 Teacher verbally gives instructions for working on a real flower, e.g., by comparing it with the drawing on the handout. Students may use the microscopes if they want.

1:39–1:45 Teacher walks around room, giving each student a real flower.

1:45–2:07 Chaos erupts. There is much confusion, with students wandering around, throwing flower parts at each other. Teacher begins writing referrals, and sends two students to the office for their misbehavior. Teacher is flustered, directs students to spend remainder of period quietly reading from their texts. Two more referrals are written.

2:05–2:07 A few students begin meandering toward the exit.

2:07   End of period (much to the delight of the teacher).

QUESTIONS FOR CLASS DISCUSSION

1. Do you think the teacher had a lesson plan? If so, what (if any) were its good points? Its problems? _____

_____

_____

_____

2. If you believed that the teacher had a lesson plan, do you believe that it was written and detailed? Explain your response. What is your evidence? _____

_____

_____

_____

3. How might the lesson have been prepared and implemented to avoid the chaos? _____

_____

_____

_____

_____

EXERCISE 6.3 (*continued*)

4. Was the format of the lesson traditional? Explain. _____

_____

_____

_____

5. Have you experienced a class such as this? Explain. _____

_____

_____

_____

6. Which teacher behaviors were probable causes of much of the chaos? (Hint: See Chapter 3.) _____

_____

_____

_____

7. What teacher behaviors could have prevented the chaos and made the lesson more effective? _____

_____

_____

_____

8. Within the 55-minute class period, students were expected to operate rather high on the Learning Experiences Ladder (see Figure 6.5). Consider this analysis: 9 minutes of silent reading; 10 minutes of listening; 6 minutes of silent reading and labeling; 2 minutes of listening; 6 minutes of action (the only direct experience); and an additional 22 minutes of silent reading. In all, there were approximately 49 minutes (89 percent of the class time) of abstract verbal and visual symbolization. Is this a problem? _____

_____

_____

_____

_____

_____

9. What have you learned from this exercise? _____

_____

_____

_____

_____

_____

_____

EXERCISE 6.4A: PREPARING A LESSON PLAN

INSTRUCTIONS: Use the model lesson format or an alternative format that is approved by your instructor to prepare a _____ -minute lesson plan (length to be decided in your class) for a grade and course of your choice. After completing your lesson plan, evaluate it yourself, modify it, and then have your modified version evaluated
by two or more peers, using Exercise 6.4B for the evaluation, before turning it in for your instructor's evaluation. This exercise may be connected with Exercise 6.5.

EXERCISE 6.4B: SELF AND PEER ASSESSMENT OF MY LESSON PLAN

INSTRUCTIONS: You may duplicate blank copies of this form for evaluation of the lesson you developed for Exercise 6.4A. Have your lesson plan evaluated by two or more of your peers and yourself. For each of the items
below, evaluators should check either "yes" or "no," and write instructive comments. Compare the results of your
self-evaluation with the other evaluations.

	No	*Yes*	*Comments*
1. Are descriptive data adequately provided?	____	____	_____
2. Are the goals clearly stated?	____	____	_____
3. Are the objectives specific and measurable?	____	____	_____
4. Are objectives correctly classified?	____	____	_____
5. Are objectives only low-order or is higher-order thinking expected?	____	____	_____
6. Is the rationale clear and justifiable?	____	____	_____
7. Is the plan's content appropriate?	____	____	_____
8. Is the content likely to contribute to achievement of the objectives?	____	____	_____
9. Given the time frame and other logistical considerations, is the plan workable?	____	____	_____
10. Will the opening (set) likely engage the students?	____	____	_____
11. Is there a preassessment strategy?	____	____	_____
12. Is there a proper mix of learning activities for the time frame of the lesson?	____	____	_____
13. Are the activities developmentally appropriate for the intended students?	____	____	_____
14. Are transitions planned?	____	____	_____
15. If relevant, are key questions written out and key ideas noted in the plan?	____	____	_____
16. Does the plan indicate how coached practice will be provided for each student?	____	____	_____
17. Is adequate closure provided in the plan?	____	____	_____
18. Are needed materials and equipment identified and are they appropriate?	____	____	_____

EXERCISE 6.4B (*continued*)

19. Is there a planned formative assessment, formal or informal? ____ ____ _____

20. Is there a planned summative assessment? ____ ____ _____

21. Is the lesson coordinated in any way with other aspects of the curriculum? ____ ____ _____

22. Is the lesson likely to provide a sense of meaning for the students by helping bridge their learning? ____ ____ _____

23. Is an adequate amount of time allotted to address the information presented? ____ ____ _____

24. Is a thoughtfully prepared and relevant student assignment planned? ____ ____ _____

25. Could a substitute who is knowledgeable follow the plan? ____ ____ _____

Additional comments: _____

_____

_____

_____

_____

_____

_____

_____

_____

_____

_____

_____

_____

_____

_____

_____

_____

_____

_____

EXERCISE 6.5: PREPARING AN INSTRUCTIONAL UNIT: BRINGING IT ALL TOGETHER

INSTRUCTIONS: The purpose of this exercise is threefold: (1) to give you experience in preparing an instructional unit, (2) to assist you in preparing an instructional unit that you can use in your teaching, and (3) to start your collection of instructional units that you may be able to use later in your teaching. This assignment will take several hours to complete, and you will need to read ahead in this resource guide. Our advice, therefore, is to start the assignment early, with a due date much later in the course. Your course instructor may have specific guidelines for your completion of this exercise; what follows is the essence of what you are to do.

First, with help from your instructor divide your class into three teams, each with a different assignment pertaining to this exercise. The units completed by these teams are to be shared with all members of the class, for feedback and possible use later.

TEAM 1

Members of this team, individually or in dyads, will develop standard teaching units, perhaps with different grade levels, grades 5–8, in mind. (You will need to review the content of Chapters 7–11.) Using a format that is practical, *each member or pair of this team* will develop a minimum two-week (10-day) unit for a particular grade level, subject, and topic. Regardless of the format chosen, each unit plan should include the following elements:

1. Identification of (a) grade level, (b) subject, (c) topic, and (d) time duration.
2. Statement of rationale and general goals.
3. Separate listing of instructional objectives for each daily lesson. Wherever possible, the unit should include objectives from all three domains—cognitive, affective, and psychomotor.
4. List of materials and resources needed and where they can be obtained (if you have that information). These should also be listed for each daily lesson.
5. Ten consecutive daily lesson plans (see Exercise 6.4A).
6. List of all items that will be used to assess student learning *during* and at *completion* of the unit of study.
7. Statement of how the unit will attend to the diversity of students one is likely to find, such as pertaining to students' reading levels, socioethnic backgrounds, and special needs.

TEAM 2

Following the steps in Exercise 8.1 (Chapter 8), *each member* of this team will develop a self-instructional module.

TEAM 3

In collaboration, members of this team will develop interdisciplinary thematic units. Depending upon the number of students in your class, Team 3 may actually comprise several teams, with each team developing an ITU. Each team should be comprised of no less than two members (e.g., a math specialist and a science specialist) and no more than four (e.g., history/social studies, English/language arts/reading, mathematics, and science).

SUMMARY

You have learned the importance of learning modalities and instructional modes. You have learned about the importance of providing an accepting and supportive learning environment, as well as about teacher behaviors that are necessary to facilitate student learning beyond that of procedural knowledge.

With this chapter in particular, you continued building your knowledge base about why planning is important and how units with lessons are useful pedagogical tools. Developing units of instruction that integrate student learning and provide a sense of meaning for the students requires coordination throughout the curriculum. Hence, for students, learning is a process of discovering how information, knowledge, and ideas are interrelated so they can make sense out of self, school, and life. Preparing chunks of information into units and units into lessons helps students to process and understand knowledge. You have developed your first unit of instruction and are well on your way to becoming a competent planner of instruction.

In Part II, you have been guided through the processes necessary to prepare yourself to teach in a classroom. Later, after you have studied Part III on specific instructional strategies, aids, media, and resources to supplement your instruction, you may choose to revisit this chapter and make revisions to your completed unit and lessons. In Part III your attention is directed to the selection and implementation of specific strategies, aids, and resources from which you may select to facilitate students' learning of particular skills and content, beginning with the use of questioning.

ADDITIONAL EXERCISES

See the companion Website http://www.prenhall. com/ kellough for the following exercises related to the content of this chapter:

- Methods of Instruction
- Generating Ideas for Interdisciplinary Units
- Initiating an ITU with a Question Map
- Integrating the Topic
- Planning Culminating Activities
- Putting Objectives, Resources, and Learning Activities Together for a Teaching Plan

QUESTIONS FOR CLASS DISCUSSION

1. In subject-field discussion groups, list and describe specific considerations you should give to student safety (a topic that this resource guide cannot adequately otherwise address) when preparing instructional plans. Share your lists with other groups.
2. Explain the importance of the notion that all middle grades teachers are teachers of literacy and of thinking, social, and learning skills. Do you agree or disagree with the notion? Why?
3. Give several reasons why both a student teacher and a first-year teacher need to prepare detailed lesson plans. Describe when, if ever, the teacher can or should divert from the written lesson plan.
4. Divide your class into subject area interest groups. Have each group devise two separate lesson plans to teach the same topic to the same group of students (grade level identified), with one plan using direct instruction and the other using indirect. Have groups share the outcomes of this activity with one another.
5. Explain why, when taught by access strategies, students learn less content but learn it more effectively? For a teacher using access strategies, could this be a problem? Explain.
6. Select one of the "Reflective Thoughts" from the introduction to Part II (page 84) that is specifically related to the content of this chapter, research it, and write a one-page essay explaining why you agree or disagree with the thought. Share your essay with members of your class for their thoughts.
7. Describe observable behaviors that would enable you to tell whether a student is learning to think critically. Describe where, specifically, in a unit plan, one would expect to find these observable behaviors.
8. Describe any prior concepts you held that changed as a result of your experiences with this chapter. Describe the changes.
9. From your current observations and field work as related to this teacher preparation program, clearly identify one specific example of educational practice that seems contradictory to exemplary practice or theory as presented in this chapter. Present your explanation for the discrepancy.
10. Do you have questions generated by the content of this chapter? If you do, list them along with ways answers might be found.

FOR FURTHER READING

Haskin, T. T. "History Repeats Itself at Yorktown Middle." *Clearing House* 72(5):285–287 (May/June 1999).

Howe, A. C., and Bell, J. "Factors Associated with Successful Implementation of Interdisciplinary Curriculum Units." *Research in Middle Level Education Quarterly* 21(2):39–52 (Winter 1998).

Johnson, A. "Fiber Meets Fibonacci; The Shape of Things to Come." *Mathematics Teaching in the Middle School* 4(4):256–262 (January 1999).

Kellough, R. D., Cangelosi, J. S., Collette, A. T., Chiappetta, E. L., Souviney, R. J., Trowbridge, L. W., and Bybee, R. W. *Integrating Mathematics and Science for Intermediate and Middle School Students.* Englewood Cliffs, NJ: Merrill/Prentice Hall, 1996.

Kellough, R. D., Jarolimek, J., Parker, W. C., Martorella, P. H., Tompkins, G. E., and Hoskisson, K. *Integrating Language Arts and Social Studies for Intermediate and Middle School Students.* Englewood Cliffs, NJ: Merrill/Prentice Hall, 1996.

Kirkwood, T. F. "Integrating an Interdisciplinary Unit in Middle School: A School-University Partnership." *Clearing House* 72(3):160–163 (January/February 1999).

Muir, M. "Planning Integrative Curriculum with Skeptical Students." *Middle School Journal* 30(2):9–17 (November 1998).

Roberts, P. L., and Kellough, R. D. *A Guide for Developing an Interdisciplinary Thematic Unit,* 2nd ed. Upper Saddle River, NJ: Prentice Hall, 2000.

Roblyer, M. D. *Integrating Technology Across the Curriculum: A Database of Strategies and Lesson Plans.* Upper Saddle River, NJ: Merrill/Prentice Hall, 1999.

Rubink, W. L., and Taube, S. R. "Mathematical Connections from Biology: 'Killer' Bees Come to Life in the Classroom." *Mathematics Teaching in the Middle School* 4(6):350–356 (March 1999).

Sandmann, A. L., Weber, W. B., Jr., Czerniak, C. M., and Ahern, J. F. "Coming Full Circuit: An Integrated Unit Plan for Intermediate and Middle Grade Students." *Science Activities* 36(3):13–20 (Fall 1999).

Sunal, C. "Semiconductors: A 21st Century Social Studies Topic." *Southern Social Studies Journal* 25(2):30–50 (Spring 2000).

Part III

STRATEGIES, AIDS, MEDIA, AND RESOURCES FOR EFFECTIVE INSTRUCTION

Part III responds to your needs concerning

- Assuring equality in the classroom.
- Developing ideas for lessons and projects.
- Employing service learning.
- Ensuring academic success for each student.
- Helping students develop a repertoire of skills for lifelong learning.
- Individualizing (personalizing) student learning.
- Making homework assignments.
- Preparing and implementing a lesson for feedback.
- Resources for free and inexpensive instructional materials.
- Teaching for thinking.

▶ Teaching toward mastery.
▶ Using electronic media and the Internet.
▶ Using games and simulations.
▶ Using inquiry and discovery learning.
▶ Using learning centers, lectures, and demonstrations.
▶ Using peer teaching and small group and cooperative learning.
▶ Using project-based learning and student exhibitions and presentations.
▶ Using questioning and discussions.
▶ Using student writing and journals.
▶ Using the writing board, the bulletin board, guest speakers, and field trips.

REFLECTIVE THOUGHTS

Your goals should include helping students to learn how to solve problems, to make decisions, to think creatively and critically, and to feel good about themselves and their learning. To do this, you will

1. *Involve students in direct experiences, both hands-on and minds-on, so they use more of their sensory modalities and develop their learning capacities. Learning is the most effective and longest lasting when all the senses are engaged.*
2. *Use questioning in a way designed to guide students to higher levels of thinking and doing.*
3. *Share in the responsibility for teaching reading, writing, thinking, and study skills.*

Today's young adolescents are used to multimillion-dollar productions on television, videodiscs, arcade games, and the movie screen. When they come into a classroom and are subjected each day to something short of a high-budget production, it is little wonder that they sometimes react in a less-than-highly motivated fashion. No doubt, today's youth are growing up in a highly stimulated instant-action society, a society that has learned to expect instant headache relief, instant meals, instant gratification, and perhaps, in the minds of many youth, instant high-paying employment for jobs that entail more fun than hard work. In light of this cultural phenomenon, we are on your side: the classroom teacher is on the firing line each day and is expected to perform—perhaps instantly and entertainingly, but most certainly in a highly competent and professional manner—in situations that are far from ideal.

Experiences afforded by inquiry help students understand the importance of suspending judgment and the tentativeness of answers and solutions. With those understandings, students eventually are better able to deal with life's ambiguities.

Teaching all students how to access and assess Internet sites adds to their repertoire of skills for lifelong learning.

7

Using Questioning for Teaching and Learning

A strategy of fundamental importance to any mode of instruction is, as introduced in Chapter 3, questioning. You will use questioning for so many purposes that you must be skilled in its use to teach effectively. Because it is so important, and because it is so frequently used and abused, this chapter is devoted to assisting you in the development of your questioning skills.

OBJECTIVES

Upon completion of this chapter, you should be able to

1. Contrast the levels of questioning and compare those with levels of thinking and doing.

2. Demonstrate developing skill in the use of questioning.
3. Demonstrate understanding of the types of cognitive questions.
4. Describe ways of helping students develop their metacognitive skills.
5. Explain the value and use of students' questions.
6. Identify categories of purposes for which questioning can be used as an instructional strategy.

PURPOSES FOR USING QUESTIONING

You will adapt the type and form of each question to the purpose for which it is asked. The purposes that questions can serve can be separated into five categories, as follows.

1. *To politely give instructions.* An example is, "Mariya, would you please turn out the lights so we can show the slides?" Although they probably should avoid doing so, teachers sometimes also use rhetorical questions for the purpose of regaining student attention and maintaining classroom control; for example, "Marcello, would you please attend to your work?" Rhetorical questions can sometimes backfire on the teacher. In this case, for example, Marcello might say "No." Then the teacher would have a problem that might have been avoided had the teacher been more direct at first and simply told Marcello to attend to his work, rather than asking him if he would. Consider the scenario that follows.

CLASSROOM SCENARIO

A Student Responds to a Teacher's Rhetorical Question

At the completion of the class opener, Jennifer, a mathematics teacher, asked, "Shall we check our homework problems now?" One of the students in the class, Mario, answered "No." Ignoring Mario's response, Jennifer continued with her planned lesson.

What are your thoughts about this scenario? Explain why you believe that Jennifer should or should not have acted differently.

---

2. *To review and remind students of classroom procedures.* For example, if students continue to talk when they should not, you can stop the lesson and say, "Class, I think we need to review the procedure we agreed on for when someone is talking. Who can tell me what is the procedure that we agreed upon?"

3. *To gather information.* Examples are "How many of you have finished the assignment?" or, to find out whether a student knows something, "Charlie, can you please explain for us the difference between a synonym and an antonym?"

4. *To discover student knowledge, interests, or experiences.* Examples might be "How many of you think you know the process by which water in our city is made potable?" or "How many of you have visited the local water treatment plant?"

5. *To guide student thinking and learning.* It is this category of questioning that is the focus of this chapter. In teaching, questions in this category are used to

- *Develop appreciation.* For example, "Do you now understand the ecological relationship between that particular root fungus, voles, and the survival of the large conifers of the forests of the Pacific Northwest?"
- *Develop student thinking.* For example, "What do you suppose the effects to the ecology are when standing water is sprayed with an insecticide that is designed to kill all mosquito larvae?"
- *Diagnose learning difficulty.* For example, "What part of the writer's argument don't you understand, Sarah?"
- *Emphasize major points.* For example, "If no one has ever been to the sun, how can we be confident that we know what it is made of?"
- *Encourage students.* For example, "OK, so you didn't remember the formula for glucose. What really impressed me in your essay is what you did understand about photosynthesis. Do you know specifically what part impressed me?"
- *Establish rapport.* For example, "We have a problem here, but I think we can solve it if we put our heads together. What do you think ought to be our first step?"
- *Evaluate learning.* For example, "Siobhan, what is the effect when two rough surfaces are rubbed together?"
- *Give practice in expression.* For example, "Yvonne, would you please share with us the examples of shadowing that you found?"
- *Help students in their metacognition.* For example, "Yes, something did go wrong in the experiment. Do you still think your original hypothesis is correct? If not, then where was the error in your thinking? Or if you still think your hypothesis is correct, then where might the error have been in the design of your experiment? How might we find out?"
- *Help students interpret materials.* For example, "Something seems to be wrong with this compass. How do you suppose we can find out what is wrong with it? For example, if the needle is marked N and S in reverse, how can we find out if that is the problem?"
- *Help students organize materials.* For example, "If you really want to test your hypothesis, then we are going to need certain materials. We are going to have to deal with some strategic questions here, such as, what do you think we will need, where can we find those things, who will be responsible for getting them, and how will we store and arrange them once we are ready to start the investigation?"
- *Provide drill and practice.* For example, "Team A has prepared some questions that they would like to use as practice questions for our unit exam, and they are suggesting that we use them to play the game of Jeopardy on Friday. Is everyone in agreement with their idea?"
- *Provide review.* For example, "Today, in your groups, you are going to study the unit review questions. After each group has studied and prepared its answers to these written questions, your group will pick another group and ask them your set of review questions. Each group has a different set of questions. Members of Team A are going to keep score, and the group that has the highest score from this review session will receive free pizza at tomorrow's lunch. Ready?"

- *Show agreement or disagreement.* For example, "Some of you believe that Gore should have been named our forty-third President. Explain why you agree or disagree with that conclusion."
- *Show relationships, such as cause and effect.* For example, "What do you suppose would be the global effect if just one inch of the total Antarctic ice shelf were to rather suddenly melt?"
- *Build the curriculum.* It is the students' questions that provide the basis for the learning that occurs in an effective inquiry-based, project centered program. More on this subject follows later in Chapter 8.

Questions to Avoid Asking

While it is important to avoid asking rhetorical questions for which you do not want a response, you should also avoid asking questions that call for little or no student thinking, such as those that can be answered with a simple yes or no or some other sort of alternative response. Unless followed up with questions calling for clarification, questions that call for simple responses such as yes or no have little or no learning and diagnostic value; they encourage guessing and inappropriate student responses that can cause classroom control problems for the teacher.

It is even more important to avoid using questions that embarrass a student, punish a student, or in any way deny the student's dignity. Questions that embarrass or punish tend to damage the student's developing self-esteem and serve no meaningful academic or instructional purpose. Questioning is an important instructional tool that should be used by the teacher only for academic reasons. Although it is not always possible to predict when a student might be embarrassed by a question, a teacher should *never* deliberately ask questions for the purpose of embarrassment or punishment. For example, avoid asking a student a content question when you know the student was not paying attention and/or does not know the answer. When done deliberately to punish or embarrass, that teacher's action borders on abuse!

TYPES OF COGNITIVE QUESTIONS: A GLOSSARY

Let us now define, describe, and provide examples for each of the *types* of cognitive (or mental) questions that you will use in teaching. Please note that although we refer to these in the traditional fashion as cognitive questions, any question type could relate to any of the three domains of learning (cognitive, affective, or psychomotor). In the section that follows, your attention is focused on the levels of cognitive questions.

Clarifying Question

The clarifying question is used to gain more information from a student to help the teacher better understand a student's ideas, feelings, and thought processes. Often, asking a student to elaborate on an initial response will lead the student to think more deeply and restructure his or her thinking, and while doing so, to discover a fallacy in the original response. Examples of clarifying questions are "What I hear you saying is that you would rather work alone than in your group. Is that correct?" "So, Denise, you think the poem is a sad one. Is that right?" There is a strong positive correlation between student learning and development of metacognitive skills (that is, their thinking about thinking), and the teacher's use of questions that ask for clarification.[1] In addition, by seeking clarification, you are likely to be demonstrating an interest in the student and her or his thinking.

Convergent-Thinking Question

Convergent thinking questions, also called *narrow questions* are low-order thinking questions that have a single correct answer (such as recall questions, discussed further in the next section). Examples of convergent questions are "What is geophagy?" "If the circumference of a circle is 31 meters, what is its radius?" "What engineering feat allowed Xerxes to invade Greece in 481 B.C.E.?" When using questions of this type, try to come back with follow-up questions so the student answering can demonstrate thinking beyond rote memory.

Cueing Question

If you ask a question to which, after sufficient **wait time** (longer than two seconds, and as long as seven),[2] no students respond or to which their inadequate responses indicate they need more information, then you can ask a question that cues the answer or response you are seeking.[3] In essence, you are going backward in your questioning sequence, to cue the students. For example, as an introduction to a lesson on the study of prefixes, a teacher asks her students, "How many legs each do crayfish, lobsters, and shrimp have?" and there is no

[1] A. L. Costa, *The School as a Home for the Mind* (Palatine, IL: Skylight Publishing, 1991), p. 63.

[2] See, for example, the work of K. G. Tobin, "The Effect of Extended Wait Time on Discourse Characteristics and Achievement in Middle School Grades," *Journal of Research in Science Teaching* 21(8):779–791 (November 1984); K. G. Tobin, "The Effects of Teacher Wait Time on Discourse Characteristics in Mathematics and Language Arts Classes," *American Educational Research Journal* 23(2):191–200 (Summer 1986); and K. G. Tobin, "The Role of Wait Time in Higher Cognitive Level Learning," *Review of Educational Research* 57(1):69–95 (Spring 1987).

[3] Studies in wait time began with the classic study of M. B. Rowe, "Wait Time and Reward as Instructional Variables, Their Influence on Language, Logic and Fate Control: Part I. Wait Time," *Journal of Research in Science Teaching* 11(2):81–94 (1974).

accurate response. She might then cue the answer with the following information and question, "The class to which those animals belong is class Decapoda. Does that give you a clue about the number of legs they have?" If that clue is not enough, and after allowing sufficient time for students to think (two to seven seconds), she might ask, "What is a decathlon?" or "What is the decimal system?" or "What is a decimeter?" or "What is a decibel?" or "What is a decade?" or "What is the Decalogue?" and so on.

When questioning students over reading material, you can use the Question Answer Relationship (QAR) strategy.[4] QAR involves asking a question and, if a student is unable to respond, providing one of three types of cues. "Right there" is used for questions for which the answer is explicitly stated in the sentence or paragraph. "Search and think" means the answer is not directly stated and therefore must be inferred. "On your own" is used for critical thinking questions for which the answers are neither explicit nor inferred in the text.[5]

Divergent-Thinking Question

Divergent-thinking questions (also known as *broad, reflective,* or *thought questions*) are open-ended (i.e., usually having no singularly correct answer), high-order thinking questions (requiring analysis, synthesis, or evaluation), that require students to think creatively, to leave the comfortable confines of the known and reach out into the unknown. Examples of questions that require divergent thinking are "Do you believe Mark Twain was a racist?" "What measures could be taken to reduce crime in our school's neighborhood?" and "What measures could be taken to improve the post-lunchtime trash problem on our campus?"

Evaluative Question

Whether convergent or divergent, some questions require students to place a value on something or to take a stance on some issue; these are referred to as *evaluative questions.* If the teacher and the students all agree on certain premises, then the evaluative question would also be a convergent question. If original assumptions differ, then the response to the evaluative question would be more subjective, and therefore that evaluative question would be divergent. Examples of evaluative questions are

"Should the United States allow clear-cutting in its national forests?" and "Should the Electoral College be abolished?"

Focus Question

This is any question that is designed to focus student thinking. For example, the first question of the preceding paragraph is a focus question when the teacher asking it is attempting to focus student attention on the economic issues involved in clear-cutting.

Probing Question

Similar to a clarifying question, the probing question requires student thinking to go beyond superficial first-answer or single-word responses. Examples of probing questions are "Why, Eloy, do you think that every citizen has the right to have a gun?"

SOCRATIC QUESTIONING

In the fifth century B.C.E., Socrates, the great Athenian teacher, used the art of questioning so successfully that to this day we still hear of the Socratic method.[6] What, exactly, is the Socratic method? Socrates' strategy was to ask his students a series of leading questions that gradually snarled them up to the point where they had to look carefully at their own ideas and to think rigorously for themselves. Today that strategy is referred to as the Socratic approach or method.

Socratic discussions were informal dialogues taking place in a natural, pleasant environment. Although Socrates sometimes had to go to considerable lengths to ignite his students' intrinsic interest, their responses were natural and spontaneous. In his dialogues, Socrates tried to aid students in developing ideas. He did not impose his own notions on the students. Rather, he encouraged them to develop their own conclusions and draw their own inferences. Of course, Socrates may have had preconceived notions about what the final learning should be and carefully aimed his questions so that the students would arrive at the desired conclusions. Still, his questions were open-ended, causing divergent rather than convergent thinking. The students were free to mentally go wherever the facts and their thinking led them.

Throughout history, teachers have tried to adapt what they believe to be the methods of Socrates to the classroom. In some situations, they have been quite successful and the methods have been a major mode of in-

[4]See, for example, M. E. McIntosh and R. J. Draper, "Using the Question-Answer Relationship Strategy to Improve Students' Reading of Mathematics Texts," *Clearing House* 69(3):154–162 (January/February 1996).

[5]J. S. Choate and T. A. Rakes, *Inclusive Instruction for Struggling Readers,* Fastback 434 (Bloomington, IN: Phi Delta Kappa Educational Foundation, 1998), p. 27.

[6]See, for example, how the Socratic seminar is used by one middle school language arts teacher in E. Schneider, "Shifting into High Gear," *Educational Leadership* 58(1): 57–60 (September 2000). See also M. L. Tanner and L. Casados, "Promoting and Studying Discussions in Math Classes," *Journal of Adolescent & Adult Literacy* 41(5): 342–350 (February 1998)

struction. However, we must remember that Socrates used this method in the context of a one-to-one relationship between the student and himself. Some teachers have adapted it for whole-class direct instruction by asking questions first of one student and then of another, moving slowly about the class. This technique may work, but it is difficult because the essence of the Socratic technique is to build question on question in a logical fashion so that each question leads the student a step closer to the understanding sought. When you spread the questions around the classroom, you may find it difficult to build up the desired sequence and to keep all the students involved in the discussion. Sometimes you may be able to use the Socratic method by directing all the questions at one student—at least for several minutes—while the other students look on and listen in. That is how Socrates did it. When the topic is interesting enough, this technique can be quite successful and even exciting, but in the long run, the Socratic method works best when the teacher is working in one-on-one coaching situations or with small groups of students, rather than in whole-class direct instruction.

In using Socratic questioning, the focus is on the questions, not the answers, and thinking is valued as the quintessential activity.[7] In essence, to conduct Socratic questioning with the student or class, identify a problem (either student- or teacher-posed) and then ask the students a series of probing questions designed to cause them to examine critically the problem and potential solutions to it. The main thrust of the questioning and the key questions must be planned in advance so that the questioning will proceed logically. To think of quality, probing questions on the spur of the moment is too difficult. You will be using the Socratic method in micro peer teaching Exercise 7.5 later in this chapter.

LEVELS OF COGNITIVE QUESTIONS AND STUDENT THINKING

Questions posed by you are cues to your students as to the level of thinking expected of them, ranging from the lowest level of mental operation, requiring simple recall of knowledge (convergent thinking), to the highest, requiring divergent thought and application of that thought. It is important that you are aware of the levels of thinking and that you understand the importance of attending to student thinking from low to higher levels of operation. What for one student may be a matter of simple recall of information, may for another require a higher-order mental activity, such as figuring something

out by deduction. (Remember the latter when you are doing Exercise 7.3 later in this chapter.)

You should structure and sequence your questions (and assist students in developing their own skill in structuring and sequencing their questions) in a way that is designed to guide students to higher levels of thinking. For example, when students respond to questions in complete sentences that provide supportive evidence for their ideas, it is fairly safe to assume that their thinking is at a higher level than if their response were an imprecise and nondescriptive single-word answer.

To help your understanding, three levels of questioning and thinking are described.[8] You should recognize the similarity between these three levels of questions and the six levels of thinking and doing from Bloom's taxonomy of cognitive objectives (Chapter 5). For your daily use of questioning, it is just as useful but more practical to think and behave in terms of these three levels, rather than of six.

1. *Lowest level: Gathering and recalling information.* At this level, questions are designed to solicit from students' concepts, information, feelings, or experiences that were gained in the past and stored in memory. Sample key words and desired behaviors are

complete, count, define, describe, identify, list, match, name, observe, recall, recite, select

Thinking involves receiving data through the senses, followed by the processing of those data. Inputting without processing is brain-dysfunctional. Information that has not been processed is stored only in short-term memory.

2. *Intermediate level: Processing information.* At this level, questions are designed to draw relationships of cause and effect, and to synthesize, analyze, summarize, compare, contrast, or classify data. Sample key words and desired behaviors are

analyze, classify, compare, contrast, distinguish, explain, group, infer, make an analogy, organize, plan, synthesize

Thinking and questioning that involves processing of information can be conscious or unconscious. When students observe the teacher thinking aloud, and when they are urged to think aloud, to think about their thinking, and to analyze it as it occurs, they are in the process of developing their intellectual skills.

At the processing level, this internal analysis of new data may challenge a learner's preconceptions (and misconceptions) about a phenomenon. The learner's brain will naturally resist this challenge to existing beliefs. The greater the mental challenge, the greater will

[7]B. R. Brogan and W. A. Brogan, "The Socratic Questioner: Teaching and Learning in the Dialogical Classroom," *Educational Forum* 59(3):288–296 (Spring 1995).

[8]This three-tiered model of thinking has been described variously by others. For example, in E. Eisner's *The Educational Imagination* (Upper Saddle River, NJ: Prentice Hall, 1979), the levels are referred to as "descriptive," "interpretive," and "evaluative." For a comparison of thinking models, see Costa, 1991, p. 44.

be the brain's effort to draw upon data already in storage. With increasing data, the mind will gradually examine existing concepts and ultimately, as necessary, develop new mental concepts.

If there is a match between new input and existing mental concepts, no problem exists. Piaget called this process **assimilation.**[9] If, however, in processing new data there is no match with existing mental concepts, then the situation is what Piaget called **cognitive disequilibrium.** The brain does not "like" this disequilibrium and will drive the learner to search for an explanation for the discrepancy. Piaget called this process **accommodation.** Although learning is enhanced by challenge, in situations that are threatening, the brain is less flexible in accommodating new ideas. As discussed in Chapter 4, that is why each student must feel welcomed in the classroom, and learners must perceive the classroom environment as challenging but nonthreatening, an environment of *relaxed alertness.*[10]

Questions and experiences must be designed to elicit more than mere recall memory responses (assimilation). Many teachers find it useful to use discrepant events to introduce concepts. *Discrepant events* are phenomena that cause cognitive disequilibrium, thus stimulating higher-level mental functioning. However, merely exposing students to a discrepant event will not in itself cause them to develop new conceptual understandings. It simply stirs the mind into processing, without which mental development does not occur. (See Figure 7.1.)

3. *Highest level: Applying and evaluating in new situations.* Questions at the highest level encourage learners to think intuitively, creatively, and hypothetically, to use their imagination, to expose a value system, or to make a judgment. Sample key words and desired behaviors are

apply, build, evaluate, extrapolate, forecast, generalize, hypothesize, imagine, judge, predict, speculate

Figure 7.1   Example of a discrepant event demonstration.

Balloon Will Not Pop

Practice this first. Partially blow up a balloon, tie it off. Take a large but sharp sewing needle and slowly push it into the balloon. Because the needle immediately plugs the hole, the balloon remains filled. Sure, you say, students have seen this done by magicians or birthday party clowns. But wait. Now for the real discrepant event: slowly remove the needle, and Voila! The balloon does not collapse. The balloon material expands to plug the hole. Make several holes. Take a long needle (as used in doll making) and push it through the balloon and out through the other side, keeping the needle in both holes. The balloon stays filled. (Hint: push the needle into the thickest portion of the balloon, opposite the opening.) If students believe you are using a fake balloon, take the same needle and quickly puncture the balloon, popping it.

You must use questions at the level best suited for the purpose and at a variety of different levels, and you must structure questions in a way intended to move the students' thinking to higher levels. When teachers use higher-level questions, their students tend to score higher on tests of critical thinking and on standardized tests of achievement.[11]

By using questions as a strategy to move students' thinking to higher levels, the teacher is facilitating the students' intellectual development. Developing your skill in using questioning requires attention to detail and practice. The following guidelines will provide that detail and some practice, but first, do Exercise 7.1 to check your understanding of the levels of questions.

---

[9]See, for example, J. Piaget, *The Development of Thought: Elaboration of Cognitive Structures* (New York: Viking, 1977).

[10]R. N. Caine, "Building the Bridge from Research to Classroom," *Educational Leadership* 58(3):59–61 (November 2000).

[11]See, for example, B. Newton, "Theoretical Basis for Higher Cognitive Questioning—An Avenue to Critical Thinking," *Education* 98(3):286–290 (March-April 1978); and D. Redfield and E. Rousseau, "A Meta-Analysis of Experimental Research on Teacher Questioning Behavior," *Review of Educational Research* 51(2):237–245 (Summer 1981).

EXERCISE 7.1: IDENTIFYING THE COGNITIVE LEVELS OF QUESTIONS— A SELF-CHECK EXERCISE

INSTRUCTIONS: The purpose of this exercise is to test your understanding and recognition of the levels of questions. Mark each of the following questions with a

1, if it is at the lowest level of mental operation, gathering and recalling data.
2, if it is at a middle level, processing data.
3, if it is at the highest level, applying or evaluating data in a new situation.

Check your answers against the key that follows. Resolve problems by discussing them with your classmates and instructor.

_____ 1. Do you recall the differences between an Asian elephant and an African elephant?

_____ 2. How are the natural habitats of the Asian and African elephants similar? How are they different?

_____ 3. Which of the elephants do you think is the more interesting?

_____ 4. For what do you think the elephant uses its tusks?

_____ 5. Do all elephants have tusks?

_____ 6. Did the trick ending make the story more interesting for you?

_____ 7. How might these evergreen needles be grouped?

_____ 8. How do these two types of pine needles differ?

_____ 9. For how many years was the Soviet Union a communist-dominated nation?

_____ 10. How many republics do you believe will be in the new Commonwealth of Independent States (the former Soviet Union) by the year 2020?

_____ 11. Why do you think the city decided to move the zoo?

_____ 12. How would the park be different today had the zoo been left there?

_____ 13. How do zoos today differ from those of the mid-nineteenth century?

_____ 14. Should a teacher be entitled to unemployment benefits during the summer or when school is not in session?

_____ 15. If $4X + 40 = 44$, what is X?

_____ 16. What happens when I spin this egg?

_____ 17. How does this poem make you feel?

_____ 18. What will happen when we mix equal amounts of the red and yellow solutions?

_____ 19. What is the capital of West Virginia?

_____ 20. What will be the long-term global effects if the rain forests continue to be removed at the present rate?

Answer Key: 1 = 1 (recall); 2 = 2 (compare); 3 = 3 (judge); 4 = 3 (imagine); 5 = 3 (extrapolate); 6 = 3 (evaluate); 7 = 2 (classify); 8 = 2 (contrast); 9 = 1 (recall); 10 = 3 (predict); 11 = 2 (explain cause and effect); 12 = 3 (speculate); 13 = 2 (contrast); 14 = 3 (judge); 15 = 1 (recall of how to work the problem); 16 = 1 (observe); 17 = 1 (describe); 18 = 3 (hypothesize); 19 = 1 (recall); 20 = 3 (speculate or generalize).

GUIDELINES FOR USING QUESTIONING

As emphasized many times in several ways throughout this resource guide, your goals are to help your students learn how to solve problems; to make decisions and value judgments; to think creatively and critically; and to feel good about themselves, their schools, and their learning—rather than simply to fill their minds with bits and pieces of information that will likely last only a brief time in the students' short-term memory. Important to the realization of these goals are how you construct your questions and how you implement your questioning strategy.

Preparing Questions

When preparing questions, consider the following guidelines.

Key cognitive questions should be planned, thoughtfully worded, and written into your lesson plan. Thoughtful preparation of questions helps to assure that they are clear and specific, not ambiguous; that the vocabulary is appropriate; and that each question matches its purpose. Incorporate questions into your lessons as instructional devices, welcomed pauses, attention grabbers, and checks for student comprehension. Thoughtful teachers even plan questions to ask specific students, targeting questions to the readiness level, interest, or learning profile of a student.

Match questions with their target purposes. Carefully planned questions allow them to be sequenced and worded to match the levels of cognitive thinking expected of students. To help students develop their thinking skills, you need to demonstrate how to do this. To demonstrate, you must use terminology that is specific and that provides students with examples of experiences consonant with the meanings of the cognitive words. You should demonstrate this every day so students learn the cognitive terminology. As stated by Brooks and Brooks, "Framing tasks around cognitive activities such as analysis, interpretation, and prediction—and explicitly using those terms with students—fosters the construction of new understandings."[12] See the three examples in Figure 7.2.

Implementing Questioning

Careful preparation of questions is one part of the skill in questioning. Implementation is the other part. Following are guidelines for effective implementation.

Ask your well-worded question before *calling on a student for a response.* A common error made is when the teacher first calls on a student and then asks the question, such

---

[12]J. G. Brooks and M. G. Brooks, *In Search of Understanding: The Case for Constructivist Classrooms* (Alexandria, VA: Association for Supervision and Curriculum Development, 1993), p. 105.

Figure 7.2 Questions that use appropriate cognitive terminology.

Instead of	*Say*
"How else might it be done?"	"How could you *apply . . .?*"
"Are you going to get quiet?"	"If we are going to hear what Joan has to say, what do you need to do?"
"How do you know that is so?"	"What evidence do you have?"

as "Sean, would you please tell us what you believe the author meant by the title 'We are one'?" Although probably not intended by the teacher, as soon as he or she calls on Sean, that signals the rest of the class that they are released from having to pay further attention and to think about the question. The preferred strategy is to phrase the question, allow time for all students to think, and then call on Sean and other students for their interpretations of the author's meaning of the title.

Avoid bombarding students with too much teacher talk. Sometimes teachers talk too much. This could be especially true for teachers who are nervous, as might be the case during the initial weeks of student teaching. Knowing the guidelines presented here will help you avoid that syndrome. Remind yourself to be quiet after you ask a question that you have carefully formulated. Sometimes, due to lack of confidence, and especially when a question has not been carefully planned, the teacher asks the question and then, with a slight change in wording, asks it again, or asks several questions, one after another. That is too much verbiage. It's called "shotgun questioning" and only confuses students, allowing too little time for them to think.

After asking a question, provide students with adequate time to think. The pause after asking a question is called *wait time* (or **think time**). Knowing the subject better than the students know it and having given prior thought to the subject, too many teachers fail to allow students sufficient time to think after they ask a question. In addition, by the time they have reached the middle grades, students have learned pretty well how to play the "game"— that is, they know that if they remain silent long enough the teacher will probably answer his or her own question. After asking a well-worded question, you should remain quiet for awhile, allowing students time to think and to respond. If you wait long enough, they usually will. You may need to rehearse your students on this procedure.

After asking a question, how long should you wait before you do something? You should wait at least two seconds, as long as seven seconds, and sometimes even longer, when it appears it is needed because students are still thinking. Stop reading now and look at your watch or a clock to get a feeling for how long two seconds is. Then, observe how long seven seconds is. Did seven seconds seem a long time? Because most of us are not used to silence in the classroom, two seconds of silence can seem quite long, while seven seconds may seem eternal. If, for some reason, students have not responded after two to seven seconds, you can ask the question again, but do not reword an already carefully worded question, or students are likely to think it is a new question. Pause for several seconds; then if you still have not received a response you can call on a student, then another, if necessary, after sufficient wait time. Soon you will get a response that can be built upon. Avoid answering your own question!

Now, to better understand the art of questioning, do Exercise 7.2.

EXERCISE 7.2: THINK TIME AND THE ART OF QUESTIONING: AN IN-CLASS EXERCISE

INSTRUCTIONS: The purpose of this exercise is to further your understanding of the art and power of questioning, the importance of well-worded questions with well-prepared and clear instructions, and the need to give students time to think.

1. Roleplay simulation: From your class ask for three volunteers. One volunteer will read the lines of Estella, a second will read the one line of the student, while the third volunteer uses a stop watch to direct Estella and the student to speak their lines at the designated times. The rest of your class can pretend to be students in Estella's English class.

   1:00:   *Estella:* "Think of a man whom you admire, perhaps a father figure, and write a three-sentence paragraph describing that person." Students begin their writing.

   1:00:05: *Estella:* "Only three sentences about someone you look up to. It might be your father, uncle, anyone."

   1:00:07: *Student:* "Does it have to be about a man?"
   Estella: "No, it can be a man or a woman, but someone you truly admire."

   1:01:   Estella works the rows, seeing that students are on task.

   1:01:10: *Estella:* "Three sentences are all you need to write."

   1:01:15: *Estella:* "Think of someone you really look up to, and write three sentences in a paragraph that describes that person."

   1:01:30: *Estella:* "Someone you would like to be like."

   1:02:   Estella continues walking around helping students who are having difficulty. All students are on task.

   1:04:   *Estella:* "Now I want you to exchange papers with the person behind or beside you, read that person's description of the person they admire, and describe a setting that you see their person in. Write a paragraph that describes that setting."

   1:04–1:05: Students exchange papers; teacher walks around seeing that everyone has received another student's paper.

   1:05:   *Estella:* "Where do you see that person being? Below the paragraph I want you to write a new paragraph describing where you see this person, perhaps in an easy chair watching a ball game, on a porch, in a car, or in the kitchen cooking."

   1:05:10: *Estella:* "Describe a scene you see this person in."

   1:05:15: *Estella:* "After you read the description I want you to create a setting for the person described."

   1:05:18: Students seem confused either about what they are reading (e.g., asking the writer what a word is or means) or what they are supposed to do.

   1:05:19: *Estella:* "Anything is fine. Use your imagination to describe the setting."

   1:05:22: *Estella:* "Describe a setting for this person."

   1:09:   *Estella:* "Now I want you to exchange papers with yet someone else, and after reading the previous two paragraphs written by two other students, write a third paragraph describing a problem you think this admired person has."

2. After the roleplay simulation, hold a whole-class discussion or small group discussions and use the following as a springboard for your discussion: Describe what you believe are the good points and weak points of this portion of Estella's lesson and her implementation of it.

Practice gender equity. To practice gender equity, follow these four rules when using questioning: (a) Avoid going to a boy to bail out a girl who fails to answer a question. Without seeming to badger, try to give the student clues until she can answer with success. (b) Avoid going to a boy to improve upon a girl's answer. Hold and demonstrate high expectations for all students. (c) Allow equal wait time regardless of student gender. (d) Call on boys and girls equally.

Practice calling on all students. Related to the last rule of the preceding paragraph, you must call on not just the bright or the slow, not just the boys or the girls, not only those in the front or middle of the room, but all of them. To do this takes concentrated effort on your part, but it is important. To ensure that students are called on equally, some teachers have in hand laminated copies of their seating charts, perhaps on bright neon-colored clipboards (gives students a visual focus). With a wax pencil or water soluble marker, they make a mark next to the name of the student each time he or she is called on. With the seating chart laminated, and using erasable markers, the marks can be erased at the end of the day and the seating chart used over and over. Additional suggestions for practicing equity in the classroom are in Chapter 8.

Give the same minimum amount of wait time (think time) to all students. This, too, will require concentrated effort on your part, but it is important to do. A teacher who waits for less time when calling on a slow student or students of one gender, is showing a prejudice or a lack of confidence in certain students. Both of these are detrimental when a teacher is striving to establish for all students a positive, equal, and safe environment for classroom learning. Show confidence in all students, and never discriminate by expecting less or more from some than from others. Although some students may take longer to respond, it is not necessarily because they are not thinking or have less ability. There may be cultural differences to think about, in that some cultures simply allow more wait time than others do. The important point here is to individualize, to allow students who need more time to have it. Variation in the length of wait time allowed should not be used to single out some students and lead to lower expectations but rather to allow for higher expectations.

Require students to raise their hands and be called on. When you ask questions, instead of allowing students to randomly shout out their answers, require them to raise their hands and be called on before they respond. Establish that procedure and stick with it. This helps ensure that you call on all students equally, fairly distributing your interactions with the students, and that you do not interact less with girls because boys tend to be more obstreperous. Even in college classrooms, male students tend to be more vocal than female students and, when allowed by the instructor, tend to

outtalk and to interrupt their female peers. Even in same-gender classrooms, some students tend to be more vocal than others and, when allowed by the instructor, tend to monopolize and control the flow of the verbal interactions. Regardless of grade level, every teacher has the responsibility to guarantee a nonbiased classroom and an equal distribution of interaction time in the classroom. That is impossible to do if students are allowed to speak out at will.

Another important reason for hand raising is to help students learn to control their impulsivity. Controlling one's impulsivity is one of the characteristics of intelligent behavior discussed in Chapter 9. One of your many instructional responsibilities is to help students develop this skill.

Actively involve as many students as possible in the questioning-answering discussion session. The traditional method of the teacher asking a question and then calling on a student to respond is essentially a one-on-one interaction. Many students, those not called on, are likely to view that as their opportunity to disengage in the lesson at hand. Even though you call on one student you do not want the other students to mentally disengage. There are many effective ways to do this. Consider the following.

To keep all students mentally engaged, call on students who are sitting quietly and have not raised their hands as well as those who have, but avoid badgering or humiliating an unwilling participant. When a student has no response, you might suggest that he or she think about it and that you will come back to assure the student eventually understands or has an answer to the original question.

By dividing a single question into several parts, the number of students involved can be increased. For example, "What are the causes of the Civil War? Who can give one reason?" followed then by "Who can give another?" Or, you can involve several students in answering a single question. For example, ask one student for an answer to the question "What was the first battle of the Civil War?" Ask a second to read the text aloud to verify the student's answer, and sometimes a third to explore the reason or thinking that makes it the accepted answer.

Carefully gauge your responses to students' responses to your questions. The way you respond to students' answers influences their subsequent participation. Responses by the teacher that encourage student participation include probing for elaboration, discussing student answers, requesting justification, asking how answers were arrived at, and providing positive reinforcement.

Use strong praise sparingly. Although a teacher's use of strong praise is sometimes okay, strong praise from a teacher tends to terminate divergent and creative thinking. It can also cause children to become dependent on external sources of praise—to become "praise junkies." (See discussion and Figure 3.3 in Chapter 3 about praise versus encouragement.)

One of your goals is to help students find intrinsic sources for motivation, that is, an inner drive of intent or desire that causes them to want to learn. Using strong praise tends to build conformity, causing students to depend on outside forces—that is, the giver of praise—for their worth rather than upon themselves. An example of a strong praise response is "That's right! Very good." On the other hand, passive acceptance responses, such as "Okay, that seems to be one possibility," keep the door open for further thinking, particularly for higher level, divergent thinking.

Another example of a passive acceptance response is one used in brainstorming sessions, when the teacher says, "After asking the question and giving you time to think about it, I will hear your ideas and record them on the board." Only after all student responses have been heard and recorded, does the class begin its consideration of each. That kind of nonjudgmental acceptance of all ideas in the classroom will generate a great deal of expression of high-level thought.

QUESTIONS FROM STUDENTS: THE QUESTION-DRIVEN CLASSROOM AND CURRICULUM

Student questions can and should be used as springboards for further questioning, discussions, and investigations. Indeed, in a constructivist learning environment, student questions often drive content. Students should be encouraged to ask questions that challenge the textbook, the process, or other persons' statements, and they should be encouraged to seek the supporting evidence behind a statement.

Being able to ask questions may be more important than having right answers. Knowledge is derived from asking questions. Being able to recognize problems and to formulate questions is a skill, and it is the key to problem solving and critical thinking skill development. You have a responsibility to encourage students to formulate questions and to help them word their questions in such a way that tentative answers can be sought. That is the process necessary to build a base of knowledge that can be drawn upon whenever necessary to link, interpret, and explain new information in new situations.

Questioning: The Cornerstone of Critical Thinking, Real-World Problem Solving, and Meaningful Learning

With real-world problem solving, there are usually no absolute right answers. Rather than "correct" answers, some are better than others. The student with a problem needs to learn how to (1) recognize the problem, (2) formulate a question about that problem (e.g., Should I date this person or not? Should I take this after-school job or not? Should I abuse drugs or not? To which col-

leges should I apply?), (3) collect data, and (4) arrive at a temporarily acceptable answer to the problem, while realizing that at some later time, new data may dictate a review of the former conclusion. For example, if a biochemist believes she has discovered a new enzyme, there is no textbook or teacher, or any other outside authoritative source to which she may refer to inquire if she is correct. Rather, on the basis of her self-confidence in problem identification, asking questions, collecting enough data, and arriving at a tentative conclusion based on those data, she assumes that for now her conclusion is safe.

Encourage students to ask questions about content and process. As emphasized in *Tried and True,* question asking often indicates that the inquirer is curious, puzzled, and uncertain; it is a sign of being engaged in thinking. And, yet, in too many classrooms too few students ask questions.[13] Students should be encouraged to ask questions. From students, there is no such thing as a "dumb" question. Sometimes students, like everyone else, ask questions that could just as easily have been looked up or are irrelevant or show a lack of thought or sensitivity. Those questions can consume precious class time. For a teacher, they can be frustrating. A teacher's initial reaction may be to quickly and mistakenly brush off that type of question with sarcasm, while assuming that the student is too lazy to look up an answer. In such instances, you are advised to think before responding and to respond kindly and professionally, although in the busy life of a classroom teacher, that may not always be so easy to remember. However, be assured that there is a reason for a student's question. Perhaps the student is signaling a need for recognition or simply demanding attention.

In large schools, it is sometimes easy for a student to feel alone and insignificant (although this seems less the case with schools that use a school-within-a-school plan and where teachers and students work together in interdisciplinary teams, or, as in looping, where one cadre of teachers remains with the same cohort of students for two or more years). When a student makes an effort to interact with you, that can be a positive sign, so gauge carefully your responses to those efforts. If a student's question is really off track, off the wall, out of order, and out of context with the content of the lesson, consider this as a possible response: "That is an interesting question (or comment) and I would very much like to talk with you more about it. Could we meet at lunch time or before or after school or at some other time that is mutually convenient?"

Avoid bluffing an answer to a question for which you do not have an answer. Nothing will cause you to lose credibility

---

[13]United States Department of Education, *Tried and True: Tested Ideas for Teaching and Learning from the Regional Educational Laboratories* (Washington, DC: Office of Educational Research and Improvement, U.S. Department of Education, 1997), p. 53.

with students any faster than faking an answer. There is nothing wrong with admitting that you do not know. It helps students realize that you are human. It helps them maintain an adequate self-esteem and realize that they are okay. What *is* important is that you know where and how to find possible answers and that you help students develop that same knowledge and those same process skills.

Now, to reinforce your understanding, do Exercises 7.3–7.8.

EXERCISE 7.3: EXAMINING COURSE MATERIALS FOR LEVEL OF QUESTIONING AND EXPECTED THINKING

INSTRUCTIONS: It is often reported that a very high percentage of the questions found in textbooks, teacher guides, student workbooks, electronic materials, and tests are low level; that is they are devoted to factual recall. The purpose of this exercise is for you to examine course materials for the levels of questions presented to students and to learn what you can do to raise the level of expected student thinking. For a subject and grade level you intend to teach, examine materials mentioned for the questions posed to the students. Complete the exercise that follows; then share your findings with your classmates. Use additional paper if necessary.

1. Materials examined (include date of publication and grade level of target students): _____

    _____

    _____

2. Questions at the recall (lowest) level: _____

    _____

    _____

    _____

    _____

3. Questions at the processing (intermediate) level: _____

    _____

    _____

    _____

    _____

4. Questions at the application (highest) level: _____

    _____

    _____

    _____

    _____

5. Approximate percentage of questions at each level: _____
    a. Recall = _____%
    b. Processing = _____%
    c. Application = _____%

6. Did you find evidence of question-level sequencing? If so, describe it. _____

    _____

    _____

    _____

    _____

☞

EXERCISE 7.3 (*continued*)

7. After sharing and discussing your results with your classmates, what do you conclude from this exercise?

_____

_____

_____

_____

8. When using instructional materials that you believe have a disproportionately high percentage of questions at the input (or recall) level, in addition to the two examples provided, what should or could you do?

Example 1: Have students scan chapter subheadings and develop higher-level cognitive questions based on the subheadings, which they would then answer through their reading.

Example 2: Require students to defend their answers to low-level cognitive chapter review and end-of-chapter questions with textual information and experience.

_____

_____

_____

_____

EXERCISE 7.4: OBSERVING THE COGNITIVE LEVELS OF CLASSROOM VERBAL INTERACTION

INSTRUCTIONS: The purpose of this exercise is to develop your skill in recognizing the levels of classroom questions. Arrange to visit a middle grades classroom. In the spaces provided here, tally each time you hear a question (or statement) from the teacher that causes students to gather or recall information, to process information, or to apply or evaluate data. In the left-hand column you may want to write additional key words to assist your memory. After your observation, compare and discuss the results of this exercise with your colleagues.

School and class visited: _____

Date of observation: _____

Level	*Tallies of Level of Question or Statement*
Recall level (key words: *complete, count, define, describe,* and so on)	
Processing level (key words: *analyze, classify, compare,* and so on)	
Application level (key words: *apply, build, evaluate,* and so on)	

FOR YOUR NOTES

EXERCISE 7.5: PRACTICE IN RAISING QUESTIONS TO HIGHER LEVELS

INSTRUCTIONS: The purpose of this exercise is to further develop your skill in raising questions from one level to the next higher level. Complete the blank spaces with questions at the appropriate levels (for the last series, create your own recall question and then vary it for the higher levels). Share and discuss your responses with your classmates.

Recall Level	*Processing Level*	*Application Level*
1. How many of you read a newspaper today?	1. Why did you read a newspaper today?	1. Do you think the time will come when nobody reads a newspaper?
2. What was today's newspaper headline?	2. Why was that so important as to be a headline?	2. Do you think that news item will be in tomorrow's paper?
3. Who is the vice president of the United States today?	3. How does the work he has done compare with that done by the previous vice president?	3. _____
4. How many presidents has the United States had?	4. _____	4. _____
5. _____	5. _____	5. _____

FOR YOUR NOTES

EXERCISE 7.6: PRACTICE IN CREATING COGNITIVE QUESTIONS

INSTRUCTIONS: The purpose of this exercise is to provide practice in writing cognitive questions. Read the following passage. Then compose three questions about it that cause students to identify, list, and recall; three that cause students to analyze, compare, and explain; and three that cause students to predict, apply, and hypothesize. Share and check your questions with your peers.

We Are One
Truth, love, peace, and beauty,
We have sought apart
    but will find within, as our
Moods—explored, shared,
    questioned, and accepted—
Together become one and all.

Through life my friends
We can travel together,
for we now know
each could go it alone.

To assimilate our efforts into one,
While growing in accepting,
and trusting, and sharing the
    individuality of the other,
Is truly to enjoy our greatest gift—
Feeling—knowing love and compassion.

Through life my friends
We are together,
for we must know
we are one.
                    —R. D. Kellough

RECALL QUESTIONS

1. To identify _____

_____

_____

_____

2. To list _____

_____

_____

_____

3. To recall _____

_____

_____

_____

☞

EXERCISE 7.6 (*continued*)

PROCESSING QUESTIONS

1. To analyze _____

_____

_____

_____

_____

2. To compare _____

_____

_____

_____

_____

3. To explain _____

_____

_____

_____

_____

APPLICATION QUESTIONS

1. To predict _____

_____

_____

_____

_____

2. To apply _____

_____

_____

_____

_____

3. To hypothesize _____

_____

_____

_____

_____

EXERCISE 7.7: A COOPERATIVE LEARNING AND MICRO PEER TEACHING EXERCISE IN THE USE OF QUESTIONING—MICRO PEER TEACHING I

INSTRUCTIONS: The purpose of this exercise is to practice preparing and asking questions that are designed to lead student thinking from the lowest level to the highest. Before class, prepare a five-minute lesson for posing questions that will guide the learner from lowest to highest levels of thinking. Teaching will be one-on-one, in groups of four, with each member of the group assuming a particular role—teacher, student, judge, or recorder. Each of the four members of your group will assume each of those roles once for five minutes. (If there are only three members in a group, the roles of judge and recorder can be combined during each five-minute lesson; or, if there are five members in the group, one member can sit out each round, or two can work together as judge.) Each member of the group should have his or her own tally sheet.

Suggested Lesson Topics

- Teaching styles

- Characteristics of young adolescents

- Learning styles of students

- Evaluation of learning achievement

- A skill or hobby

- Teaching competencies

- A particular teaching strategy

- Student teaching and what it will really be like

Each of your group members should keep the following role descriptions in mind:

- *Teacher (sender).* Pose recall (input), processing, and application (output) questions related to one of the topics above or to any topic you choose.

- *Student (receiver).* Respond to the questions of the teacher.

- *Judge.* Identify the level of each question or statement used by the teacher *and* the level of the student's response.

- *Recorder.* Tally the number of each level of question or statement used by the teacher (S = sender) as indicated by the judge; also tally the level of student responses (R = receiver). Record any problems encountered by your group.

EXERCISE 7.7 (*continued*)

TALLY SHEET

	Minute	Input	Processing	Output
Sender _____	1 S			
Receiver _____	R			
	2 S			
	R			
	3 S			
	R			
	4 S			
	R			
	5 S			
	R			

TALLY SHEET

	Minute	Input	Processing	Output
Sender _____	1 S			
Receiver _____	R			
	2 S			
	R			
	3 S			
	R			
	4 S			
	R			
	5 S			
	R			

EXERCISE 7.8: IDENTIFYING TEACHING BEHAVIORS IN CLASSROOM INTERACTION— A SELF-CHECK EXERCISE*

INSTRUCTIONS: The purpose of this exercise is to assess your understanding of the teacher's use of certain facilitative behaviors, including the use of questioning. It is a synthesis of what you have learned not only from this chapter but from previous chapters as well. (You may want to refer to Chapter 3.) The following is a sample classroom interaction, which includes examples of various levels of questions and structuring and responsive behaviors. See if you can identify them. Your answers should be from this list: *structuring, facilitating, active acceptance, passive acceptance, clarifying, input questioning, process questioning,* and *application questioning.* (An answer key is found at the end of this exercise.) Discuss and resolve any problems with your classmates and instructor.

	Interaction	**Teacher's Behavior**
Joyce:	Ms. Clarion, here's a picture that shows how a magnet works.	
Teacher:	Okay, Joyce, would you please share this with the rest of the group? Tell us what you think is happening.	1. _____
Joyce:	Well, this girl is in the garage using a magnet to pick up things, and over here it shows all the things a magnet will pick up.	
Teacher:	What kind of things are they, Joyce?	2. _____
Joyce:	Nails, paper clips, spoons, screws, screwdr—	
Molly:	It will not pick up spoons, Joyce. I've tried it.	
Joyce:	It will too. It shows right here.	
Olivia:	I picked up a spoon with a magnet that my uncle gave me.	
Joyce:	Sure it will.	
Sarah:	No it won't, 'cause—	
Teacher:	Just a minute. We'd like to hear everyone's idea, but we can't if we all talk at once. If you'll raise your hand, then I'll know who to call on next.	3. _____
Teacher:	Now, Joyce says a magnet will pick up spoons. Sarah says that a magnet can't pick it up.	4. _____
Teacher:	Yes, Sarah, what do you think?	5. _____
Sarah:	I'm not sure, but I think it has to be metal.	
Linda:	I think it depends upon the kind of spoon. Some spoons have metal, and some are plastic and other stuff.	
Teacher:	That's another possibility.	6. _____
Teacher:	How can we solve this problem as to whether a magnet will pick up the spoons?	7. _____
Molly:	We can get some spoons and try it with our magnet.	
Teacher:	All right. Anybody know where we can get some spoons?	8. _____
José:	There's a spoon in my lunch bag.	
Olivia:	There are some spoons in the lunchroom. Can we go get them?	
Teacher:	Yes, José, would you get yours? Olivia, would you get some from the lunchroom? Be sure you ask the cook. Joyce, would you get the magnet?	9. _____

☞

EXERCISE 7.8 (*continued*)

[*Later*]

Teacher:	Now, because this is José's spoon, what do you think would be the fair thing to do?	10. _____
David:	Let him try the magnet on his own spoon.	
Teacher:	All right, José, what do you think will happen when we touch the magnet to your spoon?	11. _____
José:	It probably won't pick it up because it's not the right kind of stuff for a magnet to pick up.	
Teacher:	What do you mean, "the right kind of stuff"?	12. _____
Sarah:	He means the right kind of metal.	
Teacher:	José, would you try it? Let's all watch.	13. _____
Molly:	See, I told you a magnet wouldn't pick up a spoon.	
Raul:	But it does pick up some spoons.	
Joyce:	I don't mean all spoons, only those made of metal. The spoon in the book is made of metal.	
Linda:	Is this pin made out of steel?	
Teacher:	No, Linda it isn't.	14. _____
Linda:	I thought it was steel or stuff like that—like a piece of car.	
Teacher:	I don't understand what you mean, Linda. What do you mean, "a piece of car"?	15. _____
Linda:	When Dad banged up our car, you could see the shining metal under the paint. He said it was steel.	
Sarah:	I think the most powerful magnet in the world might be able to pick it up.	
David:	An electromagnet, I think, is the strongest magnet that was ever invented.	
Teacher:	Are you saying, David, that you think a stronger magnet would pick up the spoon?	16. _____
David:	Um-hm. I think so.	
Teacher:	What would you want to do to find out?	17. _____
David:	We could set up our electromagnet and try it.	
Teacher:	Okay.	18. _____

Answer Key for Exercise 7.8: 1. Structuring; 2. Input questioning (listening); 3. Structuring; 4. Active acceptance; 5. Process questioning; 6. Passive acceptance; 7. Process question (problem solving); 8. Input question (locating); 9. Data acquisition (this might also be interpreted as a structuring behavior since the teacher directs the students to perform a task); 10. Application question (evaluation); 11. Application question (predicting); 12. Clarifying); 13. Data acquisition; 14. Data acquisition; 15. Clarifying; 16. Clarifying; 17. Process question (planning); 18. Passive acceptance.

*Adapted and modified from A. L. Costa, *The Enabling Behaviors* (Orangevale, CA: Search Models Unlimited, 1989) pp. 71–77. By permission of Arthur L. Costa.

SUMMARY

This chapter presented a great deal of information about one teaching strategy, which will be perhaps the most important one in your teaching repertoire. Questioning is the cornerstone to meaningful learning, thinking, communication, and real-world problem solving. The art of its use is something you will continue to develop throughout your teaching career.

In the next two chapters, your attention is directed to how teachers group students and to the selection and implementation of specific instructional strategies to facilitate students' meaningful learning of skills and content of the curriculum.

QUESTIONS FOR CLASS DISCUSSION

1. Have you ever noticed that some teachers seem to anticipate a lower level response to their questions from particular students? Discuss your answer with your peers.
2. Should a teacher verbally respond to every student's verbal comment or inquiry? Explain why or why not. If not, on what basis does the teacher decide when and how to respond?
3. Describe when, if ever, and how, a teacher could use strong praise. Explain the difference, if any, between strong praise and positive reinforcement.
4. Explain why it is important to wait after asking students a content question? How long should you wait? What should you do if, after waiting a certain amount of time, there is no student response?
5. To what extent should (or can) a classroom teacher allow student questions to determine content studied? To what extent should students' initial interest, or lack of interest, in a topic determine whether the topic gets taught?
6. Explain the meaning of the following statement: We should look not for what students can reiterate but for what they can demonstrate and produce. Explain why you agree or disagree with the concept.
7. Select one of the "Reflective Thoughts" from the introduction to Part III (page 232) that is specifically related to the content of this chapter, research it, and write a one-

page essay explaining why you agree or disagree with the thought. Share your essay with members of your class for their thoughts.
8. Describe any prior concepts you held that changed as a result of your experiences with this chapter. Describe the changes.
9. From your current observations and field work as related to this teacher preparation program, clearly identify one specific example of educational practice that seems contradictory to exemplary practice or theory as presented in this chapter. Present your explanation for the discrepancy.
10. Do you have questions generated by the content of this chapter? If you do, list them along with ways answers might be found.

FOR FURTHER READING

Brualdi, A. C. *Classroom Questions.* ERIC/AE Digest 422407 (Washington, DC: ERIC Clearinghouse on Assessment and Evaluation, 1998).

Chappell, M. F., and Thompson, D. "Modifying Our Questions to Assess Students' Thinking." *Mathematics Teaching in the Middle School* 4(7):470–474 (April 1999).

Cuccio-Schirripa, S., and Steiner, H. E. "Enhancement and Analysis of Science Question Level for Middle School Students." *Journal of Research in Science Teaching* 37(2):210–224 (February 2000).

Gober, D. A., and Mewborn, D. S. "Promoting Equity in Mathematics Classrooms." *Middle School Journal* 32(3):31–35 (January 2001).

Good, T. L., and Brophy, J. E. *Looking in Classrooms,* 8th ed. Chapter 9. New York: Addison Wesley Longman, 2000.

Harpaz, Y., and Lefstein, A. "Communities of Thinking." *Educational Leadership* 58(3):54–57 (November 2000).

Marzano, R. J., Pickering, D. J., and Pollock, J. E. *Classroom Instruction That Works: Research-Based Strategies for Increasing Student Achievement.* Chapter 10, "Cues, Questions, and Advance Organizers," Alexandria, VA: Association for Supervision and Curriculum Development, 2001.

Ochoa-Becker, A. S. "Decision Making in Middle School Social Studies: An Imperative for Youth and Democracy." *Clearing House* 72(6):337–340 (July 1999).

Using Grouping and Assignments for Positive Interaction and Quality Learning

Rather than diluting standards and expectations, exemplary schools and teachers believe in the learning potential of every student and effectively modify the key variables of time, methodology, and grouping to help individual students achieve mastery of the curriculum. In Chapter 1 we discussed ways in which time is modified. Throughout the book, we talk about ways to vary the methodology. In this chapter, we focus on ways of grouping students to enhance positive interaction and quality learning.

In the most effective instructional environments, during any given week or even day of school, a student might experience a succession of group settings. The initial topic of this chapter is ways of grouping young adolescent learners for quality instruction—from individualized instruction to working with dyads, small groups, and large groups. You also will learn how to ensure equality in the classroom, how to use assignments and homework, and how to coordinate various forms of independent and small-group, project-based study.

OBJECTIVES

Upon completion of this chapter, you should be able to

1. Describe the meaning of *mastery learning* and its implications for middle grades teaching.

2. Explain the advantages and disadvantages of various ways of grouping students for quality learning.
3. Explain how the teacher can personalize the instruction to ensure success for each student.
4. Demonstrate an understanding of the meaning and importance of classroom equity and how it can be achieved.
5. Demonstrate a theoretical and practical understanding of how to effectively use each of these instructional strategies: assignments, homework, written and oral reports, cooperative learning, learning centers, problem-based learning, and projects.

MASTERY LEARNING AND PERSONALIZED INSTRUCTION

Learning is an individual or personal experience. Yet as a middle level classroom teacher, you will be expected to work effectively with students on other than an individual basis—often with 30 or more students at a time. Much has been written of the importance of individualizing instruction for learners. Virtually all the research concerning effective instructional practice emphasizes greater individualization, or personalization, of instruction. We know about the individuality of the learning experience, and we know that while some young adolescent students are primarily verbal learners, many more are primarily visual, tactile, or kinesthetic learners. As the classroom teacher, though, you find yourself in the difficult position of simultaneously "treating" many separate and individual learners with individual learning capacities, styles, and preferences.

To individualize the instruction, exemplary middle level schools and teachers use a variety of strategies—exploratory programs, cooperative learning groups, project-based learning, and independent study—to respond to individual student competencies, interests, needs, and abilities. As was emphasized in Chapter 1, they also use nonconventional scheduling so that teaching teams can vary the length of time in the periods, the size of the instructional groups, and the learning strategies within a given time period.

Common sense tells us that student achievement in learning is related to both the quality of attention and the length of time given to learning tasks. In 1968, Benjamin Bloom, building upon a model developed earlier by John Carroll, developed the concept of individualized instruction called **mastery learning,** saying that students need sufficient time on task (i.e., engaged time) to master content before moving on to new content.[1]

From that concept, Fred Keller developed an instructional plan called the *Personalized System of Instruction* (PSI), or the *Keller Plan,* which by the early 1970s enjoyed popularity and success, especially at many two-year colleges. PSI involves the student's learning from printed modules of instruction (which, today, would likely be presented as computer software programs) that allow the student greater control over the learning pace.[2] The instruction is mastery oriented; that is, the student demonstrates mastery of the content of one module before proceeding to the next.

Today's Emphasis: Quality Learning for Every Student

Emphasis today is on mastery of content, or quality learning, for every student.[3] By mastery of content, we mean that the student demonstrates his or her use of what has been learned. Because of that emphasis and the research that indicates that quality learning programs positively affect achievement, the importance of the concept of mastery learning has resurfaced and is becoming firmly entrenched. For example, two approaches—*Results-Driven Education* (RDE), also known as *Outcome-Based Education* (OBE), and the *Coalition of Essential Schools* (CES)—use a goal-driven curriculum model with instruction that focuses on the construction of individual knowledge through mastery and assessment of student learning against the anticipated outcomes.[4] In some instances, unfortunately, attention may be on the mastery of only minimum competencies; thus, students are not encouraged to work and learn to the maximum of their talents and abilities.

Assumptions about Mastery, or Quality, Learning

Today's concept of mastery, or quality, learning is based on six assumptions:

1. Mastery learning can ensure that students experience success at each level of the instructional process, which provides incentive and motivation for further learning.

[1]See B. Bloom, *Human Characteristics and School Learning* (New York: McGraw-Hill, 1987), and J. Carroll, "A Model of School Learning," *Teachers College Record* 64(8):723–733 (May 1963).

[2]See, for example, I. R. Hambleton; W. H. Foster; and J. T. E. Richardson, "Improving Student Learning Using the Personalized System of Instruction," *Higher Education* 35(2):187–203 (March 1998).

[3]See, for example, the discussion "ensuring success for every student" on page 30 of A. W. Jackson and G. A. Davis, *Turning Points 2000: Educating Adolescents in the 21st Century* (New York: A Report of Carnegie Corporation of New York, Teachers College Press, 2000).

[4]Sample CES middle schools are: James Lick MS, San Francisco, CA; Rippowam Magnet MS, Stamford, CT; and Carpentersville MS, Carpentersville, IL. Information about CES, including a directory of participating schools, can be obtained from http://www.essentialschools.org.

2. Mastery of content, or quality learning, is possible for every student.

3. Although all students can achieve mastery, to master a particular content some students may require more time than others—the teacher and the school must provide for this difference in time needed to complete a task successfully.

4. For quality learning to occur, it is the instruction that must be modified and adapted, not the students—tracking and ability grouping do not fit with the concept of mastery learning.

5. Most learning is sequential and logical.

6. Most desired learning outcomes can be specified in terms of observable and measurable performance.[5]

Components of Any Mastery Learning Model

Any instructional model designed to teach toward mastery (quality) learning will contain the following components: (a) clearly defined target learning objectives, (b) a preassessment of the learner's present knowledge, (c) an instructional component, with a rich variety of choices and options for students, (d) frequent practice, reinforcement, and comprehension checks, with corrective instruction at each step to keep the learner on track, and (e) a postassessment to determine the extent of student mastery of the learning objectives.

Strategies for Personalizing the Instruction

You can immediately provide personalized instruction by (a) starting study of a topic from where the students are in terms of what they know (or think they know) and what they want to know about the topic (see "think-pair-share" discussed in later section titled "Learning in Pairs"), (b) providing students with choices from a rich variety of pathways and hands-on experiences to learn more about the topic, (c) providing multiple instructional approaches (that is, using multilevel instruction in a variety of settings, from learning alone to whole-class instruction), and (d) empowering students with responsibility for decision making, reflection, and self-assessment.

LEARNING ALONE

While some young adolescents learn well in pairs (dyads), others learn well with their peers in groups—collaboratively, cooperatively, or competitively—or collaboratively with adults, and still others learn well in combinations of these patterns, researchers tell us that more than 10 percent of students learn best alone. Learning-alone students often are gifted, nonconforming, able to work at their own pace successfully, comfortable using media, or seemingly underachieving but potentially able students for whom unconventional instructional strategies, such as *contract learning packages* (agreements between the teacher and individual students to proceed with tasks appropriate to their readiness, interests, or learning profiles in a sequence and at a pace each student selects) or multisensory instructional packages, encourage academic success.[6]

The Self-Instructional Module

One technique that can be used to ensure mastery of learning is the self-instructional module (SIM), which is a learning package (written, on audio- or videotape, or on computer) specifically designed with an individual student in mind. It uses small sequential steps, with frequent practice and immediate learning feedback to the student. It is designed to teach a relatively small amount of material, at the mastery level, requiring a brief amount of learning time (about 30 minutes for middle grades students). The SIM can be designed to teach any topic, at any grade level, in any subject, for any domain or combination of domains of learning. Exercise 8.1 is a self-instructional module designed to guide you through the completion of your first SIM.

As instructed by your course instructor, do Exercise 8.1.

---

[5]See J. Battistini, *From Theory to Practice: Classroom Application of Outcome-Based Education* (Bloomington, IN: ERIC Clearinghouse on Reading, English, and Communication, 1995), and L. Horton, *Mastery Learning*, Fastback 154 (Bloomington, IN: Phi Delta Kappa Educational Foundation, 1981).

[6]R. Dunn, *Strategies for Diverse Learners*, Fastback 384 (Bloomington, IN: Phi Delta Kappa Educational Foundation, 1995), p. 15.

EXERCISE 8.1: PREPARING A SELF-INSTRUCTIONAL MODULE*

INSTRUCTIONS: The purpose of this exercise is to guide you through the process of preparing a self-instructional module for use in your own teaching. The exercise continues for several pages; it is important that you follow it step by step, beginning with the following boxed-in "cover page."

Self-Instructional Module Number: 1
Instructor's Name: Professor Richard D. Kellough
School: California State University, Sacramento
Course: Methods of Teaching Young Adolescents
Intended Students: Students in Teacher Preparation
Topic: How to Write a Self-Instructional Module
Estimated Working Time: 10 hours

For the challenge of today's classroom . . .

THE SELF-INSTRUCTIONAL MODULE

You are about to embark upon creating and writing a perfect lesson plan. The result of your hard work will be an instructional module in which you will take a lot of pride. More important, you will have learned a technique of teaching that ensures learning takes place. For what more could you ask?

Let us get to the essence of what this self-instructional module (SIM) is: This SIM is about how to write an SIM. The general objective is to guide you gently through the process of preparing and writing your first SIM. Let's begin the experience with background about the history of the SIM.

*Copyright 2003 and 1991 by Richard D. Kellough.

EXERCISE 8.1 (*continued*)

A History

Research evidence indicates that student achievement in learning is related to time and to the *quality of attention* being given to the learning task. You knew that already! In 1968, Benjamin Bloom developed a concept of individualized instruction called mastery learning, based on the idea that students need sufficient time on task to master content before moving on to new content. Did you know that? _____. (Please read along with a pencil, and fill in the blanks as you go.)

Although Bloom is usually given credit for the concept of mastery learning, the idea did not originate with him. He reinforced and made popular a model developed earlier by John Carroll. In 1968, Fred Keller developed a similar model called the Keller Plan, or the Personalized System of Instruction (PSI). The PSI quickly became a popular teaching technique in the community and four-year colleges. In about 1972, enter Johnson and Johnson (not of the Band-Aid family, but Rita and Stuart Johnson), who developed their model of mastery learning and called it the Self-Instructional Package (SIP). Since 1972, I (Richard D. Kellough) have been developing my version, the Self-Instructional Module, which you are now experiencing. As you will learn, *frequent comprehension checks and corrective instructions* are important to the effectiveness of the SIM.

One other thing. There are several devices available to individualize instruction, but the SIM has the flexibility to be adaptable for use at all grade levels, from kindergarten through college. I believe the following to be the reasons for the popularity of this strategy:

- The SIM allows the teacher to *create an experience that ensures learning.* Creating makes you feel good; when your students learn, you feel good—two reasons for the SIM's popularity.
- The SIM is truly *individualized,* because it is a module written for an individual student, with that student in mind as it is being written.
- Although it takes time to prepare, the SIM *requires little financial expenditure,* a fact important to today's teacher.
- Once you have prepared your first SIM, you might see that you have begun a series. Subsequent modules are easier to do, and you may see the value in having a series available.
- With today's emphasis on the *basics,* the SIM is particularly helpful for use in remediation.
- When you finish your SIM, you will have collected the content that could be used for a computer program.
- With today's *large and mixed-ability classes,* teachers need help! Here is time and cost-effective help!
- With emphasis today on competency-based instruction, the SIM makes sense.

How are we doing so far? _____ Are your interests and curiosity aroused? _____

_____ Do you have questions? _____ If so, write them down, then continue.

Questions: _____

_____

_____

_____

_____

What Is the Self-Instructional Module and Why Use It?

The SIM is a learning module designed for an individual student; it is self-instructional (i.e., if you, the teacher, drop dead—heaven forbid—the student can continue to learn), and *it requires about 30 minutes of learning time.* The final module can be recorded on tape, video, or computer disc; it can be written in booklet form; or it can exist in any combination of these.

EXERCISE 8.1 (*continued*)

Here are ways that teachers have found the SIM to be useful:

- As an *enrichment* activity for an accelerated student.
- As a strategy for make-up for a student who has been absent.
- As a strategy for a student in need of *remediation*.
- As a strategy for introducing basic information to an entire class, freeing the teacher to work with individual students, making the act of teaching more *time-efficient,* a particularly significant value of the SIM.
- As a learning experience especially coordinated with manipulatives, perhaps in connection with a science experiment, library work, a computer, a tape recording, a videotape, a DVD, hands-on materials for an activity, or any combination of these.

One other point before we stop and check your comprehension: *The single most important characteristic of the SIM is that it uses small sequential steps followed by immediate and corrective feedback to the learner.* In that respect, the SIM resembles programmed instruction.

   Stop the action!

Let's check your learning with the review questions and instructions that follow.

Comprehension Check 1

   Answer the following three questions, then check your responses by reviewing Feedback Check 1. If you answer all three questions correctly, continue the package; otherwise, back up and review.

---

1. How would you define a SIM? _____

_____

_____

2. What is the single most important characteristic of the SIM? _____

_____

3. What is one way that the SIM could be used in your own teaching, a way that currently stands out in your

   thinking? _____

_____

_____

EXERCISE 8.1 (*continued*)

Feedback Check 1

1. Although we will continue development of the definition, at this point it should resemble this: The SIM is an individualization of learning—teaching strategy that teaches toward mastery learning of one relatively small bit of content by building upon small, sequential steps and providing corrective feedback throughout.
2. Referring to the small, sequential steps, followed by immediate and corrective feedback.
3. Your answer is probably related to one of those listed earlier but it could differ.

How Does the SIM Differ from Other Kinds of Learning Packages?

Another characteristic of the SIM is the *amount of learning contained in one module.* Each SIM is designed to teach a relatively small amount of material, but to do it well. *This is a major difference in the SIM from other types of learning activity packages.*

And, in case you have been wondering about what the SIM can be designed to teach, I want to emphasize that it *can be designed*

- For any topic,
  - At any grade level,
    - In any discipline,
      - For cognitive understanding,
        - For psychomotor development, and
          - For affective learning.

That probably brings to your mind all sorts of thoughts and questions. Hold them for a moment, and let's do another comprehension check.

Stop the action and check your learning.

Comprehension Check 2

Answer the following two questions, then check your responses in the feedback box that follows.

---

1. How does the SIM differ from other self-contained learning packages?

_____

_____

_____

EXERCISE 8.1 (*continued*)

2. Although teachers frequently emphasize learning that falls within the cognitive domain, is it possible for the

    SIM to be written to include learning in the psychomotor and affective domains? Yes or no? _____

Feedback Check 2

1. Length of learning time is shorter for the SIM, and it is written with an individual student in mind. It is written to teach one thing well, to one student.
2. The SIM *can* be written for any domain, although evaluation is trickier for the affective and for the highest-level psychomotor.

Perhaps we should now say a word about what we mean when we use the expression *teach one thing well*—that is, to explain what is meant by mastery learning. Theoretically, if the package is being used by an individual student, performance level expectation is 100%. In reality, performance level will most likely be between 85 and 95%, particularly if you are using the SIM for a group of students rather than an individual. That 5–15% difference allows for human errors that can occur in writing and in reading.

Now that you have learned what the SIM is—and how this learning strategy differs from other learning activity packages—it is time to concentrate on developing your SIM. Please continue.

SIM DEVELOPMENT

How Do I Develop a SIM?

As with any good lesson plan, it takes time to develop an effective SIM. Indeed, preparation of your first SIM will test your imagination and writing skills! Nevertheless, it will be time well spent; you will be proud of your product. *It is important that you continue following this module, step by step; do not skip parts, or I will assume no responsibility for your final product! Understand?* _____ Development of your SIM emphasizes the importance of

- Writing the learning objectives clearly, precisely, and in behavioral terms.
- Planning the learning activities in small, sequential steps.
- Providing frequent practice and learning comprehension checks.
- Providing immediate feedback, corrective instruction, and assurance to the learner.
- Preparing evaluative questions that measure against the learning objectives.

As you embark on preparing what may be the perfect lesson plan, keep in mind the following two points:

1. Prepare your first SIM so it will take no more than

---

30 minutes for young adolescents

---

2. Use a *conversational tone* in your writing. Write in the first person, as though you are talking directly to the student for whom it is intended. For example, when speaking of the learning objectives, use *You will be able to* rather than *The student will be able to*. Keep in mind that you are communicating with one person rather than with an entire class (even though you may be preparing your package for entire class use). It helps to pretend that you are in a one-on-one situation tutoring the student at the writing board.

☞

EXERCISE 8.1 (*continued*)

Stop the action, and again check your learning.

Comprehension Check 3

Answer the following two questions; then check your responses in Feedback Check 3.

---

1. What maximum learning-time duration is recommended? _____

2. What major item of importance has been recommended for you to keep in mind as you write your

   SIM? _____

   _____

Feedback Check 3

1. Approximately 30 minutes.
2. Write in the first person, as if you are speaking directly to the student.

Now that I have emphasized the *length of learning time* and *the personalization of your writing*, here are other important reminders.

1. Make your SIM attractive and stimulating. Consider using cartoons, puns, graphics, scratch-and-sniff stickers, and interesting manipulatives. Use your creative imagination! Use both cerebral hemispheres!

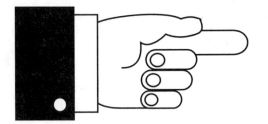

Add sketches, diagrams, modules, pictures, magazine clippings, humor, and a conversational tone, as students appreciate a departure from the usual textbooks and worksheets.

EXERCISE 8.1 (*continued*)

2. Use colleagues as resource persons, brainstorming ideas as you proceed through each step of module production.

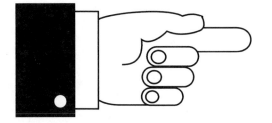

During production, use your best cooperative learning skills.

3. The module should not be read (or heard) like a lecture. It *must* involve small sequential steps with frequent practice and corrective feedback instruction (as modeled in this module).

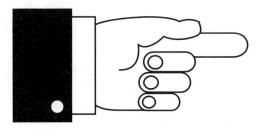

". . . and with the course material broken down into small self-instructional units, students can move through at individual rates."

4. The module should contain a variety of activities, preferably involving all four learning modalities—*visual, auditory, tactile, and kinesthetic.*

☞

EXERCISE 8.1 (*continued*)

5. Vary margins, indentations, and fonts

so the final module does not have the usual textbook or worksheet appearance with which students are so familiar. Build into your module the "Hawthorne Effect."

Note about the cosmetics of your SIM: My own prejudice about the SIM is that it should be spread out more than the usual textbook page or worksheet. Use double-spaced lines, varied margins, and so on. Make cosmetic improvements after finishing your final draft. Write, review, sleep on it, write more, revise, add that final touch. This modular packet that you are using has been "toned down" and modified for practical inclusion in this textbook.

6. Your SIM does not have to fit the common 8 1/2″ × 11″ size. You are encouraged to be creative in the design of your SIM's shape, size, and format.
7. Like all lesson plans, the SIM is subject to revision and improvement after use. Use your best creative writing skills. *Write, review, sleep on it, write more, revise, test, revise. . . .*

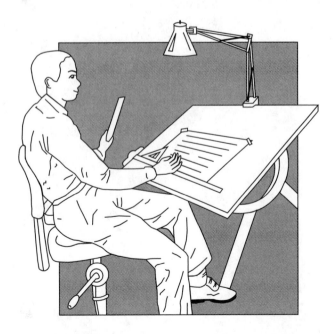

EXERCISE 8.1 (*continued*)

Perhaps before proceeding, it would be useful to review the preceding points. Remember, too, the well-written module *will ensure learning*. Your first SIM will take several hours to produce, but it will be worth it!

Proceed with the steps that follow.

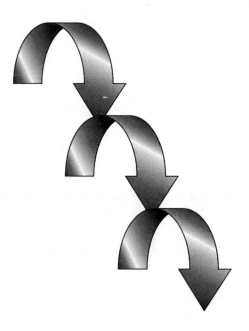

STEPS FOR DEVELOPING YOUR SIM

Instructions: It is important that you proceed through the following module development step by step. One thing you will notice is that immediately after writing your learning objectives, you will prepare the evaluative test items; both steps precede the preparation of the learning activities. That is not the usual order followed by a teacher when preparing lessons, but it does help to ensure that test items match objectives. Now, here we go! *Step-by-step,* please.

Note: From here on, write on separate paper for draft planning.

Step 1. Prepare the cover page. It should include the following items:

- Instructor's name (that is you)
  - School (yours)
    - Class or intended students (whom it's for)
      - Topic (specific but not wordy)
        - Estimated working time

For a sample, refer to the beginning of this module. You can vary the design of the cover page according to your needs.

☞

EXERCISE 8.1 (*continued*)

Step 2. Prepare the instructional objectives. For now, these should be written in specific behavioral terms. Later, when writing these into your module introduction, you can phrase them in more general terms.

Recommended is the inclusion of at least one attitudinal (affective) objective, such as "Upon completion of this module, you will tell me your feelings about this kind of learning."

Step 3. **Comprehension Check 4**

Share with your colleagues what you have accomplished (with steps 1 and 2) to solicit their valuable feedback and input.

Step 4. Depending on feedback (from step 3), *modify items 1 and 2,* if necessary. For example, after listing the learning instructions, you may find that you really have more than one module in preparation, and within the list of objectives you may find a natural cut-off between modules 1 and 2. You may discover that you have a *series* of modules begun.

Step 5. Prepare the pretest. If the learner does well on the pretest, there may be no need for the student to continue the module. Some modules (like this one) may not include a pretest, though most will. And if this is your first SIM writing experience, I think you *should* include a pretest.

Suggestion: The pretest need not be as long as the posttest but should include a limited sample of questions to determine whether the student already knows the material and need not continue with the module. A pretest also serves to set the student mentally for the SIM.

Step 6. Prepare the posttest. The pretest and posttest could be identical, but usually the pretest is shorter. It is important that both pretest and posttest items actually test against the objectives (of step 2). Try to keep the items objective (e.g., multiple-choice type), avoiding as much as possible the use of subjective test items (e.g., essay type), but do include at least one item measuring an affective objective (see boxed item in step 2).

Important reminder: If your module is well written, the student should achieve 85–100% on the posttest.

Step 7. **Comprehension Check 5**

Share with colleagues your pretest and posttest items (providing a copy of your objectives) for suggested improvement changes before continuing to the next step.

EXERCISE 8.1 (*continued*)

Use the following space to write notes to yourself about ideas you are having and regarding any materials you may need to complete your module.

Dear Self—

Good work so far! Before continuing, take a break.

It is time to stop working for a while . . .   . . .and go play!

Step 8. Okay, enough play; it is time to prepare the text of your SIM. This is the "meat" of your module—what goes between the pretest and the posttest. It is the INSTRUCTION. *Reminder:* For the SIM to be self-instructional, the learner should be able to work through the module with little or no help from you.

EXERCISE 8.1 (*continued*)

An important ingredient in your module is the *directions.* The module should be self-directed and self-paced. Therefore, each step of the module should be clear to the learner, making you, the instructor, literally unnecessary. *Everything needed by the learner to complete the module should be provided with the module.*

Use small, sequential steps with frequent practice cycles, followed by comprehension checks and corrective feedback. Make it fun and interesting with a variety of activities for the student, activities that provide for learning in several ways, from writing to reading, from viewing a video tape to drawing, from listening to a tape recording to doing a hands-on activity. And be certain the activities correlate with the learning objectives. The learning cycles should lead to satisfaction of the stated objectives, and the posttest items *must* measure against those objectives.

Step 9. **Comprehension Check 6**

Test your package. Try it out on your colleagues as they look for content errors, spelling and grammar errors, and clarity, as well as offer suggestions for improvement. Duplicate and use the SIM Assessment Form provided at the end of this exercise.

Stop the Action!
Congratulations on the development of your first SIM!
However, two additional steps need your consideration.

Step 10. Revise if necessary. Make appropriate changes to your SIM as a result of the feedback from your colleagues. Then you are ready to give your SIM its first real test—try it out on the student for whom it is intended.

Step 11. Further revisions. This comes later, after you have used it with the student for whom it was originally intended. Like any other well-prepared lesson or unit plan, it should always be subject to revision and to improvement, never "set in concrete."

SIM ASSESSMENT FORM

1. Module identification

   Author: _____

   _____

   _____

   Title of SIM: _____

   _____

   _____

2. Module Objectives: Do they tell the student

   a. What the student will be able to do? _____

      _____

      _____

      _____

      _____

   b. How the student will demonstrate this new knowledge or skill? _____

      _____

      _____

      _____

      _____

   Is there a clear statement (overview or introduction) of the importance, telling the learner what will be learned by completing the module?

   _____

   _____

   _____

   _____

3. Pretest

   _____

   _____

   _____

   _____

   _____

   _____

☞

4. Activities (practice cycles)

   Are small sequential steps used? _____

   _____

   _____

   _____

   _____

   Are there frequent practice cycles, with comprehension checks and corrective feedback to the learner?

   _____

   _____

   _____

   _____

5. Posttest: Does it test against the objectives? _____

   _____

   _____

   _____

   _____

6. Clarity and continuity of expression: _____

   _____

   _____

   _____

   _____

7. Is the module informative, attractive, and enjoyable? _____

   _____

   _____

   _____

   _____

8. Additional comments useful to the author of this module: _____

   _____

   _____

   _____

   _____

LEARNING IN PAIRS

It is sometimes advantageous to pair students (dyads) for learning. Four types of dyads are described as follows.

Peer Tutoring, Mentoring, and Cross-Age Coaching. Peer mentoring, tutoring, or peer-assisted learning (PAL) is a strategy whereby one classmate tutors another. It is useful, for example, when one student helps another who has limited proficiency in English or when a student skilled in math helps another who is less skilled. For many years, it has been demonstrated repeatedly that peer tutoring is a significant strategy for promoting active learning. Cross-age coaching is a strategy whereby one student coaches another from a different, and sometimes lower, grade level. This is similar to peer tutoring, except that the coach is from a different age level than the student being coached.[7] As discussed in Chapter 1 and in the last section of this chapter, many middle level schools have service learning projects that involve students mentoring younger children.

Paired Team Learning. Paired team learning is a strategy whereby students study and learn in teams of two. Students identified as gifted work and learn especially well when paired. Specific uses for paired team learning include drill partners, reading buddies,[8] book report pairs, summary pairs, homework partners,[9] project assignment pairs, and elaborating and relating pairs.

Think-Pair-Share. Think-pair-share is a strategy where students, in pairs, examine a new concept or topic about to be studied. After the students of each dyad discuss what they already know or think they know about the concept, they present their perceptions to the whole group. This is an excellent technique for discovering student's **misconceptions** (also called **naïve theories**) about a topic. Introducing a writing step, the modification called *think-write-pair-share*, is when the dyad thinks and writes their ideas or conclusions before sharing with the larger group.

The Learning Center

Another significantly beneficial way of pairing students for instruction (as well as of individualizing the instruction and learning alone and integrating the learning) is by using the learning center (LC) or learning station. [*Note:* Whereas each learning center is distinct and un-related to others, learning stations are sequenced or in some way linked to one another, as discussed in the TEAMS approach below.] The LC is a special station located in the classroom where one student (or two, if student interaction is necessary or preferred at the center, or as many as 4 or 5 students in the case of learning stations) can quietly work at his or her own pace to learn more about a special topic or to improve specific skills. All materials needed are provided at the center, including clear instructions for operating the center. The use of LCs and SIMs in tandem works especially well.

Whereas the LC used to be thought of as belonging to the domain of elementary school teachers with self-contained classrooms, now, with block scheduling and longer class periods, the LC has special relevance for all teachers, regardless of grade level. In the words of a teacher of French and Spanish at Bailey Middle School (Austin, TX),

> As other teachers in our district have begun to use center techniques, I hear comments such as, "The students are so excited," and "There was none of the chaos I was afraid of." In using centers as a teaching tool, I have found that students are eager to participate in all class work and excited about speaking a new language both inside and outside the classroom.[10]

The value of learning centers as instructional devices undoubtedly lies in the following characteristics. LCs can provide instructional diversity. While working at a center, the student is giving time and quality attention to the learning task (learning toward mastery) and is likely to be engaging her most effective learning modality, or integrating several modalities or all of them.

Learning centers are of three types. In the *direct-learning center,* performance expectations for cognitive learning are quite specific and the focus is on mastery of content. In the *open-learning center,* the goal is to provide opportunity for exploration, enrichment, motivation, and creative discovery. In the *skill center,* as in a direct-learning center, performance expectations are quite specific but the focus is on the development of a particular skill or process.

Although in all instances the primary reason for using a learning center is to individualize—that is, to provide collections of materials and activities adjusted to the various readiness levels, interests, and learning profiles of students, there are additional reasons. Other reasons to use an LC are to provide (a) a mechanism for learning that crosses discipline boundaries, (b) a special place for a student with special needs, (c) opportunities for creative work, enrichment experiences, multisensory experiences, and (d) opportunity to learn from learning packages that use special equipment or media that may be in limited supply in your classroom (e.g., science materials, a microscope, a computer, a videodisc player, or some combination of these).

[7]See, for example, J. Wagmeister and B. Shifrin, "Thinking Differently, Learning Differently," *Educational Leadership* 58(3):45–48 (November 2000), and L. Thrope and K. Wood, "Cross-Age Tutoring for Young Adolescents," *Clearing House* 73(4):239–242 (March/April 2000).

[8]See, for example, C. C. Block and R. J. Dellamura, "Better Book Buddies," *The Reading Teacher* 54(4): 364–370 (December 2000/January 2001).

[9]See, for example, C. Kaplan, "Homework Partners," *Mathematics Teaching in the Middle School* 2(3):168–169 (January 1997).

[10]L. Voelzel, "Making Foreign Language Instruction the Center of Attention," *Middle Ground* 4(2):44–46 (October 2000).

To adapt instruction to the curriculum and to students' individual needs and preferences, it is possible to design a learning environment that includes several learning stations, each of which uses a different medium and modality or focuses on a special aspect of the curriculum. Students then rotate through the various stations according to their needs and preferences. For example, several schools in Florida use the TEAMS (Technology Enhancing Achievement in Middle School) approach, in which at least four learning stations are set up in a classroom: a Technology Station for computer-based instruction; an Exploration Station I for creative activities involving student-created products; Exploration Station II for learning in a game-like format; and a Text Station for written work.[11]

When constructing an LC, you can be as elaborate and as creative as your time, imagination, and resources allow. Students can even help you plan and set up learning centers, which will relieve some of the burden from your busy schedule. Following are guidelines for setting up and using this valuable instructional tool.

The center should be designed with a theme in mind, preferably one that integrates the student's learning by providing activities that cross discipline boundaries. Decide the purpose of the center and give the center a name, such as "the center for the study of wetlands," "walking tour of Florence," "traveling to Quebec City," "structure and function," "patterns in nature," "the United Nations," "sound editing," "the center for world-wide communication," or "headquarters for our class newspaper," and so on. The purpose of the center should be clearly understood by the students. Learning centers should always be used for educational purposes, *never* for punishment.

The center should be designed to be attractive, purposeful, and uncluttered, and should be identified with an attractive sign. Learning centers should be activity-oriented (i.e., dependent on the student's manipulation of materials, not just paper-and-pencil tasks).

Topics for the center should be related to the instructional program—for review and reinforcement, remediation, or enrichment. It should be self-directing (i.e., specific instructional objectives and procedures for using the center should be clearly posted and understandable to the student user). An audio- or videocassette or a computer program is sometimes used for this purpose. The center should also be self-correcting (i.e., student users should be able to tell by the way they have completed the task whether or not they have done it correctly and have learned).

The center should contain a variety of activities geared to the varying abilities and interest levels of the students. A choice of two or more activities at a center is one way to provide for this.

Materials to be used at the center should be maintained at the center, with instructions for use provided to the students. Again, using SIMs with LCs works well. Materials should be safe for student use, and you or another adult should easily supervise the center. Some centers may become more or less permanent centers, that is, remain for the school term or longer, whereas others may change according to what is being studied at the time.

LEARNING IN SMALL GROUPS

Small groups are those involving three to five students, in either a teacher- or a student-directed setting. Using small groups for instruction, including the cooperative learning group (CLG), enhances the opportunities for students to assume greater control over their own learning, sometimes referred to as *empowerment*.

Purposes for Using Small Groups

Small groups can be formed to serve a number of purposes. They might be useful for a specific learning activity (e.g., reciprocal reading groups, where students take turns asking questions, summarizing, making predictions about, and clarifying a story). Or they might be formed to complete an activity that requires materials that are in short supply, or to complete a science experiment or a project, and last only as long as the project does. Teachers have various rationales for assigning students to groups. Students can be grouped according to (a) personality type (e.g., sometimes a teacher may want to team less-assertive students to give them the opportunity for greater management of their own learning), (b) social pattern (e.g., sometimes it may be necessary to break up a group of rowdy friends, or it may be desirable to broaden the association among students), (c) common interest, (d) learning styles (e.g., forming groups of either mixed styles or of styles in common), or (e) their abilities in a particular skill or their knowledge in a particular area. One specific type of small group instruction is the cooperative learning group.

COOPERATIVE LEARNING

Lev Vygotsky (1896–1934) studied the importance of a learner's social interactions in learning situations. Vygotsky argued that learning is most effective when learners cooperate with one another in a supportive learning environment under the careful guidance of a teacher. Cooperative learning, group problem solving, problem-based learning, and cross-age tutoring are instructional strategies used by teachers that have grown in popularity as a result of research evolving from the work of Vygotsky.

---

[11]R. A. Reiser and S. M. Butzin, "Using Teaming, Active Learning, and Technology to Improve Instruction," *Middle School Journal* 32(2):21–29 (November 2000).

The Cooperative Learning Group (CLG)

The *cooperative learning group* is a heterogeneous group (i.e., mixed according to one or more criteria, such as ability or skill level, ethnicity, learning style, learning capacity, gender, and language proficiency) of three to five students who work together in a teacher- or student-directed setting, emphasizing support for one another. Often times, a CLG consists of four students of mixed ability, learning styles, gender, and ethnicity, with each member of the group assuming a particular role. Teachers usually change the membership of each group several to many times during the year.

THE THEORY AND USE OF COOPERATIVE LEARNING

The theory of cooperative learning is that when small groups of students of mixed backgrounds and capabilities work together toward a common goal, members of the group increase their friendship and respect for one another. As a consequence, each individual's self-esteem is enhanced, students are more motivated to participate in higher order thinking, and academic achievement is accomplished.[12]

There are several techniques for using cooperative learning. Of special interest to teachers are general methods of cooperative learning, such as "student team-achievement division" (STAD) where the teacher presents a lesson, students work together in teams to help each other learn the material, individuals take quizzes, and team rewards are earned based on the individual scores on the quizzes; "teams-games-tournaments" (TGT) where tournaments (rather than quizzes) are held in which students compete against others of similar academic achievements and then winners contribute toward their team's score; and group investigations.[13] Yet the primary purpose of each is for the groups to learn—which means, of course, that individuals within a group must learn. Group achievement in learning, then, is dependent upon the learning of individuals within the group. Rather than competing for rewards for achievement, members of the group cooperate and help one another learn, so that the group reward will be a good one.

ROLES WITHIN THE COOPERATIVE LEARNING GROUP

It is advisable to assign roles (specific functions) to each member of the CLG. (The lesson plan shown in the unit plan of Figure 6.12, Chapter 6, shows the use of a CLG activity using assigned roles for a lesson in science.) These roles should be rotated, either during the activity or from one time to the next. Although titles may vary, five typical roles are

- *Group facilitator*—role is to keep the group on task.
- *Materials manager*—role is to obtain, maintain, and return materials needed for the group to function.
- *Recorder*—role is to record all group activities and processes, and perhaps to periodically assess how the group is doing.
- *Reporter*—role is to report group processes and accomplishments to the teacher and/or to the entire class. When using groups of four members, the roles of recorder and reporter can easily be combined.
- *Thinking monitor*—role is to identify and record the sequence and processes of the group's thinking. This role encourages metacognition and the development of thinking skills.

It is important that students understand their individual roles, and that each member of the CLG performs her or his tasks as expected. No student should be allowed to ride on the coattails of the group. To give significance to and to reinforce the importance of each role, and to be able to readily recognize the role any student is playing during a CLG activity, one teacher went to an office supplier and had permanent badges made for the various CLG roles. During CLGs, then, each student attaches the appropriate badge to her or his clothing.

WHAT STUDENTS AND THE TEACHER DO WHEN USING COOPERATIVE LEARNING GROUPS

Actually, for learning by CLGs to work, each member of the CLG must understand and assume two roles or responsibilities—the role he or she is assigned as a member of the group, and that of seeing that all others in the group are performing their roles. Sometimes this requires interpersonal skills that young adolescents have yet to learn or to learn well. This is where the teacher must assume some responsibility, too. Simply placing students into CLGs and expecting each member and each group to function and to learn the expected outcomes may not work. In other words, skills of cooperation must be taught, and if some of your students have not yet learned the skills of cooperation, then you will have to teach them. This does not mean that if a group is not functioning you immediately break up the group and reassign members to new groups. Part of group learning is learning how to work out conflict. For a group to work out a conflict may require your assistance. With your guidance, the group should be able to discover

---

[12]See, for example R. E. Slavin, "Cooperative Learning in Middle and Secondary Schools," *Clearing House* 69(4):200–204 (March/April 1996).

[13]For details about these CLG strategies and others, see R. E. Slavin, *Student Team Learning: A Practical Guide for Cooperative Learning,* 3rd ed. (Washington, DC: National Education Association, 1991); E. Coelho, *Learning Together in the Multicultural Classroom* (Portsmouth, NH: Heinemann, 1994); and Y. Sharan and S. Sharan, *Expanding Cooperative Learning through Group Investigation* (New York: Teachers College Press, 1992).

what is causing the conflict, then identify some options and mediate at least a temporary solution. If a particular skill is needed, then with your guidance, students identify and learn that skill.

WHEN TO USE COOPERATIVE LEARNING GROUPS

CLGs can be used for problem solving, investigations, opinion surveys, experiments, review, project work, test making, or almost any other instructional purpose. Just as for small group work in general, you can use CLGs for most any purpose at any time, but as with any other type of instructional strategy, it should not be overused.

OUTCOMES OF USING COOPERATIVE LEARNING GROUPS

When the process is well-planned and managed, the outcomes of cooperative learning include (a) improved communication and relationships of acceptance among students of differences, (b) quality learning with fewer off-task behaviors, and (c) increased academic achievement. For example, for the latter, students who practice in cooperative groups demonstrate greater long-term memory of problem-solving strategies in mathematics.[14] In the words of Good and Brophy,

> Cooperative learning arrangements promote friendships and prosocial interaction among students who differ in achievement, sex, race, or ethnicity, and they promote the acceptance of mainstreamed handicapped students by their nonhandicapped classmates. Cooperative methods also frequently have positive effects, and rarely have negative effects, on affective outcomes such as self-esteem, academic self-confidence, liking for the class, liking and feeling liked by classmates, and various measures of empathy and social cooperation.[15]

COOPERATIVE GROUP LEARNING, ASSESSMENT, AND GRADING

Normally, the CLG is rewarded on the basis of group achievement, though individual members within the group can later be rewarded for individual contributions (see Figure 8.1). Because of peer pressure, when using CLGs you must be cautious about using group grading.[16] Some teachers give bonus points to all members of a group to add to their individual scores when everyone in

the group has reached preset criteria. In establishing preset standards, the standards can be different for individuals within a group, depending on each member's ability and past performance. It is important that each member of a group feel rewarded and successful. For determination of students' report card grades, individual student achievement is measured later through individual results on tests and other sources of data.

WHY SOME TEACHERS HAVE DIFFICULTY USING CLGs

Sometimes, when they think they are using CLGs, teachers have difficulty and either give up trying to use the strategy or simply tell students to divide into groups for an activity and call it cooperative learning.[17] As emphasized earlier, for the strategy to work, each student must be given training in and have acquired basic skills in interaction and group processing and must realize that individual achievement rests with that of their group. And, as is true for any other strategy, CLGs must not be overused—teachers must vary their strategies.

For CLGs to work well, advance planning and effective management are a must. Students must be instructed in the necessary skills for group learning. Each student must be assigned a responsible role within the group and be held accountable for fulfilling that responsibility. And, when a CLG activity is in process, groups must be continually monitored by the teacher for a possible breakdown of the process within a group. In other words, while students are working in groups the teacher must exercise skills of withitness. When a potential breakdown is noticed, the teacher quickly intervenes to help the group get back on track.

LEARNING IN LARGE GROUPS

Large groups are those that involve more than five students, usually the entire class. Most often, they are teacher-directed. Student presentations and whole-class discussions are two techniques that involve large groups.

Student Presentations

Students should be encouraged to be presenters for discussion of the ideas, opinions, and knowledge obtained from their own independent and small-group study. Several techniques encourage the development of certain skills, such as studying and organizing material, discovery, discussion, rebuttal, listening, analysis, suspending judgment, and critical thinking. Possible

[14]See, for example, P. E. Duren and A. Cherrington, "The Effects of Cooperative Group Work versus Independent Practice on the Learning of Some Problem-Solving Strategies," *School Science and Mathematics* 92(2):80–83 (February 1992).

[15]T. L. Good and J. E. Brophy, *Looking in Classrooms*, 8th ed. (New York: Addison Wesley Longman, 2000), p. 291.

[16]See S. Kagan, "Group Grades Miss the Mark," *Educational Leadership* 52(8):68–71 (May 1995), and D. W. Johnson and R. T. Johnson, "The Role of Cooperative Learning in Assessing and Communicating Student Learning," Chapter 4 in T. R. Guskey (Ed.), *Communicating Student Learning*, ASCD Yearbook (Alexandria, VA: Association for Supervision and Curriculum Development, 1996).

[17]See, for example, C. A. Tomlinson, et al., "Use of Cooperative Learning at the Middle Level: Insights from a National Survey," *Research in Middle Level Education Quarterly* 20(4):37–55 (Summer 1997).

Figure 8.1 Sample scoring rubric for assessing individual students in a cooperative learning group project. (Source: Courtesy of Susan Abbott, Pam Benedetti, and Carleen Smith, Elk Grove School District, Elk Grove, California.) Explanation for use: Possible score = 50. Scorer marks a relevant square in each of the five categories (horizontal rows), and student's score for that category is the small number in the top right corner within that square.

	9–10	8	7	1–6
Goals	Consistently and actively helps identify group goals; works effectively to meet goals.	Consistently communicates commitment to group goals; carries out assigned roles.	Sporadically communicates commitment to group goals; carries out assigned role.	Rarely, if ever, works toward group goals or may work against them.
Interpersonal Skills	Cooperates with group members by encouraging, compromising, and/or taking a leadership role without dominating; shows sensitivity to feelings and knowledge of others.	Cooperates with group members by encouraging, compromising, and/or taking a leadership role.	Participates with group but has own agenda; may not be willing to compromise or to make significant contributions.	May discourage others, harass group members, or encourage off-task behavior. Makes significant changes to others' work without their knowledge or permission.
Quality Producer	Contributes significant information, ideas, time, and/or talent to produce a quality product.	Contributes information, ideas, time, and/or talent to produce a quality product.	Contributes some ideas, though not significant; may be more supportive than contributive; shows willingness to complete assignment but has no desire to go beyond average expectations.	Does little or no work toward the completion of group product; shows little or no interest in contributing to the task; produces work that fails to meet minimum standards for quality.
Participation	Attends daily; consistently and actively utilizes class time by working on the task.	Attends consistently; sends in work to group if absent; utilizes class time by working on the task.	Attends sporadically; absences or tardies may hinder group involvement; may send in work when absent; utilizes some time; may be off task by talking to others, interrupting other groups, or watching others do the majority of the work.	Frequent absences or tardies hinder group involvement; fails to send in work when absent; wastes class time by talking, doing other work, or avoiding tasks; group has asked that member be reproved by teacher or removed from the group.
Commitment	Consistently contributes time out of class to produce a quality product; attends all group meetings as evidenced by the group meeting log.	Contributes time out of class to produce a quality product; attends a majority of group meetings as evidenced by the group meeting log.	Willing to work toward completion of task during class time; attends some of the group meetings; may arrive late or leave early; may keep inconsistent meeting log.	Rarely, if ever, attends group meetings outside of class or may attend and hinder progress of the group; fails to keep meeting log.

forms of discussions involving student presentations are described in the following paragraphs.

- *Debate.* The debate is an arrangement in which oral presentations are made by members of two opposing teams, on topics preassigned and researched. The speeches are followed by rebuttals from each team.[18]
- *Jury Trial.* The jury trial is a discussion approach in which the class simulates a courtroom, with class members playing various roles of judge, attorneys, jury members, bailiff, and court recorder.
- *Panel.* The panel is a setting in which four to six students, with one designated as the chairperson or moderator, discuss a topic about which they have studied, followed by a question-and-answer period involving the entire class. The panel usually begins with each panel member giving a brief opening statement.
- *Research Report.* One or two students or a small group of students gives a report on a topic that they have investigated, followed by questions and discussions by the entire class.
- *Roundtable.* The roundtable is a small group of three to five students, who sit around a table and discuss among themselves (perhaps with the rest of the class listening and later asking questions) a problem or issue that they have studied. One member of the panel may serve as moderator.
- *Symposium.* Similar to a roundtable discussion but more formal, the symposium is an arrangement in which each student participant presents an explanation of his or her position on a preassigned topic researched by the student. Again, one student should serve as moderator. After the presentations, questions are accepted from the rest of the class.

To use these techniques effectively, students may need to be coached by you—individually, in small groups, or in whole class sessions—on how and where to gather information; how to listen, take notes,[19] select major points, and organize material; how to present a position succinctly and convincingly (see Figure 8.2); how to play roles; and, how to engage in dialogue and debate with one another.

Whole Class Discussion

Direct whole-class discussion is a teaching technique used frequently by most or all teachers. On this topic, you should consider yourself an expert. Having been a student in formal learning for at least fifteen years, you are undoubtedly knowledgeable about the advantages and disadvantages of whole-class discussions, as least from your personal vantage point. Explore your knowledge and share your experiences by responding to Exercise 8.2.

---

[18]See, for example, M. Koenig, "Debating Real-World Issues," *Science Scope* 24(5):19–23 (February 2001).

[19]For the importance of and information about helping students develop the study of skill of notetaking, see pp. 43–48 of R. J. Marzano, D. J. Pickering, and J. E. Pollock, *Classroom Instruction That Works: Research-Based Strategies for Increasing Student Achievement* (Alexandria, VA: Association for Supervision and Curriculum Development, 2001).

Figure 8.2   Sample scoring rubric for small group or individual presentation.

PRESENTATION SCORING RUBRIC

5. Presentation was excellent. Project clearly understood and delivery organized.
   - Made eye contact throughout presentation.
   - Spoke loud enough for all to hear.
   - Spoke clearly.
   - Spoke for time allotted.
   - Stood straight and confidently.
   - Covered at least five pieces of important information.
   - Introduced project.
   - All members spoke.

4. Presentation was well thought out and planned.
   - Made eye contact throughout most of presentation.
   - Spoke loud enough and clearly most of the time.
   - Spoke nearly for time allotted.
   - Covered at least four pieces of important information.
   - Introduced project.
   - All members spoke.

3. Adequate presentation. Mostly organized.
   - Made eye contact at times.
   - Some of audience could hear the presentation.
   - Audience could understand most of what was said.
   - Spoke for about half of time allotted.
   - At least half of team spoke.
   - Covered at least three pieces of important information.
   - Project was vaguely introduced.

2–1. Underprepared presentation. Disorganized and incomplete information.
   - No eye contact during presentation.
   - Most of audience were unable to hear presentation.
   - Information presented was unclear.
   - Spoke for only brief time.
   - Covered less than three pieces of information.
   - Project was not introduced or only vaguely introduced.

EXERCISE 8.2A: WHOLE-CLASS DISCUSSION AS A TEACHING STRATEGY: WHAT DO I ALREADY KNOW?

INSTRUCTIONS: It is the purpose of this exercise to build your knowledge about using whole-class discussions by sharing experiences and knowledge with your classmates. Answer the following questions, and then share your responses with classmates, perhaps first in small discussion groups and then in the large group.

1. Your subject field: _____

2. For what reasons would you hold a whole-class discussion? _____

_____

_____

_____

_____

3. Assuming that your classroom has movable seats, how would you arrange them? _____

_____

_____

_____

4. What would you do if the seats were not movable? _____

_____

_____

_____

5. What rules would you establish before starting the discussion? _____

_____

_____

_____

6. Should student participation be forced? Why or why not? If so, how? _____

_____

_____

_____

7. How would you discourage a few students from dominating the discussion? _____

_____

_____

_____

_____

☞

EXERCISE 8.2A (*continued*)

8. What preparation should the students and the teacher be expected to make before beginning the discussion?

_____

_____

_____

9. How would you handle digression from the topic? _____

_____

_____

_____

10. Should students be discussion leaders? Why or why not? If so, what training, if any, should they receive, and how? _____

_____

_____

_____

_____

11. What teacher roles are options during a class discussion? _____

_____

_____

_____

_____

12. When is each of these roles most appropriate? _____

_____

_____

_____

13. When, if ever, is it appropriate to hold a class meeting for discussing class procedures, not subject matter?

_____

_____

_____

14. Can brainstorming be a form of whole-class discussion? Why or why not? _____

_____

_____

_____

_____

EXERCISE 8.2A (*continued*)

15. What follow-up activities would be appropriate after a whole-class discussion? On what basis would you decide to use each? _____

_____

_____

_____

_____

16. What sorts of activities should precede a class discussion? _____

_____

_____

_____

_____

17. Should a discussion be given a set length? Why or why not? If so, how long? How is the length to be decided?

_____

_____

_____

_____

18. Should students be graded for their participation in class discussion? Why or why not? If so, how? On what basis? By whom? _____

_____

_____

_____

_____

19. For effective discussions, 10 to 12 feet is the maximum recommended distance between participants. During
a teacher-led discussion, what can a teacher do to keep within this limit? _____

_____

_____

_____

_____

20. Are there any pitfalls or other points of importance that a teacher should be aware of when planning and implementing a whole-class discussion? If so, explain them and how to guard against them. _____

_____

_____

_____

FOR YOUR NOTES

EXERCISE 8.2B: WHOLE-CLASS DISCUSSION AS A TEACHING STRATEGY: BUILDING ON WHAT I ALREADY KNOW

INSTRUCTIONS: Having shared your responses to Exercise 8.2A with your classmates, now individually answer the first two questions below. Then, as a group, use all three questions to help you generate a list of five general guidelines for the use of whole-class discussion as a strategy for teaching young adolescent students in the classroom. Share your group's guidelines with the whole class. Then, finally, as a class, derive a final list of general guidelines.

1. How effective was your small-group discussion in sharing Exercise 8.2A? _____

_____

_____

_____

_____

_____

_____

_____

_____

_____

2. What allowed for or inhibited the effectiveness of that small-group discussion? _____

_____

_____

_____

_____

_____

_____

_____

_____

_____

3. How effective is this small-group discussion? Why? _____

_____

_____

_____

_____

_____

_____

_____

EXERCISE 8.2B (*continued*)

GENERAL GUIDELINES GENERATED FROM SMALL-GROUP DISCUSSION

1. _____

   _____

2. _____

   _____

3. _____

   _____

4. _____

   _____

5. _____

   _____

GENERAL GUIDELINES: FINAL LIST DERIVED FROM WHOLE CLASS

_____

_____

_____

_____

_____

_____

_____

_____

_____

_____

_____

_____

_____

_____

_____

_____

_____

_____

_____

_____

_____

_____

EQUALITY IN THE CLASSROOM

Especially when conducting direct whole-group discussions, it is easy for a teacher to fall into the trap of interacting with only "the stars," or only those in the front of the room or on one side, or only the most vocal and assertive. You must exercise caution and avoid falling into that trap. To ensure a psychologically safe and effective learning environment for every person in your classroom, you must attend to all students and try to involve all students equally in all class activities. You must avoid any biased expectations about certain students, and you must avoid discriminating against students according to their gender or some other personal characteristic.

You must avoid the unintentional tendency of teachers of *both* sexes to discriminate on the basis of gender. For example, teachers, along with the rest of society, tend to have lower expectations for girls than for boys in mathematics and science. They tend to call on and encourage boys more than girls. They often let boys interrupt girls but praise girls for being polite and waiting their turn. To avoid such discrimination may take special effort on your part, no matter how aware of the problem you may be. Some researchers believe the problem is so insidious that separate courses about it are needed in teacher training.[20]

To guarantee equity in interaction with students, many teachers have found it helpful to ask someone to secretly tally classroom interactions between the teacher and students during a class discussion. After an analysis of the results, the teacher arrives at decisions about his or her own attending and facilitating behaviors. Such an analysis is the purpose of Exercise 8.3. You are welcome to make blank copies and share them with your teaching colleagues.

In addition to the variables mentioned at the beginning of Exercise 8.3, the exercise can be modified to include responses and their frequencies according to

other teacher-student interactions. These might include calling on all students equally for responses to your questions, calling on students equally to assist you with classroom helping jobs, chastising students for their inappropriate behavior, or asking questions to assume classroom leadership roles.

Ensuring Equity

In addition to the advice given in Chapter 7 about using questioning, there are many other ways of assuring that students are treated fairly in the classroom, including the following:

- Encourage students to demonstrate an appreciation for one another by applauding all individual and group presentations.
- Have and maintain high expectations, although not necessarily identical expectations, for all students.
- Insist on politeness in the classroom. For example, a student can be shown appreciation—such as with a sincere "thank you" or "I appreciate your contribution," or with a whole-class applause, or with a genuine smile—for her or his contribution to the learning process.
- Insist students be allowed to finish what they are saying, without being interrupted by others. Be certain that you model this behavior yourself.
- During whole-class instruction, insist that students raise their hands and be called on by you before they are allowed to speak.
- Keep a stopwatch handy to unobtrusively control the wait time given for each student. Although at first this idea may sound impractical, it works.
- Use a seating chart attached to a clipboard; next to each student's name, make a tally for each interaction you have with a student. This also is a good way to maintain records about which students to reward for their contributions to class discussion. Again, it is workable at any grade level. The seating chart can be laminated so it can be used day after day simply by erasing the marks of the previous day.

Now, do Exercise 8.3, through which you will examine a teacher's behavior with students according to gender.

---

[20]See, for example, S. Zaher, "Gender and Curriculum in the School Room," *Education Canada* 36(1):26–29 (Spring 1996), and S. M. Bailey, "Shortchanging Girls and Boys," *Educational Leadership* 53(8):75–79 (May 1996). For information on how to identify equity problems and develop programs to help schools achieve academic excellence for all students, contact EQUITY 2000, 1233 20th St. NW, Washington, DC 20056-2304; Phone 202-822-5930.

FOR YOUR NOTES

EXERCISE 8.3: TEACHER INTERACTION WITH STUDENTS ACCORDING TO STUDENT GENDER

INSTRUCTIONS: The purpose of this exercise is to provide a tool for analysis of your own interactions with students according to gender. To become accustomed to the exercise, you should do a trial run in one of your university classes, then use it during your student teaching and again during your first years of teaching. The exercise can be modified to include (1) the amount of time given for each interaction, (2) the response time given by teacher according to student gender, and (3) other student characteristics, such as ethnicity.

Prior to class, select a student (this will be you during the trial run recommended above) or an outside observer, such as a colleague, to do the tallying and calculations, as follows. Ask the person to tally secretly the interactions between you and the students by placing a mark after the name of each student (or on the student's position on a seating chart) with whom you have verbal interaction. If a student does the tallying, he or she should not be counted in any of the calculations.

Exact time at start _____

Exact time at end _____

Total time in minutes _____

CALCULATIONS BEFORE TALLYING

a. Total number of students _____

b. Number of female students _____

c. Number of male students _____

d. Percentage of students who are female _____ (= b divided by a)

e. Percentage of students who are male _____ (= c divided by a)

(Check: d + e should = 100%)

CALCULATIONS AFTER TALLYING

f. Total females interacting _____

g. Total males interacting _____

h. Percentage of students interacting _____ (f + g divided by a)

i. Total female tallies _____

j. Total male tallies _____

k. Total of all tallies (i + j) _____

l. Percentage of interacting students who are female _____ (i divided by k)

m. Percentage of interacting students who are male _____ (j divided by k)

n. Most tallies for any one male _____

o. Percentage of class interactions directed to most frequently addressed male _____ (n divided by k)

p. Most tallies for any one female _____

q. Percentage of class interactions directed to most frequently addressed female _____ (p divided by k)

☞

EXERCISE 8.3 (*continued*)

TEACHER CONCLUSIONS

LEARNING FROM ASSIGNMENTS AND HOMEWORK

An assignment is a statement of *what* the student is to accomplish and is tied to a specific instructional objective. Assignments, whether completed at home or at school, can ease student learning in many ways, but when poorly planned, they can discourage the student and upset an entire family. *Homework* can be defined as any out-of-class task that a student is assigned as an extension of classroom learning. Like everything else you do as a teacher, it is your professional responsibility to think about and plan carefully any and all homework assignments you give to students. Consider how you would feel if you were given the assignment and about how much out-of-class time you expect the assignment to take. The time a student needs to complete assignments beyond school time will vary. Very generally, students of middle grades may spend a total of anywhere from 45 minutes to an hour or two on homework each school night.[21]

Purposes for Assignments

Purposes for giving homework assignments can be any of the following: to constructively extend the time that students are engaged in learning, to help students to develop personal learning, to help students develop their research skills, to help students develop their study skills, to help students organize their learning, to individualize the learning, to involve parents and guardians in their children's learning, to provide a mechanism by which students receive constructive feedback, to provide students with opportunity to review and practice what has been learned, to reinforce classroom experiences, and to teach new content.

Guidelines for Using Assignments

Consider the guidelines in the following paragraphs. While an assignment is a statement of *what* the student is to accomplish, procedures are statements of *how* to do something. Although students may need some procedural guidelines, especially regarding your expectations on an assignment, generally, you will want to avoid supplying too much detail on how to accomplish an assignment.

Plan early and thoughtfully the types of assignments you will give (e.g., daily and long-range; minor and major; in class, at home, or both; individual, paired, or group),[22] and prepare assignment specifications. Assignments must correlate with specific instructional objectives and should *never* be given as busy work or as punishment. For each assignment, let students know what the objectives are; for example, whether the assignment is to prepare the student for what is to come in class, to practice what has been learned in class, to extend the learning of class activities.

Use caution in giving assignments that could be controversial or that could pose a hazard to the safety of students. In such cases (especially if you are new to the community), before giving the assignment it is probably a good idea to talk it over with members of your teaching team, the departmental chair, or an administrator. Also, for a particular assignment, you may need to have parental or guardian permission and even support for students to do it. You may also need to be prepared to give an alternate assignment for some students.

Provide differentiated, tiered, or optional assignments—assignment variations given to students or selected by them on the basis of their interests and learning capacities.[23] Students can select or be assigned different activities to accomplish the same objective, such as read and discuss, or they can participate with others in a more direct learning experience. After their study, as a portion of the assignment, students share what they have learned. This is an example of using multilevel teaching.

Teachers have found it beneficial to prepare individualized study guides with questions to be answered and activities to be done by the student while reading textbook chapters as homework. One advantage of a study guide is that it can make the reading more than a visual experience. A study guide can help organize student learning by accenting instructional objectives, emphasizing important points to be learned, providing a guide for studying for tests, and encouraging the student to read the homework assignment.

Beginning teachers need to understand that not only can homework help students learn factual information, develop study skills, and involve parents as facilitators in their child's education, it can also overwhelm students and cause them to dislike learning, encourage them to take shortcuts such as copying others' work, and prevent them from participating in extracurricular activities. Teachers sometimes underestimate just how long it

---

[21]See Figure 5.2, "Recommended Total Minutes Per Day for Homework," page 62 of R. J. Marzano; D. J. Pickering; and J. E. Pollock, *Classroom Instruction that Works* (Alexandria, VA: Association for Supervision and Curriculum Development, 2001). See also several articles about using homework, H. Cooper, "Homework for All-in Moderation," N. T. Glazer and S. Williams, "Averting the Homework Crisis," and E. Kralovec and J. Buell, "End Homework Now," all in *Educational Leadership* 58(7):34–38, 43–45, and 39–42 respectively (April 2001).

[22]See, for example, C. Kaplan, "Homework Partners," *Mathematics Teaching in the Middle School* 2(3):168–169 (January 1997).

[23]See, for example, M. H. Sullivan and P. V. Sequeira, "The Impact of Purposeful Homework on Learning," *Clearing House* 69(6):346–348 (July/August 1996).

will take a student to complete a homework assignment. With these facts in mind, think carefully about all homework assignments before you make them.

Some students find homework and assignments very difficult, especially those who have limited English proficiency, special needs, and little to no support from home. As an aide to these students in particular and to any student in general, many teachers use student volunteers to serve as homework helpers who assist other students both during class and after school by exchanging telephone numbers. In some middle level schools, teachers also use high school students and even paid college students and adults as mentors.

As a general rule, homework assignments should stimulate thinking by arousing a student's curiosity, raising questions for further study, and encouraging and supporting the self-discipline required for independent study.

Determine the resources that students will need to complete assignments and check the availability of these resources. This is important; students cannot be expected to use what is unavailable to them, and many will not use what is not readily available.

Avoid yelling out assignments as students are leaving your classroom. Write assignments on a special place on the writing board, require that each student write the assignment into his or her assignment folder, or include them in the course syllabus, taking extra care to be sure that assignment specifications are clear to students. Allow time for students to ask questions about an assignment. It is important that your procedure for giving and collecting assignments be consistent throughout the school year.

Students should be given sufficient time to complete their assignments. In other words, avoid announcing an assignment that is due the very next day. Try to avoid changing assignment specifications after they are given. Especially avoid changing them at the last minute, since this can be very frustrating to students who have already completed the assignment and shows little respect for them.

Allow time in class for students to begin work on homework assignments, so you can give them individual attention (guided or coached practice). Your ability to coach students is *the reason* for in-class time to begin work on assignments. As said in earlier chapters, the benefits of this coached practice include being able to (a) monitor student work so that a student does not go too far in a wrong direction, (b) help students reflect on their thinking, (c) assess the progress of individual students, and (d) discover or create a teachable moment. For example, while monitoring students doing their work, you might discover a commonly shared student misconception. Then, taking advantage of this teachable moment, you could stop and talk about it and attempt to clarify the misconception.

Timely, constructive, and corrective feedback from the teacher on the homework—and the grading of homework—increases the positive contributions of

homework.[24] If the assignment is important for students to do, then you must give your full and immediate attention to the product of their efforts. Read almost everything that students write. Students are much more willing to do homework when they believe it is useful, when it is treated as an integral part of instruction, when it is read and evaluated by the teacher, and when it counts as part of the grade.

Provide feedback about each student's work, and be positive and constructive in your comments. Always think about the written comments that you make to be relatively certain they will convey your intended message to the student. When writing comments on student papers, consider using a color other than red, such as green or blue. Although this may sound trite, red brings a host of negative connotations to many people (e.g., blood, hurt, danger, stop), and children often perceive it as punitive.

Most routine homework assignments should not be graded for accuracy, only for completion. Rather than give a percentage or numerical grade, with its negative connotations, teachers often prefer to mark assignment papers with constructive and reinforcing comments and symbols they have created for this purpose.

Regardless of the subject taught, you must give attention to the development of students' reading, listening, speaking, and writing skills. Attention to these skills must also be obvious in your assignment specifications and your assignment grading policy. Reading is crucial to the development of a person's ability to write. For example, to foster high-order thinking, students in any subject can and should be encouraged to write in their journals (as discussed in Chapter 5 and later in this chapter) or draw representations of their thoughts and feelings about the material they have read.

Opportunities for Recovery

The concept of mastery (quality) learning would seem to us to necessitate a policy whereby students are able to revise and resubmit assignments for reassessment and grading. Although it is important to encourage good initial efforts by students, sometimes, for a multitude of reasons, a student's first effort is inadequate or is lacking entirely. Perhaps the student is absent from school without legitimate excuse, or the student does poorly on an assignment or fails to turn in an assignment on time, or at all. Accepting late work from students is extra work for the teacher, and allowing the resubmission of a marked or tentatively graded paper increases the amount of paperwork. However, many teachers report that it is worthwhile to give students the opportunity for recovery and a day or so to make corrections and resubmit an assign-

---

[24]H. J. Walberg, "Productive Teaching and Instruction: Assessing the Knowledge Base," *Phi Delta Kappan* 71(6):472 (February 1990).

CLASSROOM VIGNETTE

Late Homework Paper from an At-Risk Student

A student turned in a class assignment several days late, and the paper was accepted by the teacher without penalty, although the teacher's policy was that late papers would be severely penalized. During the week that the assignment was due, the student had suffered a miscarriage. In this instance, her teacher accepted the paper late sans penalty because the student carried a great deal of psychological baggage and the teacher felt that turning in the paper at all was a positive act. If the paper had not been accepted, or had been accepted only with severe penalty to her grade, then, in the teacher's opinion, the student would have simply quit trying and probably dropped out of school altogether.

ment for an improved score. Out of regard for students who do well from the start, though, you are advised against allowing a resubmitted paper to receive an *A* grade (unless, of course, it was an *A* paper originally).

Some teachers and schools provide recovery methods that encourage students by recognizing both achievement and improvement on report cards and by providing students with second opportunities for success on assignments, although at some cost to encourage a good first effort.

Students sometimes have legitimate reasons for not completing an assignment by the due date. (Consider the classroom vignette "Late Homework Paper from an At-Risk Student.") The teacher should listen and exercise professional judgment in each instance. As someone once said, there is nothing democratic about treating unequals as equals. The provision of recovery options seems a sensible and scholastic tactic.

How to Avoid Having So Many Papers to Grade That Time for Effective Planning Is Restricted

A waterloo for some beginning teachers is that of being buried beneath mounds of homework to be read and marked, leaving less and less time for effective planning. To keep this from happening to you, consider the following suggestions. Although, in our opinion, the teacher should read almost everything that students write—papers can be read with varying degrees of intensity and scrutiny, depending on the purpose of the assignment. For assignments that are designed for learning, understanding, and practice, students can check them themselves using either self-checking or peer checking. During the checking, you can walk around the room, monitoring the activity, and recording whether a student did the assignment or not, or, when the checking is finished, you can collect the papers and do your recording. Besides reducing the amount of paperwork for you, student self- or peer-checking provides other advantages: (a) it allows students to see and understand their errors, (b) it encourages productive peer dialogue, and (c) it helps them develop self-assessment

techniques and standards. If the purpose of the assignment is to assess mastery competence, then the papers should be read, marked, and graded only by you.

CAUTION ABOUT USING PEER CHECKING*

Peer-checking can, however, be a problem. During peer-checking of student work, students may spend more time watching the person checking their paper than accurately checking the one given to them. And this strategy does not necessarily allow the student to see or understand his or her mistakes.

Of even greater concern is the matter of privacy. When Student A (the checker) has knowledge about the academic success or failure of Student B, Student A could cause emotional or social embarrassment to Student B. Peer checking of papers should perhaps be done only for the editing of classmates' drafts of stories or research projects; making suggestions about content and grammar, but not assigning a grade or marking answers right or wrong. To protect students' privacy rights, using peers to grade each other's papers also should be avoided. Harassment and embarrassment have no place in a classroom; they do not provide a safe learning environment.

PROJECT-CENTERED LEARNING: GUIDING LEARNING FROM INDEPENDENT AND GROUP INVESTIGATIONS, PAPERS, AND ORAL REPORTS

For the most meaningful student learning to occur, independent study, individual writing, student-centered projects, and oral reports should be major features of your instruction. There will be times when the students are interested in an in-depth inquiry of a topic and will want to pursue a particular topic for study. This undertaking of a learning project can be flexible—an individual student, a

---

*Regarding this caution, you and your students should know that on February 19, 2002, the U.S. Supreme Court ruled unanimously that students may grade each other's work in class without violating federal privacy law.

Figure 8.3   Sample choices for culminating presentation.

After reading *(name of novel)*, students make a culminating presentation that is focused on representing various themes and events as depicted in the novel. Students may choose from the following:

1. Story in a shoebox	A representation of major events in the novel through the presentation of various symbolic objects.
2. Poster board presentation	A poster board designed with at least five different events depicted and titled appropriately. May use miniature drawings or graphics.
3. Sketching/drawing	A collection of detailed drawings depicting at least five major events in the novel.
4. Model	A model depicting the geography that serves as the setting of the novel.
5. Play or skit	A 5 to 8 minute play or skit performed by the student(s) in class with a script for the teacher to follow. Must involve at least one major event from the novel.

team of two, a small group, or the entire class can do the investigation. The *project* is a relatively long-term investigative study from which students produce something called the culminating presentation, which usually includes an oral and written report accompanied by a hands-on item of some kind (e.g., a display, play or skit, book, song or poem, multimedia presentation, diorama, poster, maps, charts, and so on). It is a way for students to apply what they are learning. See the sample in Figure 8.3.

Values and Purposes of Project-Centered Learning

The values and purposes of encouraging project-centered learning are to develop individual skills in cooperation and social interaction; develop student skills in writing, communication, and higher-level thinking and doing; foster student engagement, and independent learning and thinking skills; optimize each student's personal meaning of the learning by considering, valuing, and accommodating individual interests, learning styles, learning capacities, and life experiences; provide opportunity for each student to become especially knowledgeable and experienced in one area of subject content or in one process skill, thus adding to the student's knowledge and experience base and sense of importance and self-worth; provide opportunity for students to become intrinsically motivated to learn because they are working on topics of personal meaning, with outcomes and even time-lines that are relatively open ended; provide opportunity for students to make decisions about their own learning and develop their skills in managing time and materials; and provide opportunity for students to make some sort of real contribution. As has been demonstrated time and again in working with young adolescents, when students choose their own projects, integrating knowledge as the need arises, motivation and learning follow naturally.[25]

GUIDELINES FOR GUIDING STUDENTS IN PROJECT-CENTERED LEARNING

In collaboration with the teacher, students select a topic for the project. You can stimulate ideas and provide anchor studies (also called model or benchmark examples) by providing lists of things students might do; by mentioning each time an idea comes up in class that this would be a good idea for an independent, small group, or class project; by having former students tell about their projects; by showing the results of other students' projects; by suggesting Internet resources and readings that are likely to give students ideas; and by using class discussions to brainstorm ideas.

Sometimes a teacher will write the general problem or topic in the center of a graphic web and ask the students to brainstorm some questions. The questions will lead to ways for students to investigate, draw sketches, construct models, record findings, predict items, compare and contrast, and discuss understandings. In essence, brainstorming such as this is the technique often used by teachers in collaboration with students for the selection of an interdisciplinary thematic unit of study.

Allow students to individually choose whether they will work alone, in pairs, or in small groups. If they choose to work in groups, then help them delineate job descriptions for each member of the group. For project work, groups of four or fewer students usually work better than groups of more than four. Even if the project is one the whole class is pursuing, the project should be broken down into parts with individuals or small groups of students undertaking independent study of these parts.

You can keep track of the students' progress by reviewing weekly updates of their work. Set deadlines with the groups and meet with them daily to discuss any questions or problems they have. Based on their investigations, the students will prepare and present their findings in culminating presentations.

Provide coaching and guidance. Work with each student or student team in topic selection, as well as in the processes of written and oral reporting. Allow students to develop their own procedures, but guide their

---

[25]See, for example, C. McCullen, "In Project-Based Learning, Technology Adds a New Twist to an Old Idea," *Middle Ground* 3(5):7–9 (April 2000).

preparation of work outlines and preliminary drafts, giving them constructive feedback and encouragement along the way. Aid students in identifying potential resources and research techniques. Your coordination with the library and other resource centers is central to the success of project-centered teaching. Frequent drafts and progress reports from the students are a must. During each of these stages, provide students with constructive feedback and encouragement. Provide written guidelines and negotiate time lines for outlines, drafts, and the completed project.

Promote sharing. Insist that students share both the progress and the results of their study with the rest of the class. The amount of time allowed for this sharing will, of course, depend upon many variables. The value of this type of instructional strategy comes not only from individual contributions but also from the learning that results from the experience and the communication of that experience with others. For project work and sharing of the outcomes, some teachers have their students use the KWHLS strategy, which is a modified version of the KWL strategy (see Chapter 5). Using the KWHLS strategy, the student identifies what he/she already *K*nows about the topic of study, *W*hat he/she wants to learn, *H*ow the student plans to learn it, what he/she *L*earned from the study, and how the student will *S*hare with others what he/she has learned from the study.

Without careful planning, and unless students are given steady guidance, project-based teaching can be a frustrating experience for both the teacher and the students—especially for a beginning teacher who is inexperienced in such an undertaking. Students should do projects because they want to and because the project seems meaningful. Therefore, students should, with guidance from you, decide *what* project to do and *how* to do it. Your role is to advise and guide students so they experience success. If the teacher lays out a project in too much detail, that project is a procedure rather than a student-centered project. There must be a balance between structure and opportunities for student choices and decision making. Without frequent progress reporting by the student and guidance and reinforcement from the teacher, a student can get frustrated and quickly lose interest in the project.

WRITING SHOULD BE A REQUIRED COMPONENT OF PROJECT-CENTERED LEARNING

Provide options but insist that writing be a part of each student's work. Research examining the links among writing, thinking, and learning has helped emphasize the importance of writing. Writing is a complex intellectual behavior and process that helps the learner create and record his or her understanding—that is, to construct meaning.

When teachers use project-centered teaching, a paper and an oral presentation are usually automatically required of all students. It is recommended that you use the *I-Search paper* instead of the traditional research paper. Under your careful guidance, the student (a) lists things that she would like to know and then selects one, which becomes her research topic; (b) conducts the study while maintaining a log of activities and findings, which, in fact, becomes a process journal; (c) prepares a booklet that presents the student's findings, which consists of paragraphs and visual representations, (d) prepares a summary of the findings including the significance of the study and the student's personal feelings; and (e) shares the project as a final oral report with the teacher and classmates.

ASSESS THE FINAL PRODUCT

The final product of the project, including papers, oral reports, and presentations should be graded. The method of determining the grade should be clear to students from the beginning, as should the weight of the project grade toward each student's term grade. Provide students with clear descriptions (rubrics) of how evaluation and grading will be done. Evaluation should include meeting deadlines for drafts and progress reports. The final grade for the study should be based on four criteria: (a) how well it was organized, including meeting draft deadlines; (b) the quality and quantity of both content and procedural knowledge gained from the experience; (c) the quality of the student's sharing of that learning experience with the rest of the class; and (d) the quality of the student's final written or oral report. For oral presentations, a sample scoring rubric and a checklist are shown in Figures 8.1 and 11.4, respectively. For scoring rubrics for research papers and other aspects of project study see Figures 11.10 and 11.11.

WRITING ACROSS THE CURRICULUM

Because writing is a discrete representation of thinking, every middle grades teacher should consider himself or herself to be a teacher of writing. In exemplary schools, student writing is encouraged in all subjects, across the curriculum. In many schools, all teachers are expected to assess students' papers using the same scoring rubric.[26]

Kinds of Writing

A student should experience a variety of kinds of writing rather than the same form, class after class, year after year. Perhaps most important is that writing should be emphasized as a process that illustrates one's thinking, rather than solely as a product completed as an

---

[26]See, for example, C. McCullen, "Using Data to Change Instruction," *Middle Ground* 4(3):7–9 (February 2001).

assignment. Writing and thinking develop best when, during any school day, a student experiences various forms of writing to express their ideas, such as the following:

Autobiographical incident. The writer narrates a specific event in his or her life and states or implies the significance of the event.

Evaluation. The writer presents a judgment on the worth of an item—book, movie, artwork, consumer product—and supports this with reasons and evidence.

Eyewitness account. The writer tells about a person, group, or event that was objectively observed from the outside.

Firsthand biographical sketch. Through incident and description, the writer characterizes a person he or she knows well.

Interpretation. The writer conjectures about the causes and effects of a specific event.

Problem solving. The writer describes and analyzes a specific problem and then proposes and argues for a solution.

Report of information. The writer collects data from observation and research and chooses material that best represents a phenomenon or concept.

Story. Using dialogue and description, the writer shows conflict between characters or between a character and the environment.

Student Journal

Many teachers across the curriculum have their students maintain journals in which the students keep a log of their activities, findings, and thoughts (i.e., a *process journal,* as discussed above) and write their thoughts about what they are studying (*response journal*). Actually, two types of response journals are commonly used: dialogue journals and reading-response journals. In *dialogue journals,* students write anything that is on their minds, usually on the right side of a page, while peers, teachers, and parents or guardians respond on the left side, thereby "talking with" the journal writer. In *response journals,* students write—and perhaps draw a "visual learning log,"—their reactions to whatever is being studied.

Purpose and Assessment of Student Journal Writing

Normally, academic journals are *not* the personal diaries of the writer's recollection of daily events and the writer's thoughts about the events. Rather, the purpose of journal writing is to encourage students to write, to think about their writing, to record their creative thoughts about *what they are learning,* and to share their written thoughts with an audience—all of which help in the development of their thinking skills, in their learning, and in their development as writers. Students are

encouraged to write about experiences, both in school and out, that are related to the topics being studied. They should be encouraged to record their feelings about what and how they are learning.

Journal writing provides practice in expression and should *not* be graded by the teacher. Negative comments and evaluations from the teacher will discourage creative and spontaneous expression by students. Teachers should read the journal and then offer constructive and positive feedback. For grading purposes, most teachers simply record whether or not a student does, in fact, maintain the required journal.

The National Council of Teachers of English (NCTE) has developed guidelines for journal writing. You can contact NCTE directly via http://www.ncte.org.

A COLLECTION OF 100 ANNOTATED MOTIVATIONAL TEACHING STRATEGIES WITH IDEAS FOR LESSONS, INTERDISCIPLINARY TEACHING, TRANSCULTURAL STUDIES, AND STUDENT PROJECTS

Today's young adolescents are used to multimillion-dollar productions on television, stage, CDs, DVDs, arcade games, and the movie screen. When they come into a classroom and are subjected each day to something short of a high-budget production, it is little wonder that they sometimes react in a less than highly motivated fashion. No doubt, today's youth are growing up in a highly stimulating instant-action society, a society that has learned to expect instant electronic communication, instant information retrieval, instant headache relief, instant meals, instant gratification, and perhaps, in the minds of many youth, instant high-paying employment with signing bonuses for jobs that entail more fun than hard work. In light of this cultural phenomenon, we are on your side: the classroom teacher is on the firing line each day and is expected to perform—perhaps instantly and entertainingly, but most certainly in a highly competent and professional manner—in situations that are far from ideal. In any case, you must gain your students' attention before you can teach them.

In this final section of the chapter, you will find an annotated list of ideas, many of which have been offered over recent years by classroom teachers. (See also Figure 8.4 at the conclusion of this chapter.) Although the ideas are organized according to discipline, and some may be more appropriate for one group of young adolescents than another, you may profit from reading all entries for each field. And an entry identified as specific to one discipline might also be useful in others (many of them can be used in interdisciplinary teaching—for example number one can clearly be combined with mathematics and science, as well as art). An entry might also stimulate a creative idea for your own stock of motivational techniques, such as a way to use the theory of multiple learning capacities or to emphasize the multicultural aspect of a lesson in math, or social studies, or some other central discipline or theme of a lesson or unit of instruction.

The Visual and Performing Arts

1. As part of a unit combining design or creativity with science, have students construct, design, and decorate their own kite. When the projects are complete, designate a time to fly them.

2. Use lyrics from popular music to influence classwork, such as putting the lyrics into pictures.

3. Use the outdoors or another environment for a free drawing experience.

4. Invite a local artist who has created a community mural to speak to the class about the mural. Plan and create a class mural, perhaps on a large sheet of plywood or in some other location approved by the school administration.

5. Use a mandala to demonstrate the importance of individual experience, as in interpreting paintings and in interpreting poetry.

6. Collect books, magazines, posters, films, videos, computer software programs, and so forth that show different kinds of masks people around the world wear. Ask students to identify the similarities and differences in the masks. Have them research the meanings that mask characters have in various cultures. Have students design and create their own masks to illustrate their own personalities, cultures, and so forth.

7. As part of a unit on the creative process, have each student draw or sketch on a piece of paper, then pass it on to the next person, who makes additions to the drawing. Instructions could include "improve the drawing," "make the drawing ugly," and "add what you think would be necessary to complete the composition."

8. Imagine that you are a bird flying over the largest city you have visited. What do you see, hear, smell, feel, taste? Draw a "sensory" map.

9. Assign a different color to each student. Have them arrange themselves into warm and cool colors and explain their decisions (why blue is cool, etc.). Discuss people's emotional responses to each of the colors.

10. Watch videos of dances from various countries and cultures. Have students identify similarities and differences. Have students research meanings and occasions of particular dances.

11. Have students discover ways in which music, art, and dance are used around them and in their community.

12. Find a popular song that students like. Transpose the melody into unfamiliar keys for each instrument. This makes the student want to learn the song, but in the process the student will have to become more familiar with his or her instrument.

13. Set aside one weekend morning a month and hold small informal recitals (workshops) allowing students to participate in and/or observe the performance situation(s) among their peers and themselves. (Students might be told beforehand about these "special days" and encouraged to prepare a selection of their own choosing.)

14. Play a rhythm game, such as the "Dutch Shoe Game," to get students to cooperate, work together, and enjoy themselves using rhythm. Participants sit in a circle, and as the song is sung, each person passes one of his or her shoes to the person on the right in rhythm to the music. Shoes continue to be passed as long as verses are sung. Those with poor rhythm will end up with a pile of shoes in front of them!

15. Choose a rhythmical, humorous poem or verse to conduct. The students read the poem in chorus, while the teacher stands before them and conducts the poem as if it were a musical work. Students must be sensitive to the intonation, speed, inflection, mood, and dynamics that the teacher wants them to convey in their reading.

16. Start a Retired Senior Citizens Volunteer Program (RSCVP) in which senior citizens present folk art workshops with students, and the students and seniors work together to create artworks for the school. For example, students at one school make tray favors, napkin rings, place mats, door decorations, and cards and treat cups for the residents of the local Veterans home.

17. Students from Elkhorn Area Middle School (Elkhorn, WI) organized an Improv Troupe, which creates and performs unscripted, improvisational skits about social issues relevant to today's young adolescents.[27]

Family and Consumer Economics, Foods, and Textiles

18. Often the foods we like originated from another part of our country or another place in the world. Have the students identify where such foods originated—foods such as spaghetti, enchiladas, fajitas, wontons, tacos, quiches, croissants, teriyaki, fried rice, pizza, hot dog, hamburger, noodle, tomato, chocolate, potato, hoagy, chop suey, ice cream cone, submarine, poor boy. Have them list the names and origins, and place pictures of the food in the proper place on a large world map.

19. Take still photos (perhaps with a digital camera) of class members at special events such as dinners, fashion shows, and field trips, and working on special projects. Build a scrapbook or bulletin board with these and display it on campus.

20. Plan thematic units on cultural foods, using the traditions, costumes, and music of a particular culture. Have the students decorate the room. Invite the

---

[27]P. A. Reedy, "Improv and the Middle School," *Principal* 80(4):52 (March 2001).

principal and perhaps community representatives for a meal and visit.

21. Have students plan and create a bulletin board displaying pictures of 100-calorie portions of basic nutritional foods and popular fad foods that contain only empty calories. The display can motivate a discussion on foods with calories and nutrients versus foods with empty calories.

22. Write the names of different garments on index cards and pin them on the backs of students. After guessing what they are, the students sort themselves into different wash loads.

23. For a clothing unit hold an "idea day." Ask each student to bring in an idea of something that can be done to give clothes a new look, a fun touch, or an extended wearing life. Ideas they may come up with include appliqués, embroidery, tie-dye, batik, colorful patches, and restyling old clothes into current or creative fashions.

24. Have the students write, practice, and present skits, for videotape presentation, on consumer fraud.

25. Once a month have students plan a menu, prepare the food, and serve it to invited senior citizens from the community.

26. Organize a program for senior citizens and students to work together on a community garden.

27. Plan a program at a senior citizens center whereby students and seniors work together to plan and decorate the center for special occasions and holidays.

28. With your students, plan a community service program. For example, at Discovery Middle School (Vancouver, WA), students provide child care, cross-age tutoring, and companionship to preschool, elementary school, and elderly clients at off-campus locations.

English, Languages, and the Language Arts

29. Organize a letter-writing activity between senior citizens and your students.

30. For a unit on the Renaissance, creating a wall-to-wall mural depicting a village of the times might be a total team project. Some students can research customs, costumes, and architecture. Others may paint or draw.

31. On a U.S. road map, have students find the names of places that sound "foreign" and categorize the names according to nationality or culture. The students might be interested in researching how the places got their names.

32. To enhance understanding of parts of speech, set up several boxes containing slips of paper with different parts of speech. Each student is to form one sentence from the fragments chosen from each box, being allowed to discard only at a penalty. The students then nonverbally make trades with other students to make coherent and perhaps meaningfully amusing sentences. A student may trade a noun for a verb but will have to keep in mind what parts of speech are essential

for a sentence. Results may be read aloud as a culmination to this activity.

33. Have students match American English and British English words (or any other combination of languages), such as cookies and biscuits; hood and bonnet; canned meat and tinned meat; elevator and lift; flashlight and torch; subway and tube; garbage collector and dustman; undershirt and vest; sweater and jumper; gasoline and petrol. Or, have students compare pronunciations and spellings.

34. English words derive from many other languages. Have students research and list some, such as ketchup (Malay), alcohol (Arabic), kindergarten (German), menu (French), shampoo (Hindi), bonanza (Spanish), piano (Italian), kosher (Yiddish), and smorgasbord (Swedish).

35. Try this for an exercise in objective versus subjective writing: After a lesson on descriptive writing, bring to the class a nondescript object, such as a potato, and place it before the class. Ask them to write a paragraph either describing the potato in detail, that is, its color, size, markings, and other characteristics, or describing how the potato feels about them.

36. Read a story to the class but without an ending. Then ask the students (as individuals or in think-write-share-pairs) to create and write their own endings or conclusions, which they will share with the rest of the class.

37. Ask students to create in groups of no more than three students each an advertisement using a propaganda device of their choice. Video record their presentations.

38. Ask students, individually or in dyads, to create and design an invention and then to write a "patent description" for the invention.

39. Using think-write-pair-share, have students write a physical description of some well-known (but unnamed) public figure, such as a movie star, politician, athlete, or musician. Other class members may enjoy trying to identify the "mystery" personality from the written description.

40. A bulletin board may be designated for current events and news in the world of writers. Included may be new books and recording releases as well as reviews. News of poets and authors (student authors and poets, too) may also be displayed.

41. Everyone has heard of or experienced stereotyping. For example, girls are not as athletic as boys, boys are insensitive, women are better cooks than men, men are more mechanical. Ask students to list some stereotypes they have heard, and examples they find in newspapers, magazines, movies, and television. Have students discuss these questions: How do you suppose these stereotypes came to be? Does stereotyping have any useful value? Is it sometimes harmful?

42. Remove the text from a Sunday newspaper comic strip and have the students work in pairs to create

a story line; or, give each pair a picture from a magazine and have the pair create a story about the picture.

43. Use newspaper want ads to locate jobs as a base for completing job application forms and creating letters of inquiry. Use videorecording equipment to record employer-employee role-play situations, interviews for jobs, or child-parent situations to develop language and listening skills.

44. Have students choose a short story from a text, write it into a play, and perform the play for parents/guardians.

45. When beginning a poetry unit, ask students to bring in the words to their favorite songs. Show how these fit into the genre of poetry.

46. Have students look for commercial examples of advertisements that might be classed as "ecopornographic," i.e., ads that push a product that is potentially damaging to our environment. Or, have students analyze advertisements for the emotions they appeal to, techniques used, and their integrity. Try the same thing with radio, teen magazines, the Internet, and other media.

47. Change the environment by moving to an outdoor location and ask students to write poetry to see if the change in surroundings stimulates or discourages their creativeness. Discuss the results. For example, take your class to a large supermarket to write, or to a lake, or into a forest, or to the school athletic stadium.

48. To introduce the concept of interpretations, use your state's seal to start the study. Have students analyze the seal for its history and the meaning of its various symbols.

49. When learning a second language, provide puppets in native costume for students to use while practicing dialogue.

50. Use the Internet to establish communication with students from another area of the country or world; establish a Web page for your school, house, or classroom.

51. Use drama to build language arts and thinking skills. Have students write dialogue, set scenes, and communicate emotions through expressive language and mime.

52. Establish a community-service learning literacy project.

Mathematics

53. Collaboratively plan with students a simulation where members role-play the solar system. Students calculate their weights, set up a proportion system, find a large field, and on the final day actually simulate the solar system, using their own bodies to represent the sun, planets, and moons. Arrange to have the event photographed.

54. Encourage students to look for evidence of Fibonacci number series (i.e., 1, 1, 2, 3, 5, 8, 13, 21, etc.),

outside of mathematics, such as in nature and in manufactured objects. Perhaps your students might like to organize a Fibonacci Club and through the Internet establish communication with similar clubs around the world.[28]

55. Have students research the history of the cost of a first-class U.S. postage stamp and ask them to devise ways of predicting its cost by the year they graduate, or are grandparents, or some other target year.

56. Give students a list of the frequencies of each of the 88 keys and strings of a piano (a local music store can provide the information). Challenge students to derive an equation to express the relationship between key position and frequency. After they have done this, research and tell them about the Bösendorfer piano (Germany) with its nine extra keys at the lower end of the keyboard. See if students can predict the frequencies of those extra keys.

57. Using a light sensor to measure the intensity of a light source from various distances, have students graph the data points and then, with their scientific calculators, find the relevant equation.

58. Students at George Washington Middle School (Alexandria, VA) participate in a parachute creation contest. Using plastic from trash bags, string, and a paperclip as the skydiver, the challenge is to design a parachute with the least surface area and longest hang time.[29]

Physical Education

59. Have students choose individually (or in dyads) a famous athlete they most (or least) admire, and have them write a short report about him or her. The student will then discuss the attributes and/or characteristics that they admire (or dislike) in the athlete, and how they feel they can emulate (or avoid) those qualities. After all pairs of students have made their presentations,

---

[28]For information about Fibonacci numbers see C. Andreasen, "Fibonacci and Pascal Together Again: Pattern Exploration in the Fibonacci Sequence," *Mathematics Teacher* 91(3):250–253 (March 1998); T. H. Garland and C. V. Kahn, *Math and Music: Harmonious Connections* (Palo Alto, CA: Dale Seymour, 1995); A. Johnson, "Fiber Meets Fibonacci; The Shape of Things to Come," *Mathematics Teacher* 4(4):256–262 (January 1999); R. Lewand, "Fibonacci Melodies," *Humanistic Mathematics Network Journal*, n14 p36–39 (November 1996); J. L. Morgan and J. L. Ginther, "The Magic of Mathematics," *Mathematics Teacher* 87(3):150–153 (March 1994); B. Rulf, "A Geometric Puzzle That Leads To Fibonacci Sequences," *Mathematics Teacher* 91(1):21–23 (January 1998); D. L. Shaw and L. Aspinwall, "The Recurring Fibonacci Sequence: Using a Pose-and-Probe Rubric," *Mathematics Teacher* 92(3):192–196 (March 1999); and M. J. Zerger, "The Dating Game," *Mathematics Teacher* 91(2):172–174 (February 1998).

[29]L. Mann, "Recalculating Middle School Math," *Education Update* 42(1):2–3, 8 (January 2000).

as a class devise two lists, one of common attributes admired, the other of qualities to avoid.

60. Have students in cooperative learning groups make up an exercise routine to their favorite music recording. Have them share it with the class and discuss how they arrived at decisions along the way.

61. Have the class divide into groups. Given the basic nonlocomotor skills, have each group come up with a "people machine." Each student within the group is hooked up to another demonstrating a nonlocomotor skill and adding some sort of noise to it. Have a contest for the most creative people machine.

62. Give students a chance to design a balance-beam routine that has two passes on the beam and must include front support mount, forward roll, leap, low or high turn, visit, chassé, and cross support dismount. These routines will be posted to show the variety of ways the different maneuvers can be put together.

63. Divide the class into groups. Have them create a new game or activity for the class, using only the equipment they are given. Let the class play their newly created games.

64. Have the students plan ways of educating the school and local community about general nutrition and regular exercise.

Science

65. Have students create and test their own microscopes using bamboo rods with a drop of water in each end.

66. Have students use the petals of flowers to create litmus indicators.

67. Use cassette-tape recorders to record sounds of the environment. Compare and write about day and night sounds.

68. On the first day of a life science class, give each student one live guppy in a test tube and one live cactus plant in a three-inch pot. Tell the students that the minimum they each need to do to pass the course is to bring their pet plant and fish back to you during the final week of school, alive.

69. Plan a year-long project where each student, or small group of students, must develop knowledge and understanding of some specific piece of technology. Each project culmination presentation must have five components: visual, oral, written, artistic, and creative.

70. If you are a life science teacher, make sure your classroom looks like a place for studying life rather than a place of death.

71. Use landlord-tenant situations to develop a simulation of predator-prey relationships.

72. With each student playing the role of a cell part, have students set up and perform a role-play simulation of cells.

73. Divide your class into groups and ask each group to create an environment for an imaginary animal, using discarded items from the environment. By asking questions, each group will try to learn about the other groups' "mystery" animals.

74. Have each student, or student pair, "adopt" a chemical element. The student then researches that element and becomes the class expert whenever that particular substance comes up in discussion. There could be a special bulletin board for putting up questions on interesting or little-known facts about the elements.

75. Milk can be precipitated and separated, and the solid product dried to form a very hard substance that was, in the days before plastic, used to make buttons. Let students make their own buttons from milk.

76. As a class or interdisciplinary team project, obtain permission to "adopt" a wetlands area near the school.

77. Have students research the composition and development of familiar objects. For example the ordinary pencil is made of cedar wood from the forests of the Pacific Northwest. The graphite is often from Montana or Mexico and is reinforced with clays from Georgia and Kentucky. The eraser is made from soybean oil and from latex from trees in South America, and is reinforced with pumice from California or New Mexico, and sulfur, calcium, and barium. The metal band is aluminum or brass, made from copper and zinc, mined in no fewer than 13 states and nine provinces of Canada. The paint to color the wood and the lacquer to make it shine are made from a variety of different minerals and metals, as is the glue that holds the wood together.

78. Have students locate information and design large posters to hang on the classroom walls that show the meanings of words used in science that are not typical of their meanings in everyday language usage—the word "theory" for example.

79. To bridge cross-cultural differences, have students design large posters to hang on the classroom walls showing potential differences in perceptions or views according to ethnoscience and formal science.

80. With your students, plan a community service project. For example, at Great Falls Middle School (Montague, MA), students research and produce television documentaries on subjects related to energy. The documentaries are broadcast on the local cable channel to promote energy literacy in the school and community. Students at Baldwyn Middle School (Baldwyn, MS) plan and care for the landscaping of the local battlefield/museum.

81. Sometimes projects become ongoing permanent endeavors with many spin-off projects of shorter duration. For example, what began as a science classroom project at W. H. English Middle School (Scottsburg, IN) has become the largest animal refuge shelter in the Midwest. While nursing animals back to health,

the students study them and learn about environmental policies. Over the years, students in the program have shared their work by making presentations in 10 states and were guests of the International Animal Rights Convention in Russia.[30]

Social Sciences

82. Organize an Intergenerational Advocacy program, in which students and senior citizens work together to make a better society for both groups.[31] For example, at Burns Middle School (Owensboro, KY) students work in collaboration with a retired senior volunteer program to develop their understanding of personal and social responsibilities.

83. Initiate a service-learning project, where for an extended period of time students work directly with community organizations and agencies. For example, at John Ford Middle School (St. Matthews, SC) students incorporate The Constitutional Right Foundation "City Youth" program into the curriculum, helping to make decisions about areas of the community that need improvement.

84. Develop a year-long, three-stage project. During the first stage students individually research the question "Who Am I?"; during the second stage, "Who Are They?"; third stage, "Who Are We?". Multimedia presentations should be part of the culminating presentations.

85. During their study of Ancient Egypt, have students create and build their own model pyramids.

86. Let students devise ways they would improve their living environment, beginning with the classroom, then moving out to the school, home, community, and world.

87. Start a pictorial essay on the development and/or changes of a given area in your community, such as a major corner or block adjacent to the school. This is a study project that could continue for years and that has many social, political, and economic implications.

88. Start a folk hero study. Each year ask, "What prominent human being who has lived during (a particular period of time) do you most and/or least admire?" Collect individual responses to the question, tally, and discuss. After you have done this for several years you may wish to share the results of your surveys of previous years with your class for discussion purposes.

89. Start a sister school program. Establish a class relationship with another similar class from another school from around the country or the world, perhaps via the Internet.

90. Role-play a family moving to the West in the 1800s. What items would they take? What would they throw out of the wagon to lighten the load?

91. Have students collect music, art, or athletic records from a particular period of history. Have them compare them with today's and predict the future.

92. Using play money, establish a capitalistic economic system within your classroom. Salaries may be paid for attendance and bonus income for work well done, taxes may be collected for poor work, and a welfare section established in a corner of the room.

93. Divide your class into small groups and ask that each group make predictions as to what world governments, world geography, world social issues, world health, world energy, or some other world issue will be like some time in the future. Let each group give its report, followed by debate and discussion. Plant the predictions in some secret location on the school grounds for a future discovery.

94. As an opener to a unit on the U.S. Constitution, have students design their own classroom's (or school's) "bill of rights."

95. One day treat your students in class as if your class were a socialist society; the next day treat them as if they were a fascist society; on another day as a communist society; etc. At the end of the simulation, have students discuss and compare their feelings about each day.

96. Using Legos™ as construction blocks and after assigning roles, have students simulate the building of the Great Wall of China or the Great Pyramids of Egypt.

97. At Indian Trail Junior High School (Addison, IL) all eighth-graders and teachers from not only social studies but various other content areas, including English, mathematics, physical education, and science, work together on a "real world" problem-based project titled the Inspector Red Ribbon Unit. It focuses on a social problem that has truly occurred too many times, the prom night automobile accident. During the study, guided by teachers of the various classes, students interview witnesses, visit and assess the scene of the accident, review medical reports, and make their recommendations in a press conference.[32]

98. Establish a caring, anti-violence program.

---

[30]Source: J. Arnold, "High Expectations For All: Perspective and Practice," *Middle School Journal* 28(3):52 (January 1997).

[31]See, for example: R. Cuevas, "I Can Help," and G. R. Hopkins, "How Important Are Intergenerational Programs in Today's Schools?" both in *Phi Delta Kappan* 82(4):316 and 317–319, respectively, (December 2000). Additional information about intergenerational programs can be obtained from the Center for Intergenerational Learning, Temple University, 1601 N. Broad St., Room 206, Philadelphia, PA 19122 (http://www/temple.edu/departments/CIL).

[32]K. Rasmussen, "Using Real-Life Problems to Make Real-World Connections," *ASCD Curriculum Update* (Summer 1997), p. 2.

99. During an interdisciplinary thematic unit of study (the history and literature of the medieval period of Europe), students study castles and build model castles.

100. With guidance from three teachers using a common philosophical approach based on Glasser's Choice Theory, Reality Therapy, and ideas from his book *The Quality School* (see Chapter 4), students of eighth-grade history at Longfellow Middle School (La Crosse, WI) designed and built their own middle school nation.[33]

---

[33]See R. Frost; E. Olson; and L. Valiquette, "The Wolf Pack: Power Shared and Power Earned—Building a Middle School Nation," *Middle School Journal* 31(5):30–36 (May 2000).

Figure 8.4 Internet sites for teaching ideas.

All subjects, lessons, units, and project ideas
- *Columbia Education Center Lesson Plans* http://www.col-ed.org/cur/
- *Global Schoolhouse* http://www.gsh.org
- *Intercultural E-Mail Classroom Connections* http://www.iecc.org/
- *K-12 Projects* http://www.eagle.ca/-matink/
- *Teachers Net Lesson Bank* http://www.teachers.net/lessons

Art
- *Crayola Art Education* http://www.crayola.com/educators
- *Eyes on Art* http://www.kn.pacbell.com/wired/art2
- *Incredible Art Department* http://homepage.mac.com/krohrer/iad/
- *World Wide Arts Resources* http://wwar.com/

Dance
- *CyberDance* http://www.cyberdance.org
- *Dance links* http://www.SapphireSwan.com/dance/

Drama and Film
- *American Alliance for Theatre & Education* http://www.aate.com/
- *Association of Theatre Movement Educators* http://www.asu.edu/cfa/atme/
- *Performing Arts Resources* http://www.educationindex.com/theater/
- *Screensite* http://www.tcf.ua.edu/screensite

Environmental issues
- *North American Association for Environmental Education* http://www.naaee.org
- *The World Bank Group* http://www.worldbank.org/depweb
- *World Resources Institute* http://www.wri.org

History/Social Studies
- *K-12 Africa Guide* http://www.sas.upenn.edu/African_Studies/Home_Page/AFR_GIDE.html
- *Mexico Online* http://www.mexonline.com/
- *FedWorld* http://www.fedworld.gov
- *Historical Text Archive* http://historicaltextarchive.com
- *The History Net* http://www.thehistorynet.com
- *History/social studies resources* http://www.execpc.com/-dboals/boals.html
- *Houghton Mifflin Social Studies Center* http://www.eduplace.com/ss/
- *The Library in the Sky* http://www.nwrel.org/sky
- *Links to lesson plans, unit plans, thematic units, and resources* http://www.csun.edu/-hcedu013/index.html
- *Medieval Life* http://www.pastforward.co.uk/
- *Scrolls from the Dead Sea* http://sunsite.unc.edu/expo/deadsea.scrolls.exhibit/intro.html
- *Social Sciences Research Network Online* http://www.ssrn.com/index.html
- *Social Science Resources Home Page* http://www.nde.state.ne.us/SS/ss.html
- U.S. History, *From Revolution to Reconstruction* http://grid.let.rug.nl/-welling/usa/usa.html
- *Women's History* http://frank.mtsu.edu/-kmiddlet/history/women.html

Language and Literacy
- *ESL/EFL links* http://www.pacificnet.net/-sperling/eslcafe.html
- *Foreign language links* http://polyglot.lss.wisc.edu/lss/lang/langlink.html

Figure 8.4   *(continued)*

Mathematics

- *Math Archives* http://archives.math.utk.edu/
- *The Math Forum* http://mathforum.org/
- *MathSource* http://mathsource.wri.com/
- *More math project ideas* http://www.luc.edu/schools/education/csimath/zmathed.htm
- *PBS Mathline* http://www.pbs.org/learn/mathline/
- *Plane Math* http://www.planemath.com/
- *Show-Me Project* http://www.showmecenter.missouri.edu

Music

- *American Music Conference* http://www.amc-music.com
- *Music Education Resource Links* http://www.isd77.k12.mn.us/resources/staffpages/shirk/k12.music.html

Science

- *BioRap* http://www.biorap.org.
- *Chemistry tutorial site* http://dbhs.wvusd.k12.ca.us/ChemTeamIndex.html
- *Cody's Science Education Zone* http://tlc.ousd.k12.ca.us/~acody/
- *Electronic Zoo* http://netvet.wustl.edu/
- *Mandel's* http://www.pacificnet.net/~mandel/Science.html
- *NASA Spacelink* http://spacelink.nasa.gov/.index.html
- *Stanford Solar Center* http://solar-center.stanford.edu
- *Windows to the Universe Project* http://www.windows.ucar.edu

SUMMARY

This chapter has continued the development of your repertoire of teaching strategies. As you know, young adolescents can be quite peer-conscious, can have relatively short attention spans for experiences in which they are uninterested, and prefer active multisensory experiences. Most are intensely curious about things that are of interest to them. Cooperative learning, student-centered projects, and teaching strategies that emphasize shared discovery and inquiry (discussed in the next chapter) within a psychologically safe environment encourage the most positive aspects of thinking and learning. Central to your strategy selection should be those strategies that encourage students to become independent thinkers and skilled learners who can help in the planning, structuring, regulating, and assessing of their own learning and learning activities.

QUESTIONS FOR CLASS DISCUSSION

1. Describe research you can find on the use of cooperation (cooperative learning groups) versus competition (competitive learning groups) in teaching. Explain why you would or would not use cooperative learning groups as they were discussed in this chapter.
2. Do you have concerns about using project-based teaching and not being able to cover all the content you believe should be covered? Think back to your own schooling. What do you really remember? Most likely you remember projects, yours and other students' presentations, the lengthy research you did and your extra effort for the art-work to accompany your presentation. Maybe you remember a compliment by a teacher or a pat on the back by peers. Most likely you do not remember the massive amount of content that was covered. Discuss your feelings about this with your classmates. Share common experiences; common concerns.
3. To learn something well students need time to practice it. There is a difference, however, between solitary practice and coached practice. Describe the difference and conditions where you would use each.
4. Divide into teams of four, and have each team develop one learning center. Set up and share the LCs in your classroom.
5. Explain how a teacher can tell when he or she is truly using cooperative learning groups for instruction as opposed to traditional small group learning.
6. When a student is said to be on task, does that necessarily imply that the student is mentally engaged? Is it possible for a student to be mentally engaged although not on task? Explain your answers.
7. Select one of the "Reflective Thoughts" from the introduction to Part III (page 232) that is specifically related to the content of this chapter, research it, and write a one-page essay explaining why you agree or disagree with the thought. Share your essay with members of your class for their thoughts.
8. Describe any prior concepts you held that changed as a result of your experiences with this chapter. Describe the changes.
9. From your current observations and field work as related to this teacher preparation program, clearly identify one specific example of educational practice that seems contradictory to exemplary practice or theory as presented in this chapter. Present your explanation for the discrepancy.

10. Do you have questions generated by the content of this chapter? If you do, list them along with ways answers might be found.

FOR FURTHER READING

Abrams, S. *Using Journals with Reluctant Writers: Building Portfolios for Middle and High School Students.* Thousand Oaks, CA: Corwin Press, 2000.

Arrington, H. J., and Moore, S. D. "Infusing Service Learning into Instruction." *Middle School Journal* 32(4):55–60 (March 2001).

Babcock, B. (Ed.). *Learning from Experience: A Collection of Service-Learning Projects Linking Academic Standards to Curriculum.* Madison, WI: Wisconsin Department of Public Instruction, 2000.

Benjamin, B., and Irwin-DeVitis, L. "Censoring Girls' Choices: Continued Gender Bias in English Language Arts Classrooms." *English Journal* 87(2):64–71 (February 1998).

Bomer, R. "Writing to Think Critically: The Seeds of Social Action." *Voices from the Middle* 6(4):2–8 (May 1999).

Buege, D. J. "The Flying Sunflower: A Seed Dispersal Project." *Science Activities* 35(4):10–12 (Winter 1999).

Carter, C. S.; Cohen, S.; Keyes, M.; Kusimo, P. S.; and Lunsford, C. *Uncommon Knowledge: Projects That Help Middle-School-Age Youth Discover the Science and Mathematics in Everyday Life.* Volume Two: Hands-On Math Projects. Charleston, WV: ED439002, ERIC Clearinghouse on Rural Education and Small Schools, 2000.

Carter, C. S.; Keyes, M.; Kusimo, P. S.; and Lunsford, C. *Uncommon Knowledge: Projects That Help Middle-School-Age Youth Discover the Science and Mathematics in Everyday Life.* Volume One: Hands-On Science Projects. Charleston, WV: ED438977, ERIC Clearinghouse on Rural Education and Small Schools, 2000.

Di Santo, G. "Building with Straw." *Green Teacher,* n16, pp. 8–13 (Spring 2000).

Fougere, M. "The Educational Benefits to Middle School Students Participating in a Student/Scientist Project." *Journal of Science Education and Technology* 7(1):25–30 (March 1998).

Gober, D. A., and Mewborn, D. S. "Promoting Equity in Mathematics Classrooms." *Middle School Journal* 32(3):31–35 (January 2001).

Harris, B.; Kohlmeier, K.; and Kiel, R. D. *Crime Scene Investigation.* Englewood, CO: Teacher Ideas Press, 1999.

Kesson, K., and Oyler, C. "Integrated Curriculum and Service Learning: Linking School-Based Knowledge and Social Action." *English Education* 31(2):135–149 (January 1999).

LaBonty, J., and Reksten, P. "Inspiring Struggling Writers with Photography." *Middle School Journal* 32(5):13–21 (May 2001).

Larson, B. E. "Influences on Social Studies Teachers' Use of Classroom Discussion." *Clearing House* 73(3):174–181 (January/February 2000).

Leloup, J. W., and Ponterio, R. "Cooperative Learning Activities for the Foreign Language Classroom." *Language Learning and Technology* 3(2):3–5 (January 2000).

Leonard, J., and McElroy, K. "What One Middle School Teacher Learned about Cooperative Learning." *Journal of Research in Childhood Education* 14(2):239–245 (Spring/Summer 2000).

Lundt, J. C., and Vanderpan, T. "It Computes When Young Adolescents Teach Senior Citizens." *Middle School Journal* 31(4):18–22 (March 2000).

Marzano, R. J.; Pickering, D. J.; Pollock, J. E. *Classroom Instruction That Works.* Chapter 7, "Cooperative Learning," pp. 84–91. Alexandria, VA: Association for Supervision and Curriculum Development, 2001.

McClure, L. J. "Wimpy Boys and Macho Girls: Gender Equity at the Crossroads." *English Journal* 88(3):78–82 (January 1999).

Means, B., and Lindner, L. *Teaching Writing in Middle Schools: Tips, Tricks, and Techniques.* Englewood, CO: Libraries Unlimited, 1998.

Mewborn, D. S. "Creating a Gender Equitable School Environment." *International Journal of Leadership in Education* 2(2):103–115 (April–June 1999).

Moutray, C. L.; Pollard, J. A.; and McGinley, J. "Students Explore Text, Themselves, and Life Through Reader Response." *Middle School Journal* 32(5):30–34 (May 2001).

Muir, M. "What Engages Underachieving Middle School Students in Learning?" *Middle School Journal* 33(2): 37–43 (November 2001).

Nelesen, K. R. "Cross-Curricular Unit Engages Students in the Presidential Election." *Middle School Journal* 32(1):26–33 (September 2000).

Nichols, W. D.; Wood, K. D.; and Rickelman, R. "Using Technology to Engage Students in Reading and Writing." *Middle School Journal* 32(5):45–50 (May 2001).

Nolan, F. "Ability Grouping Plus Heterogeneous Grouping: Win-Win Schedules." *Middle School Journal* 29(5):14–19 (May 1998).

Paulu, N., and Darby, L. B., eds. *Helping Your Students with Homework: A Guide for Teachers.* Washington, DC: U.S. Office of Educational Research and Improvement, U.S. Government Printing Office, 1998.

Randall, V. "Cooperative Learning: Abused and Overused?" *Gifted Child Today Magazine* 22(2):14–16 (March/April 1999).

Rillero, P.; Gonzalez-Jensen, M.; and Moy, T. "Moon Watch: A Parental-Involvement Homework Activity." *Science Activities* 36(4):11–15 (Winter 2000).

Sadker, D. "Gender Equity: Still Knocking at the Classroom Door." *Educational Leadership* 56(7):22–26 (April 1999).

Scales, P. C. "Increasing Service-Learning's Impact on Middle School Students." *Middle School Journal* 30(5):40–44 (May 1999).

Shepard-Tew, D., and Forgione, J. "A Collaborative Mentor-Training Program for Learning-Disabled Middle-Grade Students." *Educational Forum* 64(1):75–81 (Fall 1999).

Smith, F. "Just a Matter of Time." *Phi Delta Kappan* 82(8): 572–576 (April 2001).

Stearns, C. J. "A Middle School Venture into Cooperative Learning: Successes and Dilemmas." *Theory into Practice* 38(2):100–104 (Spring 1999).

Walters, L. S. "Putting Cooperative Learning to the Test." *Harvard Education Letter* 16(3):1–5 (May/June 2000).

Wiest, L. R. "Mathematics That Whets the Appetite: Student-Posed Problems." *Mathematics Teaching in the Middle School* 5(5):286–291 (January 2000).

Wyatt, F. R. "Publishing Biographies to Learn About History, Writing, and Research." *Middle School Journal* 32(5):7–12 (May 2001).

Zinn, B.; Gnut, S.; and Kafkafi, U. "First-Rate Crops from Second-Rate Water: Classroom Activities Model a Real-World Problem." *Science Activities* 35(4):27–30 (Winter 1999).

9

Using Teacher Talk, Demonstrations, Thinking, Inquiry, and Games

Perhaps no other strategy is used more by teachers than teacher talk, so this chapter begins by presenting guidelines for using that vital and significant instructional strategy. A strategy related to teacher talk is the demonstration, which is addressed later in the chapter, followed by guidelines for other important strategies, namely, thinking, inquiry, discovery, and games.

OBJECTIVES

Upon completion of this chapter, you should be able to

1. Give an effective demonstration.
2. Help students learn to think and behave intelligently.
3. Describe the relationship among thinking, problem solving, discovery, and inquiry.

TEACHING VIGNETTE

A Precious Moment in Teaching with Advice to Beginning Teachers

We share with you this teaching vignette that we believe to be both humorous and indicative of creative thinking. While teaching a history class, the teacher began her lesson with the question, "What comes to mind when you hear the words 'Puritan' and 'Pilgrim'?" Without hesitation, a rather quiet student voice from somewhere near the rear of the room replied, "Cooking oil and John Wayne." To us, that represented one of those rare and precious moments in teaching, reaffirming our belief that every teacher is well advised to maintain throughout his or her teaching career a journal in which such intrinsically rewarding moments can be recorded to be reviewed and enjoyed again years later.

---

4. Integrate strategies for integrated learning.
5. Demonstrate when and how to use student inquiry.
6. Determine when and how to use teacher talk for instruction.
7. Describe the advantages and disadvantages of each of seven categories of games for learning.

TEACHER TALK: FORMAL AND INFORMAL

Teacher talk encompasses both lecturing *to* students and talking *with* students. A lecture is considered formal teacher talk, whereas a discussion with students is considered informal teacher talk.

Cautions in Using Teacher Talk

Whether your talk is formal or informal, there are certain cautions that you need to be mindful of. Perhaps the most important is that of *talking too much*. If a teacher talks too much, the significance of the teacher's words may be lost because some students will tune the teacher out.

Another caution is to avoid *talking too fast*. Students can hear faster than they can understand what they hear. Remind yourself to talk slowly and to check frequently for student comprehension of what you are talking about. It is also important to remember that your one brain is communicating with many student brains, each of which responds to sensory input (auditory in this instance) at different rates. Because of this, you will need to pause to let words sink in and during transitions from one point or activity to the next.

A third caution is to be sure you are being *heard and understood*. Sometimes teachers talk in a pitch that is too low or use words that are not understood by many of the children, or both. You should vary the pitch of your voice, and you should stop and help students with their understanding of vocabulary that may be new to them.

A fourth caution is to remember that just *because students have heard something before does not necessarily mean that they understood it or learned it*. From our earlier discussions of learning experiences (such as "The Learning Experiences Ladder" in Chapter 6), remember that verbal communication is an important form of communication, but because it relies on the use of ab-

stract symbolization, it is not a very reliable form of communication. Teacher talk relies on words and on skill in listening—a skill that is not mastered by many young adolescents (or for that matter, even many adults). For that and other reasons, to ensure student understanding, it is good to reinforce your teacher talk with either direct or simulated learning experiences.

A related caution is to *resist believing that students have attained a skill or have learned something that was taught previously by you or by another teacher*. During any discussion (formal or informal), rather than assuming that your students know something, you should make sure they know it. For example, if the discussion and student activity involve a particular math skill or thinking skill, make sure that students know how to use that skill (thinking skills are discussed later in this chapter).

Still another problem is *talking in a humdrum monotone*. Students need teachers whose voices exude enthusiasm and excitement (although not overdone) about the subject and about teaching and learning. Such enthusiasm and excitement for learning are contagious. A voice that demonstrates genuine enthusiasm for teaching and learning, is more likely to motivate students to learn.

A final caution is *just because your speaking channel is engaged does not mean that you should disengage your sensory input channels*. This is another time when the exemplary teachers' skills of withitness and overlapping (discussed in Chapter 3) are apparent. While an exemplary teacher is talking, he or she is still seeing and listening and capable of changing physical location in the classroom.

Keep those cautions in mind as you study the general principles and specific guidelines for the productive and effective use of teacher talk.

Teacher Talk: General Guidelines

Certain general guidelines should be followed whether your talk is formal or informal. First, begin the talk with an advance organizer. Advance organizers are introductions that mentally prepare students for a study by helping them make connections with material already learned or experienced—a *comparative organizer*—or by providing students with a conceptual arrangement of what is to be learned—an *expository organizer.*[1] The value of using advance organizers is well documented by research.[2] An advance organizer can be a brief introduction or statement about the main idea you intend to convey, and how it is related to other aspects of the students' learning (an expository organizer), or it can be a presentation of a discrepancy to arouse curiosity (a comparative organizer, in this instance causing students to compare what they have observed with what they already knew or thought they knew). Preparing an organizer helps you plan and organize the sequence of ideas, and its presentation helps students organize their own learning and become motivated about it. An advance organizer can also make their learning meaningful by providing important connections between what they already know and what is being learned.

Second, *your talk should be planned so that it has a beginning and an end, and a logical order between.* During your talk, you should reinforce your words with visuals (discussed in the specific guidelines that follow). These visuals may include writing unfamiliar terms on the board; (helping students learn new vocabulary), visual organizers; and prepared graphs, charts, photographs, and various audiovisuals.

Third, *pacing is important.* Your talk should move briskly, but not too fast. The ability to pace the instruction is a difficult skill for many beginning teachers (the tendency among many beginning teachers is to talk too fast and too much), but one that will improve with experience. Until you have developed your skill in pacing lessons you probably will need to constantly remind yourself to slow down during lessons and provide silent pauses (allowing for think-time) and frequent checks for student comprehension. Specifically, your talk should

- Be brisk, though not too fast, with occasional slowdowns to change the pace and to check for student comprehension. Allow students time to think, ask questions, and to make notes.[3]
- Have a time plan. A talk planned for 10 minutes, if it is interesting to students, will probably take longer. If it is not interesting to them, it will probably take less time.
- Always be planned with careful consideration to the characteristics of the students. For example, if you have a fairly high percentage of LEP students or students with special needs, your teacher talk may be less brisk, and sprinkled with even more visuals, repeated statements, and frequent checks for student comprehension.

Fourth, *encourage student participation.* Their active participation enhances their learning. This encouragement can be planned as questions that you ask, as time allowed for students to comment and ask questions, or as some sort of a visual and conceptual outline that students complete during the talk.

Fifth, *plan a clear ending (closure).* Be sure your talk has a clear ending, followed by another activity (during the same or next class period) that will help secure the learning. As for all lessons, strive for planning a clear and mesmerizing beginning, an involving lesson body, and a firm and meaningful closure.

Teacher Talk: Specific Guidelines

Understand the various purposes for using teacher talk. Teacher talk, formal or informal, can be useful to discuss the progress of a unit of study, explain an inquiry, introduce a unit of study, present a problem, promote student inquiry or critical thinking, provide a transition from one unit of study to the next, provide information otherwise unobtainable to students, share the teacher's experiences, share the teacher's thinking, summarize a problem, summarize a unit of study, and teach a thinking skill by modeling that skill.

Clarify the objectives of the talk. Your talk should center around one idea. The learning objectives, which should not be too numerous for one talk, should be clearly understood by the students.

Choose between informal and formal talk. Although an occasional formal "cutting edge" lecture may be appropriate for some middle grades classes, spontaneous interactive informal talks of 5 to 12 minutes are preferred. You should *never* give long lectures with no teacher-student interaction. A formal period-long noninteractive lecture, common in some college teaching, is developmentally inappropriate when teaching most groups of young adolescents. On the other hand, to arouse student interest and to provide new information in relatively small and intellectually digestible chunks, the lecture may be appropriate. If, during your student teaching, you have doubts or questions about your selection and use of a particular instructional strategy, discuss it with your cooperating teacher, your university supervisor, or both. When you have doubts about the appropriateness of a particular strategy, trust your intuition—without some modification, the strategy probably is inappropriate.

Remember also, today's youth are of the "media, or light, generation," and are used to video interactions as well as "commercial breaks." For many lessons, especially those that are teacher-centered, after about 10 minutes student attention is likely to begin to stray. For that eventuality you need elements planned to recapture student attention. These planned elements can include: analogies to help connect the topic to students' experiences; verbal cues, such as voice inflections; pauses to allow information to sink in; humor; visual cues, such as the use of slides, overhead transparencies, charts, board drawings, exerpts from videodisks, real objects (**realia**), or body gestures;

---

[1]D. P. Ausubel, *The Psychology of Meaningful Learning* (New York: Grune & Stratton, 1963).

[2]T. L. Good and J. E. Brophy, *Looking in Classrooms*, 8th ed. (New York: Addison Wesley Longman, 2000), pp. 252–253.

[3]See "Research and Theory on Note Taking," pp. 43–48, in R. J. Marzano, et al., *Classroom Instruction That Works* (Alexandria, VA: Association for Supervision and Curriculum Development, 2001).

and sensory cues, such as eye contact and proximity (as in moving around the room, or casually and gently touching a student on the shoulder without interrupting your talk).

Vary strategies and activities frequently. Perhaps most useful as a strategy for recapturing student attention is to change to an entirely different strategy or learning modality. For ex-ample, from teacher talk (a teacher-centered strategy) you would change to a student activity (a student-centered strategy). Notice that changing from a lecture (mostly teacher talk) to a teacher-led discussion (mostly more teacher talk) would not be changing to an entirely different modality. Figure 9.1 provides a comparison of different changes.

Figure 9.1   Recapturing student attention by changing the instructional strategy.

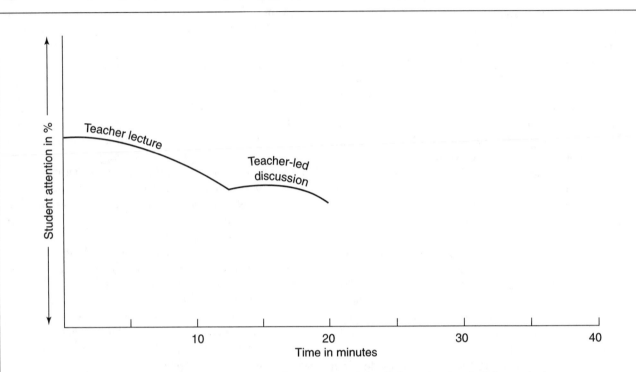

Example 1: Changing from teacher talk (lecture) to more teacher talk (e.g., teacher-led discussion).

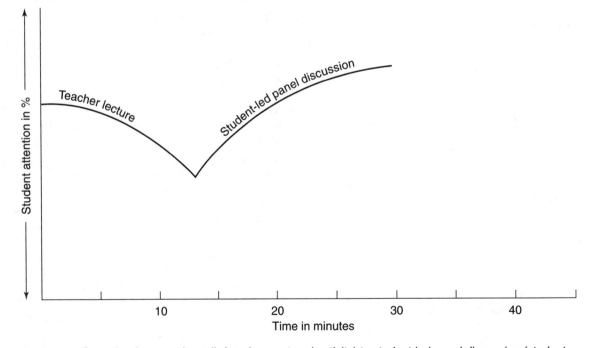

Example 2: Changing from teacher talk (teacher-centered activity) to student-led panel discussion (student-centered activity).

Figure 9.1   (*continued*)

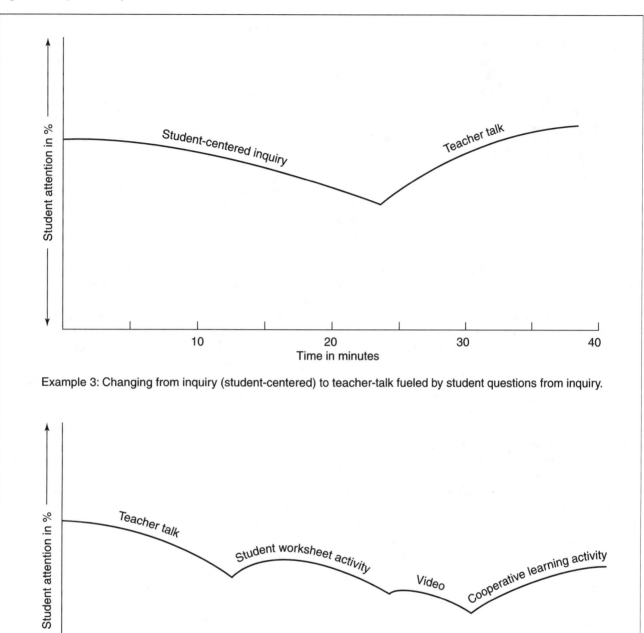

Example 3: Changing from inquiry (student-centered) to teacher-talk fueled by student questions from inquiry.

Example 4: Changing from teacher talk (teacher-centered activity) to cooperative learning activity (student-centered activity).

In general, when using teacher-centered direct instruction, with most classes you will want to change the learning activities about every 10 to 15 minutes. (That is one reason that, in the sample lesson plan format of Chapter 6, you find space for at least four activities, including the introduction and closure.) This means that in a 50- or 60-minute time block (the length of traditional class periods), for example, you should probably plan three or four *sequenced* learning activities, with some that are teacher-centered and many others that are more student-centered. In a 90-minute block, plan five or six learning activities.

In exemplary middle grades classrooms, rather than using teacher-centered direct instruction, teachers often have several activities being performed *concurrently* by individuals, dyads, and small groups of students—that is, the teachers use multitasking or multilevel instruction. Multilevel instruction is particularly important for use during long block periods, called macroperiods (discussed in Chapter 1). Macroperiods provide more time for student inquiry and for interactive and interdisciplinary thematic instruction that might otherwise be difficult or impossible to accomplish in shorter class periods.

Prepare and use notes as a guide for your talk. Planning your talk and preparing notes to be used during formal and informal teacher talk is important—just as important as implementing the talk with visuals. There is absolutely nothing wrong with using notes during your teaching. You can carry them on a clipboard, perhaps a brightly colored one that gives students a visual focus, as you move around the room. Your notes for a formal talk can first be prepared in narrative form; for class use, though, they should be reduced to an outline form. *Talks to students should always be from an outline, never read from prose.* The only time it is appropriate for a teacher to read aloud to students from prose is when reading a brief published article (such as in science or social studies) or portions of a story or a poem (such as in reading/ English/language arts).

In your outline, use color coding with abbreviated visual cues to yourself. You will eventually develop your own coding system—but keep whatever coding system you use simple so that you will not forget what the codes are for. Consider these examples of coding: where transitions of ideas occur and you want to allow silent moments for ideas to sink in, mark *P* for *pause,* *T* for a *transition,* and *S* for moments of *silence;* where a slide or other visual aid will be used, mark *AV* for *audiovisual;* where you intend to stop and ask a question, mark *TQ* for *teacher question,* and mark *SQ* or *?* where you want to stop and allow time for *student questions;* where you plan to have a discussion, mark *D; or* mark *SG* where you plan *small-group work* and *L* where you plan to switch to a *laboratory investigation;* for *reviews* and *comprehension checks,* mark *R* and *CS.*

Share your note organization with your students. Sharing with them how you organize your work is important modeling for them for their organization of their learning. Teach the students how to take notes and what kinds of things they should write down. Use colored chalk or markers to outline and highlight your talk; encourage your students to use colored pencils for notetaking, so their notes can be color-coded to match your writing board notes.

Rehearse your talk. Using your lesson plan as your guide, rehearse your talk using a camcorder or an audiorecorder, or rehearse it while talking into a mirror or to a roommate. You may want to include a time plan for each subtopic to allow you to gauge your timing during implementation of the talk.

Avoid racing through the talk solely to complete it by a certain time. It is more important for students to understand some of what you say than for you to cover it all and have them understand little or none of it. If you do not finish, continue it later.

Augment your talk with multisensory stimulation and allow for think-time. Your presentation should not overly rely on verbal communication. When using visuals, such as video excerpts or overhead transparencies, you do not need to be constantly talking. After clearly explaining the purpose of a visual, give students sufficient time to look at it, to think about it, and to ask questions about it. The visual is new to the students, so give them time to take it in.

Carefully plan the content of your talk. The content of your talk should supplement and enhance that found in the student textbook rather than simply rehash content from the textbook. Students may never read their book if you tell them in an interesting and condensed fashion everything that they need to know from it.

Monitor your delivery. Your voice should be pleasant and interesting to listen to rather than a steady, boring monotone or a constantly shrieking, irritating, high pitch. On the other hand, it is good to show enthusiasm for what you are talking about, for both teaching and learning. Occasionally use dramatic voice inflections to emphasize important points and meaningful body language to give students a visual focus. To not appear phony, practice these skills so they become second nature.

As is always the case when teaching, *avoid standing in the same spot for long periods of time.* (We consider standing for 10 minutes in the same spot to be a long time.) Be mobile! Even during direct instruction, you need to monitor student behavior and to use proximity (moving closer to a student) and signal interference (e.g., eye contact, body language, smile or frown, thumbs up or down) as a means of keeping students focused. It is especially during extended periods of direct instruction that a beginning teacher's skills in withitness and overlapping behaviors are likely to be put to the test (see Chapter 3).

View the vocabulary of the talk as an opportunity to help students with their word morphology. Words you use should be easily understood by the students, though you should still model professionalism and help students develop their vocabulary—both the vocabulary of your special discipline and the more general vocabulary of the English language. During your lesson planning, predict when you are likely to use a word that is new to most students, and plan to stop to ask a student to help explain its meaning and perhaps demonstrate its derivation. Help students with word meaning, which helps them remember. Regardless of subject or grade level, keep in mind that *all teachers are language arts teachers.* Knowledge of word morphology is an important component of skilled reading and includes the ability to generate new words from prefixes, roots, and suffixes. For some students, nearly every subject in the curriculum is like a foreign language. That is certainly true for some LEP students, for whom teacher talk, especially formal teacher talk, should be used sparingly, if at all. Every teacher has the responsibility of helping students learn how to learn, and that includes helping students develop their word comprehension skills, reading skills, thinking and memory skills, and their motivation for learning.

Give thoughtful and intelligent consideration to student diversity. During the preactive phase of planning, while preparing your talk, consider students in your classroom who are culturally and linguistically different and those who have special needs. Personalize the talk for them by choosing your vocabulary carefully and appropriately, speaking slowly and methodically, and repeating often, and by planning meaningful analogies and examples, and relevant audio and visual displays.

Use familiar examples and analogies to help students make relevant connections (bridges). Although this sometimes takes a great deal of creative thinking as well as action during the preactive planning phase, it is important that you attempt to connect the talk with ideas and events with which the students are already familiar. The most effective talk is one that makes frequent and meaningful connections between what students already know and what they are learning, which bridges what they are learning with what they have experienced in their lives. Of course, this means you need to know your students. (See section of Chapter 4 titled, "Get to Know the Students as People to Build Intrinsic Motivation for Learning.")

Establish eye contact frequently. Your primary eye contact should be with your students—always! That important point cannot be overemphasized. Only momentarily should you look at your notes, your visuals, the projection screen, the writing board, and other adults or objects in the classroom. Although you will probably raise your eyebrows in doubt when you read this, it is true and it is important that with practice you can learn to scan a classroom of 30 students, establishing eye contact with each student about once a minute.

To *establish* eye contact means that the student is aware that you are looking at him or her. Frequent eye contact can have two major benefits. First, as you *read* a student's body posture and facial expressions, you obtain clues about that student's attentiveness and comprehension. Second, eye contact helps to establish rapport between you and a student. A look with a smile or a wink from the teacher to a student can say so much! Be alert, though, for students who are from cultures where eye contact is infrequent or unwanted and could have negative consequences. In other words, don't push it!

Frequent eye contact is easier when using an overhead projector than when using the writing board. When using a writing board, you have to turn at least partially away from your audience; you may also have to pace back and forth from the board to the students in order to retain that important proximity to them.

While lecturing on a topic, you must remain aware and attentive to everything that is happening in the classroom (that is, to student behavior as well as to the content of your lecture). No one ever said that good teaching is easy, or if they did, they did not know what they were talking about. But don't dismay; with the knowledge of the preceding guidelines and with practice, experience, and intelligent reflection, in time you will develop the necessary skills.

DEMONSTRATION

Most students like demonstrations because the person doing the demonstration is actively engaged in a learning activity rather than merely verbalizing about it. Demonstrations can be used to teach any subject and for a variety of purposes. The teacher demonstrates role-playing in preparation for a social studies simulation. A teacher demonstrates steps in solving a mathematics problem. A language arts/English teacher demonstrates clustering to students ready for a creative writing assignment. A science teacher demonstrates the effect of combining an acid and a base to form saltwater. The physical education teacher demonstrates the proper way to serve in volleyball.

Purposes of Demonstrations

A demonstration can be designed to serve any of the following purposes: to assist in recognizing a solution to an existing problem; to bring an unusual closure to a lesson or unit of study; to demonstrate a thinking skill; to model a skill used in conflict resolution; to establish problem recognition; to give students an opportunity for vicarious participation in active learning; to illustrate a particular point of content; to introduce a lesson or unit of study in a way that grabs the students' attention; to reduce potential safety hazards (where the teacher demonstrates with materials that are too dangerous for students to handle); to review; to save time and resources (as opposed to the entire class doing what is being demonstrated); and to set up a discrepancy recognition.

Guidelines for Using Demonstrations

When planning a demonstration, you should consider the following guidelines.

Decide the most effective way to conduct the demonstration. It might be a verbal or a silent demonstration, by a student or by the teacher, by the teacher with a student helper, by a student with the teacher as helper, to the entire class or to small groups, or by some combination of these such as first by the teacher followed by a repeat of the demonstration by a student or a succession of students.

Practice with the materials and procedure before demonstrating to the students. During your practice, try to prepare for anything that could go wrong during the real demonstration; if you don't, as "Murphy's Law" states, if anything can go wrong, it probably will. Then, if something does go wrong during the live demonstration, use that as an opportunity for a teachable moment; engage the students in working with you to try to figure out what went wrong, or if that is not feasible, then go to Plan B (see Chapter 10).

Consider your pacing of the demonstration, allowing for enough student wait-see and think time. At the start of the demonstration, explain its purpose and the learning objectives. Remember this adage: tell them what you are going to do, show them, and then help them understand what they saw. As with any lesson, plan your closure and allow time for questions and discussion. During the demonstration, as in other types of teacher talk, use frequent stops to check for student understanding.

Consider using special lighting to highlight the demonstration. For example, a slide projector can be used as a spotlight.

Be sure that the demonstration table and area are free of unnecessary objects that could distract, be in the way, or pose a safety hazard. With potentially hazardous demonstrations, such as might occur in physical education, science, or shop classes, you must *model* proper safety precautions. Wear safety goggles, have fire-safety equipment at hand, and position a protective transparent shield between the demonstration table and nearby students.

TEACHING THINKING FOR INTELLIGENT BEHAVIOR: DEVELOPING A SENSE OF "I CAN" AND THE FEELING OF "I ENJOY"

Pulling together what has been learned about adolescent learning and brain functioning, teachers are encouraged to integrate explicit thinking instruction into daily lessons. In other words, teachers should help students develop their thinking skills. As their thinking skills develop students develop a sense of "I can," with an accompanying feeling of "I enjoy."

In teaching for thinking, we are interested not only in what students know but also in how students behave when they do not know. Gathering evidence of the performance and growth of intelligent behavior requires observing students as they try to solve the day-to-day academic and real-life problems they encounter. By collecting anecdotes and examples of written, oral, and visual expressions, we can see students' increasingly voluntary and spontaneous performance of intelligent behaviors.

Characteristics of Intelligent Behavior

Characteristics of intelligent behavior that you should model, teach for, and observe developing in your students, as identified by Costa,[4] are described in the following paragraphs.

Persistence. Persistence is sticking to a task until it is completed. Consider the following examples.

- *Amelia Earhart.* Born in 1898, Earhart demonstrated from the time that she was a young girl that she was creative, curious, and persistent. Learning to fly in 1920, in just eight more years she became the first woman to fly the Atlantic Ocean, thereby paving the way for other women to become active in aviation.
- *Thomas Edison.* In his effort to develop the electric light bulb, Edison tried more than 3,000 filaments before finding one that worked to his satisfaction.
- *Wilma Rudolf.* As the result of childhood diseases, Wilma Rudolf, at the age of 10, could not walk without the aid of leg braces. Just ten years later, at the age of 20, she was declared to be the fastest running woman in the world, having won three gold medals in the 1960 World Olympics.
- *Babe Ruth.* For years Ruth owned not only the highest number of home runs in professional baseball but also the highest number of strikeouts.

---

[4]A. L. Costa, *The School as a Home for the Mind* (Palatine, IL: Skylight Publishing, 1991), pp. 20–31. See also D. Shein, "Intelligent Behavior, Art Costa, and the Role of the Library Media Specialist," *School Library Media Activities Monthly* 15(5):28–30 (January 1999). Costa has expanded the list to include "thinking and communicating with clarity and precision" and "remaining open to continuous learning." See A. L. Costa and B. Kallick, *Discovering and Exploring Habits of Mind*, Book 1 of *Habits of Mind: A Developmental Series* (Alexandria, VA: Association for Supervision and Curriculum Development, 2000). See also Armstrong's 12 qualities of genius— curiosity, playfulness, imagination, creativity, wonderment, wisdom, inventiveness, vitality, sensitivity, flexibility, humor, and joy—in T. Armstrong, *Awakening Genius in the Classroom* (Alexandria, VA: Association for Supervision and Curriculum Development, 1998), pp. 2–15; and, Project Zero's seven dispositions for good thinking— the disposition (1) to be broad and adventurous; (2) toward wondering, problem finding, and investigating; (3) to build explanations and understandings; (4) to make plans and be strategic; (5) to be intellectually careful; (6) to seek and evaluate reasons; and (7) to be metacognitive—at http://pzweb.harvard.edu/HPZpages/PatThk.html.

Managing impulsivity. When students develop impulse control, they think before acting. Impulsive behavior can worsen conflict and can inhibit effective problem solving.[5] Students can be taught to think before shouting out an answer, before beginning a project or task, and before arriving at conclusions with insufficient data. One of several reasons that teachers should routinely expect a show of student hands before a student is acknowledged to respond or question is to help students develop control over the impulsive behavior of shouting out in class.[6]

Listening with understanding and empathy. Some psychologists believe that the ability to listen to others, to empathize with and to understand their point of view, is one of the highest forms of intelligent behavior. Empathic behavior is considered an important skill for conflict resolution. Piaget refers to this behavior as *overcoming egocentrism.* In class meetings, brainstorming sessions, think tanks, town meetings, advisory councils, board meetings, and legislative bodies, people from various walks of life convene to share their thinking, to explore their ideas, and to broaden their perspectives by listening to the ideas and reactions of others.

Thinking interdependently. Real-world problem solving has become so complex that seldom can any person go it alone. As stated by Elias, "We live in an interdependent world; there is no such thing, in any practical sense, as independence and autonomy. We live lives of synergy and linkage."[7] Not all middle grade students come to school knowing how to work effectively in groups. They may exhibit competitiveness; narrowmindedness; egocentrism; ethnocentrism; or criticism of others' values, emotions, and beliefs. Listening, consensus seeking, giving up an idea to work on someone else's, empathy, compassion, group leadership, cooperative learning, knowing how to support group efforts, and altruism are all behaviors indicative of intelligent human beings, and they can be learned by students at school and in the classroom.

Thinking flexibly. Sometimes referred to as *lateral thinking,* flexibility in thinking is the ability to approach a problem from a new angle, using a novel approach. With modeling by the teacher, students can develop this behavior as they learn to consider alternative points of view and to deal with several sources of information simultaneously.

Metacognition. Learning to plan, monitor, assess, and reflect on one's own thinking is another characteristic of intelligent behavior. Cooperative learning groups, journals, student-led portfolio conferences, self-assessment, thinking aloud in dyads, are strategies that can be used to help students develop this intelligent behavior. Thinking aloud is good modeling for your students, helping them to develop their own cognitive skills of thinking, learning, and reasoning.[8]

Striving for accuracy and communicating with precision. Teachers can observe students growing in this behavior when students take time to check over their work, review the procedures, refuse to draw conclusions with only limited data, and use concise and descriptive language.

Sense of humor. The positive effects of humor on the body's physiological functions are well established: a drop in the pulse rate, an increase of oxygen in the blood, the activation of antibodies that fight against harmful microorganisms, and the release of gamma interferon, a hormone that fights viruses and regulates cell growth. Humor liberates creativity and provides high-level thinking skills, such as anticipation, finding novel relationships, and visual imagery. The acquisition of a sense of humor follows a developmental sequence similar to that described by Piaget[9] and Kohlberg.[10] Initially, young children and immature youth may find humor in all the wrong things—human frailty, ethnic humor, sacrilegious riddles, ribald profanities. Later, creative young people thrive on finding incongruity and will demonstrate a whimsical frame of mind during problem solving.

Questioning and problem posing. Young adolescents are usually full of questions, and, unless discouraged, they do ask them. As educators, we want students to be alert to, and recognize, discrepancies and phenomena in their environment and to freely inquire about their causes. In exemplary middle level programs, students are encouraged to ask questions (see Chapter 7) and, from those questions, to develop a problem-solving strategy to investigate their questions.

Drawing on knowledge and applying it to new situations. A major goal of formal education is for students to apply school-learned knowledge to real-life situations. To develop skills in drawing on past knowledge and applying that knowledge to new situations, students must be given the opportunity to practice doing that very thing. Problem recognition, problem solving, and project-based

---

[5]See, for example, M. Goos and P. Galbraith, "Do It This Way! Metacognitive Strategies in Collaborative Mathematics Problem Solving," *Educational Studies in Mathematics* 30(3):229–260 (April 1996).

[6]For further reading about the relation of impulse control to intelligence, see D. Goleman, *Emotional Intelligence: Why It Can Matter More Than IQ* (New York: Bantam Books, 1995); R. Brandt, "On Teaching Brains to Think: A Conversation with Robert Sylwester," *Educational Leadership* 57(7):72–75 (April 2000), p. 73; and D. Harrington-Lueker, "Emotional Intelligence," *High Strides* 9(4):1, 4–5 (March/April 1997).

[7]M. J. Elias, "Easing Transitions With Social-Emotional Learning," *Principal Leadership* 1(7) [Online 4/1/01, http://www.nassp.org/news/pl_soc_emo_lrng_301.htm, on page 2 of 4].

[8]See, for example, J. W. Astington, "Theory of Mind Goes to School," *Educational Leadership* 56(3):46–48 (November 1998).

[9]J. Piaget, *The Psychology of Intelligence* (Totowa, NJ: Littlefield Adams, 1972).

[10]I. Kohlberg, *The Meaning and Measurement of Moral Development* (Worcester, MA: Clark University Press, 1981).

learning are significantly important ways of providing that opportunity to young adolescents.

Taking risks: venturing forth and explore ideas beyond the usual zone of comfort. Such exploration, of course, must be done with thoughtfulness; it must not be done in ways that could put the student at risk psychologically or physically. Using the analogy of a turtle going nowhere until it sticks its neck out, middle level teachers should model this behavior. They should provide opportunities for students to develop this intelligent behavior by using techniques such as brainstorming strategies, divergent-thinking questioning, think-pair-share, cooperative learning, inquiry, and project-based learning.

Using all the senses. As discussed in previous chapters, especially Chapter 6, as often as is appropriate and feasible, students should be encouraged to use and develop all their sensory input channels to learn (i.e., verbal, visual, tactile, and kinesthetic).

Ingenuity, originality, insightfulness = Creativity. All students must be encouraged to do, and discouraged from saying "I can't." Students must be taught in such a way as to encourage intrinsic motivation rather than reliance on extrinsic sources. Teachers must be able to offer criticism so that the student understands the criticism is not a criticism of self. In exemplary educational programs, students learn the value of feedback. They learn the value of their own intuition, of guessing—they learn "I can."

Wonderment, inquisitiveness, curiosity, and the enjoyment of problem solving-A sense of efficacy as a thinker. Young children express wonderment, an expression that should never be stifled. Through effective teaching, young adolescents can recapture that sense of wonderment as they are guided by an effective teacher into a sense of "I can," and express a feeling of "I enjoy."

We should strive to help our own students develop these characteristics of intelligent behavior. In Chapter 3 you learned of specific teacher behaviors that facilitate this development. Now, let's review additional research findings that offer important considerations in the facilitation of student learning and intelligent behaving.

Direct Teaching for Thinking and Intelligent Behavior

The curriculum of any school includes the development of skills that are used in thinking—skills such as *classifying, comparing* and *contrasting, concluding, generalizing, inferring,* and others. Because the academic achievement of students increases when they are taught thinking skills directly, many researchers and educators concur that direct instruction should be given to all students on how to think and behave intelligently.[11] Several research perspectives have influenced today's interest in the direct teaching of thinking. The *cognitive view of intelligence* asserts that intellectual ability is not fixed but can be developed. The *constructivist approach to learning* maintains that learners actively and independently construct knowledge by creating and coordinating relationships in their mental repertoire. The *social psychology view of classroom experience* focuses on the learner as an individual who is a member of various peer groups and a society. The *perspective of information processing* deals with the acquisition, elaboration, and management of information.[12]

Rather than assuming that young adolescent students have developed thinking skills, teachers should devote classroom time to teaching them directly. When teaching a thinking skill directly, the subject content becomes the vehicle for thinking. For example, a social studies lesson can teach students how to distinguish between fact and opinion; a language arts lesson instructs students how to compare and analyze; and a science lesson can teach students how to set up a problem for their inquiry. Inquiry teaching and discovery learning are both useful tools for learning and for teaching thinking skills.[13]

INQUIRY TEACHING AND DISCOVERY LEARNING

Intrinsic to the effectiveness of both **inquiry** and **discovery** is the assumption that students would rather actively seek knowledge than receive it through traditional expository (i.e., information delivery) methods such as lectures, demonstrations, and textbook reading. Although inquiry and discovery are important teaching tools, there is sometimes confusion about exactly what inquiry teaching is and how it differs from discovery learning. The distinction should become clear as you study the following descriptions of these two important tools for teaching and learning.

Problem Solving

Perhaps a major reason why inquiry and discovery are sometimes confused is that, in both, students are actively engaged in problem solving. **Problem solving** is the ability to recognize, identify, define, or describe a problem; determine the preferred resolution; identify potential

---

[11]See, for example, A. Whimbey, "Test Results From Teaching Thinking," in A. L. Costa (Ed.). *Developing Minds: A Resource Book for Teaching Thinking* (Alexandria, VA: Association for Supervision and Curriculum Development, 1985), pp. 269–271.

[12]B. Z. Presseisen, *Implementing Thinking in the School's Curriculum,* unpublished paper presented at the third Annual Meeting of the International Association for Cognitive Education, Riverside, CA, on February 9, 1992.

[13]For products for teaching thinking, contact Critical Thinking Books & Software, PO Box 448, Pacific Grove, CA 93950. http://www.criticalthinking.com

solutions; select strategies; test solutions; evaluate outcomes; and revise any of these steps as necessary.

Inquiry Versus Discovery

Problem solving is *not* a teaching strategy but a high-order intellectual behavior that facilitates learning. What a teacher can and should do is provide opportunities for students to identify and tentatively solve problems. With the processes involved in inquiry and discovery, teachers can help students develop the skills necessary for effective problem solving. Two major differences between discovery and inquiry are (a) who identifies the problem and (b) the percentage of decisions that are made by the students. Table 9.1 shows three levels of inquiry, each level defined according to what the student does and decides.[14]

[14]The levels of inquiry are adapted from "the three different levels of openness and permissiveness . . . for laboratory enquiry" by Joseph J. Schwab, *The Teaching of Science as Enquiry* (Cambridge, MA: Harvard University Press, 1962), p. 55.

It should be evident from Table 9.1 that *Level I inquiry* is actually traditional, didactic, "cookbook" teaching, where both the problem and the process for resolving it are identified and defined for the student. The student then works through the process to its inevitable resolution. If the process is well designed, the result is inevitable—the student "discovers" what was intended by the writers of the program. This level is also called *guided inquiry* or *discovery,* because the students are carefully guided through the investigation to (the predicable) "discovery."

Level I is, in reality, a strategy within the *delivery mode,* the advantages of which were described in Chapter 6. Because Level I inquiry is highly manageable and the learning outcome is predictable, it is probably best for teaching basic concepts and principles. However, students who never experience learning beyond Level I are missing an opportunity to engage their highest mental operations, and they seldom (or never) get to experience more motivating, real-life problem solving. Furthermore, those students may come away with the false notion that problem solving is a linear process, which it is not. As illustrated in Figure 9.2, true inquiry

Table 9.1 Levels of Inquiry

	Level I	*Level II*	*Level III*
Problem Identification	By teacher or textbook	By teacher or textbook	By student
Process of Solving the Problem	Decided by teacher or text	Decided by student	Decided by student
Identification of Tentative Solution	Resolved by student	Resolved by student	Resolved by student

Figure 9.2 The inquiry cycle.

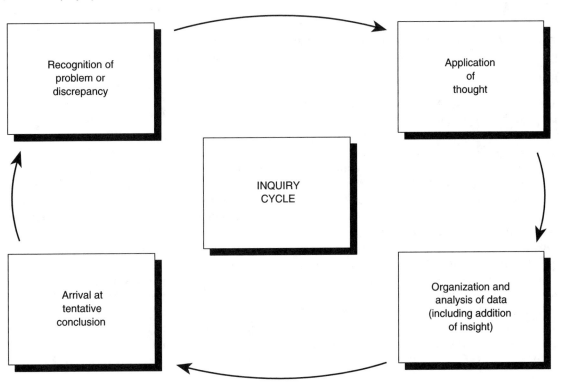

REAL-LIFE SCENARIO

Problem Solving and Decision Making in the Real World Is an Integrated and Interdisciplinary Inquiry Activity

During any given day or specified time period, teacher and students can look at a problem or subject of study from the point of view of many separate disciplines. Such an interdisciplinary approach has been adopted not only by educators but by other professionals as well. It is the mode of meaningful learning and real-life problem solving.

For example, consider the fact-finding and decision-making approach of public officials in Colorado when confronted with making decisions about projects proposed for watersheds in their state. While gathering information, the officials brought in Dave Rosgen, a state hydrologist. Rosgen led the officials into the field to demonstrate specific ways by which he helped control erosion and rehabilitate damaged streams. He took the officials to Wolf Creek, where they donned high waders. Rosgen led the group down the creek to examine various features of that complex natural stream. He pointed out evidence of the creek's past meanders—patterns that he had incorporated into his rehabilitation projects. In addition to listening to this scientist's point of view, the public officials listened to other experts to consider related economic and political issues; for example, before making final decisions about projects that had been proposed for watersheds in that state.

During interdisciplinary thematic units, students study a topic and its underlying ideas as well as related knowledge from various disciplines on an ongoing basis. The teacher, sometimes with the help of students and other teachers and adults, introduces experiences designed according to ideas and skills from various disciplines—just as Rosgen introduced information from hydrology—to develop literacy skills through the unit. For instance, the teacher might stimulate communication skills through creative writing and other projects. Throughout the unit, the students are guided in exploring ideas related to different disciplines, to integrate their knowledge.

---

is cyclical rather than linear. For that reason, Level I is *not* true inquiry, because it is linear. Real-world problem solving is cyclical rather than linear. One enters the cycle whenever a discrepancy or problem is observed and recognized, and that can occur at any point in the cycle.

True Inquiry

By the time students are in the middle grades, they should be provided experiences for true inquiry, which begins with *Level II*, where students actually decide and design processes for their inquiry. In true inquiry, there is an emphasis on the tentative nature of conclusions, which makes the activity more like real-life problem solving, where decisions are always subject to revision if and when new data so prescribes.

At *Level III* inquiry, students recognize and identify the problem; decide the processes, and reach a conclusion. In *project-centered teaching*, as has been discussed and described throughout this resource guide, especially in Chapter 8, students are usually engaged at this level of inquiry. By the time students are in middle grades, Level III inquiry should be a major strategy for instruction, which is often the case in schools that use cross-age teaching and interdisciplinary thematic instruction. But, it is not

easy; like most good teaching practices, it is a lot of work, but the intrinsic rewards make the effort worthwhile. As exclaimed by one middle school teacher using interdisciplinary thematic instruction with student-centered inquiry, "I've never worked harder in my life, but I've never had this much fun, either."

The Critical Thinking Skills of Discovery and Inquiry

In true inquiry, students generate ideas and then design ways to test those ideas. The various processes used represent the many critical thinking skills. Some of those skills are concerned with generating and organizing data; others are concerned with building and using ideas. Figure 9.3 provides four main categories of these thinking processes and illustrates the place of each within the inquiry cycle.

Some processes in the cycle are discovery processes; others are inquiry processes that include the more complex mental operations (including all of those in the idea-using category). Project-centered teaching provides an avenue for doing that, as does problem-centered teaching.

Inquiry is a higher-level mental operation that introduces the concept of the discrepant event, some-

Figure 9.3 Inquiry cycle processes.

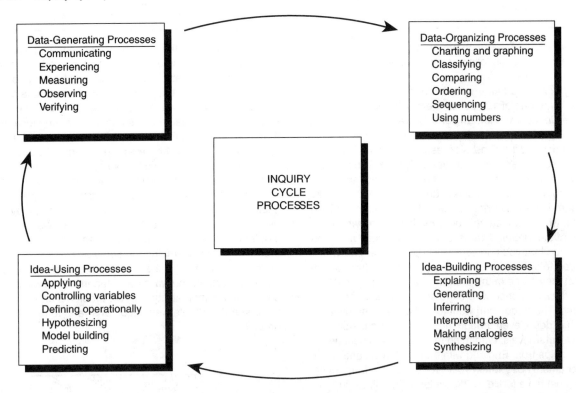

thing that establishes cognitive disequilibrium (using the element of surprise to challenge their prior notions) to help students develop skills in observing and being alert for discrepancies. Such a strategy provides opportunities for students to investigate their own ideas about explanations. Inquiry, like discovery, depends upon skill in problem solving; the difference between the two is in the amount of decision-making responsibility that is given to students. Experiences afforded by inquiry help students understand the importance of suspending judgment, and the tentativeness of answers and solutions. With those understandings, students eventually are better able to deal with life's ambiguities. When students are not provided these important educational experiences, their education is incomplete.

One of the most effective ways of stimulating inquiry is to use materials that provoke students' interest. These materials should be presented in a nonthreatening, noncompetitive context, so students think and hypothesize freely. The teacher's role is to encourage students to form as many hypotheses as possible and then to support their hypotheses with reasons. After the students suggest several ideas, the teacher should begin to move on to higher-order, more abstract questions that involve the development of generalizations and evaluations. True inquiry problems have a special advantage in that they can be used with almost any group of students. Members of a group approach the problem as an adventure in thinking and apply it to whatever

background they can muster. Background experience may enrich a student's approach to the problem, but is not crucial to the use or understanding of the evidence presented to him or her. Locating a colony, Figure 9.4, is a Level II inquiry. As a class, do the inquiry now.

INTEGRATING STRATEGIES FOR INTEGRATED LEARNING

In today's exemplary middle level classrooms, instructional strategies are combined to establish the most effective teaching-learning experience. For example, in an integrated language arts program, teachers are interested in their students' speaking, reading, listening, thinking, study, and writing skills. These skills (and not textbooks) form a holistic process that is the primary aspect of integrated language arts.

In the area of speaking skills, oral discourse (discussion) in the classroom has a growing research base that promotes methods of teaching and learning through oral language. These methods include cooperative learning, instructional scaffolding, and inquiry teaching.

In cooperative learning groups, students discuss and use language for learning that benefits both their content learning and skills in social interaction. Working in heterogeneous groups, students participate in their own learning and can extend their knowledge base and cultural awareness with students of different backgrounds. When students share information and ideas, they are

Figure 9.4 Locating a colony: A Level II inquiry. (*Source:* Adapted by permission from unpublished material provided by Jennifer Devine and Dennis Devine.)

Presentation of the Problem. In groups of three or four, students receive the following information.

Background. You (your group is considered as one person) are one of 120 passengers on the ship, the *Prince Charles.* You left England 12 weeks ago. You have experienced many hardships, including a stormy passage, limited rations, sickness, cold and damp weather, and hot, foul air below deck. Ten of your fellow immigrants to the New World, including three children, have died and been buried at sea. You are now anchored at an uncertain place, off the coast of the New World, which your captain believes to be somewhere north of the Virginia Grants. Seas are so rough and food so scarce that you and your fellow passengers have decided to settle here. A landing party has returned with a map they made of the area. You, as one of the elders, must decide at once where the settlement is to be located. The tradesmen want to settle along the river, which is deep, even though this seems to be the season of low water levels. Within ten months they expect deep-water ships from England with more colonists and merchants. Those within your group who are farmers say they must have fertile, workable land. The officer in charge of the landing party reported seeing a group of armed natives who fled when approached. He feels the settlement must be located so that it can be defended from the natives and from the sea.

Directions, step one: You (your group) are to select a site on the attached map that you feel is best suited for a colony. Your site must satisfy the different factions aboard the ship. A number of possible sites are already marked on the map (letters *A–G*). You may select one of these locations or use them as reference points to show the location of your colony. When your group has selected its site, list and explain the reasons for your choice. When each group has arrived at its tentative decision, these will be shared with the whole class.

Directions, step two: After each group has made its presentation and argument, a class debate is held about where the colony should be located.

Notes to teacher: For the debate, have a large map drawn on the writing board or on an overhead transparency, where each group's mark can be made for all to see and discuss. After each group has presented its argument for its location and against the others, we suggest that you then mark on the large map the two,

three, or more hypothetical locations (assuming that, as a class, there is no single favorite location yet). Then take a straw vote of the students, allowing each to vote on her or his own independently, rather than as members of groups. At this time you can terminate the activity by saying that if the majority of students favor one location, then that, in fact, is the solution to the problem—that is, the colony is located wherever the majority of class members believe it should be. No sooner will that statement be made by you than someone will ask, "Are we correct?" or "What is the right answer?" They will ask such questions because, as students in school, they are used to solving problems that have right answers (Level I inquiry teaching). In real-world problems, however, there are no "right" answers, though some answers may seem better than others. It is the process of problem solving that is important. You want your students to develop confidence in their ability to solve problems and understand the tentativeness of "answers" to real-life problems.

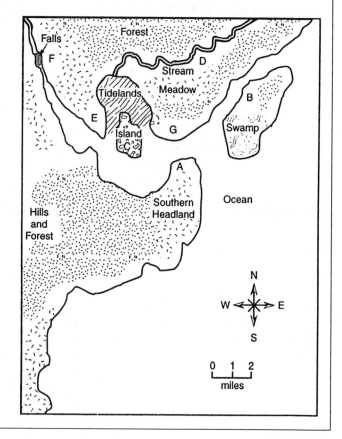

completing difficult learning tasks, using divergent thinking and decision making, and developing their understanding of concepts. As issues are presented and responses are challenged, student thinking is clarified. Students assume the responsibility for planning within the group and for carrying out their assignments. When needed, the teacher models an activity with one group in front of the class that, when integrated with student questions, can become inquiry teaching. Activities can include a variety of heuristics (a heuristic is a tool used in solving a problem or understanding an idea), such as the following:

Brainstorming. Members generate ideas related to a key word and record them. Clustering or chunking, mapping, and the Venn diagram (discussed later) are variations of brainstorming.

Think-pair-share. The teacher presents a concept, and students are paired to discuss the concept. They share what they already know or have experienced about that concept, and then share that information with the rest of the class. This strategy is an excellent technique for preassessing and discovering students' prior notions.

Chunking or clustering. Groups of students apply mental organizers by clustering information into chunks for easier manipulation and remembering.

Memory strategies. The teacher and students model the use of acronyms, mnemonics, rhymes, or clustering of information into categories to promote learning. Sometimes one must learn by rote information that is not connected to any prior knowledge, such as in memorizing a social security number. To do that, it is helpful to break the information to be learned into smaller chunks, such as dividing the nine digit social security number into smaller chunks of information (with, in this instance, each chunk separated by a hyphen). Learning by rote is also easier if one can connect what is being memorized to some prior knowledge. Strategies such as these are used to bridge the gap between rote learning and meaningful learning, and are known as *mnemonics.*[15] Sample mnemonics are:

- The notes on a treble staff are *FACE* for the space notes and *Empty Garbage Before Dad Flips* (*EGBDF*) for the line notes. The notes on the bass staff are *All Cows Eat Granola Bars* or *Grizzly Bears Don't Fly Airplanes* (*GBDFA*).
- The order of the planets from the Sun are *My Very Educated Mother Just Served Us Nine Pizzas* (*M*ercury, *V*enus, *E*arth, *M*ars, *J*upiter, *S*aturn, *U*ranus, *N*eptune, and *P*luto—although, in reality, Pluto and Neptune alternate in this order because of their elliptical orbits).

- The names of the Great Lakes: *HOMES* for *H*uron, *O*ntario, *M*ichigan, *E*rie, and *S*uperior.
- Visual mnemonics are useful too, such as remembering that Italy is shaped in the form of a boot.

Comparing and contrasting. Similarities and differences between items are found and recorded.

Visual tools. There are a variety of terms for the visual tools useful for learning (some of which are synonymous), such as brainstorming web, mindmapping web, spider map, cluster, thinking process map, semantic map, Venn diagram, visual scaffold, and graphic organizer. Visual tools are separated into three categories, according to purpose: (a) *brainstorming tools* (such as mind mapping, webbing, and clustering) for developing one's knowledge and creativity; (b) *task-specific organizers* (such as life cycle diagrams used in biology, decision trees used in mathematics, and text structures in reading); and (c) *thinking process maps* for encouraging cognitive development across disciplines.[16] It is the latter that we are interested in here.

Based on Ausubel's theory of meaningful learning,[17] thinking process mapping has been found useful in helping students change prior misconceptions, sometimes referred to as *naïve views*. It can help students organize and represent their thoughts, and connect new knowledge to their past experiences and precepts.[18] Simply put, concepts can be thought of as classifications that attempt to organize the world of objects and events into a smaller number of categories. In everyday usage, the term *concept* means idea, as when someone says, "My concept of love is not the same as yours." Concepts embody a meaning that develops in complexity with experience and learning over time. For example, the concept of love that is held by a second-grader is unlikely to be as complex as that held by an eleventh-grader. Thinking process mapping is a graphical way of demonstrating the relationship among concepts.

Typically, a thinking process map refers to a visual or graphic representation of concepts with bridges (connections) that show relationships. Figure 9.5 shows a partially complete thinking process map in social studies, where students have made connections of concept relationships related to fruit farming and marketing. The general procedure for thinking process mapping is to have the students (1) identify important concepts in

---

[15]See, for example, M. A. Mastropieri, et al., "Using Mnemonic Strategies to Teach Information about U.S. Presidents: A Classroom-Based Investigation," *Learning Disability Quarterly* 20(1):13–21 (Winter 1997), and J. G. van Hell and A. C. Mahn, "Keyword Mnemonics versus Rote Rehearsal: Learning Concrete and Abstract Foreign Words by Experienced and Inexperienced Learners," *Language Learning* 47(3):507–546 (September 1997).

[16]D. Hyerle, *Visual Tools for Constructing Knowledge* (Alexandria, VA: Association for Supervision and Curriculum Development, 1996).

[17]D. P. Ausubel, *The Psychology of Meaningful Learning* (New York: Grune & Stratton, 1963).

[18]About thinking process mapping, see J. D. Novak, "Concept Maps and Venn Diagrams: Two Metacognitive Tools to Facilitate Meaningful Learning," *Instructional Science* 19(1):29–52 (1990); J. D. Novak and B. D. Gowin, *Learning How to Learn* (Cambridge, England: Cambridge University Press, 1984); and E. Plotnick, *Concept Mapping: A Graphical System for Understanding the Relationship Between Concepts.* (ED407938, 1997.)

Figure 9.5 Partially completed thinking process map.

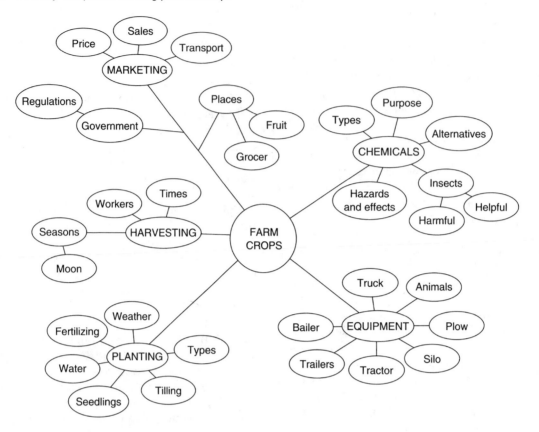

the materials being studied, often by circling those concepts; (2) rank order the concepts from the most general to the most specific; and (3) arrange the concepts on a sheet of paper, connect related ideas with lines, and define the connections between the related ideas.

Inferring. For instance, students assume the roles of people (real or fictional) and infer their motives, personalities, and thoughts.

Outlining. Each group completes an outline that contains some of the main ideas but with subtopics omitted.

Paraphrasing. In a brief summary, each student restates a short selection of what was read or heard.

Reciprocal teaching. In classroom dialogue, students take turns summarizing, questioning, clarifying, and predicting.[19]

Study strategies. Important strategies that should be taught explicitly include vocabulary expansion; reading

and interpreting graphic information; locating resources; using advance organizers; adjusting one's reading rate; and skimming, scanning, and study reading.[20]

Textbook study strategies. Students use the *SQ4R* or related study strategies (see Figure 5.3 in Chapter 5).

Vee mapping. A kind of V-shaped road map is completed by students, as they learn, showing the route they follow from prior knowledge to new and future knowledge.

prognostication about what may be known in the future

listing of what is known today

what we knew when we began our quest

Venn diagramming. This is a technique for comparing two concepts or, for example, two stories, to show similarities and differences. Using stories as an example, a student is asked to draw two circles that intersect and to mark the circles one and two and the area where they intersect three. In circle one, the student lists characteristics of one story, and in circle two she or he lists the characteristics of the second story. In the area of the in-

[19]See A. S. Palincsar and A. L. Brown, "Reciprocal Teaching: Activities to Promote Reading with Your Mind," in T. L. Harris and E. J. Cooper (Eds.), *Reading, Thinking and Concept Development: Strategies for the Classroom,* (New York: The College Board, 1985); C. J. Carter, "Why Reciprocal Teaching?" *Educational Leadership* 54(6):64–68 (March 1997); and R. J. Marzano; D. J. Pickering; and J. E. Pollock, *Classroom Instruction That Works* (Alexandria, VA: Association for Supervision and Curriculum Development, 2001).

[20]J. S. Choate and T. A. Rakes, *Inclusive Instruction for Struggling Readers,* Fastback 434 (Bloomington, IN: Phi Delta Kappa Educational Foundation, 1998).

CLASSROOM SCENARIO

Science Students Write and Stage a One-Act Play

Early in the year, in preparation for a unit on the study of oxygen and other gases, Robert told the 28 students in his seventh-grade physical science class that, if they were interested, he would like for them to plan, write, and stage a one-act play about the life of Joseph Priestley, the theologian and scientist who in 1774 discovered what he called "dephlogisticated air," later named *oxygen* by Lavoisier. Furthermore the students would be given one week to plan. The play would be presented and videotaped in class. The students accepted Robert's idea with enthusiasm and immediately went about the task of organizing and putting their ideas into motion. They took on the challenging task with such vigor and seriousness that they asked Robert for an additional three days to prepare. Sean, a bright student who was really more interested in theatre than science, was selected by the students to play the role of Priestley and to be the producer. Other students played lesser roles. Students with special interest in writing wrote the play. Those with interest in art and stagecraft assumed the task of designing and preparing the set, while another assumed the role of sound stage manager. The resulting 60-minute presentation was more successful than Robert, and perhaps the students, could ever have anticipated. By request of the school principal, the students put on the play two more times, once for the entire student body, and a second time for the school's parent-teacher-student organization. Both performances resulted in standing ovations. During the performance before the PTO, the student production was simultaneously recorded by the local cable television network and later played several times over the community cable channel. Robert later said that during this experience the students learned far more content than they ever would have via his traditional approach to the topic. In addition, these students were highly motivated in learning science for the entire rest of the year. Several years later, Sean graduated with honors from the University of California with a degree major in theatre and a minor in chemistry.

---

tersection, marked three, the student lists characteristics common to both stories.

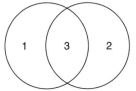

Visual learning log (VLL). This is another kind of road map completed by students showing the route they follow from prior knowledge to new and future knowledge. However, the VLL consists of pictograms (free-form drawings) that each student makes and that are maintained in a journal.

LEARNING BY EDUCATIONAL GAMES

Devices classified as educational games include a wide variety of learning activities, such as simulations, role-play and sociodrama activities, mind games, board games, computer games, and sporting games, all of which provide valuable learning experiences for participants. That is, they are experiences that tend to involve several senses and several learning modalities, tend to engage higher-order thinking skills, and tend to be quite effective as learning tools.

Of all the arts, drama involves the learner-participant most fully—intellectually, emotionally, physically, verbally, and socially. Interactive drama, or role-playing, is a simplified form of drama through which students can become involved with literature. Studies show that students' comprehension increases, and they are highly motivated to read if they are involved in analyzing and actively responding to the characters, plot, and setting of the story being read.[21]

Simulations, a more complex form of drama, serve many of the developmental needs of young adolescents. They provide for interaction with peers and allow students with differences to work together on a common project. They engage students in physical activity and provide an opportunity to try out different roles, which helps them to better understand themselves. Role-play

---

[21]R. Coney and S. Kanel, "Opening the World of Literature to Children through Interactive Drama Experiences." Paper presented at the Annual International Conference and Exhibition of the Association for Childhood Education (Portland, OR, April 9–12, 1997).

Table 9.2 Classification of Educational Games

Type	Characteristics	Examples
1. Pure game*	Fun	*Ungame, New Games*
2. Pure contest	Stimulates competition; built-in inefficiency[†]	Political contests, e.g., U.S. presidential race
3. Pure simulation*	Models reality	Toddler play
4. Contest/game	Stimulates competition; fun; built-in inefficiency	Golf; bowling; *Trivial Pursuit*
5. Simulation/game*	Models reality; fun	*SIMCITY; Our Town's Planning Commission Meeting* [§]
6. Contest/simulation	Stimulates competition; models reality; built-in inefficiency	Boxcar Derby of Akron, OH
7. Simulation/game/contest	Models reality; fun; stimulates competition; built-in inefficiency	*Careers, Life, Monopoly*

*These game types do not emphasize competition and, therefore, are particularly recommended for use in the classroom as learning tools.

[†]This means that rules for accomplishing the game objective make accomplishment of that objective less than efficient. For example, in golf the objective is to get the ball into the hole with the least amount of effort; but to do that, one has to take a peculiarly shaped stick (the club) and hit the ball, find it, and hit it again, continuing that sequence until the ball is in the hole. Yet, common sense tells us that the best way to get the ball into the hole with the least amount of effort would be to simply pick up the ball and place it by hand into the hole.

[§] See J. V. Vort, "Our Town's Planning Commission Meeting," *Journal of Geography* 96(4):183–190 (July–August 1997).

simulations can provide concrete experiences that help students understand complex concepts and issues, and they provide opportunities to explore values and develop skill in decision making.

Educational games can play an integral role in interdisciplinary teaching and serve as valuable resources for enriching the effectiveness of students' learning. As with any other instructional strategy, the use of games should follow a clear educational purpose, have a careful plan, and be congruent with the instructional objectives.

Classification of Educational Games

What are educational games? Seven types of games fall under the general heading of "educational games." Table 9.2 shows the seven types, with characteristics and examples of each. Certain types have greater educational value than others. Games that do not emphasize the element of competition—that are not "contests"—are particularly recommended for use in the academic classroom. This includes types 1, 3, and 5 in Table 9.2.

Purposes of Educational Games

Games can be powerful tools for teaching and learning. A game can have from one to several of the following purposes: (a) add variety and change of pace, (b) assess student learning, (c) enhance student self-esteem, (d) motivate students, (e) offer a break from the usual rigors of learning, (f) provide learning about real-life issues through simulation and role-playing, (g) provide learning through tactile and kinesthetic modalities, (h) provide problem-solving situations and experiences, (i) provide skill development and motivation through computer usage, (j) provide skill development in inductive thinking, (k) provide skill development in verbal communication and debate, (l) reinforce convergent thinking, (m) review and reinforce subject matter learning, (n) encourage learning through peer interaction, (o) stimulate critical thinking, (p) stimulate deductive thinking, (q) stimulate divergent and creative thinking, and (r) teach both content and process.

Sources of Educational Games

Sources for useful educational games include professional journals (see Figure 9.6) and the Internet. Sources of commercially available educational games for use in teaching are shown in Figure 9.7. Now do Exercise 9.1.

Figure 9.6   Professional journals with educational games.

- J. Bassett, "The Pullman Strike of 1894," *OAH Magazine of History* 11(2):34–41 (Winter 1997). Role-play simulation.
- D. Bogan and D. Wood, "Simulating Sun, Moon, and Earth Patterns," Science Scope 21(2):46, 48 (October 1997). Role-play simulation.
- C. Collyer, "Winter Secrets: An Instant Lesson Plan," *Pathways: The Ontario Journal of Outdoor Education* 9(2):18–20 (April 1997). Instructions for two games about predator-prey relationships.
- S. A. Farin, "Acting Atoms," *Science Scope* 21(3):46 (November/December 1997). Role play.
- J. Gorman, "Strategy Games: Treasures from Ancient Times," *Mathematics Teaching in the Middle School* 3(2):110–116 (October 1997). Games for integrating history and mathematics.
- S. Hightshoe, "Sifting Through the Sands of Time: A Simulated Archaeological Special Feature," *Social Studies and the Young Learner* 9(3):28–30 (January/February, 1997).
- M. J. Howle, "Play-Party Games in the Modern Classroom," *Music Educators Journal* 83(5):24–28 (March 1997). Introduces games that were popular on the nineteenth-century American frontier.
- T. Levy, "The Amistad Incident: A Classroom Reenactment," *Social Education* 59(5):303–308 (September 1995).
- T. M. McCann, "A Pioneer Simulation for Writing and for the Study of Literature," *English Journal* 85(3):62–67 (March 1996).
- H. Morris, "Universal Games from A to Z," *Mathematics Teaching in the Middle School* 5(5):300–305 (January 2000).
- K. D. Owens, et al., "Playing to Learn: Science Games in the Classroom," *Science Scope* 20(5):31–33 (February 1997).
- K. D. Owens and R. L. Sanders, "Travel the World—An Addition Game," *Mathematics Teaching in the Middle School* 5(6):392–396 (February 2000).

Figure 9.7   Sources of educational games.

- Ampersand Press, 750 Lake St., Port Townsend, WA 98368. 800-624-4263; http://www.ampersandpress.com
- Aristoplay, 450 S. Wagner Rd., Ann Arbor, MI 48103. 800-GR8-GAME; http://www.aristoplay.com
- Creative Teaching Associates, P.O. Box 7766, Fresno, CA 93747. 800-767-4282; http://www.mastercta.com
- Dawn Publications, 14618 Tyler-Foote Rd., Nevada City, CA 95959. 800-545-7475; http://www.dawnpub.com
- Harcourt Brace School Publishers, 6277 Sea Harbor Dr., Orlando, FL 32887. 800-346-8648; http://www.harcourt.com
- Higher-Order Thinking Company, 1733 N. E. Patterson Dr., Lee's Summit, MO 64086. 816-524-2701
- Latz Chance Games, P.O. Box 72308, Marietta, GA 30007-2308. 888-LCH-GAME
- Novostar Designs, 317 S. Main St., P.O. Box 1328, Burlington, NC 27216-1328. 800-659-3197
- Optical Data School Media, 512 Means St., NW, Atlanta, GA 30318. 800-524-2481; http://www.opticaldata.com
- Other Worlds Educational Enterprises, P.O. Box 6193, Woodland Park, CO 80866-6193. 719-687-3840; http://www.otherworlds-edu.com
- Summit Learning, P.O. Box 493, Fort Collins, CO 80522. 800-777-8817; http://www.summitlearning.com
- Teacher Created Materials, 6421 Industry Way, Westminster, CA 92683. 800-662-4321; http://www.teachercreatedmaterials.com

FOR YOUR NOTES

EXERCISE 9.1: DEVELOPING A LESSON USING INQUIRY LEVEL II, THINKING SKILL DEVELOPMENT, A DEMONSTRATION, OR AN INTERACTIVE LECTURE—MICRO PEER TEACHING II

INSTRUCTIONS: The purpose of this exercise is to provide an opportunity for you to create a brief lesson (about 20 minutes of instructional time, but to be specified by your instructor) designed for a specific grade level and subject and to try it out on your peers for their feedback in an informal (i.e., nongraded) micro peer teaching demonstration.

Divide your class into four groups. The task of the members of each group is to prepare lessons (individually) that fall into one of the four categories: Level II inquiry, thinking level, demonstration, interactive lecture. Schedule class presentations so that each class member has an opportunity to present his or her lesson and to obtain feedback from class members about it. For feedback, class members who are the "teacher's" audience can complete the assessment rubric shown after this exercise (by circling one of the three choices for each of the 10 categories) and give their completed forms to the teacher for use in analysis and self-assessment. Before your class starts this exercise, you may want to review the scoring rubric and make modifications to it that the class agrees on.

To structure your lesson plan, use one of the sample lesson plan formats presented in Chapter 6; however, each lesson should be centered on one major theme or concept and should be planned for about 20 minutes of instructional time.

Group 1: Develop a Level II inquiry lesson.

Group 2: Develop a lesson designed to raise the level of student thinking.

Group 3: Develop a lesson that involves a demonstration.

Group 4: Develop a lesson that is an interactive lecture.

EXERCISE 9.1 (*continued*)

PEER AND SELF-ASSESSMENT RUBRIC FOR USE WITH EXERCISE 9.1

For: _____   Group: _____

	1	0.5	0
1. Lesson beginning	effective	less effective	not effective
Comment:			
2. Sequencing	effective	less effective	rambling
Comment:			
3. Pacing of lesson	effective	less effective	too slow or too fast
Comment:			
4. Audience involvement	effective	less effective	none
Comment:			
5. Motivators (e.g., analogies, verbal cues, humor, visual cues, sensory cues)	effective	less effective	not apparent
Comment:			
6. Content of lesson	well chosen	interesting	boring or inappropriate
Comment:			
7. Voice of teacher	stimulating	minor problem	major problems
Comment:			
8. Vocabulary used	well chosen	appropriate	inappropriate
Comment:			
9. Eye contact	excellent	average	problems
Comment:			
10. Closure	effective	less effective	unclear/none
Comment:			

Other Comments:

SUMMARY

Central to your selection of instructional strategies should be those that encourage students to become independent thinkers and skilled learners who can help in the planning, structuring, regulating, and assessing of their own learning and learning activities.

Important to helping students construct their understandings are the cognitive tools available for their use. There is a large variety of useful and effective aids, media and resources from which to draw as you plan your instructional experiences, which is the topic of the next and final chapter of Part III.

QUESTIONS FOR CLASS DISCUSSION

1. Many cognitive researchers agree that students should spend more time actively using knowledge to solve problems and less time reading introductory material and listening to teachers. Describe the meaning of this statement and how you feel about it with respect to your decision to become a middle level classroom teacher.

2. With an example, explain the meaning of the statement: just because your speaking output channel is engaged does not mean that you should disengage your sensory input channels.

3. Explain the meaning of integrating strategies for integrated learning.

4. Are there any cautions that teachers need to be aware of when using games for teaching? If there are, describe them.

5. Explain some specific ways you can help students develop their skills in thinking and learning. Explain how you will determine that students have raised their skill level in thinking and learning.

6. Select one of the characteristics of intelligent behavior and (for a grade level of your choice and time limit as decided by your class) write a lesson plan for helping students develop that behavior. Share or teach your lesson to others in your class for their analysis and suggestions.

7. Select one of the "Reflective Thoughts" from the introduction to Part III (page 232) that is specifically related to the content of this chapter, research it, and write a one-page essay explaining why you agree or disagree with the thought. Share your essay with members of your class for their thoughts.

8. Describe any prior concepts you held that changed as a result of your experiences with this chapter. Describe the changes.

9. From your current observations and field work as related to this teacher preparation program, clearly identify one specific example of educational practice that seems contradictory to exemplary practice or theory as presented in this chapter. Present your explanation for the discrepancy.

10. Do you have questions generated by the content of this chapter? If you do, list them along with ways answers might be found.

FOR FURTHER READING

Allsopp, D. H. "Using Modeling, Manipulatives, and Mnemonics with Eighth-Grade Math Students." *Teaching Exceptional Children* 32(2):74–81 (November/December 1999).

Baroody, A. J. and Bartels, B. H. "Using Concept Maps To Link Mathematical Ideas." *Mathematics Teaching in the Middle School* 5(9):604–609 (May 2000).

Battista, M. T. "How Many Blocks?" *Mathematics Teaching in the Middle School* 3(6):404–411 (March/April 1998).

Beamon, G. W. "Guiding the Inquiry of Young Adolescent Minds." *Middle School Journal* 33(2):19–27 (January 2002).

Bockler, D. "Let's Play Doctor: Medical Rounds in Ancient Greece." *American Biology Teacher* 60(2):106–111 (February 1998).

Boston, J. A. "Using Simulations." *Social Studies Review* 37(2):31–32 (Spring/Summer 1998).

Callison, D. "Inquiry." *School Library Media Activities Monthly* 15(6):38–42 (February 1999).

Clemens-Walatka, B. "Amusement Park Inquiry." *Science Teacher* 65(1):20–23 (January 1998).

Collom, J. "Illot-Mollo and Other Games." *Teachers & Writers* 30(5):12–13 (May/June 1999).

Como, R. M. and O'Connor, J. S. "History on Trial: The Case of Columbus." *OAH Magazine of History* 12(2):45–48 (Winter 1998).

Eflin, J. C. and Eflin, J. T. "Thinking Critically about Global Environmental Issues." *Journal of Geography* 98(2):68–78 (March/April 1999).

Fong, R. "Making the Connection: Using Experiential Learning to Bridge the Classroom and the 'Real World'." *Social Studies Review* 37(2):83–84 (Spring/Summer 1998).

Ford, B. "Critically Evaluating Scientific Claims in the Popular Press." *American Biology Teacher* 60(3):174–180 (March 1998).

Foster, S. J. and Padgett, C. S. "Authentic Historical Inquiry in the Social Studies Classroom." *Clearing House* 72(6):357–363 (July 1999).

Hannel, G. I. and Hannel, L. "The Seven Steps to Critical Thinking: A Practical Application of Critical Thinking Skills." *NASSP* (National Association of Secondary School Principals) *Bulletin* 82(598):87–93 (May 1998).

Harris, B.; Kohlmeier, K.; and Kiel, R. D. *Crime Scene Investigation.* Englewood, CO: Teacher Ideas Press, 1999.

Jongsma, K. "Vocabulary and Comprehension Strategy Development." *Reading Teacher* 53(4):3190–3192 (December 1999/January 2000).

Koirala, H. P. and Goodwin, P. M. "Teaching Algebra in the Middle Grades Using Mathmagic." *Mathematics Teaching in the Middle School* 5(9):562–566 (May 2000).

Martino-Brewster, G. "Reversing the Negative." *Voices from the Middle* 6(3):11–14 (March 1999).

Marzano, R. J.; Pickering, D. J.; and Pollock, J. E. Chapter 9, "Generating and Testing Hypotheses." *Classroom Instruction that Works: Research-Based Strategies for Increasing Student Achievement.* Alexandria, VA: Association for Supervision and Curriculum Development, 2001.

Mayer, R. H. "Two Actors in Search of a Story: Using Primary Documents to Raise the Dead and Improve History Instruction." *OAH Magazine of History* 13(3):66–72 (Spring 1999).

Myers, R. E. *Mind Sparklers. Fireworks for Igniting Creativity in Young Minds.* Book 2 for Grades 4–8. Waco, TX: Prufrock Press, 1998.

Perkins, D. N. "Schools Need to Pay More Attention to 'Intelligence in the Wild'." *Harvard Education Letter* 16(3):8, 7 (May/June 2000).

Presseisen, B. Z., ed. *Teaching for Intelligence: A Collection of Articles.* Arlington Heights, IL: Skylight, 1999.

Quinn, R. J. and Wiest, L. R. "Exploring Probability through an Evens-Odds Dice Game." *Mathematics Teaching in the Middle School* 4(6):358–362 (March 1999).

Renzulli, J. S. "Academies of Inquiry and Talent Development," *Middle School Journal* 32(2):5–14 (November 2000).

Richardson, T. L. "The Importance of Emotional Intelligence During Transition into Middle School." *Middle School Journal* 33(2):55–58 (January 2002).

Rulf, B. "A Geometric Puzzle That Leads to Fibonacci Sequences." *Mathematics Teacher* 91(1):21–23 (January 1998).

Schug, T. "Teaching DNA Fingerprinting Using a Hands-on Simulation." *American Biology Teacher* 60(1):38–41 (January 1998).

Shiveley, J. M. and VanFossen, P. J. "Critical Thinking and the Internet: Opportunities for the Social Studies Classroom." *Social Studies* 90(1):42–46 (January/February 1999).

Sweeney, E. S. and Quinn, R. J. "Concentration: Connecting Fractions, Decimals, and Percents." *Mathematics Teaching in the Middle School* 5(5):324–328 (January 2000).

CHAPTER 10

Using Media and Other Instructional Aids and Resources

Important to helping students construct their understandings are the cognitive tools available for their use. You will be pleased to know that there is a large variety of useful and effective media, aids, and resources from which to draw as you plan your instructional experiences. On the other hand, you could become overwhelmed by the sheer quantity of materials available—textbooks, supplementary texts, pamphlets, anthologies, paperbacks, encyclopedias, tests, programmed instructional systems, dictionaries, reference books, classroom periodicals, newspapers, films, records and cassettes, computer software, transparencies, realia, games, filmstrips, audio- and videotapes, slides, globes, manipulatives,

CD-ROMs, DVDs, and graphics. You could spend a great deal of your time reviewing, sorting, selecting, and practicing with these materials and tools. Although nobody can make the job easier for you, information in this chapter may expedite the process.

OBJECTIVES

Upon completion of this chapter, you should be able to

1. Demonstrate an awareness of the variety of materials and resources for use in your teaching.
2. Demonstrate knowledge of copyright laws for using printed and media materials for teaching.

3. Demonstrate an understanding about using community resources, speakers, and field trips.
4. Demonstrate an awareness of electronic media available for teaching your subject field, how they can be evaluated and used, and how and where they can be obtained.
5. Demonstrate competency in using standard classroom tools for teaching.

PRINTED MATERIALS, VISUAL DISPLAYS, AND THE INTERNET

Historically, of all the materials available for instruction, the printed textbook has had, and still has, the most influence on teaching and learning (discussed in Chapter 5). In addition to the student textbook and perhaps an accompanying workbook, there is a vast array of other printed teaching materials available, many without cost. (See "Sources of Free and Inexpensive Materials" that follows). Printed materials include books, workbooks, pamphlets, magazines, brochures, newspapers, professional journals, periodicals, duplicated materials, and those copied from Internet sources.

In reviewing printed materials, factors to be alert for include (a) appropriateness of the material in both content and reading level; (b) articles in newspapers, magazines, and periodicals related to the content that your students will be studying or the skills they will be learning; (c) assorted workbooks available from tradebook publishers that emphasize thinking and problem solving rather than rote memorization—using an assortment of workbooks students can work on similar but different assignments depending upon their interests and abilities, an example of multilevel teaching; (d) pamphlets, brochures, and other duplicated materials that students can read for specific information and viewpoints about particular topics; and (e) inexpensive paperback books that would provide multiple book readings for your class and that make it possible for students to read primary sources.

Sources of Free and Inexpensive Printed Materials

Look for sources of free and inexpensive printed materials in your college, university, or public library; in the resource center at a local school district; and through connections on the Internet (see Figure 10.1). When considering the use of materials that were free or inexpensive, make sure that the materials are appropriate for use with your students, and that they are free of bias or unwanted messages. The National Education Association (NEA) has published guidelines for teachers to consider before purchasing or using commercial materials; for a free copy, contact NEA communications, 1201 16th Street, NW, Washington, DC 20036; phone 202-822-7200; or online at http://www.nea.org/.

Figure 10.1   Resources for free and inexpensive printed materials.

- Educators Progress Service, Inc., 214 Center Street, Randolph, WI 53956. 414-326-3126. *Educator's Guide to Free Materials; Educator's Guide to Free Teaching Aids.*
- *Freebies: The Magazine with Something for Nothing.* PO Box 5025, Carpenteria, CA 93014-5025.
- *Video Placement Worldwide (VPW).* Source of free sponsored educational videos and print materials on the Internet at http://www.vpw.com.

The Internet

Originating from a Department of Defense project in 1969 (called ARPANET) to establish a computer network of military researchers, its successor, the federally funded Internet, has become an enormous, steadily expanding, worldwide system of connected computer networks. The Internet provides literally millions of resources to explore, with thousands more added nearly every day. Today you can surf the Internet to find sources about how to use it, and you can walk into most any bookstore and find hundreds of recent titles, most of which give their authors' favorite Websites. However, new technologies are steadily emerging and the Internet is changing every day. Some sites and resources have disappeared or are not kept current, others have changed their location or undergone reconstruction, and new ones continue to appear. Therefore, it would be superfluous for us, since this book will be around for a few years, to make too much of sites that we personally have viewed and can recommend as teacher resources. Nevertheless, Figure 10.2 shows Internet resources that we recently have surfed and can recommend. Sites have been mentioned in the text throughout this resource guide, and others are listed in figures of Chapters 1 and 8 respectively. Perhaps you have found others that you can share with your classmates—and with us.

CAUTIONS AND GUIDELINES FOR USING THE INTERNET

If you have yet to learn to use the Internet, we shall leave the mechanics of that to the many resources available to you, including the experts that can be found among your peers, on your college or university staff, and among members of any public school faculty. The remaining pages of this section address the how of using the Internet from an academic perspective. Let's begin with the fictitious, although feasible, Teaching Scenario: Natural Disasters.

Figure 10.2   Additional Internet sites: materials and technology.

- *Education World* http://www.education-world.com
- *Electronic Reference Formats Recommended by the American Psychological Association* http://www.apastyle.org/elecref.html
- *ERIC Documents Online* http://ericir.syr.edu
- *International Telementor Program* http://www.telementor.org
- *Mathematics Archives* http://archives.math.utk.edu/
- *MLA-Style Citations of Electronic Sources* http://www.columbia.edu/cu/cup/cgos/idx_basic.html
- *National Archives and Records Administration* http://www.nara.gov
- *National Education Association (NEA)* http://www.nea.org/teaching/refs.html
- *National Endowment for the Arts Home Page* http://www.arts.endow.gov
- *National Geographic Map Machine* http://www.nationalgeographic.com
- *School Match* http://schoolmatch.com
- *School Page* http://www.theschoolpage.com
- *Science Stuff* http://www.sciencestuff.com/nav
- *Telementoring Young Women in Science, Engineering, and Computing* http://www.edc.org/CCT/telementoring
- *Teacher's Network* http://www.teachnet.org
- *United States Copyright Office* http://lcweb.loc.gov/copyright
- *WWW4Teachers* http://4teachers.org/home/index.shtml

TEACHING SCENARIO

Natural Disasters

Let us suppose that the students from your "house" have been working nearly all year on an interdisciplinary thematic unit titled "surviving natural disasters" (returning to the discussion in Chapter 5 regarding ITU themes). As a culmination to their study, they "published" a document titled *Natural Disaster Preparation and Survival Guide for (name of their community)* and proudly distributed the guide to their parents and members of the community.

Long before preparing the guide, however, the students had to do research about the history of various kinds of natural disasters that had occurred or might occur locally and about the preparations a community should take for each kind of disaster. Students searched sources on the Internet, such as federal documents, scientific articles, and articles from newspapers around the world where natural disasters had occurred. They also searched in the local library and the local newspaper's archives to learn about floods, tornadoes, and fires that had occurred during the past 200 years. Much to their surprise, they also learned that their community is located very near the New Madrid Fault and did, in fact, experience a serious earthquake in 1811, although they have had none since. As a result of that earthquake, two nearby towns completely disappeared; the Mississippi River flowed in reverse; and the river's course changed and caused the formation of a new lake.

From published and copyrighted sources, including Websites, the students found many useful photographs, graphics, and articles that they included in whole or in part in their "Natural Disaster Preparation and Survival Guide." They did so without obtaining permission from the original copyright holders or even citing those sources.

You and the other members of your teaching team and other people in the community were so impressed with the student's work that the students were encouraged to publish the document on the school's Website. In addition, the students decided to place it for sale in local retail outlets. This would help defray the original cost of duplication and enable them to continue to supply the guides.

To the Natural Disasters scenario, there is both a desirable aspect and a not-so-desirable aspect. The students used a good technological tool (the Internet) to research a variety of sources, including many primary ones. But when they published their document on the Internet and made copies of their guide to sell, they did so without the permission of original copyright holders, and thus were infringing copyright law. Although it would take an attorney to say for certain, it is probable that the students, teacher, school, and school district would be liable. As is true for other documents (such as published photos, graphics, and text), unless there is a clear statement that materials taken from the Internet are public domain, it is best to assume that they are copyrighted and should not be republished for profit or on another Website.

With such a proliferation of information today from both printed materials and information on the Internet—except for obviously reliable sites such as the *New York Times* and the Library of Congress—how can a person determine the validity and currency of a particular piece of information? When searching for useful and reliable information on a particular topic, how can one avoid wasting valuable time sifting through information? Just because information is found on a printed page or is published on the Internet does not necessarily mean that the information is accurate or current. Using a checklist, such as those found on the Internet at http://www.infopeople.org/bkmk/select.html or http://lib.nmsu.edu/instruction/eval.html, and with examples of materials that meet and do not meet the criteria of the checklist, students can learn how to assess materials and information found on the Internet.

Teaching all students how to access and assess Websites adds to their repertoire of skills for lifelong learning. Consider allowing each student or teams of students to become experts on specific sites during particular units of study. It might be useful to start a chronicle of student-recorded log entries about Websites to provide comprehensive long-term data about those sites.

When students use information from the Internet, have them print copies of sources of citations and materials so you can check for accuracy. These copies may be maintained in their portfolios.

Student work published on the Internet should be considered as intellectual material and protected from plagiarism by others. You may be interested to know that the prevention of plagiarism by students of materials found on the Internet is now offered as a service to teachers by several Internet providers.[1]

Most school districts now post a copyright notice on their home page. Usually, someone at the school or from the district office is assigned to supervise the school Website to see that district and school policy and legal requirements are observed.

Professional Journals and Periodicals

Figure 10.3 lists examples of the many professional periodicals and journals that can provide useful teaching ideas and Website information and that carry information about instructional materials and how to get them. Some of these may be in your university or college li-

---

[1] See, for example, L. Renard, "Cut and Paste 101: Plagiarism and the Net," *Educational Leadership* 57(4):38–42 (December 1999/January 2000).

Figure 10.3   Selected professional journals and periodicals for middle school teachers.

The American Biology Teacher	*The Mathematics Teacher*
American Educational Research Quarterly	*Mathematics Teaching in the Middle School*
The American Music Teacher	*The Middle School Journal*
American Teacher	*Modern Language Journal*
The Art Teacher	*Music Educator's Journal*
The Computing Teacher	*NEA Today*
Creative Classroom	*The Negro Educational Review*
The Earth Scientist	*The New Advocate*
Educational Horizons	*Phi Delta Kappan*
Educational Leadership	*Physical Education*
English Journal	*The Reading Teacher*
English Language Teaching Journal	*Reading Today*
The Good Apple Newspaper	*School Arts*
Hispania	*School Library Journal*
The History Teacher	*The School Musician*
The Horn Book	*School Science and Mathematics*
Instructor	*School Shop*
Journal of Home Economics	*Science*
Journal of Learning Disabilities	*Science Scope*
Journal of the National Association of Bilingual Educators	*Social Education*
	The Social Studies
Journal of Physical Education and Recreation	*Teacher Magazine*
Journal of Reading	*TESOL Quarterly*
Journal of Teaching in Physical Education	*Theory and Research in Social Education*
Language Arts	*Voices from the Middle*
Language Learning	*Writing Teacher*
Learning	

brary and may be accessible through Internet sources. Check there for these and other titles of interest to you.

The ERIC Information Network

The Educational Resources Information Center (ERIC) system, established by the United States Office of Education, is a widely used network providing access to information and research in education. Selected clearinghouses and their addresses are shown in Figure 10.4.

Copying Printed Materials

As a teacher, you must be familiar with the laws about using copyrighted materials, printed and nonprinted, including those obtained from sources on the Internet. Remember that, although on many Web pages there is no notice, the material is still copyrighted. Copyright law protects original material; that is just as true for the intellectual property created by a minor as it is for that of an adult.

Space here prohibits full inclusion of U.S. legal guidelines, but your local school district should be able to provide a copy of current district policies for compliance with copyright laws. District policies should include guidelines for teachers and students in publishing materials on the Internet. If no district guidelines are available, when using printed materials adhere to the guidelines shown in Figure 10.5.[2]

_____

[2]See also the *Copyright and Fair Use* Website of Stanford University, at http://fairuse.stanford.edu/.

When preparing to make a copy, you must find out whether the laws under the category of "permitted use" permit the copying. If it is not allowed under "permitted use," then you must obtain written permission from the holder of the copyright to reproduce the material. If the address of the source is not given on the material, addresses may be obtained from various references, such as *Literary Market Place, Audio-Visual Market Place,* and *Ulrich's International Periodical's Directory.*

The Classroom Writing Board

As is true for an auto mechanic or a brain surgeon or any other professional, a teacher needs to know when and how to use the tools of the trade. One of the tools available to most every classroom teacher is the writing board. Can you imagine a classroom without a writing board? In this section, you will find guidelines for using this important tool.

They used to be, and in some schools still are, slate blackboards, a type of metamorphic rock. In today's classroom, however, the writing board may be a board that is painted plywood (chalkboard), which, like the blackboard, is also quickly becoming obsolete, at least in part because of concern about the dust created from using chalk. More often, the writing board is a white or colored (light green and light blue are common) *multipurpose dry-erase board* that is written on with special marking pens and erased with any soft dry cloth. The multipurpose board can also be used as a projection screen and as a surface to stick figures cut

Figure 10.4   Selected ERIC Addresses.

- *Assessment and Evaluation.* University of Maryland, College Park, Department of Measurement, Statistics, and Evaluation, 1129 Shriver Laboratory, College Park, MD 20742. URL: http://ericae.net/
- *Counseling and Student Services.* University of North Carolina at Greensboro, School of Education, 201 Ferguson Building, P.O. Box 26171, Greensboro, NC 27402-6171. URL: http://ericcass.uncg.edu/
- *Disabilities and Gifted Education,* The Council for Exceptional Children (CEC), 1920 Association Drive, Reston, VA 20191-1589. URL: http://ericec.org/
- *Elementary and Early Childhood Education,* University of Illinois at Urbana-Champaign, Children's Research Center, 51 Gerty Drive, Champaign, IL 61820-7469. URL: http://ericeece.org/
- *Information & Technology.* Syracuse University, 621 Skytop Road, Suite 160, Syracuse, NY 13244-5290. http://ericir.syr.edu/ithome/
- *Languages and Linguistics.* Center for Applied Linguistics (CAL), 4646 40th Street, NW, Washington, DC 20016-1859. URL: http://www.cal.org/ericcll/
- *Reading, English, and Communication.* Indiana University, Smith Research Center, 2805 East 10th Street, Suite 140, Bloomington, IN 47408-2698. URL: http://www.indiana.edu/-eric_rec/
- *Rural Education and Small Schools.* Appalachia Educational Laboratory, Inc. (AEL, Inc.), 1031 Quarrier Street, P.O. Box 1348, Charleston, WV 25325-1348. URL: http://www.ael.org/eric/
- *Science, Mathematics, and Environmental Education.* Ohio State University 1929 Kenny Road, Columbus, Ohio 43210-1080. URL: http://www.ericse.org/
- *Service Learning.* University of Minnesota, R-460 VoTech Building, 1954 Bufford Avenue, St. Paul, MN 55108. URL: http://nicsl.jaws.umn.edu/
- *Social Studies/Social Science Education.* Indiana University Social Studies Development Center, 2805 East 10th Street, Suite 120, Bloomington, IN 47408-2698 URL: http://www.indiana.edu/-ssdc/eric-chess.html
- *Urban Education.* Teachers College, Columbia University, Institute for Urban and Minority Education, Main Hall, Room 303, Box 40, New York, NY 10027-6696. URL: http://eric-web.tc.columbia.edu/

Figure 10.5 Guidelines for copying printed materials that are copyrighted. (*Source:* Section 107 of the 1976 Federal Omnibus Copyright Revision Act.)

Permitted Uses—You May Make

1. Single copies of
   - A chapter of a book.
   - An article from a periodical, magazine, or newspaper.
   - A short story, short essay, or short poem whether or not from a collected work.
   - A chart, graph, diagram, drawing, or cartoon.
   - An illustration from a book, magazine, or newspaper.
2. Multiple copies for classroom use (not to exceed one copy per student in a course) of
   - A complete poem if less than 250 words.
   - An excerpt from a longer poem, but not to exceed 250 words.
   - A complete article, story, or essay of less than 2,500 words.
   - An excerpt from a larger printed work not to exceed 10 percent of the whole or 1,000 words.
   - One chart, graph, diagram, cartoon, or picture per book or magazine issue.

Prohibited Uses—You May Not

1. Copy more than one work or two excerpts from a single author during one class term (semester or year).
2. Copy more than three works from a collective work or periodical volume during one class term.
3. Reproduce more than nine sets of multiple copies for distribution to students in one class term.
4. Copy to create, replace, or substitute for anthologies or collective works.
5. Copy "consumable" works (e.g., workbooks, standardized tests, or answer sheets).
6. Copy the same work year after year.

---

from colored transparency film. It may also have a magnetic backing.

Extending the purposes of the multipurpose board and correlated with modern technology is an *electronic whiteboard* that can transfer information written on it to a connected computer monitor, which in turn can save it as a computer file. The electronic whiteboard uses dry-erase markers and special erasers with optically encoded sleeves that enable the device to track their position on the board. The data are then converted into a display for the computer monitor, that may be printed, cut and pasted into other applications, sent as an e-mail or fax message, or networked to other sites.

Each day, each class, and even each new idea should begin with a clean board, except for announcements that have been placed there by you or another teacher. At the end of each class, clean the board, especially if another teacher follows you in that room. This is simple professional courtesy.

Use colored chalk or marking pens to highlight your board talk. This is especially helpful for students with learning difficulties. Beginning at the top left of the board, print or write neatly and clearly, with the writing intentionally positioned to indicate content relationships (e.g., causal, oppositional, numerical, comparative, categorical, and so on).

Use the writing board to acknowledge acceptance and to record student contributions. Print instructions for an activity on the board, in addition to giving them orally. At the top of the board frame you may find clips for hanging posters, maps, and charts.

Learn to use the board without turning your back entirely on students and without blocking their view of the board. When you have a lot of material to put on the board, do it before class and then cover it, or better yet, put the material on transparencies and use the overhead projector rather than the board, or use both. Be careful not to write too much information.

The Classroom Bulletin Board

Bulletin boards are found in nearly every classroom, and, although sometimes poorly used or not used at all, they can be relatively inexpensively transformed into attractive and valuable instructional tools. Among other things, the bulletin board is a convenient location for posting reminders, assignments and schedules, and commercially produced materials, and to celebrate and display model student work and anchor papers.

To plan, design, and prepare bulletin board displays, some teachers use student assistants or committees, giving those students guidance and responsibility for planning, preparing, and maintaining bulletin board displays. When preparing a bulletin board display, keep these guidelines in mind: the display should be simple, emphasizing one main idea, concept, topic, or theme, and captions should be short and concise; illustrations can accent learning topics; verbs can vitalize the captions; phrases can punctuate a student's thoughts; and alliteration can announce anything you wish on the board. Finally, as in all other aspects of the classroom learning environment, make sure that the board display reflects gender and ethnic equity.

Figure 10.6   Community resources for speakers, materials, and field trips.

Airport	Highway patrol station
Apiary	Historical sites and monuments
Aquarium	Industrial plant
Archeological site	Legislature session
Art gallery	Levee and water reservoir
Assembly plant	Library and archive
Bakery	Mass transit authority
Bird and wildlife sanctuary	Military installation
Book publisher	Mine
Bookstore	Museum
Broadcasting and TV station	Native American Indian reservation
Building being razed	Newspaper plant
Building under construction	Observatory
Canal lock	Oil refinery
Cemetery	Park
Chemical plant	Poetry reading
City or county planning commission	Police station
Courthouse	Post office and package delivery company
Dairy	Recycling center
Dam and floodplain	Retail store
Dock and harbor	Sanitation department
Factory	Sawmill or lumber company
Farm	Shopping mall
Fire department	Shoreline (stream, lake, wetland, ocean)
Fish hatchery	Telecommunications center
Flea market	Town meeting
Foreign embassy	Universities and colleges
Forest and forest preserve	Utility company
Freeway under construction	Warehouse
Gas company	Water reservoir and treatment plant
Geological site	Weather bureau and storm center
Health department and hospital	Wildlife park and preserve
Highway construction site	Zoo

THE COMMUNITY AS A RESOURCE

One of the richest resources for learning is the local community and the people and places in it. You will want to build your own file of community resources—speakers, sources for free materials, and field trip locations. Your school may already have a community resource file available for your use, but it may need updating. The file (see Figure 10.6) should contain information about (a) possible field trip locations, (b) community resource people who could serve as guest speakers or mentors, and (c) local agencies that can provide information and instructional materials.

There are many ways to use community resources, and quite a variety have been demonstrated by the schools specifically mentioned throughout this resource guide (see "Schools" in index). Here, the discussion is limited to two instructional tools that are often used, and sometimes abused, (a) guest speakers and (b) out-of-classroom and off-campus excursions, commonly called *field trips*.

Guest Speakers

Bringing outside speakers into your classroom can be a valuable educational experience for students, but it is not automatically so. In essence, guest speakers can be classified within a spectrum of four types, two of which should not be used. They include (a) a speaker who is both informative and inspiring, (b) a speaker who may be inspiring but has nothing substantive to offer, except possibly diversion from the usual rigors of classroom work, (c) a speaker who might be informative but boring to students, and (d) at the worst end of this spectrum, a guest speaker who is both boring and uninformative. So, just like any other instructional experience, to make a guest-speaker experience most effective takes careful planning on your part. To make sure that the experience is beneficial to student learning, consider the following guidelines.

- If at all possible, meet and talk with the guest speaker in advance to inform him or her about your students and your expectations for the presentation, and to gauge how motivational and informative the speaker might be. If you believe the speaker might be informative but boring, then perhaps you can help structure the presentation in some way to make the presentation a bit more inspiring. For example, stop the speaker every few minutes and involve the students in questioning and discussions of points made.

- Prepare students in advance with key points of information that you expect students to obtain.
- Prepare students in advance with questions to ask the speaker, things the students want to find out, and information you want them to inquire about.
- Follow up the presentation with a thank-you letter to the guest speaker and perhaps with further questions that developed during class discussions subsequent to the speaker's presentation.

Field Trips

Can you recall the most memorable field trip that you were ever on as a young adolescent student? What made it memorable? You may want to discuss these questions and others like them with your classmates.

Today's schools often have very limited funds for the transportation and liability costs for field trips. In some cases, there are no funds at all. At times, parent-teacher groups, or business and civic organizations help by providing financial resources so students can get the valuable first-hand experiences that field trips can offer.

To prepare for and implement a successful field trip, there are three important stages of planning—before, during, and after-and critical decisions to be made at each stage. Consider the following guidelines.

BEFORE THE FIELD TRIP

When the field trip is your idea (and not the students') discuss the idea with your teaching team, principal, or department chair (especially when transportation will be needed) *before* mentioning the idea to your students. There is no cause served by getting students excited about a trip before you know if it is feasible.

Once you have obtained the necessary, but tentative, approval from school officials, take the trip yourself (or with team members), if possible. A previsit allows you to determine how to make the field trip most productive and what arrangements will be necessary. For this previsit, you might consider taking a couple of your students along for their ideas and help. If a previsit is not possible, you still need to arrange for travel directions; arrival and departure times; parking; briefing by the host, if there is one; storage of students' personal items, such as coats and lunches; provisions for eating and rest rooms; and fees, if any.

If there are fees, you need to talk with your administration about who will pay the fees. If the trip is worth taking, the school should cover the costs. If that is not possible, perhaps students can plan a fund-raising activity or financial assistance can be obtained from some other source. If this does not work, you might consider an alternative experience that does not involve costs.

Arrange for official permission from the school administration. This usually requires a form for requesting, planning, and reporting field trips. After permission has been obtained, discuss the field trip with your students and arrange for permissions from their parents or guardians. You need to realize that although parents or guardians sign official permission forms allowing their children to participate in the trip, these only show that the parents or guardians are aware of what will take place and give their permission for their child to participate. Although the permission form should include a statement that the parent or guardian absolves the teacher and the school from liability should an accident occur, it *does not* lessen the teacher's and the school's responsibilities should there be negligence by a teacher, driver, or chaperone.

Arrange for students to be excused from their other classes while on the field trip. Using an information form prepared and signed by you and perhaps by the appropriate administrator, the students should then assume responsibility for notifying their other teachers of the planned absence from classes or other school activities and assure them that they will make up whatever work is missed. In addition, you will need to make arrangements for your own teaching duties to be covered. In some schools, teachers cooperate by filling in for those who will be gone. In other schools, substitute teachers are hired. Sometimes teachers have to hire their own substitutes.

Arrange to have a cell phone available for your use during the trip. Some schools have a cell phone for just that purpose. If not, and if you do not have one yourself, perhaps one of the drivers or other adult chaperones might.

Arrange for whatever transportation is needed. Your principal, or the principal's designee, will help you with the details. In many schools, someone else takes care of this detail. In any case, the use of private automobiles is ill advised, because you and the school could be liable for the acts of the drivers.

Arrange for the collection of money that is needed for fees. If there are out-of-pocket costs to be paid by students, this information needs to be included on the permission form. No student should ever be excluded from the field trip because of a lack of money. This can be a tricky issue, because some students might rather steal the money for a field trip than say they do not have it. Try to anticipate problems; if the school or some organization can pay for the trip, fees need not be collected from students and potential problems of this sort are avoided.

Plan details and monitor student safety from departure to return. This should include a first-aid kit and a system of student control, such as a "buddy system" whereby students must remain paired throughout the trip. The pairs sometimes are given numbers that are recorded and kept by the teacher and the chaperones. The numbers are then checked at departure time, periodically during the trip, when departing the field trip site, and again upon return. Use adult chaperones. As a very general rule, there should be one adult chaperone for every 10 students. Some districts have a policy regarding this. While on a field trip, all students should be under the direct supervision of an adult at all times.

Plan the complete route and schedule, including any stops along the way. If transportation is being provided, you will need to discuss the plans with the provider.

Establish and discuss, to the extent you believe necessary, the rules of behavior your students should follow. Included in this might be details of the trip, its purpose, directions, what they should wear and bring, academic expectations of them (consider, for example, giving each student a study guide), and follow-up activities. Information should also be included about what to do if anything should go awry, for example, if a student is late for the departure or return, loses a personal possession along the way, gets lost, is injured, becomes sick, or misbehaves. *Never* send a misbehaving student back to school alone, such as via the city's transit system or a taxi. Involve the adult chaperones in the previsit discussion. All of this information should also be included on the parental permission form.

If a field trip is intended to promote some kind of learning, as is probably the case, then to avoid leaving it to chance, the learning expectations need to be clearly defined and the students given an explanation of how and where they may encounter the learning experience. Before the field trip, students should be asked questions such as, "What do we already know about _____? What do we want to find out about _____? How can we find out?" and then, with their assistance, an appropriate guide can be prepared for the students to use during the field trip.

To further ensure learning and individual student responsibility for that learning, you may want to assign different roles and responsibilities to students, just as you would in cooperative learning, ensuring that each student has a role with responsibility.

You may want to take recorders and cameras so the field trip experience can be relived and shared in class upon return. If so, rules and responsibilities for the equipment, and its care and use can be assigned to students as well.

DURING THE FIELD TRIP

If your field trip has been carefully planned according to the preceding guidelines, it should be a valuable and safe experience for all. Enroute, while at the trip location, and on the return to school, you and the adult

chaperones should monitor student behavior and learning just as you do in the classroom.

AFTER THE FIELD TRIP

Plan the follow-up activities. As with any other lesson plan, the field trip lesson is complete only when there is both a proper introduction and a well-planned closure. All sorts of follow-up activities can be planned as an educational wrap-up to this educational experience. For example, a bulletin board committee can plan and prepare an attractive display summarizing the trip. Students can write about their experiences in their journals or in papers. Small groups can give oral reports sharing what they did and learned. Their reports can then serve as springboards for further class discussion, and perhaps further investigations. Finally, for future planning, all who were involved should contribute to an assessment of the experience.

MEDIA TOOLS

Your attention is now directed to teaching tools that depend upon electricity to project light and sound, and to focus images on screens. Included are projectors of various sorts, computers, CD-ROMs, video recorders, and DVDs. The aim here is *not* to provide instruction on how to operate modern equipment but to help you develop a philosophy for using it and to provide strategies for using media tools in your teaching. Consequently, to conserve space in this book, other than for the overhead projector we devote no attention to traditional AV equipment, such as 16-mm film, opaque, and slide projectors. There are staff members on any school faculty who will gladly assist you in locating and using those tools.

It is important to remember that the role of media tools is to aid student learning, not to teach *for* you. You must still select the objectives, orchestrate the instructional plan, tweak the instruction according to the needs of individual students, assess the results, and follow up the lessons, just as you have learned to do with various other instructional strategies. If you use media tools prudently, your teaching and your students' learning will both benefit. Like a competent brain surgeon or a competent auto mechanic, a competent teacher knows when and how to select and use the right tools at the right time. Would you want your child operated on by a surgeon who was unfamiliar with the tools used in surgery? The education of youth should be no less important.

When Equipment Malfunctions

When using media equipment, it is usually best to set up the equipment and have it ready to go before students arrive. That helps avoid problems in classroom management that can occur when there is a delay because the equipment is not ready. After all, if you were a surgeon ready to begin an operation and your tools and equipment were not ready, your patient's life would likely be placed in extra danger. Like any other competent professional, a competent teacher is ready when the work is to begin.

Of course, delays may be unavoidable if equipment breaks down or a videotape breaks. Remember "Murphy's law," which says if anything can go wrong, it will? It is particularly relevant when using audiovisual equipment. You want to be prepared for such emergencies. Effectively planning for and responding to this eventuality is a part of your system of movement management that takes place during the preactive stage of your planning (see Chapter 3). That preparation includes consideration of a number of factors.

When equipment malfunctions, three principles should be kept in mind: (a) you want to avoid dead time in the classroom; (b) you want to avoid causing permanent damage to equipment; (c) you want to avoid losing content continuity of a lesson. So, what do you do when equipment breaks down? Again, the answer is: Be prepared for the eventuality.

If a projector bulb goes out, quickly insert another. That means that you should have an extra bulb on hand. As simplistic as this seems, when the bulb goes, unless you have a replacement bulb, so goes an effective part of the lesson. If a tape breaks, you can do a quick temporary splice with cellophane tape; that means tape should be readily available. If you must do a temporary splice, do it on a section of the film or videotape that has already run through the machine rather than on the end yet to go through, so as not to damage the machine or the film. Then, after class or after school, be sure to notify the person in charge of the tape that a temporary splice was made, so the tape can be permanently repaired before its next use. If the computer screen freezes during direct, whole-class instruction you should probably quickly move to an alternate activity. If it is during multilevel instruction, you can probably take the time to treat this as a teachable moment and, while maintaining your classroom withitness, show the student who is working on the computer what to do, which probably would be simply how to restart the computer.

If, during surgery, a patient's cerebral artery suddenly and unexpectedly breaks, the surgeon and the surgical team are ready for that eventuality and make the necessary repair. If, while working on an automobile, a part breaks, the mechanic gets a replacement part. If, while teaching, a computer program freezes or aborts on the screen, or if a fuse blows or you lose power for some other reason, and you think there is going to be too much dead time before the equipment is working again, it is time to go to an alternate lesson plan. You have probably heard the expression "go to Plan B." It is a useful phrase; what it means is that without missing a beat in the lesson, to accomplish the same instructional objective or another objective, you immediately and smoothly switch to an alternate learning activity. For you, the beginning teacher, it does not mean that you must plan *two* lessons for every one, but when planning a lesson that uses media equipment, you should plan an alternative activity, just in case. Then, you can move your students into the planned alternative activity quickly and smoothly.

The Overhead Projector

In addition to a writing board and a bulletin board, nearly every classroom is equipped with an overhead projector. The overhead projector is a versatile, effective, and reliable teaching tool. Except for the bulb burning out, not much else can go wrong with an overhead projector. There is no film to break or program to crash.

The overhead projector projects light through objects that are transparent (see Figure 10.7). A properly functioning overhead projector usually works quite well in a fully lit room. Truly portable overhead projectors are available that can be carried easily from place to place in their compact cases.

Other types of overhead projectors include rear-projection systems that allow the teacher to stand off to the side rather than between students and the screen, and overhead video projectors that use video cameras to send images that are projected by television monitors. Some schools use overhead video camera technology that focuses on an object, pages of a book, or a demonstration, while sending a clear image to a video monitor with a screen large enough for an entire class to clearly see.

In some respects, the overhead projector is more practical than the writing board, particularly for a beginning teacher who is nervous. Using the overhead projector rather than the writing board can help avoid tension by decreasing the need to pace back and forth to the board. And by using an overhead projector rather than a writing board, you can maintain both eye contact and physical proximity with students, both of which are important for maintaining classroom control.

GUIDELINES FOR USING THE OVERHEAD PROJECTOR

As with any projector, find the best place in your classroom to position it. If there is no classroom projection screen, you can hang white paper or a sheet, or use a white multipurpose board, or a white or near-white wall.

Have you ever attended a presentation by someone who was not using an overhead projector properly? It can be frustrating to members of an audience when the image is too small, out of focus, partially off the screen, or partially blocked from view by the presenter. To use this teaching tool in a professional manner

- *Turn on the projector (the switch is probably on the front).* Place it so the projected white light covers the entire screen and hits the screen at a 90-degree angle; then focus the image to be projected.

Figure 10.7   An overhead projector consists of a glass-topped box that contains a light source and a vertical post mounting a head that contains a lens. To use it, place an acetate transparency on the glass top (some overhead projectors are equipped with acetate rolls to use as transparencies), switch on the light, and adjust the focus by moving the head, which contains the lens, up and down.

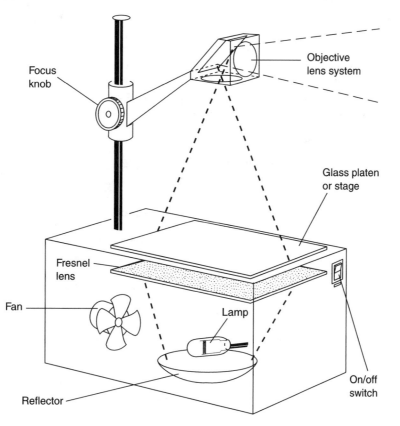

- *Face the students while using the projector.* The fact that you do not lose eye contact with your audience is a major advantage of using the overhead projector rather than a writing board. What you write as you face your students will show up perfectly (unless it is out of focus or off the screen).
- *Lay a pencil flat onto the transparency with the tip of the pencil pointing to the detail being emphasized* rather than tilting the pencil, using your finger to point to detail, or pointing directly to the screen (thereby turning away from your students).
- *To lessen distraction, turn the overhead projector off when you want the students to shift attention back to you.*

To preserve the life of the projector's bulb, it is best not to move the projector until the bulb has cooled. In addition, bulbs will last longer if you avoid touching them with your fingers.

For writing on overhead projector transparencies, ordinary felt-tip pens are not satisfactory. Select a transparency-marking pen available at an office supply store. The ink of these pens is water-soluble, so keep the palm of your hand from resting on the transparency or you will have ink smudges on your transparency and on your hand.

Non-water-soluble pens—permanent markers—can be used, but the transparency must be cleaned with an alcohol solvent or a plastic eraser. When using a cleaning solvent, you can clean and dry with paper toweling or a soft rag. To highlight the writing on a transparency and to organize student learning, use pens in a variety of colors. Transparency pens tend to dry out quickly, and they are relatively expensive, so the caps must be taken on and off frequently, which is something of a nuisance when working with several colors. Practice writing on a transparency and also practice making overlays. You can use an acetate transparency roll or single sheets of flat transparencies. Flat sheets of transparency come in different colors—clear, red, blue, yellow, and green—which can be useful in making overlays.

Some teachers prepare lesson outlines in advance on transparencies, which allows more careful preparation of the transparencies and means they are ready for reuse at another time. Some teachers use an opaque material, such as a 3 × 5 notecard, to block out prewritten material and then uncover it at the moment it is being discussed. For preparation of permanent transparencies, you will probably want to use permanent marker pens, rather than those that are water-soluble and easily smudged.

Heavy paper frames are available for permanent transparencies; marginal notes can be written on the frames. Personal computers with laser printers and thermal processing (copy) machines, which are probably located in the teacher's workroom or in the school's main office, can be used to make permanent transparencies.

Other transparent objects can be shown on an overhead projector, such as transparent rulers, protractors, and clear glass dishes; even opaque objects can be used if you want simply to show silhouette, as you might in math and art activities. Calculators, too, are available specifically for use on the overhead projector, as is a screen that fits onto the platform and is circuited to a computer, so whatever is displayed on the computer monitor is also projected onto the classroom screen.

Commercial transparencies are available from a variety of school supply houses. For sources, check the catalogs available in your school office or at the audio-visual and resource centers in your school district.

The overhead projector can also be used for tracing transparent charts or drawings on larger paper or on the writing board. The image projected onto the screen can be made smaller or larger by moving the projector closer or farther away, respectively, and then traced when you have the size you want. Also, an overhead projector (or a filmstrip projector) can be used as a spotlight to highlight demonstrations or presentations by you or students.

Multimedia Program

A multimedia program is a collection of teaching/learning materials involving more than one type of medium and organized around a single theme or topic. The types of media involved vary from rather simple kits—perhaps a videotape, a game, activity cards, student worksheets, and a manual of instructions for the teacher—to very sophisticated packages involving building-level site licensed computer software, student handbooks, reproducible activity worksheets, classroom wall hangings, and an on-line subscription to a telecommunication network. Some kits are designed for a teacher's use, others for individuals or small groups of students, and many more for the collaborative use of students and teachers. Teachers sometimes incorporate multimedia programs with learning activity centers.

Many multimedia programs are available on CD-ROM; they are designed principally as reference resources for students and teachers but include other aspects as well. One example is National Geographic's *Mammals: A Multimedia Encyclopedia*, which provides a lesson-planning guide, facts on more than 200 animals, 700 still color photos, range maps, animal vocalizations, full-motion movie clips, animal classification game, glossary, and a printing capability. Selected programs sources are shown in Figure 10.8.

Figure 10.8   Selected Internet resources for videotapes, computer software, CD-ROM's, and interactive multimedia.

- **A. D. A. M. Software, Inc.** http://www.adam.com
- **Agency for Instructional Technology** http:www.ait.net
- **AIMS Multimedia** http://www.aimsmultimedia.com
- **Bigchalk** http://www.bigchalk.com
- **Boxer Learning** http://www.boxerlearning.com
- **Broderbund Software** http://www.broderbund.com
- **Cognitive Concepts** http://www.earobics.com
- **Educational Insights** http://www.educationalinsights.com
- **Pitsco, Inc.** http://www.pitsco.com
- **Riverdeep Interactive Learning** http://www.riverdeep.net
- **Sunburst.Com** http://www.sunburst.com
- **SVE & Churchill Media** http://www.SVEmedia.com
- **Tom Snyder Productions** http://www.tomsnyder.com
- **Videodiscovery** http://www.videodiscovery.com

Everyone knows that television, videos, and videodiscs represent a powerful medium. Their use as teaching aids, however, may present scheduling, curriculum, and physical problems that some school systems are not yet able to handle adequately.

For purposes of professional discussion, television programming can be divided into three categories: instructional television, educational television, and general commercial television. Instructional television refers to programs specifically designed as classroom instruction. Educational television refers to cable television programs and public broadcasting programs designed to educate in general, but not aimed at classroom instruction. Commercial television programs include the entertainment and public service programs of the television networks and local stations.

Watch for announcements of special educational programs in professional journals. And, of course, television program listings can be obtained from your local commercial, educational, or cable companies, or by contacting network stations. Some networks sponsor Internet Websites.

Combined with a television monitor, the VCR (videocassette recorder) is one of the most popular and frequently used tools in today's classroom. Videotaped programs can do nearly everything that 16-mm films could do. In addition, the VCR, combined with a video camera, makes it possible to record student activities, practice, projects, and demonstrations—as well as yourself when teaching. It gives students a marvelous opportunity to self-assess as they see and hear themselves in action.

Entire course packages, as well as supplements, are now available on videocassettes or computer discs. The schools where you student teach and those where you eventually are employed may have a collection of such programs. Some teachers make their own.

Carefully selected programs, tapes, discs, films, and slides enhance student learning. For example, videodiscs and CD-ROMs offer quick and efficient accessibility to thousands of visuals, thus providing an appreciated boost to teachers of students with limited language proficiency. With the use of frame control, students can observe phenomena in detail that previous students only read about.

Check school supply catalogs and Internet resources for additional titles and sources for videodiscs. Generally, companies that sell computer software and CD-ROMs, also sell videodiscs. Figure 10.8 provides sample Web addresses from which you may obtain information.

COMPUTERS AND COMPUTER-BASED INSTRUCTIONAL TOOLS

As a teacher, you must be computer literate—you must understand and be able to use computers as well as you can read and write. The computer can be valuable to you in several ways. For example, the computer can help you manage the instruction by obtaining information, storing and preparing test materials, maintaining attendance and grade records, and preparing programs to aid in the academic development of individual students. This category of uses of the computer is referred to as **computer-managed instruction (CMI).**

The computer can also be used to employ various instructional software programs, to teach about computers, and to help students develop their metacognitive skills and their skills in computer use.[3] When the computer is used to assist students in their learning, it is called **computer-assisted instruction (CAI)** or *computer-assisted learning (CAL).*

The Placement and Use of Computers: The On-line Classroom

Teachers looking to make their classrooms more student-centered, collaborative, and interactive, increasingly turn to telecommunications networks. Webs of connected computers allow teachers and students from around the world to reach each other directly and to gain access to quantities of information previously unimaginable. Students using networks learn new inquiry and analytical skills in a stimulating environment, and they gain an increased awareness of their role as world citizens.

How you use the computer for instruction is determined by several factors, including your knowledge of and skills in its use, the number of computers that you have available for instructional use, where computers are placed in the school, the software that is available, printer availability, and the telecommunications capabilities (that is, wiring and phone lines, modems, and servers).

Schools continue to purchase or to lease computers and to upgrade their telecommunications capabilities. Some school districts are beginning to purchase handheld computers. Regarding the more traditional desktop computer placement and equipment available, following are some possible scenarios and how classroom teachers work within each.

SCENARIO 1. With the assistance of a computer lab and the lab technician, computers are integrated into the whole curriculum. In collaboration with members of interdisciplinary teaching teams, students use computers, software, and sources on the Internet in a computer lab as tools to build their knowledge, to write stories with word processors, to illustrate diagrams with paint utilities, to create interactive reports with hypermedia, and to graph data they have gathered using spreadsheets.

SCENARIO 2. In some schools, students take "computer" as an elective or an exploratory. Students in your classes who are simultaneously enrolled in such a course may be given special computer assignments by you that they can then share with the rest of the class.

SCENARIO 3. Some classrooms have a computer connected to a large-screen video monitor. The teacher or a student works the computer, and the entire class can see the monitor screen. As they view the screen, students can verbally respond to and interact with what is happening on the computer.

SCENARIO 4. You may be fortunate enough to have one or more computers in your classroom for all or for a part of the school year—computers with Internet connections, CD-ROM playing capabilities, a DVD player, an overhead projector, and an LCD (liquid crystal display) projection system. Coupled with the overhead projector, the LCD system allows you to project onto your large wall screen (and TV monitor at the same time) any image from computer software or a videodisc. With this system, all students can see and verbally interact with the multimedia instruction.

SCENARIO 5. Many classrooms have at least one computer with telecommunications capability, and some have many. When this is the case in your classroom, you most likely will have one or two students working at the computer while others are doing other

---

[3]See, for example, X. Bornas, et al., "Preventing Impulsivity in the Classroom: How Computers Can Help Teachers," *Computers in the Schools* 13(1–2):27–40 (1997).

Figure 10.9   Resources for free and inexpensive audio-visual materials.

- Best freeware and shareware at http://www.zdnet.com/pccomp/1001dl/html/1001.html
- Professional periodicals and journals.
- *Catalog of Audiovisual Materials: A Guide to Government Sources* (ED 198 822). Arlington, VA: ERIC Documents Reproduction Service.
- Educator's Progress Service, Inc., 214 Center Street, Randolph, WI 53956 (414-326-3126): *Educator's Guide to Free Audio and Video Materials; Educator's Guide to Free Films; Educator's Guide to Free Filmstrips; Guide to Free Computer Materials; Educator's Guide to Free Science Materials.*
- *Video Placement Worldwide (VPW).* Source of free sponsored educational videos on Internet at http://www.vpw.com.

learning activities (multilevel teaching). Computers can be an integral part of a learning center and an important aid in your overall effort to personalize the instruction within your classroom.

Programs are continually being developed and enhanced to meet the new and more powerful computers being made available. DVDs, computer software, and CD-ROMs are usually available from the same companies, addresses of which are listed in Figure 10.9. For evaluating computer software programs and testing them for their compatibility with your instructional objectives, there are many forms available—usually from the local school district or state department of education, and from professional associations.

For computers there are three types of storage disks—floppy disks of various storage capacities, the hard disk, and the CD-ROM, which is an abbreviation for "compact disc-read only memory." Use of a CD-ROM disc requires a computer and a CD-ROM drive. Newer computers have built-in CD-ROM drives, while others may be connected to one. As with floppy and hard disks, CD-ROMs are used for storing characters in a digital format, while images on a videodisc are stored in an analog format. The CD-ROM is capable of storing some 20,000 images or the equivalent of approximately 250,000 pages of text—the capacity of 1,520 360K floppy disks or eight 70MB hard disks. Therefore, it is ideal for storing

large amounts of information such as dictionaries, encyclopedias, and general reference works full of graphic images that you can copy and modify.

Having superior sound and visual performance, the DVD may replace CDs, VCR tapes, and computer CD-ROMs. Although in appearance it resembles the CD-ROM, the DVD can store nearly 17 gigabytes of information (a minimum of 7X the amount of data stored by a CD), provide faster retrieval of data, and be made interactive.

Sources of Free and Inexpensive Audio-visual Materials

For free and inexpensive audio-visual materials, check the Internet and your college or university library for sources listed in Figure 10.9.

USING COPYRIGHTED VIDEO, COMPUTER, AND MULTIMEDIA PROGRAMS

You must be knowledgeable about the laws concerning the use of copyrighted videos and computer software materials. Although space here prohibits full inclusion of U.S. legal guidelines, your local school district undoubtedly can provide a copy of current district policies to ensure your compliance with all copyright laws. As with printed materials that are copyrighted, when preparing to make any copy you must find out whether it is permitted by law under the category of "permitted use." If not allowed under "permitted use," then you must get written permission to reproduce the material from the holder of the copyright. Figures 10.10 and 10.11 present guidelines for copying videotapes and computer software.

Usually, when you purchase CD-ROMs and other multimedia software packages intended for use by schools, you are also paying for a license to modify and use its contents for instructional purposes. However, not all CD-ROMs include copyright permission, so always check the copyright notice on any disc you purchase and use. Whenever in doubt, do not use it until you have asked your district media specialists about copyrights or have obtained necessary permissions from the original source.

As yet, there are no guidelines for fair use of films, filmstrips, slides, and multimedia programs. A general rule of thumb for using any copyrighted material is to treat the work of others as you would want your own material treated were it protected by a copyright (see Figure 10.12).

Figure 10.10   Copyright law for off-air videotaping. *Note:* From *Instructional Media and Technologies for Learning,* 6th ed., p. 389, by R. Heinich, M. Molenda, J. D. Russell, and S. E. Smaldino, 1999, Copyright 1999 by Merrill/Prentice Hall, Upper Saddle River, NJ: Merrill/Prentice Hall. Reprinted by permission.

Permitted Uses—You May

1. Request your media center or audiovisual coordinator to record a program for you if you cannot or if you lack the equipment.
2. Keep a videotaped copy of a broadcast (including cable transmission) for 45 calendar days, after which the program must be erased.
3. Use the program in class once during the first 10 school days of the 45 calendar days, and a second time if instruction needs to be reinforced.
4. Have professional staff view the program several times for evaluation purposes during the full 45 day period.
5. Make a few copies to meet legitimate needs, but these copies must be erased when the original videotape is erased.
6. Use only a part of the program if instructional needs warrant.
7. Enter into a licensing agreement with the copyright holder to continue use of the program.

Prohibited Uses—You May *Not*

1. Videotape premium cable services such as HBO without express permission.
2. Alter the original content of the program.
3. Exclude the copyright notice on the program.
4. Videorecord before a request for use is granted—the request to record must come from an instructor.
5. Keep the program, and any copies, after 45 days.

Figure 10.11   Copyright law for use of computer software. *Source:* December, 1980, Congressional amendment to the 1976 Copyright Act.

Permitted Uses—You May

1. Make a single back-up or archival copy of the computer program.
2. Adapt the computer program to another language if the program is unavailable in the target language.
3. Add features to make better use of the computer program.

Prohibited Uses—You May *Not*

1. Make multiple copies.
2. Make replacement copies from an archival or back-up copy.
3. Make copies of copyrighted programs to be sold, leased, loaned, transmitted, or given away.

Figure 10.12   Fair use guidelines for using multimedia programs.

---

1. For portions of copyrighted works used in your own multimedia production for use in teaching, follow normal copyright guidelines (e.g., the limitations on the amount of material used, whether it be motion media, text, music, illustrations, photographs, or computer software).
2. You may display your own multimedia work using copyrighted works to other teachers, such as in workshops. However, you may *not* make and distribute copies to colleagues without obtaining permission from copyright holders.
3. You may use your own multimedia production for instruction over an electronic network (e.g., distance learning) provided there are limits to access and to the number of students enrolled. You may *not* distribute such work over any electronic network (local area or wide area) without expressed permission from copyright holders.
4. You must obtain permissions from copyright holders before using any copyrighted materials in educational multimedia productions for commercial reproduction and distribution or before replicating more than one copy, distributing copies to others, or for use beyond your own classroom.

SUMMARY

You have learned of the variety of tools available to supplement your instruction. When used wisely, these tools will help you to reach more of your students more of the time. As you know, teachers must meet the needs of a diversity of students—many who are linguistically and culturally different. The material selected and presented in this chapter should be of help in doing that. The future will undoubtedly continue bringing technological innovations that will be even more helpful—compact discs, computers, and telecommunications equipment are only the beginning of a revolution for teaching. As we enter a new millennium, new instructional delivery systems made possible by microcomputers and multimedia workstations will likely fundamentally alter what had become the traditional role of the classroom teacher during the twentieth century.

You should remain alert to developing technologies for your teaching. Digital videodiscs (DVDs), CD-ROMs interfaced with computers (i.e., the use of multimedia), telecommunications, digitized textbooks, and portable handheld computers offer exciting technologies for learning. New instructional technologies are advancing at an increasingly rapid rate. You and your colleagues must maintain vigilance over new developments, constantly looking for those that will not only help make student learning meaningful and interesting, and your teaching effective, but that are cost effective as well.

ADDITIONAL EXERCISES

See the companion Website http://www.prenhall. com/ kellough for the following exercises related to the content of this chapter:

- Collecting and Evaluating Free Materials
- Observations of Teacher's Use of Audio-visual Materials
- The Classroom Teacher and the Purchase of Materials for Teaching

QUESTIONS FOR CLASS DISCUSSION

1. Explain how your effective use of the writing board and bulletin board can help students see relationships among verbal concepts or information.
2. Describe what you should look for when deciding whether material that you have obtained free or inexpensively is appropriate for use in your teaching.
3. Share with others in your class your knowledge, observations, and feelings about the use of multimedia and telecommunications for teaching. From your discussion, what more would you like to know about the use of multimedia and telecommunications for teaching? How might you learn more about these things?
4. In 1922 Thomas Edison predicted that "the motion picture is destined to revolutionize our educational system and . . .

in a few years it will supplant largely, if not entirely, the use of textbooks." In 1945 William Levenson of the Cleveland public schools' radio station claimed that "the time may come when a portable radio receiver will be as common in the classroom as is the blackboard." In the early 1960s B. F. Skinner believed that with the help of the new teaching machines and programmed instruction, students could learn twice as much in the same time and with the same effort as in a standard classroom. Did motion pictures, radio, programmed instruction, and television revolutionize education? Will computers become as much a part of the classroom as writing boards? What do you predict the public school classroom of the year 2050 will be like? Will the role of a teacher be different in any way than it is today?
5. Select and identify one instructional tool that is *not* discussed in this chapter and explain to your classmates its advantages and disadvantages for use in teaching.
6. Has the purchase of new textbooks and library books become stagnated as schools increase their spending on leading-edge technology? Have music and art programs suffered as a result of increased expenditures on technology? How are school districts finding the funds necessary for the cost of technology, such as for wiring classrooms for networking and for updated computers; and for the planning, installation, and maintenance of complex computer networks? Or are districts finding the necessary funds? In this respect, are some districts worse off or better off than others? Is this an issue?
7. Select one of the "Reflective Thoughts" from the introduction to Part III (page 232) that is specifically related to the content of this chapter, research it, and write a one-page essay explaining why you agree or disagree with the thought. Share your essay with members of your class for their thoughts.
8. Describe any prior concepts you held that changed as a result of your experiences with this chapter. Describe the changes.
9. From your current observations and field work as related to this teacher preparation program, clearly identify one specific example of educational practice that seems contradictory to exemplary practice or theory as presented in this chapter. Present your explanation for the discrepancy.
10. Do you have questions generated by the content of this chapter? If you do, list them along with ways answers might be found.

FOR FURTHER READING

Abdullah, M. H. *Guidelines for Evaluating Websites.* ERIC Digest426440 98. Bloomington, IN: ERIC Clearinghouse on Reading, English, and Communications, 1998.

Bernhard, J.; Lernhardt, M. M.; Miranda-Decker, R. "Evaluating Instructional Materials." *Mathematics Teaching in the Middle School* 5(3):174–178 (November 1999).

Brogan, P. "The Good, the Bad, and the Useless: Recognizing the Signs of Quality in Educational Software." From the *American School Board Journal* [On-line 3/26/01, http://www.electronic-school.com/2001/03/0301f3.html]

Churma, M. *A Guide to Integrating Technology Standards into the Curriculum.* Upper Saddle River, NJ: Merrill/Prentice Hall, 1999.

Ertmer, P. A.; Hruskocy, C.; and Woods, D. M. *Education on the Internet.* Upper Saddle River, NJ: Merrill/Prentice Hall, 2000.

Gardiner, S. "Cybercheating: A New Twist on an Old Problem." *Phi Delta, Kappan* 83(2):172–174 (October 2001).

Gruber, S., ed. *Weaving a Virtual Web: Practical Approaches to New Information Technologies.* Urbana, IL: National Council of Teachers of English, 2000.

McCullen, C. "Copyright Issues in a Digital World." *Middle Ground* 3(2):7–9, 52 (October 1999).

———. "The Hows and Whys of Conducting Desktop Teleconferences." *Middle Ground* 2(3):7–8 (February 1999).

McLeod, J., and Kilpatrick, K. M. "Exploring Science at the Museum." *Educational Leadership* 59–63 (April 2001).

Newby, T. J.; Stepich, D. A.; Lehman, J. D.; and Russell, J. D. *Instructional Technology for Teaching and Learning,* 2nd ed. Upper Saddle River, NJ: Merrill/Prentice Hall, 2000.

Nichols, W. D.; Wood, K. D.; and Rickelman, R. "Using Technology to Engage Students in Reading and Writing." *Middle School Journal* 32(5):45–50 (May 2001).

Owens, K. D. "Scientists and Engineers in the Middle School Classroom." *Clearing House* 73(3):150–152 (January/February 2000).

Renard, L. "Cut and Paste 101: Plagiarism and the Net." *Educational Leadership* 57(4):38–42 (December 1999/January 2000).

Roblyer, M. D., and Edwards, J. *Integrating Educational Technology into Teaching,* 2nd ed. Upper Saddle River, NJ: Merrill/Prentice Hall, 2000.

Rowlands, K. D. "Alice in Web Wonderland: Internet Resources for Middle Schoolers and Their Teachers." *Voices from the Middle* 7(3):49–54 (March 2000).

Tanner, C. K. "Into the Woods, Wetlands, and Prairies." *Educational Leadership* 64–66 (April 2001).

Wassermann, S. "Curriculum Enrichment With Computer Software." *Phi Delta Kappan* 82(8):592–597 (April 2001).

Weinman, J., and Haag, P. "Gender Equity in Cyberspace." *Educational Leadership* 56(5):44–49 (February 1999).

Wilhelm, J. "Literacy by Design: Why Is All This Technology So Important?" *Voices from the Middle* 7(3):4–14 (March 2000).

Part IV

ASSESSMENT AND CONTINUING PROFESSIONAL DEVELOPMENT

Part IV responds to your needs concerning

- Assessing student learning.
- Finding a teaching job.
- Grading and reporting student achievement.
- Meeting with parents and guardians.
- Performance assessment.
- Portfolio assessment.
- Remaining an alert and effective teacher.
- More sample rubrics for scoring student work.
- Self-assessment through micro-peer teaching.
- Student teaching.

REFLECTIVE THOUGHTS

When assessing for student achievement, it is important to use procedures that are compatible with the instructional objectives.

Performance-based assessment procedures require students to produce rather than to select responses.

What separates the professional teacher from "anyone off the street" is the teacher's ability to go beyond mere description of a student's behavior.

For the continued intellectual and emotional development of your students, your comments about their work should be useful, productive, analytical, diagnostic, and prescriptive.

You must provide opportunities for students to think about what they are learning, how they are learning it, and how far they have progressed in learning it.

It is unprofessional to place a student teacher into a "sink-or-swim" situation.

Teaching is such an electrifying profession that it is not easy to remain energetic and to stay abreast of changes and trends in research and practice.

A teacher's concern should not be with deciding which students are better than others but with helping all of them succeed.

A student should never need to ask the question, "What's going to be on the test?"

Important decisions that affect an individual child's educational career should not rest on just one test score but on multiple sources of data.

Assessing and Reporting Student Achievement

Whereas the preceding parts of this resource guide addressed the *why* (Part I), *what* (Part II), and *how* (Part III) of teaching, Part IV focuses on the fourth and final component—the *how well*, or assessment, component. Together, these four components are the essentials of effective instruction.

Teaching and learning are reciprocal processes that depend on and affect one another. Thus, the assessment component deals with both how well the students are learning and how well the teacher is teaching. This chapter addresses the former.

Assessment is an integral part of an ongoing process in the educational arena. Curricula, buildings, materi-

als, specific courses, teachers, supervisors, administrators, and equipment all must be periodically assessed in relation to student learning, which is the purpose of the school. When gaps between anticipated results and student achievement exist, efforts are made to eliminate the factors that seem to be limiting the educational output or, in some other way, to improve the situation. Thus, educational progress occurs.

Much concern today is expressed over the use of *high-stakes assessments*. An assessment is called *high stakes* if its results carry serious consequences, such as a student's grade promotion resting on his performance on one test, or the student's graduation from high school resting on her performance on one test. We agree with the many educators who argue that important decisions affecting an individual student's educational career should not rest on just one test score but on multiple sources of data. In our opinion, placing a too-high reliance on a single source of data is likely to result in an increase, rather than an improvement, in the school dropout rate.

Albeit, to learn effectively, students need to know how they are doing. Similarly, to be an effective teacher, you must be informed about what the student knows, feels, and can do so that you can help the student build on her or his skills, knowledge, and attitudes. Therefore, you and your students need continuous feedback on their progress and problems to plan appropriate learning activities and to make adjustments to those already planned. If this feedback says that progress is slow, you can provide alternative activities; if it indicates that some or all of the students have already mastered the desired learning, you can eliminate unnecessary activities and practice for some, or all, of the students. In short, assessment provides a key for both effective teaching and learning.

The importance of continuous assessment mandates that you are knowledgeable about various principles and techniques of assessment. This chapter explains some of those and shows you how to construct and use assessment instruments. It defines terms related to assessment, suggests procedures to use in the construction of assessment items, points out the advantages and disadvantages of different types of assessment items and procedures, and explains the construction and use of alternative assessment devices.

In addition, this chapter discusses grading (or marking) and reporting student achievement, two responsibilities that can consume much of a teacher's valuable time. Grading is time-consuming and frustrating for many teachers. What should be graded? Should grades or marks represent student growth, level of achievement in a group, effort, attitude, general behavior, or a combination of these? What should determine grades—homework, tests, projects, class participation and group work, or some combination of these? And, what should be their relative weights? These are just a few of the questions that plague teachers, parents, and, indeed the profession, and have for a century or more of education in this country.

Still today, in too many middle level schools, the grade progress report and final report card are about the only communication between the school and the student's home. Unless the teacher and the school have clearly determined what grades or marks represent and unless such understanding is periodically reviewed with each set of new parents or guardians, these reports may create unrest and dissatisfaction on the part of parents, guardians, and students and prove to be alienating devices. Then, instead of informing parents and guardians, the grading system and reporting scheme may separate even further the home and the school, which do have a common concern—the intellectual, physical, social, and emotional development of the student.

The development of the student encompasses growth in the cognitive, affective, and psychomotor domains. Traditional objective paper-and-pencil tests provide only a portion of the data needed to indicate student progress in those domains. Many experts today, as indeed they have in the past, question the traditional sources of data and encourage the search for, development of, and use of alternative means to assess more authentically the students' development of thinking and higher-level learning. Although much is not yet clear, one thing that is clear is that various techniques of assessment with the resultant multiple kinds of data must be used to determine how the student works, what the student is learning, and what the student can produce as a result of that learning. As a teacher, you must develop a repertoire of means of assessing learner behavior and academic progress.

Marks and grades have been a part of school for about 100 years, but it is clear to many experts that the conventional report card with marks or grades falls short of being a developmentally appropriate procedure for reporting the academic performance or progress of learners. Although some schools are experimenting with other ways of reporting student achievement in learning, letter grades for middle level schools still seem to be firmly entrenched—parents, students, colleges, and employers have come to expect grades as evaluations. Today's interest is (or should be) more on what the student can do (performance testing) as a result of learning than merely on what the student can recall (memory testing) from the experience.

In addition, there have been complaints about subjectivity and unfair practices. As a result of these concerns, a variety of systems of assessment and reporting has evolved, is still evolving, and will likely continue to evolve throughout your professional career.

When teachers are aware of alternative systems, they may be able to develop assessment and reporting processes that are fair and effective for particular situations. So, after beginning with assessment, the final focus in this chapter is on today's principles and practices in grading and reporting student achievement.

OBJECTIVES

Upon completion of this chapter, you should be able to

1. Demonstrate an understanding of the importance of assessment in teaching and learning.
2. Describe the concept of authentic assessment.

3. Explain the value of and give an example of a performance assessment that could be used in teaching your subject.

4. Explain why criterion-referenced grading is preferred over norm-referenced grading.

5. Explain how rubrics, checklists, portfolios, and journals are used in the assessment of student learning.

6. Differentiate between diagnostic assessment, summative assessment, and formative assessment, with examples of when and how each can be used.

7. Describe the importance of self-assessment in teaching and learning.

8. Describe the importance of and manner by which parents or guardians can be involved in the education of their children.

9. Describe guidelines for meeting with an angry parent.

PURPOSES AND PRINCIPLES OF ASSESSMENT

Assessment of achievement in student learning is designed to serve several purposes. They include the following:

1. *To assist in student learning.* This is the purpose that is usually thought of first when speaking of assessment, and it is the principal topic of this chapter. For the classroom teacher, it is (or should be) the most important purpose.

2. *To identify students' strengths and weaknesses.* Identification and assessment of students' strengths and weaknesses are necessary for two reasons: to structure and restructure the learning activities and to restructure the curriculum. Concerning the first, for example, data on student strengths and weaknesses in content and process skills are important in planning activities appropriate for *both* skill development and intellectual development. This is *diagnostic assessment,* known also as preassessment. For the second, data on student strengths and weaknesses in content and skills are useful for making appropriate modifications to the curriculum.

3. *To assess the effectiveness of a particular instructional strategy.* It is important for you to know how well a specific strategy helped accomplish a specific goal or objective. Exemplary teachers continually reflect on and evaluate their strategy choices, using a number of sources: student achievement as measured by assessment instruments, their own intuition, informal feedback given by the students, and, sometimes, informal feedback given by colleagues, such as members of a teaching team or mentor teachers. (Mentor teachers are discussed in Chapter 12).

4. *To assess and improve the effectiveness of curriculum programs.* Committees composed of teachers and administrators, and sometimes parents, students, and other members of the school and community, continually assess components of the curriculum. The assessment is done while students are learning (*formative assessment*) and afterward (*summative assessment*).

5. *To assess and improve teaching effectiveness.* To improve student learning, teachers are periodically evaluated on the basis of (a) their commitment to working with middle grades students; (b) their ability to cope with students at a particular age, developmental, or grade level; (c) the achievement of subject matter knowledge by the students they teach; and (d) their ability to show mastery of appropriate instructional techniques articulated throughout this resource guide.

6. *To provide data that assist in decision making about a student's future.* Assessment of student achievement is important in guiding decision making about course and program placement, promotion, school transfer, class standing, eligibility for honors and scholarships, and career planning.

7. *To provide data to communicate with and involve parents and guardians in their children's learning.* Parents and guardians, communities, and school boards all share in an accountability for the effectiveness of the learning of the children. Today's middle level schools are reaching out more than ever before and engaging parents, guardians, and the community in their children's education. All teachers play an important role in the process of communicating with, reaching out to, and involving parents, guardians, and the community.

Because the welfare and, indeed, the future of so many people depend on the outcomes of assessment, it is impossible to overemphasize its importance. For a learning endeavor to be successful, the learner must have answers to basic questions: Where am I going? Where am I now? How do I get where I am going? How will I know when I get there? Am I on the right track for getting there? These questions are integral to a good program of assessment. Of course, in the process of teaching and learning, the answers may be ever changing, and the teacher and students continue to assess and adjust plans as appropriate and necessary. As you have been reminded many times in this resource guide, the exemplary school is in a mode of continuous change and progress.

Based on the preceding questions, the following are principles that guide the assessment program and that are reflected in the discussions in this chapter.

- A teacher's responsibility is to facilitate student learning and to assess student progress in that learning, and for that, the teacher is, or should be, held accountable.
- Assessment is a continuous process. The selection and implementation of plans and activities requires continuing monitoring and assessment to check on progress and to change or adopt strategies to promote desired behavior.
- Assessment is a reciprocal process, which includes assessment of teacher performance, as well as student achievement.

- Evidence and input data concerning how well the teacher and students are doing should come from a variety of sources and types of data-collecting devices.
- Reflection and self-assessment are important components of any successful assessment program. Reflection and self-assessment are important if students are to develop the skills necessary for them to assume increasingly greater ownership of their own learning. Reflection and self-assessment are important for the continued and increasing effectiveness of a teacher.
- Students need to know how well they are doing.
- Teachers need to know how well they are doing.
- The program of assessment should aid teaching effectiveness and contribute to the intellectual, social, and psychological growth of young adolescents.

TERMS USED IN ASSESSMENT

When discussing the assessment component of teaching and learning, it is easy to be confused by the terminology used. The following clarification of terms is offered to aid your reading and comprehension.

Assessment and Evaluation

Although some authors distinguish between the terms **assessment** (the process of finding out what students are learning, a relatively neutral process) and **evaluation** (making sense of what was found out, a subjective process), in this text we do not. We consider the difference too slight to matter; we consider the terms to be synonymous.

Measurement and Assessment

Measurement refers to quantifiable data about specific behaviors. Tests and the statistical procedures used to analyze the results are examples. Measurement is a descriptive and objective process; that is, it is relatively free from human value judgments.

Assessment includes objective data from measurement but also other types of information, some of which are more subjective, such as information from anecdotal records, teacher observations, and ratings of student performance. In addition to the use of objective data (data from measurement), assessment includes arriving at value judgments made on the basis of subjective information.

An example of the use of these terms is as follows. A teacher may share the information that Penny Brown received a score in the 90th percentile on the eighth-grade state-wide achievement test in reading (a statement of measurement) but may add that "according to my assessment of her work in my language arts class, she has not been an outstanding student" (a statement of assessment).

Validity and Reliability

The degree to which a measuring instrument actually measures what it is intended to measure is the instrument's **validity.** For example, when we ask if an instrument (such as a performance assessment instrument) has validity, key questions concerning that instrument include the following: Does the instrument adequately sample the intended content? Does it measure the cognitive, affective, and psychomotor knowledge and skills that are important to the unit of content being tested? Does it sample all the instructional objectives of that unit?

The accuracy with which a technique consistently measures what it does measure is its **reliability.** If, for example, you know that you weigh 118 pounds, and a scale consistently records 118 pounds when you stand on it, then that scale has reliability. However, if the same scale consistently records 105 pounds when you stand on it, we can still say the scale has reliability (producing similar results when used again and again) but it is not necessarily valid. The scale is not measuring what it is supposed to measure, so it is reliable, but not valid. A technique must have reliability before it can have validity. The greater the number of test items or situations on a particular content objective, the higher the reliability. The higher the reliability, the more consistency there will be in students' scores measuring their understanding of that objective.

Authentic Assessment: Advantages and Disadvantages

When assessing for student achievement, it is important that you use procedures that are compatible with the instructional objectives. This is referred to as **authentic assessment.** Other terms used for *authentic* assessment are *accurate, active, aligned, alternative,* and *direct.* Although the term *performance* assessment is sometimes used, **performance assessment** refers to the type of student response being assessed, whereas authentic assessment refers to the assessment situation. So, not all performance assessments are authentic, but assessments that are authentic are most assuredly performance assessments.

In language arts, for example, it may seem fairly easy to develop a criterion-referenced test, administer it, and grade it, but tests often measure language *skills* rather than language use. It is extremely difficult to measure students' communicative competence with a test. Tests do not measure listening and talking very well, and a test on punctuation marks, for example, does not indicate students' ability to use punctuation marks correctly in their own writing. Instead, tests typically evaluate students' ability to add punctuation marks to a set of sentences created by someone else or to proofread and spot punctuation errors in someone else's writing. An alternative and far better approach is to examine how students use punctuation marks in their own writing.[1] An authentic assessment of punctuation, then, would be an assessment of a performance item that involves students in writing and in punctuating their own writing. For the authentic assessment of the student's understanding of what he or she has been learning, you would use a performance-based assessment procedure.

Consider another example: "If students have been actively involved in classifying objects using multiple characteristics, it sends them a confusing message if they are then required to take a paper-and-pencil test that asks them to 'define classification' or recite a memorized list of characteristics of good classifications schemes."[2] An authentic assessment technique would be a performance item that actually involves the students in classifying objects. In other words, to obtain an accurate assessment of a student's learning, the teacher uses a performance-based assessment procedure that requires students to produce rather than to select a response.

Advantages claimed for the use of authentic assessment include (a) the direct (also known as performance-based, criterion-referenced, outcome-based) measurement of what students should know and can do and (b) an emphasis on higher order thinking. On the other hand, disadvantages of authentic assessment include a higher cost; difficulty in making results consistent and usable; and problems with validity, reliability, and comparability.

Unfortunately, a teacher may never see a particular student again after a given school semester or year is over, and the effects he or she has had on the student's values and attitudes may never be observed by that teacher at all. In schools where groups or teams of teachers remain with the same cohort of students—as in the house concept and looping programs—teachers are often able to observe the positive changes in their students' values and attitudes.

Diagnostic, Formative, and Summative Assessment

Assessing a student's achievement is a three-stage process, involving (1) *diagnostic assessment* (preassessment)—the assessment of the student's knowledge and skills *before* the new instruction; (2) *formative assessment*—the assessment of learning *during* the instruction; and (3) *summative assessment*—the assessment of learning *after* the instruction, ultimately represented by the student's final term, semester, or year's achievement grade.

Grades (or marks) shown on unit tests, progress reports, deficiency notices, and interim reports are examples of formative evaluation reports. However, an end-of-chapter test or a unit test is summative when the test represents the absolute end of the student's learning of material for that instructional unit.

ASSESSING STUDENT LEARNING: THREE AVENUES

Three general avenues are available for assessing a student's achievement in learning: (1) assess what the student *says*—for example, the quantity and quality of a student's contributions to class discussions; (2) assess what the student *does*—for example, a student's performance (the amount and quality of a student's participation in the learning activities); and (3) assess what the student *writes*—for example, items in the student's portfolio (homework assignments, checklists, project work, and written tests).

Importance and Weight of Each Avenue

Although your own situation and personal philosophy will dictate the levels of importance and weight you give to each avenue of assessment, you should have a strong rationale if you value and weigh them differently than one-third each.

Assessing What a Student Says and Does

When evaluating what a student says, you should listen to the student's oral reports, questions, responses, and interactions with others, and observe the student's attentiveness, involvement in class activities, creativeness, and responses to challenges. Notice that we say you should *listen* and *observe*. While listening to what the student says, you should also observe the student's nonverbal behaviors. For this you can use narrative observation forms (see Figure 11.1) and you can use observations with checklists and scoring rubrics (see sample checklists in Figures 11.2, 11.4, 11.5, 11.6, and 11.12 and sample scoring rubrics in Figures 8.1, 11.2, 11.3, 11.10, and 11.11), and periodic conferences with the student.

With each technique used, you must proceed from your awareness of anticipated learning outcomes (the instructional objectives) and assess a student's progress toward meeting those objectives. That is referred to as **criterion-referenced** assessment.

OBSERVATION FORM

Figure 11.1 illustrates a sample generic form for recording and evaluating teacher observations of a student's verbal and nonverbal behaviors. With modern technology, such as the software program *Learner Profile* a

---

[1] G. E. Tompkins and K. Hoskisson, *Language Arts: Content and Teaching Strategies* (Upper Saddle River, NJ: Prentice Hall, 1991) p. 63.

[2] S. J. Rakow, "Assessment: A Driving Force," *Science Scope* 15(6):3 (March 1992).

Figure 11.1   Form for evaluating and recording student verbal and nonverbal behaviors.

Student			Course		School	

Observer _____   Date _____   Period _____

Objective	Desired Behavior	What Student Did, Said, or Wrote

Teacher's (Observer's) comments:

---

teacher can record observations electronically anywhere at any time.[3]

CHECKLIST VERSUS SCORING RUBRIC

As you can see from the sample rubric and checklist shown in Figure 11.2, there is little difference between a checklist and a rubric. The difference is that rubrics show the degrees for the desired characteristics, and checklists usually show only the desired characteristics. The checklist could easily be made into a scoring rubric and the rubric could easily be made into a checklist.

GUIDELINES FOR ASSESSING WHAT A STUDENT SAYS AND DOES

When assessing a student's verbal and nonverbal behaviors in the classroom you should

- Maintain an anecdotal record (teacher's log) book or folder, with a separate section for your records of each student.
- For a specific activity, list the desirable behaviors.
- Check the list against the specific instructional objectives.
- Record your observations as quickly as possible following your observation. Audio or video recordings, and, of course, computer software programs, can

help you maintain records and check the accuracy of your memory. If this is inconvenient, you should spend time during school, immediately after school, or later that evening recording your observations while they are still fresh in your memory.
- Record your professional judgment about the student's progress toward the desired behavior, but think it through before transferring it to a permanent record.
- Write comments that are reminders to yourself, such as, "Discuss observation with the student," "Check validity of observation by further testing," "Discuss observations with student's mentor" (e.g., an adult representative from the community), and "Discuss observations with other teachers on the teaching team."

Assessing What a Student Writes

To assess what a student writes, use worksheets, written homework and papers, student journal writing, student writing projects, student portfolios, and tests (all discussed later in this chapter). In many schools, portfolios, worksheets, and homework assignments are the tools usually used for the formative evaluation of each student's achievement. Tests, too, should be a part of this evaluation, but tests are also used for summative evaluation at the end of a unit and for diagnostic purposes.

Your summative evaluation of a student's achievement and any other final judgment made by you about a student can have an impact on the psychological and intellectual development of that student. Special atten-

---

[3]For information about *Learner Profile,* contact Sunburst, 101 Castleton Street, PO Box 100, Pleasantville, NY 10570-0100. Phone 800-321-7511. See http://www.sunburst-store.com.

Figure 11.2   Checklist and rubric compared.

Sample rubric for assessing a student's skill in listening.

Score Point 3—Strong listener:

Responds immediately to oral directions

Focuses on speaker

Maintains appropriate attention span

Listens to what others are saying

Is interactive

Score Point 2—Capable listener:

Follows oral directions

Usually attentive to speaker and to discussions

Listens to others without interrupting

Score Point 1—Developing listener:

Has difficulty following directions

Relies on repetition

Often inattentive

Has short attention span

Often interrupts the speaker

Sample checklist for assessing a student's skill in map work:

Check each item if the map comes up to standard in this particular category.

_____ 1. Accuracy

_____ 2. Neatness

_____ 3. Attention to details

Figure 11.3   Scoring rubric for assessing student writing. (*Source:* Texas Education Agency, *Writing Inservice Guide for English Language Arts and TAAS* (Austin, TX: Author, 1993.)

Score Point 4—correct purpose, mode, audience; effective elaboration; consistent organization; clear sense of order and completeness; fluent

Score Point 3—correct purpose, mode, audience; moderately well elaborated; organized but possible brief digressions; clear, effective language

Score Point 2—correct purpose, mode, audience; some elaboration; some specific details; gaps in organization; limited language control

Score Point 1—attempts to address audience; brief, vague, unelaborated; wanders off topic; lack of language control; little or no organization; wrong purpose and mode

tion is given to this later in the section titled "Recording Teacher Observations and Judgments."

GUIDELINES FOR ASSESSING STUDENT WRITING

Use the following guidelines when assessing what a student writes.

Student writing assignments, test items, and scoring rubrics (see Figure 11.3) *should be criterion-referenced.* They should correlate with and be compatible with specific instructional objectives. Regardless of the avenue chosen and the relative weights you give them, you must evaluate against the instructional objectives. Any given objective may be checked using more than one method and more than one instrument. Subjectivity, inherent in the assessment process, may be reduced as you check for validity, comparing results of one measuring strategy against those of another.

Read nearly everything a student writes. [*Note:* We are not talking here about student diaries and private journals which are just that—private—and, in our opinion, should be left at home, not brought to school.] Regarding schoolwork, if it is important for the student to do the work, then it is equally important that you give your professional attention to the product of the student's efforts. Of course, as emphasized in Chapter 8, in deference to the teacher's productive and efficient use of valuable time, student papers can be read with varying degrees of intensity and scrutiny, depending on the purpose of the assignment.

Provide written or verbal comments about the student's work, and be positive in those comments. Rather than just writing "good" on a student's paper, briefly state what it was that, in your opinion, made it good. Rather than simply saying or pointing out that the student did not do it right, tell or show the student what is acceptable and how to achieve it. For reinforcement, use positive comments and encouragement as frequently as possible.

Think before writing a comment on a student's paper, asking yourself how you think the student (or a parent or guardian) will interpret and react to the comment and whether that is your intended interpretation.

Avoid writing evaluative comments or grades in student journals.[4] Student journals are for encouraging students to write, to think about their thinking, and to record their creative thoughts. In journal writing, students should be encouraged to write about their experiences in school and out of school, and especially about their experiences related to what is being learned. They should be encouraged to write how they feel about what

---

[4]See, for example, A. Chandler, "Is This for a Grade? A Personal Look at Journals," *English Journal* 86(1):45–49 (January 1997).

is being learned and about how they are learning it. Writing in journals gives them practice in expressing themselves in written form and in connecting their learning, and should provide nonthreatening freedom to do it. Comments and evaluations from teachers might discourage creative and spontaneous expression. You can write simple empathic comments such as "Thank you for sharing your thoughts," or "I think I understand what makes you feel that way."

When reading student journals, talk individually with students to seek clarification about their expressions. Student journals are useful to the teacher (of any subject) in understanding the student's thought processes and writing skills (diagnostic assessment), and should not be graded. For grading purposes, teachers may simply record whether the student is maintaining a journal and, perhaps, an assessment regarding the quantity of writing in it, but no judgment should be made about the quality.

When reviewing student portfolios, discuss with students individually the progress in their learning as shown by the materials in their portfolios. As with student journals, the portfolio should not be graded or compared in any way with those of other students. Its purpose is for student self-assessment and to show progress in learning. For this to happen, students should keep all or major samples of papers related to the course in their portfolios. (Student portfolios are discussed later.)

Assessment for Affective and Psychomotor Domain Learning

While assessment of cognitive domain learning lends itself to traditional written tests of achievement, the assessment of learning within the affective and psychomotor domains is best suited to the use of performance checklists where student behaviors can be observed in action. However, many educators today are encouraging the use of alternative assessment procedures (i.e., alternatives to traditional paper-and-pencil written testing). After all, in the learning that is most important and that has the most meaning to students, the domains are inextricably interconnected. Learning that is meaningful to students is not as easily compartmentalized as the taxonomies of educational objectives would imply. Alternative assessment strategies include the use of projects, portfolios, skits, papers, oral presentations, and performance tests.

STUDENT INVOLVEMENT IN ASSESSMENT

Students' continuous self-assessment should be planned as an important component of the assessment program. If students are to progress in their understanding of their own thinking (*metacognition*) and in their intellec-tual development, then they must receive instruction and guidance in how to become more responsible for their own learning. During that empowerment process, they learn to think better of themselves and of their individual capabilities. To achieve this self-understanding and improved self-esteem requires the experiences afforded by successes, along with guidance in self-understanding and self-assessment.

To meet these goals, teachers provide opportunities for students to think about what they are learning, how they are learning it, and how far they have progressed. Specifically, to engage students in the assessment process, you can provide opportunities for the students to identify learning targets that they especially value; help in the design of assessment devices for the units of study; evaluate the tests that are furnished by the textbook publisher in terms of how well they match learning targets identified by you and the students; and help interpret assessment results. To aid in the interpretation of results, students can maintain portfolios of their work, use rating scales or checklists periodically to self-assess their progress, and discuss their self-assessments with their parents or guardians and teacher.

Using Student Portfolios

Portfolios are used by teachers as a means of instruction and by teachers and students as one means of assessing student learning. Although there is little research evidence to support or refute the claim, educators believe the instructional value comes from the process of the student's assembling and maintaining a personal portfolio. During that creative process, the student is expected to self-reflect, to think critically about what has and is being learned, and to assume some responsibility for his or her own learning.

Student portfolios fall into three general categories, but the purpose in a given situation may transcend some combination of all three. The categories are (a) *selected works portfolio,* in which students maintain samples of their work as prompted by the teacher, (b) *longitudinal* or *growth portfolio,* which is oriented toward outcome-driven goals and includes samples of student work from the beginning and the end of the school term (or thematic unit of study) to exemplify achievement toward the goals, and (c) *passport* or *career portfolio,* which contains samples of student work that will enable the student to transition, such as from one school grade level to the next or from school to work.

Student portfolios should be well organized and, depending on the purpose (or category), should contain assignment sheets, class worksheets, the results of homework, project binders, forms for student self-assessment and reflection on their work, and other class materials thought to be important by the students and teacher.[5] As a model of a real-life portfolio, you can show students your personal career portfolio (see Chapter 12).

PORTFOLIO ASSESSMENT: KNOWING AND DEALING WITH ITS LIMITATIONS

Although portfolio assessment as an alternative to traditional methods of evaluating student progress has gained momentum in recent years, establishing standards has been difficult. Research on the use of portfolios for assessment indicates that validity and reliability of teacher evaluation are often quite low. In addition, portfolio assessment is not always practical for every teacher. For example, a sole art teacher for a school who is responsible for teaching art to every one of the 400 students is unlikely to have the time or storage capacity for 400 portfolios. For that teacher's assessment of student learning, the use of checklists, rubrics, and student self-assessment may be more practical.

Before using portfolios as an alternative to traditional testing, you are advised to carefully consider and clearly understand the reasons for doing it and its practicality in your situation. Then decide on portfolio content carefully, establish rubrics or expectation standards, anticipate grading problems, and consider and prepare for reactions from parents and guardians.

While emphasizing the criteria for assessment, rating scales and checklists provide students with a means of expressing their feelings, and they give the teacher still another source of input data for use in assessment. To provide students with reinforcement and guidance to improve their learning and development, teachers can meet with individual students to discuss their self-assessments. Such conferences should provide students with understandable and achievable short-term goals as well as help them develop and maintain adequate self-esteem.[6]

Although almost any instrument used for assessing student work can be used for student self-assessment, in some cases it might be better to construct specific instruments with the student's understanding of the instrument in mind. Student self-assessment and self-reflection should be done on a regular and continuing basis so comparisons can be made periodically by the student. You will need to help students learn how to analyze these comparisons. Comparisons should provide a student with information not previously recognized about his or her own progress and growth.

Using Checklists

One of the items that can be maintained by students in their portfolios is a series of checklists. Checklist items can be used easily by a student to compare with previous self-assessments. Items on the checklist will vary depending on your purpose, subject, and grade level. (See sample forms, Figures 11.4 and 11.5.) Open-ended questions allow the student to provide additional information and to do some expressive writing. After a student has demonstrated each of the skills satisfactorily, a check is made next to the student's name, either by the teacher alone or in conference with the student.

---

[5]Software packages for the development of student electronic portfolios are available, such as *Classroom Manager* from CTB Macmillan/McGraw-Hill (Monterey, CA), *Electronic Portfolio* from Learning Quest (Corvallis, OR), and *Grady Profile* from Aurbach and Associates (St. Louis, MO).

[6]For a discussion of the biological importance and educational benefits of positive feedback, student portfolios, and group learning, see R. Sylwester, "The Neurobiology of Self-Esteem and Aggression," *Educational Leadership* 54(5):75–79 (February 1997).

Figure 11.4   Checklist: oral report assessment.

Oral Report Assessment Checklist			
Did the student	Yes	No	Comments
1. Speak so that everyone could hear?	_____	_____	_____
2. Finish sentences?	_____	_____	_____
3. Seem comfortable in front of the group?	_____	_____	_____
4. Give a good introduction?	_____	_____	_____
5. Seem well informed about the topic?	_____	_____	_____
6. Explain ideas clearly?	_____	_____	_____
7. Stay on the topic?	_____	_____	_____
8. Give a good conclusion?	_____	_____	_____
9. Use effective visuals to make the presentation interesting?	_____	_____	_____
10. Give good answers to questions from the audience?	_____	_____	_____

Figure 11.5 Checklist: student learning assessment for use with interdisciplinary thematic instruction.

Checklist: Interdisciplinary Thematic Unit Learning

Student _____   Date _____

Teacher _____   Time _____

The student	Yes	No	Comments/Evidence
1. Can identify theme, topic, main idea of the unit	_____	_____	_____
2. Can identify contributions of others to the theme	_____	_____	_____
3. Can identify problems related to the unit study	_____	_____	_____
4. Has developed skills in:	_____	_____	_____
Applying knowledge	_____	_____	_____
Assuming responsibility	_____	_____	_____
Classifying	_____	_____	_____
Categorizing	_____	_____	_____
Decision making	_____	_____	_____
Discussing	_____	_____	_____
Gathering resources	_____	_____	_____
Impulse control	_____	_____	_____
Inquiry	_____	_____	_____
Justifying choices	_____	_____	_____
Listening to others	_____	_____	_____
Locating information	_____	_____	_____
Metacognition	_____	_____	_____
Ordering	_____	_____	_____
Organizing information	_____	_____	_____
Problem recognition/identification	_____	_____	_____
Problem solving	_____	_____	_____
Reading text	_____	_____	_____
Reading maps and globes	_____	_____	_____
Reasoning	_____	_____	_____
Reflecting	_____	_____	_____
Reporting to others	_____	_____	_____
Self-assessing	_____	_____	_____
Sharing	_____	_____	_____
Studying	_____	_____	_____
Summarizing	_____	_____	_____
Thinking	_____	_____	_____
Using resources	_____	_____	_____
Working with others	_____	_____	_____
Working independently	_____	_____	_____
(Others unique to the unit)			

Additional teacher and student comments:

GUIDELINES FOR USING PORTFOLIOS FOR ASSESSMENT

Following are general guidelines for using student portfolios in the assessment of learning:

- Contents of the portfolio should reflect course goals and objectives.
- Determine what materials should be kept in the portfolio and announce clearly (post schedule in room) when, how, and by what criteria portfolios will be reviewed by you.
- Give responsibility for maintenance of the portfolios to the students.
- Portfolios should be kept in the classroom.
- Students should be allowed and encouraged to personalize their portfolios, such as with brightly decorated exteriors or the student's personal photo.
- Students should date everything that goes into their portfolios.
- The portfolio should not be graded or compared in any way with those of other students. Its purpose is for student self-assessment and for showing progress in learning. For this to happen, students should keep all papers, or major sample papers, related to the course in their portfolio. For grading purposes, you can simply record whether or not the portfolio was maintained and use a checklist to determine whether all items required are in the portfolio.

MAINTAINING RECORDS OF STUDENT ACHIEVEMENT

You must maintain well-organized and complete records of student achievement. You may do this in a written record book or on an electronic record book. At the very least, the record book should include attendance records and all records of scores on tests, homework, projects, and other assignments.

Daily interactions and events occur in the classroom that may provide informative data about a student's intellectual, emotional, and physical development. Maintaining a dated log of your observations of these interactions and events can provide important information that might otherwise be forgotten. At the end of a unit and again at the conclusion of a grading term, you will want to review your records. During the course of the school year, your anecdotal records (and those of other members of your teaching team) will provide important information about the development of each student and ideas for attention to be given to individual students.

Recording Teacher Observations and Judgments

You must think carefully about any written comments that you intend to make about a student. Young adolescents can be quite sensitive to what others say about them, and most particularly to comments made by a teacher.

Additionally, we have seen anecdotal comments in students' permanent records that said more about their teachers who made the comments than about the recipient students. Comments that have been carelessly, hurriedly, and thoughtlessly made can be detrimental to a student's welfare and progress in school. Teacher comments must be professional; that is, they must be diagnostically useful to the continued intellectual and psychological development of the student. This is true for any comment you make or write, whether on a student's paper, on the student's permanent school record, or on a message sent to the student's home.

As an example, consider the following unprofessional comment observed in one student's permanent record. A teacher wrote, "John is lazy." Describing John as "lazy" could be done by anyone; it is nonproductive, and it is certainly not a professional diagnosis. How many times do you suppose John needs to receive such negative descriptions of his behavior before he begins to believe that he is lazy and as a result acts that way even more often? In addition, comments like that may be read by the teacher who next has John in class and may lead that teacher to perpetuate the same expectation of John. To say that John is lazy merely describes behavior as judged by the teacher who wrote the comment. A better and more professional approach would be for the teacher to try to analyze why John is behaving that way, then to *prescribe* activities that are likely to motivate John to assume more constructive charge of his own learning behavior.

For students' continued intellectual and emotional development, your comments should be useful, productive, analytical, diagnostic, criterion-referenced, and prescriptive. The professional teacher makes diagnoses and prepares prescriptions; a professional teacher does not label students as "lazy," "vulgar," "slow," "stupid," "difficult," or "dumb." The professional teacher sees the behavior of a student as being goal-directed. Perhaps "lazy" John found that particular behavioral pattern won him attention. John's goal, then, was attention (don't we all need attention?), and John assumed negative, perhaps even self-destructive, behavioral patterns to reach that goal. The professional task of any teacher is to facilitate the learner's understanding (perception) of a goal and help the student identify acceptable behaviors positively designed to reach that goal.

What separates the professional teacher from "anyone off the street" is the teacher's ability to go beyond mere description of behavior. Always keep that in mind when you write comments that will be read by students, by their parents or guardians, and by other teachers.

GRADING AND MARKING STUDENT ACHIEVEMENT

If conditions were ideal (which they are not), and if teachers did their job perfectly well (which many of us do not), then all students would receive top marks (the ultimate in mastery or quality learning), and there would be less need to talk about grading and marking. Mastery learning implies that some end point of learning is attainable, but there probably is no end point. In any case, because conditions for teaching are never ideal and teachers are mere humans, let us continue with this topic of grading, which is undoubtedly of special interest to you, your students, and their parents or guardians; to school counselors, administrators, and school boards; to potential employers; and to providers of scholarships and college admissions officers.

The term *achievement* is used frequently throughout this resource guide. What is the meaning of the term? Achievement means accomplishment, but is it accomplishment of the instructional objectives against preset standards, or is it simply accomplishment? Most teachers probably choose the former, where the teacher subjectively establishes a standard that must be met in order for a student to receive a certain grade for an assignment, project, test, quarter, semester, or course. Achievement, then, is decided by degrees of accomplishment.

Preset standards are usually expressed in percentages (degrees of accomplishment) needed for marks or *ABC* grades. If no student achieves the standard required for an *A* grade, for example, then no student receives an *A*. On the other hand, if all students meet the preset standard for the *A* grade, then all receive *As*. Determining student grades on the basis of preset standards is referred to as *criterion-referenced grading*.

Criterion-Referenced versus Norm-Referenced Grading

While criterion-referenced (or competency-based) grading is based on preset standards, norm-referenced grading measures the relative accomplishment of individuals in the group (e.g., one classroom of tenth-grade English students) or in a larger group (e.g., all students enrolled in tenth-grade English) by comparing and ranking students. It is commonly known as "grading on a normal curve." Because it encourages competition and discourages cooperative learning, determining student grades with *norm-referenced grading is not recommended*. Norm-referenced grading is educationally dysfunctional. For your personal interest, after several years of teaching, you can produce frequency-distribution studies of grades you have given over a period of time, but *do not* give students grades that are based on a curve. The fact that grading and reporting should always be done in reference to learning criteria and never "on a curve" is well supported by research studies and authorities on the matter.[7] Grades for student achievement should be tied to performance levels and determined on the basis of each student's achievement toward preset standards. As stated by Stiggins, "Teachers who develop success-oriented partnerships with students have no use for grading on a curve. They know they are not the best teacher they can be until every student attains an A—demonstrating the highest possible achievement on rigorous, high-quality assessments."[8]

In criterion-referenced grading, the aim is to communicate information about an individual student's progress in knowledge and work skills in comparison to that student's previous attainment, or in the pursuit of an absolute, such as content mastery. Criterion-referenced grading is featured in continuous-progress curricula, competency-based curricula, and other programs that focus on quality learning and individualized education.

Criterion-referenced grading is based on the level at which each student meets the specified objectives (standards) for the course or grade level. The objectives must be clearly stated to represent important student learning outcomes. This approach implies that effective teaching and learning result in high grades (*As*) or marks for most students. In fact, when a mastery concept is used, the student must accomplish the objectives before being allowed to proceed to the next learning task. The philosophy of teachers who favor criterion-referenced procedures recognizes individual potential. Such teachers accept the challenge of finding teaching strategies to help students progress from where they are to the next designated level. Instead of wondering how Sally compares with Juanita, the comparison is between what Sally could do yesterday and what she can do today and how well these performances compare to the preset standard.

Most school systems use some combination of norm-referenced and criterion-referenced data usage. Sometimes both kinds of information are useful. For example, a report card for a student in the eighth grade might indicate that the student is meeting certain criteria, such as an *A* grade for addition of fractions. However, another entry might show that this mastery is expected in the sixth grade. Both criterion- and norm-referenced data may be communicated to the parents or guardians, and the student. Appropriate procedures

---

[7]See, for example, T. R. Guskey (Ed.), *Communicating Student Learning* (Alexandria, VA: ASCD Yearbook, Association for Supervision and Curriculum Development, 1996), pp. 18–19; R. J. Stiggins, *Student-Involved Classroom Assessment*, 3rd ed. (Upper Saddle River, NJ: Prentice Hall, 2001), pp. 443–444; and R. L. Linn and N. E. Gronlund, *Measurement and Assessment in Teaching*, 8th ed. (Upper Saddle River, NJ: Merrill/Prentice Hall, 2000), p. 392.

[8]Stiggins, *Student-Involved Classroom Assessment*, p. 444.

should be used: a criterion-referenced approach shows whether or not the student can accomplish the task, and if so, to what degree, and a norm-referenced approach shows how well that student performs compared to the larger group to which the student belongs. The latter is important data for college admissions officers and for committees that appropriate academic scholarships.

Determining Grades

Once entered onto school transcripts, grades have a significant impact on students' futures. When determining achievement grades for student performance, you must make several important and professional decisions. Although in a few schools, and for certain classes or assignments, only marks such as *E, S,* and *I* or *pass/no pass,* are used, percentages of accomplishment and letter grades are used for most middle level schools.[9] For determining student grades, consider the guidelines presented in the following paragraphs.

At the start of the school term, explain your marking and grading policies *first to yourself,* then to your students and their parents or guardians at "back-to-school night," in a written explanation that is sent home, or both. Share sample scoring and grading rubrics with students and parents. In addition, include your grading policy in the course syllabus (Chapter 6).

When converting your interpretation of a student's accomplishments to a letter grade, be as objective as possible. For the selection of criteria for *ABC* grades, select a percentage standard, such as 92 percent for an *A,* 85 percent for a *B,* 75 percent for a *C,* and 65 percent for a *D.* The cutoff percentages used are your decision, although the district, school, program area, or department may have established guidelines that you are expected to follow.[10]

For the determination of students' final grades, many teachers use a point system, in which things that students write, say, and do are given points (but not journals or portfolios, except, perhaps, for whether the student does one or not). The possible point total is the factor then used to determine grades. For example, if 92 percent is the cutoff for an *A* and 500 points are possible, then any student with 460 points or more (500 × .92) has achieved an *A.* Likewise, for a test or other assignment with a value of 100 points, the cutoff for an *A* is 92 (100 × .92). With a point system and preset standards, the teacher and students, at any time during the

grading period, know the current points possible and can easily calculate a student's current grade standing. That way, students always know where they stand in the course.

Build your grading policy around degrees of accomplishment rather than failure, where students proceed from one accomplishment to the next. This is *continuous promotion,* not necessarily the promotion of the student from one grade level to the next, but within the classroom. Some schools have eliminated grade-level designation and, in its place, use the concept of continuous promotion from the time a student enters the school until he or she graduates or exits from it.

Remember that "assessment" and "grading" are *not* synonymous. Assessment implies the collection of information from a variety of sources, including measurement techniques and subjective observations. These data, then, become the basis for arriving at a final grade, which in effect is a final value judgment. Grades are one aspect of evaluation and are intended to communicate educational progress to students and to their parents or guardians. To be valid as an indicator of that progress, you *must* use a variety of sources of data for determination of a student's final grade.

Decide beforehand your policy about makeup work. Students will be absent and will miss assignments and tests, so it is best that your policies about late assignments and missed tests be clearly communicated to students and to their parents or guardians. For makeup work, please consider the remainder of this section.

Homework Assignments. As discussed in Chapter 8, we recommend that after due dates have been negotiated or set for assignments, no credit or reduced credit be given for work that is turned in late. Sometimes, however, a student has legitimate reasons for not being able to complete the assignment by the due date, and the teacher must exercise a professional judgment in each instance. Although it is important that teachers have rules and procedures—and that they apply them consistently—the teacher must consider all aspects of a student's situation and then show compassion, caring, and regard for the human situation. (Refer to the discussion titled "Opportunities for Recovery" in Chapter 8.)

Tests. If students are absent when tests are given, there are several options. Some teachers allow students to miss or discount one test per grading period. Another technique is to allow each student to substitute a written homework assignment or project for one missed test. Still another option is to give the absent student the choice of either taking a makeup test or having the next test count double. When makeup tests are given, the makeup test should be taken within a week of the regular test unless there is a compelling reason (e.g., medical or family problem) why this cannot happen.

Sometimes students miss a test, not because they are absent from school but because of involvement in other

[9]For other methods being used to report student achievement see J. Bailey and J. McTighe, "Reporting Achievement at the Secondary Level: What and How," Chapter 10 in T. R. Guskey, *Communicating Student Learning.*

[10]See the discussion in T. R. Guskey, "High Percentages Are *Not* The Same as High Standards," *Phi Delta Kappan* 82(7):534–536 (March 2001).

school activities. In those instances, the student may be able to take the test during another of your class periods, or during your prep period, on that day or the next. If a student is absent during performance testing, the logistics and possible diminished reliability of having to re-administer the test for one student may necessitate giving the student an alternate paper-and-pencil test or some other kind of test.

Quizzes. Many teachers give frequent, brief quizzes, as often as every day. As opposed to tests (see next section), quizzes are usually brief (perhaps taking only five minutes of class time) and are intended to reinforce the importance of frequent study and review. Quizzes should be prepared with the same care and precision as presented in the guidelines for testing and preparation of assessment items. When quizzes are given at frequent intervals, no single quiz should count very much toward the student's final grade; therefore, you will probably want to avoid scheduling and giving make-up quizzes for students who were absent when a quiz was given. The following are reasonable options to administering make-up quizzes and are presented here in order of our preference, number one being our preferred choice. (1) Give a certain number of quizzes during a grading period, say ten, but allow a student to discount a few quiz scores, say two of the ten, thereby allowing the student to discount a low score or a quiz missed due to absence or both. (2) Count the next quiz double for a student who missed one due to absence. About the only problem with this option is when a student misses several quizzes. If that happens, (3) count the unit test a relative percentage greater for any student who missed a quiz during that unit. By the way, we see absolutely no educational value in giving "pop" or unannounced graded quizzes.

Caution about assigning zero credit. Be very cautious about ever assigning a score of zero to a student for a missed or incomplete assignment, test, or quiz, or for cheating, specially when using a point system for grading. Depending on the weight of the assignment in relation to the total points possible for the grading period, assigning a zero grade can have an extremely negative effect on the student's total grade. Thus, it becomes an act of punishment by the teacher rather than a fair representation of the grade earned (or, in this instance, not earned) by the student. This is another example where you, the teacher, must exercise your professional judgment. Other alternatives to using a zero grade include ignoring the missing grade and calculating the student's final (quarter or semester) percentage grade using fewer total possible points for that student. If not counter to school policy, you might assign a grade of "incomplete" and give the student some additional time to complete the work.

TESTING FOR ACHIEVEMENT

One source of information for determining grades is data obtained from testing for student achievement. There are two kinds of tests—those that are standardized and those that are not.

Standardized and Nonstandardized Tests

Standardized tests are constructed and published by commercial testing bureaus and used by states and districts to determine and compare student achievement, principally in the core subjects of reading, mathematics, and science. Norms for particular age groups of children are established, usually on a state or national level, by administering it to large groups of children. Standardized norm-referenced tests are best for diagnostic purposes and should *not* be used for determining student grades.

As mentioned in Chapter 1, the administration of standardized achievement tests and the use of their results have become major concerns to classroom teachers and school administrators in particular. In some locales, for example, their salaries and, indeed, their jobs are contingent on the results of student scores on standardized achievement tests. We do not mean to minimize the concern you will have for high-stakes standardized norm-referenced achievement testing as a classroom teacher. However, it is not our purpose nor does space allow an in-depth consideration of standardized achievement testing in this guide. Rather, our focus is on nonstandardized criterion-referenced tests, ones that you design (or collaboratively design) for your own unique group of young adolescent students to determine their level of learning on particular instructional objectives. (For more on standardized testing, see the recommended readings at the end of this chapter.)

Competent planning, preparing, administering, and scoring of tests is an important professional skill. You may want to refer to the guidelines that follow while you are student teaching, and again, occasionally, during your initial years as an employed teacher.

Purposes for Testing

Tests can be designed for several purposes. A variety of kinds of tests and alternate test items will keep your testing program interesting, useful, and reliable. As a college student, you are probably most experienced with testing for measuring for achievement, but as a middle level classroom teacher you will use tests for other reasons as well. Tests also assess and aid in curriculum development; help determine teaching effectiveness; help students develop positive attitudes, appreciations, and values; help students increase their understanding and retention of facts, principles, skills, and concepts; motivate students; provide diagnostic information to plan for individualization of the instruction; provide review and drill to enhance teaching and learning; and serve as informational data for students and parents or guardians.

Frequency of Testing

Assessment for student learning should be continual; it should be going on every minute of every class day. For grading or marking purposes, it is difficult to generalize about how often to formally test for student achievement, but we believe that testing should be cumulative and frequent. By cumulative, we mean that each assessment should assess for the student's understanding of previously learned material as well as for the current unit of study; that is, it should assess for connected learning. By frequent, we mean as often as once a week for classes that meet daily. Advantages of cumulative assessment include the review, reinforcement, and articulation of old material with the most recent. Advantages of frequent assessment include a reduction in student anxiety over tests and an increase in the validity of the summative assessment.

Test Construction

After determining the reasons for which you are designing and administering a test, you need to identify the specific instructional objectives the test is being designed to measure. (As you learned in Chapter 5, your written instructional objectives are specific so that you can write assessment items to measure against those objectives; this is referred to as criterion-referenced assessment.) Therefore, the first step in test construction is identification of the purpose(s) for the test. The second step is to identify the objectives to be measured, and the third step is to prepare the test items. The best time to prepare draft items is after you have prepared your instructional objectives, while the objectives are fresh in your mind, which means before the lessons are taught. After a lesson is taught, you will rework the first draft of test items related to that lesson to make any modifications that are necessary as a result of the instruction that occurred.

Administering Tests

For many young adolescents, test taking can be a time of high anxiety. Students demonstrate test anxiety in various ways. Just before and during testing some are quiet and thoughtful, while others are noisy and disruptive. To more accurately measure student achievement, you will want to take steps to reduce their anxiety. To control

or reduce student anxieties, consider the following guidelines for administering tests.

Since many people respond best to familiar routine, plan your assessment program so tests are given at regular intervals and administered at the same time and in the same way.

Avoid tests that are too long and that will take too much time. Sometimes beginning teachers have unreasonable expectations about the attention span of young adolescents during testing. Frequent testing with frequent sampling of student knowledge is preferred over infrequent and long tests that attempt to cover everything.

Attend to creature comforts. Try to arrange the classroom so it is well-ventilated; the temperature is comfortable; and, when giving paper-and-pencil tests individually, the seats are well-spaced. If spacing is a problem, consider using individual privacy protectors (see Consider the Physical Layout in Chapter 4) made by the students, group testing, or using alternate forms of the same test for students seated adjacent to one another (for example, multiple choice answer alternatives are arranged in different order).

Before distributing the test, explain to students what they are to do when finished, such as quietly beginning an anchor activity (see Chapter 4), because not all of the students will finish at the same time. It is unreasonable to expect most young adolescent students to just sit quietly after finishing a test; they need something to do.

When you are ready to test, do not drag it out. Distribute tests quickly and efficiently. Once testing has begun, avoid interrupting the students. (It is amazing to us how often we see teachers interrupt students once the students are at a task, while those same teachers resent being interrupted themselves.) Items or announcements of important information can be written on the board or, if unrelated to the test, held until all are finished with the test. Stay in the room and visually monitor the students. If the test is not going to take an entire class period (and most should not) and it is a major test, give it at the beginning of the period, if possible, unless you are planning a test review just prior to it (although that seems rather late to conduct a meaningful review; a review just prior to giving the test is likely to upset those children who discover they do not know the material like they thought they did). It is improbable that any teacher can effectively teach a lesson and maintain a reasonable degree of student interest just prior to a major test or immediately after it.

Controlling Cheating

Whatever the causes, some students will try to cheat on tests. There are steps you can take to discourage cheating or to reduce the opportunity and the pressure that causes students to cheat on tests. Consider the following.

Preventing Cheating. As mentioned before, space students, use alternate forms of the test, or use space dividers (see the "Physical Layout" in Chapter 4). Frequent testing and not allowing a single test to count too much toward a term grade reduces test anxiety and the pressure that can cause cheating. Prepare test questions that are clear and unambiguous, thereby reducing student frustration caused by a question or instructions that students do not understand. Avoid tests that are too long and that will take too much time. During long tests, some students get discouraged and restless, and then classroom management problems can occur.

By their sheer nature, performance tests can cause even greater pressure on students and can also provide greater opportunity for cheating. When administering performance tests to an entire class, it is best to have several monitors, such as members of your teaching team. If that is not possible, consider testing groups of students rather than individuals. Evaluation of test performance, then, would be based on group rather than individual achievement. However, we tend to agree with those who argue against using any kind of assessment of an individual based to any degree on group process and functioning. It is very difficult, if not impossible, to rationalize giving a student a grade based on a group assignment.

Consider using open-text and open-notebook tests or allowing each student to prepare a page of notes to use during the test. When students can use their books and notes, it not only reduces anxiety but helps them organize information and retain what has been learned. Open note and open book testing are useful adaptations that are appreciated by many students.[11]

Stopping Cheating. The preceding paragraphs provide hints to prevent student cheating. If you suspect cheating *is* occurring, move and stand in the area of the suspected student. Usually that will stop it.

Dealing with Cheating. When you suspect cheating has occurred, you are faced with a dilemma. Unless your suspicion is backed by solid proof, you are advised to forget it, but to keep a close watch on the student during the next test to prevent cheating. Think of your job not as catching students being dishonest but of discouraging dishonesty. If you have absolute proof that a student has cheated, then you are obligated to proceed with school policy on student cheating. That may call for a session with the counselor or the student and the student's parent or guardian, or perhaps an automatic *F* grade on the test.

Table 11.1 Approximate Time to Allow for Testing as Determined by the Types of Items*

Type of Test Item	Time Needed Per Item
Matching	30 seconds per matching item
Completion	30 seconds per item
Multiple-choice	1 minute per item
Completion drawing	2–3 minutes
Arrangement	2–3 minutes
Identification	2–3 minutes
Short explanation	2–3 minutes
Essay and performance	10 or more minutes

(*Students with disabilities and ELL students, of course, may need more time per item, or you may need to administer the test in briefer sessions or provide some other accommodation, depending on the individual's special needs situation.)

Determining the Time Needed to Take a Test

Again, avoid giving tests that are too long and that will take too much time. For most classes, a testing duration of 30 to 40 minutes should be long enough. Preparing and administering good tests is a skill that you will develop over time. In the meantime, it is best to test frequently and to use tests that sample student achievement rather than try for a comprehensive measure of that achievement.

Some students take more time on the same test than do others. You want to avoid giving too much time, because classroom management problems will result. On the other hand, you do not want to cut the time short for students who can do well but need more time to think and to write. As a very general guide, use the table of time needed for different types of test items (Table 11.1). This is only a guide for determining the approximate amount of time to allow students to complete a test. For example, for a test made up of 10 multiple-choice items, five arrangement items, and two short-explanation items, you would want to plan about 30 minutes for students to complete the test.

PREPARING ASSESSMENT ITEMS

Preparing and writing good assessment items is yet another professional skill. To become proficient at it takes study, time, practice, feedback, and reflection. Because of the importance of an assessment program, please assume this professional charge seriously and responsibly. Although poorly prepared items take no time at all to construct, they will cause you more trouble than you can ever imagine. As a professional, you should take time to study different types of assessment items and how best to write them, and then practice writing them. Remember, when

---

[11]J. S. Nelson, et al., "Student Preferences for Adaptations in Classroom Testing," *Remedial and Special Education* 21(1):41–52 (January/February 2000).

preparing assessment items, be sure they match and sufficiently cover the instructional objectives. In addition, prepare each item carefully enough to be reasonably confident that it will be understood by the student in the manner that you intended. With the diversity of students in today's school classroom, especially with respect to their proficiency in oral and written English language and the inclusion of students with special needs, this is an especially important point. For high-stakes tests, such as unit tests, ask a trusted colleague or friend to read your test for clarity and errors and to check the test's key for accuracy. Finally, after administering a test you must take time to analyze the results and reflect on the value of each item before ever using that item again.

Classification of Assessment Items

Assessment items can be classified as verbal (oral or written words), visual (pictures and diagrams), and manipulative or performance (handling of materials and equipment; performing). Written verbal items are the ones that have traditionally been used most frequently in testing. However, visual items and visual tests are useful; for example, when working with students who lack fluency with the written word or when testing students who have limited or no proficiency in the English language.

Performance items and tests are useful when measuring for psychomotor skill development. Common examples are performance testing of a student's ability to carry a microscope or hold a jumping rope in place (gross motor skill) or to focus a microscope or to jump rope (fine motor skill). Performance testing also can and should be part of a wider testing program that includes testing for higher-level thinking skills and knowledge. For example, a student or small group of students are given the problem of creating from discarded materials a habitat for an imaginary animal and then displaying, writing about, and orally presenting their product to the rest of the class.

As noted often throughout this resource guide, educators have an interest in the last described form of performance testing as a means of assessing learning that is closer to measuring for the real thing—that is, authentic. In a program for teacher preparation, micro peer teaching and student teaching are examples of performance assessment; that is, assessment practices used to assess the teacher candidate's ability to teach (to perform). It seems axiomatic that assessment of student teaching is a more authentic assessment of a candidate's ability to teach than would be a written (paper-and-pencil test) or verbal (oral test) form of assessment. Although less direct and perhaps less reliable than a checklist observation and analysis of a student teacher actually teaching, observing a student teacher's analysis of a video recorded episode of another teacher's performance is another way to more authentically assess a teacher's ability to teach than would be a paper-and-pencil response item test.

Performance Testing: Potentially Expensive And Time-Intensive

Performance testing is usually more expensive and time-consuming than is verbal testing, which in turn is more time demanding and expensive than is written testing. However, a good program of assessment will use alternate forms of assessment and not rely solely on one form (such as written) and one type of written item (such as multiple choice).

The type of test and items that you use depend upon your purpose and objectives. Carefully consider the alternatives within that framework. To provide validity checks and to account for the individual differences of students, a good assessment program should include items from all three types, which is called **alternative assessment.** Rather than the traditional heavy reliance on objective items such as multiple-choice questions, multiple assessment items should be used.

General Guidelines for Preparing to Assess Student Learning

Every test that you administer to your students should represent your best professional effort. It should be clean and sans spelling and grammar errors. A quickly and poorly prepared test can cause you more grief than you can imagine. One that was obviously prepared in a hurry and is wrought with spelling and grammar errors will be frowned upon by discerning parents or guardians. If you are a student teacher, such sloppiness and unprofessional output will certainly bring about an admonishment from your university supervisor and, if it continues, your speedy release from the teacher preparation program. Consider the following general guidelines when preparing to assess for student learning.

- Assure that content coverage is complete (i.e., that all objectives or relevant standards are being measured).
- Assure that each item is clear and unambiguous to all students.
- Assure that each item is reliable; that it measures the intended objective. One way to check item reliability is to have more than one item measure for the same objective.
- Because it is time-consuming to write good assessment items, you are advised to maintain a bank of items, each coded according to its matching instructional objective, its domain of learning (cognitive, affective, or psychomotor), and perhaps its level within the hierarchy of a particular domain. Another code could indicate whether the item requires thinking that is recall, processing, or application. Computer software programs are available for this. Ready-made test item banks are available on computer disks and accompany many programs or textbooks. If you use them, be certain that the items match your course objectives and that they are well written. It does not follow that

because they were published they are well written or that they match what students were supposed to have learned. When preparing items for your test bank, use your creative thinking and best writing skills. Prepare items that match your objectives, put them aside, think about them, then work them over again.

- Include several kinds of items and assessment instruments (see 12 types that follow).
- Plan each item to be difficult enough for the poorly prepared student but easy enough for the student who is well prepared.

Attaining Content Validity

To ensure that your test measures what is supposed to be measured, you can construct a table of specifications. A two-way grid indicates behavior in one dimension and content in the other (see Figures 11.6 and 11.7).

In this grid, behavior relates to the three domains: cognitive, affective, psychomotor. In Figure 11.6, the cog-

nitive domain is divided, according to Bloom's taxonomy, into six categories: knowledge or simple recall, comprehension, application, analysis, synthesis (often involving an original product in oral or written form), and evaluation. The specifications table in Figure 11.6 does not specify levels within the affective and psychomotor domains.

To use a table of specifications, the teacher examining objectives for the unit decides what emphasis should be given to the behavior and to the content. For example, if vocabulary development is a concern for this sixth-grade study of matter and energy, then probably 20 percent of the test on vocabulary would be appropriate, but 50 percent would be unsuitable. This planning enables the teacher to design a test that fits the situation rather than a haphazard test that does not correspond to the objectives either in content or behavior emphasis. Since this is to be an objective test and it is so difficult to write objective items to test affective and psychomotor behaviors, this table of specifications calls for no test items in these areas. If these areas are included in the

Figure 11.6 Table of specifications I.

CONTENT	BEHAVIORS								TOTAL
SOCIAL STUDIES GRADE 8	COGNITIVE						AFFEC-TIVE	PSYCHO-MOTOR	
Ancient Greece	Knowledge	Compre-hension	Appli-cation	Analysis	Synthesis	Evaluation			
I. Vocabulary development		2 (1,2)	1 (2)						3
II. Concepts		2 (3,4)	2 (4)						4
III. Applications	1 (5)	1 (5)	1 (5)	1 (5)	1 (5)	1 (5)			6
IV. Problem solving		1 (6)		1 (6)					2
TOTAL	1	6	4	2	1	1			15

Figure 11.7 Table of specifications II.

CONTENT	BEHAVIORS							TOTAL
	COGNITIVE			AFFECTIVE		PSYCHOMOTOR		
	Input	Processing	Application	Low	High	Low	High	
I.								
II.								
III.								
IV.								
TOTAL								

unit objectives, some other assessment devices must be used to test learning in these domains. The teacher could also show the objectives tested, as indicated with parentheses in Figure 11.6. Then, a check later on inclusion of all objectives is easy.

Preferred by some teachers is the alternative table shown in Figure 11.7. Rather than differentiating among all six of Bloom's cognitive levels, this table separates cognitive objectives into just three levels: those that require simple low-level recall for knowledge, those that require information processing, and those that require application of new knowledge. In addition, the affective and psychomotor domains each are divided into low- and high-level behaviors. A third alternative, not illustrated here, is a table of specifications that shows all levels of each of the three domains.

ASSESSMENT ITEMS: DESCRIPTIONS, EXAMPLES, AND GUIDELINES FOR PREPARING AND USING 12 TYPES

This section presents descriptions, advantages and disadvantages, and guidelines for preparing and using 12 types of assessment items. You will notice that some types are appropriate for use in direct or performance assessment, while others are not.

Arrangement

Description: Terms or real objects (realia) are to be arranged in a specified order.

Example 1: Arrange the following list of events on a time line in order of their occurrence: Maximilian I elected King of Germany; Maximilian I becomes Holy Roman Emperor; Diet of Augsburg establishes Council of Regency, divides Germany into six regions; Charles I of Spain becomes Holy Roman Emperor; Ferdinand I assumes the title of Holy Roman Emperor.

Example 2: The assortment of balls on the table represents the planets in our solar system. [*Note:* The balls are of various sizes, such as marbles, golf balls, tennis balls, basketballs, and so on, each labeled with a planetary name. A large beach ball is labeled *Sun.*] Arrange the balls in their proper order around the sun.

Advantages: This type of item tests for knowledge of sequence and order, and is good for review, for starting discussions, and for performance assessment. Example 2 is also an example of a performance test item.

Disadvantages: Scoring could be difficult, so be cautious, meticulous, and open to lateral thinking (see Chapter 9) when using this type for grading purposes. For instance, in example 2 the student could rightfully place either Neptune or Pluto as the outermost planet in the solar system (because of the extreme oval shape of their orbits, Pluto and Neptune alternate in their relative positions from the Sun), or even omit Pluto (most scientists today believe that Pluto is actually the largest

or nearest member of a group of icy asteroids found in the outer solar system).

Guideline for use: To enhance reliability, you may need to have students include the rationale for their arrangement on an answer sheet, making it a combined arrangement and short-explanation type of assessment. This is useful for small, heterogeneous group assessment to allow students to share and learn from their collaborative thinking and reasoning.

Completion Drawing

Description: An incomplete drawing is presented and the student is to complete it.

Example 1: Connect the following items with arrow lines to show the stages from introduction of a new bill until it becomes law (items not included here).

Example 2: In the following food web (not included here), draw arrow lines indicating which organisms are consumers and which are producers.

Advantages: This requires less time than would a complete drawing that might be required in an essay item. Scoring is relatively easy although you should be alert and allow for lateral thinking.

Disadvantages: Care needs to be exercised in the instructions so students do not misinterpret the expectation.

Guidelines for use: Use occasionally for diversion, but take care in preparing. This type of assessment can be instructive when assessing for student thinking and reasoning as it can measure conceptual knowledge. Consider making the item a combined completion-drawing, short-explanation type by having students include their rationales for the thinking behind their drawing completion. Be sure to allow space for their explanations. This is useful for small, heterogeneous group assessment to allow students to share and learn from their collaborative thinking and reasoning.

Completion Statement

Description: Sometimes called a "fill-in" item, an incomplete sentence is presented and the student is to complete it by filling in the blank space(s).

Example 1: A group of words that have a special meaning, such as "a skeleton in the closet," is called a(n) _____.

Example 2: To test their hypotheses, scientists and social scientists conduct _____.

Advantages: This type is easy to devise, take, and score.

Disadvantages: When using this type, there is a tendency to emphasize rote memory and to measure procedural knowledge only. Providing a word bank of possible answers is sometimes useful, especially with mainstreamed students, to reduce dependency on rote memory. It is difficult to write this type of item to measure for conceptual knowledge and higher levels of cognition. You must be alert for a correct response that is different from the expected. For instance, in Example 2, although the teacher's key has *experiments* as the correct answer, a student might answer the question with *research, investigations,* or *tests* or some other response that is equally valid.

Guideline for use: Use occasionally for review or for preassessment of student knowledge. Avoid using this for grading unless you can write quality items that extend student thinking beyond mere recall. In all instances, avoid copying items verbatim from the student book. As with all types, be sure to provide adequate space for students' answers, and large spaces for students with motor control difficulties. Try to use only one blank per item and to write so the blank is at the end of the sentence (the reason it is called *completion*) rather than at the front or in the middle. Try also to keep the blanks equal in length. This is useful for small, heterogeneous group assessment to allow students to share and learn from their collaborative thinking and reasoning. Rewriting the item as a statement makes the item a short-answer type, which students might prefer over the completion statement type. Rewritten as short-answer questions, the two examples above would appear as (a) What do we call a group of words that have a special meaning, such as "a skeleton in the closet?" (b) What is it that scientists and social scientists conduct to test their hypotheses?

Correction

Description: This is similar to the completion type, except that sentences or paragraphs are complete but with italicized or underlined words that can be changed to make the sentences correct.

Example 1: The work of the TVA was started by building <u>sand castles.</u> A <u>sand castle</u> is a wall built across a <u>kid</u> to stop its flow. The <u>sand castle</u> holds back the <u>football</u> so the <u>kids</u> do not overflow their <u>backpacks</u> and cause <u>tears.</u>

Example 2: 1, 1, 2, 3, 5, 8, <u>12</u>, 21, 34, <u>87</u>, 89.

Advantages: Writing this type can be fun for the teacher for the purpose of preassessment of student knowledge or for review. Students may enjoy this type, especially when used only occasionally, for the tension relief afforded by the incorrect absurdities. It is useful for introducing words with multiple meanings.

Disadvantages: As with completion, correction tends to measure for low-level recall and rote memory (although this is not necessarily the case in Example 2; if a student is unfamiliar with the Fibonacci number series in mathematics, it would be a relatively high-level question). The underlined incorrect items could be so whimsical that they might cause more classroom disturbance than you want.

Guidelines for use: Use occasionally for diversion and discussion. Try to write items that measure for higher-level cognition. Consider making it a combined correction, short-explanation type. Be sure to allow space for student explanations.

Essay

Description: A question or problem is presented, and the student is to compose a response in the form of sustained prose, using his or her own words, phrases, and ideas, within the limits of the question or problem.

Example 1: In the story just read does the author elaborate the setting in great detail or barely sketch it? Explain your response.

Example 2: A healthy green coleus plant sitting in front of you has been planted in fertile soil and sealed in a glass jar. If we place the jar on the window sill, where it will receive strong sunlight, and if we maintain a temperature inside the jar of 60 to 80 degrees Fahrenheit, how long do you predict the plant will live? Justify your prediction.

Advantages: This type of question measures conceptual knowledge and higher mental processes, such as the ability to synthesize material and express ideas in clear and precise written language. It is especially useful in integrated thematic teaching. It provides practice in written expression and can be used in performance assessment, as in the case of Example 2.

Disadvantages: Essay items require a good deal of time to read and score. They tend to provide an unreliable sampling of achievement and are vulnerable to teacher subjectivity and unreliable scoring. Furthermore, they tend to punish the student who writes slowly and laboriously, or who has limited proficiency in the written language but may have achieved as well as a student who writes faster or is more proficient in the language. Essay items tend to favor students who have fluency with words but whose achievement may not necessarily be better. In addition, unless the students have been given instruction in the meaning of key directive verbs and how to respond to them, the teacher should not assume that all students understand such verbs (such as *explain* in the first example and *justify* in the second).

GUIDELINES FOR USING AN ESSAY ITEM

1. When preparing an essay-only test, many questions, each requiring a relatively short prose response (see the short-explanation type, page 372), are preferable to a smaller number of questions requiring long prose responses. Briefer answers tend to be more precise, and using many items provides a more reliable sampling of student achievement. When preparing a short prose response, avoid using words verbatim from the student textbook.

2. Allow students adequate test time for a full response.

3. Different qualities of achievement are more likely to be comparable when all students must answer the same questions, as opposed to selecting which they answer from a list of essay items.

4. After preparing essay items, make a tentative scoring key. Decide what key ideas you expect students to identify and how many points you will allot to each.

Figure 11.8   Meaning of key directive verbs for essay item responses.

Compare asks for an analysis of similarity and difference, but with a greater emphasis on similarities or likenesses.

Contrast asks more for differences than for similarities.

Criticize asks for the good and bad of an idea or situation.

Define means to express clearly and concisely the meaning of a term, as from a dictionary or in the student's own words.

Diagram means to put quantities or numerical values into the form of a chart, graph, or drawing.

Discuss means to explain or argue, presenting various sides of events, ideas, or situations.

Enumerate means to name or list one after another, which is different from "explain briefly" or "tell in a few words."

Evaluate means to express worth, value, and judgment.

Explain means to describe, with emphasis on cause and effect.

Generalize means to arrive at a valid generalization from specific information provided.

Identify means to state recognizable or identifiable characteristics.

Infer means to forecast what is likely to happen as a result of information provided.

Illustrate means to describe by means of examples, figures, pictures, or diagrams.

Interpret means to describe or explain a given fact, theory, principle, or doctrine within a specific context.

Justify means to show reasons, with an emphasis on correct, positive, and advantageous.

List means just that, to simply name items in a category or to include them in a list, without much description.

Outline means to give a short summary with headings and subheadings.

Prove means to present materials as witnesses, proof, and evidence.

Relate means to tell how specified things are connected or brought into some kind of relationship.

Summarize means to recapitulate the main points without examples or illustrations.

Trace means to follow a history or series of events, step by step, by going backward over the evidence.

5. Students should be informed about the relative test value for each item. Point values, if different for each item, can be listed in the margin of the test next to each item.

6. Inform students of the role of spelling, grammar, and sentence structure in your scoring of their essay items.

7. When reading student essay responses, read all student papers for one item at a time in one sitting, and, while doing that, make notes to yourself; then repeat and while reading that item again, score each student's paper for that item. Repeat the process for the next item but modify the order of the pile of papers so you are not reading them in the same order by student. While scoring essay responses, keep in mind the nature of the objective being measured, which may or may not include the qualities of handwriting, grammar, spelling, punctuation, and neatness.

8. To nullify the "halo effect" that can occur when you know whose paper you are reading, have students put their name on the back of the paper or use a number code rather than names on essay papers, so while reading the papers, you are unaware of whose paper is being read.

9. While having some understanding of a concept, many young adolescents are not yet facile with written expression, so you must remember to be patient, tolerant, positive, and prescriptive. Mark papers with positive and constructive comments, showing students how they could have explained or responded better.

10. Prior to using this type of test item, give instruction and practice to students in responding to key directive verbs that will be used (see Figure 11.8).

Grouping

Description: Several items are presented, and the student is to select and group those that are in some way related.

Example 1: Separate the following words into two groups (words are not included here); those that are homonyms, place in group A and those that are not homonyms, place in group B.

Example 2: Circle the figure that is least like the others (showing a wrench, screwdriver, saw, and swing).

Advantages: This type of item tests knowledge of grouping and can be used to measure conceptual knowledge, for higher levels of cognition, and to stimulate discussion. As Example 2 shows, it can be similar to a multiple-choice type item.

Disadvantage: Remain alert for the student who has an alternative but valid rationale for her or his grouping.

Guideline for use: To allow for an alternative correct response, consider making the item a combination grouping and short-explanation type, being certain to allow adequate space to encourage student explanations.

Identification

Description: Unknown "specimens" are to be identified by name or some other criterion.

Example 1: Identify each of the trees on our school campus (the trees have been numbered) as to whether it is evergreen or deciduous.

Example 2: Identify by style each of the three poems shown on the screen.

Advantages: Verbalization (i.e., the use of abstract symbolization) is less significant, as the student is working with real materials; it should measure for higher-level learning than simple recall. The item can also be written to measure for procedural understanding, such as for identification of steps in booting up a computer program. This is another useful type for authentic and performance assessments.

Disadvantages: Because of a special familiarity with the material, some students may have an advantage over others; to be fair, "specimens" used should be equally familiar or unfamiliar to all students. This type takes more time than many of the other items types, both for the teacher to prepare and for students to do.

Guidelines for use: Whatever "specimens" are used, they must be familiar to all or to none of the students, and they must be clear, not confusing. For example, fuzzy photographs or unclear photocopies, dried and incomplete biological specimens, and garbled music recordings can be confusing and frustrating to try to discern. Consider using dyad or team rather than individual testing.

Matching

Description: Students are to match related items from a list of numbered items to a list of lettered choices or in some way to connect the items that are the same or related. To eliminate the paper-and-pencil aspect and make the item more direct, use an item such as, "Of the materials on the table, pair up those that are most alike."

Example 1: In the blank space next to each description in Column A (stem or premises column) put the letter of the correct answer from Column B (answer or response column).

A (stem column)	B (answer column)
_____ 1. Current president of the United States	A. George W. Bush
_____ 2. Most recent past president of the United States	B. Bill Clinton
_____ 3. U.S. president at the conclusion of WW II	C. Thomas Jefferson
_____ 4. First president of the United States (etc.)	D. Harry Truman
	E. George Washington (etc.)

Example 2: Match items in Column A (stem column) to those in Column B (answer column) by drawing lines connecting the matched pairs.

Column A	Column B
ann/enn	conquer
auto	large
min	self
vic/vinc	small
(etc.)	year
	(etc.)

Advantages: Matching items can measure for ability to judge relationships and to differentiate between similar facts, ideas, definitions, and concepts. They are easy to score and can test a broad range of content. They reduce guessing, especially if one group (e.g., answer column) contains more items than the other; are interesting to students; and are adaptable for performance assessment.

Disadvantages: Although the matching item is adaptable for performance assessment, items are not easily adapted to measuring for higher cognition. Because all parts must be homogeneous, it is possible that clues will be given, thus reducing item validity.

Guidelines for use: The number of items in the response or answer column should exceed the number in the stem or premises column. The number of items in the stem column to be matched should not exceed 10. Fewer is better. Matching sets should have high homogeneity (i.e., items in both columns or groups should be of the same general category; avoid, for example, mixing dates, events, and names). Answers in the response column should be kept short, to one or two words each and should be ordered logically, such as alphabetically. If answers from the response column can be used more than once, which is advised to avoid guessing by elimination, the directions should so state. Be prepared for the student who can legitimately defend an "incorrect" response. To eliminate the paper-and-pencil aspect and make the item more direct, use an item such as "of the materials on the table, pair up those that are most alike."

Multiple Choice

Description: This is similar to the completion item in that statements are presented (the stem)—sometimes in incomplete form—but with several options or alternatives, requiring recognition or even higher cognitive processes rather than mere recall.

Example 1: Of four cylinders with the following dimensions, the one that would cause the highest-pitched sound would be

(a) 4 inches long and 3 inches in diameter
(b) 8 inches long and 3 inches in diameter
(c) 4 inches long and 1 inch in diameter
(d) 8 inches long and 1 inch in diameter

Example 2: Which one of the following is a pair of antonyms?

(a) loud—soft
(b) halt—finish
(c) absolve—vindicate
(d) procure—purchase

Advantages: Items can be answered and scored quickly. A wide range of content and higher levels of cognition can be tested in a relatively short time. This type is excellent for all testing purposes—motivation, review, and assessment of learning.

Disadvantages: Unfortunately, because multiple-choice items are relatively easy to write, there is a tendency to write items measuring only for low levels of cognition. Multiple-choice items are excellent for major testing, but it takes care and time to write quality questions that measure higher levels of thinking and learning.

GUIDELINES FOR USING MULTIPLE-CHOICE ITEMS

1. If the item is in the form of an incomplete statement, it should be meaningful in itself and imply a direct question rather than merely lead into a collection of unrelated true and false statements.

2. Use a level of language that is easy enough for even the poorest readers and those with limited proficiency in English to understand; avoid unnecessary wordiness.

3. If there is much variation in the length of alternatives, arrange the alternatives in order from shortest to longest. For single-word alternatives, consistent use of arrangement of alternatives is recommended, such as by length of answer or alphabetically.

4. Arrangement of alternatives should be uniform throughout the test and listed in vertical (column) form rather than horizontal (paragraph) form.

5. If there is more than one correct response, students should be instructed to identify all responses they believe are correct. Questions that have more than a single correct response should each be worth more than one point, such as a point for each correct response.

6. Incorrect responses (distracters) should be plausible and related to the same concept as the correct alternative. Although an occasional humorous distracter may help relieve text anxiety, along with absurd distracters they should generally be avoided. They offer no measuring value and increase the likelihood of the student guessing the correct response.

7. It is not necessary to maintain a fixed number of alternatives for every item, but the use of less than three is not recommended. Although it is not always possible to come up with four or five plausible responses, using four or five reduces chance responses and guessing, thereby increasing reliability for the item. If you cannot think of enough plausible distracters, include the item on a test the first time as a completion item. As students respond, wrong answers will provide you with a number of plausible distracters that you can use the next time to make the item a multiple-choice type item.

8. Some mainstreamed students may work better when allowed to circle their selected response rather than writing its letter or number in a blank space.

9. Responses such as "all of these" or "none of these" should be used only when they will contribute more than another plausible distracter. Care must be taken that such responses answer or complete the item. "All of the above" is a poorer alternative than "none of the above" because it needs to have four or five correct answers; also, if it is the right answer, knowledge of any two of the distracters will cue it.

10. Every item should be grammatically consistent. For example, if the stem is in the form of an incomplete sentence, it should be possible to complete the sentence by attaching any of the alternatives to it.

11. The stem should state a single and specific point.

12. The stem must mean the same thing to every student.

13. The item should be expressed in positive form. A negative form can present a psychological disadvantage to students. Negative items are those that ask what is *not* characteristic of something, or what is the *least* useful. Discard the item if you cannot express it in positive terminology.

14. The stem must not include clues that would clue the correct alternative. For example, A four-sided figure whose opposite sides are parallel is called _____.

    (a) a triangle
    (b) an octagon
    (c) a trapezoid
    (d) a parallelogram

Use of the word "parallel" clues the answer.

15. There must be only one correct or best response. However, this is easier said than done (refer to guideline 20).

16. Measuring for understanding of definitions is better tested by furnishing the name or word and requiring a choice among alternative definitions than by presenting the definition and requiring a choice among alternative words.

17. Avoid using alternatives that include absolute terms such as *never* and *always*.

18. Multiple-choice items need not be entirely verbal. Consider the use of realia, charts, diagrams, videos, and other visuals. They will make the test more interesting, especially to students with low verbal abilities or limited proficiency in English. Consequently, they will make the assessment more direct.

19. Once you have composed a series of multiple-choice items or a test comprised completely of this item type, tally the position of answers to be sure they are evenly distributed. This avoids the common psychological habit

(when there are four alternatives) of having the correct alternative in the third position. In other words, when alternative choices are A, B, C, and D, or 1, 2, 3, and 4, unless the test designer is aware and avoids it, more correct answers will be in the "C" or "3" position than in any other.

20. Consider providing space between test items for students to include their rationales for their response selections, thus making the test a combination of multiple-choice and short-explanation items. This measures higher levels of cognition and encourages writing. It also provides for the student who can rationalize an alternative that you had not considered plausible, especially possible today with the diversity of cultural experiences represented by students. For example, we recall the story of a math question on a test that asked if a farmer saw eight crows sitting on a fence and shot three of them, how many would be left. Of course, the "correct" response on the answer key was "5." However, one critical thinking student chose "none" as his response, an answer that was marked wrong by the teacher. However, the student was thinking that those crows that were not shot would be frightened and would all fly away, thus he selected "none" as his answer.

21. While scoring, on a blank copy of the test, tally the incorrect responses for each item. Analyze incorrect responses for each item to discover potential errors in your scoring key. If, for example, many students select B for an item for which your key says the correct answer is A, you may have made a mistake on your scoring key or in teaching the lesson.

22. Sometimes teachers attempt to discourage cheating by preparing several versions of the multiple-choice exam with the questions in different order. This could give one group of students an unfair advantage if the order of their questions was in the same sequence that the information was originally presented and learned, and in random order for another group of students. To avoid this, questions should be in random order on every version of the exam.

Performance

Description: Provided with certain conditions or materials, the student solves a problem or accomplishes some other action.

Example 1: Write a retelling of your favorite fable and create a diorama to go along with it.

Example 2: As a culminating project in physical science for a unit on sound, groups of students were challenged to design and make their own musical instruments. The performance assessment included the following:

1. Play your instrument for the class.
2. Show us the part of the instrument that makes the sound.
3. Describe the function of other parts of your instrument.
4. Demonstrate how you change the pitch of the sound.
5. Share with us how you made your instrument.

Example 3: (see Example 2 in "Essay," earlier in this section).

Example 4: Measure and calculate to the nearest centimeter the within-bounds square footage of our basketball court.

Advantages: Performance test item types come closer to direct measurement (authentic assessment) of certain expected outcomes than do most other types. As has been indicated, other types of questions can actually be prepared as performance-type items, that is, where the student actually does what he or she is being tested for.

Disadvantages: This type of test can be difficult and time-consuming to administer to a group of students. Adequate supply of materials could be a problem, scoring may tend to be subjective, and it could be difficult to give make-up tests to students who were absent.

Guidelines for use: Use your creativity to design and use performance tests, as they tend to measure well the important objectives. To reduce subjectivity in scoring, set up a performance assessment situation as shown in Figure 11.9 and prepare distinct scoring guidelines (rubrics) as discussed in scoring essay-type items and as shown in Figures 11.10 and 11.11.

Short Explanation

Description: The short explanation question is like the essay-type question but requires a shorter answer.

Example 1: Briefly explain in a paragraph why the patriot/colonists were rebelling against England.

Example 2: Briefly explain why organ pipes are made to vary in length.

Advantages: As with the essay type, student understanding is assessed, but this type takes less time for the

Figure 11.9 Procedure for setting up a performance assessment situation.

1. Specify the performance objective.
2. Specify the test conditions.
3. Establish the standards or criteria (scoring rubric) for judging the quality of the process and/or product.
4. Prepare directions in writing, outlining the situation, with instructions that the students are to follow.
5. Share the procedure with a colleague for feedback before using it with students.

Figure 11.10 Sample of a scoring rubric for student project presentation. Possible score = 100. Scorer marks a relevant square in each of the six categories (the horizontal rows), and the student's score for that category is the number within that square. (*Source:* Elk Grove School District, Elk Grove, California.)

Professional Presentation	14–15 Well organized; smooth transitions between sections; all enthusiastically participate and share responsibility.	12–13 Well organized with transitions; students confer/present ideas; group shows ability to interact; attentive discussion of research.	11 Shows basic organization; lacks transitions; some interaction; discussion focuses mostly on research.	1–10 Unorganized, lacks planning; no transitions; reliance on one spokesperson; little interaction; disinterest; too brief.
Engagement of Audience	14–15 Successfully and actively engages audience in more than one pertinent activity; maintains interest throughout.	12–13 Engages audience in at least one related activity; maintains attention through most of presentation.	11 Attempts to engage audience in at least one activity; no attempt to involve *entire* audience. May not relate in significant way.	1–10 Fails to involve audience; does not maintain audience's attention; no connection with audience. No relationship between activity and topic.
Use of Literature	18–20 Strong connection between literature and topic; significant, perceptive explanation of literature; pertinent to topic. At least two pieces used.	16–17 Clear connection between literature and topic; clear explanation; appropriate to topic. Two pieces used.	14–15 Weak connection to topic; unclear explanation; one genre; one piece used.	1–13 No connection to topic; no explanation; inappropriate literature; no literature.
Knowledge of Subject	18–20 Strong understanding of topic; knowledge factually relevant, accurate, and consistent; solution shows analysis of evidence.	16–17 Good understanding of topic; uses main points of information researched; builds solution on examination of major evidence.	14–15 Shows general understanding; focuses on one aspect, discusses at least one other idea; uses research, attempts to add to it; solution refers to evidence.	1–13 Little understanding or comprehension of topic; uses little basic information researched; forms minimal solution; relies solely on own opinions without support.
Use of Media	18–20 Effectively combines and integrates three distinct forms with one original piece; enhances understanding; offers insight into topic.	16–17 Combines two forms with one original piece; relates to topic; connection between media and topic is explained.	14–15 Includes two or three forms but no original piece; media relates to topic. Explanation may be vague or missing.	1–13 One form; no original piece; connection between media and topic is unclear.
Speaking Skills	9–10 Clear enunciation; strong projection; vocal variety; eye contact with entire audience; presentation posture; solid focus with no interruptions.	8 Good enunciation; adequate projection; partial audience eye contact; appropriate posture.	7 Inconsistent enunciation; low projection with little vocal variety; inconsistent posture.	1–6 Difficult to understand; inaudible; monotonous; no eye contact; inappropriate posture; interruptions and distractions.

Figure 11.11   Sample of a scoring rubric for student research paper. Possible score = 100. Scorer marks a relevant square in each of the six categories (the horizontal rows), and the student's score for that category is the number within that square.
(*Source:* Elk Grove School District, Elk Grove, California.)

Parenthetical References	**14–15** All documented correctly. Paper's references document a wide variety of sources cited—at least five from bibliography.	**12–13** Most documented correctly. Few minor errors. At least three sources from bibliography are cited.	**11** Some documented correctly. Some show no documentation at all. May not correlate to the bibliography.	**1–10** Few to none are documented. Does not correlate to the bibliography. May be totally absent.
Bibliography and Sources	**14–15** Strong use of library research. Exceeds minimum of five sources. Bibliography is correctly formatted.	**12–13** Good use of library research. Exceeds minimum of five sources. Bibliography has few or no errors in format.	**11** Some use of library research. Meets minimum of five sources. Bibliography is present but may be problematic.	**1–10** Fails to meet minimum standards for library research. Bibliography has major flaws or may be missing.
Mechanics/Format	**14–15** Correct format and pagination. Neat title page, near-perfect spelling, punctuation, and grammar.	**12–13** Mostly correct format and pagination. Neat. Few errors in title page, spelling, punctuation, and grammar.	**11** Errors in format and pagination. Flawed title page. Distracting errors in spelling, punctuation, and grammar.	**1–10** Incorrect format. Title page is flawed or missing. Many errors in spelling, punctuation, and grammar. Lack of planning is obvious. Paper is difficult to read.
Thesis	**9–10** An original and comprehensive thesis that is clear and well thought out. All sections work to support it.	**8** Comprehensive and well-focused thesis, which is clearly stated. All sections work to support it.	**7** Adequate thesis that is understandable but may be neither clear nor focused. It covers the majority of the issues found in the sections.	**1–6** Inadequate thesis that is disconnected from the research or may be too broad to support. May be convoluted, confusing, or absent.
Completeness/ Coherence	**18–20** Paper reads as a unified whole. There is no repetition of information. All sections are in place, and transitions between them are clearly developed.	**16–17** Paper reads as a unified whole with no repetition. All sections are in place, but transitions between them are not as smooth.	**14–15** Paper has required sections. Repetitions may be evident. The paper does not present a unified whole. Transitions are missing or inadequate.	**1–13** Paper lacks one or more sections and makes no attempt to connect sections as a whole unit. Sections may be grossly repetitive or contradictory.
Thinking/Analyzing	**23–25** Strong understanding of the topic. Knowledge is factually relevant, accurate, and consistent. Solutions show analysis of research discussed in paper.	**20–22** Good understanding of the topic. Uses main points of information researched. Solutions build on examination of research discussed in paper.	**17–19** General understanding of topic. Uses research and attempts to add to it; solutions refer to some of the research discussed.	**1–16** Little understanding of topic. Uses little basic information researched. Minimal examination of the topic. Solutions may be based solely on own opinions, without support.

teacher to read and to score. By using several questions of this type, a greater amount of content can be covered than with a lesser number of essay questions. This type of question is good practice for students to learn to express themselves succinctly in writing.

Disadvantages: Some students will have difficulty expressing themselves in a limited fashion or in writing. They need practice, coaching, and time.

Guidelines for use: This type is useful for occasional reviews and quizzes and as an alternative to other types of questions. For scoring, establish a scoring rubric and follow the same guidelines as for the essay-type item.

True-False

Description: A statement is presented that students are to judge as being accurate or not.

Example 1: A suffix is any bound morpheme added to the end of a root word. T or F?

Example 2: Christopher Columbus discovered America in 1492. T or F?

Advantages: Many items can be answered in a relatively short time, making broad content coverage possible. Scoring is quick and simple. True-false items are good as discussion starters, for review, and for diagnostic evaluation (preassessment) of what students already know or think they know.

Disadvantages: It is sometimes difficult to write true-false items that are purely true or false or to write them without qualifying them in such a way that clues the answer. In the second sample question, for example, the student may question whether Columbus really did discover America or he or she might misunderstand the meaning of "discovering America." Weren't there people already there when he landed? Where, in fact, did he land? What is meant by "America?" Example 2 is poor also because it tests for more than one idea—Columbus, America, and 1492.

Much of the content that most easily lends itself to the true-false type of test item is trivial. Students have a 50 percent chance of guessing the correct answer, thus giving this item type both *poor validity and poor reliability.* Scoring and grading give no clue about why the student missed an item. Consequently, the disadvantages of true-false items far outweigh the advantages; *pure true-false items should not be used for arriving at grades.* For grading purposes, you may use modified true-false items (see guideline 11 following), where space is provided between items for students to write in their explanations, thus making the item a combined true-false, short explanation type.

GUIDELINES FOR USING TRUE-FALSE ITEMS

1. For preparing a false statement, first write the statement as a true statement, then make it false by changing a word or phrase.
2. Try to avoid using negative statements since they tend to confuse students.
3. A true-false statement should include only one idea.
4. Use close to an equal number of true and false items.
5. Try to avoid using specific determiners (e.g., "always," "all," or "none"), because they usually clue that the statement is false. Avoid also words that may clue that the statement is true (e.g., "often," "probably," and "sometimes").
6. Avoid words that may have different meanings for different students.
7. Avoid using verbatim language from the student textbook.
8. Avoid trick items, such as a slight reversal of numbers in a date.
9. Do not use symbols for the words *true* and *false* (such as + and −) that might be confusing, or have students write the letters *T* and *F* (sometimes a student does not write the letters clearly enough for the teacher to be able to distinguish which it is). Instead, have students either write out the words *true* and *false* or, better yet, have them simply circle *T* and *F* as indicated by the two previous examples.
10. Proofread your items (or have a friend do it) to be sure that the sentences are well constructed and free from typographical errors.
11. To avoid "wrong" answers caused by variations in thinking, and to make the item more valid and reliable, students should be encouraged to write in their rationale for selecting true or false, making the item a *modified true-false* item. For example,

> When a farmer saw eight crows sitting on the fence surrounding his corn field, he shot three of them. Five were left on the fence. T or F?
>
> Explanation: _____

In addition to the combined true-false, short-explanation question, modified true-false "sometimes-always-never" items may be used for grading. Here, a third alternative, "sometimes," is introduced to reduce the chance for guessing.

Now do Exercise 11.1 to start developing your skill in writing assessment items. As you work on Exercise 11.1 you may want to correlate it with your previous work on Exercises 5.12, 6.4, and 6.5.

FOR YOUR NOTES

EXERCISE 11.1: PREPARING MY ASSESSMENT ITEMS

INSTRUCTIONS: The purpose of this exercise is to practice your skill in preparing the different types of assessment items discussed in this section. For use in your own teaching, select one specific instructional objective and write assessment items for it. When completed, share this exercise with your colleagues for their feedback. (See Exercises 5.12, 6.4, and 6.5.)

Objective: _____

Grade and subject: _____

1. Arrangement item: _____

   _____

   _____

   _____

   _____

2. Completion-drawing item: _____

   _____

   _____

   _____

   _____

3. Completion-statement item: _____

   _____

   _____

   _____

   _____

4. Correction item: _____

   _____

   _____

   _____

   _____

5. Essay item: _____

   _____

   _____

   _____

   _____

6. Grouping item: _____

   _____

☞

EXERCISE 11.1 (*continued*)

_____

7. Identification item: _____

_____

8. Matching item: _____

_____

9. Multiple-choice item: _____

_____

10. Performance item: _____

_____

11. Short-explanation item: _____

_____

12. *Modified* true-false item: _____

_____

REPORTING STUDENT ACHIEVEMENT

One of your responsibilities as a classroom teacher is to report student progress in achievement to parents or guardians as well as to the school administration for record keeping. In some schools, the reporting is of student progress and effort as well as of achievement. As described in the discussions that follow, reporting is done in at least two, and sometimes more, ways. However, for middle level schools, letter grades on report cards are still the most widely used method for reporting student learning.[12]

The Grade Report

Periodically a grade report (report card) is issued—generally from four to six times a year, depending upon the school, its purpose, and its type of scheduling. Grade reports may be distributed during an advisory period or they may be mailed to the student's home. This grade report represents an achievement grade (formative evaluation). The final report of the semester is also the semester grade, and for courses that are only one semester long, it is also the final grade (summative evaluation). In essence, the first and sometimes second reports are progress notices; the semester grade is the one that is transferred to the student's transcript of records.

In addition to the student's academic achievement, you must report his or her social behaviors (classroom conduct) while in your classroom. Whichever reporting form is used, you must separate your assessments of a student's social behaviors from the student's academic achievement. Academic achievement, or accomplishment, is represented by a letter or number grade (A through E or F; E, S, and U; 1 to 5, and sometimes with minuses and pluses). Social behavior is marked "satisfactory" or "unsatisfactory," or with a more specific designation, or it may be supplemented by teacher-written or computer-generated comments. There may also be a place on the reporting form for teachers to check whether basic grade-level standards have been met in the core subjects.

TEACHER PARENTAL/GUARDIAN CONNECTIONS

Study after study shows that when parents or guardians are involved in their child's school and schoolwork, students learn better and earn better grades, and teachers experience more positive feelings about teaching. As a result, as said in Chapter 1, schools constantly are searching for new and better ways to communicate with and to involve parents/guardians. What follows are additional suggestions and resources.

Contacting Parents/Guardians

Although it is not always obligatory, some teachers purposefully contact parents or guardians by telephone or by e-mail, especially when a student has shown a sudden turn for either the worse or the better in academic achievement or in classroom behavior. That initiative and contact by the teacher is usually welcomed by parents/guardians and can lead to productive conferences with the teacher. An electronic conference (telephone or e-mail) can save valuable time for both the teacher and the parent/guardian.

Another way of contacting parents/guardians is by letter, which gives you time to think and make clear your thoughts and concerns and to invite them to respond at their convenience by letter or phone, or by arranging to have a conference with you.

Progress Reporting to Parents/Guardians

In the absence of a computer-link assignment/progress report hotline, or in addition to that, most middle level schools have a progress report form that, upon request by a parent/guardian, can be sent home as often as agreed upon by the teacher and the parent/guardian. For example, parents of children at Kernersville Middle School (Winston-Salem NC) receive weekly academic updates.[13]

The form for progress reporting may be similar to the one shown in Figure 11.12, which shows the student's progress in each of the core subjects, or it might be like the one in Figure 11.13, which requires student self-evaluation, teacher assessment, office signature, and parental/guardian response and signature.

Meeting Parents/Guardians

You will meet some of the parents/guardians early in the school year during "Back to School" (or "Meet the Teacher" or "Curriculum" night, as it is variously called), throughout the year in individual conferences, and later in the year during spring open house. For the beginning teacher, these meetings with parents/guardians can be anxious times. The following paragraphs provide guidelines to help you with those experiences.[14]

Back-to-School night is the evening early in the school year when parents and guardians come to the school and meet their children's teachers. The parents and guardians arrive either at the student's homebase

---

[12]T. R. Guskey, *Communicating Student Learning*, p. 121.

[13]M. E. L'Esperance and D. Gabbard, "Empowering *All* Parents," *Middle Ground* 4(3):17–18 (February 2001).

[14]For suggestions from a school administrator for "delivering powerful presentations to parents," see W. B. Ribas, "Tips for Reaching Parents," *Educational Leadership* 56(1):83–85 (September 1998).

Figure 11.12 Weekly assessment checklist: Sample with teacher input only.

Weekly Assessment Checklist for _____

	Math	Social Studies	Science	Language Arts
Number of tardies				
Number of absences				
Academic grade				
Citizenship grade				

	Usually	Sometimes	Rarely	Never
Homework turned in on time				
Class work satisfactorily completed				
Exhibits acceptable classroom behavior				
Exhibits acceptable use of time in class				
Skill level is adequate to do work				
Participates orally in class discussions				
Participates in classroom learning activities				
Assumes responsibilities for own actions				
Avoids talking excessively or out of turn				
Comes to class prepared with supplies				
Is ready to start working when class begins				
Performs well on quizzes and tests				
Is attentive and focused during class				
Shows good listening skills				
Shows good organizational skills				
Reports for assigned detentions				
Respects the property of others and of the school				
Respects the rights of others				

Other comments or concerns _____

_____

_____

_____

_____

_____

_____

_____

_____

_____

Figure 11.13 Progress report: Subject-specific sample with student and parent input.

Progress Report: Marina Del Rey Middle School

Student: _Anthony von Hauser_   Course: _Algebra 1_   Date: _September 14, 2003_

This progress report form incorporates evaluation by student, teacher, and parent. The form will be completed by the student on Wednesday and by the teacher on Thursday and reviewed by the office and returned to the student on Friday. The student will take the form home for parental review, comments, and signature.

Section I: Self-Assessment: The student is asked to evaluate progress in the course in terms of goals and how closely these goals are being achieved. Do you feel you have made progress since the last progress report?

By taking this algebra class I achieved a greater understanding of it. I feel I have made a lot of progress since I took the class in 8th grade. It is also taught much better, which makes it easier.

Section II: Teacher Assessment: The teacher is asked to assess the student's entry, competency, and achievement to date and make recommendations.

Anthony is doing quite well. He has had to make some adjustments from previous work habits (ie, showing work), but he has made an excellent transition. Anthony has great skills and strong understanding of concepts.

	Present Status: (Rated A–F)		*What Is Needed*
B+ Class work/ participation	A = Excellent	✔ Emphasis on homework	
C+ Homework	B = Above average	____ Improve class participation	
A Portfolio	C = Average	____ More careful preparation for tests	
A Quizzes	D = Below average	✔ Keep up the good work	
A– Tests	F = Failing	____ Contact teacher	
A– Overall		____ Improve portfolio	
		____ Other _____	
		Office initial *CM*	

Section III: Parent Evaluation and Comments: Parents are asked to respond and sign this progress report.

I thank you for this timely report. I am delighted that Anthony has started off well and is liking the class. He talks at home a lot about the class and the interesting activities, a tribute to good teaching. I can tell from our conversations at home that he is feeling much better about his math capability. I thank you

Eric von Hauser

---

or in the auditorium for a greeting and a few words from various school officials and then proceed through a simulation of their sons' or daughters' school day; as a group, they meet each class and each teacher for a few minutes. Later, in the spring, many schools host an "open house" where parents and guardians may have more time to talk individually with teachers, although the major purpose of the open house is for the school and teachers to celebrate and display the work and progress of the students.

At Back-to-School night, parents/guardians are anxious to learn as much as they can about their children's teachers. You will meet each group of parents/guardians for a brief time, usually about 10 minutes. During that meeting you will provide them with a copy of the course syllabus; make some straightforward remarks about yourself; and talk about the course, its requirements, your expectations of the students, and how the students' parents and guardians, might help.

Although there will be precious little time for questions from the parents/guardians during your introduction, the adults will be delighted to learn that you have your program well planned and that you appreciate their interest and welcome their participation. They will be happy to hear about your willingness to communicate with them and pleased to know that you are "from the school of the three Fs"—that is, that you are firm, friendly, and fair. If a parent/guardian indicates an urgent need to talk with you just as soon as possible, try to schedule a mutually convenient private conference time in person or via telephone for later that evening or during the next few days.

Specifically, parents/guardians will expect to learn about your curriculum: goals and objectives, any long-term projects, class size, schedules for tests, and grading procedures. They will want to know what you expect of them: Will there be homework, and if so, should they help their children with it? [*Note:* The answer to the preceding question is in the nature of the help given; parents and other family members should encourage and help facilitate their children doing homework, but they "should be careful, however, not to solve content problems for students."[15]] How can parents/guardians contact you? Try to anticipate other questions. Your principal, department chair, or colleagues can help you anticipate and prepare for these questions. Of course, you can never prepare for the question or comment that comes from left field. Just remain calm (or at least appear so) and avoid being flustered. Ten minutes will fly by quickly, and parents and guardians will be reassured to know you are an in-control person.

Parent/Guardian Conference

When meeting parents or guardians for conferences, you should be as specific as possible when explaining the progress of their child in your class. Express your appreciation for their interest, be helpful to his or her understanding, and do not saturate the parent/guardian with more information than he or she needs. Resist any tendency to talk too much. Allow time for the parent or guardian to ask questions. Keep your answers succinct. Never compare one student with another or with the rest of the class. If the parent or guardian asks a question for which you do not have an answer, tell the person you will try to find an answer and will phone him or her as quickly as you can. And do it. Have the student's portfolio and other work with you during the parent/guardian conference so you can show them examples of what is being discussed. Also, have your grade book or a computer printout of it on hand, but be prepared to protect the names and records of the other students.

Sometimes it is helpful to have a three-way conference with the parent or guardian, the student, and you, or a conference with the parent/guardian, the principal or counselor, and several or all of the student's teachers.

If, especially as a beginning teacher, you would like the presence of an administrator at a parent/guardian-teacher conference as backup, do not be hesitant to arrange that.

Some educators prefer a *student-led conference,* arguing that "placing students in charge of the conference makes them individually accountable, encourages them to take pride in their work, and encourages student-parent/guardian communication about school performance."[16] For example, from Derby Middle School (Derby, KS) a teacher reports that "I can't imagine going back to the previous way we met with parents. The preparatory time and work that this alternative takes is worth it, especially when you hear a struggling student explaining what he or she learned from an assignment, and taking responsibility for the score he or she achieved."[17] At Talent Middle School (Talent, OR), parent/guardian attendance at conferences increased from just 40% to 95% after students were put in charge of the conferences.[18] And, during the 1999–2000 and 2000–2001 school years, 90% of the parents attended the student-led conferences at Conway Middle School (Louisville, KY).[19,20]

The paragraphs that follow offer suggestions for when a parent or guardian asks how she or he may help in the student's learning. Many schools have made special and successful efforts to link home and school. At some schools, through homework hotlines, parents/guardians have phone access to their children's assignment specifications and to their progress in their schoolwork, and those with a personal computer and modem have access to tutorial services to assist students with assignments.

---

[15]R. J. Marzano, D. J. Pickering, and Jane E. Pollock, *Classroom Instruction That Works* (Alexandria, VA: Association for Supervision and Curriculum Development, 2001), p. 63.

[16]D. W. Johnson and R. T. Johnson, "The Role of Cooperative Learning in Assessing and Communicating Student Learning," page 43 in T. R. Guskey, *Communicating Student Learning.* (Alexandria, VA: ASCD Yearbook, Association for Supervision and Curriculum Development, 1996), pp. 18–19.

[17]L. Hayden, "Letting Student Lead Parent Conferences," from *Middle Matters,* NAESP (National Association of Elementary School Principals) *Principal Online* [online 3/20/01 http://www.naesp.org/comm/mmf98b.htm], Fall 1998, p. 3.

[18]P. Farber, "Speak Up: Student-Led Conference Is a Real Conversation Piece," *Middle Ground* 2(4):21–24 (April 1999).

[19] A. Downs, "It's All in the Family: Middle Schools Share the Secrets of Parent Engagement," *Middle Ground* 4(3):10–15 (February 2001), p. 10.

[20]For further information about student-led conferences, see P. Kinney, M. B. Munroe, and P. Sessions, *A School-Wide Approach to Student-Led Conferences* (Westerville, OH: National Middle School Association, 2000); B. Cesarone, "Parent-Teacher Conferences," *Childhood Education* 76(3):180 (Spring 2000); and D. G. Hackmann, *Student-Led Conferences at the Middle Level,* ERIC Digest (Champaign, IL: ED407171, ERIC Clearinghouse on Elementary and Early Childhood Education, 1997), online http://www.ed.gov/databases/ERIC_Digests/ed407171.html.

Figure 11.14   Resources for developing home-school partnerships.

- Alliance for Parental Involvement in Education, PO Box 59, East Chatham, NY 12060-0059 (518-392-6900).
- *A School-Wide Approach to Student-Led Conferences: A Practitioner's Guide,* by P. Kinney, M. B. Munroe, and P. Sessions, National Middle School Association, 2000 (800-528-NMSA).
- Center on Families, Communities, Schools & Children's Learning, 3505 N. Charles St., Baltimore, MD 21218 (410-516-8800).
- *How To Help Your Child with Homework: Every Caring Parent's Guide to Encouraging Good Study Habits and Ending the Homework Wars (For Parents of Children Ages 6–13)* by M. C. Radencich and J. S. Schumm. Revised and Updated. Free Spirit Publishing, Minneapolis, MN, 1997 (612-338-2068).
- *Keys to Re-engaging Families in the Education of Young Adolescents,* by H. Loucks and J. E. Waggoner, National Middle School Association, 1998 (800-528-NMSA).
- National Coalition for Parent Involvement in Education, Box 39, 1201 16th St., NW, Washington, DC 20036.
- National Community Education Association, 3929 Old Lee Highway, Suite 91A, Fairfax, VA 22030-2401 (703-359-8973).
- National PTA, 330 North Wabash Ave., Suite 2100, Chicago, IL 60611-3690 (312-670-6782).
- Parents for Public Schools, PO Box 12807, Jackson, MS 39236-2807 (800-880-1222).
- *School, Family, and Community Partnerships: Your Handbook for Action,* by J. Epstein, et al, Corwin Press, Thousand Oaks, CA, 1997 (805-499-9734).

Helping students become critical thinkers is one of the aims of education and one that parents and guardians can help with by reinforcing the strategies being used in the classroom. Ways to do this are to ask "what if" questions; to think aloud as a model for the student's thinking development; to encourage the student's own metacognition by asking questions such as, "How did you arrive at that conclusion?" or "How do you feel about your conclusion now?" and asking questions about the student's everyday social interactions, topics that are important to the student; and to ask the student to elaborate on his or her ideas accepting the fact that the student may make mistakes but encouraging the student to learn from them.

Many resources are available for parents/guardians to use at home. The U. S. government, for example, has a variety of free or low-cost booklets available. For information contact the Consumer Information Center, Department BEST, Pueblo, CO 81009 or the website at http://www.pueblo.gsa.gov. Figure 11.14 presents addresses for additional ideas and resources for home-school partnerships.

Dealing with an Angry Parent or Guardian

The following paragraphs offer guidelines for dealing with a parent or guardian who is angry or hostile toward you and the school.

Remain calm in your discussion with the adult, allowing the parent or guardian to talk out his or her hostility while you say very little; usually, the less you say the better off you will be. What you do say must be objective and to the point of the student's work in your classroom.

The parent or guardian may just need to vent frustrations that might have very little to do with you, the school, or even the student.

Do *not* allow yourself to be intimidated, put on the defensive, or backed into a verbal corner. If the parent/guardian tries to do so by attacking you personally, do not press your defense at this point. Perhaps the parent/guardian has made a point that you should take time to consider. Arrange for another conference with the parent/guardian for about a week later. In a follow-up conference, if the parent/guardian agrees, you may want to consider bringing in a mediator, such as another member of your teaching team, an administrator, or a school counselor.

You must *not* talk about other students; keep the conversation focused on the progress of this parent or guardian's child. The adult is *not* your rival, or should not be. You both share a concern for the academic and emotional well-being of the parent or guardian's child. Use your best skills in critical thinking and problem solving, trying to focus the discussion by identifying the problem, defining it, and then arriving at some decision about how mutually to go about solving it. To this end, you may need to ask for help from a third party, such as the student's school counselor. If agreed to by the parent, please take that step.

Parents and guardians do *not* need to hear about how busy you are, about your personal problems, or about how many other students you are dealing with on a daily basis, unless, of course, a parent or guardian asks. Parents and guardians expect you to be the capable professional who knows what to do and is doing it.

SUMMARY

Whereas preceding parts of this resource guide addressed the *why, what,* and *how* components of teaching, this chapter has focused your attention on the fourth and final component—the *how well* component—and on the first of two aspects of that component. Assessment is an integral and on-going factor in the teaching-learning process; consequently, this chapter has emphasized the importance of including the following in your teaching performance:

• Use a variety of instruments to collect a body of evidence that most reliably assesses the learning of students and that focuses on their individual development.

• Involve students in the assessment process and keep them informed of their progress. Return tests promptly, review answers to all questions, and respond to inquiries about marks given.

• Consider your assessment and grading procedures carefully, plan them, and explain your policies to the students.

• Make sure to explain any ambiguities that result from the terminology used, and base your assessments on the target objectives and the material that has been taught.

• Strive for objective and impartial assessment as you put your assessment plan into operation.

• Try to minimize arguments about grades, cheating, and teacher subjectivity by involving students in the planning; reinforcing individual student development; and providing an accepting, stimulating learning environment.

• Maintain accurate and clear records of assessment results so that you will have an adequate supply of data on which to base your judgmental decisions about achievement.

Because teaching and learning work hand in hand and because they are reciprocal processes where one depends on and affects the other, the how-well component deals with the assessment of both how well the students are learning and how well the teacher is teaching. This chapter has dealt with the first. In the next and final chapter of this resource guide, your attention is directed to techniques designed to help you develop your teaching skills and to assess that development, a process that is just beginning and will continue throughout your teaching career. As a teacher you are a learner among learners.

ADDITIONAL EXERCISE

See the companion Website http://www.prenhall. com/kellough for the following exercise related to the content of this chapter:

• Evaluating Written Teacher Comments—A Self-Check Exercise.

QUESTIONS FOR CLASS DISCUSSION

1. Identify a problem in grading that you personally experienced as a student in school. What was your perceived cause of the problem? How might it have been avoided? What was the resolution and how was that resolution arrived at? Was the resolution satisfactory to all concerned? Why or why not?

2. Other than a paper-and-pencil test, identify three alternative techniques for assessing student learning during or at completion of an instructional unit.

3. Investigate various ways that schools housing middle grades are experimenting today with assessing and reporting student achievement. Share what you find with your classmates. With your classmates, discuss the pros and cons of various systems of assessing and reporting.

4. When using a point system for determining student grades, is it educationally defensible to give a student a higher grade than that student's points call for? A lower grade? Give your rationale for your answers.

5. Describe any student learning activities or situations that you believe should *not* be graded but should or could be used for assessment of student learning.

6. If, you were a parent of a young adolescent, list five things you would like to hear from your child's teachers at Back-to-School night. Share and compare your list with those of your classmates. What were the commonalities?

7. Select one of the "Reflective Thoughts" from the introduction to Part IV (page 348) that is specifically related to the content of this chapter, research it, and write a one-page essay explaining why you agree or disagree with the thought. Share your essay with members of your class for their thoughts.

8. Describe any prior concepts you held that changed as a result of your experiences with this chapter. Describe the changes.

9. From your current observations and field work related to this teacher preparation program, clearly identify one specific example of educational practice that seems contradictory to exemplary practice or theory as presented in this chapter. Present your explanation for the discrepancy.

10. Do you have questions generated by the content of this chapter? If you do, list them along with ways answers might be found.

FOR FURTHER READING

Andrade, H. G. "Using Rubrics to Promote Thinking and Learning." *Educational Leadership* 57(5):13–18 (February 2000).

Asp, E. "Assessment in Education: Where Have We Been? Where Are We Headed?" Chapter 6 of R. S. Brandt, ed. *Education in a New Era.* Alexandria, VA: ASCD Yearbook, Association for Supervision and Curriculum Development, 2000, pp. 123–157.

Bond, B. "Using Standards-Based Performance Assessment with At-Risk Students." *Middle Ground* 4(3):36–39 (February 2001).

Bracey, G. W. *A Short Guide to Standardized Testing.* Fastback 459. Bloomington, IN: Phi Delta Kappa Educational Foundation, 2000.

Carr, J. F., and Harris, D. E. *Succeeding with Standards: Linking Curriculum, Assessment, and Action Planning.* Alexandria, VA: Association of Supervision and Curriculum Development, 2001.

Cizek, G. J. *Cheating on Tests: How To Do It, Detect It, and Prevent It.* Mahway, NJ: Lawrence Erlbaum, 1999.

Colby, S. A. "Grading in a Standards-Based System." *Educational Leadership* 56(6):17–21 (March 1999).

Cole, K. A. "Walking Around: Getting More from Informal Assessment." *Mathematics Teaching in the Middle School* 4(4):224–227 (January 1999).

Conway, K. D. "Assessing Open-Ended Problems." *Mathematics Teaching in the Middle School* 4(8):510–514 (May 1999).

Downs, A. "It's All in the Family: Middle Schools Share the Secrets of Parent Engagement." *Middle Ground* 4(3):10–15 (February 2001).

Kelly, K. "Retention vs. Social Promotion: Schools Search for Alternatives." *The Harvard Education Letter* 15(1):1–3 (January/February 1999).

Kinney, P.; Munroe, M. B.; and Sessions. P. *A School-Wide Approach to Student-Led Conferences.* Westerville, OH: National Middle School Association, 2000.

Langer, J. A. "Turning Obstacles into Opportunity." *Harvard Education Letter* 17(2):6–7 (March/April 2001).

Leon, S., and Elias, M. "A Comparison of Portfolio, Performance, and Traditional Assessment in the Middle School." *Research in Middle Level Education Quarterly* 21(2):21–37 (Winter 1998).

Lockledge, A., and Hayn, J., eds. *Using Portfolios Across the Curriculum.* Westerville, OH: National Middle School Association, 2000.

Marzano, R. J. *Transforming Classroom Grading.* Alexandria, VA: Association for Supervision and Curriculum Development, 2000.

Murdock, T. B. "Discouraging Cheating in Your Classroom." *Mathematics Teacher* 92(7):587–591 (October 1999).

Oosterhof, A. *Classroom Applications of Educational Measurement,* 3rd ed. Upper Saddle River, NJ: Merrill/Prentice Hall, 2001.

Popham, J. W. *The Truth About Testing.* Alexandria, VA: Association for Supervision and Curriculum Development, 2001.

Ronis, D. *Brain Compatible Assessments.* Arlington Heights, IL: Skyline, 2000.

Schmoker, M. *The Results Fieldbook: Practical Strategies from Dramatically Improved Schools.* Alexandria, VA: Association for Supervision and Curriculum Development, 2001.

Stephens, D., and Story, J. (Eds.). *Assessment as Inquiry: Learning the Hypothesis-Test Process.* Urbana, IL: National Council of Teachers of English, 2000.

Stiggins, R. J. *Student-Involved Classroom Assessment,* 3rd ed. Upper Saddle River, NJ: Merrill/Prentice Hall, 2001.

Stix, A. "Bridging Standards Across the Curriculum with Portfolios." *Middle School Journal* 32(1):15–25 (September 2000).

Wormeli, R. "Aim for More Authentic Assessment." *Middle Ground* 4(3):25–28 (February 2001).

Assessing Teaching Effectiveness and Continued Professional Development

Most of us are not born with teaching skills, but teaching skills can be learned and steadily improved. Teachers who wish to improve their teaching can do so and, in addition to this resource guide, there are many resources that can help.

This chapter addresses the assessment and development of your effectiveness as a classroom teacher, a process that continues throughout your professional career. Teaching is such an electrifying profession that it is not easy to remain energetic and to stay abreast of changes and trends that result from research and practice. You will need to make a continu-

ous and determined effort to remain an alert and effective teacher.

Whether you are a beginning or experienced teacher, one way to collect data and improve your effectiveness is through periodic assessment of your teaching performance. This can be done either by an evaluation of your teaching in the real classroom or, if you are in a teacher preparation program, by a technique called micro peer teaching. The latter is the focus of the final section of this chapter and is an example of a type of final performance (authentic) assessment for this resource guide.

OBJECTIVES

Upon completion of this chapter, you should be able to

1. Demonstrate knowledge about the field components of teacher preparation.
2. Demonstrate knowledge about how to find a teaching job.
3. Demonstrate knowledge about how to remain an alert and effective classroom teacher throughout your teaching career.

PROFESSIONAL DEVELOPMENT THROUGH STUDENT TEACHING

You are probably excited about the prospect of being assigned as a student teacher to your first classroom, but you are probably also concerned. Questions linger in your mind. Will your host (cooperating) teacher(s) like you? Will you get along? Will the students accept you? Will you be assigned to the school, grade level, and subjects you want? What will the students be like? Will there be many classroom management problems? What about mainstreamed students, and students with only limited English proficiency? Your questions will be unending.

Indeed, you *should* be excited and concerned, because student teaching is one of the most significant and important facets of your program of teacher preparation. In some programs, this practical field experience is planned as a co-experience with the college or university theory classes. In other programs, student teaching is the culminating experience. Different sequences are represented in different programs. For example, at some colleges, field teaching extends over two or three semesters. In other programs, teacher candidates take a theory class followed by a full second semester of student teaching. Regardless of when and how your student teaching occurs, the experience is a bright and shining opportunity to hone your teaching skills in a real classroom. During this time, you will be supported by an experienced college or university supervisor and by carefully selected cooperating teachers, who will share their expertise. Once you have started your student teaching, it can help establish a feeling of community, prevent a sense of isolation, and encourage reflection if you and your college or university supervisor can communicate by e-mail.

Everyone concerned in the teacher preparation program—your cooperating teacher, your university instructors, the school administrators, and your university supervisor—realize that this is your practicum in learning how to teach. During your student teaching, you will no doubt make errors and, with the understanding and guidance of those supervising your work, you will benefit and learn from those errors. Sometimes your fresh approach to motivation, your creative ideas for learning activities, and your energy and enthusiasm make it possible for the cooperating teacher to learn from you. After all, teaching and learning are always reciprocal processes. What is most important is that the students who are involved with you in the teaching-learning process will benefit from your role as the teacher candidate in the classroom. The following guidelines are offered to help make this practical experience beneficial to everyone involved.

Student Teaching Is the Real Thing

Because you have a classroom setting for practicing and honing your teaching skills with active, responsive, young adolescents, student teaching *is* the real thing. On the other hand, student teaching is *not* real in the sense that it is your cooperating teacher, not you, who has the ultimate responsibility and authority for the classroom.

Getting Ready for Student Teaching

To prepare yourself for student teaching, you must study, plan, practice, and reflect. You should become knowledgeable about your students and their developmental backgrounds. In your theory classes, you learned a great deal about students. Review your class notes and textbooks from those courses, or select some readings suggested in Part I. Perhaps some of the topics will have more meaning for you now.

First Impressions

First impressions are often lasting impressions. You have heard that statement before, and now, as you ready for this important phase of your professional preparation, you hear it again. Heed it, for it is crucial to your success. Remember it as you prepare to meet your school principal and cooperating teacher for the first time; remember it as you prepare to meet your students for the first time; remember it as you prepare to meet parents and guardians for the first time; remember it as you prepare for your university supervisor's first observation of your teaching; remember it as you prepare for your school principal's first visit to see you teach. Remember it again as you prepare for your first teaching job interview. In each case, you have only one opportunity to make a first impression.

Continuing to Get Ready for Student Teaching

In addition to the aforementioned preparations, you will need to be knowledgeable about your assigned school and the community that surrounds it. Review the subject areas you will be teaching and the curriculum content and standards in those areas. Carefully discuss with your cooperating teacher (or teachers, as you may have more than one) and your university supervisor all of the responsibilities that you will be expected to assume.

As a student teacher you may want to run through each lesson verbally, perhaps in front of a mirror, the night before teaching the lesson. Some student teachers read through each lesson, record the lesson, play it back, and evaluate whether the directions are clear, the instruction is mind-grabbing (or at least interesting), the sequence is logical, and the lesson closure is concise. Still other student teachers always have a "Plan B" in mind in case "Plan A" turns out to be inappropriate.

Student Teaching from the Cooperating Teacher's Point of View

Information about student teaching from the viewpoint of a cooperating teacher is presented here in a question-and-answer format. You may wish to share this section with your cooperating teacher.

What is my role? As the cooperating teacher, your role is to assist when necessary: to provide guidance, to review lesson plans *before* they are taught, to facilitate the learning and skill development of your student teacher, and to help your student teacher become and feel like a member of the school faculty and of the profession.

How can I prepare for the experience? Get to know your student teacher *before* he or she begins teaching. Develop a collegial rapport with the student teacher.

Who is my student teacher? Your student teacher is a person who is making the transition from another career or from the life of a college student to the profession of teaching. Your student teacher may be your age, older, or younger. In any case, he or she may be scared to death, anxious, knowledgeable, and, when it comes to teaching philosophy, somewhere between a romantic idealist and a pragmatic realist. Do not destroy the idealism—help the student teacher to understand and deal with the realism of everyday teaching.

It is important that you learn about the kinds of teaching experiences your student teacher has had prior to this assignment so together you may build from those experiences. For example, this may be your student teacher's very first teaching experience; he or she may have substitute teaching experience or experience teaching in another country; or he or she may have student taught at another school prior to this term.

What kind of support, criticism, and supervision should I give? Much of this, you will have to decide for yourself. On the other hand, some teacher preparation programs include seminars that train the cooperating teachers in techniques for supervising student teachers. Cooperating teachers are often selected not only because of their effectiveness in teaching but also because of their skill in

working with other adults. It is likely that you will be working as a member of a team that includes you, the student teacher, and the university supervisor. Your student teacher may have more than one cooperating teacher, who should then also be included as a member of this professional team. Whatever the situation, your student teacher needs support, helpful suggestions, and productive monitoring. It is unprofessional to place a student teacher into a total "sink-or-swim" situation.

What danger signs should I be alert for? Your student teacher may be quite different from you in both appearance and style of teaching but may be potentially just as effective as a teacher. Be slow and cautious in judging your student teacher's effectiveness. Offer suggestions, but do not make demands.

A student teacher who is not preparing well is likely to be heading for trouble. The saying stands: Failing to prepare is preparing to fail. Be certain to ask for and to receive lesson plans before they are taught, especially in the beginning and whenever you feel the student teacher is not preparing well.

Another danger signal is when the student teacher seems to show no real interest in the school and the students beyond the classroom. The student teacher should be prompt, should be eager to spend extra time with you, should attend faculty meetings, and should be aware of the necessity of performing school clerical tasks. If you feel there is a lurking problem, let the student teacher or the university supervisor know immediately. Trust your intuition. Poor communication between members of the teaching team is another danger signal.

What else should I know? Your student teacher may be employed elsewhere and have other demands on his or her time. Become aware of these other demands, but keep the educational welfare of your students paramount in your mind.

See that your student teacher is treated as a member of the faculty and invited to faculty functions. He or she should have a personal mailbox (or share yours, with his or her name on it as well) and should understand school policies, procedures, and curriculum documents.

Once your student teacher is well grounded, he or she should be ready to gradually be alone with the students for increasingly longer periods of time. For a specified time, a student teacher's goal is to work toward a competency level that enables him or her to assume increasing responsibility for everything. This means that you are nearby and on call in case of an emergency, but out of sight of the students.

Comments from the University Supervisor

When is the supervisor coming? Is the supervisor going to be here today? Do you see a university or a college supervisor's observation of your student teaching as a pleasant experience or a painful one? Do you realize that classroom observations of your teaching continue during your beginning years of teaching? Being observed and evaluated does not have to be a painful, nerve-racking experience for you. You do not have to become a bundle of raw nerve endings when you realize the supervisor is coming to see you. Whether you are a student teacher being observed by your university supervisor or a probationary teacher being evaluated by your principal, some professional suggestions may help you turn an evaluating observation into a useful, professionally satisfying experience.

What to Do Before an Observation

Successful teachers seem to be able to ameliorate tension and get through an evaluation with skill and tact. Prepare for your evaluative visit by deciding what you do well and plan to demonstrate your best skills. Decorate your room and bulletin boards, especially displaying student work. Make sure your work area is orderly (this shows good organization), and select an academic aspect of the teaching day that demonstrates some of your best teaching skills. If your university supervisor has previously targeted some areas that need strengthening, plan to demonstrate growth in those teaching abilities.

What to Do During an Observation

Some supervisors and administrators choose to preannounce their visits. This is certainly true for clinical supervision practices. Clinical supervision is based on shared decision making between the supervisor and teacher, and is focused on improving, rather than evaluating, teaching behaviors. For clinical supervision, you will know when the supervisor or administrator is coming, and you will probably look forward to the visit because of the rapport that has been established between members of your triad (in student teaching situations, your triad is composed of you, your cooperating teacher, and your university or college supervisor).

Features of clinical supervision include a preobservation conference, observation of teaching, and a postobservation conference. In the preobservation conference, the student teacher, cooperating teacher, and supervisor meet to discuss goals, objectives, teaching strategies, and the evaluation process. During the observation, the supervisor collects data on the classroom students' performance of objectives and on the student teacher's performance of the teaching strategies. In the postobservation conference, the student teacher, cooperating teacher, and supervisor discuss the performances. They may compare what happened with what was expected, make inferences about students' achievement of objectives, and discuss relationships between teaching performance and student achievement.

The supervisor and cooperating teacher act as educational consultants and may discuss alternative strategies for teaching at this conference or at a later one.

Sometimes your supervisor or administrator may drop in unannounced. When that happens you can take a deep breath, count to 10 (quietly), and then proceed with your lesson. You will undoubtedly do just fine if you have been following the guidelines set forth in this book. Additional guidelines for a classroom observation include the following: allow the observer to sit wherever he or she wishes; do not interrupt your lesson to introduce the observer unless the observer requests it, but *do* prepare your students in advance by letting them know who may be visiting and why; do not put the observer on the spot by suddenly involving him or her in the lesson, but *do* try to discern in advance the level of participation desired by your observer.

If you have been assigned to a classroom for a student teaching experience, your university supervisor will meet with you and explain some of the tasks you should attend to when the supervisor visits your class. These may vary from the list presented. For instance, some supervisors prefer to walk into a classroom quietly and not interrupt the learning activities. Some prefer not to be introduced to the class or to participate in the activities. Some supervisors are already well known by the students and teaching staff from prior visits to the school. Other supervisors may give you a special form to be completed before he or she arrives for the visit. This form often resembles a lesson plan format and includes space for your objectives, lesson procedures, motivational strategies, related activities, and method of assessing how well the students learned from the lesson. Remember, keep the line of communication open with your supervisor so you have a clear understanding of what is expected of you when she or he visits your classroom to observe your teaching. Without "missing a beat" in your lesson, you may walk over and quietly hand the observer a copy of the lesson plan and the textbook (or any other materials being used), opened to the appropriate page.

In some teacher preparation programs the student teacher is expected to maintain a *student teaching binder* in the classroom. (A similar expectation is common in beginning teacher mentor programs.) The binder is kept in a particular location so the cooperating teacher may refer to it and the college or university supervisor (or mentor) can pick it up upon entering the classroom and refer to it during the observation. Organized in the binder is the current lesson plan, the current unit plan, previous lessons with reflections, tests and their results, assignments, the classroom management plan, and a current seating chart with the student's names. The student teaching binder can, in fact, represent the start of your *professional portfolio* (discussed later in this chapter).

Soon after the observational visit, there should be a conference in which observations are discussed in a nonjudgmental atmosphere. You may need to make sure that a conference is scheduled. The purpose of this post-observation conference is for you and the observer(s) to discuss, rather than to evaluate, your teaching; and for you to exit the conference with agreements about areas for improvement and how to accomplish those improvements. Sometimes, because of conflicting schedules, conferences may be electronic, via e-mail or phone.

What to Do During an Observation Conference

When a supervisor arranges to have a conference with you, as a teacher or teacher candidate, you should be professional during this meeting. For instance, some student teachers ask for additional help by requesting resources. Others take notes and suggest developing a cooperative plan with the supervisor to improve teaching competencies. Still others discuss visiting other classrooms to observe exemplary teachers.

During other conferences, student teachers may ask for assistance in scheduling additional meetings with the supervisor. At such meetings, the teacher (or teacher candidate) views videos of selected teaching styles or methods, listens to audiotapes, or visits an outside educational consultant or nearby resource center.

Almost all supervisors conclude their conferences by leaving something in writing with the teacher or teacher candidate. This written record usually includes a summary of teaching strengths or weaknesses, with a review of classroom management; the supervisor's recommendations; and, perhaps, steps in an overall plan for the teacher's (or student teacher's) continued professional growth and development.

What to Do After the Supervisor Leaves

In addition to observing the classes of other teachers, attending workshops and conferences, and conferring with college and university authorities, the following are ways to implement your plan for improvement. Be sure you debug your lesson plans by walking through them before implementing them in the classroom. Do what you and your supervisor have agreed on. Document your activities in a record or diary with dated entries. If you maintain a supervisor's binder, this documentation may be kept in the binder along with the supervisor's written comments. If you have a problem with classroom management or organization, review your written classroom management plan and procedures, comparing your plan with the guidelines presented in Chapter 4. Review your plan and procedures with your cooperating teacher, a trusted teaching colleague, or your university supervisor. Obtain help when you need it. Write comments to parents or guardians about students' progress, and leave space for

a return message from the adult (see, for example Figure 11.13 in Chapter 11). Keep positive responses that you receive from these adults and share them with your supervisor at your next conference.

FINDING A TEACHING POSITION

As your successful student teaching experience draws to a close, you will embark upon finding your first paid teaching job. The guidelines that follow are provided to help you accomplish your goal.

Guidelines for Locating a Teaching Position

To prepare for finding the position you want, you should focus on (a) letters of recommendation from your cooperating teacher(s), your college or university supervisor, and, in some instances, the school principal; (b) your professional preparation as evidenced by your letters of recommendation and other items in your professional portfolio (discussed next); and (c) your job-interviewing skills.

First, consider the recommendations about your teaching. Most colleges and universities have a career center, usually called a *job* (or *career*) *placement center.* There is usually a counselor who can advise you on how to open the job placement file that will hold your professional recommendations. This enables prospective personnel directors or district personnel who are expecting to employ new teachers to review your recommendations. Sometimes there are special forms for writing these. It is your responsibility to request letters of recommendation and, when appropriate, to supply the person with the blank form and an appropriately addressed stamped envelope. Sometimes job placement files are confidential, in which case your recommendations will be mailed directly to the placement office. If the files are not confidential, when possible, you may want to maintain your own copies of letters of recommendation and include them in your professional portfolio.

The letters of recommendation from educators at the school(s) where you did your student teaching should include the following information: the name of the school and district where you did your student teaching; the grade levels and subjects you taught; your proven skills in managing students of diversity in the classroom; your ability to teach the relevant subject(s); your skills in assessing student learning, reflecting on your teaching performance, and learning from that reflection; and your skills in communicating and interacting with students and adults.

Second, consider your preparation as a teacher. Teachers, as you have learned, represent a myriad of specialties. Hiring personnel will want to know how you see yourself—for example, as a specialist in core, as a music teacher, or as a social studies teacher who would also like to coach basketball. Perhaps your interest is only in teaching science. You may indicate a special interest or skill, such as competency in teaching English as a second language. Or, perhaps, your teaching field is mathematics, but you also are bilingual and have had rich and varied crosscultural experiences. Have you had experiences that would allow you to feel comfortable being hired and placed in the one assignment in which you were least interested? The hiring personnel who consider your application will be interested in your sincerity and will want to see that you are academically and socially impressive.

Finally, consider your in-person interview with a district official. Sometimes, you will have several interviews or you will be interviewed simultaneously with other candidates. There may be an initial screening interview by an administrative panel from the district, followed by an interview by a department chairperson, a school principal, or a school team composed of one or more teachers and administrators from the interested school or district. In all interviews, your verbal and nonverbal behaviors will be observed as you respond to various questions, including (a) factual questions about your student teaching, or about particular curriculum programs with which you would be expected to work, and (b) hypothetical questions, such as "What would you do if . . .?" Often these are questions that relate to your philosophy of education; your reasons for wanting to be a teacher, particularly a teacher for the middle grades; your approach to handling a particular classroom situation; and perhaps specifically your reasons for your interest in teaching at this particular school and in this district. Interview guidelines follow later in this section.

The Professional Career Portfolio (or How to Get Hired by Really Trying)

One way to be proactive in your job search is to create a personal professional portfolio to be shared with persons who are considering your application for employment. That is the objective of Exercise 12.1.

EXERCISE 12.1: DEVELOPMENT OF MY PROFESSIONAL PORTFOLIO

INSTRUCTIONS: The purpose of this exercise is to guide you in the creation of a personal professional portfolio that will be shared with persons who are considering your application for employment as a credentialed teacher.

Because it would be impractical to send a complete portfolio with every application you submit, you should consider developing a minimum portfolio (portfolio B) that could be sent with each application, in addition to a complete portfolio (portfolio A) that you could make available upon request and take with you to an interview. However it is done, the actual contents of the portfolio will vary depending on the specific job being sought; you will continually add to and delete materials from your portfolio. Suggested categories and subcategories, listed in the order that they may be best presented in portfolios A and B are as follows.

1. Table of contents of portfolio (not too lengthy)—portfolio A only.
2. Your professional résumé—both portfolios.
3. Evidence of your language and communication skills (evidence of your use of English and of other languages, including American Sign)—portfolio A. (Also state this information briefly in your letter of application. See the résumé section that follows.)
   a. Your teaching philosophy (written in your own handwriting to demonstrate your handwriting). (See Exercise 3.4.)
   b. Other evidence to support this category.
4. Evidence of teaching skills—portfolio A.
   a. For planning skills, include instructional objectives, a syllabus, and a unit plan. (See Exercises 5.12 and 6.5.)
   b. For teaching skills, include a sample lesson plan and a video of your actual teaching. (See Exercises 6.4, 9.1, and 12.2.)
   c. For assessment skills, include a sample personal assessment and samples of student assessment. (See Exercises 9.1, 11.1, and 12.2.)
5. Letters of recommendation and other documentation to support your teaching skills—both portfolios.
6. Other (for example, personal interests related to the position for which you are applying)—portfolio A.

The professional career portfolio is organized to provide clear evidence of your teaching skills and to make you professionally desirable to a hiring committee. A professional portfolio is not simply a collection of your accomplishments randomly tossed into a folder. It is a deliberate, current, organized collection of your skills, attributes, experiences, and accomplishments.

It might be advisable to have both a complete portfolio (portfolio A) and a minimum portfolio (portfolio B). Exercise 12.1 explains the portfolios in more detail and suggests categories and subcategories for portfolios A and B.[1]

Resources for Locating Teaching Vacancies

To locate teaching vacancies, contact any of the following resources.

Academic Employment Network. A network employment page on the Internet http://www.academploy.com/. Contact AEN, 2665 Gray Road, Windham, ME 04062 (800-890-8283). E-mail info@academploy.com.

College or university placement office. Establishing a career placement file with your local college or university placement service is an excellent way to begin the process of locating teaching vacancies.

Local school or district personnel office. You can contact school personnel offices to obtain information about teaching vacancies and sometimes about open job interviews.

County educational agency. Contact local county offices of education about job openings.

State departments of education. Some state departments of education maintain information about job openings statewide.

Independent schools. You can contact non–public-supported schools that interest you, either directly or through educational placement services such as the following:

- IES (Independent Educational Services), 20 Nassau Street, Princeton, NJ 08540 (800-257-5102).
- European Council of Independent Schools, 21B La-vant St., Petersfield, Hampshire, GU32 3EL, England.

Commercial placement agencies. Nationwide job listings and placement services are available from such agencies as the following:

- Carney, Sandoe & Associates, 136 Boylston Street, Boston, MA 02116 (800-225-7986).
- National Education Service Center, PO Box 1279, Department NS, Riverton, WY 82501-1279 (307-856-0170).
- National Teachers Clearinghouse-SE, PO Box 267, Boston, MA 02118-0267 (617-267-3204).

Out-of-country teaching opportunities. Information regarding teaching positions outside the United States can be obtained from the following:

- American Field Services Intercultural Programs, 313 East 43rd St., New York, NY 10017.
- Department of Defense Dependent Schools, 4040 N. Fairfax Dr., Arlington, VA 22203-1634.
- European Council of Independent Schools, 21B La-vant St., Petersfield, Hampshire, GU32 3EL, England.
- International Schools Service, PO Box 5910, Princeton, NJ 08543.
- Peace Corps, Recruitment Office, 806 Connecticut Ave. NW, Washington, DC 20526.
- Teachers Overseas Recruitment Centers, National Teacher Placement Bureaus of America, Inc., PO Box 09027, 4190 Pearl Rd., Cleveland, OH 44109.
- YMCA of the USA, Attn: Teaching in Japan and Taiwan, 101 N. Wacker Dr., Chicago, IL 60606.

Professional educational journals and other publications. Professional teaching journals often run advertisements of teaching vacancies, as do education newspapers such as *Education Week*. These can be found in your college or university library. See also *Education Week's* site on the Internet at http:// www.edweek.org/.

STATE (AND TERRITORIAL) SOURCES FOR INFORMATION ABOUT CREDENTIAL REQUIREMENTS

If you are interested in the credential requirements for other states and U.S. territories, check at the appropriate office of your own college or university teacher preparation program for information about requirements for states of interest to you. Find out whether the credential that you are about to receive has reciprocity with other states. Addresses and contact numbers for information about state credentials are available on the Internet at http://www.ed.gov/Programs/bastmp/SEA.htm.

The Professional Résumé

Résumé preparation is the subject of how-to books, computer programs, and commercial services, but a teacher's résumé is specific. Although no one can tell you exactly what will work best for you, a few basic guidelines are especially helpful in preparing a teacher's résumé:

---

[1] For further information, see K. Wolf, "Developing an Effective Teaching Portfolio," *Educational Leadership* 53(6):34–37 (March 1996), and Chapter 4, "Creating a Professional Portfolio," in C. Danielson, *Enhancing Professional Practice: A Framework for Teaching* (Alexandria, VA: Association for Supervision and Curriculum Development, 1996). See also the Internet at http://www.teachnet.com/. Preservice teachers in particular may be interested in several articles about portfolios in the theme issue of *Teacher Education Quarterly*, 25(1) (Winter 1998).

- The résumé should be no more than *two pages* in length. If it is any longer, it becomes a life history rather than a professional résumé.
- The presentation should be neat and uncluttered.
- Page size should be standard 8 1/2 × 11 inches. Oversized and undersized pages can get lost.
- Stationery color should be white or off-white.
- Do *not* give information such as your age, height, weight, marital status, or number or names of your children, and do not enclose a photograph of yourself, because including personal data may make it appear that you are trying to prejudice members of the hiring committee, which is simply unprofessional.

- Sentences should be clear and concise; avoid educational jargon, awkward phrases, abbreviations, or unfamiliar words.
- Organize the information carefully, in this order: your name, address, and telephone number, followed by your education, professional experience, credential status, location of placement file, professional affiliations, and honors.
- When identifying your experiences—academic, teaching, and life—do so in *reverse chronological order,* listing your most recent degree or your current position first. (See sample résumé in Figure 12.1.)

Figure 12.1   Sample professional résumé.

JENNIFER DAWSON
510 Newcomb Street, #309, Davis, CA 95616
(916) 552-8996
jdaw@aol.com

CREDENTIALS

January 2001	California Preliminary Single Subject Credential in English
	Supplemental Authorization in Social Studies
May 2001	CLAD (Culture and Language Academic Development) Certificate
	California State University, Sacramento

EDUCATION

May 1995	Bachelor of Arts Degree in English Literature
	Saint Olaf College, Northfield, Minnesota

TEACHING EXPERIENCE

September 2001 through
January 2002
(Student Teaching III)

Douglass Junior High School (Woodland, CA). *Two 7th-grade 2-hour block interdisciplinary core classes, English and Social Studies.*
- Worked with a team to develop interdisciplinary thematic lessons.
- Conducted student-led parent conferences.
- Employed hands-on learning techniques and simulations.

February 2001 through
May 2001
(Student Teaching II)

Davis High School (Davis, CA). *One period of college preparatory English Literature for juniors.*
- Developed book clubs, small-group forums for discussing three novels.
- Developed poetry unit in which students published their own poems for class collection.

September 1999 through
May 2000 (Student Teaching I)

Los Cerros Middle School (Danville, CA). *One period ESL—13 culturally diverse 7th and 8th graders.*
- Bilingual stories and activities; reader's theater presentations.

RELATED EXPERIENCE

Summer of 2001

- Developed and taught a Summer Writing Workshop for small groups of 3rd- through 10th-grade students. Met with students and parents to establish goals.

September 1999–May 2000

- Reader for English department at Valley High School.

OTHER EXPERIENCE

- Volunteer in Juarez, Mexico, through YWAM (Youth with a Mission).
- Coordinator in Glacier National Park for the group, A Christian Ministry in the National Parks.

- Be absolutely truthful; avoid any distortions of facts about your degrees or experiences, or any other information that you provide on your résumé.
- Take time to develop your résumé, and then keep it current. Do not duplicate hundreds of copies; produce a new copy each time you apply for a job. If you maintain your résumé on a computer disc, it is easy to make modifications and print a current copy each time one is needed.
- Prepare a cover letter to accompany your résumé that is written *specifically* for the position for which you are applying. Address the letter personally but formally to the personnel director. Limit the cover letter to one page, and emphasize yourself, your teaching experiences and interests, and reasons that you are best qualified for the position. Show a familiarity with the particular school or district. Again, if you maintain a generic application letter on a computer disc, you can easily modify it to make it specific for each position.
- Have your résumé and cover letter edited by someone familiar with résumé writing and editing, perhaps an English-teaching friend. A poorly written, poorly typed, or poorly copied résumé fraught with spelling and grammar errors will guarantee that you will not be considered for the job.
- Be sure that your application reaches the personnel director by the announced deadline. If, for some reason, it will be late, telephone the director, explain the circumstances, and request permission to submit your application late.

The In-Person Interview

If your application and résumé are attractive to the personnel director, you will be notified and scheduled for a personal or small-group interview, although in some instances the hiring interview may precede the request for your personal papers. Whichever the case, during the interview you should be honest, and you should be yourself. Practice an interview, perhaps with the aid of a videocamera. Ask a friend to role-play an interview with you and to ask you some tough questions. Plan your interview wardrobe and get it ready the night before. Leave early for your interview so that you arrive in plenty of time. If possible, long before your scheduled interview, locate someone who works in the school district and discuss curriculum, classroom management policies, popular programs, and district demographics with that person. If you anticipate a professionally embarrassing question during the interview, think of diplomatic ways to respond—ways to turn your weaknesses into strengths. For instance, if your cooperating teacher has mentioned that you need to continue to develop your room environment skills (meaning that you were sloppy), admit that you need to be more conscientious about keeping supplies and materials neat and tidy, but mention your concern about students and learning and that you have a tendency to interact with students more than with objects. Assure them that you will work on this skill, and then do it. The paragraphs that follow offer additional specific guidelines for preparing for and handling the in-person interview. As you peruse these guidelines, please remember that what may seem trite and obvious to one reader is not necessarily obvious to another.

You will be given a specific time, date, and place for the interview. Regardless of your other activities, accept the time, date, and location suggested, rather than trying to manipulate the interviewer around a schedule more convenient for you.

As a part of the interview you may be expected to do a formal but abbreviated (10–15 minutes) teaching demonstration. You may or may not be told in advance of this expectation. So, it is a good idea to thoughtfully develop and rehearse a model one that you could perform on request. Just in case it might be useful, some candidates carry to the interview a videotape of one of their best real teaching episodes made during student teaching.

Dress for success. Regardless of what else you may be doing for a living, take the time necessary to make a professional and proud appearance.

Avoid coming to the interview with small children. If necessary, arrange to have them taken care of by someone.

Arrive promptly, shake your dry hands firmly with members of the committee, and initiate conversation with a friendly comment based on your personal knowledge, about the school or district.

Be prepared to answer standard interview questions. Sometimes school districts will send candidates the questions that will be asked during the interview; at other times, these questions are handed to the candidate upon arrival at the interview. The questions that are likely to be asked will cover the following topics:

- *Your experiences with students of the relevant age.* The committee wants to be reasonably certain that you can effectively manage and teach at this level. You should answer this question by sharing specific successes that demonstrate that you are a decisive and competent teacher.
- *Hobbies and travels.* The committee wants to know more about you as a person to ensure that you will be an interesting and energetic teacher to the students, as well as a congenial member of the faculty.
- *Extracurricular interests and experiences.* The committee wants to know about all the ways in which you might be helpful in the school and to know that you will promote the interests and co-curricular activities of students and the school community.

- *Classroom management techniques.* You must convince the committee that you can effectively manage a classroom of diverse learners in a manner that will help the students to develop their self-esteem.
- *Knowledge of the curriculum standards and the subject taught at the level for which you are being considered.* The committee needs to be reasonably certain that you have a command of the subject and its place within the developmental stages of students at this level. This is where you should show your knowledge of national standards and of state and local curriculum documents.
- *Knowledge of assessment strategies that are relevant for use in teaching at this level.* This is your place to shine with your professional knowledge about using rubrics and performance assessment.
- *Commitment to teaching at this level.* The committee wants to be assured that you are knowledgeable about and committed to teaching and learning at this level, as opposed to just seeking this job until something better comes along.
- *Your ability to reflect on experience and to grow from that reflection.* Demonstrate that you are a reflective decision maker and a life-long learner.
- *Your perceived weaknesses.* If you are asked about your weaknesses, you have an opportunity to show that you can effectively reflect and self-assess, that you can think reflectively and critically, and that you know the value of learning from your own errors and how to do it. Be prepared for this question by identifying a specific error that you have made, perhaps while student teaching, and explain how you turned that error into a profitable learning experience.

Throughout the interview, you should maintain eye contact with the interviewer while demonstrating interest, enthusiasm, and self-confidence. When an opportunity arises, ask one or two planned questions that demonstrate your knowledge of and interest in the position and the community and school or district.

When the interview has obviously been brought to a close by the interviewer, that is your signal to leave. Do not hang around; this is a sign of lacking confidence. Follow the interview with a thank-you letter addressed to the personnel director or interviewer. Even if you do not get the job, you will be better remembered for future reference.[2]

Once you are employed as a teacher, your professional development continues. The sections that follow demonstrate ways in which that can happen.

PROFESSIONAL DEVELOPMENT THROUGH REFLECTION AND SELF-ASSESSMENT

Beginning now and continuing throughout your career, you will reflect on your teaching (reflection is inevitable), and you will want to continue to grow as a professional as a result of those reflections (growth is not so inevitable unless it is self-initiated and systematically planned). The most competent professional is one who is proactive; that is, one who takes charge and initiates his or her own continuing professional development. One useful way of continuing to reflect, self-assess, and grow professionally is by maintaining a professional journal, much as your students do when they maintain journals reflecting on what they are learning. Another is by continuing to maintain the professional career portfolio that you began assembling early in your preservice program and finalized for your job search (as discussed earlier in this chapter). Some teachers maintain professional logbooks, which serve not only as documentations of their specific professional contributions and activities, but also as documentation of the breadth of their professional involvement. Some teachers maintain research logs as a way to record questions that come up during the busy teaching day, and to establish a plan for finding answers.[3] The research log strategy can be of tremendous benefit to you in actively researching and improving your classroom work, but it can also be of interest to colleagues. Finally, working in teams and sharing your work with team members is still another way of continuing to reflect, self-assess, and grow as a teacher.

PROFESSIONAL DEVELOPMENT THROUGH MENTORING

Mentoring, one teacher facilitating the learning of another teacher, can aid in professional development.[4] In what is sometimes called *peer coaching*, a mentor teacher volunteers or is selected by the teacher who wishes to improve, or he or she is selected by a school administrator, formally or informally. The mentor observes and coaches the teacher to help him or her to improve in

---

[2] For additional suggestions for preparing for a teaching job interview, see Internet Website http://www.teachnet.com/.

[3] For more on the professional portfolio and logs, see Chapter 4, "Creating a Professional Portfolio," of C. Danielson, *Enhancing Professional Practice: A Framework for Teaching* (Alexandria, VA: Association for Supervision and Curriculum Development, 1996), pp. 38–50.

[4] For additional information, see "The International Center for Information About New Teacher Mentoring and Induction" at http://www.teachermentors.com/MCenter%20Site/AdviceBegTchr.html, and a description of California's Beginning Teacher Support and Assessment (BTSA). Program at http://www.ccoe.k12.ca.us/coe/curins.sbtsa/description. See also A. Gratch, "Beginning Teacher and Mentor Relationships," *Journal of Teacher Education* 49(3):220–227 (May/June 1998).

teaching. Sometimes the teacher simply wants to learn a new skill. In other instances, the teacher being coached remains with the mentor teacher for an entire school year, developing and improving old and new skills or learning how to teach with a new program. In many districts, new teachers are automatically assigned to mentor teachers for their first, and sometimes second, year, as a program of induction.

PROFESSIONAL DEVELOPMENT THROUGH INSERVICE AND GRADUATE STUDY

Inservice workshops and programs are offered for teachers at the school level, by the district, and by other agencies such as a county office of education or a nearby college or university. Inservice workshops and programs are usually designed for specific purposes, such as to train teachers in new teaching skills, to update their knowledge in content, and to introduce them to new teaching materials or programs. For example, Baltimore City Public School (MD) provides a system-wide professional development program for teachers of middle grades, administrators, and staff at its Lombard Learning Academy Demonstration Center. The Lombard Learning Academy is a school-within-a-school located at Lombard Middle School. Cohorts of five to ten teachers from other schools in the district visit the Academy for five-day periods to observe instruction, practice strategies, and hone their skills in using technology.

University graduate study is yet another way of continuing your professional development. Some teachers pursue master's degrees in academic teaching fields, while many others pursue master's degrees in curriculum and methods of instruction or in educational administration or counseling. Some universities offer a Master of Arts in Teaching (MAT), a program of courses in specific academic fields that are especially designed for teachers.

PROFESSIONAL DEVELOPMENT THROUGH PARTICIPATION IN PROFESSIONAL ORGANIZATIONS

There are many professional organizations—local, statewide, national, and international. Except for the National Middle School Association, the organizations for middle school teachers are usually discipline-specific, such as the National Council of Teachers of Mathematics, the National Council for the Social Studies, the National Council of Teachers of English, and the National Science Teachers Association (see Chapter 5). In most states, there is a statewide organization, usually affiliated with a national organization. In addition, there are national teachers organizations, such as the

Figure 12.2 National professional associations for teachers.

- American Federation of Teachers (AFT), AFL-CIO, 555 New Jersey Avenue NW, Washington, DC 20001 http://www.aft.org
- Association of American Educators (AAE), 26012 Marguerite Parkway #333, Mission Viejo, CA 92692 http://www.aaeteachers.org/info.html#board
- National Association of Professional Educators (NAPE), Suite 300, 900 17th Street, Washington, DC 20006 http://www.teacherspet.com/napeindx.htm
- National Education Association (NEA), 1201 16th Street NW, Washington, DC 20036-3290 http://www.nea.org

ones shown in Figure 12.2. The NEA is the oldest and the AAE and NAPE are more recent. The NEA and AFT have merged state wide in a few states and in a few large metropolitan areas.[5]

Local, district, state, and national organizations have meetings that include guest speakers, workshops, and publishers' displays. Professional meetings of teachers are educational, enriching, and fulfilling for those who attend. In addition, many other professional associations, such as those for reading teachers, supply speakers and publish articles in their journals that are often of interest to teachers other than the target audience.

Professional organizations publish newsletters and journals for their members that will likely be found in your college or university library. Sample periodicals were listed in Figure 10.3 (Chapter 10). Many professional organizations have special membership prices for teachers who are still college or university students, a courtesy that allows for an inexpensive beginning affiliation with a professional association. For information on special membership prices and association services, contact those that are of interest to you.

PROFESSIONAL DEVELOPMENT THROUGH COMMUNICATIONS WITH OTHER TEACHERS

Visiting teachers at other schools; attending inservice workshops, graduate seminars, and programs; participating in teacher study groups[6] and meetings of professional organizations; and participating in teacher

---

[5] See A. Bradley, "Teachers' Unions To Merge in Two More States," *Education Week*, April 5, 2000, p. 3.

[6] See, for example, A. Jolly, "Improving Instruction Through Collaboration," *Middle Ground* 4(3):29–31 (February 2001).

networks[7] and sharing with teachers by means of electronic bulletin boards are all valuable experiences, if for no other reason than for talking and sharing with teachers from across the country and around the world. These discussions include not only a sharing of "war stories" but of ideas and descriptions of new programs, books, materials, and techniques that work.

As in other process skills, the teacher practices and models skill in communication, both in and out of the classroom. This includes communicating with other teachers to improve one's own repertoire of strategies and knowledge about teaching as well as sharing one's experiences with others. Teaching other teachers about your own special skills and sharing your experiences are important components of the communication and professional development processes.

PROFESSIONAL DEVELOPMENT THROUGH SUMMER AND OFF-TEACHING WORK EXPERIENCE

In many areas of the country, there are special programs of short-term employment available to interested teachers. These are offered by public agencies, private industry, foundations, and research institutes. These institutions are interested in disseminating information and providing opportunities for teachers to update their skills and knowledge, with the ultimate hope that the teachers will stimulate in more students a desire to develop their physical fitness, to understand civic responsibilities, and to consider careers in science and technology. Participating industries, foundations, governments, and institutes provide on-the-job training with salaries or stipends to teachers who are selected to participate. During the program of employment and, depending on the nature of the work, a variety of people (e.g., scientists, technicians, politicians, businesspersons, social workers, and sometimes university educators) meet with teachers to share experiences and discuss what is being learned and its implications for teaching and curriculum development.

Some of the programs for teachers are government-sponsored, field-centered, and content-specific. For example, a program may concentrate on geology,

anthropology, mathematics, or reading. At another location, a program may concentrate on teaching, using a specific new or experimental curriculum. These programs, located around the country, may have university affiliation, which means that university credit may be available. Room and board, travel, and a stipend are sometimes granted to participating teachers.

Sources of information about the availability of programs include professional journals, the local chamber of commerce, and meetings of the local or regional teacher's organization. In areas where there are no organized programs of part-time work experience for teachers, some teachers have had success in initiating their own by establishing contact with management personnel of local businesses or companies.

PROFESSIONAL DEVELOPMENT THROUGH MICRO PEER TEACHING

Micro peer teaching (MPT) is a skill-development strategy used for professional development by both preservice (prior to credentialing) and inservice (credentialed and employed) teachers. Micro peer teaching (to which you were introduced in Exercises 7.7 and 9.1) is a scaled-down teaching experience involving a

- Limited objective.
- Brief interval for teaching a lesson.
- Lesson taught to a few (8 to 10) peers (as your students).
- Lesson that focuses on the use of one or several instructional strategies.

Micro peer teaching can be a predictor of later teaching effectiveness in a regular classroom. More importantly, it can provide an opportunity to develop and improve specific teaching behaviors. A videotaped MPT allows you to see yourself in action for self-evaluation and diagnosis. Evaluation of an MPT session is based on

- The quality of the teacher's preparation and lesson implementation.
- The quality of the planned and implemented student involvement.
- Whether the instructional objective(s) was reached.
- The appropriateness of the cognitive level of the lesson.

Whether a preservice or inservice teacher, you are urged to participate in one or more MPT experiences. Formatted differently from previous exercises in this resource guide, Exercise 12.2 can represent a summative performance assessment for the course for which this book is being used.

---

[7] See, for example, A. Lieberman and M. Grolnick, "Networks, Reform, and the Professional Development of Teachers," Chapter 10 of A. Hargreaves (Ed.), *Rethinking Educational Change With Heart and Mind* (Alexandria, VA: ASCD 1997 Yearbook, Association for Supervision and Curriculum Development, 1997), pp. 192–215.

FOR YOUR NOTES

EXERCISE 12.2: PULLING IT ALL TOGETHER—MICRO PEER TEACHING III

INSTRUCTIONS: The purpose of this exercise is to learn how to further develop your own MPT experiences. You will prepare and teach a lesson as a presentation for your peers, at their level of intellectual maturity and understanding (i.e., as opposed to teaching the lesson to peers pretending that they are public school students).

This experience has two components:
1. Your preparation and implementation of a demonstration lesson.
2. Your completion of an analysis of the summative peer assessment and the self-assessment, with statements of how you would change the lesson and your teaching of it were you to repeat the lesson.

You should prepare and carry out a 15- to 20-minute lesson to a group of peers. The exact time limit for the lesson should be set by your group, based on the size of the group and the amount of time available. When the time limit has been set, complete the time-allowed entry (item 1) of Form A of this exercise. Some of your peers will serve as your students; others will be evaluating your teaching. (The process works best when "students" do not evaluate while being students.) Your teaching should be videotaped for self-evaluation.

For your lesson, identify one concept and develop your lesson to teach toward an understanding of that concept. Within the time allowed, your lesson should include both teacher talk and a hands-on activity for the students. Use Form A for the initial planning of your lesson. Complete a lesson plan, selecting a lesson plan format as discussed in Chapter 6. Then present the lesson to the "students." The peers who are evaluating your presentation should use Form B of this exercise.

After your presentation, collect your peer evaluations (the Form B copies that you gave to the evaluators). Then review your presentation by viewing the videotape. After viewing the tape, prepare

- A tabulation and statistical analysis of peer evaluations of your lesson.
- A self-evaluation based on your analysis of the peer evaluations, your feelings after having taught the lesson, and your thoughts after viewing the videotape.
- A summary analysis that includes your selection and a description of your teaching strengths and weaknesses as indicated by this peer-teaching experience and how you would improve were you to repeat the lesson.

TABULATION OF PEER EVALUATIONS

The procedure for tabulating the completed evaluations received from your peers is as follows:

1. *Use a blank copy of Form B for tabulating.* In the left margin of that copy, place the letters N (number) and σ (total) to prepare for two columns of numbers that will fall below each of those letters. In the far right margin, place the word *Score*.
2. *For each item (a through y) on the peer evaluation form, count the number of evaluators who gave a rating (from 1 to 5) on the item.* Sometimes an evaluator may not rate a particular item, so although there may have been 10 peers evaluating your MPT, the number of evaluators giving you a rating on any one particular item could be less than 10. For each item, the number of evaluators rating that item we call N. Place this number in the N column at the far left margin on your blank copy of Form B, next to the relevant item.
3. *Using a calculator, obtain the sum of the peer ratings for each item.* For example, for item a, "Lesson preparation evident," you add the numbers given by each evaluator for that item. If there were 10 evaluators who gave you a number rating on that item, then your sum on that item will not be more than 50 (5×10). Because individual evaluators will make their X marks differently, you must sometimes estimate an individual evaluator's number rating—that is, rather than a clear rating of 3 or 3.5 on an item, you may have to estimate it as being a 3.2 or a 3.9. In the left-hand margin of your blank copy of Form B, in the σ column, place the sum for each item.
4. *Now obtain a score for each item, a through y.* The score for each item is obtained by dividing σ by N. Your score for each item will range between 1 and 5. Write this result in the column in the right-hand margin under the word *Score* on a line parallel to the relevant item. This is the number you will use in the analysis phase.

☞

EXERCISE 12.2 (continued)

PROCEDURE FOR ANALYZING THE TABULATIONS

Having completed the tabulation of the peer evaluations of your teaching, you are ready to proceed with your analysis of those tabulations.

1. To proceed, you need a blank copy of Form C of this exercise, your self-analysis form.
2. On the blank copy of Form C, there are five items: Implementation, Personal, Voice, Materials, and Strategies.
3. In the far left margin of Form C, place the letter σ for the sum. To its right and parallel with it, place the word *Average*. You now have arranged for two columns of five numbers each—a σ column and an *Average* column.
4. For each of the five items, get the total score for that item, as follows:
    a. *Implementation.* Add all scores from the right-hand margin of blank Form B for the four items a, c, x, and y. The total should be 20 or less (4 × 5). Place this total in the left-hand margin under σ (to the left of "1. Implementation").
    b. *Personal.* Add all scores from the right-hand margin of blank Form B for the nine items f, g, m, n, o, p, q, s, and t. The total should be 45 or less (9 × 5). Place this total in the left-hand margin under σ (to the left of "2. Personal").
    c. *Voice.* Add all scores from the right-hand margin of blank Form B for the three items h, i, and j. The total should be 15 or less (3 × 5). Place this total in the left-hand margin under σ (to the left of "3. Voice").
    d. *Materials.* Add all scores from the right-hand margin of blank Form B for item k. The total should be 5 or less (1 × 5). Place this total in the left-hand margin under σ (to the left of "4. Materials").
    e. *Strategies.* Add all scores from the right-hand margin of blank Form B for the eight items b, d, e, l, r, u, v, and w. The total should be 40 or less (8 × 5). Place this total in the left-hand margin under σ (to the left of "5. Strategies").
5. Now, for each of the five categories, divide the sum by the number of items in the category to get your peer evaluation average score for that category. For item 1 you will divide by 4; for item 2, by 9; for item 3, by 3; for item 4, by 1; and for item 5, by 8. For each category you should then have a final average peer evaluation score of a number between 1 and 5. If correctly done, you now have average scores for each of the five categories: Implementation, Personal, Voice, Materials, and Strategies. With those scores and evaluators' comments you can prepare your final summary analysis.

The following table includes three sample analyses of MPT lessons based *only* on the scores—that is, without reference to comments made by individual evaluators, although peer evaluators' comments are important considerations for actual analyses.

Sample Analyses of MPTs Based Only on Peer Evaluation Scores

Teacher	Category/Rating					Possible Strengths and Weaknesses
	1	2	3	4	5	
A	4.2	2.5	2.8	4.5	4.5	Good lesson, weakened by personal items and voice
B	4.5	4.6	5.0	5.0	5.0	Excellent teaching, perhaps needing a stronger start
C	2.5	3.0	3.5	1.0	1.5	Poor strategy choice, lack of student involvement

EXERCISE 12.2: FORM A—MPT PREPARATION

Form A is to be used for initial preparation of your MPT lesson. (For preparation of your lesson, study Form B.) After completing Form A, proceed with the preparation of your MPT lesson using a lesson plan format as discussed in Chapter 6. A copy of the final lesson plan should be presented to the evaluators at the start of your MPT presentation.

1. Time allowed: _____

2. Title or topic of lesson I will teach: _____

3. Concept: _____

4. Specific instructional objectives for the lesson:

_____

_____

_____

_____

_____

_____

_____

5. Strategies to be used, including approximate time plan:

Set introduction _____

_____

Transitions _____

_____

Closure _____

_____

Others _____

_____

6. Student experiences to be provided (i.e., specify for each—visual, verbal, kinesthetic, and tactile experiences):

_____

_____

_____

_____

7. Materials, equipment, and resources needed: _____

_____

_____

_____

_____

_____

FOR YOUR NOTES

EXERCISE 12.2: FORM B—PEER EVALUATION

Evaluators use Form B, making an *X* on the continuum between 5 and 1. Far left (5) is the highest rating; far right (1) is the lowest. Completed forms are collected and given to the teacher upon completion of that teacher's MPT and are reviewed by the teacher prior to reviewing his or her videotaped lesson.

To evaluators: Comments as well as marks are useful to the teacher.

To teacher: Give one copy of your lesson plan to the evaluators at the start of your MPT. [*Note:* It is best if evaluators can be together at a table at the rear of the room.]

Teacher: _____ Date: _____

Topic: _____

Concept: _____

1. Organization of Lesson	5	4	3	2	1
a. Lesson preparation evident	very		somewhat		no
b. Lesson beginning effective	yes		somewhat		poor
c. Subject-matter knowledge apparent	yes		somewhat		no
d. Strategies selection effective	yes		somewhat		poor
e. Closure effective	yes		somewhat		poor

Comments:

_____

_____

_____

_____

_____

_____

_____

_____

_____

_____

_____

_____

_____

_____

_____

_____

_____

EXERCISE 12.2 (*continued*)

2. Lesson Implementation

	5	4	3	2	1
f. Eye contact excellent	yes		somewhat		poor
g. Enthusiasm evident	yes		somewhat		no
h. Speech delivery	articulate		minor problems		poor
i. Voice inflection; cueing	effective		minor problems		poor
j. Vocabulary use	well chosen		minor problems		poor
k. Aids, props, and materials	effective		OK		none
l. Use of examples and analogies	effective		needs improvement		none
m. Student involvement	effective		OK		none
n. Use of overlapping skills	good		OK		poor
o. Nonverbal communication	effective		a bit confusing		distracting
p. Use of active listening	effective		OK		poor
q. Responses to students	personal and accepting		passive or indifferent		impersonal and antagonistic
r. Use of questions	effective		OK		poor
s. Use of student names	effective		OK		no
t. Use of humor	effective		OK		poor
u. Directions and refocusing	succinct		a bit vague		confusing
v. Teacher mobility	effective		OK		none
w. Use of transitions	smooth		a bit rough		unclear
x. Presentation motivating	very		somewhat		not at all
y. Momentum (pacing) of lesson	smooth and brisk		OK		too slow or too fast

Comments:

_____

_____

_____

_____

_____

_____

_____

_____

_____

_____

_____

_____

_____

EXERCISE 12.2 FORM C—TEACHER'S SUMMATIVE PEER EVALUATION

See instructions within Exercise 12.2 for completing this form.

1. Implementation (items a, c, x, y)	5	4	3	2	1
2. Personal (items f, g, m, n, o, p, q, s, t)	5	4	3	2	1
3. Voice (items h, i, j)	5	4	3	2	1
4. Materials (item k)	5	4	3	2	1
5. Strategies (items b, d, e, l, r, u, v, w)	5	4	3	2	1

Total = _____

Comments:

_____

_____

_____

_____

_____

_____

_____

_____

_____

_____

_____

_____

_____

_____

_____

_____

_____

_____

_____

_____

_____

_____

_____

_____

_____

_____

FOR YOUR NOTES

SUMMARY

Because teaching and learning go hand in hand, and the effectiveness of one affects that of the other, the final two chapters of this resource guide have dealt with both aspects of the *how well* component of teacher preparation—how well the students are learning and how well the teacher is teaching.

In addition, you have been presented with guidelines about how to obtain your first teaching job and how to continue your professional development. Throughout your teaching career you will continue improving your knowledge and skills in all aspects of teaching and learning.

We wish you the very best in your new career. Be the very best teacher that you can be. The nation and its young adolescents need you.

—Richard Kellough and Noreen Kellough

ADDITIONAL EXERCISE

See the companion Website http://www.prenhall.com/kellough for the following exercise related to the content of this chapter:

- Attending a Back-to-School Night

QUESTIONS FOR CLASS DISCUSSION

1. Discover what professional teacher organizations there are in your geographical area. Share what you find with others in your class. Attend a local, regional, or national meeting of a professional teachers' association and report to your class what it was like and what you learned. Share with your class any free or inexpensive teaching materials you obtained.
2. Talk with experienced teachers and find out how they remain current in their teaching fields. Share what you find with others in your class.
3. Select one of the "Reflective Thoughts" from the introduction to Part IV (page 348) that is specifically related to the content of this chapter, research it, and write a one-page essay explaining why you agree or disagree with the thought. Share your essay with members of your class for their thoughts.
4. Describe any prior concepts you held that changed as a result of your experiences with this chapter. Describe the changes.

5. From your current observations and field work related to this teacher preparation program, clearly identify one specific example of educational practice that seems contradictory to exemplary practice or theory presented in this chapter. Present your explanation for the discrepancy.
6. Congratulations! You have reached the end of this resource guide, but there may be questions lingering in your mind. As before, list them and try to find answers.

FOR FURTHER READING

Bradford, J. J. "How to Stay in Teaching (When You Really Feel Like Crying)." *Educational Leadership* 56(8):67–68 (May 1999).

Close, E., and Ramsey, K., eds. "Planning for the Job Interview." *English Journal* 89(5):143–146 (May 2000).

Cramer, G., and Hurst, B. *How to Find a Teaching Job: A Guide for Success.* Upper Saddle River, NJ: Merrill/Prentice Hall, 2000.

Duck, L. "The Ongoing Professional Journal." *Educational Leadership* 57(7):42–45 (May 2000).

Graham, P., et al., eds. *Teacher/Mentor.* New York: Teachers College Press, 1999.

Keller, J. D. "Deciphering Teacher Lounge Talk." *Phi Delta Kappan* 81(4):328–329 (December 1999).

Kellough, R. D. *Surviving Your First Year of Teaching: Guidelines for Success,* 2nd ed. New Jersey: Merrill/Prentice Hall, 2001.

Kramer, M. C. "Triumph Out of the Wilderness: A Reflection on the Importance of Mentoring." *Phi Delta Kappan* 82(5):411–412 (January 2001).

Lowenhaupt, M. A., and Stephanik, C. E. *Making Student Teaching Work: Creating a Partnership.* Fastback 447. Bloomington, IN: Phi Delta Kappa Educational Foundation, 1999.

Martin, D. B. *The Portfolio Planner: Making Professional Portfolios Work for You.* Upper Saddle River, NJ: Merrill/Prentice Hall, 1999.

McEwan, E. K. *How To Deal with Parents Who Are Angry, Troubled, Afraid, or Just Plain Crazy.* Thousand Oaks, CA: Corwin Press, 1998.

Notman, T. S., and Megyeri, K. A. "To Student Teach." *English Journal* 88(4):20–25 (March 1999).

Sparks, D. "What Teachers Know and Don't Know Matters." *Harvard Education Letter* 15(4):8 (July/August 1999).

Torreano, J. M. *500 Q&A for New Teachers: A Survival Guide.* Norwood, MA: Christopher-Gordon, 2000.

Willman, K., and Smith, T. "Creating a Professional Development Opportunity within the Supervisor-Student Teacher Relationship." *Science Educator* 9(1):19–26 (Spring 2000).

Glossary

ability grouping The assignment of students to separate classrooms or to separate activities within a classroom according to their perceived academic abilities. *Homogeneous grouping* is the grouping of students of similar abilities, while *heterogeneous grouping* is the grouping of students of mixed abilities.

accommodation The cognitive process of modifying a schema or creating new schemata.

accountability Reference to the concept that an individual is responsible for his or her behaviors and should be able to demonstrate publicly the worth of the activities carried out.

adolescence The period of life from the onset of puberty to maturity and terminating legally at the age of majority; generally from the ages of 12 to 20.

advance organizer Preinstructional cues that encourage a mental set, used to enhance retention of materials to be studied.

advisor-advisee A homebase or advisory program that provides each student the opportunity to interact with peers about school and personal concerns and to develop a meaningful relationship with at least one member of the school staff.

affective domain The area of learning related to interests, attitudes, feelings, values, and personal adjustment.

alternative assessment Assessment of learning in ways that are different from traditional paper-and-pencil objective testing, such as a portfolio, project, or self-assessment. See *authentic assessment*.

anticipatory set See *advance organizer*.

articulation Term used when referring to the connectedness of the various components of the formal curriculum. *Vertical articulation* refers to the connectedness of the curriculum K–12; *horizontal articulation* refers to the connectedness across a grade level.

assessment The relatively neutral process of finding out what students are learning or have learned as a result of instruction. See also *evaluation*.

assignment A statement telling the student what he or she is to accomplish.

assimilation The cognitive process by which a learner integrates new information into an existing schema.

at risk General term given to a student who shows a high potential for not completing school.

authentic assessment The use of evaluation procedures (usually portfolios and projects) that are highly compatible with the instructional objectives. Also referred to as *accurate, active, aligned, alternative, direct,* and *performance assessment*.

behavioral objective A statement of expectation describing what the learner should be able to do upon completion of the instruction. See also *curriculum standards*.

behaviorism A theory that equates learning with changes in observable behavior.

block scheduling The school programming procedure that provides large blocks of time (e.g., two hours) in which individual teachers or teacher teams can organize and arrange groupings of students for varied periods of time, thereby more effectively individualizing the instruction for students with various needs and abilities.

brainstorming   An instructional strategy used to create a flow of new ideas, during which judgments of the ideas of others are forbidden.

CD-ROM (compact disc-read only memory)   Digitally encoded information (up to 650 MB of data that can include animation, audio, graphics, text, and video) permanently recorded on a compact disc that is 4.72 inch or 12 cm in diameter.

character education   Focuses on the development of the values of honesty, kindness, respect, and responsibility.

classroom control   The process of influencing student behavior in the classroom.

classroom management   The teacher's system of establishing a climate for learning, including techniques for preventing and handling student misbehavior.

closure   In a lesson, the means by which a teacher brings the lesson to an end.

coaching   See *mentoring*.

cognition   The process of thinking.

cognitive disequilibrium   The mental state of not yet having made sense out of a perplexing (discrepant) situation.

cognitive domain   The area of learning related to intellectual skills, such as retention and assimilation of knowledge.

cognitive psychology   A branch of psychology devoted to the study of how individuals acquire, process, and use information.

cognitivism   A theory that holds that learning entails the construction or reshaping of mental schemata and that mental processes mediate learning. Also known as *constructivism*.

common planning time   A regularly scheduled time during the school day when teachers who teach the same students meet for joint planning, parent conferences, materials preparation, and student evaluation.

competency-based instruction   See *performance-based instruction*.

comprehension   A level of cognition that refers to the skill of understanding.

computer-assisted instruction (CAI)   Instruction received by a student when interacting with lessons programmed into a computer system. Known also as computer-assisted learning (CAL).

computer literacy   The ability at some level on a continuum to understand and use computers.

computer-managed instruction (CMI)   The use of a computer system to manage information about learner performance and learning-resources options in order to prescribe and control individual lessons.

constructivism   See *cognitivism*.

continuous progress   An instructional procedure that allows students to progress at their own pace through a sequenced curriculum.

convergent thinking   Thinking that is directed to a preset conclusion.

cooperative learning   A genre of instructional strategies that use small groups of students working together and helping each other on learning tasks, stressing support for one another rather than competition.

core curriculum   Subject or discipline components of the curriculum considered as being absolutely necessary. Traditionally these are English/language arts, mathematics, science, and social science.

covert behavior   A learner behavior that is not outwardly observable.

criterion   A standard by which behavioral performance is judged.

criterion-referenced assessment   Assessment in which standards are established and behaviors are judged against the preset guidelines, rather than against the behaviors of others.

critical thinking   The ability to recognize and identify problems and discrepancies, to propose and to test solutions, and to arrive at tentative conclusions based on the data collected.

curriculum   Originally derived from a Latin term referring to a race course for the chariots, the term still has no widely accepted definition. As used in this text, curriculum is what is planned and encouraged for teaching and learning. This includes both school and nonschool environments, overt (formal) and hidden (informal) curriculums, and broad as well as narrow notions of content—its development, acquisition, and consequences.

curriculum standards   Statements of the essential knowledge, skills, and attitudes to be learned.

deductive learning   Learning that proceeds from the general to the specific. See also *expository learning*.

detracking   An effort to minimize or eliminate separate classes or programs for students according to their differing abilities.

developmental characteristics   A set of common intellectual, psychological, physical, and social characteristics that, when considered as a whole, indicate an individual's development relative to others during a particular age span.

developmental needs   A set of needs unique and appropriate to the developmental characteristics of a particular age span.

diagnostic assessment   See *preassessment*.

didactic teaching   See *direct teaching*.

direct experience   Learning by doing (applying) what is being learned.

direct instruction   Teacher-centered instruction, typically with the entire class, where the teacher controls student attention and behaviors as opposed to permitting students to have greater control over their own learning and behaviors.

direct intervention   Teacher use of verbal reminders or verbal commands to redirect student behavior, as opposed to nonverbal gestures or cues.

direct teaching   See *direct instruction*.

discipline   The process of controlling student behavior in the classroom. The term has been largely replaced by the terms *classroom control* or *classroom management*. It is also used in reference to the subject taught (e.g., language arts, science, mathematics, and so forth).

discovery learning   Learning that proceeds from identification of a problem, through the development of a hypotheses and the testing of the hypotheses, to a conclusion. See also *critical thinking*.

divergent thinking   Thinking that expands beyond original thought.

downshifting   Reverting to earlier learned, lower cognitive level behaviors.

DVD (digital versatile disc)   Like CD-ROMs but with a greatly increased storage capacity.

early adolescence   The developmental stage of young people as they approach and begin to experience puberty. This stage usually occurs between 10 and 15 years of age and deals with the successful attainment of the appropriate developmental characteristics for this age span.

eclectic   Using the best from a variety of sources.

effective school   A school where students master basic skills, seek academic excellence in all subjects, demonstrate achievement, and display good behavior and attendance. Known also as an *exemplary school*.

elective   High-interest or special-needs courses that are based on student selection from various options.

elementary school   Any school that has been planned and organized especially for children of some combination of grades kindergarten through 6. There are many variations; for example, a school might house preschool children through grades 7 or 8 and still be called an elementary school.

empathy   The ability to understand the feelings of another person.

equality   Considered to be the same in status or competency level.

equilibration   The mental process of moving from disequilibrium to equilibrium.

equilibrium   The balance between assimilation and accommodation.

equity   Fairness and justice, with impartiality.

evaluation   Like assessment, but includes making sense out of the assessment results, usually based on criteria or a rubric. Evaluation is more subjective than is assessment.

exemplary school   See *effective school*.

exceptional child   A child who deviates from the average in any of the following ways: mental characteristics, sensory ability, neuromotor or physical characteristics, social behavior, communication ability, or multiple handicaps. Also known as a *special-needs child* and *special education student*.

exploratory course   A course designed to help students explore curriculum experiences based on their felt needs, interests, and abilities.

expository learning   The traditional classroom instructional approach that proceeds as follows: presenting information to the learners, referring to particular examples, and applying the information to the learner's experiences.

extended-year school   Schools that have extended the school year calendar from the traditional 180 days to a longer period, such as 200 days.

extrinsic motivators   Motivation of learning by rewards outside of the learner, such as parent and teacher expectations, gifts, certificates, and grades.

facilitating behavior   Teacher behavior that makes it possible for students to learn.

facilitative teaching   See *indirect teaching*.

family   See *school-within-a-school*.

feedback   Information sent from the receiver to the originator that provides disclosure about the reception of the intended message.

flexible scheduling   Organization of classes and activities in a way that allows for variation from day to day, as opposed to the traditional fixed schedule that does not vary from day to day.

formative assessment   Evaluation of learning in progress.

goal, course   A broad generalized statement about the expected outcomes of a course.

goal, educational   A desired instructional outcome that is broad in scope.

goal, teacher   A statement about what the teacher hopes to accomplish.

hands-on learning   Learning by doing, or active learning.

Hawthorne effect   Says that trying something new will show positive effects at first simply because of the interest demonstrated when something new is tried. Name derived from first notice of the effect in 1962 at the Hawthorne plant of Western Electric in Cicero, IL.

heterogeneous grouping   A grouping pattern that does not separate students into groups based on their intelligence, learning achievement, or physical characteristics.

high school   A school that houses students in any combination of grades 9 to 12.

holistic learning   Learning that incorporates emotions with thinking.

homogeneous grouping   A grouping pattern that usually separates students into groups based on their intelligence, school achievement, or physical characteristics.

house   See *school-within-a-school*.

inclusion   The commitment to the education of each special-needs learner, to the maximum extent appropriate, in the school and classroom he or she would otherwise attend.

independent study   An instructional strategy that allows a student to select a topic, set the goals, and work alone to attain them.

indirect teaching   Student-centered teaching using discovery and inquiry instructional strategies.

individualized instruction   See *individualized learning*.

individualized learning   The self-paced process whereby individual students assume responsibility for learning through study, practice, feedback, and reinforcement with appropriately designed instructional packages or modules.

inductive learning   Learning that proceeds from specifics to the general. See also *discovery learning*.

inquiry learning   Like discovery learning, except here the learner designs the processes to be used in resolving the problem, thereby requiring higher levels of cognition.

inservice teacher   Term used when referring to credentialed and employed teachers.

instruction   Planned arrangement of experiences to help a learner develop understanding and to achieve a desirable change in behavior.

instructional module   Any freestanding instructional unit that includes these components: rationale, objectives, pretest, learning activities, comprehension checks with instructive feedback, and posttest.

instructional objective   See *behavioral objective*.

integrated (interdisciplinary) curriculum   Curriculum organization that combines subject matter traditionally taught separately.

interdisciplinary team   An organizational pattern of two or more teachers representing different subject areas. The team shares the same students, schedule, areas of the school, and the opportunity for teaching more than one subject.

interdisciplinary thematic unit (ITU)   A thematic unit that crosses boundaries of two or more disciplines.

intermediate grades   Term sometimes used to refer to grades 4 through 6. An intermediate school, for example, is an elementary school that houses children of grades 4 through 6.

internalization   The extent to which an attitude or value becomes a part of the learner. That is, without having to think about it, the learner's behavior reflects the attitude or value.

interscholastic sports   Athletic competition between teams from two or more schools.

intervention   A teacher's interruption to redirect a student's behavior, either by direct intervention (e.g., by a verbal command) or by indirect intervention (e.g., by eye contact or physical proximity).

intramural program   Organized activity program that features events between individuals or teams from within the school.

intrinsic motivation   Motivation of learning through the student's internal sense of accomplishment.

intuition   Knowing without conscious reasoning.

junior high school   A school that houses grades 7 through 9 or 7 and 8 and that has a schedule and curriculum that resembles those of the traditional senior high school (grades 9 through 12 or 10 through 12) more than those of the elementary school.

lead teacher   The member of a teaching team who is designated to facilitate the work and planning of that team.

learning   The development of understandings and the change in behavior resulting from experiences. For different interpretations of learning, see *behaviorism* and *cognitivism*.

learning center (LC)   An instructional strategy that uses activities and materials located at a special place in the classroom and is designed to allow a student to work independently at his or her own pace to learn one area of content.

learning modality   The way a person receives information. Four modalities are recognized: visual, auditory, tactile (touch), and kinesthetic (movement).

learning resource center   The central location in the school where instructional materials and media are stored, organized, and accessed by students and staff.

learning style   The way a person learns best in a given situation.

looping   An arrangement in which the cohort of students and teachers remain together as a group for several or for all the years a child is at a particular school. Also referred to as multiyear grouping, multiyear instruction, multiyear placement, and teacher-student progression.

magnet school   A school that specializes in a particular academic area such as science, mathematics and technology, the arts, or international relations. Also referred to as a *theme school.*

mainstreaming   Placing an exceptional child in regular education classrooms for all (inclusion) or part (partial inclusion) of the school day.

mandala   A diagram, usually circular, with spiritual and ritual significance.

mastery learning   The concept that a student should master the content of one lesson before moving on to the content of the next.

measurement   The process of collecting and interpreting data.

mentoring   One-on-one coaching, tutoring, or guidance to facilitate learning.

metacognition   The ability to plan, monitor, and evaluate one's own thinking.

micro peer teaching (MPT)   Teaching a limited objective for a brief period to a small group of peers for the purpose of evaluation and improvement of particular teaching skills.

middle grades   Grades 5 through 8.

middle level education   Any school unit between elementary and high school.

middle school   A school that has been planned and organized especially for students ages 10 to 14, and that generally includes grades 5 through 8, with grades 6 through 8 being the most popular grade-span organization—although many varied patterns exist. For example, a school might include only grades 7 and 8 and still be called a middle school.

minds-on learning   Learning in which the learner is intellectually active, thinking about what is being learned.

misconception   Faulty understanding of a major idea or concept. Also known as a *naïve theory* and *conceptual misunderstanding.*

modeling   The teacher's direct and indirect demonstration, by actions and by words, of the behaviors expected of students.

multicultural education   A deliberate attempt to help students understand facts, generalizations, attitudes, and behaviors derived from their own ethnic roots as well as others. In this process, students unlearn racism and biases and recognize the interdependent fabric of society, giving due acknowledgment for contributions made by its members.

multilevel teaching   See *multitasking.*

multimedia   The combined use of sound, video, and graphics for instruction.

multiple intelligences   A theory of several different intelligences, as opposed to just one general intelligence. Other intelligences that have been described are verbal/linguistic, musical, logical/mathematical, naturalist, visual/spatial, bodily/kinesthetic, interpersonal, and intrapersonal.

multipurpose board   A writing board with a smooth plastic surface used with special marking pens rather than chalk. Sometimes called a visual aid panel, the board may have a steel backing and then can be used as a magnetic board as well as a screen for projecting visuals.

multitasking   The simultaneous use of several levels of teaching and learning in the same classroom, with students working on different objectives or different tasks leading to the same objective. Also called *multilevel teaching.*

naïve theory   See *misconception.*

norm-referenced   Individual performance is judged relative to overall performance of the group (e.g., grading on a curve), as opposed to being criterion-referenced.

orientation set   See *advance organizer.*

overlapping   A teacher behavior where the teacher is able to attend to more than one matter at once.

overt behavior   A learner behavior that is outwardly observable.

peer tutoring   An instructional strategy that places students in a tutorial role in which one student helps another learn.

performance assessment   See *authentic assessment.*

performance-based instruction   Instruction designed around the assessment of student achievement against specified and predetermined objectives.

performance objective   See *behavioral objective.*

portfolio assessment   An alternative approach to evaluation that assembles representative samples of a student's work over time as a basis for assessment.

positive reinforcer   A means of encouraging desired student behaviors by rewarding those behaviors when they occur.

preassessment   Diagnostic assessment of what students know or think they know prior to the instruction.

preservice Term used when referring to teachers in training, as opposed to inservice teachers or teachers who are employed.

probationary teacher An untenured teacher. After a designated number of years in the same district, usually three, upon rehire the probationary teacher receives a tenure contract.

procedure A statement telling the student how to accomplish a task.

psychomotor domain The domain of learning that involves locomotor behaviors.

realia Real objects used as visual props during instruction, such as political campaign buttons, plants, memorabilia, art, balls, and so forth.

reciprocal teaching A form of collaborative teaching where the teacher and the students share the teaching responsibility and all are involved in asking questions, clarifying, predicting, and summarizing.

reflection The conscious process of mentally replaying experiences.

reflective abstraction See *metacognition*.

reliability In measurement, the consistency with which an item or instrument is measured over time.

rubric An outline of the criteria used to assess a student's work.

rules In classroom management, rules are the standards of expectation for classroom behavior.

schema (plural: schemata) A mental construct by which the learner organizes his or her perceptions of situations and knowledge.

school-within-a-school Sometimes referred to as a *house, cluster, village, pod,* or *family,* it is a teaching arrangement where one team of teachers is assigned to work with the same group of about 125 students for a common block of time, for the entire school day, or, in some instances, for all the years those students are at that school.

secondary school Traditionally, any school housing students for any combination of grades 7 through 12.

self-contained classroom Commonly used in the primary grades, it is a grouping pattern where one teacher teaches all or almost all subjects to one group of children.

self-paced learning See *individualized learning*.

senior high school Usually a high school that houses only students in grades 9 to 12 or 10 to 12.

sequencing Arranging ideas in logical order.

simulation An abstraction or simplification of a real-life situation.

special-needs student See *exceptional child*.

standards See *curriculum standards*.

student teaching A field experience component of teacher preparation, traditionally the culminating experience, where the teacher candidate practices teaching children while under the supervision of a credentialed teacher and a university supervisor.

summative assessment Assessment of learning after instruction is completed.

teacher leader See *lead teacher*.

teaching See *instruction*.

teaching style The way teachers teach; their distinctive mannerisms complemented by their choices of teaching behaviors and strategies.

teaching team A team of two or more teachers who work together to provide instruction to the same group of students, either alternating the instruction or team teaching simultaneously.

team teaching Two or more teachers working together to provide instruction to a group of students.

tenured teacher After serving a designated number of years in the same school district (usually three) as a probationary teacher, upon rehire the teacher receives a tenure contract. This means the teacher is automatically rehired each year thereafter unless the contract is revoked by either the district or the teacher for specific and legal reasons.

terminal behavior What has been learned as a direct result of instruction.

thematic unit A unit of instruction built on a central theme or concept.

theme school See *magnet school*.

think time See *wait time*.

tracking The practice of the voluntary or involuntary placement of students in different programs or courses according to their ability and prior academic performance.

traditional teaching Teacher-centered direct instruction, typically using lectures, discussions, textbooks, and worksheets.

transescence A no-longer-popular term referring to the stage of human development, usually thought of as ages 10 to 14. It is the middle school years, which begins before the onset of puberty and extends through the early stages of adolescence. Students in this stage of development have been referred to variously as the *transescent, preadolescent, pre-teen, in-betweenager,* and *tweenager.*

transition In a lesson, the planned procedures that move student thinking from one idea to the next or that move their actions from one activity to the next.

untracking   See *detracking*.

validity   In measurement, the degree to which an item or instrument measures what it is intended to measure.

village   See *school-within-a-school*.

wait time   In the use of questioning, the period of silence between the time a question is asked and the inquirer (teacher) does something, such as repeats the question, rephrases the question, calls on a particular student, answers the question him- or herself, or asks another question.

whole-language learning   A point of view with a focus on seeking or creating meaning that encourages language production, risk-taking, independence in producing language, and the use of a wide variety of print materials in authentic reading and writing situations.

withitness   The teacher's timely ability to intervene and redirect a student's inappropriate behavior.

year-round school   A school that operates for the traditional 180 school days, but spreads the days out over 12 months rather than the more traditional 10. Most common is a nine weeks on, three weeks off format.

young adolescent   The 10 to 14 year old experiencing the developmental stage of early adolescence.

Name Index

Subject Index